Les Carlyon was born in northern Victoria in 1942. He has been editor of the Melbourne *Age* and editor-in-chief of the Herald and Weekly Times group, as well as the winner of two Walkley awards. His *Gallipoli* was published in 2001 to enormous critical and commercial success in Australia, New Zealand and Great Britain and is now widely regarded as the definitive history of the campaign. *Gallipoli* won the Queensland Premier's Literary Award for Best History Book and the Australian Publishers' Association Readers' Choice Award.

Les Carlyon's *The Great War* was published in 2006 to universal acclaim and became one of Australia's biggest non-fiction bestsellers. It won the inaugural Prime Minister's Prize for History in 2007, and was also honoured by the Australian Book Industry Awards, winning the Australian Book of the Year, as well as the Best General Non-fiction Book.

By the same author

Gallipoli
Heroes in Our Eyes
True Grit
Chasing a Dream
Paperchase: The Press
Under Examination

LES CARLYON

THE GREAT WAR

PICADOR
Pan Macmillan Australia

Imperial measurements have been used in this book as they were in documents and letters from the Great War. Exceptions to this are some gun calibres, which were measured in centimetres.

1 inch	25.4 millimetres		1 centimetre	0.394 inches
1 foot	30.5 centimetres		1 metre	3.28 feet
1 yard	0.914 metres		1 metre	1.09 yards
1 mile	1.61 kilometres		1 kilometre	0.621 miles
1 acre	0.405 hectares		1 hectare	2.47 acres

First published 2006 in Macmillan by Pan Macmillan Australia Pty Ltd
This Picador edition published 2010 by Pan Macmillan Australia Pty Ltd
1 Market Street, Sydney

National Library of Australia
Cataloguing-in-Publication data:

Carlyon, Les.
The Great War/Les Carlyon

New ed.

ISBN 978 0 330 42496 7 (pbk).

1. Australia. Army. Australian and New Zealand Army Corps – History.
2. World War, 1914–1918 – Campaigns – France.
3. World War, 1914–1918 – Campaigns – Western Front.
4. World War, 1914–1918 – Participation, Australia. I. Title.

940.4144

Typeset in Sabon by Post Pre-press Group
Printed in Australia by McPherson's Printing Group
Cover photograph: courtesy of the Australian War Memorial (E00033)
Maps by Map Illustrations (maps@mapillustrations.com.au)

Papers used by Pan Macmillan Australia Pty Ltd are natural, recyclable products made from wood grown in sustainable forests. The manufacturing processes conform to the environmental regulations of the country of origin.

The author and publisher have made every effort to contact copyright holders for material used in this book. Any person or organisation that may have been overlooked should contact the publisher.

Contents

Part Two: 1917

Part Three: 1918

Aftermath

List of maps

Key to maps

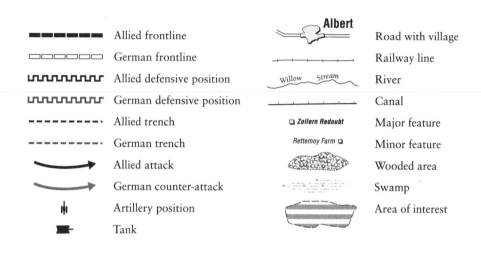

▬▬▬▬▬▬▬▬	Allied frontline
▭▭▭▭▭▭	German frontline
⎍⎍⎍⎍⎍⎍	Allied defensive position
⎍⎍⎍⎍⎍⎍	German defensive position
- - - - - - - -	Allied trench
- - - - - - - -	German trench
➤	Allied attack
➤	German counter-attack
ⵖ	Artillery position
▆►	Tank

Albert

	Road with village
	Railway line
Willow *Stream*	River
	Canal
❑ **Zollern Redoubt**	Major feature
Rettemoy Farm ❑	Minor feature
	Wooded area
	Swamp
	Area of interest

Military symbols

✕	Army group
	Army
	Corps
	Division
	Brigade
	Battalion

Abbreviations

UK	United Kingdom	AUS	Australia
FR	France	NZ	New Zealand
BEL	Belgium	US	United States
GER	Germany	CDN	Canada

Examples

35 ▷ AUS	35th Battalion Australia
8 ◀ AUS	8th Brigade Australia
4 ▣ UK **RAWLINSON**	4th Army Rawlinson (commander) United Kingdom

Hypsometric tints

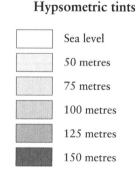

	Sea level
	50 metres
	75 metres
	100 metres
	125 metres
	150 metres

The trench stalemate, July, 1916

GREAT BRITAIN

Dover

Strait of Dover

Ostend
Bruges
Antwerp

XXXVI FR Nieuport
4 GER

Dunkirk
1 BEL Dixmude
Ghent
Brussels

Calais
Roulers
Passchendaele

Ypres

BELGIUM

Boulogne
St Omer
2 UK PLUMER
Armentières
Lille
Mons

GHQ UK
Lys River

HAIG
Montreuil
1 UK MONRO
Loos
6 GER

Arras
Vimy

Abbeville
3 UK ALLENBY
2 GER
Cambrai

Dieppe
Somme
4 UK RAWLINSON

RESERVE ARMY
UK GOUGH
Albert
Péronne

Amiens
6 FR
St Quentin
Guise

ARMY GROUP NORTH FR FOCH
Villers-Bretonneux
10 FR
7 GER

GQG FR JOFFRE
3 FR
Compiègne
Aisne
Soissons
3 GER

Chantilly
5 FR
Reims

Château Thierry
Epernay
Chalons
4

Seine

Paris

Marne River

Fontainebleau

Troyes

Aube

SCALE	30 miles
0	50 kilometres
0	

FRANCE

German frontline   OHL   Oberste Heeresleitung
German Supreme Command
(General von Falkenhayn)

French frontline

British frontline   GQG   French Grand Quartier Général
(General Joffre)

Belgian army frontline   GHQ   British General Headquarters
(General Haig)

PROLOGUE

In the gloaming

Here dead lie we because we did not choose
To live and shame the land from which we sprung.
Life, to be sure, is nothing much to lose;
But young men think it is, and we were young.

A. E. Housman

There were so many of them, more than three hundred thousand, and we never really saw them. Not when it mattered to see them anyway, not when they were doing the things that marked them as different, then and now, from the rest of us.

Here they are resting during a lull in one of the Somme battles, their boots sprinkled with white dust. Some drag on cigarettes, lumpy and hand-rolled. One daydreams and another, eyes big, face like a slab of marble, just stares, not at the landscape, not at the shell holes that sit lip to lip like sores, but at some panorama that exists only in his mind and now holds him prisoner. One re-reads a cutting that his mother has sent him from the *Ballarat Courier*. Another scribbles with an indelible pencil worn so short that it needs to be gripped with the thumb and forefinger in a taut circle. He adds three or four lines to what he wrote the night before. It seems important to write things down. It makes the absurd seem real. You *could* see the German shells in the sky at the top of their arc. Others saw them too. And writing makes events seem less terrible. If you can write about them, they are at least imaginable. One man, propped on his elbow, tries to doze, his helmet tilted over his eyes, a sprig of hair fluffing out one side. Another peers at the tear in his trousers as though it is a personal insult. The barbed wire has brought up a blood-stippled welt on his thigh. In this war it is nothing much. Some of the men's faces carry the soft contours of youth but sometimes the eyes look older than the faces.

They are stretched out on the downs, these men, on those red-brown earths shot through with lumps of chalk, rich dirt, soft country, nothing like home. Back there the soils were thin and hungry, as if some earlier civilisation had worn them out and left, so that all the ground could push up now was scraggy gums. But at least Australian soils smelled sweet. They didn't reek of explosives and wet sandbags and decomposing bodies that would swell up, then turn black and, if left, become huddles of khaki or grey that hid a jumble of bones, joined here and there by scraps of gristle and blown by the winter winds.

Anyone coming upon this group resting on the Somme would know at once that they were Australians. They had a look to them. There was a lankiness, a looseness in the way they moved that was occasionally close to elegance but not quite soldierly. War and the old world of Europe had failed to impose all of its formalities on them. They were good at war but in a way that offended the keepers of the orthodoxies: lots of dash, not much discipline away from the battlefield. They were good at war but they didn't want to stay in the army once the fighting ended. They were all volunteers. This was an interlude, not a career. When it was over they would go back to being commercial travellers and science teachers, farmers and bank clerks. In 1918 two architects, an orchardist and a grazier commanded four of the five Australian divisions. The corps commander, an engineer from a family of Jewish immigrants that had settled in Melbourne, also had degrees in law and arts, played the piano, sketched and wrote.

We, their kin and countrymen, didn't see the Australians when they were roistering in the cafés of Poperinghe, behind the Belgian front, where *vin blanc* was rhymed into plonk and used to wash down eggs and chips. We didn't see them when they sauntered around Horse Guards in London, eyes wide, because these were men from a land where the most ancient public buildings were little more than 100 years old and weren't well loved anyway, since they belonged to a convict society that was best not talked about. We didn't see them queuing outside the theatres or riding in taxis, carelessly spending their pay, which was much higher than that of their British cousins. We didn't see them watching the morning horsemanship in Hyde Park and smiling at the primness of it all. These tourists wore slouch hats and woollen tunics that ballooned over their hips, partly because the pockets always seemed to be full of tins and pouches. They tended to be taller than Englishmen and used slang words that had no currency outside their homeland. They seemed to be alive with the hopes of the New World and careless when it came to the protocols of the old. They didn't expect too much from life: that was the way of people then. They wore shoulder badges that said 'Australia', and these really weren't necessary. Their look, those languid poses, gave them away. They didn't call themselves 'Diggers': that came later.

They didn't much like saluting: it didn't seem democratic. A British officer once rebuked an Australian for failing to salute him.

'I'm a colonel!' he said.

'Best job in the army,' said the Australian. 'You keep it.'

We didn't hear these men the way the British and French did. In the night behind the Ypres front an Englishman heard a voice say: 'Get *over*, ya bastard.' It was said casually – there might even have been a hint of affection – and the Englishman knew at once that it was an Australian driver whose horse had shied at some obscenity in a shell hole.

On the Somme front in 1918 an English major observed a 'curious procession of two – an Australian private soldier, cigarette in mouth, and before him a miserable-looking German shambling along carrying the Aussie's kit and rifle'. The Australian had stumbled, drunk, into the British line the previous night. Upon being told where he was he muttered: 'Hell, I can't go back to my mob like this. What'll they say to me?' He ventured into no-man's land and half-an-hour later returned with a German. He had crept up to a German post and offered to toss a grenade in unless one man gave himself up. Now the Australian was heading back to his division. He would tender the prisoner in mitigation of being absent without leave. He had a hangover and it was good that the German was there to carry his rifle. Still, he would take it off him as they approached the Australian line. Might look bad.

On that same front in the same year Australians had asked a staff captain of a British formation for more hand grenades, or 'bombs' as they were called then. The bombs didn't come. The Australian commander found the staff captain playing bridge. The Australian threatened to take his men out of the line if the bombs didn't arrive in half-an-hour. The staff captain got up and ordered the bombs delivered at once. The Australian left. The staff captain returned to the bridge game. 'By jove,' he said, 'stout fellers, these Australians, but *socially* – im*poss*ible.'

The French watched these Australians as they stood, heads uptilted, puzzling over the cathedral in Amiens, a Gothic stab at the heavens, so fussy in all its tracery, so intimidating with its gargoyles and grotesques, and like nothing at Ballarat or Wagga Wagga, where the divine rights of clerics and kings had hardly played at all. The French saw them coming out of the battle for Pozières, white-faced and looking as if they had been drugged. They saw them squatting under the willows that line the Somme canals while four of their mates played cricket nearby, using a stick as a bat. The French saw them offering a farmer's wife a few coins if she would make them coffee laced with brandy. They would stand in front of her kitchen fire and stare at the crucifixes on the wall, then leave to doss down on straw in one of the barns. They had an easy-going way about them and spoke French badly and in between giggles. They seemed to like farms, although it puzzled them that holdings so small could produce so much, and even more that cows should spend the nights in brick barns, filling them with the ammonia fumes of urine on straw.

The French saw Australians slapping horses with the reins to drive them through a bog, saw them stamping their feet against the frost and snow that seemed so *foreign*, saw them rolling up their sleeves on a summer's day before tossing a grenade into a canal in the hope of stunning a few fish. They are still there, so many of these men. Those who were found are in the archipelago of cemeteries that stretches from Villers-Bretonneux to Passchendaele; and those who weren't lie under fields of corn and sugar beet.

The men spoke of this place in terms of villages, roads and rivers. To them, the names of these created their own imagery. It was enough to say that a man had been at Bullecourt. It was enough to speak of the Menin Road at Ypres and the Stations of the Cross above it, Polygon Wood and Broodseinde. The men knew the rivers well, because they kept crossing them. The Somme dawdled and the Ancre tinkled. Both might have been thought beautiful in other circumstances.

For three years these Australians, youths of seventeen and balding men of forty-five, tramped up and down the Somme downland and the Flanders plain, past wayside shrines and clusters of brick barns, sometimes marching twenty miles in a day, haversacks and scabbards slapping against their thighs, going up to the war and coming out again, taking in reinforcements and going back again.

We didn't see them when they won their great battle in front of Amiens in 1918 or when they later broke through the Hindenburg Line, where their leader, Lieutenant-General John Monash, also had two American divisions under his command. In 1918 the world seemed so weary of war and so suspicious of official dispatches that even victories sounded like more of the same and needed to be questioned. By 1918 people knew that the newspapers had not been telling them the truth about the war. We still don't know much about those successes and the skill with which they were arranged. Lieutenant Cyril Lawrence wrote to his mother: 'You will never know, you people in Australia, what the boys have done – even the people of England do not know because they call us *British troops* in the paper.' We didn't know until years later how badly the Australians had suffered in 1916 and 1917, at Fromelles and

Pozières, Bullecourt and Passchendaele. As the Australian historian Robin Prior has written, those men engaged the main army of the main enemy in the main theatre of war. This has not happened with Australian troops since.

We saw these men leave, full of derring-do, for a war that would turn out nothing like they expected, and indeed nothing like anyone expected. And we saw some of them come back, many haunted and secretive, and for the next twenty years the country went through a long grieving, and now it was the turn of women and children to suffer and to wonder what demons had come unbidden into their world. They knew these men before and after they went across the sea. They never saw them when, for three years, they did things Australians have never done since.

WHEN YOU TRY to write about these men it is better if you can see the ground, better if you can walk around alone for a while. You mostly end up doing the same things. You work out which way is east and which is west because these are the directions that matter most. The British and the French usually attacked from the west and the Germans for most of the war usually shot them down from trenches and blockhouses in the east. Between east and west is no-man's land and that's where you invariably find the shrapnel ball, grey and heavy in the hand, and proof that this field of corn, now sappy with life, was once a place where men from a faraway land cried out for water and their mothers. You hear the barking of unseen dogs and this leads you to identify the village on the river-bank. You can't see the houses and barns because of the plane trees, but you can see the church spire and one navigates by spires here. God is everywhere in the lands of the Somme and Flanders, and in the Great War that passeth understanding both sides drew comfort from the certainty that He was with them.

Eventually you are tempted to try something that almost always ends in bathos. You try to redraw the landscape. You blot out the round hay bales and the tractor with a cloud of grey-brown dust boiling behind it. You try to draw in trench lines and observation balloons and khaki bundles hung up on barbed wire. You take that field of sugar beet and try to turn it into thousands of shell holes, each with a slimy puddle at the bottom. You take that copse, soft and leafy, and try to transform it into stumps, outraged and blackened. It hardly ever works; yet you always try.

It is better to see the ground. It doesn't necessarily lead you to the truth. Often there is no truth about these battles, just a clamour of voices. But it can be the start of understanding, this walking around. There are other roads to the same end. All have potholes and some are cul-de-sacs.

There are official documents, operational and intelligence reports and the diaries and memoirs of generals. These mostly sound like disembodied voices. They are discreet and careful; they do not admit to chaos or fear; ineptitude is often dressed up as bad luck. The general staff is seldom taken by surprise and the passive voice is almost strident. Failure is often explained by saying that the frontline troops, 'though they attacked in a most gallant manner' were 'inexperienced'. Generals are never said to be inexperienced, and of course they were. But we must also try to be fair to the generals. We should not blame them for not knowing things that we know now.

The diaries of Douglas Haig for 1917 leave the reader convinced that the commander-in-chief of the British and dominion forces didn't understand that his troops, far away to the east, were stalled in front of Passchendaele village mainly because they were waist-deep in mud and the wounded were drowning. Haig is *here*, disembodied at GHQ, with sheafs of maps and other pieces of paper that say the war is orderly, almost as orderly as the field-marshal's daily routine; and the soldiers are *there*, in an ocean of mud. They no longer know quite where they are or what they are supposed to be doing. They are in the same war as Haig, but their war is a shambles. The generals William Birdwood and Alexander Godley commanded the two Anzac corps for most of the Great War and both afterwards wrote autobiographies. Neither book mentioned a battle in France in 1916 near a village called Fromelles. Omission is also part of the game.

As a counterpoint there are the letters and diaries of ordinary soldiers. The diary may be a Collins Paragon Diary No. 181, black-bound and dimpled, or scraps of paper that have been cut into small squares and bound with string. These chronicles are usually written with an indelible pencil and sometimes with fountain pens that leave blots when the hand pauses at the end of a sentence. Nothing matches them for verisimilitude. An Australian lieutenant writes in 1916: 'I have one puttee, a dead man's helmet, another dead man's gas protector, a dead man's bayonet. My tunic is rotten with other men's blood and partly splattered with a comrade's brains.' Read that and you know what it was like to be on the gentle rise above Pozières village in 1916.

The vigour and directness of soldiers' prose also tells us much about the Australian idiom of the day, which was almost free of Americanisms and home-grown in a way that today's language is not. Men occasionally talked about their mates or pals, but more often they wrote of their *cobbers*. Seldom does one come upon a soldier saying he went over the top; he *hopped the bags*. He doesn't take part in an attack but a *stunt*. When some of his cob-bers are killed he says they are *knocked*. The place where they are knocked is a *very warm corner*. Leave in Paris or London is said to be *bonzer*. High-ranking officers are *heads* and some of them are thought to be *duds*. One feels *queer* when a hot piece of shrapnel tears into one's arm. After that one looks for a *cushy* job. A man who is carefree is *gay*. Things are not stolen but *half-inched*. *Coves*, *beggars* and *coots* make up the passing parade.

Yet there are sometimes problems with soldiers' letters too. Troops on a battlefield can see only so far, maybe as little as twenty yards, but they are quick to blame the soldiers on their flanks for any reverses. A soldier writes his account of the battle of Polygon Wood; the date that he gives tells you that he is fighting the battle that preceded it, on Menin Road ridge. We need to remember that there was still a Victorian sensibility, even in private letters. There were things one did not talk about. Fear and despair and doubt were three of them. Pat Barker wrote of English soldiers of the Great War in her novel *Regeneration*. She has one of her characters say in an interior monologue: 'They'd been trained to identify emotional repression as the essence of manliness.' So too it was with the Australians.

There is another trouble with soldiers' letters. They touch you in a way that official documents do not. They drag you in when you are trying to stand back. You follow a man to Egypt and Gallipoli and on to Pozières and Passchendaele. You gain a sense of him, of where he came from and of the people to whom he is writing. You come to like him, his rough sense of humour and his acceptance of outrageous events. And then his letters end and you look him up on a file and it says 'Killed in action', followed by a date, and you feel a loss.

And there are maps. A map is sometimes as much an abstraction as a graph about poverty: all the numbers are there, but you can't smell the boiled cabbage. Detractors pursued General Monash in life and in death. He wasn't the true article, they whispered: too cerebral, not swashbuckling enough. Some of these critics point to Monash's failure at Gallipoli in August, 1915, when the brigade he led failed to take the heights above the Anzac beachhead. The battle plan looks reasonable when drawn on a map, and at least one critic has suggested that the poor leadership Monash is supposed to have shown there might be explained by the fact that he was overweight, which he then was. When you try to follow his steps, in daylight and with no-one shooting at you from the heights, you realise that the swell of Monash's girth had nothing to do with anything. The country there is mad. There is no grain to it. It rears and plunges in a jumble of ravines and razorbacks. And, as you blunder on, you realise that the scheme, that flourish of arrows stabbing into the Turkish hills, could never have worked. It looked right only on a map owned by an officer on the general staff.

It is always better if you can see the ground.

SO WE ARE here on a plain in French Flanders, near the village of Fromelles. That's its church spire you can see to the east and further along the same rise is the village of Aubers, which gives its name to the ridge, little more than a frown on the horizon, but high enough for observation. The ground on the plain is heavy clay, nothing like as sweet as the chalky loams of the Somme to the south, and as flat as a tabletop. All that breaks it is a ditch, not much more than six-feet across, sullen and splotched with algae, the nettles along its banks proclaiming its sourness. On the trench maps of the Great War this drain rejoiced in the name of the Laies River. Dusk is almost upon us. The sky is pastel blue and streaked with contrails and the east wind blows clouds of butterflies this way and that over a patch of pumpkins. Children sit straight-backed on ponies at the riding school next to the Australian cemetery and the voice of the instructress, bubbly and cheery, echoes across the empty plain and argues with what once went on here.

This is where the Australians in 1916 fought their first battle in France. Several thousand of them died within a few minutes' walk either side of where you are standing. They died in a single night, many of them before the sun had properly set. Some were Gallipoli men and others had never been in battle before. Some were still wearing felt hats rather than metal helmets. None of them knew much about how the war was being fought on the western front. They quite likely thought, as they had been taught to think, that winning was about 'character' and 'the spirit of the bayonet', when in truth the world had changed. Winning was about firepower, which meant artillery, but another year would pass before this notion began to take on. It was, after all, a form of heresy. It went against just about everything a fifty-year-old British general had been taught at his public school, at the staff college and on the job in India, Egypt and South Africa. It reeked of intellectualism – all those calculations about the weight of shells required to take so many yards of trench – and the British armies of the Victorian and Edwardian eras had been uncomfortable with intellectuals. They understood and admired officers who fearlessly put their horses at stone walls on the hunting fields. Field-Marshal Wolseley wrote in 1897: 'I hope the officers of Her Majesty's Army may never degenerate into bookworms.' There was no sign of this happening, he conceded, before going on to hint that too much reading could be unmanly.

Fromelles may be the most tragic battlefield in Australia's history. Yet it had no place in Australian folklore during the Great War and none now. The register at the cemetery shows thirty-five visitors for the previous month. Fromelles refuses to lodge in the Australian consciousness. One reason for this may be that Pozières, a much bigger battle in which three Australian divisions fought, began four days later down on the Somme. Another may be that Australians at home weren't told much about Fromelles. And another is almost certainly that the British and Australian commanders didn't much want to talk about it, because what they ordered done there was afterwards hard to explain.

The Australians and a British division left their breastworks (the ground was too wet to dig conventional trenches) and attacked from the north across the open plain at about 6 pm in bright daylight. The Germans waited for them on the flat ground to the south, where they had built concrete bunkers and blockhouses, notably at a place known as the Sugarloaf, which bulged out as a salient and bristled with machine guns. Other German divisions were behind, up on that ridge where Fromelles nestles, up where you can see everything that moves on the plain. That was the way of the western front for most of the war: the Germans were on the high ground and the British and French were trying to get up there.

SOMEWHERE IN FRONT of the Australians at Fromelles in 1916, somewhere behind the Sugarloaf, probably a mile or so from the front, there was a German corporal who fussed over a white terrier he called Foxl. The dog had strayed over from the British lines and the corporal had taught it tricks. We don't know whether this soldier was in the fighting against the Australians around the Sugarloaf, although one account – not to be relied upon – has him running through trenches clogged with dead and mutilated men. He was a dispatch runner in the Bavarian division that held the front and had been awarded the Iron Cross, second class, in 1914.

This man stares at us from a photograph taken at Fromelles in April, 1916. He is lank and pale and looks older than his twenty-seven years. He has a thick moustache, droopy and lop-sided, and his neck rears out of a baggy jacket. His eyes are hooded and dull, as though the mind behind them is so run down it can put out no light. There is much of the bumpkin about him: he is not so much a soldier as the man who collects the tickets at an alpine railway station. His comrades thought him odd. He would throw a tantrum if the barrack-room talk about the war turned glum. He was too literal-minded to enjoy jokes. He didn't smoke. He spurned alcohol and the French girls in the back-area villages. He had decided long ago that life was a fearful struggle. Why try to make it pleasanter? The little terrier gave him affection and, unlike the French girls, made no demands on his honour. He was annoyed when, during the Christmas of 1914, German and British troops met in no-man's land to sing carols and swap cigarettes. He thought such things gave war a bad name.

It would have been better for the world if a stray shell had landed on him at Fromelles during that British-Australian attack of July 19, 1916. He was a nobody then. Later, as Adolf Hitler, the world would come to know him better.

WE NEED TO find the Sugarloaf so that we have a reference point from which we can pencil in the rest of the battlefield. Martial Delebarre, from Fromelles, knows the ground as well as anyone. In 1992 he found a bone-handled table knife here. The blade was broken and rusted. Scratched on the handle was 'G. Blake'. Private George Francis Blake, a carpenter from Footscray, Victoria, died near the Sugarloaf, aged twenty-six. A year after his death his wife inserted an 'In Memoriam' notice in the *Age* that ended: 'Each day I miss his footsteps/As I walk through life alone.'

Now Delebarre has to find the Sugarloaf again, and the navigation has to be precise because there isn't much of the strong point left. You follow him across the wheat stubble, keeping the fetid ditch on the right. You plunge into a field of ripened corn to be swiped by the hairy tassels on the cobs. On the ground you see shrapnel balls and cartridge cases spotted with green mould. Then into a field of potatoes, where you follow the furrows to avoid stepping on the wilting plants. Then into another field of corn, then into wheat stubble that reeks from a dressing of cattle manure. You turn right across a small bridge over the ditch and into a bigger field of stubble. Now Delebarre's eyes are searching for the Sugarloaf. Eventually it identifies itself. Weeds spout from a strip of unploughed land, the only untouched soil in the field, just a few feet wide and fifteen-feet long. Iron stakes rise out of the weeds. That's all that remains. Nearby a rusty cylinder, a shrapnel shell from a British field gun, sits up on the stubble and German rifle rounds are everywhere, most spent, a few not. A farmer ploughs the field as we stand talking. The tines of his plough will bury those German cartridges and bring up other war debris, maybe something exotic, a toffee-apple mortar shell perhaps, or a tin of Three Nuns pipe tobacco.

So you stand there, at the centrepiece of this battlefield, and look back towards the allied line that you can now start to sketch in. Somewhere near that patch of thistles there died a wool buyer from Geelong, a medical student from Colac, a Duntroon graduate, a detective from Sydney, an architecture student from Melbourne. Just north of where we are standing the Australian wounded lay in the open, among knee-high weeds that had sprung up in the unplanted fields. Some remained there for five days and nights, several for three weeks. They scrounged food and water from the dead and watched maggots squirming in their wounds. One man cried out 'Bill, Bill' all night and at dawn was heard no more. Some raised their arms and legs or rolled from one side to the other in the hope of shifting the pain. An Australian bringing in broken men from no-man's land heard a voice about thirty yards away. 'Don't forget me, cobber,' it said. So many friendships ended within a couple of hundred yards of here: over in that stubble, behind the riding school, in and around that ditch, near the patches of pumpkins and cabbages and where the hay bales lie bleaching in the sun.

It is too much for the imagination to take in on this pretty summer's night with the horizon now blushing with soft pinks. This place was an open-air abattoir for most of the Great War.

About 20,000 Germans, Britons, Frenchmen, Indians, Australians, Canadians and Portuguese died in these few acres. Most have no known grave. Now this ground is a food bowl again, bleak and sticky in winter, but kind: no droughts, no bushfires.

Fromelles is a typical village in French Flanders, smart and clean the way the Somme villages to the south are dowdy and charming. Red geraniums explode out of window boxes and elderly couples potter in their vegetable gardens before locking up the ducks for the night. Many of Fromelles' residents now work in the nearby city of Lille but the village is still about the land and its rhythms. Australians moving up for the attack here in 1916 recalled passing labourers, men and women with old and inscrutable faces, hoeing mangolds as shells shrieked across the sky. Eighty-seven years on, in the gloaming, you hear the diesel knock of a tractor making a last pass before night closes in.

The land healed itself and life went on as before. Yet the world changed here, and along the line that led north for twenty miles to Passchendaele in Belgium and fifty miles south to the still waters of the Somme, and on from there to the madness of Verdun, where the land has not healed and probably never will. The nature of war changed in these soft fields. War lost its romantic glow here, and let's not worry that this imagery was false because war has always been about the grubby business of killing people. War here was no longer pretty: no red-and-blue uniforms, no pipeclay, no rushes of cavalry, none of the panoply of the fox hunt, no generals issuing orders from the saddle and needing nothing other than their voice to pass them on. The new colours were khaki and field grey, the right hues for the industrial age and its armies of conscripts. The war here was about machines: howitzers and mortars, machine guns and trains, wafer-like aircraft and tanks so ponderous that one could outpace them on foot, poisonous gas and flamethrowers. Wars had always been romantic to those who didn't go, which meant most of the people. Henry V had 7000 men at Agincourt and those who returned made play of a victory against the odds and only whispered about the dysentery and the murder of French prisoners. Shakespeare did the rest.

This was different. It touched more people. One way or another everyone in the British Isles was caught up in the Great War. After the opening of the British attack on the Somme in 1916, with its 57,000 casualties on the first day, whole streets and suburbs fell into mourning. Just about every family, high and low, was touched by death. There seemed more death than glory. The French lost 330,000 men killed or taken prisoner in less than a month early in the war. This was about mass armies and, by mid-1916, there seemed no end to it. Vladimir Lenin, the Bolshevik firebrand living in exile in Switzerland, wrote at the outbreak of war in 1914: 'The epoch of the bayonet has begun.' He was wrong. Bayonets caused less than one per cent of deaths on the western front. This was the epoch of the howitzer.

The year before the Australian attack at Fromelles the British had tried to take Aubers Ridge by attacking through the village of Neuve Chapelle. The opening artillery barrage lasted thirty-five minutes and more than eighty aircraft helped direct the fire. More shells were fired in that opening barrage than for all of the Boer War, yet one reason the attack failed was that the barrage was too light. At Verdun in 1916 the Germans brought up 1000 heavy guns and two million shells – for a front of only eight miles. By 1918 Britain's armies included half-a-million gunners, twice as many men as the whole expeditionary force it had sent to France in 1914.

Australian life was changed by that same line of trenches, but with a difference. Just about alone among the warring powers, Australia did not introduce conscription. A young nation with a population of just under five million at the outbreak of war sent 324,000 volunteers overseas to fight. Most of the 61,000 who died and the 155,000 who were wounded fell along the line that stretched northwards from the Somme to Passchendaele. Those casualties work out at around two-thirds of all who went overseas, the highest rate among the British empire forces. Why did a country so far away from the conflict give up so much? Why did it bury so much of its future under the chalk of the Somme and the clay of Flanders? How many young men who might have been prime ministers or professors, novelists or scientists, lie in the ground here?

FRANCE AND BELGIUM still give up their dead from the Great War. The headstone of Sergeant John James White, a blacksmith from the high country of East Gippsland, is paler and cleaner than the others in a cemetery near Bullecourt. A tractor driver turned up White's remains in 1995. A metal detector turned up his effects. These included a wallet that contained a photograph of the ten-month-old daughter he had left behind. Myrtle went to her father's funeral in France as an eighty-year-old.

In 1998, near the Windmill above Pozières village, a farmer felt his plough strike something and stopped his tractor. He climbed down to make sure it wasn't a shell. He had uncovered the body of Private Russell Bosisto, a baker from South Australia, lying in heavy clay. He was on his back and clutching a rifle in his right hand. He had died there in August, 1916, most likely killed by a machine gun. All his effects were with him, including a pipe, a penknife and an identity disc that was still legible. They buried him in a military cemetery down the hill. Mourners gathered blood-red poppies from the nearby fields and dropped them into his grave. There are few fences on the Somme. When you do see one it is usually around a cemetery from the Great War. And the cemeteries are everywhere, laid out like formal English gardens, the hardness of the headstones offset by the gentleness of roses and daisies and willows.

The grave of Fred Tubb, a farmer from Longwood in Victoria's north-east, lies near Poperinghe, west of Ypres, in Belgium. There was a hospital here, so it was inevitable that the hop field nearby became a graveyard. Tubb had won the Victoria Cross in the grottoes of Lone Pine on Gallipoli after being wounded in the head and arm. His time came two years later in the battle of Menin Road, just east of Ypres. A pink rose blooms near his grave. Beyond the cemetery Friesian cattle crop the short grass around a shed, the walls of which are marked with soldiers' graffiti. The war is gone and it is still here. The past is gone but it isn't dead. Only the men are dead.

Phillip Schuler lies south of here, just across the border in France, on a rich plain broken by red-brick farmhouses. He was a journalist at the *Age*. His father edited the paper and suffered throughout the war because of his German name and birthplace. Phillip Schuler was handsome and outgoing. He loved books and plays and everyone seemed to like him. He went to Gallipoli as a war correspondent, saw Lone Pine and the August offensive and wrote a book, *Australia in Arms*. Schuler had a sensitive ear and a light touch; it was an astonishingly good book from someone in his mid-twenties. One might have thought that, after Gallipoli, Schuler would have realised that it is always better to be a reporter than a soldier. But in 1916 he enlisted, not as an officer, as he could have been, but as a driver. And, not long after the battle of Messines in Belgium, he died of wounds to the left arm, the right leg, the face and the throat. He was just short of twenty-eight years old and he had literally been shot to pieces.

And here he is now, lying in the ground at Trois Arbres cemetery at Steenwerck with a crab apple tree next to his grave. Each spring the blossom comes out pink for the shining youth who is no more. Schuler lies with 469 Australians, 997 Britons, 214 New Zealanders, twenty-two Canadians, one South African and one Indian. Here, under a grey sky, is a lost generation. There were so many, and they were ours, and we never really saw them.

PART ONE: 1916

In viewing 1914–1916 I feel that I must remember that from the highest to the lowest we were all amateurs.
        – Brigadier-General Sir James Edmonds,
        British official historian, writing in 1928

1

Verdun's bitter fruits

An Australian brigade commander, burly and ruddy cheeked, took a British staff officer out into no-man's land five days before the attack at Fromelles. He wanted to show him the Sugarloaf salient and the ground the Australians would have to cross. Four hundred yards of it: rank grass, that ditch they called a river, shell holes filling with stinking water, barbed wire twitched to iron stakes, then the German bunkers, squat and inscrutable.

The Australian was Harold 'Pompey' Elliott; the staff officer was Major H. C. L. Howard from General Haig's headquarters. The three brigades of the 5th Australian Division were to attack to the left of the Sugarloaf and the 61st British Division to the right and at the salient itself. Howard had come up to report on preparations for the attack.

As the pair walked back from the frontline Elliott produced a circular that had been sent out by Haig's headquarters. This tried to distil some of the lessons of two years of trench warfare. It recommended that no assault should be made where the breadth of no-man's land exceeded 200 yards. Elliott's 15th Brigade was being asked to cover twice that distance. Elliott conceded to Howard that he didn't know much about tactics on the western front. He had been here only ten days and it was nothing like the crazy escarpment at Gallipoli, where neither side had much heavy artillery and the trench lines were often only a few yards apart. Then he told Howard what he thought. Elliott liked to tell people what he thought.

The attack would fail, he said. What did Howard think? Howard knew much more about artillery than Elliott. He said he thought it would be 'a bloody holocaust'. Elliott asked him to tell Haig this. Howard agreed to do so.

Elliott and Howard were alone. Howard never spoke publicly of the conversation. We have only Elliott's account and this is a pity: it would have been interesting to know what Howard made of the Australian. Elliott wasn't like other generals, English or Australian. Loud and dishevelled and cocksure, he was one of the true eccentrics of the Australian army. Pompey (the nickname came from the big-hearted Carlton footballer Fred 'Pompey' Elliott) was admired and feared down the line, by the enlisted men he roared at like 'a bull thirsting for gore', by the men he arrested or threatened to shoot (Elliott was forever on the edge of drawing a revolver, often for such heinous offences as smoking while on a route march), and by the junior officers he taunted by telling them they weren't 'a wart on a soldier's arse', and who cared if corporals and privates could hear what he was saying. He bullied and blustered, but there was said to be a fatherly quality to it. As several contemporaries observed, other commanders tried to be disciplinarians and ended up being hated. Elliott did the same thing and mostly found respect, and sometimes affection. His men had their own fun with him. They paid newsboys in Egypt to stand outside his tent in the early morning and shout: 'Egyptian Times – very good news – death of Pompey the bastard.'

Maybe his men sensed that he cared, and he did. If there was bombast, there was also generosity. Elliott wrote to his wife Kate, a soft beauty, that a private had died from pneumonia and 'he was such a good fellow'. These tender letters to Kate sit curiously with his ravings on the parade grounds of Australia and Egypt. He wanted to gaze into her 'dear, bright eyes and sunshine face' and kiss her 'dear lips and cheek and chin'. He liked children and referred to his young son and daughter as 'our dear little pets'.

Elliott luxuriated in that power, often tyrannical, that devolves on some men in wartime, but he had not been a career-soldier. When war broke out he was a suburban man who found content-ment in his family and his garden, a solicitor who had done lots of part-time soldiering and read much about war. He admired Stonewall Jackson, the Confederate general, and dreamed of glory. It is not clear whether Elliott, even by early 1916, had begun to understand modern war, where heroics alone were not enough and indeed sometimes caused thousands of men to be butchered for no gain.

Elliott had been an outstanding student at Melbourne University, where he took degrees in law and arts and shared the Supreme Court Prize for the top student in final-year law. He liked poetry, particularly Kipling. But he had also known poverty in the red dust of the family farm at Charlton, in Victoria's north-west, where he attended a one-teacher school and lived in a two-room hut of iron and bark. He won the Distinguished Conduct Medal for bravery as a corporal in the Boer War after he ran off enemy horses. On Gallipoli, where he commanded the 7th Battalion, he was the old-fashioned leader, straight out of military romance, at the front with his men, leading by example. He was shot in the ankle on the morn-ing of the landing at Anzac Cove and lay for hours on the shingle of the beach, his foot throbbing. He fought at Lone Pine in August. The man next to him was shot and his head exploded. Elliott led his men covered head to foot in blood and brains.

Elliott certainly fascinated his men because of the way he looked. He had just turned thirty-eight at the time of Fromelles. He stood five foot ten inches, maybe a little more, and was particularly heavy in the shoulders and upper arms. His head was huge and the chin jutted; he would lift it at the end of a sentence, sometimes as a form of intimidation. His hair had receded at the temples, leaving a tuft of grey standing up over his forehead. People said it stood up because of all the frantic energy inside his head. The cheeks were pink and unlined, like those of a boy, and they turned to puce when he was angry. His brown eyes were loaded with mischief. The face was plump and open. Elliott was heavy through the hips and his uniform hung on him like a bag.

He looked the typical fighting leader: bull-like, sure of himself, full of menace, big of heart. He seemed even more impressive when he was on Darkie, his black horse with a white star. Unafraid – that was the word most people used to describe him. Elliott was clearly unafraid of Turks and Germans, his pettifogging superiors at corps headquarters and foppish English staff officers. But demons were running around in his head, and they had been there long before Gallipoli. Elliott demanded to be taken seriously. If he felt he wasn't, he could be high-handed and petty. He imagined slights and let them eat away at him; he wanted to 'arrest' too many people for things that didn't matter. Elliott only looked sure of himself.

Lieutenant-General Sir William Birdwood, the head of the Anzac forces, and his Australian chief-of-staff, Brigadier-General Brudenell White, thought Elliott lacked judgement and tact. He knew how to come barging through the front door, red-faced and affronted; he had no idea of how to pick the lock on the back door. Birdwood had considered sending Elliott home.

Birdwood and White knew how to play political games up the line, all the way to General Haig's headquarters. They knew the rules. They would dissent from time to time, but politely. They would push, but only so far. They were temperate and subtle. They were against the plan to attack in front of Fromelles and said so. Finally, though, they agreed to hand over the 5th Division to a British corps commander for the assault. Elliott would help carry the plan out. He was good at the frontline. He wasn't subtle and neither was the plan.

UNLIKE ELLIOTT, THE commander of the 5th Division was disliked by just about everyone for most of his adult life. When James Whiteside McCay (he pronounced his name to rhyme with sky and sometimes spelt it M'Cay) died in 1930 the *Bulletin* first acknowledged that he was a 'born soldier and a brave man', then ran up to the point it really wanted to make: 'Nevertheless, he became about the most detested officer in the A.I.F. [Australian Imperial Force] at an early stage of the World War, and remained so to the end.' McCay's career was unusual. Here he was at Fromelles, fifty-one years old, tall and with a wilting moustache, a major-general commanding a division, and having spent only five-or-so weeks of his life in action. Yet those weeks were tumultuous. They showed him to be about as brave as a soldier can be, and also as a commander with a genius for alienating his men.

He had gone ashore with the 1st Division at Gallipoli and walked into a shambles. His 2nd Brigade was supposed to go left. Lieutenant-Colonel Ewen Sinclair-MacLagan, who had landed first with his 3rd Brigade, told McCay to go to the right. McCay reluctantly agreed and walked into a bigger shambles. Battalions were mixed up, command structures had broken down and some men had gone too far forward. McCay became crankier than usual. When Major-General William Bridges, the divisional commander, came ashore with Brudenell White around 7.30 am, he found McCay unstrung. White said that McCay was 'completely lost'. Bridges 'wanted to know what the hell he was doing'. Bridges grew angrier and White said he saw McCay's face change. 'He began to get a grip on himself and before long he was in complete control.'

We should not judge McCay for this. The shambles would have tested any commander. Two bullets passed through McCay's cap that morning and another through his sleeve. But he did not help himself. He accused rankers of cowardice and threatened them with a revolver. It was the style of the man that offended: the threats, the sarcasm, the prissiness of the schoolmaster and the pedantry of the lawyer. McCay could put the wind up men; he could not inspire.

Early in May the 2nd Brigade was sent south to the British beachhead at Cape Helles. Major-General Aylmer Hunter-Weston, the senior British officer there, wanted to try again to capture the village of Krithia. Hunter-Weston was one of the Great War's spectacular incompetents. Haig called him an 'amateur'. Others said he was a 'music-hall general'. At least twice during the war he went 'off his head'. He bubbled with cheery humour and threw troops away as lesser men tossed away socks. Hunter-Weston sent McCay's Australians into the battle late on the third day, telling them to advance on Krithia. There was no time to organise anything, not that this would have made much difference. The attack was suicidal. Half of the Australians involved in it were killed or wounded. McCay's brigade took more than 1000 casualties. Broken men lay in the darkness and cried out for water. It was heroic – and futile.

The Australians blamed McCay, which was unfair. Hunter-Weston wrote the orders. McCay showed much grit. He took his headquarters closer to the frontline than was usual. A bullet smashed into his leg, breaking it. His wound healed, then the leg snapped again. McCay was invalided home.

Two Australian divisions had fought at Gallipoli. The 1st Division, plus John Monash's 4th Brigade, had been there from the start; the bulk of the 2nd Division arrived in September and missed the worst fighting. After the abandonment of Gallipoli these two divisions and Monash's brigade returned to Egypt, where large numbers of Australian reinforcements were training. Out of this pool four new divisions were created: the 1st, 2nd, 4th and 5th. The 3rd Division was meanwhile being formed from new recruits in Australia. Birdwood, in Egypt, had to find two new divisional commanders. He didn't believe there were any obvious candidates among the Australians. This dismayed Senator George Pearce, the Australian Minister of Defence, who sent a telegram saying that McCay should command one of the two new divisions. So McCay came to command the 5th, mainly it seems because he was deemed to be an 'Australian', even though he had been born in Ireland. He arrived in Egypt in late March, 1916, just in time to alienate himself from his new command.

McCay, the son of a Presbyterian minister, had come to Australia as an infant. Young James was a brilliant student. He was dux of Scotch College, Melbourne, where he was a contemporary of Monash, before taking masters degrees in arts and law and winning the Supreme Court Prize (as Elliott later would), even though, the story goes, he didn't attend a single lecture. Before he graduated he had bought Castlemaine Grammar School, where he was said to be a good teacher, although one of his aids was a birch, which he used often. He became a lieutenant-colonel in the militia, won a seat in the Victorian Parliament and then in the new Federal Parliament. He was not popular among politicians because of his scornful wit, but briefly became Minister of Defence, before losing his seat.

McCay had no sooner returned to Egypt to command the 5th Division when he received orders to march two of the three brigades nearly forty miles to the Suez Canal. McCay appears to have made 'some objection' to this order but agreed to carry it out. His 14th Brigade suffered frightfully in the heat, which topped 100 degrees Fahrenheit, and deep sand. McCay composed a rant against the 14th Brigade and had it read out to the troops. He didn't seem to care about the men he commanded and they didn't care for him.

So here, now, was McCay on the plain in front of Fromelles, carrying the burden of his own personality and the blame for Krithia and the desert march, and eager to get this one right, even if the battle plan seemed slanted towards heroics rather than good sense. As with Krithia, it wasn't his plan. As with Krithia, he and his men had been loaned out to the British. This scheme belonged to Lieutenant-General Richard Haking, also a son of a clergyman and possessed of a doleful moustache. Haking commanded the British XI Corps and Aubers Ridge, where Fromelles lay, kept beckoning to him.

THE 5TH WAS the last of the Australian divisions to arrive in France. If the men didn't know much about Haking, they were doubtless pleased to be leaving General Sir Archibald Murray, the British commander-in-chief in Egypt. Murray was politely called a 'conventional' soldier. Haig in private called him an 'old woman'. Murray had a nervy disposition and collapsed from strain during the battle of Le Cateau in 1914. The following year he became Chief of the Imperial General Staff, which might have been the most important post in the army.

It couldn't be so in 1915 because Lord Kitchener was Secretary of

State for War. Kitchener, cross-eyed and cranky and unknowable, a man who lived in an 'Arctic loneliness', was thought to be a distinguished soldier. He had routed the Mahdists near Khartoum in 1898, but this left him several battles short of being a military genius. Kitchener didn't understand Cabinet government. He wanted to hold a political office and run the day-to-day affairs of the army as well, to be a politician and a field-marshal at the same time. He had run the Boer War as a one-man band; he was now trying to run the Great War the same way and his Cabinet colleagues were tiring of him. But they had a problem: how did they sack a public idol? Kitchener regarded the Chief of the Imperial General Staff as his flunkey and Murray didn't let him down. Murray then became commander-in-chief in the Middle East in March, 1916. His replacement as Chief of the Imperial General Staff, Lieutenant-General Sir William Robertson, was never going to be Kitchener's flunkey.

Murray's dislike of the Australians had nothing to do with their fighting essay at Gallipoli. Murray alighted on something his Victorian and Edwardian past told him was more important: a certain lack of discipline and, specifically, the failure of these civilian-soldiers to take saluting seriously. As Charles Bean, Australia's official historian, wrote, Britain's political system at this time was democratic in form but largely feudal in tradition. Bean said saluting came more naturally to English soldiers because most had been brought up to see themselves as inferior, socially and mentally, to their officers. The Australians came from a quirky new democracy. Officers, the colonials contended, had to earn respect, like the boss in the shearing shed.

Murray hinted to the Australian commanders that he could not recommend that their troops be sent to France. Saluting and other courtesies would be matters of real consequence there, he said.

Then, on February 21, the Germans attacked at Verdun. France needed men. Whether the Australians were good at saluting suddenly didn't seem important. Murray told London he would send the Australian divisions, even though they were the 'most backward in training and discipline'.

So the Australians sailed for France. Saluting, however, would remain a problem. The poet John Masefield told how in early 1917 a British staff captain reprimanded an Australian for failing to salute. The Australian patted him on the shoulder. 'Young man,' he said, 'when you go home, you tell your mother that today you've seen a real bloody soldier.'

BY THE END of 1915, a disappointing year for the allies even though Italy had come in on their side, France had already run up 1.9 million casualties (including 50,000 officers). One million of these were dead. British casualties (including those from dominions and other empire lands) now topped half-a-million. It was bad enough that a generation of young men was being sacrificed; worse still was the realisation that there didn't seem to be any end to it. The stalemate, that line of trenches running from the Belgian coast to Switzerland, couldn't be broken. The French had carried out the big offensives, above the Somme in Artois and below it in the Champagne. These produced long casualty lists for gains of a thousand yards here and a thousand yards there that changed the nature of the war not one whit. The British had tried smaller assaults in Artois, at Neuve Chapelle, Aubers Ridge and Loos. All failed. The British generals were still learning the new ways of war. And they didn't have enough modern weapons. The Victorian and Edwardian manuals had stressed the importance of 'character' and 'the offensive spirit' and the wonders of bayonets and cavalry. What the generals needed in France and Belgium were more howitzers and high-explosive shells. Character was fine and of course it mattered; but firepower mattered more.

The British politicians were learning even more slowly than their generals. They had split into two camps: the 'westerners' who believed the war could only be won on the western front against the main German army, and the 'easterners' (who included David Lloyd George and Winston Churchill) who wanted to knock away Germany's 'props', the Austrian and Ottoman empires. Gallipoli was an easterners' adventure; so was Salonika. There was a flaw in the easterners' argument, although it is easier to see from a distance of ninety years. Austria and Turkey were not propping up Germany; she was propping up them. Much of the time the Austro-Hungarian army was a shambles and it only avoided setbacks in the east because the Russian army was a grander shambles. As someone said, the easterners were like a boxer who tries to win the fight by knocking out his opponent's seconds. But the easterners would be around for the whole war, always looking for the quick fix, the sly flanking movement, in the Balkans or the Middle East or indeed anywhere but on the western front. Haig was a westerner. He predicted that Gallipoli would fail weeks before the troops landed. He had tentatively agreed late in 1915 to a joint offensive with the French on the Somme the following year, even though he would have preferred to attack around Ypres in Belgium.

The German generals had also been thinking about how to break the stalemate. They had spent most of 1915 on the defensive on the western front while they propped up the Austrians in the east. General Erich von Falkenhayn, the chief-of-staff of the German army, a ruthless and secretive man, now came up with a scheme that was wondrous in its cynicism. He understood the importance of firepower. He would build up a stockpile of high-explosive shells and launch them at one spot, a narrow front where the French would be compelled, for reasons of honour, to pour in more and more men and watch them be blown to pieces. The idea, Falkenhayn explained, was to make France 'bleed to death'.

He would play Dracula at Verdun, the ring of forts that had long been the eastern gateway to France. The forts had been built for older forms of warfare. And they hadn't mattered much in this war, because the Germans had come not from the east, as the French had expected, but from the north, spearing out of Belgium in great hook-like formations that were supposed to sweep around either side of Paris and crush the French army in six weeks. Even so, the French people saw the Verdun forts as symbolic. This was the sentiment Falkenhayn was working on. The French could give up Verdun and be humiliated; or they could fight for it and be slaughtered, division after division, fed into that narrow front like sheep clattering up the ramp of an abattoir.

Verdun sits astride the River Meuse, 140 miles east of Paris, inside a ring of hills, and in those days it was only a day's march from the German frontier. The forts surrounded the town, most of them on the eastern side of the river, facing Germany, and the strongest of these was Douaumont. Falkenhayn threw in his stockpile of two million shells and 1000 heavy guns on a front of only eight miles after first establishing air superiority so as to spot the French artillery batteries. Here was the new warfare: killing at a distance, killing from places where the enemy couldn't see you, so that the old infantry tactics, the close-order drills that had been taught in the previous century, no longer had much meaning. The muzzles of the heavier guns looked like sewer outlets. The shells for the seventeen-inch howitzers each weighed a ton. The first shell fired in the battle, from a fifteen-inch howitzer twenty miles away, hit the bishop's palace in Verdun. It was meant to hit a bridge but the French and British propagandists seized upon it as proof that the Hun was godless. On that first day about 80,000 shells fell on a 100-acre rectangle just behind the French frontline before the first German infantryman was seen.

That day was February 21 and in the next few days the German 5th Army, commanded by Kaiser Wilhelm II's son, the Crown Prince of Prussia, advanced five miles and took Fort Douaumont and the chalk and clay in front of Verdun became a hell. The Germans used flamethrowers for the first time. Both sides used gas. Shell craters were so thick that aerial photographs of the battlefield looked like a wasps' nest, a rash of cysts. Men simply disappeared, blown into thousands of pieces. The luckier ones lived in a pall of black smoke. Kaiser Wilhelm arrived behind the battlefield; this, he thought, had the feel of a victory.

Church bells rang out across Germany and France slipped into despondency. General Henri-Philippe Pétain took command at Verdun. He had been a colonel when war broke out and thought a heretic because he didn't believe, as most did, that attack was virtually the only tactic worth studying. Pétain was cautious and taciturn – some said he was without charm – but he understood that this war was about firepower. Haig and Joseph Joffre, the

French commander-in-chief, were like lions locked in a cage: they longed to break out, to escape to the open plains and get back to the war of movement they had been taught as young men and which was about the only form of war they understood. They seemed to think some collective act of 'character', some display of Napoleonic heroics, could get them out there, wheeling and turning, pennants fluttering and saddles creaking. As much as one can tell, the people of France and England thought much the same. They knew about Napoleon and Wellington; they didn't yet perceive that this war was as much about the science of artillery as it was about the human spirit.

Pétain, a bachelor, was fifty-nine at the time of Verdun, straightbacked and aloof, a man of some presence, mainly because of his glacial stare. His eyes were said to be the same colour as his uniform, horizon blue. Women found him charming. On the night before he took command at Verdun he was finally found at a Paris hotel. His boots stood outside the bedroom door next to a pair of ladies' shoes. Pétain explained to his aide that he had other duties to attend to at this moment; he would deal with Verdun tomorrow.

A week into the battle, which was to last ten months, Falkenhayn's scheme was in trouble. Because he had insisted on a narrow front, his troops were soon exposed to flanking fire. Pétain had seen that weakness and exploited it. Falkenhayn began to widen his front and the scheme started to lose its point. If it was 'bleeding' France, it was bleeding Germany too. The French rotated divisions through Verdun, which meant the horror of the place was felt through most of the French army. The Germans pushed their artillery closer to the front over wet ground and on one day 7000 horses, French and German, were killed, ninety-seven by a single shell.

The Germans captured a French captain who had a bayonet wound in the thigh. Charles de Gaulle spent the rest of the war as a prisoner. The German expressionist painter Franz Marc, famous for his 'Blue Horses', wrote from Verdun: 'For days I have seen nothing but the most terrible things that can be painted from a human mind.' The agonies of the horses particularly upset him. A shell killed him the next day.

Pétain saved French honour at Verdun and became a national hero, but by April his superiors privately thought him too cautious and promoted him so as to install General Robert Nivelle at Verdun. Nivelle, a fifty-nine-year-old artilleryman, had one of the best gifts a general can own: he could charm politicians. He was confident and outgoing and spoke excellent English. At Verdun he thought that he had discovered the formula for winning the war, a combination of artillery and infantry known only to him, and this made him popular with politicians. They all wanted to know a man who thought he had found the formula.

The Germans ground on towards the town. By now more than twenty million shells had been fired into the battlefield and each side had run up about 200,000 casualties. A German lieutenant had joined in the battle. He could not have conceived that one day he would command in a battle just as cruel. Lieutenant Friedrich Paulus would twenty-seven years later surrender a Germany army at Stalingrad.

The Germans now had other things to worry about. General Alexei Brusilov had run the first successful Russian offensive of the war, routing the Austro-Hungarian forces in Galicia, taking 400,000 prisoners, and forcing the Germans to send reinforcements to prop up the empire that was supposed to be propping them up. And the French and British were clearly preparing to do something on the Somme.

In October, when the Somme battle had been going three months, the French recaptured Fort Douaumont and began to push the Germans back along the main line of their advance. Falkenhayn had fallen. He had got things wrong too many times and the Germans had the good sense to see Verdun as a failure. Falkenhayn in August was sent to command an army in Rumania. He had not found the formula, just a way to run up 300,000 casualties on both sides, maybe more. No-one knows precisely. An ossuary at Verdun contains the bones of more than 130,000 unknown soldiers, French and German. Some of the villages in front of the town were never rebuilt and fields thick with bones and shells have been left unploughed to this day.

Many claim Verdun was the worst battle of the Great War and this perhaps underestimates what happened in the Ypres salient of Belgium over four years. But the world changed at Verdun. It brought to prominence Pétain and Nivelle. It satisfied French pride but it seared the souls of French soldiers. They had been asked to do too much. Verdun saw off Falkenhayn and brought forth two Prussians, Paul von Hindenburg and Erich Ludendorff, who would command the German armies for the rest of the war. And it put pressure on Haig and the British to achieve something worthwhile on the Somme, to shift the German gaze off Verdun. Which was why the Australian 5th Division was at Fromelles. The battle planned for there, under the control of General Haking, was supposed to stop the Germans sending reinforcements south to the Somme.

THE MEN OF the Australian 1st and 2nd divisions began arriving in Marseilles from Egypt in late March. As the trains took them through the south of France they thought they had wandered into the Elysian Fields. No more Egyptian sandstorms, no more Gallipoli flies. These men had grown up on the thin soils of Australia. They were used to paddocks bleached pale yellow and dotted with skinny merinos grazing with their noses into the wind. Here was something from a picture-book: fat cattle and green meadows and old farmhouses with stone barns. The land seemed to smile at them.

Arthur Thomas, a thirty-seven-year-old tailor from Melbourne, arrived with the 1st Division.

From Marseilles we trained across France, & a more lovely sight I have never seen, the South of France is beautiful, forest, meadows, glorious roads, delightful homesteads, little wonder the Frenchman is proud of his country, every available bit of land is tilled & gardened & no waste ground is left, no fearful hoardings like Melbourne, very little advertising is allowed over the country . . . all along the line the people gave us a very warm welcome & one noted the number of people in black & beautiful women in their widow's weeds, hundreds of them.

Lieutenant Gordon Maxfield from the 2nd Division had just turned twenty-seven. He had bright eyes, an unlined face and a crisp moustache. An accountant from the gritty soils of Longwood, in Victoria's north-east, he had fought at Gallipoli. He told his father that France seemed like paradise. 'We wanted to climb out of the train and bury our faces in the green, green grass, and roll about in the fields like toil-weary old horses just unharnessed after a hard day's work.'

John Raws, slightly built but a good cricketer at school in Adelaide, was the head of the parliamentary reporting team for the Melbourne *Argus* when he joined up in 1915. His father, a clergyman, apparently demurred. Raws, gentle and sensitive, replied that he wasn't one for heroics and claimed no great patriotism. He simply believed that 'the only hope for the salvation of the world is a speedy victory for the Allies'.

Raws was thirty-two and unmarried. He had been born in Manchester and had come to Australia as a twelve-year-old. His younger brother Robert (known as 'Goldy') had already joined up and had fought at Gallipoli. Now both were in France, lieutenants in the 2nd Division. John (known as 'Alec') wrote to his niece that French girls threw kisses to the Australians passing on the trains. 'It seemed such a pity that we couldn't get out of the train, so that they needn't have had to throw them. Because kisses get spoiled being thrown, don't you think?'

English officers puzzled him. They put on 'a frightful amount of dog . . . they appear to be absurdly mincing and effeminate, and to have an extraordinary desire to look foppish. I think they really try to put it on, because whenever one scratches one of them he does seem to be all right inside.'

Ivor Margetts, a captain in the 1st Division, had splashed ashore from one of the first boats to land at Gallipoli. He was a schoolteacher from Hobart, twenty-four years old, six foot four inches tall, a big handsome man with a whimsical turn of phrase and a pipe clenched in his teeth. He loved Australian rules football and even played at Gallipoli. 'Beautiful match. Led at three-quarter time, lost by seven points.' France, he wrote to his parents, was much better than Gallipoli.

John Monash arrived in northern France with his 4th Brigade in June. He explained how billets were arranged. 'You pull up at a large farm house, demand inspection of the accommodation available (rooms, barns, stables and kitchens), make friends with the children, or the dog, or in one case the pet pig; curry favour with the old dame who cannot understand my Parisian French, as she speaks only a Flemish-French patois; and finally after much gesticulation and remonstrance you chalk up on the various doors: "3 officers and six batmen", "Mess for 4 officers", "1½ platoons" (in the barns) . . .' Monash was astonished to see a pretty French girl selling the London papers just behind the front as shells burst nearby.

One of the first things Sergeant Cyril Lawrence, an engineer in the 1st Division, noticed in Marseilles were the public urinals. A man was relieving himself against a wall even though a tram 'with any amount of ladies aboard' had pulled up a few yards away. When Lawrence reached the front there was a scare about a gas attack. One of his men, in thrall to the folklore of Ned Kelly, came rushing up, eyes standing out like doorknobs. 'God! sergeant,' he said, 'I'm done, I'm done, it's got me, tell them at home I died game.' The horror was in his mind: there had been no gas attack.

The 5th Division arrived last, at the end of the spring flush. William Barry, a private, liked the cafés, or *estaminets*. He could buy wine and beer for a penny a glass, 'and one good thing about the beer was you could drink a ship load and it would not take any effect'. Barry's battalion had to march nineteen miles over cobbled roads to the front. The men's feet were blistered 'like raw meat', Barry wrote in his diary. 'I noticed that all through the march Mr McKie [Major-General James McCay], the Commander of the Division, was riding up and down the line in his motor car . . . [The next day] Mr McKie said that he was disgusted at the way the men marched and if in the future any man fell out while he was on the march, he was liable to be immediately shot . . .' Few of McCay's men had any time for him, Barry said.

Major Geoffrey McCrae, also of the 5th, strong-jawed and conventionally handsome, had been badly wounded at Gallipoli. He liked to write poetry, which was right enough considering his line-age. His father, George, had been close to Henry Kendall, Adam Lindsay Gordon and Marcus Clarke. Kendall regarded George as the finest poet in Australia. 'This is a most gorgeous country where it has not been devastated by the Hun,' Geoffrey McCrae wrote. 'I always thought Australia was the only place on God's earth until I came here.' McCrae's only complaint was that he had hay fever.

Fromelles, July 19, 1916

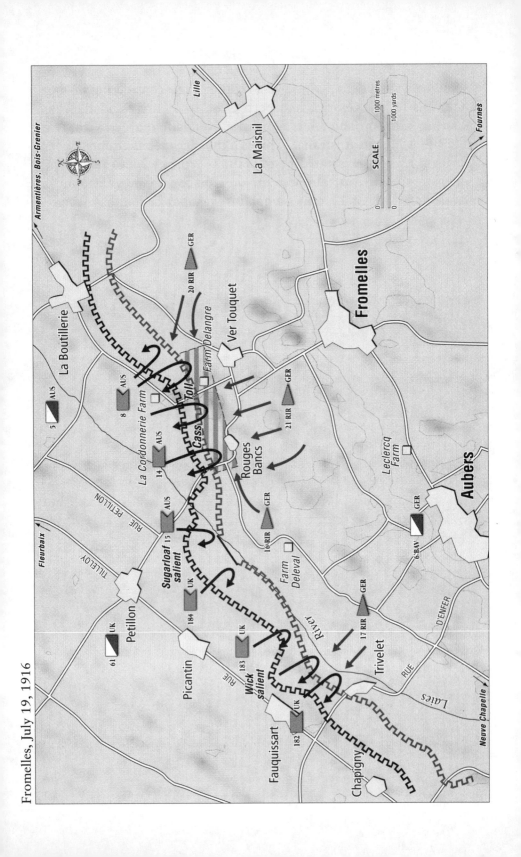

2

An unprepared little show

One lesson of the Great War is that any nation, even in times that suggest peace and tranquillity are the norm, needs to cull its military commanders ruthlessly. If it does not, it will one day go off to a big war – most likely one that comes out of nowhere – with its young men being directed by commanders who are out of time and place. Thinking in the upper reaches of the British army had begun to change by 1916. The old generation, the men who were in power, began to realise that an era, and a way of life, leisured and ordered, was ending, although they probably didn't go about saying so, because that would have also been to say that so much of their lives had been in vain, that the verities they had learned and lived by had diminished relevance in the trenches of the western front. One British regular is supposed to have said: 'I'll be glad when this war is over and we can get back to proper soldiering.' By which he meant horse sports and boisterous nights in the mess, rather than waking before dawn to the smell of whale oil on feet and mildew on sandbags.

The regulars' world had changed so abruptly. Soldiers in helmets and khaki looked like miners, drab and careworn. The scale of killing was without precedent. Bordino, seventy miles west of Moscow, was the bloodiest battle of the Napoleonic wars with

75,000 casualties. Most of the battles of the 100-or-so years before 1914 had been fought on narrow fronts. Mostly they ended quickly, whereupon the winner imposed a deal on the loser. Mass armies conscripted from millions of civilians were not the norm, least of all in Britain. Neither was attrition. Napoleonic battles had been about colour and lightness of movement, both of which tended to distract from the brutishness that happened at close quarters. Cavalry and infantry had been more important than artillery. Killing was done with muskets at eighty yards and needle bayonets at arm's length. Communications were seldom a problem. Generals could see where their troops were and direct battles from near the front, often without the need for written orders.

The Great War was a new thing in the world: attrition on a front of 400 miles, hardly any movement, lots of horses but mostly only as baggage animals, killing done from a distance (sometimes as far as twenty miles), men blown into so many pieces that there was nothing to pick up, trenches and tunnels and galleries and saps, massed artillery, mass armies, millions of civilian soldiers, nightmares of supply, administration and communication. The problem of communications was perhaps the worst. Commanding generals, as the historian John Keegan has noted, were now not even spectators. They tried to direct battles they could not see and seldom understood, because the messages coming back from the front were always late and often wrong or ambiguous.

And, as well, there were all these inventions from the industrial age: quick-firing artillery and high-explosive shells, machine guns, railways, traction engines, barbed wire, poison gas, aircraft, telephones, submarines. War, the older generation of soldiers felt, was losing its 'human element'. Control was passing from gentlemen to technicians. Once the war of movement ended late in 1914 Kitchener said: 'I don't know what is to be done – this isn't war.'

Most of Britain's generals were in thrall to abstract notions they had absorbed at schools such as Eton, Harrow and Clifton and carried into the army, ideas about pluck and manliness and, above all, the importance of character and the power of will. They were not too much interested in down-to-earth matters, such as how to configure an artillery barrage.

Most were born between 1860 and 1870 and had grown up (and they can hardly be blamed for this) with Victorian values. They were predominately from the upper class (with the exception of Robertson, who came up through the ranks) and, while most had attended the famous public schools, few had gone to university. They liked sports, particularly polo and fox-hunting. Many had been to the staff college at Camberley and perhaps overestimated the quality of the scholarship there. They were not much interested in books or theories. In 1902 the assistant commandant at Woolwich, the academy for officers who would become engineers and artillerymen, said:

> We would rather have a classically educated boy than one who has given his mind very much up to Electricity and Physics and those kinds of subjects. We want them to be leaders in the field first . . . I think the man who has a strong turn for science does not at the same time develop the soldierly side of his nature. Power of command and habits of leadership are not learned in the laboratory . . . Our great point is character; we care more about that than subjects.

The old guard believed in the cult of the offensive, masses of men closing in with bayonets, even though the Russo–Japanese war of 1904–05 had told them that future wars were going to be about firepower. In 1910 Sir Ian Hamilton, who later commanded at Gallipoli, wrote: 'War is essentially the triumph, not of a chassepot [a breech-loading rifle closed with a bolt] over a needle-gun, not of a line of men entrenched behind wire entanglements and fireswept zones over men exposing themselves in the open, but of one will over another weaker will.' Hamilton, courtly, brave, intelligent, a writer of sweet prose, was a poor commander at Gallipoli, weak even. It wasn't that he didn't understand modern war. He didn't *want* to understand it: to do so would be a betrayal of the human qualities he held dear, an admission that the world of his youth had changed. The old guard was suspicious of citizen and dominion armies and many clung to this prejudice throughout the war, much like unionists forced to work with scabs.

The French generals at the outbreak of war were a touch older on average than their British counterparts, and more reactionary. They believed in attack: that was about the extent of their theory. Their plan, in the event of a German invasion, was to rush east, into their lost province of Lorraine. Charles de Gaulle was there when this happened in August, 1914. 'With affected calm,' he wrote, 'the [French] officers let themselves be killed standing up, some obstinate platoons stuck their bayonets in their rifles, bugles sounded the charge, isolated heroes made fantastic leaps, but all to no purpose. In an instant it had become clear that not all the courage in the world could withstand this fire.' De Gaulle, a soldier in the line, knew at once that a machine gun spitting out 500 rounds a minute could kill a lot of character. The French went to war dressed for Napoleon: turned-back blue greatcoats and red trousers. Eventually they turned to horizon blue uniforms, which still left them a little more conspicuous than the British in khaki and the Germans in field grey.

Before the Great War was over it would throw up 'modern' men, notably the Canadian Arthur Currie and the Australian John Monash. But in 1916, and even though it had seen what machine guns and howitzers could do to men advancing in extended lines, the British army was still running on Victorian and Edwardian values. Among these were courage and high moral purpose, and also cronyism, rivalries that sometimes had a feline edge, and patronage. Birdwood and Ian Hamilton were 'Kitchener men'; Hubert Gough (commander of the Reserve Army) and Haking were 'Haig men'.

HAIG WAS FOREVER saying that he liked 'straight' men, yet he had worked patronage more deftly than most all through his career. His best patron was King George V, who sometimes put aside the constitutional niceties to support him. The two men were clearly comfortable with each other. 'No-one would have described

George V as an intellectual,' the historian Robert Rhodes James wrote, 'indeed he would have been outraged by such a slur, but he was no fool.' The same things might have been said of Haig. Both were men of simple tastes and a rigid sense of the proprieties. Neither possessed much curiosity. Both could keep their nerve. Both thought the side that showed the most character would win the war. Both were suspicious of 'clever' men like Winston Churchill and David Lloyd George and of liberal thought generally. The King had trouble with spelling and punctuation. Haig wrote with economy and a cold clarity, often reducing an argument to three or four numbered points, but he was inarticulate of speech. Haig and the King exchanged 'secret' letters throughout the war. When in 1915 Haig was intriguing to have Sir John French dumped as commander-in-chief on the western front 'for the sake of the empire', Gough and Haking were looking after *their* patron. Both had been to see the King and told him that French was unfit, which he undoubtedly was.

HAKING WENT TO war in 1914 as a brigade commander and was soon wounded. Before the war he had lectured on tactics at the staff college and written a book, *Company Training*. Haking was the son of a clergyman and passages of his book could have been taken from a homily. Haking was concerned with the battle going on in men's hearts: the struggle to go forward when one's instincts were saying it was best to flee. The tone of the book was cool but the message was unmistakeable: attack was everything; attack was the way to victory. Haking even argued that if the attackers were weaker than the defenders, the attackers 'will win as sure as there is a sun in the heavens'.

Haking's book was read and reprinted during the Great War, probably because, for a few years anyway, it was somewhere near majority opinion. By 1918 majority opinion was closer to the theories of Monash. The true role of infantry, Monash was to write, 'was not to expend itself on heroic physical effort, nor to wither away under merciless machine-gun fire, nor to impale itself on hostile bayonets, nor to tear itself to pieces in hostile entanglements . . . but, on the contrary, to advance under the maximum possible protection of the maximum possible array of mechanical resources'. Monash came from another place and, when it came to war, he was no mystic.

Haking was fifty-four at the time of Fromelles. After nearly two years he didn't appear to understand that the Germans had thought about tactics much more intelligently than he had. They were on the ridges: at Aubers, at Pozières above the Somme, at Messines and Passchendaele in Belgium. They could see the British and French on the flats. They had lots of howitzers and machine guns; they had built concrete blockhouses and bunkers and galleries. They could be tossed off those ridges only by superior firepower. Haking seemed to believe they could be tossed off by force of character.

Haking, now promoted to command of the British 1st Division, was involved in the attack on Aubers Ridge in May, 1915. The preliminary bombardment was too light. When it 'lifted' to the support trenches the Germans rushed back to their machine guns in the frontline and shot down Haking's troops as they left their trenches. In a few minutes the attack had failed. Several generals told Haig, who was then commanding the 1st Army, that fresh assaults in daylight would fail. Haking argued to push on. Haig agreed with him. An Indian brigade was sent in and lost 1000 men in a few minutes.

In *Goodbye to All That* Robert Graves, who was in Haking's division, tells of the general going around the survivors, shaking hands with tears in his eyes. Graves quotes a sergeant saying: 'Bloody lot of use that is: busts up his bloody division, and then weeps over what's bloody left.'

The attack was called off. The British and Indians in the 1st Army had taken 11,600 casualties for no gain. The Germans may have lost less than 1000. The lesson was obvious. These attacks were pointless unless the British could bring up more heavy guns firing high-explosive shells. Eighteen-pounder field guns firing shrapnel could not be relied upon to cut wire.

Haking was promoted to command a corps and four months after Aubers Ridge he had charge of the reserve divisions at the battle around the slag heaps of Loos, south of Aubers Ridge, where the British used poison gas for the first time. Haking sent up two of his divisions on the second day. Both were made up of volunteers from Kitchener's New Army. They had never been in action before. Somehow they ended up marching on the Germans, without covering fire, as if carrying out a parade-ground drill. The German machine gunners, less than a mile away, couldn't believe what they were seeing. They shot down Haking's troops without risk. The casualties in Haking's two divisions came to about 8000, or roughly half the men involved.

Loos dragged on for a fortnight or so. By then the British had run up more than 40,000 casualties, including eight generals, Rudyard Kipling's son, and Harold Macmillan, a future British prime minister, wounded in the head and shot through the right hand, so that decades later people who did not know about his war service would make fun of his weak handshake.

Robert Graves was there too, aged twenty. In *Goodbye to All That* he tells of a brother-officer who whistled for his platoon, which had gone forward twenty yards, to resume its advance. No-one moved. The officer jumped up and waved. No movement.

'You bloody cowards,' the officer shouted, 'are you leaving me to go on alone?'

His sergeant, his shoulder broken, gasped: 'Not cowards, sir. Willing enough. But they're all f---ing dead!' A machine gun had caught them as they rose to the first whistle.

Loos was a defeat, proof of the power of the machine guns and the insanity of attackers parading in front of them as though they were at Waterloo. Haig had said five months before Loos that the machine gun was 'a much over-rated weapon'. He was being forced to change his mind. He had brought up cavalry at Loos in the hope of sending it through a gap. Cavalry in its traditional form had no place near machine guns. Here Haig would never change. One criticism of him, made so often that it has become a cliché, is that he lacked imagination. This needs qualification. All through the war he dreamed of cavalrymen galloping through gaps in the German lines.

LOOS, AND PARTICULARLY the massacre of Haking's troops, also demonstrated that some British staff work was poor, and this went all the way to Sir John French. Just before the battle he moved to a château that had no telephone line to Haig, who was running the battle. Wounded men from Loos went home and said they had been asked to do too much. Politicians in London began talking about a string of defeats – Neuve Chapelle, Aubers, Loos – and began wondering about the men who were running the war for them, particularly Kitchener and French.

Haig felt that French had taken too long to hand over the reserve divisions to him at Loos. Haig became furious when French wrote a dispatch in which he claimed to have handed the reserves to Haig hours earlier than he had. Haig had been writing in his diary that French had an 'unreasoning brain', that his temperament was too flighty for command on the western front. Now he began openly to campaign against his one-time friend and benefactor, and French had no hope. Haig was aloof and unloved, mainly because he allowed hardly anyone to know him, and was laced up so tightly that in all his photographs he seems to be holding his breath. His speech was often a succession of grunts. He didn't much understand political life and looked down on it as a calling. But he knew how to run an intrigue. He knew exactly where to plant doubts, what to say and what not to say.

King George V visited France a month after the opening of Loos. Haig told the King that French was obstinate and conceited and that he had handled the reserves badly at Loos. 'I therefore thought strongly, that, for the sake of the Empire, French ought to be removed. I, personally, was ready to do my duty in any capacity, and of course would serve under anyone who was chosen for his military skill to be C. in C.' When he said that, he was making a job application that he knew would be approved. The King told Haig that he had seen Gough and Haking that afternoon and, according to Haig's diary, they had imparted 'startling truths of French's unfitness for the command'. The King had also seen Sir William Robertson, French's chief-of-staff, who had told him that his commander's mind was never the same for two consecutive minutes.

French had little leverage. Defeat, as someone said, is an orphan, and French throughout 1915 had lurched from one setback to another. Kitchener was implicated in all of them, and Gallipoli too, and most Cabinet members were more disenchanted with him than they were with French, but Kitchener couldn't be sacked because he was a public idol. French was simply a soldier with a ruddy face, a white moustache and a skittish manner who seemed to fail a lot. Asquith sacked him in December and replaced him with Haig.

French had been unnerved by the destruction of the seven divisions of regulars he had taken to France in 1914 for a war that many thought would be over by Christmas. He often went to the hospitals to talk to the wounded; he couldn't come to terms with the scale of the killing or the frightful wounds caused by shells. He belonged to the old colonial army and the hunting field, to good times in the mess and restless natives outside. He didn't really understand what was happening in France. Haig hardly ever visited the wounded. His diary is a cold place, hardly about the real war at all. Seldom does he show any warmth for the young men from Manchester and Bendigo and Calgary who, thirty miles away, are dying in the mud for him. There is a kingly quality to him: he seems to imply that it is their duty to be there, at the grubby end, and his to be here, running a political salon. Haig's son would later explain that he believed his father felt it was his 'duty' to refrain from going to casualty clearing stations because the visits made him physically ill.

THERE IS NO doubt Haig was better qualified to command than French. He was a more methodical soldier and, above all, steady and predictable. Haig never became fluttery. He didn't torture himself with doubts, probably because he saw the world in monochrome. He had defined the task: Germany had to be beaten in the main theatre. That was the way, the only way, to win the war. Gallipoli, Salonika, Palestine, Italy: these were the dreams of the feeble-minded. He seemed to believe that God had put him in charge. He would therefore not be deflected by the antics of politicians who had merely been anointed by the people. What he couldn't quite see was that this had to be a 'political' war. It touched everyone in Britain in a way other wars had not. It could not be left to the professionals like some punitive expedition up the Nile. Of course the politicians would meddle in it; they would have been derelict if they had not.

As French fell so did Archibald Murray, the Chief of the Imperial General Staff. Robertson, Haig's co-conspirator, replaced Murray. Robertson, known as 'Wully', was an exotic in the British army. He was the son of a village tailor and had worked as a domestic servant before enlisting as a trooper. Eleven years later he became an officer and after that his rise was relentless. Like Haig, he wrote with directness and clarity and was a hopeless speaker. Unlike Haig, he dropped his aitches. Like Haig, he was a 'westerner': he had no time for sideshows away from France. Unlike Murray, he was not going to be Kitchener's flunkey and obtained a piece of paper from Asquith that said just that.

Robertson became the main adviser to the government with direct access to Cabinet. He was a hard man, particularly when it came to dealing with politicians, whom he saw as amateur strategists, but he tended to defer to Haig, always treating him gently. Anyone reading letters between the two might assume that Robertson was working for Haig.

HAKING MIGHT HAVE failed all through 1915 but so did many British generals. Haking remained one of Haig's favourites. His failures were of the best sort. When an attack failed with light casualties there was a suspicion at GHQ that someone may not have tried too hard and a general or brigadier might be sent home for failing to show enough of the offensive spirit. On the other hand blood sacrifices with long casualty lists were seen as evidence of enthusiasm. Haking, like Hubert Gough, was known as a 'thruster'. Haig liked thrusters.

Haking is a difficult man to find. He didn't tell much about himself. The *Who's Who* entry he submitted didn't mention his place of birth, his parents or his education. Bean called him 'experienced and distinguished'. Philip Game, a regular officer, served in a division under Haking. In a letter to his wife late in 1915 Game said he didn't trust Haking 'halfway across the road'. Two days later Game told her that Haking was 'a bad man, though I think a good soldier'. Ten days later Game called Haking a 'vindictive bully'. Game won the Distinguished Service Order and the *Legion d'Honneur* during the war and was five times mentioned in dispatches. As Sir Philip Game he became Governor of New South Wales and in 1932 reluctantly dismissed the Premier, Jack Lang. Game, a liberal, admired some of Lang's ideals. If many disagreed with what Game called his 'assassin's stroke', they also saw the governor as a man of integrity.

IN JULY, 1916, Haking commanded XI Corps, the northernmost corps of the 1st Army, on the flats below Aubers Ridge and Fromelles. He was confident that he could succeed in an attack on the Sugarloaf, pin down the Germans and prevent them sending reinforcements south to the battle of the Somme. In the previous month he had been confident about another similar, if smaller, attack he had thought up for Boar's Head, a German salient two miles south-west of the Sugarloaf. This, like the coming battle of Fromelles, was a feint. It too was to stop the Germans sending reserves to the Somme, where the British build-up was becoming obvious.

Two Sussex battalions made the attack on June 29, when the Australians of the 5th Division were finding billets behind the lines and, being fresh from Gallipoli and Egypt, thinking that they had arrived at a kinder place. Two Sussex battalions: here was the first flaw in Haking's plan of attack. Why would the Germans think a charge by less than 2000 men constituted anything but a gesture? The attack went in on June 29. The British artillery shot badly. 'Come on Sussex,' the Germans shouted as they opened up with their machine guns. The Sussex were not short on courage: they came on all right and briefly held parts of the German frontline. Then they had to retreat. When it was over the Sussex had lost 1153 men, a shocking casualty rate for a two-battalion attack. A communiqué dressed up the slaughter as a 'successful raid'.

Edmund Blunden, the poet and critic, then nineteen, watched the madness of Boar's Head. The salient was to be 'bitten off', he was told – 'no doubt to render the maps in the châteaux of the mighty more symmetrical'. The German machine gunners had been presented with 'hideously simple targets'; most of the men died against the uncut wire. Blunden thought the communiqué a travesty. A few days later he passed a lance-corporal making a cup of tea. A shell fell. Blunden went back to find the lance-corporal reduced to gobbets of blackening flesh, the earth wall sotted with blood and flesh, and an eye under the duckboard. 'At this moment, while we looked with dreadful fixity at so isolated a horror, the lance-corporal's brother came round the traverse.'

Most of the Australians taking part in Haking's new attack towards Fromelles knew nothing of his debacle at Boar's Head.

As the 5th Australian Division took over the frontline on the plain below Fromelles the composition of the two Anzac corps also changed. The 1st, 2nd and 4th divisions left the area for the Somme and the sorrows of Pozières Ridge. These three divisions became the new I Anzac Corps under General Birdwood, who also had administrative control over all Australian forces. The 5th and the New Zealand Division (which had gone into the line near Armentières in May) now became II Anzac Corps under Lieutenant-General Alexander Godley. The 5th was made up of three brigades, each of four battalions. Brigadier-General Elliott's 15th Brigade was on the right, looking at the Sugarloaf; the 14th Brigade was in the centre and the 8th on the left. About one quarter of the men in the 14th and 15th brigades and most of the officers had fought at Gallipoli. The 8th had never been under fire anywhere.

The three Australian divisions heading for the Somme had fought no big engagements during their stay in the line near Armentières but they raided the German lines often in June. The idea was to grab prisoners, identify the enemy units opposite, create havoc by killing as many Germans as possible during a few minutes of madness and bring back any papers they might be carrying. The raiders carried revolvers rather than rifles and knobkerries, short clubs with nails or bolts driven horizontally through the head, so that they looked like instruments that hang on the walls of torture chambers.

THE 5TH DIVISION, unlike the other three that were headed for the Somme, hadn't been in France long enough to launch any raids or even to discover where the holes and horrors lay in no-man's land. Its 17,800 men had taken over the frontline on the nights of July 10 and 11, just as Haking and others were cobbling up the scheme to attack towards Fromelles. Captain A. D. Ellis, who later wrote the history of the 5th Division, walked up the sap towards the frontline when he became aware of a 'novel smell' that he later realised was common to all trenches on the western front. 'It is a mixture of damp earth, high explosive, and perhaps of other things.' Godley handed the 5th Division over to Haking for the attack, which was to be over the very ground where the British, and Haking, had failed in the battle of Aubers Ridge the previous year. Why, someone might well have asked, was an attack going to succeed this time?

Sergeant Walter 'Jimmy' Downing arrived at the front and noticed the graves of Englishmen everywhere. The inscriptions on the little crosses had almost faded but he made out dates in 1914 and 1915. Charles Bean, Australia's official war correspondent, wrote that by the time the 5th Division came to the front the stories of Aubers Ridge and Loos (when a British division again attacked towards Fromelles) had been almost forgotten: '. . . it remained only in the vague rumour that, quiet though the sector now was, certain famous British regiments spoke of it with dreadful memories of some futile and tragic attack.'

Godley apparently had no qualms about what was happening. He was a robotic soldier, tall and thin-lipped, made for drill and good order and peacetime. He was prickly and hidebound and thought all citizen-soldiers amateurs. His main interests seemed to be horses, hunting, fishing and garden parties. He took orders without question and expected his subordinates to do the same. On

Gallipoli he had developed the skill of somehow not being seen to be responsible for anything that didn't turn out well, which was most of the things he touched.

Birdwood and White did have qualms about Fromelles. Two days before the battle White said: 'I hate these unprepared little shows. What do we do? We may deceive the enemy for two days; and, after that, he knows perfectly well that it is not a big attack, and that we are not in earnest there.'

HAKING'S PLAN FOR the attack now went through a series of hurried changes. Haking's immediate superior, Sir Charles Monro, commander of the 1st Army, kept changing his mind about whether there should be an infantry assault. McCay seemed pleased that his would be the first Australian division to make a big attack in France. This may have caused him to brush aside the risks involved. After the battle Pompey Elliott wrote home that McCay wanted to lead the first Australian attack in France 'and so get a big splash'. The other players, Haig and his staff at GHQ, were not only far away but also preoccupied with the battle of the Somme. Fromelles was always a sideshow and the staff at GHQ didn't appear to share Haking's confidence that the attack would succeed.

On July 5, a fortnight before the attack went in at Fromelles, Haig was confident of a breakthrough on the Somme. He wanted his northern armies to prepare to break into the German lines opposite them. Monro and the commander of the 2nd Army, Sir Herbert Plumer, thought the most prospective place for an attack was where their two armies met, roughly in front of Fromelles. On July 8 Monro asked Haking to draw up a scheme for an attack. Haking didn't want merely to break into the German lines on the plain; he wanted to surge on, through the German support lines, through all the concrete fortifications that had been thrown up in the past year, and on to Aubers Ridge itself, where he would take the villages of Fromelles and Aubers. Monro next day rejected the plan, not because it was starry-eyed but because he thought capturing Aubers would not be much help if the British broke through on the Somme.

The British didn't break through there. Haig had been too optimistic, as he so often was, and he didn't know the true extent of his casualties. And now there was another problem on the Somme: the Germans were reinforcing their front there with troops drawn from the north. The Germans had to be pinned down in the north. Haig's staff now thought an attack at Fromelles should be 'an artillery demonstration' only with the idea of making the Germans think an infantry attack was imminent. Then, around July 13, Monro and the GHQ staff decided the infantry should be part of the assault. Haking was not to try for Aubers Ridge. He was simply to break into the frontline and tell the Germans, in effect, that they could not afford to thin it out. The attack was set down for July 17. Haking would use the borrowed 5th Australian Division (Godley's II Anzac Corps was then part of Plumer's 2nd Army) plus two divisions of his own. There would be no secrecy. The preliminary bombardment was to make the Germans think an infantry attack was coming. This was going to make things particularly hard for the foot soldiers.

Haking decided to attack on a 6000-yard front. Then he realised that he didn't have the artillery support and ammunition he had hoped for. He reduced the front to 4000 yards and the attacking force to two divisions, the Australians and the British 61st Division, a territorial outfit that was under strength. Each division would be supported by two divisional artilleries (in the case of the Australians the guns of the 5th and 4th divisions) plus about thirty heavy guns and several batteries of trench mortars. The attackers were to go no further than the German support lines.

McCay learned of the new plan on July 14, which meant he had just two-and-a-half days to prepare his division for a major attack. And his men had just two-and-a-half days to lay duckboards and tramways to the front and to bring up rifle and machine-gun ammunition, bombs, bundles of sandbags, scaling ladders, hundreds of picks and shovels, duckboards and light bridges. Telephone cables had to be buried and regimental aid posts set up.

Artillery batteries recently brought up had to find firing positions. It was all too frantic: the men would be exhausted before they hopped the bags.

Haking thought the support trenches would be found about 100 to 150 yards behind the German frontline. There were four battalions in British and Australian brigades. Haking was so confident that he thought only two battalions in each brigade would be needed for the assault; the other two battalions were not to be committed without his consent, although some of these men could be used to provide carrying parties. McCay must have been confident too: he apparently thought his men should rush across no-man's land two yards apart. This would only make sense if the Germans could not man their machine guns. McCay now issued an order that looked innocuous enough but which was to matter greatly. The first wave was to take the German frontline. The second wave would then pass through the first and go on to take the support trenches. Then the first wave was to also go on to the supports.

ON JULY 16, THE day before the assault was supposed to begin, Major-General Richard Butler, the deputy chief of the general staff, visited 1st Army headquarters and told Monro, Plumer and Haking that there was now no urgent need for the attack. Haig, he said, did not wish it to go ahead unless the commanders on the spot were satisfied they had enough artillery and ammunition to hold the enemy trenches they were going to capture. GHQ clearly didn't believe in the attack or didn't think Haking had the means to pull it off. Haking was 'most emphatic' he had the resources; he was 'quite confident' of success; he thought he had enough ammunition to put infantrymen in the German trenches and keep them there. Monro said he was satisfied the attack should go in. Monro and Haking said the troops' morale would suffer if the attack was called off. Butler agreed it could go ahead.

Then heavy rain began to fall, which meant the artillerymen had difficulty registering on their targets. Butler now returned to

Monro's headquarters. He said that Monro had the power to postpone or cancel the attack, either because of the bad weather or indeed for any other reason. A political game seemed to be going on. GHQ didn't really think the attack a good idea, but it wanted Monro to say so.

Early on the morning of the 17th, the day set down for the assault, a heavy mist lay over the front. Haking wrote to Monro that, with reluctance, he would have to postpone the attack. Did Monro wish him to carry it out the following day? 'It is important with these new troops that this information should be given to me as early as possible, so that I can issue such instructions as will minimise any loss of moral [sic] owing to postponement.'

This was nonsense, although Haking probably believed it. The men of the Australian and British divisions were tired out from carrying ammunition and ladders along narrow and wet communication trenches; they were pleased to hear of the postponement. They had been worried about the haste with which the operation was being rushed forward. Haking was out of touch. A few days earlier he had discovered that some of the gunners in the heavy batteries had never fired in France before.

Monro's attitude now changed. He refused Haking permission to attack on the following day. Monro told Haig he wanted to postpone the attack. Back came this dispatch from GHQ:

> The Commander-in-Chief wishes the special operation mentioned in the above letter to be carried out as soon as possible, weather permitting, provided always that General Sir Charles Monro is satisfied that the conditions are favourable, and that the resources at his disposal, including ammunition, are adequate both for the preparation and the execution of the enterprise.

The generals were playing with words. Haig, as the British official historian put it, 'did nothing to relieve the 1st Army commander of his responsibility'. Yet he left him with an escape: Monro could call it off if he thought his resources inadequate. We really don't know what was happening here, although we know army and corps commanders didn't like to be thought timid. Monro didn't take the escape route offered. The attack was on for the 19th. The artillery bombardment would begin at 11 am; the infantry would go over at 6 pm, three hours before dusk.

3

A night of horror and doubt

Jimmy Downing's battalion, the 57th, part of Pompey Elliott's 15th Brigade, spent the night before the attack sleeping in a mill on the outskirts of the village of Sailly-sur-la-Lys. Downing, a law student at Melbourne University, had tried to enlist shortly after war broke out but was rejected eight times because he was too short. For his ninth attempt Downing had friends hoist him up by the shoulders while weights were tied to his feet. He then went off to be measured before he reverted to his normal height.

Downing woke up at the mill and didn't think too much about what might happen that day. 'One accepts the immediate present in the army. We woke with the birds, reminded of friendly magpies in the morning back in Australia. Here were only twitterings under the eaves, but at least it was a cheerful sound, pleasant on a lazy summer morning when the ripening corn was splashed with poppies, and the clover was pink, and the cornflowers blue under the hedges.'

At the mill old women and small girls were selling gingerbread and sweets laced with cognac. At 1.45 pm the battalion moved off for the front.

Shelling commenced. These were the days of long and casual bombard-ments. Labourers were hoeing in the mangold fields. Stooping men and women watched us pass, without ceasing their work. It may have been courage, or stolidity, or the numbness of the peasant bound to the soil, or else necessity, that held the sad tenacious people here in such an hour of portent. Their old faces were inscrutable. They tilled the fields on the edge of the flames, under the arching trajectory of shells. Bees hummed in the clear and drowsy sunshine. There was little smoke about the cottages, where the creepers were green . . . We battalions came to the four cross-roads where there were trenches in the corn, by a crucifix of wood in a damaged brick shrine . . . Late in the afternoon we were ordered forward. From his crucifix the Man of Sorrows watched our going. One wondered if His mild look was bent especially on those marked for death that day.

Downing headed down a communications trench leading to the front. He saw a bald man with a red moustache lying dead on a duckboard. The sap had been blown up in parts; splintered wood and iron poked from burnt earth. Downing dashed through a shrapnel barrage to the Australian front trench. A sad-faced man was sitting beside a body. He said: 'Sniper – my brother – keep under the parapet.'

The 59th and 60th battalions were already in the line. They were the two assaulting battalions for the 15th Brigade. Downing's 57th was the reserve. The order for the assaulting battalions to attack was passed along the line: 'Over the bags in five minutes . . . over the bags in five minutes.' Then: 'Over you go.' The 60th went over first, carrying bags of bombs, scaling ladders, picks and shovels.

THE AUSTRALIAN FRONTLINE was a sandbagged breastwork, built eight to nine feet above the plain, which itself was only about fifty feet above sea level. Traverses were notched into the breastwork every ten to fifteen yards, giving the line a zigzag look. The ground here was too wet for trenches and the heavy clay, about a foot or so down, turned blue and sticky when damp. The support trench, also a breastwork, stood 300 yards back. The road to the front was a series of conventional communication trenches, narrow and muddy-bottomed, running at right angles to the frontline. Ammunition and reinforcements went one way along these trenches, wounded the other. The Germans could see most of this system from the heights of Aubers Ridge.

The German frontline, 120 to 450 yards away, was also a breast-work but more elaborate, eight-feet high and up to twelve-feet thick. The 16th Bavarian Reserve Infantry Regiment, Hitler's regiment, held the breastwork in front of Elliott's 15th Brigade and the two British brigades to his right. In this section of the front alone – it was only about 1500 yards – the Bavarians had built seventy-five shelters into the parapet, each protected by nine to twelve inches of concrete. The Germans were good at what came to be called defence in depth. Immediately behind the frontline were roomy dugouts with about five feet of earth for a roof. Ten yards back again were deep chambers, twenty feet down in the clay, lit by electricity and kept reasonably dry by pumps. Troops sheltering in these were pretty much safe from heavy artillery. The Germans had dug support trenches 100 yards behind the front but these had been abandoned after becoming waterlogged. The support troops were now 250 to 400 yards behind the frontline, in wrecked farmhouses and strong points reinforced with concrete.

The ground at Fromelles was a typical German defensive position. Aubers Ridge was only 120-feet high but that was high enough for the Germans to see everything on the plain. The German front ran back to the ridge in tier after tier. It was formidable.

THE ARTILLERY BOMBARDMENT began at 11 am on a fine and clear day and Elliott was up at the frontline with his men. 'Boys,' he said, 'you won't find a German in those trenches when you get there.' He may have been trying to make his men feel better. Or he may have truly believed that the artillery was doing what Haking said it could do. This was the first time Elliott had watched a bombardment in France. He had seen nothing like this on Gallipoli: hundreds of guns firing, great tails of earth and sandbags and the doll-like bodies of men soaring high above the German front, holes opening up in the parapet, smoke and dust and shrieking shells. And Elliott didn't know about those deep German dugouts just behind the front. Hell didn't reach down there. Men would come out of them coated with dust and shaken, but still able to fire machine guns.

The barrage was working in some places and failing in others. The gaps in the German breastwork looked impressive. What the gunners didn't know was that of those seventy-five concrete shelters in the front of the 16th Bavarian Regiment, sixty remained intact. The wire was cut in some places and intact at others. Artillery observers were worried about the Sugarloaf redoubt: after hours of shelling it didn't seem badly damaged. Neither side did much counter-battery work – that is, firing on the enemy's gun positions. Both aimed nearly all their shells at infantry.

The German gunners waited several hours until the British and Australian lines were thick with troops. Then, around 2.15 pm, they began to bombard the Australian and British front and support lines, smothering them in smoke, catching the troops packed into trenches, blowing up piles of ammunition, cutting telephone wires and starting small fires. The pattern in allied attacks on the western front was for a shambles to begin once the attackers reached the German frontline and communications broke down. This time the shambles began at the jump-off points.

Shrapnel burst over the 15th Brigade on the right of the Australian line. The 14th Brigade, in the centre, and the 8th, on the left, suffered worse. The 8th was also hit by allied shells, which were dropping short.

The allied bombardment sounded better than it was. Private Leslie Martin, a machine gunner in the 8th Brigade, wrote home to his brother, Jack: 'The row was deafening. I put wadding in my ears while we were down in the supports waiting to go forward and take our place in the fighting.' Martin saw dead and wounded everywhere when he reached the parapet. 'I had to sit on top of a dead man as there was no picking or choosing where to sit, for if you dallied at all you were likely to catch one.' Shortly afterwards Martin caught one – two actually. Fragments of shell hit him in the leg and the tongue, 'which stung a good deal at the time'. He saw a shell-burst lift two men six feet in the air 'and they simply rolled back dead, killed instantly'. He saw a man die in a few minutes after having both legs blown off.

Martin was twenty-six, a warehouseman from Dulwich Hill, Sydney. And now he saw something that in those days was little written about: shell-shock. The military and its medical arm understood men carried back soaked in blood: these were wounded. The army didn't yet understand psychological trauma, panic attacks and catatonia. Martin saw these things at Fromelles and understood.

> One or two of the chaps got shell shock and others got really frightened. It was piteous to see them. One great big chap got away as soon as he reached the firing line and could not be found when he was wanted. I saw him in the morning in a dug-out, he was white with fear and shaking like a leaf. One of our lieutenants got shell shock, and he literally cried like a child. Some that I saw carried down out of the firing line were struggling and calling for their mother, while others were blabbering sentences one could not make out. For one to get shell shock it is worse than a wound, a wound will heal, but a chap when he has lost control of his nerves takes a lot before he has got mastery of them again, and it is doubtful if he would ever be able to be relied on again. It is a thing everyone has to fight against, and if he gives in at all he is practically done for as a fighter.

The German artillery also hit the British 61st Division hard and this mattered greatly because its battalions were under strength at about 550 men each, compared with around 900 in the Australian force. The two assaulting battalions in the 184th Brigade had the hardest task in the whole attack. They had to take the Sugarloaf. They lost 140 men to artillery fire before they set out.

Many Australians who fought at Fromelles afterwards talked of spies who had somehow passed Haking's plans to the Germans. There was talk of farm horses of a certain colour being put in certain pastures as a signal to German pilots. There had to be spies, the

Australians contended, because the Germans seemed to foresee everything the Allies did. The Germans didn't need spies. From Aubers Ridge they could see everything that happened in the allied lines. They knew an attack was coming when on July 18 they saw men bringing up boxes of hand-grenades and rolled mats that were used to cross barbed wire.

The Germans simply read the script that had been thrust under their eyes. They set out to destroy the attack before it began. Had they owned more guns – they had less than half as many as the British and Australians – they might have done so.

THE AUSTRALIAN LINE, spread out over about a mile, ran from right to left like this:

Brigade:	15th	14th	8th
Commander:	Elliott	Pope	Tivey
Assaulting battalions:	59th, 60th	53rd, 54th	31st, 32nd
Support and 'carrying' battalion:	58th	55th	30th
Reserve battalion:	57th	56th	29th

The 15th had to cover up to 400 yards to reach the German line; if the allied artillery failed, its men would be exposed to flanking fire from the Sugarloaf. The 14th had to cover about 250 yards and the 8th about 120. The 8th were exposed to a German salient to the north, outside the battle zone, called the Tadpole.

At 5.45 pm, when the bombardment of the German frontline still had fifteen minutes to run, the men of the 59th and 60th battalions climbed over the parapet into no-man's land and headed off through the long grass towards oblivion. Thirty yards out the 59th came under rifle fire from the Sugarloaf. Then a machine gun opened up. The battalion moved through the orchard of an old farm, heading towards a line of willow stumps and the Laies ditch. The German fire grew heavier as the allied artillery lifted its bombardment off the German frontline. The Australians peered through the smoke haze and saw Germans manning the parapet. Nothing was as it should be. Australians fell all along the line. Lieutenant-Colonel E. A. Harris, the battalion commander, sent his second-in-command, Major Bert Layh, back to tell Elliott that the battalion was pinned down halfway to the German line. Then Harris came down with shell-shock. Meanwhile wounded from the 60th had returned to the Australian lines to say that their battalion had broken into the German breastwork. Elliott concluded that the attack was succeeding and ordered the 59th to make another attempt.

The attack was failing, quickly and horribly. The waves of the 60th crossed the Laies and came under heavy fire, much of it from the Sugarloaf. A few from the 59th may have reached the German parapet. Mostly the survivors of the 59th and 60th were out beyond the German wire, in shell holes or hastily dug scrapes. Most of the officers had been killed or wounded.

Lieutenant Tom Kerr of the 60th got close enough to the enemy line to see Germans 'standing out shoulder high . . . looking as if they were wondering what was coming next'. He lay in a shell hole and decided to send a message back. The only paper that could be found was the fly-leaf from a New Testament carried by a private. Kerr wrote: 'Here with 4 men, a few yards from parapet. Must have reinforcements. Useless going on without.' No reinforcements came. Kerr and his three men crawled back after midnight. Kerr had been wounded in the shoulder and the ribs. He refused to leave the battlefield.

Major Tom Elliott, second-in-command of the 60th, was a twenty-two-year-old Duntroon graduate whom Pompey Elliott (no kin) regarded as a brilliant soldier. Pompey wanted Tom to stay at brigade headquarters and help him. Tom wanted to go with his battalion and went. He died from a wound to the chest. Geoff McCrae, the poet and architecture student who led the 60th, died from a bullet to the neck only eighty yards from the Australian trench. That morning he had written:

Dearest Mother Father and Helen,

Today I lead my Battalion in our assault on the German lines and I pray God I may come through alright and bring honour to our name. If not I will at least have laid down my life for you and my country which is the greatest privilege one can ask for.
Farewell dear people the hour approacheth.

Love from
Geoff.

Pompey Elliott had written to his wife, Kate, the same day.

. . . we hope to so pound the enemy's trenches that we won't have much loss at all . . . I am going to watch the assault from our front line. I cannot stay back here. If mischance comes I can only say God bless and keep you my own dear little true wife and helpmate and [may] our dear little pets comfort you always . . . My will is in the safe at the office.

Tom Elliott wrote to his sister. 'Some operations are pending . . . Don't worry about me, I'll be alright.'

Pompey Elliott wrote to McCrae's parents two days after the battle. Elliott told them he believed 'from the commencement that an attack as such was doomed to failure for we had no sufficient reserves & the artillery Bombardment was far from being sufficient'. He likened the assault to the charge at the Nek on Gallipoli, but 'on a tenfold scale'. In his sloping handwriting with its dramatic downstrokes Elliott explained that Australians searching for wounded in no-man's land had found McCrae's body. 'He was quite dead kneeling on one knee with his pistol pointing towards the enemy.'

Two days later Elliott wrote again. The body had been brought in and buried. 'An examination . . . disclosed conclusively that he was shot through the head . . . & evidently died instantly as he knelt behind the lines directing operations.' Geoff was 'a true soldier & gentleman. The only fault I have ever had to find with him was that he was too gentle & kindly & hated to *tell off* those who thoroughly deserved it but this fault (if fault it was) was rapidly being remedied as he grew older & more experienced.'

McCrae's father could not reconcile himself to the death of a son he had loved so dearly and who had promised so much. For years afterwards he wrote to Elliott, seeking such small details as the location of the farmhouse in which Geoff had spent his last night and the name of his batman. The McCraes left their son's bedroom as it was and placed his military cap on the pillow.

IN THE CENTRE the two assaulting battalions of the 14th Brigade had to cover only about half as much ground as the 15th to reach the German line. Two hundred and fifty yards was still a long way across open ground in daylight, and part of the 53rd Battalion, which was on the right of the line, was hit by the same fire from the Sugarloaf that had stopped, and was now wiping out, the two assaulting battalions of the 15th. Both battalions of the 14th took rifle and machine-gun fire from the front. The allied artillery had blown gaps in the German breastwork but it had neither demolished it nor 'frightened' the Germans still alive, as Haking predicted it would.

The two battalions of the 14th nevertheless stormed the front-line. The first wave stayed there briefly to flush Germans out of their dugouts. The three waves following went on to look for their objective, the German support lines. Here was a success, of sorts, but the battle had been going only thirty minutes and the toll of officers had been frightful. The men in the German lines were looking for someone to tell them what to do.

A German machine gunner killed Lieutenant-Colonel Ignatius Norris, a thirty-five-year-old Sydney barrister who was well liked by his men, as he went forward looking for the support trenches. His last words were: 'Here, I'm done, will somebody take my papers?' He had received Holy Communion from a Catholic priest that morning. His wife, along with his infant son, had several weeks earlier sailed to London to be near him. Captain Charles Arblaster, a twenty-one-year-old Duntroon graduate, found himself commanding the 53rd Battalion.

The 54th, commanded by Lieutenant-Colonel Walter Cass, a veteran of the Boer War and Gallipoli, suffered even worse. It lost all its company commanders and a string of junior officers in the first half-hour, many of them before the battalion had left its own lines. Cass had been shot twice in twenty minutes during the second battle of Krithia on Gallipoli. Nearly five hours passed before, shivering from the cold wind, he was put on a stretcher to be 'dressed & plugged up'. Now, fourteen months later, and unlike most of his brother officers, he had made the German frontline without a wound. Cass set up his temporary headquarters in a German dugout that had a table, an armchair, a stove, electric light, an electric bell and paper-covered walls decorated with gold moulding similar to that used on picture frames. His long night was just beginning.

Cass's men pushed on looking for the support trenches. They saw the white walls of a ruined farm ahead and passed ditches filled with water. Now they were perhaps 300 yards inside the German frontline. Where were these support trenches that they were supposed to occupy? Where were those lines that showed like veins on the aerial photographs? The truth began to soak in. There *was* no support line, not in the form of a trench system anyway. And these ditches half full of water? They were probably old trenches, perhaps from 1915. And the water? The Germans might have been using the old trenches as holding ponds for water pumped out of the deep dugouts on the frontline. So what were the men to do? They couldn't consolidate a position that didn't exist. They began building a new frontline, shovelling mud into sandbags alongside the farthest ditch. The mud was so heavy with clay that it sometimes had to be pushed off the spade by hand.

Meanwhile engineers were digging a sap across no-man's land and the 55th, the 'carrying' battalion, was bringing across sandbags and ammunition. The first wave, having cleared out the German frontline and sent prisoners back, moved on to help the men building the new frontline at the ditch.

ON THE LEFT the 8th Brigade had been badly shot up by the German artillery and 'drop shorts' from Australian guns while waiting to attack. The facts are unclear, but one of the assaulting battalions, the 31st, appears to have suffered hundreds of casualties from this. Lieutenant-Colonel Frederick Toll, commander of the 31st, was bleeding from a head wound but that didn't stop him leading his troops to the German line. What then happened to the men of the 31st and 32nd battalions was almost identical to what happened to the two battalions in the centre. The artillery had not done what it was supposed to do. As the men began to cross no-man's land they ran into rifle and machine-gun fire from the front and their left flank. Corporal Richard Kennedy of the 32nd wrote to his sister that the first thing he saw on emerging from an opening in the parapet 'was the man in front of me blown to atoms, and then on the ground hundreds of my mates dead and wounded . . . They were in all positions, and piled in heaps . . .' Kennedy was hit twice in the first forty yards, but crawled to the German lines and five hours later crawled back again. He ended up in a hospital in England where the bed linen was branded 'Chorlton House Workhouse'.

Many officers fell in no-man's land, but the two battalions took the German frontline, captured prisoners and watched other Germans fleeing across the grassland behind. The Australians moved on but couldn't find the support trench, mainly because it didn't exist. All they found were flooded ditches.

Toll left a few men in the old German frontline and went on. His men came upon a ditch filled with water to waist height and containing several dead Germans and one who was frantically alive. On a footbridge across the ditch an Australian soldier stood prodding at this German with a bayonet. The German would duck completely under the water, then at intervals bring his head out to say 'Officer'. He was rescued by an Australian lieutenant and sent back as a prisoner.

Toll sent a message back to his brigade commander, Brigadier-General Edwin Tivey: '6.30 pm. Four waves well over 200 yards beyond enemy's parapets. No enemy works found yet, so am digging in.' Accompanied by a lieutenant and a messenger Toll went on another 200 yards, looking for the support trenches, then returned. Shells started to land among his men and German troops appeared to be massing in front. Toll sensibly concluded that the position was too vulnerable. As dusk came he led the 31st back to the old German frontline. There was a chance it was at least defensible. Out in no-man's land wounded men from the assaulting and carrying battalions lay groaning and weeping in shell holes. Engineers began to dig a trench across no-man's land.

Private Les Martin, the machine gunner in the 8th Brigade, crossed no-man's land around this time. 'You could hear the moans of the wounded and dying wherever you went,' he said. He thought the German frontline 'much superior to ours'. Behind the German frontline he found himself 'floundering in muck and water in places up to our waist, other places it was just mud and took us all our time to get along'.

AT DUSK THE truth about the Australian attack at Fromelles went something like this. The artillery had failed to subdue the Germans and their machine guns. Haking had never possessed the means to demolish the German line. Elliott's attack on the right had failed. Those still unwounded in his two attacking battalions, and they were few, were pinned down in no-man's land. The attacks in the centre and on the left had succeeded, in the formal sense anyway. The infantrymen had reached their objectives. But could they hold them? Four battalions were digging in several hundred yards behind the old German frontline. Most of the officers in these battalions had been killed or wounded. The new line was not continuous; it amounted to four islands in a sea of Germans. Contact between the four battalions was either intermittent or non-existent. The men had followed orders and left the old German frontline unoccupied, except at the points where Cass and Toll had established themselves. This meant that the Germans could creep around the flanks of the 'islands', reoccupy their front breastwork and cut off the Australians. The islands were not good defensive positions anyway. They were being built up by filling sandbags with mud. There were no German support trenches to occupy. Here was a final truth: the British general staff had much to learn about the interpretation of aerial photographs.

Of course these truths were not apparent at dusk that night. The pattern in these battles was for divisional and corps commanders to begin to lose control the moment the infantry hopped the bags. Modern artillery killed at long range and this meant that headquarters had to be set up well back from the front. Modern artillery meant that the telephone lines to the front were invariably blown up. Modern artillery meant that the frontline was invariably wreathed in smoke, so that observers could only guess at what was happening. Brigadiers tried to work out what was happening from a mile or so behind the front (although Elliott at Fromelles was only 300 yards back); divisional commanders issued fresh orders from several miles further back; corps commanders were several miles back again. And Haig, the commander-in-chief? He might be twenty or thirty miles away. Misinformation flowed up this line and back down it. Everyone in the chain of command wanted to give the impression that they actually knew what was happening behind the smoke some of them couldn't even see. None wanted to be thought timid.

So the 'truths' that General McCay, the 5th Division commander, thought he saw around dusk were rather different to those above. He was entitled to think there was some chance of success. Pigeons from Cass and Toll had been his main informants. The messages they carried spoke of difficulties and the need for reinforcements. But the men were 'in'. And they were holding on. McCay and Elliott knew they had problems on the right with the 15th Brigade. They didn't know how bad these problems were. The trouble here was the Sugarloaf and its ever-twinkling machine guns. The British infantry had failed to take the position and it was hardly their fault.

THE BRITISH 61ST Division, badly under strength, had attacked on a front of about a mile. On the extreme right the British quickly broke into the German line and took about eighty prisoners, but those going directly for the Wick Salient found the wire mostly intact and were shot to pieces by machine guns. Much the same thing happened to the brigade in the centre. Brigadier-General Charles Carter's 184th Brigade, on the left, went for the Sugarloaf after being hit hard by German artillery before its advance began. Those attacking just to the right of the salient found the wire uncut. Those going directly for the Sugarloaf came under heavy shrapnel fire.

Major-General Colin Mackenzie, the British divisional commander, believed his brigade in the centre had made a 'small lodgement' in the German line and that 'a footing had been gained in the Sugarloaf'. Mackenzie decided to resume the bombardment where the attack had failed. All three brigades would attack again. Haking issued an order around 7.30 pm saying he wanted to strengthen the hold on the Sugarloaf to help the Australians. Then the British discovered that they had no hold on the Sugarloaf. They decided to make a fresh assault at 9 pm.

SHORTLY AFTER 8 PM Elliott received a message from General Carter: 'Am attacking at 9 pm. Can your right battalion co-operate?' The message had passed through both divisional headquarters. About twenty minutes earlier McCay had given Elliott permission to use half of the 58th battalion (the 'carrying' battalion) to reinforce the 59th and 60th. Elliott now decided to throw in these two companies from the 58th at 9 pm to help the new English attack on the Sugarloaf.

They set off under Major Arthur Hutchinson, a twenty-one-year-old Duntroon graduate and son of a Tasmanian clergyman. All the Sugarloaf's machine guns seemed to be turned on Hutchinson's two companies, but they kept going and apparently carried on some men of the 59th who had been sheltering in no-man's land. Ellis, the historian of the 5th Division, wrote:

At the enemy wire the fire became hellish, irresistible. Major Hutchinson, his body riddled with bullets, perished gloriously, close to the German parapet. The attack melted into nothingness – passed in a few quivering moments from the realm of man's high endeavour to the record of his deathless failures . . . The ground was covered with [the brigade's] dead and dying, among whom the wounded dragged themselves painfully, seeking the fearful security of a shell hole or a mound that might give some protection from the machine gun fire that still enveloped them . . . the fruitlessness of further sacrifice was now apparent to all. After a couple of hours the remnants of all three battalions commenced to drift back to their old front line, wounded assisting wounded, those still unscathed bearing some comrade too badly stricken to aid himself.

Hutchinson's body was never found. Elliott unsuccessfully recommended him for the Victoria Cross. And the sacrifice had been for nothing. The British had not attacked at 9 pm: that's why it seemed all the firepower of the Sugarloaf had been directed at Hutchinson's two companies.

Around 8.20 pm Haking had discovered a little more, all of it discouraging, about the true position of the 61st Division. When, shortly afterwards, he heard about Carter's proposed attack on the Sugarloaf he ordered it cancelled. Haking had not told the 5th Division HQ of this, possibly because he was unaware that Elliott had been asked to participate. Nevertheless around 8.35 the 5th Division HQ received this message from the 61st Division: 'Under instructions from corps commander am withdrawing from captured enemy line after dark.' McCay's headquarters did not immediately pass this to Elliott. We have to consider the possibility here that McCay may have been unaware that Elliott was using Hutchinson's two companies to help Carter. At 9.10 pm McCay received a message from Haking saying that the 61st Division was withdrawing from no-man's land and would renew its attack next day. Now McCay's staff apparently thought that Elliott should be told what was happening. He was sent this message: '9.25 pm. 61st Division not attacking tonight. General Elliott may withdraw 59th Battalion and its reinforcements if he thinks attack is not likely to succeed.' It was, as we know, too late. Hutchinson and his men had gone off to their deaths sharply at 9 pm in support of a non-existent attack.

Soldiers and historians have argued for close to ninety years about this incident. McCay and his staff have most usually been blamed, directly or by innuendo. McCay was always going to be an attractive target because he was so easy to dislike. And yet, to be fair, it is hard to blame him alone for the sacrifice of Hutchinson and the two companies. Bean wrote that there was 'a failure at the headquarters of the 5th Australian Division to grasp either the meaning of the message [from the 61st Division] or the importance of sending it on to General Elliott'. Ross McMullin, Elliott's biographer, puts the blame on Carter and his staff in the 184th Division. 'They asked for the assistance in the first place; they should have ensured that the 15th Brigade was informed that they no longer required it.'

AROUND 11 PM ELLIOT was still unaware of how completely things had failed on his front or of the carnage among the two-and-a-half battalions he had sent out. He thought the 60th was in the German breastwork and the 59th almost there; he didn't know where Hutchinson's men were. Then at 12.30 am he received a message from Major Charles Denehy of the 58th:

> Men of all battalions are coming back from No-Man's Land and I expect that they will gradually drift back to the line. Many men are wounded, many are not. Very many officers are casualties, including Majors McCrae, Elliott and Hutchinson, all of whom are reported dead, and seems impossible to organise . . . Report seems unanimous that not a single man of 15th Brigade has now arrived in enemy's trench, as enemy's flares are coming from the whole of the front allotted to this brigade. I am now organising the defence of our original trenches . . .

There it was: the truth, long delayed and awful.

AND NOW THE wounded were coming back. Some crawled. Others were dragged in. They lay on the firesteps and the duckboards in the bays and traverses and along the saps that led away from the front. Red and green signal rockets burst in the black sky. Blood was splashed and smeared everywhere and lay in dark patches on the clayey ground and the air smelled of fire and ashes and failure. Jimmy Downing wrote that the smell of blood was still in his nostrils four years later. The communications trenches became congested. Stretcher-bearers, their knuckles bleeding from repeatedly being barked against trench walls, sometimes took hours to carry a man 1000 yards. The wounded cried out from no-man's land, as they would for days. Downing heard one man in delirium singing a marching song. A machine gun opened up, then stopped. The wounded man continued singing. The machine gun rattled again and the man sang no more. 'The interminable hours wore on,' Downing wrote. 'It was a night of horror and doubt.'

In the morning it was worse. The men could see what no-man's land was like. Charles Bean borrowed Brudenell White's car to drive from the Somme to the battlefield, arriving early in the afternoon. He wrote in his official history: 'Especially in front of the 15th Brigade, around the Laies, the wounded could be seen everywhere raising their limbs in pain or turning hopelessly, hour after hour, from one side to the other.'

And in the morning the sums were done. The 60th battalion had been wiped out as a fighting force. It went out 877-strong and now, on the morning after, Lieutenant Tom Kerr, wounded in the shoulder and ribs and the only officer present, abruptly found himself in charge of a 'battalion'. Sixty-one men answered the roll; another forty or so turned up later. The 59th had suffered nearly as badly.

The brigade had gone into the line about 3750-strong. Now it was down to about 2000. The most common wounds were to the lower limbs, followed by wounds to the upper limbs, then head and neck wounds. The ratio of dead to wounded was unusually high. Arthur Butler, author of the official history of the Australian medical services in the Great War, said that this was because many men were shot while lying wounded in no-man's land or simply died there from lack of help. One man, wounded in both legs and one arm, was brought in after spending nine or ten days out in no-man's land. He had survived by sucking on a strip of tunic that he soaked, hour after hour, day after day, in the muddy water in the bottom of a shell hole.

In the morning Elliott went to the frontline. Lieutenant J. D. Schroder went with him.

> What had been ordinary sandbagged trenches were now heaps of debris, and it was impossible to walk far without falling over dead men. Although the Hun had a barrage down and there must have been dozens of machine guns operating from the Sugarloaf, Pompey never thought of ducking, but went from battalion to company headquarters and so on right along the line. A word for a wounded man here, a pat of approbation to a bleary-eyed digger there, he missed nobody. He never spoke a word all the way back . . . but went straight inside, put his head in his hands and sobbed his heart out.

Private William Boyce returned from no-man's land early that morning. 'This was when Pompey Elliott disclosed his true self,' he said. '[He] was there with tears running down his face, apologising for the mix up . . . He was very, very upset . . . "don't blame me for this," he said, "this is wrong, it's not my fault", he was definitely very upset.'

Strange words for a brigade commander to offer in the presence of a private. Such men were supposed to at least pretend to infallibility. They were supposed to be stoic in the face of outrageous casualties. This was what the Great War had come to be about: stoicism at the top and casualties, millions of them, at the bottom. Tears and doubts were for wives and mothers in Manchester and Ballarat. But then few senior officers went to the front immediately after a battle. Few stepped around the gore and looked into the eyes, bug-like and white, of men who had been dragged back without arms and legs. And Elliott was truly 'very upset'. The memory of that morning would burn in his brain for the rest of his life. On that day in front of Fromelles he didn't know that much about the battle beyond what had happened to his own brigade. He didn't know about the failure at Boar's Head a few weeks earlier. He didn't know that much about the on-again, off-again prelude to the battle and the sinuous game played by Monro and Haig. He was new to the western front and knew little about artillery. When over the next few years he learned about these things the memory of that morning would turn him to anger.

Bean saw Elliott some time that afternoon and wrote in his diary: 'Old Elliott was dead asleep when I called – but McCay came in and woke him up. When Elliott came out I felt almost as if I were in the presence of a man who had just lost his wife. He looked down and could hardly speak – he was clearly terribly depressed and over wrought.'

4

The morning after

An Australian soldier – some said he was an officer – wandered about near the German lines after the battle of Fromelles. He had been hit in the forehead and skin hung over his eyes. He was blinded and out of his mind. He would blunder around in circles, hands outstretched, then fall down. Then he would get up and stumble around again. This went on for days. Some said the Germans were using him as a decoy. The Germans eventually killed him. It is unclear whether they did this with a bomb or a bullet. It is also unclear whether they did this out of cussedness or kindness. This was the Great War and men did terrible things and did not always understand why they did them.

AROUND MIDNIGHT ON July 19 the generals running the Fromelles battle from a few miles back were being ambushed by reality – but slowly, teasingly, by one scrap of paper after another. Amid the accounts of failures and – that quaint military noun – retirements, there were also reports of local successes. It was lost and it wasn't lost. This battalion was 'in' and that one wasn't.

The confusion was profound, but a rough profit-and-loss

account was starting to take form. Six brigades – three Australian, three British – had rushed the German lines six hours earlier. It was now clear that four of these assaults had failed: those of the three British brigades and Elliott's 15th. Which meant the right-hand side of the attack and part of the centre was lost. On the left four battalions of Australians – two from the 14th Brigade and two from the 8th – were still scrapping behind the German lines, helped by reinforcements that had been sent over later. These battalions were not joined up; there was a big gap where one brigade ended and the other started.

And now the Germans were counter-attacking, working their way between the Australian strong points. There had been no order to leave men behind in the German frontline trench while the main body of Australians went forward. This meant that the Germans could creep between the Australian positions, re-occupy their own frontline and shoot the Australians down from behind.

The generals simply knew that their men were 'in'. The Australians behind the old German frontline didn't know that much either, except that they lived in chaos and from moment to moment. Globs of mud stuck to their boots. Some were often up to their waists in water. They took rifles from dead men and laid them down nearby so that they had spares if their own weapon became clogged. They tried to move German sandbags from one side of a position to the other and found that the bags were rotten and fell apart in their hands. They looked out through mist and artillery smoke and now and then saw the spiked helmets of Bavarians pricking the night sky, some in front, some moving towards the flanks. They heard the squelch of shovels going into sodden clay and the cries of the wounded behind them in no-man's land. They heard German officers shouting orders up ahead. They looked for their own officers, most of whom were either dead or wounded. They looked at the ground and tried to work it out; the Germans knew it and they didn't. They looked to the sky and saw flare after flare. What did these mean? They tried to light cigarettes with soggy matches, then ran out of cigarettes. They were also running out of bombs and ammunition. They had done the job, broken into the German front, well in, but they couldn't hold on unless reinforcements arrived.

The string of Australian 'islands' ran something like this. In the centre there was Captain Arblaster and the remnants of the 53rd Battalion, about 100 yards inside the old German frontline. Next to him, but not always in touch, were the 54th and some of the 55th, who had been sent over as reinforcements. Behind them, in the old German frontline, was Colonel Cass of the 54th. This was the 14th Brigade's front.

East of Cass, also in the old frontline, was Colonel Toll, bleeding from a head wound and trying to direct his 31st Battalion, which was 100 to 150 yards ahead. And on the extreme left, frightfully exposed, its flank hinged to thin air, was the 32nd. This was the front of the 8th Brigade.

MEN FROM THE 'carrying' and reserve battalions had drifted into the fight on the 8th Brigade's front. Sapper Fred Strode went out to help dig the communication trench across no-man's land to the new front. Just before he was due to climb the ladder and go over the parapet 'we was told to read a verse out of our bible, because a lot of us, won't be coming back'.

Private William Barry, from the 8th Brigade's reserve battalion, went over after the infantry attack had been going about three hours. He handed over the bombs and ammunition he was carrying and went back for more.

I was in 'no man's land', near the German parapet when a lad in my platoon came up and asked me to show him the way across the wires as he was wounded in the head and bleeding freely. After helping him on his way I returned, only to meet another poor lad with his arm shattered and he wanted to know if there were any Red Cross men about. During all that night I never saw any. I helped him as far as the barbed wire and again returned. The enemy was now shelling us unmercifully and everybody was running amok with himself, for by the way they were shouting out, there was nobody in charge of the men. The German artillery fire was growing fiercer every minute, in fact it was hellish and their shells were landing with great accuracy and killing the boys like flies. About ten o'clock I shifted my position . . . and was able to get into the German trench. No sooner was I there, when a shell struck the top of the parapet with a terrific explosion. Two boys standing alongside of me started to cry for their mother and I told them to cut that out, but pray to god to get them out of this hole. No sooner were the words out of my mouth, when another shell hit the parapet just above my head and I remembered nothing more.

The two assaulting battalions on Barry's front had called for reinforcements about 8.50 pm. They were being swept by machine-gun fire from three distant German strong points and bombed from the flanks. A sap was dug across no-man's land and eventually became blocked with Australian dead just short of the German frontline. The 32nd Battalion, at the extreme left of the Australian line, appeared to suffer worse in the German counter-attacks. At 9.40 it sent back a message: 'Frontline cannot be held unless strong reinforcements are sent. Enemy's machine-gunners are creeping up . . . The artillery is not giving support. Sandbags required in thousands. Men bringing sandbags are being wounded in the back. Water urgently required.' Twenty minutes later the 32nd reported that it was being forced back. It fell back further around 2.30 am when the Germans attacked again. The Germans were behind the 32nd and men from the 29th – Private Barry's battalion – who had been drawn into the fight. The Australians here were just about surrounded.

They decided their only chance to avoid death or captivity was to make a rush, through the Germans, back to their own frontline. This they did at 3.45 am. There were about 150 men in the charge. They fought the Germans with bayonets and bombs; German machine guns fired at them from all four sides, but some of these men made it into no-man's land and eventually scrambled into the Australian frontline. By 4 am the battle here was lost.

WE LEFT PRIVATE Barry unconscious in the German breastwork, hit by a shell. Around daybreak he felt Germans pulling at his leg.

Barry pretended to be dead, then passed out again. He regained consciousness several hours later. He felt no pain but couldn't move. Several Australians, stripped of their equipment, came up and told Barry they were all prisoners. Barry wrote that the Germans were 'bumping' the Australians with rifle butts and prodding them with bayonets. A German sighted his rifle at Barry but was sent away by a German officer. The officer cut open Barry's trousers and exposed a terrible wound to his right knee and another in the calf. The officer bandaged Barry's leg and began to question him. Barry answered with 'the most awful lies imaginable'.

The German wanted to know how many Australians were in France. Barry told him three to five million, with the conscripts yet to come.

'Wass you a fria willie, a volunteer, eh?'

'Yes,' said Barry.

'You Australians are b----- cowards. We are not at war with you, but you came over here last night and went *hough* [he imitated a bayonet thrust] while we always fight a long way off.'

By now, Barry wrote, the German was angry with him. No, Barry would not be sent to a doctor. As he left the officer said something to several German soldiers standing nearby 'and I got one of the worst beltings it was possible to give a man'. Barry lapsed back into unconsciousness. He was beaten again as the Germans dragged him to the rear. A German Red Cross man gave him a piece of black bread and a German military coat. 'It was wet with blood, but that didn't matter.'

Barry, to his horror, found that he was at a place where the dead were being stacked. 'I was sitting on the edge of a hole about forty feet long, twenty feet wide and fifteen feet deep and into this hole the dead were being thrown without any fuss or respect. Friend and Foe being treated alike, it was pitiful to see the different expressions on their faces, some with a peaceful smile while others showed they had passed away in agony.'

Three months later the Germans amputated Barry's leg.

MAJOR MUIR PURSER of the 30th, the 8th Brigade's 'carrying' battalion, lost the last subaltern left in his company to shellfire as the remnants of the brigade returned to the Australian front about 5 am. 'Dawn showed our trenches to be a shambles – breastworks badly damaged; dead, wounded and blood everywhere . . . I met General Tivey [Brigadier-General Edwin Tivey, commander of the 8th Brigade] on his way to the front line. His lip showed a spot of blood, as though he had been biting it, and he remarked to me that it had been a "great fight".' Purser called the roll of his company. He was the only one of six officers left; only about thirty of the 181 other ranks who had gone into the fight answered the roll.

Bean saw Tivey that afternoon and wrote in his diary: 'Poor old Tivey looked quite overdone – with eyes like boiled gooseberries. He had been up two nights . . .' Tivey told Bean: 'Men who were at Anzac said that the shell fire at Gallipoli was child's-play to this.'

Ellis, the 5th Division's historian, said Tivey had gone to the frontline as soon as he could get away from headquarters. He stood there silent with grief. Then he 'picked his way carefully through the frontline among the bodies of the men he had loved so well'.

Toll was the last to leave the German trench. He strode back proudly. A man who was near him said: 'Col Toll's head was covered in blood. I don't know how he got back to our lines.' Private William Miles was near Toll just before the retreat. Toll said: 'Well, men, no-one could ask you to do more – get back to our lines, but don't bunch up.' Miles wrote that he was halfway across no-man's land when another Australian passed him 'flying'. The man yelled out to him: 'Never knew I won a Stawell Gift, did you Billy?'

Private Les Martin had been wounded before he left the Australian lines. Now he was coming back as machine-gun bullets fizzed around him. In no-man's land he fell on a German spike that gashed his leg to the bone. Then a small piece of shell, about the size of a three-pence, hit him in the leg. He told his brother that the Australian lines that morning were ghastly. He headed for the dressing station.

Several bodies I passed had been burned by fires igniting their clothing, wounded were crawling about here and there but mainly lying as near the parapet as possible waiting for stretcher bearers who never seemed to come, a lot of them hardly uttering a sound although they had been badly hit. One passed here and there hands, arms, legs, quite detached from the bodies. One chap had his head cut clean off by a shell. He was bending at the time and the shell caught him right at the back of the neck. A lot of the wounded were continuously crying out with pain, others were calling for water, water, water . . . Some of the chaps down at the dressing station appeared to be all bandages – some of their faces were unrecognisable, especially those who had been hit about the mouth. Their cheeks were risen to an enormous size. Others had great holes in their sides or backs you could almost put your hands into. Some were minus both feet, others with hands or arms off.

Private Martin went to a hospital in England. By early 1918 he had been made a lieutenant. A few months later a shell blew off his right arm. He returned home and eventually bought three grocery shops. He drove back and forth to them, steering his car with one hand.

Sapper Fred Strode had been digging the sap across no-man's land for the 8th Brigade. An officer told him and two others to try to hold the line while the others carried two machine guns back. Each of the men had four hand grenades. The officer gave Strode an extra three or four in a Malvern Star tucker bag and wished the men luck. Strode and his two companions were in the German front trench. The Germans advanced in columns of twenty and the bomb fight began. Strode said the three Australians scattered the first row of Germans, then let fly at the second.

. . . we lost the man on the right, he toss a hand grenade over and forgot to pull out the pin, but one of the Germans pull the pin out and let fly at him, and a piece of the casen hit him in the forehead just between the eyes, and he fell back into my arms. I could see he was going very white, and he died straight away. And then they [the Germans] called for the bombers again to shift us, so my mate said he will have a look to see how far back they were, and then he got shot in the belly, he said it was burning like hell. I said to him I will carry you back, he said get back, while the going is good, but I did not leave him, and then I saw him fall over, that was the end of him. I could see they were coming into the trench again, so by that time I had only 1 bomb left so I let them have it, and then I made my run back, when I was just about ½ way back, the ground was just like a hail storm hitting the ground, all around me, how I got back I do not know . . .

Sometime after 5 am General McCay was told that the 8th Brigade, what was left of it, was back in the Australian lines. The 14th Brigade, the men under Cass and Arblaster, were now alone in the German trenches. After eleven hours they were all that was left of Haking's grand vision.

IT HAD BEEN the worst night of Colonel Walter Cass's life and now, as the golden lights of dawn began to stipple this place of death and smoke, he knew things would only become worse. Before long the Germans would be able to see everything. They would see him vulnerable and isolated. Cass was wet and cold. He had lost most of his officers. He had indeed lost a large part of his 54th battalion. From his position in the old German frontline he didn't really know who was alive and who wasn't, or where those who were alive were. He didn't know with any certainty what was happening on his flanks. The 53rd, under Captain Arblaster, was on his right; the 8th Brigade was on his left. Cass knew that both these formations were in trouble and could collapse at any time.

At 3 am he had sent a message back saying the 53rd appeared to be giving way and the Germans were coming in. Twenty minutes later he wrote that his position was 'serious'. His men had no grenades and the Germans were massing again. Twenty minutes later again he sent a message saying the position was 'very serious'. The 53rd was retiring. The Germans were re-occupying their own frontline on either side of him. At 4.20 am he reported: 'Position almost desperate. Have got 55th [the 'carrying' battalion] and a few of the 54th together and have temporarily checked enemy. But do get our guns to work at once, please. The 53rd have lost confidence temporarily and will not willingly stand their ground. Some appear to be breaking across No-Man's Land. If they give way to my right rear, I must withdraw or be surrounded.'

All through he remained calm and resolute. We don't know whether he had time to reflect on the great quest of his life, a Canadian woman named Helena Holmes, a chiselled beauty who was ten years his junior. He had been courting her for five years – by letter. He had met her on a liner crossing the Indian Ocean in 1911 while she was on a world tour with a chaperone. Cass went ashore when the ship docked in Western Australia and bought her an armful of yellow roses. Then the correspondence, tender and flirtatious, began. Cass sent her petals of roses and violets by post. He hinted at marriage and finally proposed and thought he had been turned down.

By now Helena had become a lieutenant in the Canadian medical corps and was heading for London. A month before the battle of Fromelles Cass wrote: 'My recollection of you is as of a beautiful queen with a "touch-me-not" air about you that made me want to take you in my arms. Oh, if only I had dared. I shouldn't have been soldiering now – would have been married and settled down into a fat old major of 40 . . .' A week before Fromelles he wrote again: 'If I get out of this war in one piece and alive you are to marry me or do please make up your mind to it.' He hoped to meet her in London. It would be his first glimpse of her in five years.

Sometime around 2 am Cass must have realised that he could expect no help on the right. That was where the 15th Brigade was supposed to be, and there was no sign of it. German flares were going up from positions where the 15th should have been. The men of the 53rd under Arblaster held the right. Around 2 am they saw figures in the mist, creeping past their flank and heading for the old German frontline. They opened fire on them, then stopped, in case the shadows were the 15th Brigade. Soon after bombs came lobbing in from the direction of those shadows. Meanwhile the Germans had attacked from the front. When the Australians tried to answer this fire some were shot in the back. The Germans were also behind them. Arblaster had just about lost contact with Cass's forward troops on his left; and he was running out of ammunition.

He decided to turn and charge the Germans behind him. His men were shot down as soon as they left their trench and had to return.

Arblaster was badly wounded. He was taken prisoner and died of septicaemia a few days later. Many of his men were taken prisoner at the same time; others tried to head back across no-man's land.

GENERAL MONRO, THE army commander, Haking, the corps commander, and McCay and Mackenzie, the two divisional generals, met at 5 am at Haking's headquarters. While the conference was going on McCay was told by telephone that the 8th Brigade was back in the Australian lines. He was also told of Cass's message of 4.20 am: 'Position almost desperate.' The 14th Brigade was all that was left of the attack. Monro and Haking decided that it should come out.

Captain Norman Gibbins, a bank manager from Ipswich, Queensland, held the left flank of the 14th Brigade after the 8th had pulled out. Gibbins was thirty-eight and had been promoted from the ranks on Gallipoli. He stood six foot four inches and Bean described him as gaunt, brave and humorous. Earlier in the night he saw a man crawling towards them. It turned out to be a German, badly wounded, covered in blood and almost unconscious. Gibbins and another Australian helped him, but when one of them let go of his hand he rose on his knees and started to pray. 'Oh, cruel, cruel!' said Gibbins. Gibbins was soon after wounded in the head.

Cass had by now received a message from Colonel Pope, his brigade commander, telling him to be ready to retreat. Cass decided that once the order came he would dribble men back through the sap across no-man's land.

Sapper William Smith had started digging that sap about 9 pm. 'The German flares were the best display I had seen, and at times one could have imagined that the battlefield was illuminated with arc lamps.' A wounded man called to Smith: 'Cobber, bring me a drink of water.' Smith gave him a drink from his water bottle. Soon the man was calling out for water again. Smith went back to the Australian breastwork and returned with water in a petrol can. The man took a long pull, even though the water reeked of petrol. He said he was cold. Smith wrapped him in sandbags and placed a bundle under his head as a pillow.

Cass decided that he needed a rearguard to cover his retreat. Captain Gibbins, his head now bandaged, was given the job. Cass still hadn't received the order to pull back. Seven runners had tried to carry the order to him; all failed to get through. The eighth runner arrived at 7.50 am and the retreat began. Inevitably it was disorderly. Some small groups were surrounded and had to surrender.

Cass was among the last to leave. Gibbins was the last. He clattered along the duckboards of the freshly dug sap until, close to the Australian line, he found it clogged with wounded. He climbed out of the trench and was killed by a bullet to the head. Some of his men claimed he died with a smile on his face. It was about 9 am. The battle was over.

Sapper Smith, in his account of Fromelles written for *Reveille* in 1936, reports an exchange between Cass and Colonel Pope near the Australian breastwork 'just before daybreak'.

> Both of these officers had been across to the enemy lines. Col. Cass was obviously over-wrought and distressed. He and Pope were having a heated argument about the attack, and Col. Cass unburdened his mind.
>
> 'I tell you that it was wholesale murder, they have murdered my boys.'
>
> 'Oh, pull yourself together man, this is war!'
>
> 'This is not war. They have murdered my boys.'

There are problems with this. There is no evidence that Pope crossed to the German lines. What evidence there is suggests that 'just before daybreak' Cass was still in the German frontline trench and Pope was at his headquarters behind the Australian lines. Yet the exchange is plausible, even if it almost certainly didn't happen when Smith said it did. Cass felt let down.

Ten days after the battle he wrote to Helena Holmes in London, telling her that he was in a 'rest home' suffering from rheumatism brought on, he said, by fourteen hours in the wet and cold of the German trenches. He had been lucky, he said. Nine of his officers were lying wounded in a London hospital, but he had escaped with a scratch on the hand.

Dear we got such a 'strafing' that I honestly thought it was certain that I should get hit as they simply rained shells on us. And then both flanks retired and left me out there to be chopped up. And I was waiting for the order to withdraw and all the time Germany was smashing in on both sides. We beat them back again and again, despite their bombs & machine guns. My men were simply splendid and only when I gave the order did they come back.

Cass never truly recovered from his long night at Fromelles. He was invalided to England, saw Helena Holmes for the first time in five years and married her in October. Cass's daughter, Angela, recorded an interview in 2001 in which she said of Fromelles: 'Some damned politician-cum-soldier was in command . . . and [Daddy] was left holding the salient with the Germans in front and on each side, and he wasn't withdrawn for a long time. And he said to this damned politician, "My lads were murdered", and the politician took against him.'

The politician-cum-soldier was clearly General McCay. Cass was one of the true heroes of Fromelles; he was also one of the few commanders who did what the battle plan said he was supposed to do. He was recommended for the Distinguished Service Order and had to settle for being mentioned in dispatches.

He fared better than his brigade commander. Colonel Pope, from Perth, was a good soldier, much admired, forty-two years old and with gentle eyes. His performance once the Fromelles battle began was just about faultless. He fell asleep at 3 pm on the afternoon after the battle. McCay tried to wake him at 4.30 and, deciding that he was drunk, sacked him and sent him home. Pope asked for a chance to clear himself at a court-martial but Birdwood, who, one suspects, was sympathetic to Pope, refused the request. Pope later returned to France to command the 52nd Battalion.

RATHER THAN HUMILIATING an exhausted brigade commander who may or may not have taken a drink, McCay should have been worrying about his wounded. Hundreds of them lay in no-man's land.

Arms could be seen waving from shell holes. On July 20, the night after the battle, 300 wounded were brought in, some of them missing limbs. When corpses were rolled over so that possessions could be recovered they gave off a short moan, much like dead lambs turned over with the foot.

Jimmy Downing said this work went on for five nights. 'Parties went out under fire in broad daylight. Some of the wounded were never found. A few crawled in three weeks later, with shattered limbs and maggoty wounds.' Downing said it took four men an hour to carry one wounded man from the Australian frontline back to safety. 'We carried till the mind refused its task and limbs sagged, and always there were hundreds for whom each minute decreased the chances of life. Release came to many of the stricken. We left the hopeless cases undisturbed for the sake of those whom the surgeons could save.'

Two Germans, Downing said, carried a wounded Australian back to his lines, saluted, then walked back towards their line. Australians in the next bay were unaware of what had happened. They shot the Germans as they walked back.

Sergeant Simon Fraser, tall and blond, a thirty-nine-year-old farmer from Victoria's Western District, spent three days bringing in wounded.

One foggy morning in particular, I remember, we could hear someone over towards the German entanglements calling for a stretcher-bearer; it was an appeal no man could stand against, so some of us rushed out and had a hunt. We found a fine haul of wounded and brought them in; but it was not where I heard this fellow calling, so I had another shot for it, and came across a splendid specimen of humanity trying to wriggle into a trench with a big wound in his thigh. He was about 14 stone weight, and I could not lift him on my back; but I managed to get him into an old trench, and told him to lay quiet while I got a stretcher. Then another man about 30 yards out sang out 'Don't forget me, cobber.'

Harry Williams, a private in the 60th, had written home two days before the battle. 'Should I fall,' he told his mother, 'I will be proud to know I did so in the cause of Righteousness and Justice . . . Dad, I have kept your wishes, neither smoked nor taken liquor.' Williams, who was eighteen, took three weeks to die in a hospital in Essex.

'Rowley' Lording, a lance-corporal, was hit in the chest, arm, spine and back. He was dragged back to the Australian line and for ten days fought tetanus. He had just turned seventeen. He didn't leave his hospital bed until early 1917. He had fifty-two operations over fifteen years and lost an arm. Through all this he married, had three children, worked as an accountant and helped limbless soldiers. But Lording had become dependent on drugs. In 1944 he died in a mental hospital.

Alfred Langan had been captain of Fort Street High School in Sydney and an original member of the Bondi Surf Lifesaving Club. Now he was the medical officer of the 30th Battalion. Three days after the battle he wrote to his father.

> For sixteen hours we worked with blood up to our elbows on the poor battered wrecks that were brought to us, in a dugout that was not wide enough to swing a cat in, nor high enough to stand in an upright position . . . Men with shattered arms staggered in carrying or dragging men with battered legs and begged us to attend to their more unfortunate mates first. Not one of them murmured or complained. God it made you humble and brought the tears to your eyes . . . I'll never forget this stunt as long as I live. If ever there was a living Hell, that night and morning was it. Won't worry you with the sights I saw, they were too awful for words. If there is a God in Heaven may he strike the bastard Kaiser and his crew dead. We lost exactly half the battalion.

MORE WOUNDED MIGHT have been saved if a truce had been allowed to go ahead on the day after the battle. William Miles, a thirty-six-year-old private, had been near Toll at the time of the retreat from the German lines. When he was back in the Australian lines, Miles saw General McCay walking along the duckboards with Tivey. Miles said McCay kept saying 'They'll get used to it.'

Miles shortly afterwards volunteered to go out and look for a captain who was thought to be lying wounded in no-man's land. He wore a Red Cross badge on his arm. He came upon a man who had been hit in the stomach and wanted a drink. Miles told him a drink would make him worse but cut his haversack off to make him more comfortable. Miles then came upon a man shot in the testicles, which had swollen terribly. He borrowed Miles' knife to rip his trousers open. His agony was so great he wouldn't let Miles touch him.

Miles slid into another shell hole and heard a voice from the German lines. He saw a German officer beckoning to him. Miles walked slowly towards him, pausing to pick up a pair of field glasses. Firing had stopped all along the line.

'What are you supposed to be doing?' the German asked in English.

Tending wounded men, Miles told him.

'You may be laying wires. This is not the usages of war.'

Miles told him the Red Cross was always allowed to work unmolested.

'What did you pick up just now?'

Field glasses.

'It might have been a bomb.'

'I'll show you,' Miles said.

The German told Miles not to put his hands in his pockets but over his head. While the German officer spoke on a field telephone several other officers asked Miles to turn this way and that so that they could photograph him.

The first German officer put the phone down and asked Miles his rank.

'Only a private, sir.'

'Well, I want you to go back to your lines and ask an officer to come over here and we will have a "parliament" [this is what Miles wrote in 1929, but it is likely the German said '*parliamentaire*'] and see if we can arrange about collecting the wounded.'

Miles returned to the Australian parapet, which was crowded with men who had watched this parley. Major Alexander Murdoch decided to accompany Miles back to the German line. A Red Cross flag was improvised from a red cushion and waved above the Australian parapet. Murdoch and Miles set out for the German lines, carrying water bottles, which they handed to the wounded. The Germans telephoned their divisional headquarters and came up with a proposal. The Australian stretcher-bearers could work only in their half of no-man's land. The Germans would clear their half. Murdoch would be blindfolded and held as a hostage behind the German lines. Murdoch said he would have to obtain his superior's approval for the truce. Both sides saluted and Murdoch and Miles headed back. An informal truce had already broken out all along the front.

McCay's headquarters (we don't know for certain whether McCay was there) refused the German proposal and also appears to have put an end to the unofficial truce. According to Miles, wounded men were lifted off stretchers in no-man's land as their would-be rescuers hurried back to the Australian line. In the Australian official history Bean writes himself into a tangle trying to exonerate McCay over this incident, and one must wonder what he is trying to do and why. Bean worshipped Brudenell White, Birdwood's chief-of-staff, who often looked over drafts of the official history. White, in turn, was one of a handful of people who saw military virtues in McCay, and in 1940 he made the preposterous suggestion that McCay was 'greater even than Monash'. Bean noted that orders from Haig's GHQ said no negotiations were to be held with the enemy. Bean said 'a divisional general could hardly be blamed for rigid adherence to the orders of the commander-in-chief.' Bean surely knew that such orders were not that rigid.

Robin Corfield's *Don't forget me, cobber*, published in 2000, is the definitive account of Fromelles. Corfield says of McCay:

> With about half of his division dead or wounded, on a stretch of ground easily accessible to stretcher-bearers, and with the battle lost, one might think that the General in charge of the 5th Australian Division might have cared, or even fought a corner for his troops. He might, had he one iota of charity, be seen to at least to show posterity that he tried. But of course McCay cared about nobody but himself ever: and all he could say to Bean is that two British generals later approved!

And later: 'It was McCay's neglect of the thousands of his men who lay dead, dying, wounded in no-man's land in those summer days that forms the most damning case against him. Hundreds of others risked their lives to bring in the wounded, and many died at this work. Nothing can pardon McCay for that neglect. Nothing.'

Bean sent a draft of his Fromelles chapters to Brigadier-General Sir James Edmonds, the British official historian, for comment. 'The mistake made,' Edmonds wrote, 'was *asking* permission to arrange a local suspension of arms. Many such suspensions were made, e.g., even during the battle of Loos, when, near Hulluch, both sides bound up and removed wounded. There was another on 3rd May 1918 at Villers-Bretonneux for half an hour.'

In a letter to Bean in 1926 McCay said he did not ask permission up the line. The diary of the 5th Division says Tivey, the commander of the 8th Brigade, sought permission. McCay is not mentioned in the diary entry, as though to suggest he was not present when the truce was requested.

THAT NIGHT AT Fromelles was one of the worst in Australian history, probably *the* worst in terms of the scale of the tragedy and the speed of it, a mere fourteen hours; but no-one back home knew this at the time, or in the weeks that followed. Bean filed a story from Amiens that appeared in the Australian newspapers of July 24. Bean had to write something that would get past the censor, and we shouldn't blame him for that, but his published story ended up a travesty. The report left readers in Australia wondering whether Fromelles had been a defeat, a fleeting victory or a draw, and whether it had been a big raid or an attack. Only the last sentence gave a clue to what had really happened: 'The losses amongst our troops engaged were severe.' It would be long after the war ended before Australians realised how severe these losses were.

Before Bean's newspaper account appeared the British authorities had put out an official communiqué: 'Yesterday evening, south of Armentières, we carried out some important raids on a front of two miles in which Australian troops took part. About

140 German prisoners were captured.' Bean wrote in his diary: 'What is the good of deliberate lying like that? The Germans know it was an attack . . .'

Some raids. The Australian casualties – dead, wounded, missing, prisoners of war – came in at 5533 and the British at 1547. The Germans estimated their casualties at between 1600 and 2000. Four hundred and seventy Australians had become prisoners of war. All this in one night, and for no gain. The Germans weren't even fooled into thinking a major attack was taking place away from the Somme.

Haking wrote a report a few days after the battle.

> The artillery preparation was adequate. There were sufficient guns and sufficient ammunition. The wire was properly cut, and the assaulting battalions had a clear run into the enemy's trenches. The Australian infantry attacked in the most gallant manner and gained the enemy's position, but they were not sufficiently trained to consolidate the ground gained. They were eventually compelled to withdraw and lost heavily in doing so. The 61st [British] Division were not sufficiently imbued with the offensive spirit to go in like one man at the appointed time . . . With two trained divisions the position would have been a gift after the artillery bombardment . . . I think the attack, although it failed, has done both divisions a great deal of good . . .

Haking had a gift for humbug that bordered on the spectacular. We need to take his assertions in order. The artillery was not *adequate*. If it had been, the machine guns at the Sugarloaf and elsewhere would not have been firing. It follows from this that there were not *sufficient guns*. The wire wasn't *properly cut*. Whether the Australians were *sufficiently trained* had nothing to do with anything; the most experienced troops in France could not have held the non-existent German second line that Haking set as the objective. The British division did not lack *the offensive spirit*; it had simply been chopped to pieces by machine guns. The position was never *a gift*; the problem here was that the artillery bombardment didn't do what it was supposed to do. Losing 7000 men for the gain of not one yard of ground did not do both divisions *a great deal of good*. When the artillery failed at Fromelles everything else had to fail; but this is the way things went on the western front in 1915 and 1916. We cannot blame Haking for failing to see the new world in perfect clarity. We cannot blame him for failing to abandon abruptly the theories he had learned over thirty years. We can blame him for timeless faults that would have got him into trouble with Napoleon or Julius Caesar. He was careless and unreasonably optimistic before the battle and less than honest afterwards. Haig tried to promote Haking to command of an army a few weeks after Fromelles. The War Office overruled Haig.

Edmonds had been on Haig's staff and knew as much about the war as anyone. He could be prickly but was in an unusually reflective mood when he wrote to Bean in September, 1928.

> In viewing 1914–16 I feel that I must remember that from the highest to the lowest we were all amateurs. The generals and staffs of the Regular army, though professionals in name, had never been trained to fight Continental armies or deal with such masses of troops . . . Economy of life did not become a principle of Haig's until, I might almost say, August 1918. I try not to judge 1915–17 by 1918 standards.

It is a fair point. The commanders of 1916 could not know what we now know, which is a pity because three Australian divisions were about to be thrown into the battle of the Somme at a village called Pozières.

POMPEY ELLIOTT WROTE a curious letter to Emily Edwards, a second cousin who lived in Wales and with whom he had stayed during the previous year.

> God knows why this enterprise was ordered apparently as a feint to distract the enemy's attention from the Somme area . . . the Division was hurled at the German Trenches without anything like adequate preparation . . . the slaughter was dreadful . . . I am glad to say that my poor boys

behaved magnificently. We attacked in four waves & there was not the least hesitation in any one of them although they saw the preceding waves going down before the machine guns like corn before the reaper . . . One of the best of my Commanding Officers was killed & practically all my best officers the Anzac men who helped to build up my brigade in Egypt are dead. I presume there was some plan at the back of the attack but it is difficult to know what it was. One can only say – It was an Order. I trust those who gave the order may be made to realise their responsibility . . . I am as you may guess not particularly happy but I am consoled by the fact that none of my own local arrangements went wrong & that the responsibility for this failure if failure it was rests entirely on higher authorities.

He wrote that four days after the battle. What was he trying to say? That it was awful but it wasn't his fault?

VC Corner Cemetery outside Fromelles is the only solely Australian war cemetery in France. The name has nothing to do with the Victoria Cross: soldiers simply referred to the intersection of two roads here as VC Corner. There are no headstones. Underfoot are the remains of 410 Australians. The bodies were picked up after the war. None could be identified.

A plastic poppy blows in the east wind, clattering against the concrete, and sparrows squabble and titter in a shrub in the corner, and all around are tranquil fields littered – still, and probably forever – with shells and shrapnel balls and cartridge cases and shards of iron. Look up to the ridge and you see the church spires of Fromelles and, to the right, Aubers. If it doesn't look much of a ridge, that's because it isn't. But when you stand on it, where the Germans were, you can count the ponies in a field near VC Corner.

The museum in the school at Fromelles smells musty, perhaps because most of what is in here has come out of the earth. There is a red tin of Oxo cubes; here an orange denture, curling at the back edge; there a purple water-canteen, the felt rotted off; here a pipe, small and neat, unbroken but bleached white.

The site of Elliott's forward headquarters, about 300 yards

behind what was the Australian frontline, is now Le Trou Aid Post Cemetery, one of the most beautiful in Flanders, with willows on four sides and a moat. Wounded Australians from Fromelles were treated here as shells dropped nearby. Now it is all about serenity. A line of ducks comes marching from a nearby farmhouse to prospect in the culvert and somewhere far away on the darkling plain a horse neighs.

5

Innocents abroad

On Easter Monday, 1916, a little more than a month after the first Australian divisions arrived in France, the Easter Rising broke out in Dublin. The revolutionaries were few, probably no more than 1000, but they took over the General Post Office and other public buildings and proclaimed a republic to the sound of breaking glass. The rebels had misread public opinion, particularly when they embraced the Germans as their 'gallant allies'. The Irish people might have longed to free themselves from the old oppressors in London, but neither did they much like the style of a new oppressor called Kaiser Wilhelm, who apparently thought he could do to Belgium and France what generations of Englishmen had done to Ireland. By the end of 1915 more than 86,000 Irishmen, mostly Roman Catholics, had volunteered for the British forces. Seventeen had won the Victoria Cross.

There was no popular rising in support of the rebels. Patrick Pearse, their leader, a headmaster and poet, was high-minded and sincere, but the proclamation he read from the portico of the Post Office sounded more like a suicide note, and it was.

The fighting in Dublin continued for about a week. By the time the rebels surrendered 450 people were dead and 2614 wounded, most of them civilians. On the Friday after the rising Lieutenant-General Sir John Maxwell, the commander of British forces in Egypt during the Gallipoli campaign, arrived to take charge of Ireland, which was now under martial rule. He tried the supposed leaders of the uprising by courts-martial, without the right to defence counsel, and fourteen were promptly executed. They were led into the jail yard blindfolded, a piece of white cloth pinned over their hearts, and shot at ten paces while sitting on a soapbox.

They died bravely, too bravely, and passed into folklore. Eamonn Ceannt was about to be led out. The priest told him: 'When you fall, Eamonn, I'll run out and anoint you.' To which Ceannt replied: 'Oh, oh, that will be a grand consolation, father.' Patrick Pearse wrote to his mother: 'We have done right. People will say hard things of us now, but later on they will praise us.'

Public opinion now swung in favour of the rebels. If they had been misguided at the Post Office, they knew how to die. The British, it was felt, had been too brutal; they had behaved as they always had. And the courts-martial gave the impression of arbitrary justice. Maxwell and Herbert Asquith, the British Prime Minister, had tried to strike a balance between deterrence and political expediency. Instead, in the best spirit of the procurator of Judea, they created new martyrs and, from this moment, from this mistimed revolution, Britain's hold on Ireland began to slip. The 'terrible beauty' had been born.

The executioners' shots echoed in Australia, where Irish Catholics were the largest minority group. Daniel Mannix, born in County Cork, was coadjutor bishop of Melbourne. His main interest was in obtaining state aid for church schools and he had taken little part in the war rhetoric, beyond approving of Britain's declaration of war in 1914. He disapproved of the Easter Rising but wept at the news of Pearse's execution. From now on he would think more about Australia's part in the Great War.

ON THE DAY the Irish rebels proclaimed their republic the Second Socialist International gathered in Switzerland. This body, set up in

Paris in 1889, was the highest moral court for socialists and trade unionists. The International saw the war as a capitalist plot and called for an immediate peace 'without annexations or indemnities' and upheld 'the right of the peoples to self-determination'. Vladimir Lenin, exiled from his native Russia, thought these words wishy-washy. He was forty-six, a formidable intellectual and theoretician and full-time revolutionary.

Lenin wanted to turn the conflict into a civil war, the working classes against the capitalists. He failed to persuade his more moderate comrades at the International to this view. He was isolated and unrepentant. It would be wrong to say a terrible beauty had been born here. Lenin had formalised his ideas on revolution long before this. He would not be deflected by a few sentimentalists.

ON JUNE 5 the cruiser *Hampshire*, on its way to Russia, hit a mine off the Orkney coast and sank. On board was Herbert Kitchener, the Secretary of State for War, on his way to see Tsar Nicholas II. Kitchener drowned. To the public this was one of the worst tragedies of the war. The people thought Kitchener knew all about war. His cross-eyed presence made them feel comfortable and his death seemed unthinkable. Kitchener too had become a martyr.

But not among his Cabinet colleagues. They knew the mythology was wrong, even though they couldn't say so. Kitchener, like Haig, had been right in predicting that the war would be long. His intimidating recruiting poster (the finger always seems to be pointing at you) flushed out 760,000 recruits in the first eight weeks after it appeared in 1914. He worked hard. Yet those in power knew that the war had exposed him: he had failed to live up to the promise he had never shown. They had wanted to get rid of him since the last days of the Gallipoli campaign, for which he and Churchill were largely responsible, but didn't know how.

John Keegan and Andrew Wheatcroft concluded their entry for Kitchener in *Who's Who in Military History* with this: 'His loss, popularly regarded as a national tragedy, was not much regretted in government and by no friends, for he never had any.'

TO THE WAR Office now came the fifty-three-year-old David Lloyd George, who during the previous thirteen months had brought his tremendous energies to the munitions ministry he had created. Lloyd George, the radical Liberal, recruited businessmen to help him divert Britain's industrial strength to the making of shells and guns and the setting up of thousands of arsenals. He coaxed trade unions to surrender many of their powers to the national interest. He brought more and more women into factory jobs. The production of munitions and guns, particularly heavy guns, rose spectacularly.

Lloyd George disliked humbug. He had little time for conventions that had outlived their time and was intolerant of people he thought 'dull' or 'plodders'. Like Churchill, he found ways to make things happen and didn't worry too much about the detail. Like Churchill, he understood political theatre. He was a dramatic speaker with a musical voice and natural wit. He had known poverty as a child in Wales and spoke easily to all people, was quick to smile and seemed truly interested in whomever he happened to be talking to, especially if it happened to be a pretty girl. He had a leonine mane, the pink cheeks of a child and clear blue eyes. He was intelligent and devious, charming and pushy. Many thought he was the war leader Britain was looking for.

And yet, with the advantage of hindsight, one can say that he was always going to have troubles in Kitchener's old job. No-one in government had done more to help the army than the former Minister for Munitions, but Lloyd George didn't understand the nature of the war. He had been an 'easterner' and would remain so. He wanted to fight at Gallipoli, Salonika and the Balkans, indeed anywhere but on the western front. His main adviser would now be the Chief of the Imperial General Staff, General Robertson, who didn't think politicians – known to the generals as 'frocks' – should interfere in military matters. Worse, Robertson's first loyalty was clearly to Haig.

There were other problems. Many of the generals that Lloyd George would now have to deal with, notably Haig, fitted the new War Minister's definition of 'dull'. These same generals, for their part, suspected that Lloyd George wasn't a 'gentleman'. By their definition he probably wasn't.

And Lloyd George didn't like visiting the front. John Grigg, his biographer, wrote that all his life Lloyd George had 'recoiled from illness, injury and death, so it was inevitable that the physical consequences of war would be so abhorrent to him that he could not trust himself to contemplate them at close quarters'. Lloyd George had lots of moral courage; he was simply born squeamish and couldn't do anything about it. Haig seldom visited the front either. Haig lacked neither physical nor moral courage. He merely thought he could run the war from a distance and sometimes he could. At other times he would not understand what was happening because he had not *seen* enough. Maps could tell you one thing and the faces of men coming out of the line another.

By the time Lloyd George's appointment was announced the Somme offensive had been going six days. Afterwards Haig would say the battle was one thing and Lloyd George would say it was another.

BRITAIN WENT INTO the war with a small regular army that fought well and suffered fearfully during the war of movement of 1914. Now, in the second year of stalemate, that original army was mostly gone. The bulk of the soldiers to be thrown into the Somme battle were volunteers who had answered Kitchener's call. Britain's first arm, its senior service, so the folklore had it, was its navy, the battle fleet that had been undefeated since Trafalgar. The navy was the symbol of empire, but its part in the war so far had been curiously passive, notably at Gallipoli, where it seemed paralysed by the fear of losing ships. The Royal Navy had not fought the big decisive battle that popular imagining had expected of it, and this was all the stranger because, while there were no flanks open on land in France and Belgium, the North Sea was one place where a breakthrough might be possible. Provided the German ships would come out, that is.

If the Kaiser's High Seas Fleet was impressive, it was also the victim of geography. Germany was an easy country to blockade. Ships leaving her ports in search of the Atlantic Ocean could turn south-west or north-west. If they turned south-west, they had to pass through the English Channel, only nineteen miles across at its narrowest point. If they turned the other way, they had to slip between Scotland and Norway, which was just about impossible because Britain's heaviest ships were at Rosyth, near Edinburgh, and Scapa Flow in the Orkneys. The North Sea was a jail and the English owned the only two keys.

Early in the war the Royal Navy had blockaded Germany so well that she could not trade with the world and this was causing shortages by 1916. German submarines ventured out to sink allied merchant ships, but the High Seas Fleet stayed in port while German soldiers died in their tens of thousands on the western and eastern fronts. This sat badly with the fleet's new commander, Admiral Reinhard Scheer. He was aggressive and busy by nature; he wanted the navy to do something that would tell the German people that it too was in the war. Late in May he took the High Seas Fleet into the North Sea and met the British Grand Fleet, commanded by Admiral Sir John Jellicoe, off the Danish coast.

Scheer brought twenty-seven capital ships, eleven cruisers and more than sixty destroyers to what would be called the battle of Jutland. He was out-gunned by Jellicoe, who brought thirty-seven capital ships, thirty-four cruisers and close to eighty destroyers. The encounter of May 31 was the stuff of legends: hundreds of ships feeling for each other in the mist, the thunder of gunfire rolling over a calm sea that was here and there dappled by sun, the smell of cordite and burning flesh. It was also inconclusive: both sides called it a victory.

The British could claim a victory by the old rules of warfare. The Germans had eventually left 'the field' and run for home. The North Sea was still a British lake. Even if the Germans defeated the British and French armies they could not invade Britain. The Germans could claim a victory on statistical grounds. The British had sunk 62,000 tons and the Germans 111,000. More than 6000 British sailors died, compared with 2500 Germans. Critics said Jellicoe had been too timid, and indeed he was a cautious man, but this time he had to be. As Churchill later wrote, had the Grand Fleet been badly damaged Britain might have lost the war.

The British people were puzzled: the 'victory' seemed too subtle; it needed too much explaining. As one historian has put it, the 'victory' was so curious that for decades a controversy raged about who was mostly to blame for it.

Jutland had failed to tip the balance of the war. Now the army would have to try again, this time on the Somme. The shape of the Somme front, a gentle bulge into the allied lines extending for more than twenty miles above the river, had been set nearly two years earlier, in late 1914, in what came to be called the race to the sea.

THE GREAT WAR didn't need to follow when Gavrilo Princip, a nineteen-year-old Bosnian Serb with a haunted face, shot dead the Austrian archduke Franz Ferdinand and his wife in Sarajevo on June 28, 1914. At worst, as someone noted, the assassination should have led to the Third Balkan War. Austria-Hungary, encouraged by Germany, threatened Serbia. Russia championed Serbia and threatened Germany and Austria-Hungary. Germany, Austria-Hungary and Russia began to mobilise their armies, millions upon millions of conscripts. Germany asked France, Russia's ally, whether she would stay out of a war. France said no and began to mobilise her three million conscripts.

Germany now had a problem and it was called the Schlieffen Plan, after Alfred von Schlieffen, chief of the German general staff for fourteen years until 1905. Schlieffen had looked at one question: what should Germany do if she had to fight simultaneously against Russia on one side and France on the other? His answer was a scheme in which thousands of trains would rush German troops to the Belgian border. The German armies would storm into France from the north, sweep in great arcs southwards through Flanders, around Paris, then eastwards towards the Franco–German border where a second, smaller, German army would be waiting. The French would be taken from the rear, pushed on to the second German army, surrounded and destroyed. It would all happen in six weeks. The time span was crucial. Schlieffen calculated that the Russians would take six weeks to move their troops into position around East Prussia. Having dealt with France, Germany would then turn east and take on Russia.

The Schlieffen plan was a gamble. The tyranny lay in the rigid timetable: the trains had to deliver the troops; Belgium had to grant them passage or else be quickly overrun; and the troops and horses had to make a set number of miles a day, whatever the opposition, as they surged through France. Its inspiration was the battle of Cannae in 216 BC, when Hannibal defeated the Romans by drawing them in on his centre as his cavalry raced around the Roman flanks, the arch example of double envelopment.

At the last moment Kaiser Wilhelm tried to change the plan. Britain could not live with German battleships in French ports, he reasoned. She would have to come into the war if Germany attacked France. So the Kaiser, ever capricious, decided he would simply attack Russia. Britain and France, he hoped, would stay neutral. It was so neat: no wonder he was the Kaiser. Wilhelm told Hellmuth von Moltke, the army chief-of-staff, that all his forces, one million men, could now be turned against Russia. No, they couldn't, said Moltke. The plan, once activated, could not be undone. Railway timetables could not be rewritten to send the army east. The trains were already taking troops west. And, anyway, how could Germany be sure France would stay neutral? The Kaiser was miffed; Moltke wept.

The Kaiser began to feel better as his troops pushed aside the Belgians. We don't know what he thought about the atrocities. In one Belgian town the Germans claimed their troops had been fired upon by civilians and, as a reprisal, shot 612 men, women and children, including a three-week-old baby. There were similar atrocities elsewhere in Belgium. The Germans had handed Britain, which had come into the war in defence of Belgium's neutrality, a propaganda weapon that would play for the rest of the war. The British exaggerated the scale of these atrocities, and a war that had grown out of balance-of-power politics, a war that was hard to explain to ordinary people, suddenly had moral form: it was the civilised

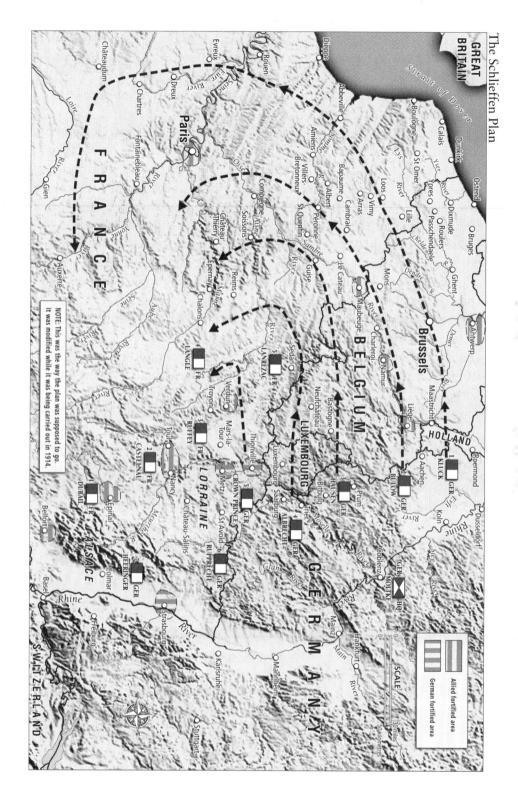

The Schlieffen Plan

NOTE: This was the way the plan was supposed to go. It was modified while it was being carried out in 1914.

GREAT BRITAIN

FRANCE

BELGIUM

Brussels

HOLLAND

LUXEMBOURG

GERMANY

LORRAINE

ALSACE

SWITZERLAND

Strait of Dover

SCALE

| | Allied fortified area |
| | German fortified area |

world against the killers of women and babies. The dreaded Hun was back.

The tiny British Expeditionary Force met the Germans amid the slag heaps and pit heads of Mons, in south-west Belgium, in late August, 1914. Two British divisions held up six German divisions for a day, then slipped away. What became known as the battle of the frontiers was soon over. The Germans were still coming on, but they had not inflicted a terrible defeat on the French and British armies that were retreating before them. General Joseph Joffre, the French commander, a hard man and a pragmatist, held his nerve throughout the long retreat and was all the time visiting his army commanders, sensing the mood, inspiring and admonishing. Von Moltke, an intellectual with a heart complaint, was at Coblenz on the Rhine, more out of touch each day and bothered by the presence of the Kaiser, who only wanted to hear good news and revelled at tales of bloodshed. The German advance across France became untidy. The men's boots were starting to fall apart and many of the horses could go no faster than a walk. Gaps opened between the formations and they were not quite where Schlieffen's plan said they should be. They had failed to envelop the French.

Victory teased when the Germans arrived at the River Marne, only thirty-or-so miles from Paris. But here the French and British armies held them up, then drove them back some forty miles. All three armies were exhausted. The Germans began to entrench, above the River Aisne and then on the heights above the valleys of the Somme and its tributary the Ancre. A line began to form as the opposing armies headed north, and an important question arose: where would the line end? At the sea obviously. But where at the sea? The armies tried to outflank each other, under the big skies of the Somme, then further north around Arras and Armentières, then at Messines in Belgium, and finally at Ypres, the walled town with its moat and brooding skies.

By mid-October, 1914, Ypres was about the only spot left where one side or the other could break through and change the northern end of the front. The Germans, who had briefly held the town, wanted to push the line towards Calais; the allies wanted to turn it back eastwards towards Roulers. The Germans threw into the first battle of Ypres eight divisions of volunteers, many of them students, who had had received two months' training. Among them was Adolf Hitler. As an Austrian living in Munich, shiftless and friendless, a painter of streetscapes, he had been exempt from the draft. The war gave him something to believe in.

British regulars shot down the student-soldiers in what the Germans called the Massacre of the Innocents. The British, French and Belgians held the Ypres salient through a series of attacks, but at a frightful cost. The British regular army that had crossed the Channel a few months earlier was wasting away. Eighteen battalions were down to less than 100 men each; most were now less than half-strength. Early in November the Kaiser came to Warneton, behind Messines, expecting Ypres to fall, yet somehow it held, a hell of smoke and rubble jutting into the German lines, taking artillery fire from three sides, and on its way to becoming what the poet Edmund Blunden would call the 'sepulchral, catacombed city'. By November 22 the battle closed down under louring winter skies. Ypres too had gone to trench warfare. Hitler wrote that First Ypres, as the battle came to be called, made him see that 'life is a constant horrible struggle'.

The frontline eventually found the sea at Nieuport, in Belgium, leaving each side with Channel ports. The line of trenches from here stretched back 475 miles to Switzerland. There were no flanks. Mobile warfare was no longer possible, hence the attraction the following year of places like Gallipoli. Napoleonic ideas were irrelevant. Here were mass armies caught in the biggest stalemate in history. New ideas were needed, and they would take years to evolve. Von Moltke's interpretation of the Schlieffen plan had failed. He had not destroyed the French army or broken the will of the French people. He wrote in September that his nerves were 'very bad'. The Kaiser quietly replaced him with Falkenhayn. But, whatever Moltke's mistakes, the Germans still finished in the stronger position. They held large parts of Belgium and northern France. They could stand on the defensive here while trying to beat the Russians in the east.

THE GERMANS TRIED to break through again at Ypres during April and May, 1915. Second Ypres is perhaps best remembered because the Germans used poison gas – chlorine – on the western front for the first time. The allies pulled back but the salient held. As we have already seen, the allies in 1915 attacked at Neuve Chapelle and Aubers in French Flanders, at Loos and Vimy Ridge in Artois, and in the Champagne. The long Somme front remained relatively quiet, but the Germans, some of whom had been there since 1914, had been busy, excavating chambers and dormitories thirty feet below ground that would render them safe from the heaviest shells.

The Somme is sweet brown dirt shot through with shards of white chalk and grows everything from root vegetables to crops of corn that rustle and shiver high above your head. The river runs roughly east to west, meandering in ponderous loops, slimy green, like the trail of a giant snail, along a marshy valley of willows, lagoons and meadows. This valley is 100 to 200 feet below the surrounding country and is more than a mile wide in places. The British front for the battle that begun on July 1 lay north of the river. This is rolling downland, broken here and there by dark copses and small farming villages. The Roman road runs west to east across the battlefield, almost dead straight, linking Albert, behind the British lines, to Bapaume, well behind the German front. The River Ancre runs roughly north to south across the battlefield, entering the Somme below Albert. For the British this coming battle was going to be more about the Ancre than the Somme. The Ancre isn't like the Somme: it hurries and sings along its little valley. The Somme says eels and the Ancre says trout; the Somme is sad and the Ancre is happy.

The highest ground, a gentle ridge rising to about 300 feet, lies roughly in the middle of the battlefield and runs southwards from Thiepval, on the frontline, to Pozières village and on to Guillemont and Ginchy. The Germans had dug a strong second line on this ridge, about two miles behind the frontline. They turned the deep cellars of houses into machine-gun posts. The ruined villages became rough forts; a machine-gun post was even built into the base of a crucifix. Concrete blockhouses, some of several storeys,

The first day of the Somme, July 1, 1916

Arras

3 UK
ALLENBY

GERMAN

SCALE
0   3 miles
0   5 kilometres

VII UK

GERMAN

Rettemoy Farm
Gommecourt

GERMAN

THIRD

Achiet le Petit

Achiet le Grand

1 GER
VON BELOW

Hebuterne

Puisieux au Mont

SECOND

Bapaume   Cambrai

Serre

Miraumont

VIII UK

Thilloy

Péronne

Beaumont Hamel

River

Pys

ROAD

Ligny Thilloy

Auchonvillers

FIRST

Grandcourt

LINE

Le Sars

2 GER
GALLWITZ

LINE

XIVR GER
STEIN

Zollern Redoubt
Courcelette

Gueudecourt

X UK

Mouquet Farm

Martinpuich

Thiepval

ROMAN

Flers

Martinsart

Pozières

Bazentin le Petit

High Wood

Deville Wood

Ancre

LINE

Bazentin le Grand

Longueval

Ginchy

Aveluy

Ovillers

La Boisselle

Contalmaison

Guillemont

4 UK
RAWLINSON

III UK

Albert

Becourt

Fricourt

Montauban

Amiens

Willow

Stream

Mametz

XV UK

Carnoy

XIII UK

Maricourt

Ancre

XX FR

German defensive lines
Allied frontline
Allied gains on first day
Haig's initial objective (not achieved)

Vaux

Hem

Suzanne

Frise

Feuillères

Bray

River

6 FR

Etinehem

Somme

Cappy

Herbecourt

sprung up where the field of fire was good. Barbed wire was strung on steel stakes in belts forty-yards thick. And a third line of defences had been started behind this second position.

The German lines were much stronger than the British and French positions facing them, and for an obvious reason. The Germans had snatched a large tract of northern France and didn't intend giving it up: they were on the defensive. The British and French, on the other hand, needed to believe their own lines were temporary; if they didn't, the Kaiser had virtually won the war.

The German position was not only deep and formidable: there was nothing of strategic value behind it, no big city, no important rail junction, just farms and orchards and churches. Haig would have preferred to attack at Ypres. He was fighting on the Somme, where the British and French fronts met, to please his French allies. The Somme campaign was as much about politics as it was about strategy.

This was going to be the biggest British attack of the war, yet Haig and General Henry Rawlinson, the infantryman who commanded the 4th Army, which would be doing most of the attacking, had different ideas on tactics. Haig became more optimistic as planning went ahead. He wanted to try for a breakthrough. If he could do this, he would send cavalry from Lieutenant-General Hubert Gough's Reserve Army through the gap and try to push the Germans northwards, towards the Belgian coast. Rawlinson wanted to attack in careful and deliberate stages, to bite off a piece of the German frontline and hold it before going on to the next step. Haig's final instructions left no doubt he wanted to break through to Bapaume, the market town seven miles inside the German lines, then turn north, but he was going to do it in stages. The first was to capture a line that runs from Serre in the north, to Pozières in the centre, and then on to Montauban in the south. The second stage would take the line out to Bapaume and Ginchy. Only then would the cavalry come in. What Haig seemed to be saying was: 'Break through – if possible.' Considering the scale of the operation, it was all rather vague, a bit of this and a bit of that, a bit of Haig and a larger bit of Rawlinson.

The infantry attack was set for Saturday, July 1. The Sunday before Haig went to the Church of Scotland and listened carefully to the sermon of the Reverend George Duncan, then summarised it, as he usually did, in his diary. Haig was a man of simple faith. Like Napoleon, he now believed that he was an instrument of destiny. Unlike Napoleon, he was not vainglorious. He was a plain and practical man, admired but unloved, perhaps because to be loved one must show human characteristics, and the Reverend Duncan's words somehow allowed him to rationalise things, to feel sure about what he was doing. Faith gave Haig an astonishing serenity throughout the Great War.

The night before the big attack Haig wrote in his diary:

> The weather report is favourable for tomorrow. With God's help, I feel hopeful. The men are in splendid spirits. Several have said that they have never before been so instructed and informed of the nature of the operation before them. The wire has never been so well cut, nor the Artillery preparation so thorough. I have seen personally all the Corps Commanders and one and all are full of confidence. The only doubt I have is regarding the 8th Corps (Hunter-Weston) which has had no experience of fighting in France and has not carried out one successful raid.

Haig was right to be worried about Hunter-Weston, who had just about proved himself the most thick-headed general in the British army. Haig was wrong about the artillery. The wire had not been well cut; and he was relying too much on field guns rather than 'heavies'.

The seven-day bombardment that preceded the infantry attack sounded tremendous. The thunder could be heard in Kent. And it looked impressive: fountains of earth rose in the air, hung there, then crashed back down again along the eighteen miles of the British front. Troops watching this doubtless said, much as their comrades had during the assaults in the north during the previous year: 'Nothing can live under that.' Men *could* live under that, terrible as it was, if they were deep enough underground. Their nerves might be frayed (rats in the German dugouts ran up the walls in panic, only to be slapped down with shovels), but once the barrage lifted every three Germans who came up from the depths with a machine gun could kill hundreds of Englishmen, and they did.

The British didn't have enough heavy guns for such a long front. Most of the guns were eighteen-pounders, field pieces, and mostly these were firing shrapnel, which could wipe out advancing infantry but did no worthwhile damage to earthworks. Five French divisions were attacking south of the British, above and below the line of the River Somme. They had one heavy gun for every twenty-one yards of trench to be attacked; the British had one to every fifty-eight yards. British ammunition was faulty: it was said that one in every three shells failed to explode. Ploughs still disinter these duds, green with mould. And there was the problem of wire-cutting. The graze-fuse was not yet in use. High-explosive shells exploded when they hit something hard. If the soil was soft, the shell might go in a few feet before detonating. This often tossed the wire coils around without cutting them.

For the Somme battle the British had a fresh army, short on experience but full of hope and, one has to say, innocence. Britain had not yet taken casualties the way France had; Britain's war still had a romantic tinge. Patriotism was a drug that linked old Etonians to coal miners in common purpose. If it was sometimes naïve, it was also genuine. The divisions for the Somme included regulars and territorials (the pre-war force of part-time volunteers), but the majority were New Army, part of the two million volunteers who had answered Kitchener's call.

Some of these volunteers had been allowed to form battalions of 'Pals' or 'Chums'. Men from certain districts or vocations could join together and serve together. Four battalions from Liverpool's business offices became the Liverpool Pals. Accrington, a Lancashire cotton town, and Grimsby, a fishing port, produced their Pals, as did Manchester. Hull threw up a Tradesman's Battalion and a Sportsmen's Battalion. Tyneside filled two brigades: the Tyneside Irish and the Tyneside Scots. Glasgow came up with a Tramways Battalion. The whole 36th Division was composed entirely of Ulstermen, men who before the war were prepared to fight England rather than be absorbed into Catholic Ireland. The Public Schools Battalion had the ill luck to be sent to the 29th Division in Hunter-Weston's corps. Also in the 29th was one of two contingents from the dominions to take part in the first day of the Somme, the Newfoundland Regiment, which had served at Gallipoli. The other dominion force was the Bermuda Volunteer Rifle Corps, eighty strong.

There was a risk with these Pals battalions that no-one seems to have foreseen. If they were to incur heavy casualties, the grief would not be spread lightly across the land. It would be concentrated in certain streets and districts, in certain offices and clubs.

The generals from the 'old army' didn't trust the New Army men, just as they were suspicious of Australians and Canadians. Many of the battalions taking part in the Somme battle were ordered to advance at the walk and in extended lines. The generals didn't think the new troops could master the fire-and-movement technique the French would use. It was also assumed that the bombardment would kill or disable all the Germans in the front trench. One senior officer told the men of a New Army battalion that they would be able to light their pipes and march all the way to Pozières without seeing a live German.

THE SOMME BATTLE took less than half-an-hour to degenerate into chaos. Haig arose on July 1 and, as he always did, tapped the barometer, which was rising. Swirls of mist hung over the valleys of the Somme and the Ancre, then began to melt as the sun rose in a clear sky. There was no wind. Between the screams of shells the soldiers could hear birds singing.

At 10.55 am Haig sent a telegram to his wife, Dorothy: 'Very successful attack this morning – captured portion of enemy second line on a front of 8000 yards – we hold the hills about Longueval and hope to get the Cavalry through – All went like clockwork . . .'

The men had followed tapes and red and green lanterns to reach the front trenches. A cook in the Ulster Division, which was to attack between Beaumont Hamel and Thiepval, produced bacon rashers, fried bread, jam and tea for breakfast. Some battalions elsewhere received nothing. Rum was plentiful. 'Real thick treacle stuff', one soldier called it. Many officers wore the rough uniforms of rankers. Others turned themselves into prime targets by carrying canes and wearing whipcord breeches, spurs and Sam Browne belts. The men were heavily loaded; most were lumping more than seventy pounds, which meant they could not have run anyway.

At 7.30 am the British guns ceased firing. The British gunners adjusted their sights to lift off the German frontline and on to the German back areas. Officers blew on silver whistles. The men from 200 battalions climbed ladders and began to make their way through the British wire, looking left and right so as to form up an extended line, walking towards the opposing trench where everyone was surely dead. Some men dribbled a football. Then the German machine guns opened up. A new massacre of the innocents had begun.

THE FIVE FRENCH divisions – two above the Somme, three below – did well. Above the river they ran through the mist at 7.30 am, going from crater to crater rather than walking in extended lines, took their objectives and fought off counter-attacks. Below the river they attacked two hours after the British at 9.30. The French here had eighty-five heavy batteries to the Germans' eight. The German frontline was just about obliterated, although machine guns further back kept firing. Here too the French took all their objectives. The five divisions sent back 4000 prisoners. The French artillery had done what it was supposed to do.

Next to the French, the two most southerly of the British divisions, both New Army and helped by the French artillery on their right, also took their objectives, including Montauban village, where crazy piles of German dead lay in the cellars and the only living creature was a fox that dashed across the main street. The wire had been well cut. Casualties in these two divisions nevertheless ran to more than 6000.

Next along, still going north, two divisions, plus an extra brigade, attacked the villages of Fricourt and Mametz. They took Mametz but not Fricourt. The casualties here were 8800.

The next two divisions up the line lost 11,500 men. The 8th Division, regulars, attacked north of the Albert–Bapaume road. The 34th, a New Army formation that included the Grimsby Chums, the Tyneside Scots and the Tyneside Irish, attacked south of the road. Ahead of them, in a dip in the road, lay La Boisselle. Just north of it sat Ovillers, and beyond both of these villages, along the Bapaume road and up the ridge, lay Pozières and, above it, the German second line. This was an exceptionally strong position: the Germans looked down from Pozières in the east and Thiepval in the north. The British set off two mines here, one at the head of Sausage Valley, south of La Boisselle, and now known as the Lochnagar crater, but these failed to rattle the Germans, who set about hacking the British divisions to pieces. The 34th Division, going for La Boisselle, lost 6380 men for a gain of perhaps 100 yards.

The 8th, going for Ovillers and Pozières, advanced over ground that was practically bare, as it still is. Battalions were wiped out in minutes by machine-gun fire from the front, from the heights of Thiepval and by artillery fire from around Pozières. Small groups made the German trenches but could not hold on. The Germans at Ovillers lost 180 men (seventy-eight killed), the 8th Division 5121 (1927 killed). A German history of this encounter says the 'English' came on in extended line and at an easy pace, 'as if expecting to find nothing alive in our front trenches'.

North of this slaughter two New Army formations – the Ulster Division and the 32nd (which included the Glasgow Tramways, the Newcastle Commercials and the Glasgow Boys' Brigade battalions) – went for Thiepval Spur. This position was just about impregnable. Thiepval village lay as rubble but it had been turned into a fort of sorts, with tunnels linking the cellars. The Ulstermen attacked with much ardour (it was the anniversary of the Battle of the Boyne), breaking into the Schwaben Redoubt and heading for Thiepval village. This was an extraordinary feat, but the German fire became intense. The Ulstermen eventually had to pull back, leaving wounded everywhere on the slopes above the River Ancre. The division had lost 5104 men. Bravery wasn't enough. The 32nd Division took and held the Leipzig Redoubt and ran up nearly 4000 casualties.

A few miles north of Thiepval, Hunter-Weston's VIII Corps went for the villages of Serre and Beaumont Hamel, on the spurs above the Ancre, which takes a swing east beyond Thiepval. This is difficult country, ridges and narrow valleys. Sappers fired a big mine at 7.20 am in front of the 29th Division's line, opening a crater sixty-feet deep, and simultaneously the British artillery lifted off the German frontline. This virtually told the Germans the infantry attack was coming. The Germans opened up a furious fire before the British hopped the bags. British dead piled up in heaps around the uncut wire. At 9.05 am the Newfoundland battalion went over. Men began to fall at once but the battalion, what was left of it, kept going and a few Newfoundlanders reached the German frontline, there to be killed. Every officer became a casualty, along with close to 700 rankers. The 4th Division also took frightful casualties.

Hunter-Weston's third division, the 31st (which included the Hull Tradesmen, the Leeds Pals, the Accrington Pals, the Hull Sportsmen and the Bradford Pals), was supposed to take Serre. A handful did make the village, only to be killed. The corps had lost 14,000 men, the heaviest casualty list for the day, for next to nothing.

Finally there was the most northerly attack, the diversion at Gommecourt. The idea was to pinch off the Gommecourt Salient with two divisions and try to draw fire that might otherwise be directed at Hunter-Weston's divisions to the south. This attack failed with another 7000 dead and wounded.

BRITISH CASUALTIES FOR that day above the Somme were eventually put at 57,470, of whom 19,240 were dead. Most of these came in the first few hours. Most fell to machine guns, not artillery. The Germans lost about 8000. It was the worst day for casualties in British military history.

'The Somme' now sits in the language like 'the Crucifixion' or 'the Depression', as though the phrase is itself self-explanatory. It is a few scraps of film, flickering and blotched: soldiers clambering up ladders to leave the trenches, little dots of men toppling over in no-man's land. It is the day thousands of young men, full of hope and trust, came to know the meaning of modern war, the day romance died. In the weeks and months afterwards just about everyone in Yorkshire and Lancashire and Ulster seemed to know someone who had lost a son, and Britain came finally to understand that war was not about cavalrymen chasing rowdy natives but thousands of men in dull khaki walking, dream-like, to their doom across a wasteland of smoke and craters. To some 'the Somme' is simply shorthand for anything that is hopelessly sad. To others it is about the day a dozen-or-so generals got most things wrong. And they did, particularly in their estimates of what artillery could do and in their faith that 'character' could triumph over technology.

The Somme didn't ruin a generation; it did, however, leave scars on two or three, as Verdun did in France and Germany. When another world war came British politicians and generals would look at maps and plans for some coming offensive or landing and announce that they didn't want a re-run of the Somme.

Thirty-two battalions each suffered casualties of more than 500, twenty of them New Army. The two Tyneside brigades, eight battalions all up, were so wrecked that they were immediately taken out of the line. Rumours spread through Accrington, in Lancashire, that only seven soldiers from the local Pals battalion had survived. The casualty lists eventually showed that some 115 had come through unwounded, which meant 585 had not. The Leeds Pals lost 528, the Public Schools Battalion 522, the Glasgow Boys' Brigade Battalion 511. In certain towns and streets death seemed to be everywhere.

But all this was known later. Communications had broken down, as they always seemed to, when the infantry went over. When dusk came on that first day no-one had a clear idea of casualties.

The realisation of what had happened came upon Haig over several days. As we have seen, he was optimistic when he telegraphed his wife on the morning of the attack. By the afternoon, when he wrote to her, he was more circumspect. The next day he wrote: 'Things are going well and I hope that, with perseverance and help from Above, a considerable success may in time result.' He thought his casualties might be 40,000. 'This cannot be considered severe in view of the numbers engaged, and the length of front attacked.' A week later he wrote: 'In another fortnight with Divine help, I hope some decisive results may be obtained.' From the second day Haig seemed to have abandoned thoughts of a breakthrough.

As with the first reports of the Gallipoli landings of the previous year, the early press accounts of the Somme were upbeat. They spoke of villages captured (few, in truth, had been) and of 9500 German prisoners (the correct figure was around 2200). Wounded soldiers arrived in Britain and told of how they had seen hundreds of their countrymen slaughtered. Crowds gathered outside newspaper offices. Then after a week or so the telegrams began arriving, thousands of telegrams for thousands of dead. Blinds were drawn and the long grieving began.

WHAT HAD GONE wrong? Two things need to be said in defence of Haig. He was attacking not at his own wish but to take the pressure off the French at Verdun. And he was doing so at a place – a formidable place, as it turned out – that the French had chosen.

All he had managed on that first day was to put a dent, about three-and-a-half miles long and a mile deep, in the southern end of the German line and a few lesser dents to the north. He had fired 1.6 million shells as an overture and the bombardment had failed. This was the nub of it: a failure of artillery. The big guns had not wiped out the German machine gunners sheltering deep in the chalk. Thus it didn't matter whether the infantrymen were regulars or well-intentioned volunteers from Glasgow: the machine gunners would get them just the same, and they did.

HAIG COULD NOT have called off the battle after it had started even if he had wanted to, which he didn't. There was a matter of honour: the French expected the English to make the same blood sacrifices that they had been making. And the battle, once started, had developed a rhythm of its own. Very early, though, and perhaps subconsciously, Haig had begun to think of it as a battle of attrition where the tactic would be to bite and hold. The best evidence of this came on the night of the first day, when he put General Hubert Gough, one of his favourites, in charge of the two infantry corps at the northern end of the 4th Army's line. Gough, a blustery cavalryman, was the commander of the Reserve Army; he had been waiting behind the front, hoping to send his three cavalry divisions galloping into 'the gap'. Haig was conceding that there was no gap and nothing for the cavalry to do. He was thinking of narrowing the front and making piecemeal attacks in those places below the Bapaume road where he had had successes on the first day.

Haig took Fricourt and La Boisselle, then Contalmaison and Mametz Wood. Falkenhayn, chief of the German general staff, suspended all offensive actions at Verdun. The Somme was not quite the failure it looked on the first day. Meanwhile the Russians, under General Alexei Brusilov, were rolling back the Austrians in Galicia in what would turn out to be the only successful Russian offensive of the war. Falkenhayn had troubles on three fronts.

On July 14 the British captured German second-line positions around Longueval and took the fighting into High and Delville woods. This battle offered a clue about the tactics that might succeed. Rawlinson used two-thirds of the artillery that had been available for July 1 but concentrated its fire on a front of just 6000 yards and used only high-explosive shells rather than shrapnel. He drove a salient into the German lines. The front now needed to be widened. That meant Pozières had to be taken on the left and Guillemont on the right. If Pozières could be taken, the British could try to take Thiepval from the rear.

Pozières was a strong position. The trenches of the German second line ran across the hill just east of the village. That hill, where the ruins of a blockhouse now lay, was one of the highest points on the Somme front, with a good view to Thiepval and fields of fire in all directions. The village had been worked into the German second-line system by a trench – marked on the maps as

Pozières Trench – that looped south of the village before heading for Mouquet Farm and Thiepval. Two British divisions tried for Pozières on the morning of July 15 and failed. The British decided to bombard it with artillery and try again at 6 pm. A British artillery observer wrote: 'This was the biggest bombardment of it [the village], by all our heavies, I have ever seen. The whole place went up in brick dust, and when it was over no trace of a building could be seen anywhere. It was a wonderful sight, huge clouds of rose-coloured, brown, bluish black, and white smoke rolling along together with flashes of bursts, the whole against a pale green-blue sky and bright evening sunlight.'

All that rose-coloured smoke and fury didn't matter. The Germans came out of the ruins and opened up with machine guns. It was the same when the British tried again on the 17th. At least ten machine guns opened up on them. Some of the fire was coming from a concrete structure at the southern end of the village.

Haig now decided to put Gough and his Reserve Army in charge of the assault on Pozières. Gough would carry it out with the 1st Australian Division, which was waiting about twelve miles behind the front.

YOU CAN SEE most of the battlefield of July 1 from the site known as the Windmill, which sits on the swell of the hill above Pozières. The French built a windmill here around 1610 and the Germans built a blockhouse out of the ruins of it. Lumps of concrete covered with grassy mould are still strewn about. Stand here, try to ignore the slap of tyres on the Bapaume road, and you can take a trip back to 1916. The first-day front curves gently before you under a summer sky.

There, away to the north, is Gommecourt. Below it is Beaumont Hamel, sitting above the line of the Ancre. And there, so close, about two-miles distant, is the British memorial at Thiepval, a triumphal arch of red brick and Portland stone, stolid and massive, squatting improbably above fields of corn and beet and somehow lacking in poignancy. Until you get up close, that is, and then you forget about the architecture and see the names, column after column of them, 73,367 men from Britain, plus a few from South Africa, who have no known grave and lie all about us, under the crops, under the red-brown fallow and the yellow stubble. To the left of Thiepval, just down the hill, is Pozières village, and behind you Fricourt, Mametz and Montauban, Delville Wood and High Wood.

What, you wonder, might a German standing here on July 1 have seen? That line from Gommecourt all the way to Montauban wreathed in smoke, British observation balloons swaying above it, the thunder of artillery rolling up the valleys, the buzzing of aircraft and the chatter of machine guns at La Boisselle. What might the German have thought? That these English would be beaten back today because they had no notion of the strength of the positions they were attacking; but that they would keep coming and that a new chapter might be opening, Verdun on the Somme.

Photographs of Pozières in 1914 show dowdy brick houses and grimy chimneys shoulder to shoulder along the Roman road, which is cambered and narrow, running dead straight to Bapaume. Rows of plane and poplar trees stand at both ends of the village. Horses and carts ply the main street and a man pushes a handcart along the footpath while another stands by his bicycle, and behind the houses are courtyards and barns and orchards and fowl pens. Elms shelter the watering-place for stock about halfway along the main street. Pozières looks careworn and honest but with few of the charms of the villages that sit so prettily along the Somme and the Ancre, and before 1916 it was never going to be famous for anything. The poet John Masefield described the pre-war village as 'poor and without glory', except for its lovely trees.

Pozières village, you just know, would have been like dozens of others above the Somme in 1914. A village would be home to 300-or-so people. These would include a mayor who would take his office very seriously, a priest who would wield even more power, if more mysteriously, a blacksmith, a carpenter, an old woman who laid out the dead and an old man who mixed up potions to cure colicky horses. The church spire would dominate the village and it might be 1100 years old. The next biggest building would be the town hall, then the school. There would be thirty or forty farms nearby. Most of the farmers would live in the village, in houses with barns and stables that were set up like small forts with a heavy door or gate that opened on to the main street. There might be one grand farm nearby, with a château topped by eight chimneys and owned by a financier from Amiens. Dairy cows would graze a common and each morning a man would drive them back to the village, dropping each cow off at its owner's barn for milking. There would be no trees in the fields and no fences: the wheat would grow right to the road, as it still does. Every mile or so there would be a copse, dark and tangled and loaded with pheasant and hare. The village would be an easy walk, maybe two miles, from the next and there would be a roadside shrine between the two.

Pozières was reduced to smoking rubble in 1916, then built again, pretty much as it had been. In the main street 'Le Tommy Café' now caters for pilgrims from Britain and Australia who come to see where a great-grandfather fought and maybe died. Behind the restaurant is an open-air museum. Here are iron pickets used to string German wire. There are shells from the German seventy-six-millimetre mortar, the dreaded *minenwerfer*. Farmers tell you that, of all the shells they unearth each year, these are the most danger-ous. And here are dozens of British eighteen-pounder shrapnel shells, duds that failed to explode. The explosive charge to burst the shrapnel is at the rear. In the middle of the shell are 200 shrapnel balls. The fuse that determines when the shell will explode in the air is in the nose cone and set by a key.

Two miles west of Pozières lies the Lochnager crater. This is where the largest mine was exploded on July 1, 1916. An Englishman now owns the land here. He has left it as it was in 1916, pockmarked with spoil and shell holes and brooding with old cruelties. Blackberries and weeds grow on the rim of the crater, which plunges ninety feet. You look down on seams of white chalk, like straggles of snow, and, at the bottom, tiny crosses left by English visitors. A wooden cross marks the spot where the body of Private George Nugent of the Tyneside Scots was found in 1998, eighty-two years after he was reported missing on the first day of the Somme. An English visitor saw a boot poking out of the earth after rain. He pulled at it and up came a shinbone.

Near Beaumont Hamel, where the Newfoundlanders of the 29th Division died so thickly, no-man's land has been left much as it was. The trenches are still here and the spoil thrown up by shells has created dozens of little mounds, grassed over like an alluvial goldfield long abandoned. The Newfoundlanders were going downhill into a cup of a valley, which meant the Germans on the low ridge ahead could pick them off easily. You know this when you go to the German lines and watch a group of Canadian tourists coming down the hill. Several graves at the bottom of the valley carry the inscription 'Two soldiers of the Great War'. One assumes the bodies could not be separated.

Beaumont Hamel, a first-day objective, finally fell four-and-a-half months later on November 13. An English officer sent out with the burial parties wrote: 'The dead Newfoundlanders looked very ragged, and the rats were running out of their chests. The rats were getting out of the rain of course, because the cloth over the rib cage made quite a nice nest . . . when you touched a body, the rats just poured out from the front . . . To think that a human being provided a nest for a rat was a pretty dreadful feeling.'

Many of the British and dominion troops coming up for the Somme battles passed through Albert and all seemed to remember the Hanging Virgin atop the basilica. Early in 1915 a German shell hit the base of the statue and it was left hanging, virtually horizontal and seemingly in defiance of gravity, like a loose tooth that would come away with one gentle push. On July 1 the basilica became a dressing station. Wounded were brought in on stretchers and wheelbarrows and soon the church was packed and slippery with blood. The church has a warmth that is lacking in the more famous and much older cathedral at Amiens. The basilica was built after the Enlightenment, the cathedral long before. The basilica, neo-Byzantine in style, says love and the cathedral says piety, with a hint of bigotry as well. The basilica was rebuilt in the 1920s. Atop the dome of gold leaf the Virgin holds the Jesus child aloft, as if to show Him to the world. The child holds His arms out, as if He owns the world.

Under those arms, for mile upon mile, north and south, in valleys and on low hills, are military cemeteries, dozens of them, each with rows of Portland stone markers and visitors' books and roses; and every day pilgrims from Britain and her former dominions come to remember young men who died in something that was so terrible and so strange it was simply called 'the Somme'.

6

The road to Pozières

Captain Ivor Margetts, a Tasmanian schoolteacher with kind eyes and the long frame of a ruckman, headed off with the 1st Australian Division for the fighting at Pozières. He passed through Albert and doubtless looked up – everyone did – at the gilded Virgin, dangling above the square. Lieutenant Charles Carrington of the British 48th Division, also on his way to Pozières, passed underneath by moonlight. The men, he wrote, were awed. 'The melodrama of it rose strongly in our hearts.' The Australians had decided the Virgin was about to dive and christened her 'Fanny', after Fanny Durack, who won a gold medal as a swimmer at the Stockholm Olympics of 1912. Margetts by now would have swapped his felt hat for a steel helmet and removed his Sam Browne belt and leggings. Only the three pips on his shoulder straps would now mark him as an officer.

Margetts had been in the big battles of Gallipoli; most of his comrades in the reconstituted 1st Division had not. They had been in the frontline at Armentières, near Fromelles, but never in a big attack. None of the Australians, neither Gallipoli veterans nor fresh recruits, was aware of what they were now marching into. Gallipoli had never been an artillery battle in the style of the western front. The

Pozières: first Australian attack, July 23, 1916

Mouquet Farm

OVILLERS–COURCELETTE ROAD

Bapaume

ROAD

Old German lines

Windmill

Cemetery

Pozières

8 ▷AUS

Munster Alley

Trench

GERMAN LINE

Mash Valley

48 ◁UK

JUL 22

Gibraltar

Pozières

Trench

ALLIED LINE

JUL 22

3 ◁AUS

Alley

III ◁UK

ROMAN

Albert

1 ◁AUS

Watch

Pearl Alley

Chalk pit

2 ◁AUS

Contalmaison Wood

Black

Sausage Valley

Casualty Corner

Bailiff Wood

Contalmaison

SCALE

0 ———— 500 metres

0 ———— 500 yards

Turks only brought up heavy howitzers, and then just four of them, a month before the allies left. And, curious as it seems, these men didn't know how cruel the twenty-day-old Somme battle had been. They, like the newspaper readers of Manchester and Sydney, thought the offensive was going well. The censors had been busy. The wider world was unaware of what Haig had been trying to achieve on that first day and that his losses had been the worst in British history. An Australian sergeant wrote home that 'a big push has been going on successfully since the 1st of July . . . Many English regiments pass us who have been relieved from the front area . . . They have been very successful and are all singing as they march along, every man wearing a German helmet.'

THE ELFIN-LIKE BILLY Hughes, all ears and crinkles and rasping adjectives, had climbed on to a wagon in an orchard near Armentières to address men from the 1st Division the previous month. Wagging a bony finger that might have been borrowed from the Grim Reaper, he told them that the thoughts of all Australians were with them. Whatever happened, Australia would not forget them or their dependents.

The Australian Prime Minister had been stumping up and down the British Isles delivering patriotic speeches. He was much feted: he understood the rough demagoguery of war in a way Herbert Asquith did not. Hughes had been given the freedom of the cities of London and Manchester, handed honorary doctorates from universities and appointed to the Privy Council. Once he had humped a swag around Queensland and the world had trampled all over him. Now the assisted migrant, born of Welsh parents in London, was a man to know. He was a trade unionist and defender of battlers, yet the war had somehow transformed him into a man who was saying the things that those in power wanted to hear.

If this was confusing to others, it wasn't to William Morris Hughes. He was now welcome at places he once would have been thrown out of as a Welsh upstart. He stayed at Windsor Castle with the King. Generals, archbishops and press barons took him seriously.

They were using him, he was using them, and Keith Murdoch, the Australian journalist now working in London, was using the entire cast to turn himself into a man of eminence. Murdoch waited on Hughes, ran his errands and literally became an arm of government, but forgot to tell his readers back in Australia that he was a player as well as an observer. Lloyd George seemed to see Hughes as a rougher version of himself, without the music or the power to make audiences nod along with his rhythms, but charged with the same energy, no gentleman, no respecter of conventions, but a man determined to have his way. As John Grigg, Lloyd George's biographer, wrote: 'Both were men of the left whose distaste for ideology and, above all, concern for national defence forced them into an alliance with the right.'

And now, on this day in France, Hughes spied from his perch on the wagon an elderly infantry private, William James Johnson, who had been a Labor member of Federal Parliament for three years until 1913. Hughes shook hands with Johnson, who quipped: 'Well, Billy, have they made you a doctor of divinity yet?'

A few months earlier, on the first anniversary of the Anzac landing, Hughes had said in London that the Gallipoli campaign 'had shown that through self-sacrifice alone could men or a nation be saved'. Then he said something that was very strange: 'And since it has evoked this pure and noble spirit, who should say that this dreadful war was wholly evil now that in a world saturated with the lust of material things came the sweet purifying breath of self-sacrifice?'

Hughes was high on the careless rhetoric of war. He was going back to the political salons of London; Private Johnson, the former parliamentarian, now aged forty-five, was going to fight Germans at Pozières, where he would die after being hit in the head by a shell fragment.

MARGETTS HAD WRITTEN home a few months before he set off for Pozières:

> I have been rather busy writing to broken hearted mothers, giving them details regards killed & missing men. It's not a nice job but I am getting a

dab at it 'every one different and quite original'. One has frequently to cut out some of the details. People ask if you can tell them the last words & who was holding their hands when they snuffed out. I could not very well say that the poor chap was cursing fairly well & was being held down on the stretcher by three or four dirty stretcher bearers who also put in an occasional curse at the Turks for doing the damage or describe some of the actual scenes which one sees.

Letters of condolence were a burden for all frontline officers: how to tell relatives enough of what had happened – but not all? As Margetts covered the last mile or so towards the Pozières front, past shell holes with muddy bottoms, past British and German corpses and with the sweet smell of German tear gas in his nostrils, it may have occurred to him that he would shortly be writing such letters again.

SERGEANT BEN CHAMPION, another 1st Division man, had given up his dental apprenticeship to enlist as an eighteen-year-old. At his first billet in France, near Hazebrouck, the farmer's wife upbraided him and other Australians for washing with soap in a pond the cows drank from. The guests pacified her by paying for coffee and cognac, and she allowed them to sit in her spotless kitchen, where the fire glowed, as did the brass work.

Now Champion was on the long march towards Pozières. Packs were discarded, except for a waterproof sheet that was rolled up and worn as a bandolier. The men received a strip of pink cotton to sew on the back of their tunics so that British pilots could identify them. Champion collected an extra 250 rounds for his .303 Lee Enfield rifle, two sandbags and two bombs before passing under the Hanging Virgin. The march through Albert was eerie, he wrote. English guides took them into Sausage Valley, which led to Pozières and was packed with artillery pieces seemingly locked wheel to wheel. The guns roared and the Australians reeled at the sound.

. . . we realised that at last that we were in a war. The Northern sector to us was just a nursery to prepare the way for this. Heaps of used ammunition, shells and war litter of all kinds, broken rifles, equipment, guns, boxes of biscuits, and ammunition were strewn everywhere. Soon we came to an area with the sickly smell of dead bodies, and half-buried men, mules and horses came into view. Here was war wastage properly. Germans and British mixed together, lying in all positions, and there wasn't a man but thought more seriously of what was ahead.

The Australians walked into gas and pulled on their masks. Some thought the smell reminded them of hyacinths. Now they could see Pozières ahead, low heaps of red-brick rubble and splintered orchards. Tired by the long march and frightened by the nearness of death, they began to dig new trenches and crack jokes.

Next day the Germans began hitting them with 5.9-inch howitzer shells, known as 'Jack Johnsons'. They exploded in black smoke, which is why they were named for the first black man to hold the world heavyweight boxing title. Australians trying to dig out comrades who had been buried by shell-bursts were hit in the arms and shoulders by machine-gun fire. Champion said the men were told that once the attack began no-one was to help a wounded man. His battalion was to go forward in waves, every fourth man in the first two companies carrying a pick or a shovel. As soon as the German trench was taken the Australians were to change its parados, or rear wall, into a parapet. The men of the first wave had their sleeves rolled up to the elbows to distinguish them from the following waves. Officers, now dressed like rankers, mingled with the men and encouraged them not to drink too much from their water bottles.

And so, on July 23, Champion hopped the bags at Pozières. 'The tension affected the men in different ways,' he wrote. 'I couldn't stop urinating . . .'

LIEUTENANT CHARLES CARRINGTON of the British 48th Division had moved up to the front earlier. His division was to attack Pozières on the left of the Australians but first it had to fight on the eastern outskirts of Ovillers. On the way, near La Boisselle, Carrington tried to sleep in a German dugout. 'This was the first German dugout we had seen, and I felt the romance of our position too strongly to sleep just then.' Carrington was nineteen, a boy from a country vicarage who had enlisted as a private in Kitchener's New Army. 'There was a strong, stale, fetid smell of sweat and decaying paper and old clothes, permeated by the solid flavour of the earth that lay fifteen-feet thick above our heads.'

Next day, after six months in France, he saw his first corpse, a German. A sergeant, pleasant-mannered and with a silky civilised voice, told Carrington that he had once pulled the teeth out of a German corpse in Belgium and made a necklace. Carrington came upon more German dead in a shell hole. 'They lay, not in picturesque attitudes, but in the stiff unreal pose of fallen tailor's dummies; they looked less human than waxworks; all the personality had faded from their faces with the life. Big men they had been: they had now a horrid plumpness. In awful fact they were bursting out of their clothes.'

On his way to the Ovillers front Carrington heard a whistling sound. The shell fell behind him. *Phut*. A dud. Then came another similar sound. The shell hit the ground like a rotten egg. Then more. Carrington smelled something. 'It was sweet, pungent, sickly, heavy. Almonds were something like it.' The smell thickened and caught at his throat. His eyes and nose began to run. The Germans were firing tear gas.

Soon Carrington was shooting at grey-clothed shadows during a bomb fight outside Ovillers. A German bullet hit one of his men in the brain. He lost consciousness at once but refused to die. His body writhed for two hours. An old corporal held his body and arms as a dozen others sat around in a ditch reeking of blood. Water came up in tins. The men swallowed it in huge draughts, even though it tasted of petrol.

Carrington looked up towards the next ridge and Pozières village, which other battalions of his division were to assault from the west while the Australian 1st Division attacked from the south.

The Australians were going in the line there to attack it, and as we stood and talked, the skyline heaved and smoked, throwing up fountains and jets of soil and grey smoke as if it were a dark grey sea breaking heavily on a reef. The bombardment grew thicker and thicker: clouds of smoke sprang up and drifted across its torn group of trees; the spurts of high explosive rose close together, till it seemed that the very contour of the hill must be changed.

GENERAL HUBERT GOUGH, the commander of the Reserve Army, had been told by Haig on July 18 to 'carry out methodical operations against Pozières with a view to capturing that important position with as little delay as possible'. Several days later Haig visited Gough 'to make sure the Australians had only been given a simple task'. He wrote in his diary that this was the first time the Australians would be 'part of a serious offensive on a big scale'. One can sense what he was trying to say, but it did rather play down what had happened at Fromelles three days earlier.

Haig wasn't sure what to think about the Australians. He liked the appearance of them. 'The men were looking splendid, fine physique, very hard and determined-looking . . . The Australians are mad keen to kill Germans and to start doing it at once! I told the Brigadier to start quietly, because so many unfortunate occurrences had happened through being in too great a hurry to win this campaign!' But Haig also worried about the Australians' reputation for rowdiness away from the front. The Australians were free spirits and Haig liked conformity. He did not equate fighting Turks with fighting Germans, which showed some failure of the imagination, since the Turks had beaten the British, French and Anzacs on Gallipoli. Haig worried about the quality of the senior Australian officers and didn't think much of his countryman Birdwood. Too indulgent of Australian ways.

Haig perhaps should have worried more about putting the Australians under Gough. The Reserve Army commander had no sooner received his order to attack Pozières – methodically, the order said – than he summoned Major-General Harold Walker, commander of the 1st Australian Division.

Gough had decided to forego the military courtesies. He would not wait for Birdwood and White and the staff of I Anzac Corps to come up. Gough and the staff of the Reserve Army would tell Walker what to do. His first words to Walker were: 'I want you to go into the line and attack Pozières tomorrow night.' Gough hadn't looked at the ground; the story goes that he had spent much time boar-hunting with his staff. He wasn't going to let 'Hooky' Walker look at the ground either.

One hesitates to say the episode is typical of Gough, but it certainly demonstrated three of his failings. He was arrogant; he was an optimist; and he was careless when it came to preparations and staff work. The cavalry charge was forever playing in his head. He wanted to gallop, to crash through; he didn't want to be held up by detail or hear the voices of doubters. He had a hot temper. Edmonds, in a letter to Bean in 1930, said Gough was a good soldier 'but too rash and headstrong'. In another letter he told Bean that he thought Gough 'first class as [a] divisional and corps commander, but his gifts of energy and dash were out of place in command of an Army . . .'

It is questionable whether Gough much understood modern war or indeed anything other than cavalry. In those days officers with his mindset were called 'thrusters'. That's why Haig seems to have favoured him, even though Haig, also a cavalryman, was by nature more prudent. Gough's rise had been fast and bore little relationship to achievements. Edmonds said Haig was 'perfectly infatuated' with Gough.

Educated at Eton, Gough had been prominent in the Curragh 'mutiny' of 1914, when British officers in Ireland refused to impose the Home Rule Bill on the Protestants of Ulster. He came to the war commanding a cavalry brigade. Soon he was running a division, then a corps and now an army. He was only forty-five and in most of his photographs a dyspeptic air seems to hover about him. His face often wears a choleric look and his eyes are without a hint of charity, but his friends insisted he was witty and charming. As the war went on his friends became fewer and his enemies, many of them dominion troops, became an army of their own.

It was lucky for Australia that Gough had tried his bluster on Walker. Hooky was not only a man who thought things out carefully: he was never going to be awed by someone like Gough. Walker was unusual among the Great War generals: he seemed to be without the conventional ambitions. Bean described him as having the style and appearance of an 'English country gentleman' but this masked a hard will. Walker didn't see the conflict as a way to promotion and honours; he was a soldier's soldier and wasn't going to defer to a superior if he thought the orders he was being handed were unsound. Australia owes this Englishman much more than it has ever acknowledged.

Walker politely told Gough he wanted a postponement. Walker had been given the choice of attacking Pozières from the south-west (along the Bapaume road, the scheme preferred by Gough) or by a flanking assault from the south-east. Walker wanted to see the ground. He also knew that no jumping-off trenches had been dug; nor was there a proper artillery plan. Gough agreed to the delay. That night Walker scribbled in his diary: 'Scrappy & unsatisfactory orders from Reserve Army – Hope I shall not be rushed into an ill prepared for operation, but fear I shall!'

Walker was arguably the best allied general on Gallipoli. He was the first officer on Birdwood's staff to land, splashing ashore around 8 am on the day before his fifty-third birthday. Three hours later he was in charge of the New Zealand Infantry Brigade after its commander had fallen ill. After dark Walker was on the beach at a panicky meeting of Birdwood's commanders. They wanted to evacuate, although they didn't quite say so. The note sent to General Sir Ian Hamilton, the allied commander-in-chief, suggested unanimity. Walker had argued against evacuation. We don't know his exact words but he is supposed to have spoken to Major-General William Bridges, the commander of the 1st Australian Division, 'in terms which could have jeopardised his career'.

Next month Walker took temporary command of the 1st Division after a sniper's bullet killed Bridges. When the Turkish attack of May 19 left 3000 of their dead lying stinking in front of the Anzac trenches, it was Walker who sauntered into no-man's land to speak to the Turks who had come out under a white flag. Walker handed out cigarettes and told the Turks they needed to arrange something formal. A few days later the famous truce of May 24 took place.

Walker became one of the 'characters' of Anzac, not tall but strongly built with a receding hairline and a neat moustache. He wore his cap at a jaunty angle and was likely to turn up anywhere. Sergeant Cyril Lawrence, the engineer who wrote perhaps the finest Australian diary of the Gallipoli campaign, said Walker would appear attended by an entourage of 'flunkeys'. He was 'a small man dressed in light khaki and shorts, and with not a sign of rank about him'. Walker, Lawrence said, seemed to enjoy the Australians uncouth replies to his questions. Walker helped shape the attack on Lone Pine and was later badly wounded by machine-gun fire. He would not allow his wound to be treated until another soldier, hit at the same time, had been taken to a dressing station.

Walker took over the 1st Division again in France in March, 1916, and about six weeks later General Haking, working on one of his schemes for an attack on Fromelles and Aubers Ridge, suggested that the 1st Australian Division, which was nearby, might be loaned to him for the assault. One of Walker's staff wrote in 1934 that Walker thought the scheme unsound and 'refused to have anything to do with it. But for his firm stand, the 1st Division might have been slaughtered on the altar of Haking's ambition, instead of the 5th Division.'

And now, two months later, Walker was standing up to Gough and his artless plan to rush at Pozières from the front. Gough, it should now be said, later disputed that he wanted to go at Pozières from the west. He said he always wanted to attack it from the south-east. In 1927 he read the proofs of Bean's account of Pozières in the Australian official history. 'I can hardly believe a word of this story about my meeting with General Walker!!' Gough harrumphed. 'I wonder if any of my staff would confirm it. I was not "temperamentally" addicted to attacks without careful reconnaissances and preparation, as the conduct of all my military operations fully bear out, including this one!' He said he always intended to attack Pozières from the flank 'but it seems the Australians wish to claim all the credit for all things'. Gough said he didn't think Walker had much to do with the choice of the direction of the attack. He also accused Bean of repeating 'camp gossip'.

In his own book *The Fifth Army* (the Reserve Army became the 5th Army) Gough gives the battle only a few pages and somehow manages to make it sound like an abstraction. He does, however, praise the Australians and their leaders, Birdwood ('always easy to work with'), White ('one of the best Staff Officers we had'), Herbert Vaughan Cox, the commander of the 4th Division, and Talbot Hobbs, the artilleryman who later took over the 5th Division. He makes no mention of Walker.

There is no reason to believe Gough's version and every reason to believe Walker's, which is corroborated by others, notably White. In a letter to Bean in 1928 Walker said that on the 20th – two days after Gough had told him to attack on the 19th – there was a conference in Albert at which Birdwood and Gough were present. There was a further conference at Gough's headquarters the next day.

> It was at the Conference on the 20th that Gough definitely wanted me to attack from the Thiepval direction . . . He wanted me to attack over the same ground which the Division commanded by I think Ingouville-Williams [of the much-battered 34th] had heroically attacked & *failed*. I said no! that the left flank was exposed to the Thiepval Ridge – Matters went so far that I asked Gough to give me a Staff Officer to accompany me up to the line where I would point out the disadvantages of attacking from the *SW* & my plan to attack by or from the *South East*.

Walker said he took a Reserve Army staff officer called Beddington up to the line and explained his plan for attack to him. 'The last words I said to Beddington were "What are you going to tell Gough" & he said – "I shall recommend your plan" – (I remember this incident absolutely).' Gough, Walker wrote, adopted his [Walker's] plan. Walker called Gough's earlier orders 'disgraceful' and suggested he was a 'cunning devil' for trying to conceal his original scheme. 'If I had not fought most strenuously for my plan & insisted on a staff officer accompanying me & being shown my plans, we should have been compelled to undertake an operation which we would have failed . . . I always look back on those days as the very worst exhibition of Army commandship that occurred in the whole campaign tho' God knows the 5th Army was a tragedy throughout.'

7

Blacker than Gallipoli

The Somme offensive began as an attempt to break through; by the time of Pozières, it had become a wearing-out battle. And not one battle either but a series of local struggles at places where Haig thought the ground vaguely prospective, little fingers poking darkly into the German lines, a village half-won here, a wood almost taken there. On a trench map Haig's advance looked like erosion, as though a leaching acid was seeping into the German lines from the west, but only south of Thiepval; north of there the German line resisted the acid. Haig hadn't intended things to go this way: they just had, because after the first day there was no other way for them to go. He couldn't let down the French; he couldn't move his army to Belgium, where he would rather have been. He had not realised how deep and elaborate the German defences were until the offensive had started.

The Germans had bought the 'wearing-out' idea too. They were under orders not to give ground anywhere; if they were driven from a position they had to counter-attack, and they did. Hamlets and woods that hardly anyone outside Picardy had ever heard of took on a life-or-death importance in newspaper headlines, as if they were Jerusalem or St Petersburg.

Haig had neither the troops nor artillery to keep pushing on a wide front. He had to attack where he perceived the enemy to be weaker. So now the assaults were on narrow fronts, a probe here, a push there, and the artillery barrages were terrific, on the scale of Verdun, hundreds of guns firing into a front that might be less than a mile across, so that the craters soon sat lip to lip, and shell-shock became common. It turned some men into zombies and others into madmen who fell into convulsions or simply ran away, although the military authorities at this time refused to concede that shell-shock could exist. On the Somme the infantryman, as the British official history acknowledged two decades later, was being worked too hard. It was honourable for him to be wounded by a shell fragment; it was inconceivable that an invisible force could enter his brain and send him mad.

Thiepval, on the same ridge as Pozières, couldn't be taken from the front. Thiepval was on the frontline; Pozières lay on the strong second line. The idea now was to use the British incursions below Thiepval to take Pozières and, from there, work back along the ridge in a hook-shaped offensive, past the strong point of Mouquet Farm, towards Thiepval, threatening it from the rear as well as the front. It was all rather untidy. Thiepval poked into the British lines; the British were now trying to thrust a salient of their own into the German salient. But Pozières, we should remember, was merely one battle of many going on here in late July. To the south, within sight of Pozières on a clear day, three British corps were going for Delville Wood, Longueval, High Wood and Guillemont.

More Australians lie in the ground at Pozières than in any other battlefield, but the carnage was spread very democratically here. If the 'colonials' suffered dreadfully, so did the Britons. If the upper classes from which British officers came sometimes mismanaged the war, they also died at a faster rate than the miners and dockworkers they led.

ROBERT GRAVES, WHO was working on his first volume of poetry, was waiting to attack High Wood a few days before the Australian assault at Pozières when a German shell burst behind him. He felt that he had been punched hard between the shoulder blades, but there was no pain. 'I've been hit,' he called out, then fell. One shell fragment had ripped into his left thigh ('I must have been at the full stretch of my stride to escape emasculation') and another entered below his shoulder blade, hitting the lung, before coming out through his chest. Graves was taken to a dressing station and, as was the practice, left in a corner because it was assumed that he would die. He stayed there, unconscious, for twenty-four hours. Graves' colonel arrived at the dressing station to be told his twenty-year-old captain was dying. Next morning, when the dead were being cleared away, Graves was found to be breathing and sent to the nearest field hospital.

Meanwhile Graves' colonel, who had lost six or seven officers at High Wood, wrote the usual notes of condolence. He told Graves' mother her son had died of wounds. There were the usual reassurances: her son was 'a very gallant soldier'; he had not been in 'bad pain' and the doctor attended to him at once. 'Please write to me if I can tell you or do anything,' the colonel concluded, before making out the official casualty list that announced that Graves had 'died of wounds'. Graves amused himself watching blood, 'like scarlet soap-bubbles', coming out of the hole in his chest.

On July 24, his twenty-first birthday, he scribbled a note to his mother: 'I am wounded, but all right.' His mother had already received the letter from the colonel. She didn't know what to think. Then she received an army telegram saying that her son was dead. *The Times* reported Graves as dead, then announced that he wasn't.

Graves left hospital and was puzzled by the mood of England. 'We could not understand the war-madness that ran wild everywhere, looking for a pseudo-military outlet. The civilians talked a foreign language; and it was newspaper language.' Graves lived to write *Goodbye to All That* and *I, Claudius*.

THE GERMANS KNEW Pozières was going to be attacked. The shelling had gone on too long. On July 23, the day of the Australian attack, a German in Pozières wrote home.

Dear Luise and children,

My darlings, the gods only know if I am writing for the last time. We have now been two days in the front trenches. It is not a trench, but a little ditch, shattered with shells, with not the slightest cover and no protection. We've made a hole, and there we sit day and night . . . We have already lost about 50 men in two days, 6 killed, the others wounded. We get nothing to eat or drink, and life is almost unendurable. Up to now I have only had a bottle of selzer. Here I have given up hope of life . . . To my last moment I will think of you. There is really no possibility that we shall see each other again. Should I fall – then farewell . . .

Walker and his chief-of-staff, Colonel Thomas Blamey, planned the Australian attack from a château with beautiful gardens in Albert. Their troops were already digging in on the southern outskirts of Pozières and watching the bombardment. The leaves had been stripped from the orchards and the trees stood up like outraged splinters. Beyond them the village was mostly rubble and the red bricks and mortar of the houses billowed away in gritty clouds of pink and grey.

Walker decided to assault on a front of about a mile with two brigades, the 3rd (the first ashore at Gallipoli) on the right and the 1st on the left. The 2nd Brigade would be in reserve. The 3rd Brigade had the worst of it: its right would be up against the German second-line trenches called OG (for Old German) 1 and 2. On the front facing the village the first objective would be Pozières Trench, which started at the OG lines and ran around the southern and western edges of the village. The second objective would be the orchards on the rim of the village. The third would be the southern shoulder of the Bapaume road. The artillery would 'lift' deeper into the village as each objective was taken. The Australians would attack in three waves, each going through the other, so that the third wave would take the farthest objective. Ivor Margetts was in the third wave; he was to dig in alongside the road.

On the day before the attack the Australians sat in their jumping-off trenches writing letters home and dozing in the warm sun, tin helmets pushed back on their heads, rifles with bayonets fixed stacked nearby. The drumfire of artillery grew louder. The 4th Army was searching the ground to the east and south in preparation for its assaults on Delville Wood, Guillemont and High Wood. And now, as night came, the shelling of Pozières became heavier. All these bombardments lit up the sky and could be seen twenty miles away. An Australian well behind the front wrote: 'Every now and then a low lurid red flush, very angry, lit the horizon.' Rockets burst with green stars and shrapnel twinkled 'like the glow of a match end'.

The Australians were to attack at 12.30 am on July 23. Long before then they had crept out into no-man's land, some to within fifty yards of the German frontline. Private Harold 'Squatter' Preston lay in no-man's land watching bullets slicing the heads off red poppies. 'In the tumult it was impossible to hear orders. My ears were ringing with the cracking of bullets. A man alongside me was crying like a baby, and although I tried to reassure him he kept on saying that we would never get out of it.' When Preston eventually rushed forward the first German he came upon turned out to be a doctor who later helped with the Australian wounded.

The Australian gunners in the last few minutes before the jump-off fired as fast as they could load, bursting shrapnel over Pozières Trench, then lifting on to the orchards at zero hour. The Australians swept forward and – here, at least – it all seemed too easy.

Few Germans were in the trench, which had been cut up by shell-fire. A German machine-gun crew got off a few shots before being wiped out. Sixty Germans quickly surrendered. Elsewhere another four tried to surrender but a fifth among them threw a bomb and all were killed. The men of the second wave passed through and headed for the next objective, the orchards.

Sergeant Champion stopped worrying about his incontinence once the final barrage came down. The ground trembled and his ears rung. The barrage in front of him was dead straight, right over the German trench. He crept towards it. The shells glowed red as they fell. Then he was rushing forward. Machine guns knocked over a row of Australians near him. 'All tiredness was forgotten, and we chased the Fritzs and got them, and then we turned round and dug like mad. We lost all our officers and soon we had NCOs and privates taking charge and doing their good work.' The next wave went through Champion's position. Some of the first wave went with them 'to be in the fun'. Afterwards 'there were trophies galore – helmets, badges, bombs, equipment, etc, enough to stock any large museum.'

The artillery lifted off the orchards and on to the village, and the Australians took their second objective. This one had been even easier but discipline now broke down. Private Archie Barwick, a farmer, wrote: 'A and B Coy [of the 1st Battalion] were supposed to stay in this trench but . . . on they went like a pack of hungry dogs now they had tasted blood . . .' More than 100 Australians took off after about thirty Germans, chasing them along the Bapaume road towards the Windmill by the light of shell-bursts and flares and eventually shooting or bayoneting them. Leaders failed to turn the men, who wanted to chase every German they spotted. Some hot heads were killed as they made their way back through the Australian barrage to where they should have been all along.

The third wave was now supposed to pass through and take the road. By 2.15 am Margetts and other 3rd Brigade men were digging in on the Bapaume road. At dawn their trench was four-feet deep. There was no sign of a German counter-attack. Snipers, however, were taking shots from across the road and, since neither side's artillery was firing, the Australians began 'ratting' in the rubble on the north side of the road, throwing phosphorous bombs into cellars to smoke out bewildered Germans. Bean wrote that 'terrified and shrieking' Germans were chased and bayoneted. Others were shot and some taken prisoner. Two or three Australians would bring in groups of twenty-or-so prisoners. The 'ratters' were also hunting for souvenirs, particularly *pickelhaubes*, the leather-covered spiked helmets that would soon be replaced by the 'coal scuttle' steel model. Champion said the prisoners looked 'shaky and rattled and only too glad to be alive'.

A German was seen waving a white handkerchief at the mouth of a dugout towards the centre of the village. He eventually came forward, hands above his head, followed by eleven others, including two medical officers, one of whom said in English: 'Well, this is a blessing!' The Germans wanted to shake hands with their captors and offered cigarettes.

The attack had not gone so well on the extreme right. The troops here were not going for the village but attacking northwards along the OG lines, heading for the Bapaume road above the village and below the Windmill. They were advancing along the German trenches rather than making a frontal attack on them and the fighting was the fiercest on the whole front. The Australian attack here ended some hundreds of yards short of where it should have been. The Germans pelted the Australians with egg-bombs (about the size of a hen's egg), which could be thrown further than the heavier British Mills grenade. Just before 1 am Private John Leak, a teamster from Rockhampton, ran forward, threw three bombs into a German stronghold, bayoneted the survivors, then wiped the blood off his bayonet with a felt hat. He was later awarded the Victoria Cross.

Around dawn Lieutenant Arthur Blackburn, a young Adelaide solicitor, seven times led bombing raids up the OG lines. Of the seventy men who went with him more than half were killed or wounded. Blackburn too won the Victoria Cross. He already had another distinction. As a private on Gallipoli, he and a South Australian lance-corporal, Phil Robin, had pushed further inland than any other Australians on the first morning.

German shells were still falling on the Australian back areas at Pozières around dawn, as they had been through the night. Private Frank Shoobridge, a stretcher-bearer, wrote in his diary:

> Shells came in about 1 or 2 a second & everything was like day with the flares that were thrown up. Wounded started coming in faster than we could get them away & the dugouts being full we had to put them out in the open where many of them got wounded again after we had dressed them . . . We were within 100 yards of the Aid post on our fifth trip . . . when a 5.9 [inch] shrapnel burst right above us. Stredwich, who was carrying in front, was hit through the thigh & the head. Doonan was hit in the head & I got a bit in the knee & splinters in the face. Doonan went on

& sent out fresh bearers to bring the patient in (who died I believe before he reached the dressing station) & I carried Stred in, who was bleeding very freely & almost unconscious. He went down straight away on a stretcher and that was the last I saw of him.

Shoobridge was sent to a collecting station. 'General Birdwood came round & talked to us – said the bearers had done good work.'

No shells were landing in the new frontline. Water, food and ammunition arrived. The Australians lay in their new trench and nearby shell holes and rested. By the standards of the Somme battles this one seemed to have gone unusually well. The bombardment had been accurate; most of the machine guns had been suppressed; and the Germans who had survived had mostly lost their will to fight. The Australians had been sent out at night, rather than as targets against the morning sunlight. They had been able to creep close to the German lines before the whistles blew, which meant most of them had a short run to the German trench. Unlike their comrades at Fromelles four days earlier, they had been given a chance to succeed. It also helped that the 1st Division men were fresh.

The British divisions attacking east of them were not. Their attacks at Delville Wood, High Wood and Guillemont failed badly. A British attack just east of the OG lines near Pozières also failed. The British 48th, Carrington's division, had attacked Pozières from the west. Its troops advanced despite heavy machine-gun fire but couldn't gain touch with the Australians in the village.

So here, at noon on July 24, was something uncommon in the Somme offensive: an attacking force, having gained all its objectives and undisturbed by German shells, dozing in the warmth of a summer's day. If it was rare, it was also a daydream. Both Australian flanks were open. The right flank was bent back because the Australian attack up the OG lines had not succeeded as well as the assault on the village. And the Germans had not begun their counterattack. Pozières had been theirs: the German artillerymen didn't have to register their guns; they knew exactly where everything was.

8

Shell-shock

Before Robert Graves was wounded at High Wood it is reasonable to assume that, like most soldiers at such moments, he was calculating the odds of mortal chance. It was just before the jump-off. Then, as he put it, 'the usual inappropriate message came through from division'. Private X was to report to Albert, under escort of a lance-corporal, for a court-martial. As Graves explained: 'Division could always be trusted to send a warning about verdigris on vermorel-sprayers, or the keeping of pets in trenches, or being polite to our allies, or some other triviality, exactly when an attack was in progress.'

On the afternoon of the Australians' first day in Pozières two colonels met on Dead Man's Road, which led back to Sausage Valley. The colonels had their maps out. They were trying to organise a second attack on a concrete blockhouse known as 'Gibraltar' on the western edge of the village. They talked (as one of them later wrote) 'amid dozens of corpses and moaning wounded, mainly German', and surrounded by blackened tree stumps that rose like stalagmites.

A messenger suddenly panted up with an envelope marked 'Urgent and secret'. Orders had changed several times that day: this could be important. The message was from Gough's headquarters. 'A number of cases have lately occurred of men failing to salute the army commander when passing in his car, in spite of the fact that the car carries his flag upon the bonnet. This practice must cease.'

GOUGH HAD MADE another rash decision that morning. Walker and Blamey had planned to capture the rest of the village by a conventional advance in the afternoon after first hitting the north side of the Bapaume road with a barrage. No, said Gough. Reports from artillery observers and airmen suggested that the north side of the village was empty. The Australians could capture it simply by sending out patrols. The British 48th Division would push in from the west and join up with them. Walker cancelled his plans, although he wasn't convinced that Gough had read the signs correctly.

He hadn't. Pozières wasn't empty. Snipers were still firing, skirmishers were creeping into the village from trench lines to the north, and huddles of Germans lay in the deep dugouts, addled and blinking after the barrages and unsure whether to fight or surrender. Germans on the edge of the village had been told they wanted to recapture it. They lay in K Trench, which ran along the village's western boundary and faced the British 48th Division, and in the OG lines on the other side of the village.

Around noon shells began falling on the left of the Australian line, near Dead Man's Road. It was from near here, earlier in the morning, that the Australians had taken the Gibraltar stronghold. Gibraltar stood out because it was white and also because it was one of the few structures in the village still standing. The Australians took the blockhouse easily enough shortly after dawn, collecting twenty-three prisoners, but they could not hold it because the British barrage falling on the nearby K Trench was too close. This is why the two colonels were in the afternoon planning a second assault when the memorandum about saluting General Gough arrived to remind them of what was truly important.

Gibraltar was taken a second time, and late in the day the patrols went out on the left and right of the Australian line, heading towards the cemetery on the northern fringe of the village. Men from the 8th Battalion, part of the 2nd Brigade, had been brought into the frontline for the sweep on the left. They went into the flattened village with bayonets fixed. The odd flare lit the night sky. They came upon the church; all that was standing was a window near where the altar had been, and soon that fell over too. Private Jack Bourke, a schoolteacher from country Victoria, came upon a heap of cake boxes in a dugout.

> The addresses [he wrote to his mother] were in a child's handwriting as were also one or two letters. In another corner was a coat rolled up. I opened it out, and found it stained with blood, and there, right between the shoulders, was a burnt shrapnel hole – shrapnel is very hot . . . The owner of the coat was a German, and, some might say, not entitled to much sympathy. Perhaps he was not, but I couldn't help thinking sadly of the little girl or boy who sent the cakes.

Around midnight the men of the 8th began to dig into the rubble about halfway between the Bapaume road and Pozières cemetery. They had met little opposition, although they could see Germans to the north-east, up towards the OG lines.

The Australians from the 3rd Brigade who went out on the right were in a black mood. They had been sniped at all day; they were going to get even. Margetts and Captain Alan Vowles sent out patrols. Lieutenant Elmer Laing of Western Australia led one and afterwards admitted that he and his men were looking for revenge. Some Germans ran away – one rode off on a bicycle as bullets hissed about him – and some tried to surrender and, one suspects, were shot or bayoneted. Laing wrote of a German in a dugout who tried to give himself up. One of Laing's men yelled at the German to come out. 'I heard him, rushed back shouting at the chap to shoot the swine or I would – so he got him. Altogether we killed 6 and captured 18 down the dugouts. The men had great sport chucking bombs down any hole they saw.'

Margetts and Vowles crossed the road to make sure the ground was safe, then returned to pick up their companies and bring them across. Vowles came back with his men; Margetts did not. A shell had burst over him. He died shortly afterwards.

Vowles, from Perth, was supervising the new forward position being dug deep in the village when he blundered into a stairway leading to a dugout. The Australians had already thrown at least one bomb down the stairs. Throw another one down, Vowles told them. There was no sound from below after the explosion. Two Australians began to descend the stairs. Then they heard voices.

'*Parlez-vous Francais?*' Vowles shouted.

'*Oui!*'

Up came seventeen Germans, some of them wounded. They said there was a captain below. These are the eighteen prisoners Laing refers to above, and they were perhaps lucky that Vowles was around. The German captain emerged from the gloom. He was smartly turned out and wore a long grey coat. Laing interpreted for Vowles. The German announced that his name was Ponsonby Lyons: his grandfather, he explained had been English. He then said: 'I am the commandant of Pozières.'

MARGETTS HAD WRITTEN so many letters of condolence. Now his family in Tasmania was receiving similar notes. And they, like the families their son had written to, wanted to know more. What had their son said before he died? Had he suffered?

Stephen Margetts wrote to Lieutenant-Colonel Charlie Elliott, his son's battalion commander. Elliott wrote back to say that he had been unable to discover further details of Ivor's death 'other than those I gave'. He said the only words Margetts spoke were: 'You boys will look after me, won't you? Tell the sergeant-major I want him.' Elliott said Ivor 'died very quickly & apparently suffered little pain'. The colonel enclosed a sketch of Pozières and marked the site of Margetts' grave with an X. He added a postscript: 'I have been unable to find out about his watch & ring, but all personal effects were sent back to the Base Records office for transmission to you.'

Stephen Margetts' letter to Elliott crossed with a letter sent to him by Private G. A. McKenzie, a stretcher-bearer from Hobart attached to Ivor's company. McKenzie wrote from a hospital in England. He had been wounded two days after Margetts' death.

It was about between 9 o'clock and ¼ past when Capt. Margetts was sitting in a *shell hole* giving orders to a sergent by the name of *Clarke* and one shell burst right in among us. I had some wounded in there as there was no room in the Trenches and could not get them down to the Aid Post. Shelling was too hot. Well it took me about half a minute to get over the shock of it, and I heard your *son* calling me. I crawled to him and he said I have got one at last. I got him into the Trench and ripped his shirt and singlet with my scissors and found a wound over his *heart* about the size of a Penny. I dressed him and gave him a drink but it was all over. He lived for about twenty minutes. I stayed with him to the end and these were the words he said before he went is that you *McKenzie* (yes Sir) if you get through this stink lad which I hope to the *God* above you do let my People know how I got hit and died thinking of them. He caught my hand and Passed Away.

I left him till the morning and got him Buried and put a *Cross* over his grave. His property he had very little on him as he had left it at our Battalion headquarters before going into action. The only part of his property that I buried him with, with of course his clothes, was a ring on his little finger which I could not get off without cutting his finger off so I left it on him . . . I was all through the Gallipoli muck with your *son* so I ought to know him well. I am only a Private myself but that is my fault, but there was never a better Officer living than *Capt Margetts*. He was the most popular man in the Batt and he never done a bad turn to anyone since we left Hobart Shore. It is the worst shock the 12th Batt has had since war started. Any one would of gave their life for to save his little toe.

McKenzie also signed a report that looks to have been made out for the Red Cross. 'I cried like a kid when I found he was dead,' he said. 'I think he went because he was too good for the beastliness of war . . .'

THE POSITION AT Pozières on the morning of Margetts' burial – July 24 – was something like this. Most of the village had been captured.

The Germans' counter-attacks had been uncharacteristically confused. There were still Germans in the centre of Pozières sheltering in artillery dugouts. The Germans also held most of K Trench, on the western fringe of the village, and this stopped the Australians joining their left flank to the British 48th Division. On the right the Australians had been unable to advance along the German second line (the two OG trenches). The British were trying to help by attacking Munster Alley, a trench that crossed the OG lines and ran away to the east, but they had been turned back, so the Australian right flank was also in the air. The troops in Pozières had a clear view to the OG lines to the north and east from where any counter-attack by German infantry would come. They would have plenty of time to shoot down the Germans in the open. But the Germans didn't have to send infantrymen on some mad downhill charge. They could plaster Pozières with high-explosive shells from Courcelette, to the north.

Most of the shelling on the 23rd, the first morning, had fallen in the Australian back areas. On the morning of the 24th the Germans began to land howitzer shells on the forward trenches. The terrible ordeal of Pozières had begun.

THE BOMBARDMENT STARTED at 7 am. The Germans concentrated on the line of the Bapaume road, and mainly on the 1st Brigade trenches at the western edge of the village. The shelling lasted all day. The Australian trenches had been hastily dug. There were no dugouts in which men could shelter and the earth was loose from the earlier British shelling. If a shell hit close to a trench, the walls fell in. Australians trying to dig out their comrades would hear the scream of the next shell and look up. Some said they could spot the shells at the top of their arc; others said they saw them in the last forty feet of their descent. A sergeant in the 1st Brigade said nearly everyone in his battalion was buried at least once.

Private Edward Jenkins, aged about forty-five and who gave his occupation as 'bushman', was always in trouble out of the line; now he became a saint. He looked after the wounded waiting to be taken away. He dragged them into a shelter he had built, gave them water from his bottle, refused to take any himself and told them the stretcher-bearers would soon be along. All these men lived. Late in the day Jenkins was blown to pieces by a shell.

Lieutenant-Colonel Owen Howell-Price, the twenty-six-year-old commander of the 3rd Battalion, one of five brothers who fought in the Great War, walked along the trenches for most of the day, trying to keep his men calm. His younger brother Philip, a captain in the 1st Battalion, later wrote home:

> ...the Huns simply poured high-explosive shells into our position. Trenches disappeared like paper in a storm. Where there had been trenches nobody could tell. The place was a series of huge shell holes, some 30-feet wide and 20-feet deep. Shells were so thick that they obscured the sun, smoke was so intense that one could not see, the row and noise was so terrific that men went mad, men simply stood and shook, their nervous system one entire wreck. Shell after shell planted itself in our lines, man after man was blown to pieces and yet not a man faltered.

Sergeant Champion wrote in his diary: 'Of course, Fritz has his own late trenches marked off to a "T" on his maps, and can shoot back on them with accuracy. We were being continually bombarded, the trenches caving in, and we were digging each other out all day long. Soon our beautiful trench was nothing but a wide ditch, each caving in making it shallower and wider... our garrison became thinner and thinner.'

Men came down with shell-shock. The Victorian mind was suspicious of this condition. Sigmund Freud's *The Interpretation of Dreams* had only appeared sixteen years earlier. Shell-shock had not figured in the Napoleonic wars or the Boer War. Was it a way for men to escape from fighting? Was it a disciplinary problem rather than a medical one? These men weren't bleeding; they weren't missing limbs or frothing from gas-filled lungs. They had been hit in the mind. Did this constitute a 'wound'?

A week or so after the Australians started to come down with shell-shock at Pozières a nineteen-year-old English private ran away from a gas attack in Belgium. He was sentenced to death. His commanding officer had told the tribunal that the youngster tended to panic under shellfire. A brigadier-general reviewing the court-martial recommended that the sentence be commuted. No, said the corps commander, cowards were a danger to the war effort. The death penalty was designed to frighten men more than the prospect of facing the enemy. The lad was shot. The corps commander was Hunter-Weston. He had had at least two 'breakdowns' of his own, one in France early in the war and another on Gallipoli.

In early 1917 the young poet Wilfred Owen fell asleep after an assault on German trenches and was blown in the air by a shell-burst. He ended up sheltering near the skewered remains of another officer, then began trembling and stammering. One of Owen's biographers wrote: 'It seems probable that his courage was called into question in some way by the CO, who may even have called him a coward.' Owen was diagnosed as having shell-shock. The following year he was decorated for bravery.

Shell-shock became relatively common during the battle of Loos in 1915 when soldiers arrived at the hospitals with 'hysterical manifestations'. Only in early 1916 did the British army recognise these men as 'wounded' rather than 'sick'.

Bean, just behind the front, understood shell-shock because he had seen it. Pozières was a 'mincing machine', he wrote in his diary early in August.

> They have to stay there while shell after shell descends with a shriek close beside them, each one an acute mental torture, each shrieking, tearing crash bringing a promise to each man instantaneous – I will tear you into ghastly wounds, I will rend your flesh and pulp an arm or a leg; fling you half a gaping, quivering man like these that you see smashed round you to lie there rotting and blackening like all the things you saw by the awful roadside.

Runners taking messages through the bombardment at Pozières suffered fearfully. One arrived worn out at 3rd Brigade head-quarters, delivered his message, went outside to lie down, then put his rifle to his head and shot himself. Brigadier-General Nevill Smyth, the Englishman commanding the 1st Brigade (he had won the Victoria Cross in the Sudan) said one of his runners came into headquarters, quietly delivered his message, and fell dead of wounds he had received on the way. Private Angel of Alexandra, Victoria, was hit in the spine while delivering a message; his legs were paralysed. He saw an officer and dragged himself forward to hand him the note. Two hours later the stretcher-bearers arrived to cart Angel away. His first words were: 'Has that message been delivered?'

CAPTAIN BERNHARDT WALTHER of the 3rd Brigade, a twenty-one year old from Perth, was shot in the abdomen on the 24th. He had trained in accountancy before the war, was a fine pianist and liked to play chess. Walther wrote a rollicking diary that ends a few days before he went to Pozières. 'I don't mind a joke but our new billet is the absolute limit. We were piloted into a dingy little shanty & received by a "fair dinkum" witch. She had one tooth, enormous boots, dirty face, clawy fingers, putrid clothes and a narrow nose.' And he had a big heart. He was in the London slums a month before Pozières. 'We passed a cartful of maimed kiddies who were being taken to school & I pulled up and gave them a handful of coppers – I don't believe I've ever saw so much appreciation in my life before.'

Walther had been born in the Victorian Wimmera; his father, Johann Gustav, had been born in Melbourne in 1857; his grandfather had arrived in Australia from Germany in 1848. Even though his son had fought at Gallipoli and was about to go to the killing grounds of the Somme, Johann Gustav had to report regularly to authorities in Perth because of his German parentage.

Australia was suspicious, sometimes hysterically so, of anyone with German antecedents. There were whispers about Monash, now training the 3rd Division in England. His father had landed at Melbourne in 1854 from a town that was then part of Prussia (it is now part of Poland). Almost as bad, Monash was Jewish and in

1916 anti-Semitism was spoken openly. Sir Ronald Munro-Ferguson, the Governor-General, privately referred to Monash as a 'competent Jew', which was a way of saying he had a fine mind but really wasn't one of us. During 1915 rumours swept around Melbourne that Monash had been shot as a German spy. Soldiers returning to Australia claimed to have been present at his execution. There were whispers too about Gottlieb Heinrich 'Frederick' Schuler, editor of the Melbourne *Age* since 1899. Schuler had arrived from Germany as a six-year-old. It didn't matter that his son, Phillip, had been at Gallipoli as a war correspondent and had since enlisted in Monash's new division.

Captain Walther died the day after he received his abdominal wound.

GENERALS GOUGH AND Walker were not thinking about shell-shock on the 24th. Neither seemed aware of the severity of the shelling at Pozières. Gough told Walker early in the day that he should promptly take the remainder of the village. Later in the day Gough explained what he was trying to do. He wanted to take the German second-line trenches on the ridge east and north of Pozières, drive north past the rubble that had been Mouquet Farm, then back towards the Ancre valley. This would cut off the German fortress at Thiepval.

On the night of July 24 the Australians were to take all of Pozières, then set up posts north-east of the village that could be used as jumping-off points for the assault on the OG lines. They were also to capture the OG lines on the southern side of the Bapaume road that they had failed to take in the initial assault. This latter attack was to be made at 2 am on the 25th by the 3rd Brigade with help from one-and-a-half battalions from the 2nd. The 1st Brigade would sweep through Pozières and beyond an hour-and-a-half later. The British would also be attacking on each flank, trying to take K Trench on the left and Munster Alley on the right. What the Australians couldn't know was that the Germans, who were still badly disorganised, were planning to recapture Pozières on the afternoon of the 25th.

THE AUSTRALIANS' NIGHT attack on the OG lines below the Bapaume road began with blunders, moved on to bravery, and ended in failure. This time, instead of bombing up the line of the OG trenches, the Australians went at them from the front. Troops from the 2nd Brigade were brought in for the frontal assault. Two companies from the 7th Battalion were supposed to attack at the Bapaume road end but became lost in the night. The 5th Battalion, which attacked at the southern end, broke into the German line and its occupants fled. Half an hour later the Australians took the second-line trench and began to dig in. Meanwhile the British again assaulted Munster Alley, just below where the Australians were digging in, but were repulsed by machine-gun fire from near the windmill site on the hill above.

The Germans now started bombing their way back down the first-line trench from the north. The Australians in the second-line trench were suddenly in danger of being cut off. They returned to the first trench and a furious bomb fight began. A bare-chested sergeant – his identity is unclear – threw bombs for an hour as German cricket-ball grenades burst about him. A German grenade exploded close to his chest and he was soon covered with blood, but he kept throwing. The Germans took ground; the Australians took it back. The fight was still going well after dawn. When it ended the Australians were still 300 yards short of the Bapaume road.

To the left of this struggle the 11th Battalion thrust into the village in the dark, seeking to link up with the 1st Brigade, which was doing the same thing at the other, or western, end of the village. On this western front the 4th Battalion attacked down K Trench while the 8th, borrowed from the 2nd Brigade, pushed through the village. The Australians in K were soon in a bomb fight, but the Germans retreated down the trench, dropping their grenades, which the Australians picked up and threw after them. The 8th pushed through the village, past the cemetery with its stone vaults and out into open country. This put them behind the Germans in K, who wanted to surrender, shouting 'Mercy, *Kamerad*'. The Australians kept firing at them. The 4th and the 8th met near the cemetery.

At 7.15 am the Germans began bombarding Pozières again. This time the shells fell all over the village. The Germans were preparing to recapture it. The shelling was heavier than on the previous day. Pozières blew away in clouds of dust that could be seen for ten miles. The British, though still dying sacrificially, were not putting enough pressure on the Germans at the other Somme fronts to the east and south. This meant the Germans could concentrate their artillery fire on Pozières. Two colonels had to lead the battalions through the barrage to take up positions on the new frontline beyond the village. Owen Howell-Price, commander of the 3rd, was twice blown off his feet and smothered in brick dust. Henry Gordon Bennett, commander of the 6th, was given a guide to take him forward. 'Ginger' Bennett later wrote:

> Bodies of hundreds of Australians were strewn along the [Bapaume] road where they had fallen. We came across some old German shelters built of pine logs, all badly battered. I stopped near one of these to have a rest. Glancing at my unfortunate guide – a runner, in his late teens – I noticed that he was scared stiff.
>
> So was I. Then one shell landed at my feet. The blast tore off the sleeve of my tunic and ripped it up the back. It did not touch me – but it was close. The runner almost panicked, but I talked to him and he quickly gained control of himself. On we went, with shells falling all around. The lad was in a bad way and wanted to leave me . . . In the end . . . I let the boy go back and he wasted no time making his way out of the inferno that was everywhere.

On his way back to bring up his battalion Bennett said he 'prayed most earnestly to the Almighty for His guidance'. Bennett, only twenty-nine, didn't frighten easily. He had rushed forward at the Gallipoli landing to Pine Ridge, a position the Australians never reached again after the first day. Bennett was shot in the wrist and shoulder there and sent to a hospital ship. Next day he discharged himself and returned to the frontline. Bennett was later in the mad charge at Krithia, where McCay and Cass had been wounded. But he had never been under a barrage like this.

Bennett managed to guide his battalion to the new frontline

during a break in the shelling. Then he set up his headquarters in a pine-log shelter occupied by several dead Germans. Blasts from exploding shells kept snuffing out the candles that provided the only light. Bennett's men outside were being shelled so heavily that their trench disappeared. Captain Percy Binns inspired them by walking along the line all day, amiably calling out: 'Buried were you?' Binns, a veteran of the Krithia charge and the winner of a Military Cross, became a victim of the new warfare. He came out of Pozières suffering from shell-shock. He was invalided back to Australia and died, aged twenty-six, on the ship taking him home.

Corporal Thomas wrote diary entries through the day.

[Early morning] For *Christ's* sake write a book on the life of an infantry-man & by so doing you will quietly prevent these shocking tragedies . . . I have seen things here that will make the bloody Military aristocrats' name stink forever.

[11 am] . . . hundreds of shells from big 12 inch howitzers are being fired at us. God! It is cruel. What humans will stand is astonishing.

[1.30 pm] . . . I turned my head sharply right & saw a decapitated man – one of ours. It is bloody gruesome – ah well, it will soon end – this awful game. Plenty of lives – just gun-fodder. Our casualties are very heavy. I picked up a German club – it will come in handy methinks. Bombs & rifles are all right but they get broken . . . This is truly the Valley of the Shadows – God help us.

Sergeant Archie Barwick wrote:

All day long the ground rocked & swayed backwards & forwards . . . men were driven stark staring mad & more than one of them rushed out of the trench over towards the Germans. Any amount of them could be seen cry-ing & sobbing like children their nerves completely gone . . . we were nearly all in a state of silliness & half dazed . . . men were buried by the dozen, but were frantically dug out again some dead and some alive.

'Squatter' Preston said that after the artillery barrages the bodies of Germans and Australians were lying side by side, some quite black, others half-buried or torn, 'and we simply had to walk over them. One well-known sergeant of our battalion lay dead on the parapet, his rosary beads across his face.'

The Germans had planned to come rolling down the hill from the Windmill at 4.30 pm. They never came. Late in the day they abandoned thoughts of retaking the village.

The Australians probably could have held off a counter-attack: their positions, particularly at the northern end of the village, were strong. But the men were spent, physically and mentally. Corporal Thomas later wrote: 'Gallipoli was a fool to this & all the old heads avow it.' The difference here was the fury of a bombardment on a narrow front. A village was ground down, then blown away. The fortunate ones under that storm were merely buried once or twice; the unlucky sometimes died with not a mark on them, killed by concussion and soft-tissue damage, or were blown into so many pieces that there was nothing large enough to bury. Men were being challenged to stay sane while madness came shrieking out of the summer sky. 'The battlefield at Pozières will baffle the smartest writer living,' Corporal Thomas wrote afterwards. 'No-one will ever describe it properly, those who have been over it now, become dazed & numb when forced to try & write about it, it has been too terrible, too fiendish . . .'

The entire 2nd Brigade, originally in reserve, had now been thrown in, but it had not suffered as much as the 'originals', the 1st and the 3rd. No-one knew the 1st Division's exact casualties, but they had to be high. It was probably time to pull the men out. One brigade of General Legge's 2nd Division was already moving along Sausage Valley, weaving around shell holes and swollen bodies. On the night of July 25–26 the 2nd Brigade began to relieve the 1st on the left. The newly arrived 2nd Division men took over from the 3rd Brigade on the right.

THE GERMAN ARTILLERY stopped firing on Pozières around dusk on July 25, then opened up again the next morning. This was the Australians' fourth day at Pozières and now a howitzer shell was landing every three seconds. Colonel Bennett, at the new frontline north of the village, reported back during mid-afternoon: 'My men are being unmercifully shelled. They cannot hold on if attack is launched. The firing line and my headquarters are being plastered with heavy guns and the town is being swept with shrapnel. I myself am OK, but the frontline is being buried.' Bennett was to later tell his wife that he was 'mortally afraid' at Pozières. If he was, it didn't show.

Bennett and others believed that the Germans were about to attack. In truth the Germans were doing something unusual: using the guns of three divisions to lay down a barrage, not as a prelude to an infantry assault but simply to create hell. Bean wrote that the fire on the 26th was probably the heaviest yet faced by Australians. The German fire eased off around 11 pm. By daybreak on the 27th most of the 1st Australian Division was out of the line. The 2nd Division came in to find Pozières smoking like Gehenna. The 1st Division men went out with memories that were hard to explain to anyone who had not been there.

SERGEANT CHAMPION SAID the 26th was his worst day. Many officers had 'gone west'. He was forced to walk over Australian corpses, and this gave him 'the creeps'. His battalion finally straggled out and headed for Sausage Valley and Albert. The men looked like scarecrows. 'What a mess of a Battalion! We felt very sad, for by the look of it, we had lost more than half of our men.' The battalion had left its packs near Albert and the survivors of Pozières now ransacked them for clean underclothes. 'There were fully half the packs unopened,' Champion wrote. The dead men's effects would be sent home. Parents and wives would months later stare at pocket knives, pipes and fountain pens and wonder whether their son or husband had suffered.

Corporal Thomas scribbled in his diary: 'We were taken out today . . . Tis a wonder any of us got out. We had no communications trench, so had to cross in the open, so a battalion of men was at stake & the silly blighters moved us out in single file, it was awful, dozens were killed, blown to bits. Never shall I forget the 26th July, 1916 . . .' On the 27th Thomas marched ten miles and slept. 'How we slept! We had not slept for three nights & had had no food.' Two days later he was issued with a new shirt and socks. Suddenly he felt comfortable.

Captain Philip Howell-Price wrote to his parents:

Last week I was fighting dirty, unshaven, sleep and tear worn and tired – today I stand a new lad with comfortable family quarters and huge mess room to myself (my other officers are casualties) a lovely bedroom with big soft single bed. How about that for war eh what? In the last engagement a shell knocked me clean head over heels and a piece of stone or iron or something entered my left cheek just below the eye. You should have seen my face a big plum pudding nothing else. There was plenty of blood and nothing very serious. The swelling has subsided but my face is very sore and the scratch is not quite healed but I am going strong. Do not worry if my name appears in the papers as I have not left my Battalion at all.

Sergeant Edgar Rule of the 4th Division watched the 1st Division men trudging back from Pozières.

. . . we had our eyes opened when we saw these men march by. Those who watched them will never forget it as long as they live. They looked like men who had been in hell. Almost without exception each man looked drawn and haggard, and so dazed that they appeared to be walking in a dream, and their eyes looked glassy and starey. Quite a few were silly, and these were the only noisy ones in the crowd . . . In all my experience [Rule served throughout the war and was twice decorated for bravery] I've never seen men so shaken up as these.

Bean saw the same men. The bright spirit had left them, he wrote. 'They were like boys emerging from a long illness.'

IT IS TIME to look at the sums. The Australians had driven a salient about 1000-yards wide and 1000-yards deep into the German lines.

They had taken Pozières village, held it, and established a line from which the next attack could be launched. They had fallen several hundred yards short of their objectives in the OG lines east of the village. By the standards of the month-old Somme offensive, this was good work. Pozières was a 'subsidiary' operation and it had mostly succeeded; the main operation, by Rawlinson's 4th Army at Guillemont and elsewhere to the south-east, had mostly failed. The 1st Australian Division had run up 5285 casualties, which, when added to the earlier losses by the 5th Division at Fromelles, meant that more than 10,800 Australians had been killed, wounded or taken prisoner in less than a fortnight. Fromelles was a failure and Pozières a success, and the cost was much the same.

THE GIBRALTAR BLOCKHOUSE, or the little that remains of it above ground, is still there. It lies, roped off, a curiosity from another age, on the western edge of the village, blocked in by shell holes that have had their rough edges smoothed over by rain so that they look like dimples. Below the rubble is the original cellar of red-and-white chalk bricks and, beyond that, the chambers the Germans dug in 1915. These have not yet been fully excavated.

Across the road hay bales lie curing in the sun beside the track along which Australian wounded were taken back to Sausage Valley. Pozières Trench, where the Australian attack began, has long ago been ploughed away. In the main street English tourists eat chips in a café before their bus takes them on to the Thiepval memorial.

We know where Margetts was buried. His battalion commander drew a map of the spot: at the eastern end of the village, below the Windmill, south of the Bapaume road. Here the stone fruits are blushing pink. Hens cackle and dogs bark. When Margetts went into the ground this was a wasteland. A visitor might have thought that the land had been so corrupted that it would never grow anything again. A photograph taken in 1916, a few months after the first Australian attack (it appears on the dust jacket of this book), shows a vista of shell holes and mounds, puddles and tree stumps;

and amid all this is a single white cross, too white really, a nod towards sentimentality in a landscape that is otherwise without pity. The cross marks Margetts' grave – or did. The grave was obliterated in later fighting. Margetts is still under the chalk of Pozières but no-one knows where.

9

Musty, dusty, god forsaken

We first met Lieutenant 'Alec' Raws, the *Argus* journalist, as he watched pretty girls from the train taking him to French Flanders. Now he was taking a train south, on his way to Pozières. Raws is unusual among the letter-writers from the Great War. His touch is light and his humour gentle. But it is his way of thinking rather than the prose itself that sets him apart. He does not write what soldiers at the Great War are expected to write. He is in a place of his own, outside the clichés. There is subtlety and ambiguity in the way he sees the war and little of the usual Australian bluntness. He believes in the war but he volunteered out of duty, not because he fell for the slogans. He sees absurdities in military rituals but amiably goes along with them.

Raws explained his duties as orderly officer:

> . . . the men are already noisily being fed in the great mess huts, 16 to a table. Past experience teaches me that it is unwise to enter, though there my duty lies. So I tell the Orderly Sergeant . . . to go in and enquire whether there are any complaints. He does so. There is a roar, like the breaking of a tidal wave upon a silent shore. The Sergeant returns in due course. 'No

169

Pozières: 2nd Australian Division attacks

Mouquet
Farm

OVILLERS-COURCELETTE ROAD

ROAD

Bapaume

Windmill

Munster
Alley

N
W   E
S

2nd Division's
start line for
July 29 attack

Cemetery

Pozières

6   AUS

7   AUS

5   AUS

K

Trench

GERMAN   LINE

JUL 22

Mash
Valley

Pozières

Trench

ALLIED   LINE   JUL 22

Alley

ROMAN

Watch

Pearl Alley

Albert

Contalmaison
Wood

Black

Sausage
Valley

Contalmaison

SCALE

0 _____ 500 metres

0 _____ 500 yards

complaints, Sir,' he says, as he salutes. 'All right, Sergeant.' We salute and proceed to other huts. The Sergeant is an old hand.

Raws said Australian soldiers disliked saluting and that he and his fellow-officers might be partly to blame, because 'it goes against our grain to make these fine fellows salute us when they somehow feel it demeans them to do so'. Many of the French girls were 'singularly beautiful, with the warmest richest of complexions . . . They seem to be charmingly free of morals.'

Raws was to join the 23rd Battalion of the 2nd Division at Pozières. Robert, his younger brother, known as 'Goldy', was a lieutenant in that battalion. Before Alec arrived he wrote to his brother-in-law:

> Tomorrow I shall be in the midst of it all . . . There is something rather humorous in the situation, when I actually come to it. John Alexander Raws, who cannot tread upon a worm; who has never struck another human being except in fun; who cannot read of the bravery of others at the Front without tears welling to his eyes; who cannot think of blood, and mangled bodies, without bodily sickness – this man, I, go forth tomorrow to kill and maim, murder and ravage. It is funny. But I am glad to go. It is what I set out for, and the mission must be fulfilled. One grows weary of this life I have been living behind the lines.

He told a friend on the *Argus* that he was no more in love with war and soldiering than when he left Melbourne:

> How we do think of home, and laugh at the pettiness of our little daily annoyances. We could not sleep, we remember, because of the creaking of the pantry door, or the noise of the tramcars, or the kids playing around and making a row. Well we can't sleep now because –
> Six shells are bursting around here every minute, and you can't get much sleep between them;
> Guns are belching out shells, with a most thunderous clap each time;
> The ground is shaking with each little explosion;
> I am wet, and the ground on which I rest is wet;

My feet are cold; in fact, I'm all cold with my two skimpy blankets;
I'm covered with cold, clotted sweat, and sometimes my person is foul;
I am hungry;
I am annoyed because of the absurdity of war;
I see no chance of anything better for tomorrow, or the day after, or the
year after.

GENERAL JAMES GORDON Legge, the commander of the 2nd
Division, at Pozières was a little like General McCay at Fromelles.
McCay was carried along by Haking, who looked longingly to
Aubers Ridge. Legge was spurred along by Gough, who wanted to
do everything at the gallop. Legge had Birdwood and White close
by, but he could no more resist Gough than McCay could Haking.
Legge wasn't Walker. He had the same rank but not the same
authority. Walker was the proven article and, as much as a soldier
could be, his own man. Legge had little battle experience. He had
been on the edge but never in the cauldron. Born in London and an
arts and law graduate from the University of Sydney, Legge was
strong on administration and organisation. Bean, ever generous,
wrote in 1957 that 'defects in judgement and experience prevented
Legge, despite his high ability, from being a good leader in battle'.
This is a little like describing a barrister as being much talented but
not very good at arguing a case in court.

Legge and McCay differed on several scores. Legge never seemed
to have the confidence of his peers or his superiors, whereas McCay
always had a network of boosters. McCay had trouble with the
men he commanded: they mostly detested him. Legge had a different problem: his men didn't know him. And here he was, being
hunted along by Gough, who wanted to push on out of Pozières,
into the OG lines north and east of the village, then on to Mouquet
Farm. John Coates, a former chief of the general staff of the
Australian army, wrote in *An Atlas of Australia's Wars* that Legge
'did not have Walker's sure touch, nor was he so well served by his
operations staff. And he succumbed to Gough's impatience in a way
that Walker had not.'

WHILE LEGGE DREW up his plans to break out of Pozières – and, like McCay at Fromelles, perhaps fleetingly dreamed of doing something grand – the German gunners continued to pound the village. The summer temperatures were now around eighty degrees Fahrenheit and Pozières had turned to ash. There was nothing above ground worth knocking over, just a few low walls. Trenches were dug, wrecked by exploding shells, then dug again. In the open areas – near Gibraltar, for instance – corpses lay in the sun, telling newcomers that this was a place of perdition. Lieutenant Clarence Wallach, from the Sydney suburb of Bondi, was at the eastern end of the village, near where Margetts had died. Wallach came from a family of German origin that sent six brothers to the war. He had played Rugby Union for Australia. He called the trench he occupied 'Blancmange Trench' because it changed shape every time he visited it.

Bean arrived at the front several days later, walked around amid the shellfire, and wrote in his diary that the dead were lying in batches of ten and twelve along the approaches to the village. He headed down K Trench. 'There were only blackened dead – and occasionally bits of men – torn bits of limbs, unrecognisable – along it.' He walked on. More dead, more wrecked trenches. He was near the cemetery at the edge of the village. 'At last I came to the end of the dead men – and into a decent trench held by the living – British, and through them to Australians – 21st Battalion at our extreme left.' At the eastern end of the village, near Wallach's Blancmange Trench, where men 'are slowly pounded to death', he left a French newspaper with the troops. 'They were delighted to get it.' On his way out Bean could recognise the Bapaume road only because of its 'curious straightness'.

A guide took him across to the southern side of the road, where there was a 'wilderness of friable grey craters, so shredded and dry that it looked most like an ancient ash-heap in which the hens have been scratching for years – musty, dusty, god-forsaken, grey potholes of grey sifted earth . . . Everywhere were blackened men – torn and whole – dead for days. About eight or ten big black shrapnel were thrown over as we went . . . I knew my way now, so the runner left me – I hope he got home safe – good chap . . .'

General White said after the war that Bean faced death more often than any other man in the AIF. Bean was shy and self-conscious, in manner and appearance nothing like the rough men from the farms and mines that he so admired, and his accent was more English than Australian. It would please him to leave a newspaper with a private in a trench; it would mortify him if a man assigned to guide him should be hurt doing so.

Bean was a thirty-four-year-old journalist with the *Sydney Morning Herald* when he won the ballot to become Australia's official war correspondent. His father, a headmaster, had been born in India and educated in England; his mother was the daughter of a Hobart solicitor. Charles grew up at Bathurst, New South Wales. In 1889 the family moved to England. Bean was educated at Clifton College (where Haig and Birdwood had been pupils) and Oxford, where he read classics and graduated with second-class honours. He turned to law and returned to Australia, aged twenty-five, as a barrister, but journalism kept beckoning. In 1910 Bean journeyed through the red country of western New South Wales, writing a series of articles about pastoral life for the *Sydney Morning Herald*. These were later collected into the book *On the Wool Track*. Bean liked the people he met in the dust. They were tough and resourceful; they lived by the code of mateship and their conversations were laced with dry humour. They seemed part of some brave adventure.

Henry Lawson had earlier made the same journey as Bean. 'The minstrel of the people' saw women standing by woodheaps with worn-out breasts and sickly children on their hips; he saw men with horny hands, and skinny dogs and cattle shrivelled up by 'the red marauder' of drought. Lawson was a pessimist and Bean a romantic.

Bean was starting to find himself. He had grown up more English than Australian and his childhood had been privileged; he came from a family steeped in the 'imperial' tradition; he believed in 'British' values and Queen Victoria's empire. In 1909 he explained what the English flag meant to him. It stood for 'generosity in sport and out of it, for a pure regard for women, a chivalrous marriage tie, a fair trial, a free speech, liberty of the subject and equality before the law, for every British principle of cleanliness – in body and mind, in trade or politics, of kindness to animals, of fun and fair play . . .'

But his travels in the bush had started him thinking rather like a breeder of livestock: he thought he could see evidence of hybrid vigour. Maybe the British race had physically improved, become taller and stronger, away from the slums of Manchester and Liverpool and under the glare of the Australian sun. Maybe 'the real Australian' was the man out in the scrub. Political ideas were also running around in his head. Australia was far from classless but it had an egalitarian streak that Bean liked. It was all rather strange: Bean admired these people, but he was not really one of them. He didn't seem to know whether he was an Australian or a Briton. And all these themes matter because they were to play through Bean's six volumes of war history.

All through these he was searching for the Australian 'character'. This interested him more than military analysis, weaponry or political strategies. The symbol of the Great War might be a howitzer rocking back as it belches fire and death but the hero of Bean's tale is the infantryman. Sir Ian Hamilton wrote in the 1920s – and he meant it kindly – that 'minor tactics' fascinated Bean. Bean's history of the Gallipoli campaign, Hamilton wrote, was all about 'the Homeric struggles of twenty men as they dwindle down to half a dozen'.

By the time he arrived at Pozières, Bean was well liked by the Australian troops, even if he was nothing like them. He was tall and thin, with a soaring forehead, blue eyes, ginger hair, a sharp beak of a nose that gave him a bird-like look and on which he balanced spectacles, and a thin mouth that was nevertheless kind. He wore khaki – he had the honorary rank of captain – but, as someone said, he cut a curiously unmilitary figure. He looked like a visiting scholar, hefting his black Corona typewriter, its keys stained pale yellow, a camera and sometimes a brass telescope. In his baggage there would be a palette and tubes of paint and sketching pencils. Bean wrote his official history from thousands of pieces of confetti: an interview here, another interview with someone else to verify the facts of the first, impressions he wrote in one of the hundreds of notebooks he filled, sketches he made while watching a bombardment, intricate little maps he drew, conversations with his friend General White. His approach was forensic rather than journalistic, all about piling up little details, and occasionally these became a tangle and blotted out the story.

His wartime journalism often suffered from this same need to try to tell all. Sometimes he forgot about the reader. The *Age* and the *Argus* stopped taking his copy. The *Bulletin* sniped at him. 'Such a man could do algebra while Rome was burning . . . Bean pants bravely along the track with a millstone about his neck and a padlock on his soul.' The troops in the frontline liked his copy better. At least he tried to tell the truth, or as much as one could under the severe gaze of censors. He didn't exaggerate or generalise, as many of the correspondents did, nor did he dress up butchery as romance. And, whenever possible, he went to the front.

Bean was hit in the thigh by a stray bullet during the August offensive at Anzac Cove. At first he thought the bullet may not have penetrated 'but presently I felt my hand greasy in my pants'. He went to a dressing station, then limped back to his dugout and flopped into bed. A doctor told him he should leave Gallipoli because of the risk of tetanus. Bean stayed. He obtained all his stuff first hand; he wasn't going to leave just because he had been shot. The bullet was still in him when he died in 1968.

And now here he was, dodging shell-bursts to see what Pozières was really like. Things might have gone differently if General Legge had made a similar reconnaissance.

LEGGE, WITH HIS headquarters in Albert, had already lost about 1500 men to the bombardment before he began his assault on the OG lines. His 2nd Division comprised the usual three brigades.

The 5th, under Brigadier-General William Holmes, a public servant, had come into the line first. Holmes had become a citizen-soldier as a ten-year-old and later fought in the Boer War, where he was decorated and wounded. Now he was fifty-three but he still liked to visit the frontline. His men were unsure what to think about this. It was good that he wanted to discover what was really happening. It was not so good that he insisted on wearing his cap with a red band rather than a helmet and thus sometimes brought on German shellfire. The 5th Brigade had come in on the right and had soon 'bought into' another furious bomb fight around Munster Alley, where a British division was still trying to break through.

The 6th Brigade, under the Tasmanian John Gellibrand, took over at the other end of the village. Bean wrote in the official history that since the 6th contained a high proportion of Victorian 'town-bred men' it might be less hardened than brigades from the 'outer' States, such as Queensland and Western Australia. This was a fantasy that assumed battles were won by men with calloused hands rather than those of bright intellect like Gellibrand, but it shows that the music of *On the Wool Track* was still playing. When war broke out Gellibrand, forty-one, tried unsuccessfully to join up in Tasmania. White knew him and suggested he come to Melbourne. He turned up in a crumpled and soiled shirt and bush trousers and didn't impress General Bridges, who accepted him, one suspects, as a favour to White.

Gellibrand was a first-rate soldier with a sharp mind and a quick wit. Though Tasmanian born, he had served as a captain in the British army, fought in the Boer War, and passed through the staff college in England with White. When Gellibrand's battalion was disbanded he resigned and returned to Tasmania to grow apples. Bean wrote of this incident: 'It was standing evidence of the hopeless defects in a system under which staffs were often appointed on the principles of a hunt-club. Gellibrand did not play polo; he was not a good rider; he had no skill at games; he kept largely to himself; he read voraciously. Men of this type found it no easy matter to achieve success in the old British Army.'

Gellibrand distinguished himself at Gallipoli, where he was twice wounded, but more conventional officers didn't know what to think of him. He baffled them with his repartee, dressed as he pleased and said pretty much what he thought. A photograph taken at Pozières shows Gellibrand breakfasting in a shell hole with several of his officers. A teapot sits on a biscuit box. All the other officers wear regulation helmets and one appears to be in a tailored jacket. Gellibrand wears a felt hat and carries no badges of rank or colour patches. Take the others out of the photograph and he looks like a stockman waiting for the horse tailer to bring in the mob. Birdwood always looked immaculate: there was an innate neatness to him, as there was to Haig. Birdwood didn't understand Gellibrand. White did.

The 7th Brigade, men from Queensland, Tasmania, South Australia and Western Australia under the New South Welshman John Paton, eventually came into the centre at Pozières and were to be the main bludgeon in Legge's coming attack. Paton had fought in New Guinea and commanded the rearguard at the Gallipoli evacuation. The three brigadiers were an impressive group. Legge was the untested quantity, and it didn't help that Gough was still spurring him along.

Legge had the confidence of the novice. His staff took over from the 1st Division on July 27. He felt he would be ready to attack the following night. Before that the artillery would cut the wire in front of the OG lines and the infantry would establish strong points near the jumping-off positions. But the artillery observers often couldn't see where their shells were landing because of the dust. The infantrymen couldn't obtain a feel for their new position, mainly because they were constantly being buried. A few took a fatalistic view and tried to play cards. The artillery was firing shrapnel rather than high explosive. Shrapnel was a poor cutter of wire. And there were no jump-off trenches within a reasonable distance of the objective. The men would have to cover more than 600 yards in places. White thought the scheme too rushed but gave way to Legge's optimism.

Legge decided to attack just after midnight on the 28th with four-and-a-half battalions. On the left, one battalion of Gellibrand's 6th Brigade would go for the Ovillers–Courcelette road. In the centre three battalions of Paton's 7th would attack the OG lines north of the Bapaume road; this was the main assault. On the right half a battalion of the 5th would go for the OG lines south of the Bapaume road and back towards Munster Alley, the stretch that had been denied them since the first day of Walker's attack.

The final artillery arrangements said much about the inexperience of the divisional staff. The artillery of the 1st and 2nd Australian divisions would continue to fire normally until 12.14 am on the 29th. They would then lay an intense barrage on the first German line for one minute before lifting to the German second line at 12.15, the moment the infantry hopped the bags. One minute's bombardment wasn't going to do that much damage. And the 'lift' at 12.15 would leave Paton's three battalions exposed as they tried to cover the 600 yards to the first German trench.

THE FLARES – THEY were the first thing the brigade staffs noticed after the attack began. German flares, dozens of them, white and red and green, falling softly through the night sky: Germans talking to Germans, infantry talking to artillerymen. The Australian brigade headquarters were in Sausage Valley and Contalmaison. The officers there didn't know what was happening, but those flares made them fretful. The Germans should have been bundled out of their trenches by now; they seemed far too busy. Just after 2 am a messenger from one of Paton's battalions arrived at brigade headquarters. He had been hit in the face. One of his eyes had been knocked out. He said his battalion had heard German rifle fire start before the final Australian bombardment came down.

An hour later the truth about the attack began to emerge as more runners arrived. Men were hung up on uncut wire. The Germans had seen them coming. The artillery barrage had been too soft. The men didn't know the ground and some had become lost in the dark. Those who had made the first German trench had been thrown out. And now the men were coming back.

As so often happened in the Great War, the commanders had drawn up an attack plan, in this case a careless one, then lost control of the battle to captains and subalterns on the spot. In this instance the junior officers had made the right decision. The attack couldn't work: all they could do was try to get their men back to safety.

Captain Walter Boys, a young draper from Maryborough,

Queensland, went out in command of 250 men from Paton's 25th Battalion 'through a perfect hell of fire'.

> I went with the first line myself & my word my men fought well. They fell around me like flies, but on we went as if in a dream, while the smell of powder & din of guns, bombs etc, nearly turned my head. I reached the German barb-wire with *some* of my men, but could not get through & the Hun brought his maxim guns on to us, & we were forced to retire. I gave the order to retire much against my will, & what remained of my men got back that night, but I had to see all my men from the German lines before I could leave & when day broke I found myself about 30 yards from his trench. What I did was to lie still and imagine I was dead from 4.0 am on one day [the 29th] to 12.10 am on following day = 20 hours and 10 minutes. I had no water & it was very hot & there [were] hundreds of dead and wounded lying all around me. It seemed years that 20 hours. The Germans came out and bound up our wounded & passed me for dead and eventually I managed to crawl to our own lines under cover of night. I was almost off my head . . . I had to be under a most terrific bombardment but somehow God watched over me . . . I received several small scratches but none serious. The Doctor says I can go to Hospital but I am going to hang on.

Captain John Nix, a journalist from Townsville, led another company in Boys' battalion. The wire in front of him had been cut and he led his men into the first German line. Most of the Germans had fled. Nix pushed on for the second trench. Here the wire had not been cut and the Germans opened up a furious fire. Nix was shot through the hand. Like Boys and other company commanders, he made the sensible decision to retreat. Nix had taken about fifty men to the second line; he returned with four. A few Australians may have broken into the second line, but nowhere was it occupied.

Lieutenant Arnold Brown went out with the battalion on Boys' right. The attack, he wrote sixteen years afterwards, was 'so complete in its stark tragedy that it should never have been undertaken'. His battalion knew nothing of the position they were attacking; none had seen it in daylight. The men's misgivings increased when 'no great shelling from our own artillery followed'. When the attack began at 12.15 am the German artillery opened up. 'The bursting shells lit up the darkness, and the advancing men fell fast under a terrific rain of shrapnel and H-E [high explosive], and a withering machine-gun fire.' The two German lines were 500 yards away. The men found the wire uncut. 'Men ran up and down in search of an opening; others tried to climb over, but all failed. The attack had ended, for the battalion was well nigh annihilated. The survivors, about forty, found their way as best they could back to the frontline . . .'

Brown predicted that the Pozières battlefield would be a sacred place for Australians. It would attract pilgrims, 'perhaps more so than any other place'. Brown had not envisioned the allure of Gallipoli or the brightness of its myths.

The Australians had everywhere suffered from the weirdness of their own artillery plan. The lack of a long and heavy barrage before the attack meant that the Germans could still man their parapets. They could see the Australians assembling. They saw the Australians, out in the open and lit up by flares, beating at wire with rifle-butts and trying to tear out steel posts with their hands. The British official history said the 7th Brigade had been set 'an almost impossible task'.

The attack on the right by the half-battalion of the 5th Brigade simply couldn't be delivered. The Germans spotted the Australians under the flares. The Australians tried to advance by running from one shell hole to another. They lay out there until 3 am, then returned.

On the left the 6th Brigade's assault with one battalion succeeded, though with casualties of 333. The men reached their objective – the Ovillers–Courcelette road – didn't recognise it, and went on another 200 yards. Here, near a German trench called Park Lane, Lieutenant Goldy Raws disappeared.

THE CASUALTIES FROM the battle came in at 2002, most of them in the three battalions of Paton's brigade in the centre. This was not particularly high in the long tragedy of the Somme: British divisions regularly ran up figures like this. But if one looked at the 2nd Division's casualties more carefully, they were frightful. Legge had attacked with only four-and-a-half battalions, not the full twelve. He had lost 2002 men in the assault and another 1500 in the bombardment of the previous two days. He had lost close to one-third of his infantry strength and all he had to show was a small finger of land on the left where Goldy Raws had disappeared. And Legge and his staff had dented the trust of the men who were left; they knew they had been misused.

Haig at first thought about 1000 men had been lost. He still resolved to talk to Gough and Birdwood. From his distance he believed the attack had been poorly planned. This of course was part of the trouble: Haig, Gough, Birdwood, White and Legge were all too far away. To them Pozières was smoke on the horizon. One of them, Legge obviously, should have taken a brief look at the ground.

The temperature rose to eighty-one degrees on the 29th. Germans carried in Australians who had fallen near the first OG line and appear to have treated them with kindness. Neither side fired on stretcher-bearers. Some wounded Australians returned three days later.

THE GERMAN OFFICIAL historian discovered an unusual reason for the success of Gellibrand's troops on the left. The Australians, he wrote, were 'inflamed with alcohol'. There had been no rum issue before the attack. No-one knows where the German historian obtained this story.

A few days after the 2nd Division's attack W. Ambrose Cull, a captain in Gellibrand's brigade, watched a batch of German prisoners trudging up Sausage Valley.

As they neared our kitchens out poured a detachment of cooks, each armed with a huge carving knife, and made a dash for their victims. The handsomest and most self-attentive man in the British army looks something of a ruffian disfigured by a few days' stubble on his face and all the stain of the trenches, but a military cook, in all his panoply of grease and rags, is the very incarnation of ruffianism. The prisoners were limp with fright. Even I for a moment thought the cooks had suddenly gone mad and contemplated murder, but it was only a dash for souvenirs, and for every button that they slashed away they considerately handed the former owner of it a cigarette.

As far as we know, the cooks had not been at the rum either.

ALEC RAWS HAD not caught up with his brother before the attack. 'Goldy is gone,' Alec wrote to another brother in Australia, 'quite probably taken prisoner and all right. If killed he could not have died in agony because our stretcher-bearers were out in no-man's land that same night and then next day, and he could not have been missed. I was out searching for him myself the next night and the German flares made it all as bright as day. Possibly, too, he may have been taken away wounded by a British brigade on our left.'

Raws said he was resting in a machine-gun post that was 'comfy', although shells were coming from all directions by the thousands. 'I've got one puttee, one and a half socks, three-quarters of a tunic, a revolver, a bayonet – no rifle – two singlets, breeches, boots, an old helmet (steel) and a gas helmet.' He didn't want to give in to grief (as he put it a fortnight later), the implication being that if he did so, he might fail in his duty on the battlefield. But if Goldy was dead, where was the body? If stretcher-bearers had picked him up, what hospital was he in? Raws didn't know what to tell his parents. Eventually he told them Goldy was wounded ('I had to tell them something') but that he didn't know where he was. A week later he hinted to his father, ever so softly, that Goldy might be dead.

Goldy Raws was officially posted as missing.

10

Treading on worms

After lunch on July 29, as the Australians at Pozières counted their dead, Haig travelled to Gough's headquarters. The Australian attack had failed, he wrote in his diary that night. 'From several reports, I think the cause was due to want of thorough preparation.' Haig told Gough and his chief-of-staff, Neill Malcolm, that they must supervise more closely the plans of the Anzac Corps. 'Some of their Divisional Generals,' Haig wrote, 'are so ignorant and (like many Colonials) so conceited, that they cannot be trusted to work out unaided the plans of attack.'

Haig journeyed on to Anzac headquarters at Contay, behind Albert, where he saw Birdwood and White. Haig wrote that White 'seems a very sound capable fellow, and assured me that they had learnt a lesson, and would be more thorough in future. Luckily, their losses had been fairly small, considering the operation and the numbers engaged – about 1000 for the whole 24 hours.'

That was Haig's version. Bean's version – and his informant was obviously White – is that Haig 'spoke strongly' to Birdwood. This would have come easily: Haig didn't like Birdwood. According to Bean, Haig told Birdwood that just because he had 'achieved success' at Gallipoli he must not assume that slapdash methods would work here. 'You're not fighting Bashi-Bazouks [mounted Turkish irregulars] now – this is serious, scientific war, and you're up against the most scientific and the most military nation in Europe.' Haig went to a wall map and pointed out errors in the attack. He said they were due to Legge's over-confidence.

Despite a warning sign from Haig's chief-of-staff, White took Haig back to the map. White politely disputed some of Haig's assertions and waited to be slapped down. Haig laid a hand on White's shoulder and said: 'I dare say you are right, young man.' White, we might note, was thirty-nine, Haig fifty-five.

What do we make of this? Haig had made a string of errors. He thought the casualties were only 1000. Birdwood had not enjoyed much 'success' at Gallipoli. He had not been fighting Turkish irregulars there. Mustafa Kemal, later to be known as Atatürk, commanded on the northern front at Anzac. Far from being a Bashi-Bazouk, he turned out one of the grander figures of the twentieth century, more significant than Haig would ever be. And if Haig felt the need to reprimand Birdwood, he should have dealt even more severely with Gough. The army commander had, after all, been pushing Legge.

But on the big issue Haig was surely right. Legge *had* been overconfident. His preparations *had* been poor: he simply didn't understand about the primacy of artillery. Birdwood and White were also at fault, but in one sense so was everyone in the line that led from Haig to Legge.

LEGGE AND BIRDWOOD had met that morning. Legge was eager to try again, and soon. He still had 10,000 infantry left. He wanted to attack again on the following night, July 30. It was all rather brave and mindless, although this time the jumping-off trenches would be 250 yards from the German lines, communication trenches would be dug and the artillery bombardment would be stronger. Legge was trying to create a new frontline of some 1400 yards in less than thirty-six hours and it would have to be dug under shellfire. He realised later in the day that this couldn't be done. The attack was put off until August 2. The men sent out to dig the new frontline suffered in a way that does not show in official accounts. Alec Raws was digging on the night of July 31.

We were shelled all the way up [Raws wrote to his sister], but got absolute hell when passing through a particularly heavy curtain of fire which the enemy was playing on [Pozières] . . . I went up from the rear, and found that we had been cut off, about half of us, from the rest of the battalion and were lost. I would gladly have shot myself . . . the shells were coming at us from, it seemed, three directions . . . Well, we lay down terror stricken along a bank. The shelling was awful. I took a long drink of neat whiskey and went up and down the bank trying to find a man who could tell where we were. Eventually I found one. He led me along a broken track and we found a trench. He said he was sure it led to our lines. So we went back and got the men. It was hard to make them move, they were so badly broken. We eventually found ourselves to the right spot, out in No Man's Land. I was so happy that I did not care at all for the danger. Our leader was shot before we arrived, and the strain had sent two other officers mad. I and another new officer [Lieutenant L. G. Short, a journalist who had worked with Raws at the *Argus*] took charge and dug the trench. We were being shot at all the time, and I knew that if we did not finish the job before daylight a new assault planned for the next night would fail. It was awful, but we had to drive the men by every possible means. And dig ourselves. The wounded and killed had to be thrown on one side. I refused to let any sound man help a wounded man. The sound men had to dig. Many men went mad.

Just before daybreak, an engineer officer out there, who was hopelessly rattled, ordered us to go. The trench was not finished. I took it on myself to insist on the men staying, saying that any man who stopped digging would be shot. We dug on and finished amid a tornado of bursting shells. All the time, mind, the enemy flares were making the whole area almost as light as day. We got away as best we could. I was again in the rear going back, and again we were cut off and lost. I was buried twice, and thrown down several times – buried with dead and dying. The ground was covered with bodies in all stages of decay and mutilation, and I would, after struggling free from the earth, pick up a body by me to try to lift him out with

me, and find him a decayed corpse. I pulled a head off – was covered with
blood. The horror was indescribable.

Alec Raws, gentle Alec Raws, had learned to tread upon a worm.

Raws went up to the front again the following night. 'We were
shelled to hell ceaselessly. My company commander went mad and
disappeared.' Raws stayed there for days. 'My nerve lasted all right
and my constitution. I had not even a coat and we had no dugouts.
I got water and biscuits from a German body. I saw many of my
friends die.'

Legge had to put the attack back another day, until August 3.
The jumping-off positions were incomplete. White had been studying aerial photographs: he still thought Legge was being optimistic.
White telephoned Gough's headquarters and said the attack would
have to be deferred again. He was told that Legge had said the
opposite. 'Well, you can order them to attack,' White replied, then
repeated that the preparations were incomplete. Gough called the
attack off until August 4, but he took affront. He wrote to Birdwood
demanding that Legge explain the postponements. Gough also
appeared to be asking Birdwood for his opinion of Legge's compe-
tence. Birdwood withheld the letter from Legge until the operation
was over.

Haig went riding with Gough on August 3. Gough told him the
attack had been postponed again. 'From what he said,' Haig wrote
in his diary, 'I concluded that the cause was due to the ignorance of
the 2nd Australian Division, and that the GOC Legge was not
much good.'

A FEW DAYS earlier Haig had received a letter from 'Wully'
Robertson, Chief of the Imperial General Staff, who was the
government's chief military adviser but behaved as if he worked for
Haig. 'The Powers that be,' Robertson wrote, 'are beginning to get
a little uneasy in regard to the situation . . . In general, what is
bothering them is the probability that we may soon have to face a
bill of 2 to 300,000 casualties with no very great gains additional

to the present. It is thought that the primary object – the relief of pressure on Verdun – has to some extent been achieved.'

The British people were as generous and patriotic as ever, but they were now starting to wonder where this war was going and what it might cost. The casualty lists from the Somme seemed unending: there had never been anything like them. Everyone, rich or poor, seemed to know someone who had lost a son or a husband. Wounded men sat up in hospitals and told stories that argued with the communiqués the newspapers published. What was being achieved by these sacrifices? Were the Germans being pushed back? Were their losses heavier than Britain's, as the newspapers said? Was their morale cracking?

The people merely wondered; the politicians were genuinely uneasy because they knew more, though not as much as they would have liked. Some felt they weren't being told enough by the military. One problem here was that Robertson couldn't tell them much because Haig didn't tell him much. Others worried whether Haig had been given too much freedom. What was he doing? The Somme attack had begun on a wide front and with the chance of a breakthrough. Now it was on a narrow front, with Pozières at the northern end; now it seemed to be about wearing down, a dance of death that would end only with the winter rains and snows.

Lloyd George, the War Minister, wondered if Haig was the right man. The two were so unlike. Lloyd George was quick-witted, eloquent, emotional, careless with conventions, a modern man. Haig was courtly and Victorian, a believer in the proprieties, distrustful of people who were more articulate than he (which sometimes meant everyone in the room) – and also a man of implacable nerve. The tensions between the two were growing. Haig had written in his diary back in January that he thought his War Minister 'shifty and unreliable'. The newspaper owner Lord Rothermere had told Lloyd George that the army communiqués were 'full of lies' and that the War Office was misleading its minister.

Churchill held no high office. Gallipoli had brought him down, but he was irrepressible, as he would be the rest of his life, and, better still, he had a way with prose that none of his colleagues could match. He wrote a paper for Cabinet members. In part it was a plea for information. No-one seemed to have accurate figures for casualties. Churchill estimated that the German losses were about half those of the British. His memorandum was mostly a polemic. Britain had not conquered in a month's fighting as much ground as it expected to gain in the first two hours of July 1. The advance of about three miles was on a front of less than 10,000 yards. This gap was too narrow to break the German line: it could be swept by artillery from both flanks. In any case Bapaume and Péronne, the original objectives, were of no strategic value. 'From every point of view, therefore, the British offensive *per se* has been a great failure.'

Before Churchill's note found its way to Haig's headquarters, the commander-in-chief replied to Robertson. Driving the enemy's best troops from strong positions had shaken the faith of the Germans, their friends and doubting neutrals, Haig said. This had shown 'the fighting power of the British race'. Haig said he had inflicted heavy losses. 'In another 6 weeks, the enemy should be hard put to it to find men.' Steady pressure would eventually result in Germany's complete overthrow. Britain had to maintain the offensive. 'Our losses in July's fighting totalled about 120,000 more than they would have been had we not attacked. They cannot be regarded as sufficient to justify any anxiety as to our ability to continue the offensive.' Haig said he would go on attacking, step by step, well into the autumn. Another campaign would be needed in 1917 to break the enemy completely.

Haig's letter was printed and circulated as an answer to the Churchill paper. Then Haig went to work on the King, who was visiting France. Haig took him into his writing room and 'explained the situation to him'. The King, according to Haig, said that generals who had been sent home from France as useless had formed a cabal that 'abused everything that was done by the British HQ on the western front'.

LEGGE'S ATTACK FINALLY went in at 9.15 pm on August 4, close to dusk but with enough light left that the men could see their objectives and the grey lump of the Windmill up the hill. So many officers had been killed or wounded in one battalion that a few hours before the attack began eleven non-commissioned officers were commissioned in the field. Three of these new lieutenants were killed that night and six wounded, two mortally.

Captain Walter Boys had lain out in no-man's land, pretending to be dead, for twenty hours after the 2nd Division's first assault on the heights. 'I expect to get a decoration out of it,' he wrote home two days before the second assault. He received no medal but died of wounds received in the second attack. He was twenty-six. Major Murdoch Mackay also died this night. His battalion became mixed up with another on the way to its jumping-off position. Mackay, a twenty-five year old from Bendigo, took charge, sorted out the confusion, urged men forward and, by his sheer energy and the force of his personality, saved a situation that could have left a dangerous gap in the Australian advance. A few yards short of the first German trench Mackay was shot through the heart. Mackay, an exceptional student, had gone to Melbourne University as a sixteen-year-old to emerge as a barrister at twenty-one. Australia was starting to lose a lot of its future at Pozières.

It was a night of extraordinary tales. Lieutenant Percy Cherry duelled with a German officer leading a counter-attack. They shot at each other at close range from shell holes. Eventually they rose and fired together. The German's bullet hit Cherry's helmet and did little harm. Cherry's bullet caused a mortal wound. Cherry bent over the German, who spoke English and pulled letters from his pockets. He asked Cherry to promise that he would post them after they had passed the censor. Cherry gave his word. The German handed over the letters and said: 'And so it ends.'

Lance-Corporal George O'Neill led a bomb fight against German counter-attackers. O'Neill's men couldn't quite reach the Germans with their grenades. The cry went up for 'Omeo'. Lance-Corporal Norman Weston came from the high country around Omeo in East Gippsland and gave his occupation as 'bushman and stockrider'. The nineteen-year-old could throw further than the others, but he decided that he couldn't reach the Germans from the trench. He climbed on to the parados and leaned back to throw his grenade. A sniper's bullet hit him in the face and knocked out an eye, which now hung by a whitish rope of nerve on his cheek. Weston fell back into the trench among half-a-dozen men.

'For God's sake, George, take this bomb,' he spluttered at O'Neill. 'The pin's out!'

O'Neill threw the grenade out of the trench. Weston fainted. And lived.

THIS TIME, AND mainly because of the careful preparation, the attack succeeded within little more than an hour. The final bombardment was so intense that few Germans had time to carry machine guns up from dugouts. With their jumping-off trench much closer to the German front, the Australians were able to creep within twenty yards of their objectives before the guns lifted.

The prelude, however, was awful. For days the German shelling had gone on and on. Men without a mark on them went mad, shivering with the fever of shell-shock as they stared at nothing. Many Australians said years later that the bombardments at Pozières were their worst memories from the war.

The brigades lined up as they had in the first assault: Holmes' 5th on the right, Paton's 7th in the centre and Gellibrand's 6th on the left.

The 5th went forward, some of the men running, as the final three-minute barrage fell on the German front. They took the first trench easily. The shelling had stunned the Germans, many of whom came blinking from their deep dugouts to surrender. The third and fourth waves went on to the second line, OG 2 on the maps. The trench had been so severely shelled they couldn't find it and kept going. Eventually someone noticed a line of stakes that had once held up a wire entanglement. This had to be OG 2, and the men were called back to it. Casualties had been light.

In the centre the 7th Brigade surprised the Germans in their dugouts. Here was evidence of one of the truths of the war. Frontal attacks *could* work if the artillery kept the defenders and their machine guns underground. Many Germans surrendered, often in groups of a dozen; others ran for their second line. Again the Australians had difficulty identifying OG 2 from all the surrounding craters and overran their objective. Lieutenant Arnold Brown, who was in this brigade, wondered afterwards why his battalion, even though it was now down to about 100 men, had not been ordered to advance further. The Germans were so disorganised the following day that they barely fired a shot, but 'we had to sit and suffer the sight of enemy gun teams limbering up and drawing their field guns to safety, later to again rain shells on us; and it was not long before that happened.'

On the left the 6th Brigade was troubled by a single machine gun that had been untouched by the barrage. This gun may have killed Murdoch Mackay; it certainly killed several officers near him. But the Australians were soon throwing bombs into the German front trench. Eric Edgerton, an acting sergeant with boyish looks, wrote laconically in his diary: 'My party capture 31 prisoners and get them safe to rear.' Edgerton had joined up as a student from Wesley College, Melbourne. He was only nineteen and had already won the Military Medal for bravery on Gallipoli.

The Australians finally had most of the OG lines, including the Windmill. The Germans knew exactly where those trenches were and around midnight began to shell them. Australian officers were in the open at this time, supervising digging in the wrecked trenches and trying to get the wounded and prisoners away. As so often happened in the Great War, a disproportionate number now became casualties. The Australians wouldn't see the little village of Courcelette until dawn but they already knew roughly where it was from the muzzle flashes of the German artillery.

In the misty light after dawn, the Australians glimpsed the trees of Courcelette and green fields beyond. But they would not be going for the village. Gough had already decided to turn them north towards Mouquet Farm the following night and Birdwood passed this news to Legge early on August 5. Which rather proved that this trio had no notion of the condition of the 2nd Division.

GOUGH SENT HIS congratulations to the 2nd Division. Haig telegraphed that the success 'opens the way to further equally valuable successes'. This, though well meant, was clumsy. Several more successes like the last one and the 2nd Division would cease to exist. Gough's order that the 2nd Division next push north towards Mouquet Farm reached the three brigades on the morning after the attack, and reality struck. The division had too many casualties and those who were left were exhausted. In the afternoon Birdwood told Gough the new attack could not go ahead. The 4th Australian Division would have to replace the 2nd.

The 2nd Division's casualties were 6848. Many of the wounded were also suffering shell-shock. Men waiting to have flesh wounds dressed were observed to be shaking uncontrollably. Paton's 7th Brigade in the centre had lost 2346 men (the normal infantry strength of a brigade was close to 4000). One of his battalions, the 25th, had run up 685 casualties, including twenty-five officers. Alec Raws' battalion, the 23rd, had lost close to half its strength.

Captain Gordon Maxfield, who, like Raws, was in Gellibrand's brigade, wrote to his father.

> We have just come out of a place so terrible that my brain prior to this could not have conjured up anything so frightful – a raving lunatic could never imagine the horrors of the last 13 days, and I will not spoil your sleep by depicting the scenes through which we lived and passed and repassed during those awful days. Our casualties you will hear of *some day*. Two of my very good friends have been killed, and five or six others wounded more or less seriously. Major Forbes, now Colonel, is now C.O. vice Colonel – who for the fifth time got 'shocked' on the 'battle eve' . . . We saw the King on our way out, and General Birdwood told him in our hearing that this Brigade had done every mortal thing that had been asked of it.

Maxfield understood better than most the nature of the Somme battle. 'Almost every inch of this country is trenched and practically fortified, and we simply have to batter the Hun from one place to another.' Maxfield was grateful for a pair of socks that arrived in the mail. He explained that he had been wearing the same pair for close to three weeks without taking his boots off.

ALEC RAWS WROTE to a Victorian parliamentarian before the attack on August 4. 'We are lousy, stinking, ragged, unshaven, sleepless. Even when we're back a bit we can't sleep for our own guns. I have one puttee, a dead man's helmet, another dead man's gas protector, a dead man's bayonet. My tunic is rotten with other men's blood and partly splattered with a comrade's brains.' Raws had met three officers in no-man's land at night, 'all rambling and mad'. Raws said that he had kept his nerve. 'Courage does not count here. It is all nerve. Once that goes one becomes a gibbering maniac.' Raws added a postscript dated August 8: 'I am still all right . . .'

Perhaps he wasn't. Eleven days later he wrote to his brother that he had 'a very bad chest'. He had fainted three times, once in public. He didn't want to report sick. It might just be nerves.

Then he wrote this:

> Before going into this next affair, at the same dreadful spot, I want to tell you, so that it may be on record, that I honestly believe Goldy and many other officers were murdered on the night you know of, through the incompetence, callousness, and personal vanity of those high in authority. I realise the seriousness of what I say, but I am so bitter, and the facts are so palpable, that it must be said. Please be very discreet with this letter – unless I should go under.

11

Jacka picks up the club

Major-General Sir Herbert Vaughan Cox, a fifty-six-year-old veteran of Britain's colonial spats, commanded the 4th Australian Division. He had led an Indian Brigade at the Cape Helles front on Gallipoli, where he eventually suffered some sort of 'breakdown', which – whatever it was – might reasonably be put down to being misused for too long in General Hunter-Weston's butcher's shop. Cox was then sent north to command the left assaulting column during the August offensive at Anzac and stayed at the front after being nicked by shrapnel. The assault on the Turkish heights failed, but it wasn't his fault, nor that of John Monash, whose 4th Brigade was part of Cox's force. Both had been presented with a scheme that made sense only on maps.

Cox at first didn't know what to think of Australians or Monash. He met both in atrocious circumstances. His left assaulting column blundered around for days in 1000 acres of the roughest country on Gallipoli and most of the time Cox didn't know where his troops were. He was steeped in the ways of the old Indian army and didn't understand citizen-soldiers or the Australian temperament. He believed in the caste system: he didn't like the idea of men who had given their occupation as 'bushman' being made officers.

Cox and Monash, who despised the military trade union, collided several times. Monash thought him 'one of those crotchety, peppery, livery old Indian officers, whom the climate has dried and shrivelled up into a bag of nerves'. Yet a few days after the August offensive ended Cox wrote to his wife that he wished he had more Australians. Cox also came to appreciate Monash's quicksilver mind and in 1916 recommended him for the command of the 3rd Division. General Godley also recommended Monash, but with a rider: 'One cannot pretend that he is as well qualified to command a division as a trained regular officer, but . . .' Godley was a member of the trade union, paid up for life.

Monash's old 4th Brigade was now part of Cox's division and under the command of Charles Brand, a veteran of the Boer War and Gallipoli. Duncan Glasfurd, commander of the 12th Brigade, had been a staff officer at Gallipoli. Thomas Glasgow, a Queensland grazier who had won the Distinguished Service Order in the Boer War, commanded the 13th Brigade and was seen as a coming man. He was forty years old and looked out on the world with blue eyes shaded by bushy eyebrows. Bean said Glasgow was not particularly articulate but had a sure sense of character and situations and could say a great deal with a frown or a shake of the head.

The 4th Division thus had a core of good officers – it probably had more than Legge's 2nd Division – as well as several crack battalions. It would be best remembered, however, not for Cox or Glasgow, but for two men, both from the bush, who had enlisted as privates.

ALBERT JACKA WAS now a twenty-three-year-old lieutenant. He commanded a platoon in the 14th Battalion. Harry Murray had become a captain in the 13th.

Jacka had won the Victoria Cross as a lance-corporal on Gallipoli. The Turks broke into the Australian line. Jacka jumped in among them, shooting five and bayoneting two. The Turks still alive thought it best to leave. An Australian officer came upon

Jacka surrounded by dead Turks and Australians, his face flushed and an unlit cigarette dangling from his lips. 'I managed to get the beggars, sir,' Jacka said.

Jacka was a forestry worker from Wedderburn, north of Bendigo. He was reckless and liked to fight. In some ways he was the soldier's soldier, a one-man epic whose style and reputation inspired not only those who knew him but also thousands who had never seen him, a man impatient with form and authority, traits admired by Australians of that era. Some said he was a natural leader, and he was, but only up to a certain level. He was cocky and outspoken and tended to see the world in monochrome.

Sergeant Edgar Rule served alongside Jacka and later wrote *Jacka's Mob*, a lively narrative of the 14th Battalion. Rule wrote: 'I often wonder to what heights Jacka would have climbed had he possessed the amiable disposition of either Harry Murray or Percy Black [Major Black, a much-decorated mining prospector and friend of Murray's, had also enlisted as a private]. I think Jacka belonged to an age when it was possible for the individual to challenge with a club the right of leadership in the tribe. In the Great War, some of his peculiar talents were a hindrance rather than a help in climbing to the higher ranks.' Ted Rule remembered the first time he saw Jacka:

> To me, he looked the part; he had a medium-sized body, a natty figure, and a determined face with crooked nose . . . At that time [Jacka was then a sergeant-major] one characteristic above all endeared him to all the under-dogs; instead of 'criming' men and bringing them before the officers, his method was: 'I won't crime you, I'll give you a punch on the bloody nose' . . . His confident, frank, outspoken personality never changed . . . the whole AIF came to look upon him as a rock of strength that never failed. We of the 14th Battalion never ceased to be thrilled when we heard our-selves referred to in the *estaminet* or by passing units on the march as 'some of Jacka's mob'.

Harry Murray was almost thirty-four when he enlisted, of average height but strong and sinewy from swinging an axe in Western

Australia, where he ran a gang of sleeper-cutters in the karri forests. He had dark green eyes and a quiet manner. Murray came from convict stock (although he didn't discover this until later in life) and grew up on a farm outside Launceston. He was a good shot by the time he was ten; possums taught him with their lives.

He had never pardoned his father for pulling him out of school to work on the farm when he was fourteen. Late in life Murray said he didn't have any time for his father: 'I have nothing to thank him for.' Who knows what a formal education might have done for Murray? He loved to read, particularly the classics, and few Australian soldiers wrote better-crafted prose in their war recollections. He wrote in 1939 of Percy Black returning to the frontline at Gallipoli with a new machine gun. 'He might have been Diomed striding back over the plains after interviewing Paris.'

Murray left the family farm for Western Australia, where he carried gold and mail for a mining company near Kalgoorlie. He travelled by bicycle or on a horse. There were hostile Aborigines and 'some bad lads with white hides' along the track 'and everyone knew what I carried'. (It was a .32 carbine.) He said long afterwards he wasn't happy in the west and we don't know why. The army seemed to give his life a point. He won the Distinguished Conduct Medal on Gallipoli and was commissioned in the field there.

He wasn't like Jacka. He wasn't so sure of things. He was tactful and understated. A young officer in the 13th wrote to his father in 1917: 'Harry Murray and I have a walk every evening in the twilight and yarn about all kinds of things – he is a wonderful character, brave to a fault, keen and quick in thought and action, gentle as a woman, a born gentleman.' Murray knew not only about courage but also about its near-relations, about how it lived next door to fear. 'I fought many a hard battle (to put it bluntly) between duty and funk,' he wrote. It didn't bother him to admit to fear, to speak of his 'shaking knees' and the urge to run away. Cowardice, he wrote, was practically the same thing as self-preservation; it was the first law of nature, 'and while some men maybe so constituted that they require no artificial stimuli, I cannot make any such claim'. Murray described himself as 'nervy and highly strung'.

Others didn't see him this way. They saw a strong man who became embarrassed when he thought others were taking him too seriously.

THE MEN OF Jacka's battalion, the 14th, thought they were being ushered into purgatory. They approached the front on the night of August 6, past the razed village and its clouds of ash, past the graves of half-buried men whose hands and feet stuck up in the loose earth, past dead men lying on stretchers and stretcher-bearers lying dead alongside. They noticed that many of the dead were unmarked, killed by concussion. They thought the 2nd Division men they were relieving looked dazed.

The new men began repairing trenches, which meant tossing the bodies of their countrymen over the parapets. At 9 pm the German artillery opened up again. Newton Wanliss, the historian of the 14th Battalion, wrote that many of those under that barrage would later say it was the worst they faced in the Great War. The men could not hear each other speak. Some sheltered in the deep German dugouts. Because of its narrowness, Pozières had become the nastiest of salients. The Germans were pounding it from Courcelette and elsewhere to the east, and from Thiepval to the west.

Ted Rule kept stumbling over dead men. His hands became wet and clammy. He thought he and his men were lost and said so to a corporal. No, said the corporal, they had to be on the right track because there were so many dead around. Eventually they found a trench near the front and the German howitzers found them. Rule and his men huddled on the floor, resting on each other's knees as clods of earth tumbled over their shoulders. Rule said the men tried to make fun of it but the jokes were feeble. As the dawn came Rule noticed that the German shells had lifted off the front trench. They were falling behind him. Was this the prelude to a German infantry attack? A lieutenant laughed and told him to sit down.

A man came running along the trench shouting: 'Jacka is killed and the Huns have got the ridge.' The lieutenant laughed again: the man was obviously mad. Rule didn't know what to think; part of the trouble was that he didn't know precisely where the frontline was. A little later he lifted his binoculars.

> ... I could see some of our boys standing up and firing point-blank at other men. Some figures I could see on their knees in front of others praying for their lives, and several were bayoneting Huns. It was one of the queerest sights I've ever seen – Huns and Aussies were scattered in ones and twos all along the side of the ridge. It was such a mix-up that it was hard to tell who were Huns and who were Aussies. Each Aussie seemed to be having a war all on his own ...

THE 48TH BATTALION, commanded by the South Australian Ray Leane, had come up the day before Jacka's battalion and took over the line from the Windmill to a bend in the OG lines called the Elbow. Lieutenant-Colonel Leane was an experienced and strong-minded soldier. He had been talking to an observer on Gallipoli when a shell carried away the man's head; Leane, though also wounded, stayed at his post. With his big shoulders, strong jaw and serious air, he was a fearsome sight and known as 'the Bull'. One of his brothers, Ben, was adjutant in the 48th, while a nephew, Allan, commanded a platoon. Another relative, from Kalgoorlie, was also in the 48th, which was known as the Joan of Arc battalion (Made of All Leanes).

Leane's men had filed into Pozières around dusk on August 5, big-eyed with apprehension as the German barrage came down on them. Glasfurd had ordered Leane to put two of his companies in the frontline and place the other two close behind. Leane didn't want the frontline crowded; he wanted to leave his reserve companies behind Pozières. Glasfurd and Leane argued. Glasfurd gave Leane a written order telling him to put his reserves in front of the village. Leane disobeyed it.

Leane described the night of August 5–6 as his worst time in the war. Shellfire carried off his men in the dark. He couldn't find the commander he was supposed to be relieving; he couldn't even find the frontline troops. When Leane visited his own frontline the next morning most of the men were dead or wounded and the trench had become a line of shell holes.

The 4th Division now found out about shell-shock. Captain Ben Leane wrote that he saw men weeping like children and cowering at every explosion. He told of a runner, not much older than a boy, going out under fire even though he showed all the symptoms of nervous collapse after being buried by a shell-burst. Eventually he told Leane: 'I *can't* face it anymore.' Leane told him not to worry; he had done well. Ben Leane was the best liked of the clan.

By mid-afternoon Ray Leane was convinced a counter-attack was coming. That night the 14th Battalion, Jacka's Mob, moved in on the left of Leane, but held the frontline lightly. Jacka was in the OG lines but Rule may have been up to 500 yards back.

Jacka sheltered with his men in a deep German dugout. Before dawn on August 7 he climbed the stairs and stared out into the darkness, looking for signs of an attack. Nothing. He went below again. Shortly after the Germans attacked from Courcelette on a narrow front.

The Australians above ground opened fire. The Germans burst into the Australian line near the Elbow, throwing bombs down dugouts, then quickly heading down the hill towards the village. Some turned and attacked Leane's men from behind. The frontline commander here was mortally wounded and his replacement told the forty men left to surrender. The Germans began to march them off.

The Germans were inside the Australians' lines and the defence was a shambles. What they couldn't know was that one man was about to challenge with a club for the leadership of this part of the battlefield. This war was about technology: artillery, machine guns, aircraft, telephones, submarines. Now, fleetingly, it reverted to a scene from Cannae.

JACKA AND HIS men were deep in the dugout when the Germans came over. Some were sleeping. The Germans threw a grenade down the stairs, wounding two men. By the time Jacka and his men had emerged from the shaft the Germans had run past. Jacka rounded up seven men. His idea was to break through the Germans behind him and get back to Pozières. Then he saw the prisoners from Leane's battalion being escorted back. Jacka charged from about thirty yards. This was the start of the mêlée that Sergeant Rule had picked up in his binoculars.

German bullets hit every man in Jacka's party. Some of the Germans threw down their rifles; Australian prisoners picked them up. Other Germans began shooting their prisoners. Australians in nearby trenches and shell holes joined in. Sergeant Cyril Beck of the 48th rushed to help Jacka from the south only to be killed. Another sergeant from the 48th joined in and had his leg blown off by a grenade. He lay in a trench, shouting encouragement until he bled to death. There were few bayonet fights in the Great War; close combat was mainly about bombs. But here, in this brawl on the hillside, men fought with bayonets and bombs and fists. Some fell to their knees and prayed. Onlookers were disinclined to shoot for fear of hitting one of their own.

More Australians came into the fray and the Germans eventually surrendered. They passed Sergeant Rule, down the hill, on their way to the cage. Then Rule saw the stretcher-bearers coming back. One of the bearers told him that Jacka was on the stretcher just ahead. 'I wouldn't give a Gyppo piastre for him,' the man said, 'he is knocked about dreadfully.'

Jacka had been wounded seven times. One bullet had entered under the right shoulder and passed through his body. He had at least two wounds to the head. He is said to have killed twenty or more Germans, some with a bayonet, although the facts are blurry. Years later Jacka told an old friend a little of what happened.

There were four Huns in a shell hole. All I could see were their heads, shoulders, and rifles. As I went towards them, they began firing point-blank at me. They hit me three times and each time the terrific impact of bullets fired at such close range swung me off my feet. But each time I sprang up like a prize-fighter, and kept getting closer. When I got up to them, they flung down their rifles and put up their hands. I shot three through the head and put a bayonet through the fourth. I had to do it – they would have killed me the moment I turned my back.

I think another fellow must have fired at me, and missed. I looked around and saw a Hun who must have weighed seventeen or eighteen stone. I aimed at his belly and he almost fell on me . . . A stretcher-bearer came, took off my tunic, and fixed me up. I asked him to go and bring a stretcher. He went away and I never saw him again. I lay there for a long time, and then began to think of the wounded that were never found. I made up my mind to try and get back by myself. I don't know how I managed it, but I got back quite a way, and some men found me.

Jacka was sent to a hospital in England. A month or so later Rule and others in France picked up a London newspaper and read that Jacka had died. It seems that Jacka was lying in bed and talking to friends when he was told that a reporter from one of the London dailies had arrived to interview him. Jacka turned to one of his mates and said: 'Go to the door and tell the beggar I'm dead.'

Jacka eventually left the hospital and spent several months as the assistant adjutant at a camp in England. A friend of Rule's did clerical work there. He told Rule that Jacka was close to a nervous breakdown. The sound of a box lid being hurriedly closed would cause him to shake for hours and so badly that he couldn't sign his name to a memorandum. When Jacka returned to the 14th Battalion in France he had contrived to hide his demons. The men thought him the same as ever.

WHO DESERVES THE Victoria Cross? The question is not easily answered. There is no formula. The British won six Victoria Crosses at W Beach on the morning of the Gallipoli landings; the Australians won seven at Lone Pine a few months later. At both these places there were enough heroics to justify the handing out of eleven medals. That was the number of Victoria Crosses awarded for the struggle at Rorke's Drift during the Zulu war of 1879, and one has to wonder how the number came to be so high there. One also has to wonder why the New Zealander Colonel William

Malone failed to receive the Victoria Cross for his rare courage at Chunuk Bair on Gallipoli, where he died. If there was a formula, or even a vague pattern, to these things one might contend that what Jacka did at Pozières was at least the equal of what he did at Courtney's Post on Gallipoli, and more inspirational, in that his audacity (as Bean put it) changed the course of the skirmish on the hillside. In other words one might argue that Jacka should have received a second Victoria Cross. He didn't. He received the Military Cross.

THE 4TH DIVISION, with just a few battalions at the front, had taken severe casualties. In two nights Leane's 48th Battalion had lost nearly two-thirds of its strength: twenty officers and 578 men. The 45th had helped the British to capture Munster Alley, which meant the line to the east was now continuous. The battalion lost 345 men, among them Major Duncan Chapman of Brisbane, who many believed was the first Australian to land at Gallipoli. Jacka's platoon went in fifty-two strong on August 6 and came out the next day with four unwounded men.

The day after that a captain in the 15th Battalion sent a runner off with a message. The runner returned almost immediately without a thumb. A shell fragment had blown it off. He refused to let the captain and another man dress the stump until he had passed his message to another runner and explained to him the route to battalion headquarters. Private George Willison was awarded the Military Medal.

12

Mad Harry

The Somme campaign lives in popular memory because of what happened on the first day. Lines of men walking to their death as if in a trance, as if they had no say in it, which they didn't. Fifty-seven thousand casualties, for a gain of three square miles. Yet it might be argued that what was happening on the Somme now, six weeks later, was worse.

The casualties from the new front – from Munster Alley, Delville Wood, High Wood, Guillemont and Pozières – were heavy, but they came in small packages, a few hundred here, a few thousand there. They also came just about every day. The war here was no longer about a wide front and the hope of breakthrough. In a sense the war here was no longer about hope of any sort, just attrition, the notion that by allowing yourself to be hurt you might hurt your enemy even more, so that when it was over there might be slightly more of you left than of him. The war here was about dozens of small fronts, perhaps only wide enough for a battalion, dozens of desperate little fights in newly created salients, repeated over and over until one side gave way. It was also about counter-attacks. The Germans were as gritty as their opponents. If they gave way, it was only because they had to. They would take a breath, then come

Mouquet Farm

Zollern Redoubt

Fabeck Graben

trench

OVILLERS-COURCELETTE ROAD

Mouquet Farm

Bapaume

OG 2

OG 1

AUS

Windmill

Cemetery

Pozières

K Trench

Mash Valley

N
W E
S

Pozières Trench

Alley

Watch

Black

Contalmaison Wood

Albert

Sausage Valley

Bailiff Wood

Contalmaison

SCALE

0   500 metres

0   500 yards

back throwing bombs. And this war was about artillery barrages more intense than anything that had gone before because the fronts were so narrow.

Pozières, and particularly the ground northwards towards Mouquet Farm, was just one of these narrow fronts, another place for men to wear each other out. Most of these fronts belonged to General Rawlinson's 4th Army to the east and south of the Australians. High Wood and Guillemont were bigger nightmares than Pozières. In their study of Rawlinson's military career, *Command on the Western Front*, Robin Prior and Trevor Wilson estimate that the 4th Army ran up 82,000 casualties between July 15 and September 14. In that time Rawlinson took two-and-three-quarter square miles from the Germans. 'That is, while capturing a somewhat smaller area than in the massed offensive of July 1, the 4th Army during six weeks of small-scale attacks sustained casualties that were 40 per cent higher.'

The problem for the 4th Australian Division, now holding the Pozières front, was that as the advance turned north towards Mouquet Farm the Australian salient became thinner and more awkward. The idea was to come at Thiepval from the rear, through Mouquet Farm, as well as from the front. It looked good on maps, neat almost. It didn't look so good on the ground.

The Pozières front had become thousands upon thousands of craters. Walking paths meandered through them, like the tracks of drunken sheep, but men still became lost. German shells screamed into the Australian salient from three sides. Runners were blown up trying to carry messages back; stretcher-bearers were buried trying to pick up wounded. The ground had once been some of the sweetest farmland in the world. Australians who had grown up on farms wrote home that it would never again grow anything but weeds. And the ground stank: of explosives, a chemical aroma relatively new in the world, and of putrefaction, a smell as old as humankind. Corpses lay everywhere, some mutilated, others untouched but for a trickle of blood from a nostril or an ear.

Pozières had developed new rhythms. It was best in the three hours before 7 am when summer mists lay on the downland and gunners from both sides took a break. It was tolerable at other times if one could shelter in the deep German dugouts. In the trenches the best a man could hope for was that the next shell would merely bury him.

Captain Allan Leane, the nephew of Ray, wrote to his mother after the 48th Battalion had lost two-thirds of its men during two nights in the line.

> You can have no idea of what the ground is like . . . All I can do in the way of description is futile & the best I can do is to say that . . . it resembles a rough sea seen from the beach, walking is imposs[ible] & no horse could cross it except where the tracks which we have made & keep in repair exist & it is only by keeping parties at work filling up fresh holes as they are made that it is possible to cross at all, this state of things exists for hundreds of acres, & so far as the eye can reach, great craters, so close together as to make traffic hopeless, these being blown in & remade incessantly till as I say the country resembles a wild sea. I cannot describe it & it is no use trying. I can only pray God that one day Father will bring you here & show you the place.

DOUGLAS HAIG DIDN'T encounter problems with the terrain when he rode his horse, which he liked to do as often as possible. Sand was sometimes spread on the road so that the horse might obtain better traction. Things went to a proper timetable at GHQ. Haig always breakfasted at 8.30 am, a gentleman's hour, even if it was long after dawn in summer. At Montreuil he was closer to the Channel ports than the Somme killing grounds. There was nothing wrong with this and much that made sense. GHQ and the commander-in-chief needed to be in a safe place. But Haig was also disinclined to visit the front and this meant that his knowledge of the conditions under which his men were fighting was sometimes poor. The Australians knew Birdwood: he always looked dapper and wanted to shake hands. The Canadians knew Arthur Currie, the commander of their 1st Division: he got about in shirt and braces and swore a lot. Haig's troops seldom saw him. He said he didn't do 'showy things' or try to be popular.

Haig was running the fray but also somehow above it. He was more like a king, mysterious, there but not there, a man who delegated and sent out emissaries and thought that God had chosen him. He was selfish like a king: his interests and those of his retinue came first. To him this was not selfishness but necessity, and he had a point. He was some sort of middle kingdom, between the Cabinet room and the frontline, and the kingdom needed to argue its case. Haig now had to convince the politicians at home that the Somme campaign was actually achieving something. He had to convince some that the British were fighting in the right place. The 'easterners' still believed the war could be won from the Balkans or Italy.

Haig's German counterparts didn't have to explain or mollify as he did. Germany wasn't a democracy. There was a federal parliament, the Reichstag, but, as someone once said, it was 'the fig-leaf of absolutism'. Kaiser Wilhelm didn't have to answer to the Reichstag. He controlled the armed forces. He had the formal powers to run Germany much as he liked. Germany was an autocracy. And, now that the Kaiser was sulking after being denied the quick victory to which he thought he was entitled, Germany was on the way to becoming a military dictatorship.

Haig looked down on politicians but when they came to his salon he brought out the brandy, fixed them with his blue eyes, and tried to put them right. Eloquent and subtle men bothered him: they might not be 'straight'. Yet he had to deal with just such men and they had names like Asquith, Churchill, Lloyd George, Balfour and Carson. He was more comfortable with King George, who, like himself, was long on character and shorter on intellect.

During the early weeks of the Somme, Haig entertained Lord Bryce, who had chaired the committee that had investigated German atrocities in Belgium. ('A nice old man,' Haig wrote, 'and very highly educated. Yet he is unable to give an opinion definitely on any subject! It is sad to think that "education" so-called will bring men to such a state of indecision.') Sir Derek Keppell, Master of the King's Household, arrived to find a suitable château for the King's visit. ('Derek is enjoying himself so much that he has asked to stay another day,' Haig said, which rather proved that Derek had not been to Guillemont or Pozières.) Lord Northcliffe, proprietor of *The Times* and the *Daily Mail*, once the cleverest popular journalist of his time but now a megalomaniac, came to lunch. ('He is most enthusiastic on all he had seen, and is very anxious to do all he can to help to win.') During his next visit, about a month later, Northcliffe told Haig that Lloyd George did everything he [Northcliffe] advised. Shortly after the King arrived. He thanked Haig for what he had done for his 'family'.

John Masefield visited Haig's GHQ. Masefield had a poet's gift for finding just the right adjective. He wrote home that Haig had a 'resolved' face. In Haig's mind all *was* resolved: it was simply a case of not losing one's nerve and wearing the Germans out.

ONE FAMILY HAD owned Mouquet Farm, where the Australians were to do their wearing out, since before the French Revolution. The house commanded the ground around it, much as the Windmill did at Pozières, and stared across to Thiepval in the west. The buildings, laid out in a square like a rustic fortress, were of red and chalk bricks. Dormer windows peeped over a courtyard that echoed with the footfalls of heavy horses. The dairy stood at the end of the square now nearest to the Australian line; there were five cellars beneath it. The main house was at the far end; it had two cellars. Mouquet Farm had been very stately. Now it was rubble and tree stumps. All the Australians could see were one or two broken beams and a patch of white cement. But the Germans had been busy in those cellars, extending and fortifying them with concrete. Now the farm truly was a fortress, a system of stairways and passages, galleries and tunnels. But it was out of sight, underground, and the British and Australians had no notion of how strong it was.

The Australians would have to fight their way through three lines of trenches before discovering the grottoes of Mouquet Farm. These lines ran roughly east to west. The first, called Park Lane and now the new German frontline, followed the highest part of the ridge north of Pozières. The next line, Skyline trench, ran across a little valley in front of Mouquet Farm and skirted around a chalk quarry. The third, Fabeck Graben, ran through Mouquet Farm itself.

BRAND'S 4TH BRIGADE took Park Lane and by August 10, amid rain, the Australians were over the ridge north of Pozières. Harry Murray came into the line with the 13th Battalion. The Australians probed at the German lines and set up outposts as German shells fell among them. Newton Wanliss said the men of the 14th Battalion were exhausted. They couldn't sleep because of the artillery barrages; several had been sent to the back areas with 'nervous disorders'. Other battalions now went for Skyline trench, with British troops on their left. The line had gone forward about 600 yards in three-and-a-half days. Gough wanted the Australians to lunge at Mouquet Farm, less than 400 yards ahead, and either take it or surround it. General Cox seemed confident this could be done; Birdwood and White had doubts. None of them knew how strong Mouquet Farm was. Then the Germans counter-attacked and took back the British section of Skyline trench. Suddenly the salient was much narrower. Cox had to change his plan. The Australians on the left would pull up short of Mouquet Farm; those on the right would go further and take the Fabeck Graben trench east of the farm. But now there was another complication. Germans near Thiepval captured British documents saying that the farm was about to be attacked. The Germans panicked: they saw every movement in the British or Australian lines as the start of an assault. They dropped a furious barrage on the waiting Australians on August 14.

The Australian attack was due to go in that night after 10 pm under a full moon. As the British official history put it, the German barrage caused 'such confusion and loss that a properly co-ordinated advance became out of the question'. The 50th Battalion was supposed to go forward on the left flank, the 13th in the centre, and the 51st and 49th on the right.

Around 8 pm a company commander in the 50th sent a message to battalion headquarters: 'We cannot move. We have few tools, few bombs, no water, and the men are badly shaken. At present we are digging a number out. I have too few men to take up the frontage, and after consulting the company commanders have decided to remain fast. Am notifying 13th Battalion.'

He told the 13th. The commander of the 13th objected: his flank would be exposed. Captain Harry Murray was commanding a company here. Just before the attack he reported: 'C Company rattled and only have 35 men.'

The commander of the 51st, on the right of the 13th, sent a message to brigade headquarters:

> Both 13th C.O. thinks, and it is my genuine (not depressed) opinion that it would be a mistake to press the offensive further locally in this salient. We are heavily shelled from due E. right round to N.W., and the communications are simply *awful*. It really requires some days' solid work. Water- and ration-carrying is most precarious. The boys are sticking it well, but are so congested that it will be most difficult to deploy tonight. Do not worry about us, but we want WATER and digging tools always. Our artillery are bombarding our own front trenches (heavies!!!).

No-one, it seemed, wanted to attack, not because of fear of the offensive itself but because they had been hit so hard by artillery before it had started. The company commanders in the 50th were promptly told they had to obey orders. The attack began at 10.30 pm.

Panic broke out in the 50th on the left. A German barrage fell on the troops just before the jump-off. Two officers managed to bring the troops under control. The line eventually went forward only to be shot down by machine guns. Those still alive dug in around the chalk quarry in front of Mouquet Farm. After half-an-hour they withdrew. The left flank was open.

On the other side of the salient the 51st, West Australians, met heavy machine-gun fire. Someone yelled 'Retire!' Confusion broke out. Some men kept going, then turned back. The right flank was open.

In the centre the 13th Battalion went forward strongly, charging the Fabeck Graben trench. The Germans there, after hesitating to weigh the odds, mostly ran. A lance-corporal threw a pick at a machine-gun post, then a bomb, and came away with eleven prisoners. A sergeant-major who was with him came away with nine bullets in his thigh. The 13th had taken its objective, but Murray soon realised he and his men were alone. The Germans were counter-attacking and his men were running out of bombs.

Murray began to think about how he would get his wounded out. He set up a line of posts along a German trench that led back to the old Australian frontline. Then he received definite news that the 51st had retreated on his right. He knew he had to leave too.

MURRAY WROTE YEARS afterwards that discipline got him through. Not the parade-ground discipline of which the English were so fond, but the discipline that said you must not give in to natural instincts like fear, that you must look after your mates, that you had a *duty*. You would feel fear. That was inevitable. You could let it tempt you. But you must not succumb. Murray knew he could not simply retreat. He had to hold off the Germans while his men fell back on the staging posts he had set up. His party was almost out of grenades and the Germans knew this. The Germans, Murray wrote, were 'cool, heady' and 'courageous'. The Australians began to fall back on the staging posts. Murray was always the last man away, with the Germans perhaps one bay behind him, throwing bombs.

Murray headed for the fifth post. 'I could hear excited, guttural voices, together with the rattle of enemy accoutrements, and I experienced the usual fierce struggle between natural promptings and duty . . . Even in those hectic moments I had experienced many a cold shiver, as I thought of the bayonets of the counter-attacking force, because it seemed to me, as I ran, that I was almost within reach of those lethal, shining blades.'

A bomb dropped one of the two men in front of him. The other man, dazed and wounded by fragments, kept running. Murray jumped over the fallen man, assuming him to be dead. As he did so he saw the man's eyes open.

215

His leg was doubled and twisted, and although he did not speak his eyes were eloquent. It was then that I fought the hardest battle of my life, between an almost insane desire to continue running and save my own life, or to comply with the sacred traditions of the AIF and stop to help a wounded comrade. Surely I must be bayoneted if I stopped for an instant. The enemy were coming up at the double, having no opposition. I often dread to think of what I might have done. I was safe enough at the time, and all I had to do was keep on going; there was only a straight run of 50 yards to my mates, and despite that poor, twisted leg, those mute lips, and pathetic eyes, it was really only the mechanical habit engendered by strict discipline, that forced me to do what I did. I dropped on to my shaking knees, caught him by the arms, and pulled him on to my back. He helped me like a hero with his one sound leg, and off we staggered, with Fritz just coming into our bay.

Murray outpaced the Germans, who, having been four times held up with Lewis-gun fire and bombs, were perhaps losing some of their zest. 'I was once more among my mates, and the wounded Digger was safe, for a little while, at all events.'

Murray's men were down to their last dozen bombs. Soon they would have to fight with their bayonets. Then Murray heard the voice of Lieutenant Bob Henderson, an electrician from Drummoyne, Sydney. Henderson was the battalion's bombing officer.

'Here I am, Bob,' Murray yelled, 'have you any bombs?'

'Any bloody amount!' said Henderson.

Henderson and his men hurled bombs and forced the Germans back 100 yards. Murray and the others were safe. Bean called this 'one of the most skilfully conducted fights in the history of the AIF'.

It said a little about the discipline that mattered, that which materialised under fire. Monash said much later in the war that 'stupid comment' had been made about the discipline of the Australians. Discipline, he wrote, was only a means to an end. 'It does not mean lip service, nor obsequious homage to superiors, nor servile observance of forms and customs, nor a suppression of individuality . . . the Australian Army is a proof that individualism is the best and not the worst foundation upon which to build up collective discipline.'

Within a week Jacka and Murray had done unusually brave things. Jacka's was a piece of madness, not at all scientific, as though the Germans had offered him a personal insult, which they undoubtedly had, and needed to be dealt with; but it was also inspired and inspiring, so frightening and elemental that it changed a local defeat into a victory. Murray's was about poise and steadiness and a courage that was profound but not reckless and only one or two degrees removed from fear. Jacka's exploit was instinctive, Murray's considered. Jacka was a natural; Murray had to screw himself up and think of duty. They called Murray 'Mad Harry' but he wasn't.

THE 4TH DIVISION was pulled out of the line the next day, to be replaced by General Walker's 1st Division, back for a second tour. In nine days the 4th had lost 4649 men, which meant the three Australian divisions had now lost 16,780 troops in a few hundred acres at Pozières. Add to that the casualties from Fromelles and the losses came in at 22,313 in just under a month.

This was a volunteer army. Enlistments for July had amounted to 6170. Billy Hughes wanted to introduce conscription.

13

Kill more Germans

Sergeant Champion, the dental apprentice from Sydney, was tramping back to Pozières, more circumspectly this time. He and the rest of the 1st Division had been gone only a fortnight, and the demons that had walked alongside them on the way out were still present, and every now and then asked them whether they were doing a rational thing, returning to this place of corruption.

Champion marched through Contay, where the sight of nurses outside the casualty stations cheered the men. If the nurses were here, the German frontline must have been pushed back a little. Champion reached Pozières village. It was dreadful, he wrote. 'We appeared to be sniped by 5.9" shells. First of all they would lob one behind us, and blow in the trench, and we would not know whether to run forward and so dodge the next one or to stop still.'

He had eaten 'marvellous food' during his rest, written home, acquired a new tunic, helped a lieutenant write letters to the families of men who had 'passed out' at Pozières and learned about the Lewis gun, the portable machine gun. He could now take one apart blindfolded. The Lewis was starting to change the tactics of the war. In 1915 there were only four to a battalion; now there were eight or more. The Germans had nothing to match it. The gun weighed only twenty-eight pounds (compared with seventy-three for the belt-fed Vickers machine gun) and the feed came from a drum magazine that held forty-seven shells. Isaac Lewis, an American army officer, had invented the gun in 1911 and brought it to Europe after his countrymen spurned it. This was a big year for American inventors. Just about every machine gun in the world traced to the original produced by Hiram Maxim, the farmer's son from Maine, in 1884. Maxim died late in 1916, the year in which his most famous invention reached its apogee. The legacy of Joseph Glidden, another American, was almost as large. Glidden had invented the first commercially successful barbed wire in 1874.

Birdwood had addressed Champion's brigade while it was out of the line. The general rubbed his hands together as if he was very pleased, then said: 'You will all be in a serious action again in a few days.' Champion said one could hear the men saying down the line: 'You old bastard, etc.' Birdwood must have heard this, Champion felt, but pretended he hadn't.

Birdwood made several similar speeches in the back areas. The division had lost nearly 5300 men during its first tour of Pozières. Reinforcements had since arrived but the 1st was still only at about two-thirds strength. The men were now wary of what new sacrifices would be asked of them. Some thought the division should not be put in a second time. Bean said Birdwood's speeches had an 'invigorating tone'. The general would say he was sure all the men were anxious to get back and kill more Germans. Bean said some of the Australians warmed to these words. Others 'called them by a harsh Australian name for idle flattery' (we may assume this had an agricultural flavour), and some suspected that the general was trying to buy himself a success with their lives. 'These – with many fine men among them – returned to the line determined to do their "job", but with deep bitterness in their hearts.'

Something had changed. Trust had not gone; but it was being tested.

OWEN HOWELL-PRICE, the young commander of the 3rd Battalion, was at one of Birdwood's speeches. Birdwood handed out a medal to Owen's brother, Philip. Three other brothers were also in the Great War. After the ceremony Birdwood told Owen he couldn't have too many Howell-Prices, 'which is very nice of him but is again one of his little ways'.

On August 17, Owen was back in the frontline, holding the most forward Australian position in front of Mouquet Farm. And he had an unusual problem. The land was so devastated that nothing stood up high enough to be a landmark. A dispute arose about where the Australian frontline actually was, and this mattered because the artillery was about to lob shells just ahead of it.

Divisional headquarters thought the front at one place, brigade headquarters another, and the difference amounted to about 300 yards. Howell-Price knew where the front really was: he was standing on it. He had to convince his superiors they were wrong. Smyth, the brigade commander, went forward and decided that, yes, the front wasn't where division thought it was. Howell-Price was worried: the Australian bombardment was to begin at 6 pm. At 5.30 pm he sent two urgent messages back. Divisional headquarters didn't think this disputation mattered much and the shelling began on time. About eighty of Howell-Price's men became casualties of their own howitzers.

It took the gunners some days to sort out where the frontline was. They sent some of their officers to Howell-Price's trenches. The ridge was so barren, so cut-up, the artillerymen couldn't find a landmark to re-register the guns on. Eventually they found a tree stump on the Mouquet Farm–Courcelette road.

THE 1ST DIVISION had taken over the front amid summer rain that left puddles in the craters and yellowy-brown mud everywhere. Rawlinson's 4th Army to the south was to attack Guillemont again on August 18 and, if this succeeded, Ginchy four days later. Haig had told Gough that the Reserve Army at Pozières and Thiepval should try to arrange its offensives around the same dates. Walker, the 1st Division commander, was thus told he was to attack north-ward, towards Mouquet Farm and also to the east, past the Windmill. The 1st Brigade would push north and the 2nd east. Which was why Howell-Price was in front of Mouquet Farm on the 17th. He was waiting to attack the next day, provided he didn't lose all his men to 'friendly' artillery fire in the meantime.

The staff work of the 1st Division during this tour seemed poor; Walker appeared to have lost his sure touch. War diaries and other official documents offer no obvious reason for this, but we do know that communications with frontline troops seemed to become worse each day. Messages took hours to get through, if they got through. Brigade headquarters often had no notion of where the front battalions were.

The Australians attacked northwards and eastwards on August 18. The 2nd Brigade was supposed to go past the Windmill behind a relatively new innovation, the creeping barrage. In a conventional barrage the artillery would fire on the German front trenches, then lift off to the second line once the infantry went over. In a creeping barrage the artillery fired just ahead of the advancing infantry, lifting anything from fifty to 150 yards every minute. The infantrymen had to know precisely when these lifts would be made and the distance of each 'creep'.

The 2nd Brigade was to attack at 9 pm. Brigade headquarters didn't receive the artillery plan until 7.40 pm. It reached the front trenches ten minutes *after* the attack was supposed to have begun. Some Australians reached the German trench but were thrown out. Brigade headquarters was still trying to work out what had happened the following morning. Three days later the brigade was pulled out. It had lost 915 men.

On the northern front Howell-Price's battalion was still being hit by its own artillery as it waited to attack. The gunners said they had made a 'most careful check': *German* shells were hitting the 3rd Battalion. The men in the frontline didn't have to check: they could see the German barrage falling on the support lines behind them. Howell-Price watched Australian shells demolish his front trench and sent a message back: 'I am doubtful whether we shall be able to carry out the stunt . . .' Howell-Price eventually sent out two assaulting parties. Both had to return.

The other battalion in the line here was the 4th, which was lucky enough to avoid being hit by its own artillery. One group of bombers drove back the Germans. They were supposed to be supported by riflemen. These turned out to be reinforcements who had joined the battalion two days earlier. They were terrified by the night-battle and baffled by the ground. Bean, with characteristic delicacy, said they could not be 'induced to come forward'. Elsewhere a company of the 4th seized two German trenches south of Mouquet Farm. This was the only gain on the northern front. The two battalions had lost 448 men.

WALKER REPLACED THE 1st Brigade with the 3rd on the northern front. The 9th, 10th and 12th battalions now took over. Not only was the front here hard to find; the communication trenches leading to it were strewn with corpses. Colonel Elliott, commander of the 12th, took a look at the frontline before bringing his men up. He had a large number of reinforcements among the two companies he intended to place there. He decided to send them up over open ground 'to minimise the possibility of their being demoralised by the revolting sights they would necessarily pass in going up by the trenches'.

'Squatter' Preston returned to Pozières with the 9th Battalion. He was taken with the German dugouts that the Australians now occupied. Some were twenty-feet deep, floored and sometimes partitioned into several rooms. One was lit by electricity generated 'by a sort of bicycle peddled by a man'. But there was a drawback: the mouths of the dugouts faced the German lines.

The 3rd Brigade attacked towards Fabeck Graben, east of the farm, on August 21 – in daylight. We don't know why this was. Perhaps it was a symptom of Gough's desperation to close in on Thiepval. The Germans watched the Australians preparing to attack and plastered them with shells. The 10th Battalion, the right wing of the attack, lost 120 of its 620 men in the hour before the attack began.

All the officers in the 10th were hit, either in the bombardment or the advance. Machine-gun fire caught Lieutenant Bert Crowle, a thirty-two-year-old builder from North Adelaide, in the buttocks. He had enlisted as a private in 1914 and had been wounded on Gallipoli. He had been an officer for just over a fortnight. Now he began the long and bumpy journey to the casualty-clearing station.

The Australians ran forward, looking for the Fabeck Graben. They may have briefly occupied sections of it, but they had to retreat around dusk. The Germans were firing at them from the flanks and from behind. The Australians had run past several well-concealed dugouts, one of them with its entrance in the roots of a tree. Some of them were cut off and surrendered.

A few men from the 12th Battalion, in the centre, actually reached the outskirts of Mouquet Farm and tossed grenades into the cellars at the southern end. They too could not hold on.

The 3rd Brigade lost 840 men on this northern ridge. Next day the 1st Division was replaced by the 2nd. In its first tour the 1st had taken Pozières village with some flair; this time it had been used as a battering ram and had mostly failed. This was the way of war here now: two hard surfaces bumping and grinding against each other, each side urged on by generals who, from a proper distance, told their men to grind harder. This time the 1st Division left behind 2650 casualties.

THEY TOOK BERT Crowle to the casualty-clearing station at Puchevillers, north-east of Amiens. On the evening of the third day after his wound he wrote to his wife Beatrice.

Dearest Beat and Bill,

Just a line you must be prepared for the worst to happen any day. It is no use trying to hide things. I am in terrible agony. Had I been brought in at once I had a hope. But now gas gangrene has set in and it is so bad that the doctor could not save it by taking it off as it had gone too far and the only hope is that the salts they have put on may drain the gangrene out otherwise there is no hope. The pain is much worse today so the doctor gave me some morphia, which has eased me a little but still it is awful. Tomorrow I shall know the worst as the dressing was to be left on for 3 days and tomorrow is the third day it smells rotten.

I was hit running out to see the other officer who was with me but badly wounded. I ran too far as I was in a hurry and he had passed the word down to return, it kept coming down and there was nothing to do but go up and see what he meant, I got two machine gun bullets in the thigh another glanced off by my water bottle and another by the periscope I had in my pocket, you will see that they send my things home.

It was during the operations around Mouquet Farm, about 20 days I was in the thick of the attack on Pozieres as I had just about done my duty. Even if I get over it I will never go back to the war as they have taken pounds of flesh out of my buttock, my word they look after us well here. I am in the officers ward and can get anything I want to eat or drink but I just drink all day changing the drinks as I take a fancy. The Stretcher Bearers could not get the wounded out any way than over the top and across the open. They had to carry me four miles with a man waving a red cross flag in front and the Germans did not open fire on us.

Well dearest I have had a rest, the pain is getting worse and worse. I am very sorry dear, but still you will be well provided for I am easy on that score. So cheer up dear I could write on a lot but I am nearly unconscious. Give my love to Dear Bill and yourself, do take care of yourself and him.

Your loving husband,
Bert.

Bert Crowle died the next day.

CROWLE LIES IN Puchevillers British Cemetery, high on a hill. Yellow roses and blue daisies sway in the north wind. Hardly anyone comes here; the cemetery registry says there have been no visitors for eight days, and few before that.

Next to Crowle lies Lieutenant Edward Butler, who had been a prominent cricketer in Tasmania. Both seem a long way from home.

All that's left of a life: bones, badges and scraps of uniform shivering in the wind. This photograph was probably taken in the summer of 1919. The priest from Fromelles kneels before the remains of a British or Australian soldier killed in the battle of July 19, 1916. Martial Delebarre from Fromelles (who supplied this photograph) in 1992 found a bone-handled knife on the old battlefield. Scratched on the handle was 'G Blake'. Private George Francis Blake, a carpenter from Footscray, Victoria, died here in 1916. Bodies from the Great War are still being found. Most cannot be identified, although buttons and badges often give a clue to the nationality of the soldier. Such men are buried under a headstone that says they are 'Known Unto God'.

Before: men of the 53rd Battalion of the 5th Australian Division waiting to 'hop the bags' at Fromelles. Because of the high water table, there were no trenches here but breastworks built above the plain. Only three of the men in this photograph came out of the battle alive, and all three were wounded. *[AWM A03042]*

After: the body of an Australian killed inside the German lines on the waterlogged plain at Fromelles. Captain Charles Mills was wounded in the hand there and taken prisoner. After the war a German officer gave him this and other photographs taken on July 20, 1916, the morning after the failed attack that resulted in 5500 Australian casualties. It was years before the extent of the Australian tragedy at Fromelles became known. [AWM A01566]

Brigadier-General 'Pompey' Elliott in a characteristic Australian pose outside a captured German headquarters late in the war. One of the true eccentrics of the Australian Imperial Force, Elliott was tyrannical and tender, blustering and subtle, cocksure and insecure. He liked to look dishevelled, particularly if there were 'foppish' English staff officers about. He was one of the fabled 'fighting' leaders of the AIF. He wept behind the Australian breastworks at Fromelles after his 15th Brigade had taken shocking casualties. *[AWM E2855]*

The monster in his formative years, long before he and Benito Mussolini (who also fought in the Great War) introduced the dress code for fascism. These German soldiers are behind the frontline at Fromelles in 1916. Corporal Adolf Hitler (right) had adopted a dog that strayed over from the allied lines and taught it tricks. He was billeted above a butcher's shop in a village near Fromelles and the old French woman who looked after him called him 'Blackie'. There is much of the bumpkin about Hitler here, aged twenty-seven and inclined to throw tantrums if the barrack-room talk turned glum. George Orwell stared at a photo of Hitler in 1940 and detected self-pity in his face. Hitler was at Fromelles when the Australians attacked on July 19.

The German blockhouse called the Windmill on a little hill east of Pozières. Some 23,000 Australians fell within a mile or so of here. The site is today the best spot from which to view the Somme battlefields of 1916.
[AWM E03375]

The knight of the doleful countenance – 1: General James McCay commanded the Australians at Fromelles. On his death the *Bulletin* described him as 'about the most detested officer' in the AIF. He showed much bravery on Gallipoli but could not inspire those under him, let alone win their affection.
[AWM H01890]

The knight of the doleful countenance – 2: Sir Richard Haking, who, more than anyone, was responsible for the madness at Fromelles and its 7080 Australian and British casualties. Haking didn't understand the new warfare and the importance of firepower. He seemed to think trenches could be taken by acts of 'character'.

Routes to a war. Above: Sausage Valley, the road to Pozières. The white dust of the road comes from the lumps of chalk in the soil here. The vehicle in the foreground is a Rolls-Royce Phantom; behind it are field kitchens. Left: Before they reached Sausage Valley, Australian and British troops passed the Hanging Virgin in Albert. The sight of it at night was eerie.

[AWM EZ0113 (above) and E167]

Hubert Gough, the British army commander under whom the Australians served at Pozières, Mouquet Farm and the two battles of Bullecourt in 1917. Gough was rash, headstrong and prickly. The cavalry charge was forever playing in his head; he didn't want to be held up by detail or doubters. Gough's rise had been fast and bore little relationship to his achievements. It owed much to the patronage of Sir Douglas Haig, the British commander-in-chief on the western front. *[AWM H12215]*

Harold Walker, an Englishman, commanded the 1st Australian Division for much of the Great War. Australia owes him more than it has ever acknowledged.

[AWM ART03349]

James Gordon Legge commanded the 2nd Australian Division at Pozières. Unlike Walker, he was unable to stand up to Gough.

[AWM C01011]

Before: the main street of Pozières in 1914. The Roman road runs away towards the Windmill on the eastern outskirts of the village. After: the same main street two years later. *[AWM G0 15341 (top) and EZ0095]*

Above: Pozières from the air just before it was destroyed by artillery fire. The Roman road runs diagonally across the photograph, from lower left to upper right; the village is in the centre. The two lines curving from top to bottom on the right of the village are the trenches known as the Old German (OG) lines, 1 and 2.

Left: Germans in a trench near Pozières. Note the white chalk thrown up from their evacuations.

[AWM J00275 (above) and J00213 (left)]

One of the shining lights that went out at Pozières. Captain Ivor Margetts, a Tasmanian schoolteacher who was killed in the early fighting for Pozières village. He had fought on the heights above Anzac Cove on the first day of the Gallipoli landing in places never again held by Australians. After he was killed a private wrote: 'I cried like a kid when I found he was dead. I think he went because he was too good for the beastliness of war . . .' Margetts was buried close to where he fell. A photograph of his grave, an over-bright white cross in a sea of shell holes, was taken in 1916 and appears on the front cover of this book. The grave was lost in later fighting. All we now know is that Ivor Margetts lies in the ground somewhere at Pozières.

The one-man epic: Captain Albert Jacka, the best-known 'fighting' soldier in the AIF. A forestry worker from northern Victoria, he won the Victoria Cross on Gallipoli, the Military Cross at Pozières (where many believed he should have received a second VC) and a bar to his MC at First Bullecourt in 1917. He was badly wounded at Pozières and gassed in 1918 at Villers-Bretonneux. A cult grew up around Jacka after the war. He died aged thirty-nine, partly as a result of his war wounds. *[AWM P02939.001]*

Before: Mouquet Farm, north of Pozières, in peacetime, a rustic fortress of red and chalk bricks. After: the farm after the fighting of 1916. All that marks the site of the farmhouse today is a small pile of German concrete and French bricks in a field grazed by sheep. *[AWM J00181 (above) and E00005]*

Stretcher-bearers bringing back a casualty during the 'terrible winter' of 1916–17. This photograph was taken near Delville Wood, just behind the Australians' winter line. The mud was so thick that stretcher-bearers sometimes took twelve hours to carry a wounded man two or three miles. Men pulled out of the mud often left their boots and trousers behind.
[AWM E00049]

Framed by icicles, a 2nd Division man in sheepskin vest and balaclava looks out on the frozen landscape that was the Australian front. Just before Christmas, 1916, German and allied troops sometimes walked about their parapets in sight of one another. Both sides were more interested in draining their trenches than shooting at each other. Australians stayed in the frontline trenches for just forty-eight hours at a time. Many came down with shivering fits and trench foot. Some said afterwards that the winter of 1916–17 was their worst memory of the war. *[AWM EZ0123]*

Charles Bean, the official Australian war correspondent, struggling along a mud-filled trench near Gueudecourt. Bean liked to obtain his material first hand. Brudenell White, the chief-of-staff of the Australian Corps, said after the war that Bean faced death more often than any man in the AIF.
[AWM E00572]

14

Hindenburg and Ludendorff

Alec Raws returned to Pozières with the 2nd Division and was killed as soon as he reached the firing line. He had been determined to go back, even though he had fainted three times during his fortnight's spell.

Lieutenant Lionel Short, a journalist who had worked with Raws on the *Argus*, said a shell burst near Raws, killing him and three others. There were no marks on his body. He had almost certainly died from concussion and at once. Short knew about the fainting fits. He wondered whether Raws' heart had been weakened by the strain of his previous tour.

Raws was buried near where he fell, another Australian body in the ground near a village that hardly anyone at home had heard of two months earlier. A wooden cross marked his grave. The grave, like that of Margetts, disappeared in later fighting. The only trace that Alec Raws and his brother Goldy were once in France is the appearance of their names on the screen wall at the Australian National Memorial at Villers-Bretonneux, on the other side of the Somme.

CAPTAIN AMBROSE CULL also returned to Pozières. He was a perceptive observer of how soldiers reacted to stress. He remembered that when the division was going in the first time the soldiers noticed a blackened arm with stiffened fingers rising out of the rim of a shell hole. A soldier placed a tin of bully beef in the hand and said: 'Get up, you loafer – we're doing your work.' Normally, Cull wrote, such a remark would have been thought 'too gross' even for war. 'But under such a strain men both do and say things that would revolt them in ordinary life, and the man who can be coarsely lighthearted, either in assault or endurance, is at the moment a greater moral asset than the quiet thinkers of finer fibre.'

IF THE AUSTRALIANS were being worn out, deliberately, division by division, they weren't alone. Haig had been wearing out his whole force on the Somme since July 23 – but democratically and, he believed, to a purpose. The losses among his British divisions were as heavy, and sometimes heavier, than those of the Australians. The British too were fighting on narrow fronts. They too were sent in, used up, pulled out, then sent back again, for gains of a hundred yards here and a hundred there. There were a dozen Pozières. Haig thought them worthwhile because he believed German morale was crumbling. He thought the crisis point on the Somme would come about mid-September. At that time he would discard the wearing-out tactics and start a new offensive against the German third-line positions. He was dreaming of breakthrough again. He had mentioned this to Gough and Rawlinson. All three wanted the hellholes with names such as Mouquet Farm, Thiepval and Guillemont cleared up before this offensive began.

Haig's casualties on the Somme were nudging 200,000. He knew that some in the Cabinet, notably Lloyd George, were starting to wonder whether he was becoming too careless with his fifty-six British and dominion divisions. He also knew that his French allies wanted him to do more. For his new offensive he had a secret weapon, the tank. It was so secret, so exotic, that Haig put quotation marks around the word 'tanks' the first time he wrote it in his diary. Quick-firing artillery, the magazine rifle, the machine gun and other automatic weapons, the submarine, aircraft, barbed wire: these all predated the Great War. The tank was born out of the war, out of the need to flatten barbed wire and steel stakes. The name was born out of the need for secrecy. People saw the great sides of the tanks being made with double rows of rivets, like ship's hulls, and asked what they were. Water tanks, they were told.

The first tanks weighed twenty-eight tons, reared up more than seven feet and groaned along, all clanking tracks and jiggling chains, at a little better than three miles an hour – when everything was right with the engine and drive mechanisms, that is, and most of the time it wasn't. No-one in 1916 saw this arthritic beast as the new form of cavalry. The 'male' tanks were armed with two six-pounder guns and four machine guns. The 'females' carried six machine guns but no artillery. Neither model had a turret; both looked like great iron monsters without a focal point, dinosaurs without heads. This machine had an appeal beyond its ability to cross trenches and flatten wire. Because it was so otherworldly, like something from a novel by Jules Verne (who had lived on the Somme at Amiens), it was a potential weapon of terror.

Haig watched the tanks being demonstrated in late August. He thought they crossed ditches and parapets with the 'greatest ease'. One entered a wood and 'walked over' trees with six-inch trunks. Haig was impressed but puzzled. What tactics did one use with these machines?

THE MEN OF the 2nd Australian Division were back in the line to capture Mouquet Farm. They still didn't know what was there. Some believed that it was lightly held. Others said the farm was a strongpoint: the Germans were simply out of sight in the tunnels and galleries. This is how unscientific the wearing-out fight had become. The infantrymen were expected to keep grinding away at the enemy in front, simply because he was in front. When they closed with him they found out precisely where he was and how strong he was. If he turned out to be particularly strong, they still ground against him, cribbing a few yards here, bombing a dugout there, until they were so depleted and addle-brained that they had to be replaced.

John Gellibrand was given the task of attacking Mouquet Farm because his 6th Brigade had suffered the least during the division's first tour. The brigade lay under barrage after barrage, waiting to attack on August 26. It was to advance on either side of the farm. The 21st and 22nd battalions were on the left. Their objectives included Point 54, which was where the farm lane met the Thiepval road, and Point 77, about halfway up the farm track. On the right the 24th Battalion would go for the farm itself and German positions along its eastern side. The men would follow a creeping barrage that would lift fifty yards every minute. Bean wrote that 'the whole area now resembled a sea of brown craters, in which the farm lay like a heap of half-submerged flotsam.'

The attack began at 4.45 am. On the right the 24th Battalion advanced towards the Fabeck Graben trench but was forced back. The troops of the 21st Battalion quickly became lost in the devastated landscape, overran their objectives and in some instances ended up under their own barrage. They fought running battles along the track leading to Mouquet Farm from the west. Some reached the rubble heaps near the north-west corner of the farm but could not get close enough to throw grenades into the dugouts. The Germans counter-attacked and the Australians retreated into shell holes. The Germans knew the Australians were cut off and called on them to surrender. Some escaped; sixty didn't.

On the left the 22nd Battalion became caught in a fight close to where the farm met the Thiepval road. Captain Harold Smith, an engineer from Geelong, was killed near here. Sadly there was nothing unusual about this – captains were being killed all the time – except that on this same day, at around the same time, some 300 yards away, Smith's brother, Richard, also a captain, was killed by shellfire. A third brother, Walter, a private, had died of wounds at Pozières three weeks earlier. They were the sons of a Bendigo policeman. Earlier, during the 2nd Division's first tour of Pozières, three brothers from the Walls family from Victoria, all privates, had been killed. Bert and John died outright. Roger lingered three days. The same shell is believed to have hit all three.

On the night of the 26th Gellibrand's brigade was relieved, having lost 896 men trying to straighten the line. The only gain was Point 77, on the western side of the farm. The 4th Division came back into the line.

Gordon Maxfield had been at the quarry south of the farm when Richard Smith was killed. A few days later he wrote to his father.

> I thought the first show was worse than anything on earth, but the last ten days have knocked out any previous ideas I ever entertained of battle and blood and death. Most of my pals have gone, and I am not exactly in the state of mind to write newsy letters. . . . I very nearly joined the great majority during a severe bombardment in which my helmet saved my life for the fifth time. I am saving that old helmet and will make you a present of it to use as a flower pot after the war. I was buried three times, but managed to scratch my way out. On another day a shell burst very close, and a piece of shrapnel as big as a large marble wounded me in the shoulder. It penetrated my tunic, shirt and singlet, and finally went through the skin, but thanks to the toughness of my hide, went no further, and barring a stiff shoulder and slight flesh wound I am as well as ever, and didn't have to leave the line . . . Just heard of Rumania, and we are consequently jubilant. Might be home sooner than we expected.

Rumania had come in on the allied side on August 27.

THREE DAYS AFTER the 2nd Division's attack a tearful Kaiser Wilhelm accepted the resignation of Eric von Falkenhayn, the chief of the German general staff. This had little to do with the Somme. The Kaiser had two years earlier envisioned quick victories over the forces of his cousins Tsar Nicholas and George V; we do not know whether he was now weeping for Falkenhayn or for himself.

In truth Falkenhayn had sacked himself: he had no supporters left that mattered. He was tall and handsome with severe eyes, a sharp intellect and a tongue that could be cruel. He did not cultivate political friendships or try to charm his critics. He was certainly a surer soldier than his predecessor Hellmuth von Moltke. He knew the war had come to be about attrition, and that the longer it went on the harder it would be for Germany to win. Falkenhayn was a loner, and he now paid the forfeit that loners pay for assuming that talent is all one needs to get along in the world. He had also been unlucky.

He carried the blame for the failure of the Austrian armies against the Russians and the Serbs, which was unfair. The Austrian military had been a multicultural shambles from the day the war opened. The Germans, on the other hand, had scored big victories in the east, but Hindenburg and Ludendorff, the generals who commanded in that theatre, took the credit for these.

Paul von Hindenburg, square-headed and blue-eyed (some said the eyes were brutal), the quintessential Prussian gentleman, a portly symbol of dignity and certainty, was a household name the way Falkenhayn wasn't. Strangers sent Hindenburg marinated eels; women sent him knitted socks; photos of him hung in beer halls. He wore the air of a superman and the Germans liked such men: they made war seem simple. Hindenburg wasn't unusually bright or energetic; he didn't work hard and preferred to shoot stags. Ludendorff did most of the work. Ludendorff was cranky because he worked too hard; Hindenburg had the comfortable look of a man who didn't.

Falkenhayn also took the blame for Verdun and that was right enough. He had been losing support long before Haig opened the Somme offensive. Theobald von Bethmann-Hollweg, the Chancellor, headed the long list of detractors. Bethmann was an intelligent but weak man, which meant he had ideal credentials for the office he occupied. Bethmann had been unstrung by the course the war had taken. Falkenhayn's answer to the stalemate was the gamble at Verdun; Bethmann's was a negotiated peace. Bethmann now smoked seventy cigarettes a day and his hair began to turn white. Falkenhayn's other enemies included Ludendorff (and thus his ventriloquist's doll, Hindenburg), several army commanders on the western front, sundry Austrian generals, as well as diplomats, politicians and industrialists, such as Gustav Krupp, who made Germany's big guns.

Rumania finished off Falkenhayn. He knew well enough that Rumania would sell herself to the side that offered her the best spoils, but he didn't think she would come into the war until after the September harvest, and this comforted the Kaiser. Rumania came in on the allied side in late August. Falkenhayn was shocked. So was the Kaiser. He was told the news while playing cards and declared the war lost. The Kaiser hadn't lost the war; like Bethmann, he had merely lost his nerve. Any little thing – and in truth Rumania was a little thing – could tip him into despondency. Falkenhayn's enemies seized on his misjudgement over Rumania and the Kaiser replaced him with Hindenburg.

Hindenburg had retired in 1911. He was sixty-eight. He had no clearly formed scheme for winning the war: he had never been a man of ideas. He became the Chief of the General Staff because his name was not Falkenhayn and because the German people had invested him with powers he did not possess. He was Germany's Kitchener.

The Kaiser wanted to give Ludendorff the title of 'second chief' of the general staff. Ludendorff didn't want to be second anything. He thought up a title of his own, First Quartermaster-General, and the Kaiser accepted it, not knowing that he had created a power that would eventually surpass his own.

Ludendorff was fifty-one, a Prussian from a relatively poor family, tall, red-faced and fleshy about the jowls. He had short-cropped hair, two or three chins (depending on how angry he was), and wore an expression that suggested he had eaten something unpleasant and was on the verge of losing his temper, which much of the time he was. He was impatient and arrogant and ran on nervous energy. He had always been an ambitious soldier, with a poor sense of how far he could push a point. At Liège in Belgium in 1914 he proved himself a brave one as well. For taking the town he received the *Pour le Mérite*. (The Kaiser had given himself the *Pour le Mérite*, as well as two Iron Crosses, presumably for feats of courage that had happened in his own mind.) Ludendorff had worked hard to bring about Germany's successes in the east but he was not the stuff of celebrity; the credit fell on Hindenburg, who was.

THE GERMAN PEOPLE needed to believe in a Siegfried. The harvest of 1915 had been poor. The British blockade was causing shortages and German civilians needed to carry up to a dozen ration cards. Black markets were common and the hospitals were crowded with wounded whose tales of life at the front (like those of their British counterparts) did not tally with the stories in the newspapers. Bread had been rationed since 1915. Clothes and shoes were now rationed, along with sugar, meat (many butcher's shops had closed), potatoes, dairy products and flour.

Caroline Cooper of Adelaide had been studying music in Leipzig when the war broke out. She decided to stay and each week wrote to her sister back home, although some of the letters were not posted. In March, 1916, she wrote that she had to visit nine grocer's shops to 'scrape together' one-eighth of a pound of butter, one pound of sugar and three eggs. Next month she wrote that she had read a long article that said crows, ravens and daws were good eating if first soaked in a thin camomile tea. She had also found two chips of wood in a breakfast roll: the flour had been mixed with sawdust. There was hardly any coal or oil for heating.

AT THE GATEWAY to Mouquet Farm, under a glade of swaying trees, you come on a scene of rustic peace. Ewes and lambs graze on the swell of a hill. The ewes are in full wool and dusty grey; the lambs are white and sappy and butt their mothers' udders before splaying their front legs to drink. There were no trees along the road in 1916, just black stumps. On the old trench maps this was Point 54. One of the three Smith brothers died just in front of here, probably near the glade of trees.

On August 26, 1916, just back a little from where we are standing, an Australian and a German stood up and parried at each other with bayonets while men from both sides stared in wonder. The war seldom ran to a duel. Then a shot was heard and the Australian fell dead. A German had shot him from somewhere on the flanks of the contest. An Australian lieutenant had been watching from up the hill towards Mouquet Farm. He was so transfixed that he hadn't thought to shoot. Now he watched the German, a big man, prod at the Australian with his foot. The lieutenant came out of his spell and fired. The German fell, presumably dead; he was still lying there at dusk.

The land where the old farmhouse stood has been fenced off into a paddock for the broad-chested Texel rams that come to the fence in the expectation that you will tip something into their feed trough. Stately trees give the paddock the air of a park. All have been planted since 1918. No trees survived the barrages of 1916. No buildings either. All that remains of the farmhouse, the dairy and the courtyard is a small pile of German concrete and a few French bricks. Somewhere underneath are the brick cellars with their high roofs and arched doorways and, beneath them, perhaps thirty-feet down, the galleries and dormitories built by the Germans, full of musty secrets and old bones.

The sensation you feel here is the same as when you look down on the Anzac position on Gallipoli: it's so *small*. In both instances a voice says to you that so many could not die in such a tiny area. It is a silly thought because they can and they did.

You stand near the point where the Fabeck Graben trench ran close to the northern end of Mouquet Farm. Men from Kalgoorlie, Subiaco, Perth and Claremont died plentifully here, right where you stand, but who remembers them now? There is no sign of the Fabeck Graben, but artillery shells, disinterred by the plough, are stacked along the fence line.

All is quiet. Suddenly there is a *thump*, a swish of grass and a flash of white belly. A rabbit has been hiding near your feet. It passes the lump of concrete that had once been Mouquet Farm with a deer-like leap. Amid death there is life.

15

A well-fertilised farm

A motif runs through the diaries and letters of the men who went to Pozières. Having been there once, in that other age, all of a fortnight ago, none much wanted to go back. They had seen something base there, something they were unready for. For the rest of their lives the word 'Pozières' would curdle their blood. But there was no point talking about it to someone who hadn't been there, because what happened above the village transcended ordinary experience and thus ordinary understanding. At the time many of the men did, however, write that they didn't want to go back, and this was unusual. Most of them had been born in the last decade of the Victorian age and its sensibilities were still playing. Stoicism was a virtue, so one pretended to enthusiasm even if trembling inside. The 'manly' thing was to say one was unfazed, and this time many of the men didn't. And a word that seldom appears in the correspondence of Gallipoli recurs through the chronicles of Pozières: 'nerves'.

Sergeant Ted Rule of the 4th Division was now going back. 'Our nerves were still rattled,' Rule wrote afterwards, 'and the thoughts of another gruelling were not very welcome.' Rule returned on a black and wet night. He didn't know where he was or what he and

his men were supposed to be doing. He went to see the senior officer. 'He seemed a bit rattled, and next morning he went out with
shell-shock.'

Rule finally received his orders. His bombers were to attack the
German post at Point 54, where the track to Mouquet Farm met the
Thiepval road. Lieutenant Archie Dean told him to go up to the
front and have a look at the position. Captain Stewart Hansen, an
architect, took Rule to the top of the quarry and they looked up
towards Point 54. When they returned an officer told Rule not to
bring back prisoners. 'They were not very popular with the heads,'
he said, 'because they ate a hole in our rations.'

Rule headed back with a corporal and a sergeant from his
platoon. The corporal said to the sergeant: 'What do you think
about taking prisoners, Jack?'

'The heads can go to hell,' the sergeant said. 'I'm not going to
shoot men down in cold blood.'

'That's what I think too,' said the corporal.

A MADNESS HAD come to the grinding match here. It was as if those
writing the orders were in a different country to those who were
supposed to carry them out. Gellibrand had attacked Point 54 and
Point 27 (on the farm track itself) with more than a battalion, and
failed. The 4th Division had taken over the line and was going to
attack the same places with one-and-a-half companies. Sergeant
Rule would attack Point 54, Lieutenant Dean Point 27. General
Brand, the commander of the 4th Brigade, was writing the orders.
He obviously didn't know what Mouquet Farm was like. Ted Rule
didn't know much about Mouquet Farm either, but he was leery of
a plan that had him capturing Point 54 with a handful of bombers.
He was sure he was going to be killed.

Rule and his men rushed the post at midnight on August 27. One
section attacked the rear, the other the front. Two platoons of
infantry were waiting in support. That was the whole of the attacking force. Rule's section penetrated about thirty yards, then the
Germans were on all sides. Rule looked around and found he had

only about four men left. He lit his red flare, the signal for the Australians in support to come up. He looked back and saw them digging a trench. They stayed in it. A bomb exploded close to Rule. His legs felt as if they had been stabbed with hot pins. Blood ran down his hand. He realised that he and his few men had to get out. 'My ears were ringing with the row of the bombs, but above it all I could hear the Huns yelling "*Ja! Ja!*" as they heaved them.'

Rule arrived back at the quarry and went to Captain Hansen's headquarters. Rule had seen two flares go up over Point 27. He assumed from these that Lieutenant Dean had taken it. Then he heard Dean's voice outside Hansen's headquarters. 'Here we are, here we are again!' Dean was saying. Then he blundered in, blood streaming down his face and into his eyes. A bullet had lifted the top of his skull. He had staggered around inside Point 27 blinded by blood. Dean insisted that the wounds of others be dressed before his.

These attacks were mere incidents in a big war. They rate one paragraph in the British official history, and this is about right, yet they tell us much about how the Somme battle was being conducted. A few men were being asked to do the jobs of battalions. Part of the problem was that the front was now so narrow that it was hard to fit a battalion into it. Another part was that those who wrote the orders didn't seem to understand the difference between being able to capture a position and being able to hold it. The Australians would take a trench. German reinforcements would arrive throwing bombs. The Australians would retreat. A day or so later the same attack would be repeated. The results would be the same. Part of the blame for these follies obviously lay in the personality of Gough. Much of it, perhaps the greater part, rested with the Australian commanders who planned the attacks without looking at the ground.

Dean received the Military Cross and died of his wound three months later. Rule received the Military Medal. He didn't get over that night at Mouquet Farm for six months. 'During that time the thought of the frontline sent me into shivers, and often at night I'd wake up, and in a dazed way live some of it over again. I know many to whom the same thing used to happen.'

THOSE IN HIGH command got over the night quickly enough, mainly because they didn't know what had happened. Next day, as more rain fell and the trenches began to ooze anew, Brand told Lieutenant-Colonel Charles Dare of the 14th Battalion that his men should go back after dark and take Mouquet Farm. Captain Hansen told Dare that the new attack would simply be a waste of lives. Dare believed in Hansen and in himself. He was only twenty-eight, an architect in his other life, and had fought in Monash's attack on the heights on Gallipoli. He told Brand the new attack was folly. We don't know whether he refused the order outright. The 13th and 16th battalions of Brand's brigade were coming into the line. It was decided they would replace Dare's 14th and take Mouquet Farm the following night, August 29.

PERCY BLACK, A big man with a drooping moustache, nearly didn't make it into the army. He was thirty-six when he joined up and had broken teeth. He was accepted 'subject to extraction of stumps'. Black was well known as a prospector in the West Australian outback, where headframes shimmered in the haze and outcrops gave off lurid colours and aroused dreams of Ophir. Everyone thought Black a 'gentleman' but, as with Harry Murray, he had been hardened by the rough bush life. Black and Murray set up their machine gun on Pope's Hill just after the Gallipoli landing. Both were wounded but kept firing. Black, Murray later said, was an intuitive soldier: he just knew what to do. After a month or so on Gallipoli he was a lieutenant. He had been born near Bacchus Marsh in Victoria, the eleventh child of immigrants from Ulster. Murray said Black was 'the bravest man I ever knew, and I knew hundreds of them'.

Black was to lead the centre of the 16th Battalion attack, going straight for the rubble of Mouquet Farm and beyond. Murray was to lead the left company of the 13th, going for the Fabeck Graben trench. The two battalions were to join up on the other side of the farm. There were now so many shell holes on this front that a pilot looking down might have thought the land had smallpox. And now it was raining and the slime was rising in the holes.

Black led his company from the front and broke into what had been the courtyard of the farm. He pushed on towards the far end. A German machine gunner was waiting there, his fingers on the buttons of the gun but his head hidden behind the earthworks. When he raised his head Black shot him, then put two more bullets into the gun to wreck it. As Black did so a bomb fragment hit him.

Black's company and another on his right went beyond the farm, knocking out German posts, throwing grenades down dugouts, engaging in hand-to-hand fights in the mud, all the time pushing forward and becoming fewer. The Germans seemed to be everywhere and, as always, fought gamely. The Australians had no idea of how the underground system connected up. They would throw bombs down one dugout entrance only to see Germans bursting from another. The farm had been captured and it hadn't. The Australians were too few to hold on, let alone to mop up. Rifles and Lewis guns became clogged with the plasticine-like mud. By 1.30 am the Australians had been driven out.

On the 13th Battalion's front Murray's company alone reached its objective. By the time he arrived there Murray had only about thirty men left and he was trying to hold roughly 150 yards of the Fabeck Graben trench. Murray and two men went looking for Black's battalion. They met Germans throwing bombs. One of Murray's men had his foot blown off; the other was hit in the eye. Two Germans attacked Murray with knobkerries. He shot both; the other three fled.

Murray's company was down to sixteen men. He moved from one to another, offering encouragement, but he knew the position was hopeless. The best the Australians could do was pick up their wounded and try to retreat. Murray was wounded in the back, lung and thigh. He eventually fainted from loss of blood and became one of 459 Australian casualties for the night. Murray ended up in a London hospital with Black and Bert Jacka. He was embarrassed when he was told he had won the Distinguished Service Order.

The attacks had failed everywhere, simply because the assaulting force was too small to hold the ground it took.

THREE BATTALIONS FROM Thomas Glasgow's 13th Brigade were now put at much the same objectives. The attack was set for just after dawn, on September 3. This would be the Australians' seventh push towards Mouquet Farm.

Captain Charles Littler was part of it and he probably shouldn't have been. He was a Tasmanian, forty-eight, too old for this soggy hill, and he had already used up a lot of lives on Gallipoli, where he was known as 'the Duke of Anzac', a flamboyant man with a beard and older than just about everybody. He had to be well known because he was in charge of the beach parties. Now, just before the seventh assault on Mouquet Farm, he came down with malaria but still lined up with his men. He decided he would not carry a revolver, just a stick. He said this would be his last fight. He was not thinking of dying, merely of being invalided out.

Three brothers from South Australia, all privates in the 52nd, came up for this final push. Edward, Hurtle and Thomas Potter would all die, the first two virtually at once, Thomas the day after. Sergeant Joseph Trotman came up too. He said his troops would be told to move back twenty yards because men were being killed in front by shells. A few minutes later they would be told to move forward because men were being killed behind. Backwards and forwards in the mud. It was cold, Trotman said, but he could feel streams of sweat running down his back. 'But the climax that surpassed all horrors was that of walking over the top of our own wounded & dead comrades.' Trotman remembered his group's first casualty that night. A shell blew a man's head off. 'The only thing we could do was to crouch in our potholes & watch the blood run down the trench.'

Trotman's battalion scrambled up the hill towards the Fabeck Graben trench and took it with bombs. To their left another battalion broke into the farm, throwing grenades down every hole they could find. The Germans were like mice in a barn: they bolted down one hole, then sneaked out another. It seemed, just briefly, that the farm had finally been captured. Then German machine gunners began firing into it. Captain Littler leaned on his stick. There was blood on his leg; he also appeared to have been hit in the chest. 'I'll reach that trench if the boys do,' he told another officer, who took Littler's stick and waved the men on. Littler died soon after.

Around 8 am more Germans began to appear north of the farm and pushed in between the Australian battalions. The German artillery began to land nine-inch shells. One battalion began to fall back. The two forward companies of another were left stranded around the north-east corner of the farm. Most were killed and others captured. A sergeant hit in both legs lay in a shell hole and wrote a letter to his brother before he died.

The Australian attack had failed, except on the ridge on the right where the Queenslanders of the 49th Battalion had dug in. About ninety men from the 52nd, under Lieutenant Duncan Maxwell, protected the 49th's flank. Maxwell's men were worn out. It was mid-afternoon and they were running out of bombs. Then they saw men in kilts coming up to reinforce them. It was a full company, 250 men, of the Royal Highlanders of Canada under Captain J. H. Lovett, an accountant from Toronto.

THE CANADIANS WOULD take over the whole front during the next few days. Major-General Arthur Currie commanded the 1st Canadian Division. Like Monash, now training the 3rd Australian Division in England, Currie was a citizen-soldier who brought a fresh and analytical mind to war. Currie was forty, a real estate speculator, rough of speech, a shambles of a man, six foot four inches tall, almost eighteen stone, heavy-hipped and big-bellied and inclined to get about in shirt and braces.

Currie carried a secret. Before the war one of his speculative schemes had gone wrong and he had stolen some $11,000 Canadian from regimental funds. He had not returned the money: he couldn't raise it. A few, including the Canadian Prime Minister, knew of the theft. Currie worried every day that a scandal would burst around him. Yet this didn't stop him from becoming one of the finest generals of the war.

AT DAWN NEXT day the Scottish Canadians and the Australians were still holding on above Mouquet Farm. Around 3.30 pm a German barrage crashed down on them. Lovett was wounded. Dead and dying lay everywhere. Those still alive needed to take their minds off what seemed inevitable. The men from the frontier societies began to compare wheat-growing methods as the carnage went on. Maxwell was down to about forty men, Australians and Canadians. Other Canadians eventually came up and took over the position. Part of the Fabeck Graben had finally been taken and held. And Glasgow's brigade had lost 1346 men.

Currie was now in charge of the front. The Canadians captured Mouquet Farm later in the month, but Germans could still be heard in the grottoes beneath. The British relieved the Canadians and the Germans crept back into the farm. The British cleared it again. Fifty-five Germans held out underground, then surrendered to a party of pioneers.

THE AUSTRALIANS LEFT for Ypres and a rest. They had taken 23,000 casualties here in less than seven weeks. They had done so in an area not much larger than 600 acres, which meant around ten Australians had died for each acre. When the casualties from Fromelles were added in, the four Australian divisions had lost 28,000 men, the same as for the eight months at Gallipoli. The British divisions had suffered on a similar scale, but Australia's was a volunteer army.

Where were the replacements to come from? Conscription? Pozières, a dowdy farming village that didn't show on many pre-war maps, had brought sadness to thousands of Australian homes. Now it was about to bring bitterness to Australian politics.

16

The black spider

The war hadn't turned out the way Australians thought it would. The country had gone to war so blithely. Australia didn't even have to declare war. Britain, as head of the family, spoke on behalf of her empire. All Australia had to decide was the extent of its participation. Most Australians saw nothing unusual about this. They also saw themselves as Britons, far from home, it was true, and in a strange land where the trees shed their bark instead of their leaves, but they were still Britons and wore three-piece suits in the pitiless sun to prove it. Alfred Deakin, the most influential politician of early Australia, called himself an 'independent Australian Briton'. Few thought him muddle-headed for saying this. The census of 1911 put the population at 4.8 million, including 590,722 who had been born in the United Kingdom and just 36,442 who had been born in Asia. Unlike the United States, which had a significant German minority, Australia was not a multicultural society. It was about ninety-six per cent 'British'.

To many Australians the prospect of war seemed exhilarating. It sounded like a titanic sporting contest that 'our side' was bound to win, and probably before Christmas. Australians rushed to join up. Before Britain declared war the Australian Government had offered

its fleet and a force of 20,000 volunteers 'to be at the complete dis-
posal of the Home Government'. Australia's new Governor-General
Sir Ronald Craufurd Munro-Ferguson cabled the Colonial
Secretary in London: 'There is indescribable enthusiasm and entire
unanimity throughout Australia in support of all that tends to provide for the security of the empire in war.' On the first day of formal
recruiting in Sydney, August 11, the new army picked up 3600 men.

Munro-Ferguson was pleased. He was a tall and handsome Scot
and he knew what he was supposed to do. The Governor-General's
office was different then. Munro-Ferguson was no figurehead: he
was a player, a true viceroy. London expected him to be a player:
he was their man. Australians also expected him to be a player: they
wanted to be part of the empire. On July 31, four days before
Britain declared war, Munro-Ferguson sent a telegraph to the
Australian Prime Minister, Joseph Cook: 'Would it not be well, in
view of latest news from Europe, that Ministers should meet in
order that Imperial Government may know what support to expect
from Australia?' By then the Governor-General knew what his main
purpose was: it was to recruit Australians, as many as possible, for
the European war.

THE WAR WAS a force for unity in Australia. The Liberals and Labor
were fighting a federal election as Australia went to war. Cook, the
Liberal Prime Minister, and Andrew Fisher, the Labor leader, had
been born in Britain. Fisher, who would win the election, caught the
mood of the times in a speech at Benalla. He was strongly opposed
to the Cook Government, he said. But 'in a time of emergency there
are no parties at all. We stand united against the common foe, and
I repeat what I said at Colac, that our last man and our last shilling
will be offered and supplied to the mother country . . .' The war
simply wasn't an election issue.

Had the war been a matter for the head rather than the heart, the
consensus would have been the same. The pragmatic case, which
Cook and Fisher didn't need to argue, would have gone something
like this: Australia could not defend itself or its sea lanes; Britain

and her fleet provided the insurance policy and Australia had to pay the premiums. There was also the matter of Japan. Australians had become suspicious of Japan's military ambitions after her humiliation of Russia in the war of 1904–05. Japan was eager to declare war on Germany in 1914 and this had nothing to do with disapproval of the Kaiser's militarism. There were spoils to be grabbed in the Pacific and Asia. By the end of 1914 Japan had acquired Germany's island possessions north of the equator: the Marshalls, the Marianas and the Carolines. In September, 1914, Australia captured Rabaul and German New Guinea. Had Australia decided against sending troops to the Great War, Japan would surely have ended up with a large chunk of New Guinea. Australians would not have wanted the Japanese so close. But these matters never came to be much talked about. Passions rather than interests led Australia deeper and deeper into the Great War. Fifty-two thousand volunteers had joined up by the end of 1914.

The nation had gone off to what would become the worst tragedy in its history in a curious way. Australia had the right to determine the extent of its participation; but, because recruitment was voluntary, the government couldn't control troop numbers, although it could decide how many would leave. The rush to enlist meant that Australia had many more men than the 20,000 it had promised before the war started. The government was happy to send the extra men overseas too. Enlistments were still averaging about 8000 a month for the first four months of 1915. Then came Gallipoli.

Censorship meant that Australians were not told the truth about the war there. The truth was that from first day the Anzacs had been clinging to a beachhead of about 400 acres. There was no prospect of breaking out of it. Casualties had been heavy. The Australian newspapers in the weeks after the landing made Gallipoli sound like an adventure. Enlistments soared. In July and August, when Gallipoli was the dominant story in the Australian press, enlistments rose to 36,575 and 25,714 respectively, heights never reached again. By the time Pozières opened enlistments had dropped to around 6000 a month. The battles in France produced no surge in enlistments. The war was now being seen as something closer to what it really was.

Those big battles of 1915 and 1916 had produced an Australian casualty list of around 56,000. Enlistments of 6000-a-month were not going to replenish the four fighting divisions. Public figures in Australia were now talking about conscription, which had been introduced in Britain in January, 1916, and in New Zealand six months later.

BILLY HUGHES INTERRUPTED his long stay in Britain in 1916 to attend an economic conference in Paris. A French journalist provided the sharpest sketch of Hughes ever written.

> He is a little man of frail appearance, narrow shouldered, rather stooped. His long face, seamed with lines, reminds one of some of our Breton peasants. We expected to see one of those powerful Australians who look capable of carrying the world on their shoulders . . . But he has only to speak to reveal in an instant the tremendous force that is embodied in that debilitated frame . . . At first he sits doubled up and lets others do the talking. The partial deafness from which he suffers and which would have discouraged any less energetic spirit, compels him to make a prodigious effort of his whole being to follow the thread of the discourse. Already he has been forgotten by the other speakers. But suddenly he straightens out, darts forward his thin arms and the double trident of his extended fingers, and projects into the centre of the flabby discussion an incisive remark. It is not only his face that carries – a distinct face, a metallic face, that cuts across all the others. His first words convince you that he is determined to push his thrust home, and that no obstacle will stop his indomitable will. One understands at once the ascendancy which this little Welshman – who resembles a black spider – has been able to obtain not only over audiences in Australia and England but over the oldest parliamentary hands in Europe.

William Morris Hughes was born in London, the son of Welsh parents. His father was a carpenter and his mother had worked as a domestic servant. She died when Hughes was seven and he went to Wales to live with an aunt. He was an intelligent boy with a love of literature and as a twelve-year-old he was back in London as a pupil teacher. He sailed for Queensland as a twenty-two-year-old assisted migrant, failed to find a teaching job, headed for the bush and became one of Henry Lawson's battlers. He worked for a pineapple grower, in a sugar factory, as a railway ganger, a boundary rider, a blacksmith's helper, a builder of rude sheds and a tally clerk. He tramped along carrying a swag, brushing away flies and coughing up dust, picking up tea and flour from sheep stations, learning the rough ways of the bush and of working men and the value of a ten-shilling note and a good feed of mutton.

Hughes arrived in Sydney two years later, broke, but not in spirit. He lived in a boarding house and married Elizabeth, the landlady's daughter. The couple eventually opened a shop in Balmain that sold green groceries, haberdashery and second-hand books. Elizabeth took in washing. Hughes did odd jobs and tramped from door to door offering to mend umbrellas. Here, in this dowdy little shop, he became captivated by the ideas of the labour movements that were emerging around the world. He was too worldly to believe in utopias; but he did believe in 'progress' and in the simple proposition that working people had as much right to happiness and a modicum of security as anyone else, and that they needed to organise themselves into a party if they were to beat the owners of factories, mines and sheep stations.

When Federation came in 1901 he won the seat of West Sydney for Labor. Three years later John Watson formed a Labor Government, the first of its kind in the world. Hughes took the foreign affairs portfolio. He also built power bases elsewhere. He became president of two unions, including the Waterside Workers' Federation. He went to London in 1907 and decided he didn't have much time for the Fabians. He had become a fixer; they were theoreticians and a little fey. They wouldn't know how to talk to shearers.

Elizabeth, his wife and mother of their six children, had died the year before. She had been cut off from his frantic life. She wrote him a letter two weeks before her death: 'Good night, Will: always remember this: that once I loved you very dearly and tho we may drift apart in the future I shall always remain, Your Faithful Wife E. Hughes.' He remarried in 1911. He had bought a car and was ranked one of the most dangerous drivers in Australia. There was no time for a honeymoon, so he took his new wife for a drive and overturned the car.

Andrew Fisher became Labor leader and won government in 1908. Hughes became Attorney-General. Fisher lost the 1913 election, then was returned a month after the outbreak of the Great War. In October, 1915, Fisher resigned to become High Commissioner in London and Hughes became Prime Minister.

And now, in 1916, here he was in London, fifty-three, the Welsh outcast who had become prime minister of a dominion, grey-haired, his face so criss-crossed with wrinkles that it looked like a trench map, cranky and deaf and dyspeptic, but still bustling with energy, cracking out abuse to his hapless typists, carried along by the fever of war. Some in Britain thought he would make a better prime minister than Asquith. Hughes was close to being as big as he would ever be. And he had also become a muddle of contradictions.

He had been a man of the Left, a socialist of sorts, a union organiser, the friend of the working man. And now the winning of the war and the preservation of imperialist ideals had taken over his soul. Some in his own party thought he was behaving like a Tory. And yet he was also an Australian nationalist, concerned that his country's voice be heard loudly in any peace settlement. He was a nationalist, yet here he was spending six months overseas when leadership was needed at home. He was a nationalist, yet had told the parliament in Melbourne late in 1915, in response to published criticisms of the Gallipoli campaign, that Australia's business was to carry out the instructions of the imperial authorities, to 'mind its own business' and supply troops. Hughes no longer fitted into any of the political compartments; he was simply Billy Hughes.

FAME OF A sort had come to Keith Murdoch, the young journalist from Melbourne, and by a curious route. By the time Hughes arrived in London in 1916 Murdoch had become well known, not for the stories he had published but for one – the so-called 'Gallipoli letter' – that had not been published. Murdoch's letter had circulated only among politicians.

It was addressed to the then Australian Prime Minister Andrew Fisher in late 1915 and circulated as a state paper in Westminster. It had helped expose the incompetence of the high command at Gallipoli. If it was larded with factual errors and the author's sense of his own importance, much of it was also true. The letter did not, of itself, result in the recall of General Sir Ian Hamilton and the evacuation of the beachheads. There were more authoritative voices: the English journalist Ellis Ashmead-Bartlett, Maurice Hankey, the secretary to the War Council, and Guy Dawnay, one of Hamilton's staff officers. But the Asquith Government was looking for a way out of Gallipoli and Murdoch's letter was a piece of ammunition it had to pick up. The politicians used Murdoch and he used them.

Murdoch's career was made, not, as journalists' careers usually are, on words he had written for newspapers, but on his unusual gifts as a manipulator of people and a seeker of power. Murdoch was in London as the head of a cable service supplying the Sydney *Sun* and the Melbourne *Herald*. His new friends included Lord Northcliffe, the proprietor of *The Times* and the *Daily Mail*, Geoffrey Dawson, the editor of *The Times*, Lloyd George and other prominent Cabinet ministers. The Gallipoli letter had opened the way to these people, along with the knowledge that Murdoch was Hughes' man.

Murdoch was only thirty years old. He was a big man with dark and generous eyes and an ardent Australian nationalist. He saw less of the war on the western front than Bean, but he certainly didn't lack courage. He was dangerous to be around at the front because of his physical awkwardness. One night early in 1917 he persuaded an Australian colonel to let him go out on a night patrol into no-man's land. The patrol had gone a few yards when Murdoch missed his footing and broke through the thin ice covering the water in a shell hole, making a prodigious noise. The party started off again. Murdoch fell into another shell hole 'splashing and threshing like a stranded whale'. Then he blundered into a third. Back at the Australian frontline Murdoch three times slipped off the duckboards into mud.

The stories Murdoch did write from the western front tended to generalisations and often had the tone of a sermon. Murdoch didn't have the day-to-day contact with the fighting troops that Bean had, and nothing like the knowledge, and he danced around this with windiness, although he was easier to read than Bean. One can only wonder what Haig, Birdwood, White and the Australian divisional commanders thought when they met Murdoch. Was this a journalist asking a question, or was this Billy Hughes' emissary? They probably knew the answer: he was both.

BIRDWOOD KNEW THAT he was running out of reinforcements before the attacks at Mouquet Farm began. He asked for larger drafts from the training camps in England. Colonel Robert Anderson was in charge of AIF headquarters in London as well as being Hughes' representative at the British War Office. Anderson told Birdwood there were only 13,408 Australian reinforcements in England; only about 4300 could be sent to France within the next three weeks. Birdwood suggested that the Australian Government should be formally told of the scale of reinforcements needed.

Colonel Anderson, meanwhile, had been called to the War Office to be told that the Army Council had decided that the reinforcements would be obtained by either breaking up Monash's 3rd Division or by borrowing from it. Without consulting Birdwood, Anderson cabled this news to Australia. Birdwood suspected that the War Office was playing at politics. The Australian Government would be appalled at being told that one of its divisions might be disbanded. Such a prospect might encourage Hughes to introduce conscription. Bonar Law, the Colonial Secretary, told Murdoch of the Army Council's resolution on the 3rd Division. 'I may tell you a piece of news which will help your conscription campaign in Australia,' he said.

The War Office also decided to adopt Birdwood's idea of asking the Australian Government to send much heavier drafts of reinforcements. The political game had taken another turn. The English authorities knew that Australia's voluntary system couldn't supply bigger drafts.

Birdwood was asked to say what reinforcements he needed. He and White came up with what Bean called a 'staggering demand'. They wanted a special draft of 20,000 men from Australia. They also asked that the monthly drafts from Australia (which normally ran at around 12,000) be increased to 16,500 for three months. This was more men than Birdwood and White needed and far more than the voluntary system could supply. The Army Council accepted the figures without demur and the Colonial Office sent a cable asking the Australian Government for the men it knew the dominion could not provide.

Hughes rose in the Parliament in Melbourne on August 30 and said he had received 'grave communications' from London. He believed the voluntary system could no longer supply sufficient reinforcements. The people would be asked at a referendum to approve compulsory overseas military service.

HUGHES HAD RETURNED to Australia on July 31, a week after the Australians had begun fighting at Pozières. A fortnight later he wrote to Murdoch.

It would be better still to have you by my side – for there are hot times ahead. Long before this reaches you the issue of 'Conscription' as they call it, will be reached in grim earnest. There is great feeling already – All or nearly all the Labour organizations – political as well as industrial – my own League included – have passed strong resolutions against compulsion. A large majority of our own party in the Parliament – are frightened out of their lives – many of course dare not call their souls their own. I'm not even sure of the *Cabinet* . . . The Party meeting is fixed for the 24th. Parliament meeting on the 30th – There will be a tug of war. I am neither hopeful or hopeless – only resolved to go on. I may go down but I shall do what I think right. *One* thing of course would turn me from compulsion – I mean a really great victory. I doubt if this is in sight.

It wasn't. Telegrams were arriving every day, telling families they had lost a husband or a son at Pozières. These casualties were different to those from Gallipoli: they were compressed into a few weeks. It was a bad time for a referendum. There was little evidence that Australians had lost faith in the rightness of the war, but some were now wondering about the scale of the sacrifice. And there was the complication caused by the aftermath to the Easter Rising in Ireland. Some 900,000 Australians were Catholics. Most seemed to have disapproved of the rebellion; many, however, disapproved even more of the British response.

HUGHES DIDN'T NEED a referendum to introduce conscription. He could have done so by regulation or legislation. He knew either of these courses would split the Labor Party, the Left wing of which had already turned against him. He knew he could push a conscription bill through the House of Representatives with the votes of the Liberal Opposition but that the bill would fail in the Senate, where Labor held a massive majority. There was also the matter of what Hughes had told Parliament in 1915: 'In no circumstances would I agree to send men out of this country to fight against their will.' The referendum was thus a gesture towards democracy. If the vote was 'Yes', Hughes could claim a mandate. Even so, the Labor Party might still split.

17

Forty days and forty nights

Billy Hughes campaigned for conscription like a man in a fever. Long fevers and short convalescences: these were the rhythms that shaped his life in politics. An idea would captivate him and he would fight for it: with rhetoric, which he did better than most, and also by threatening and prodding and wheedling and fixing, so that the cause became a crusade. And when the crusade was over, whether successful or not, Hughes would suffer some form of breakdown and hide in his crab's shell for days or weeks. Then he would come out to fight anew. He loved political theatre and big themes. He only looked frail.

Shortly after announcing the referendum he told Parliament: 'For myself, I say that I am going into this referendum campaign as if it were the only thing for which I lived.' He began the crusade in Sydney on September 18, which gave him forty days and forty nights to win the people over. We do not know whether he rebuffed Satan three times. We do know that he thought he was going to win. We may also assume he knew he was going to wreck the Labor Party, which had made him as he had helped to make it. It was as though Hughes had outgrown Labor and its gentle socialism. Hughes thought he had found a larger constituency.

As Donald Horne wrote in *Billy Hughes*:

Hughes allowed himself to be deceived by the British about the number of reinforcements required: accepting estimates which had doubled the number needed to keep the Australian divisions going, he passed these figures on to the voters and magnified the distortion by understating the success of voluntary recruiting. The combination of his lionising in Britain and the encouraging sound of his own voice in the guild halls and banqueting rooms had turned his head. He later told a secretary that he was talked into conscription by the British authorities and by powerful pressures in Australia. Whatever the reason for his change of view, having made the decision, he committed himself to it with the zealous fixedness of a charging rhinoceros. He had a new brief; he had therefore become a new person. Not only did it not occur to him that he could lose the referendum; neither did it occur to him that if he won the referendum, and tried to enforce conscription, even if the majority had said 'yes', within the minority there might be violent resistance – that, as Henry Lawson had put it, blood might stain the wattle.

Hughes toured the country by train. He would alight and make a tremendous speech. Then he would get back on and, with a cigarette in one hand and a fountain pen in the other, run the country from his rocking carriage, scribbling tart notes on state papers, dispatching cables to London, drafting his next speech, niggling at secretaries and helpers. Each time he alighted from the train messengers arrived with bundles of urgent telegrams. Ernest Scott wrote in his official history of the home front: 'As a sheer feat of physical and mental exertion, Mr Hughes' expenditure of himself in those forty days and forty nights . . . was as remarkable an achievement as he ever performed . . . few could have reached his limits of exertion.' Billy Hughes only looked frail.

THE REFERENDUM, SET down for October 28, would ask the people: 'Are you in favour of the Government having, in this grave emergency, the same compulsory powers over citizens in regard to requiring their military service, for the term of this war, outside the Commonwealth, as it now has in regard to military service within the Commonwealth?' Hughes' over-confidence showed in these words. Note the loaded phrase 'in this grave emergency'. And note the clunky wording, the repetition of 'in regard too', as though the people were being asked to vote on some bureaucratic abstraction.

People were being asked to define the nature of the threat that first appeared in August, 1914. That part was relatively easy. It was not in Australia's interests for Britain to lose the war, or to make a bad peace that left Australia's sea lanes endangered. It was not in Australia's interests, nor in those of any country of enlightened or liberal values, for Germany to occupy Belgium and France; it was not in the interests of the liberal democracies that Prussian militarists were saying that might was right. But then one had to move on to trickier questions. What was a reasonable contribution from a faraway land with a population of fewer than five million? Was it right that young men be compelled to fight, particularly since, on the experience of Gallipoli, Fromelles and Pozières, these men stood a high chance of being killed or wounded? Was it right, on the other hand, that the burden be carried entirely by those generous enough to volunteer?

There was a terrible flaw in the process. People didn't truly know what was happening at the war. They didn't know much beyond official dispatches and censored news items. The *War Precautions Act* banned the publication of material that might interfere with recruiting. The historian Joan Beaumont wrote of the censorship regime that began in 1914: 'Progressively it was used by the Hughes Government not only to restrict the publication of sensitive military information but to muzzle any opposition to conscription, or indeed any reporting in the press of opinions embarrassing or threatening to the Government.' People were to decide a life-or-death question by referendum, which sounded very democratic; but they also had to form their opinions from a flow of information controlled by Hughes.

The Universal Service League had been set up to push for conscription. Members included Chris Watson, the first Labor prime minister, William Holman, Premier of New South Wales and one-time debater at Hughes' Balmain bookshop, the barrister John Latham, who would later become Chief Justice of the High Court, Dr J. C. Wright, the Anglican Primate of Australia, and Michael Kelly, Irish born and the Roman Catholic Archbishop of Sydney.

A few unions supported conscription, but most didn't. It was much the same with Labor parliamentarians. Some were prepared to soften their opposition if there was also to be a conscription of wealth. And then there were the Catholics. Some, notably Archbishop Kelly, believed in conscription; many lay people, however, had turned against it in the aftermath of the Easter Rising. Daniel Mannix spoke for these people and exercised an influence disproportionate to his place in the Catholic hierarchy. He didn't speak often, but when he did his gifts were obvious. He paused at just the right moment, never dissembled, kept it simple, and said exactly what he wanted to say.

The referendum forced people in public life to choose. The New South Wales Political Labor League chose quickly. It expelled Hughes and withdrew the endorsement of Holman. Hughes said no secret junta would tell him what to do.

The forces for conscription looked formidable. The Chief Justice of Victoria put aside the rules about judicial independence to come out publicly for compulsion. Nellie Melba, the famous soprano and socialite, was also in favour. She said that if Germany won the war, the first thing the Kaiser would demand would be Australia. The *Age*, perhaps the most liberal of the dailies, called those who failed to enlist 'muddy-mettled wastrels who disgrace the country in which they skulk and shirk and play the dunghill cock'. The *Bulletin* had long been advocating conscription, even though it also called Hughes a buffoon. The mainstream press, city and country, was all for conscription, but not the labour and Catholic newspapers.

The historian Lloyd Robson wrote that 'Australia in September and October 1916 could be described as paranoic'. Uniformed soldiers broke up anti-conscription meetings. A Labor Party poster showed a small boy telling his mother to vote 'No', because 'they'll take Dad next'. A cartoon in the *Bulletin* showed two 'shirkers' leaving a wounded Australian soldier as vultures circled. Cartoons put out by the Victorian Government showed the Kaiser standing on a pile of corpses. The Kaiser and his soldiers were invariably portrayed as ape-like creatures wearing *pickelhaube* helmets several sizes too small; crouching before them would be a terrified woman, clothes in disarray, breasts exposed, clutching a child. The suggestion was that a man who refused to enlist didn't care to protect women and children.

Hughes was over-confident and now made a serious mistake. He wanted to ship his reinforcements overseas as soon as possible once the referendum was passed. Early in October the government issued an order calling up all unmarried men between the ages of twenty-one and thirty-five for service *within* Australia. These men knew that, should the referendum pass, they would be among the first sent off to the western front, whether they wanted to go or not. Some could apply for exemption: a sole surviving son, for instance, or a man who provided the sole support for aged parents, or someone whose job was thought to be in the national interest. Special courts were set up to rule on exemptions. Men called up were to be fingerprinted. This was to stop any traffic in exemption certificates. It also made decent men feel like criminals.

Hughes sent flurries of cables to London. He wanted the British Government to make a conciliatory gesture towards Ireland, so that he might secure more of the Catholic vote. He wanted the soldiers' vote to be 'Yes'. He wanted them to be seen to be calling out for help. (Voting among the troops in France was to begin almost a fortnight before polling day in Australia.) Hughes wanted Haig, Birdwood and British and French labour leaders to publicly support what he was doing.

ON AUGUST 30, the day Hughes announced the referendum, he sent Murdoch a cable in code. He was 'quite certain' the referendum would be carried. He would be able to supply the reinforcements requested. He would call up men for home service and they would be trained by the time the referendum was passed. 'Absolutely

CONFIDENTIAL Labour organisation and large section of Labour [sic] Party hostile to conscription any kind or sort. Proposal of Government was forced through all Parties in face of bitter opposition. Men already pledged to organisation which threatens them with refusal endorsement any one daring to vote in favour of proposals.' He ended by telling Murdoch to stress 'that Australia most democratic government in world and first in history to give masses of Nation opportunity to freely express opinion. Be quite sure Australia will not fail Britain. I am quite sure she will do her duty.'

Hughes prepared a 'manifesto' for Australian soldiers and on September 30 cabled Murdoch, telling him to 'please arrange widest possible publication in press and give Brigadier-General Anderson for issue direct every Australian soldier'. A week later Murdoch cabled Hughes, saying the manifesto was 'excellent'. He was distributing it to every soldier. Publicity was assured. 'Large numbers soldiers possibly majority against conscription because misunderstand exemption. Working hard and hopeful of substantial yes majority.'

Three days later Hughes replied. 'It is absolutely imperative that the voice from the Trenches calling on Australia to vote yes to send reinforcements be heard.' This could only be done, he said, through mass meetings of soldiers in France.

> I have asked Capt. Elliott to arrange with other French soldiers who speak English to address Australian Imperial Force. Get in touch with him and get this done and also get men addressed by British soldiers who are very strong Conscriptionists. I am quite certain it will be easy to get such resolutions as I want carried by large meetings of soldiers and this cabled to me will have profound effect. Please see General Birdwood immediately re permission to address soldiers and for any further facilities necessary for the purpose. Resolution must be passed this week. Am telegraphing you 250 pounds expenses and at your discretion if not enough let me know . . . Please accept my best thanks. Best wishes – Do not fail.

Hughes next day told Murdoch the campaign in Australia was causing 'tremendous excitement'. He had addressed 'great meetings' everywhere. There was 'extraordinary enthusiasm'. Hughes said the opposition came from Irish elements.

Ten days later Murdoch cabled Hughes. He said he had obtained messages of support from Birdwood and British trade unionists and Labour parliamentarians. Then this: 'Strongly urge you to prevent publication now or in future of AIF voting. General Headquarters is very strong on this. It would be equal to serious military defeat if partial army opposition to reinforcements was known, therefore suggest you announce without delay that Army Council prohibits publication men's voting – you can then submerge army's vote amongst the States.' Here was something unusual: a journalist telling a politician to suppress a news story, and, better still, a story that would have been of real interest to the journalist's constituents.

Murdoch had read the mood of the men at the front well. There was no certainty they would vote 'Yes'. Murdoch and Lloyd George had both asked Birdwood to appeal to the Australian people and he had refused. He told a friend he wanted to avoid 'doing the politician'. Then Hughes appealed to him personally. Birdwood, as was his way, immediately 'did the politician' and put out a statement in which he managed to tell soldiers to vote according to their consciences and that conscription was a good idea. His troops at this time were returning from Flanders to the Somme and General Gough, two prospects unlikely to put them in good humour.

How was it that men at the front might have been against conscription when, in their letters home, they so often referred to shirkers and loafers? Some, Bean thought, didn't want to serve with conscripts. Some perhaps feared that conscription could open the way to the introduction of the death penalty for Australian soldiers. Bean also thought that many Labor supporters among the troops would have voted against conscription. But the best reason for voting 'No', he suggested, was one of nobility. These men had not known the horrors of war when they enlisted; now they did, and they didn't want to force others to suffer as they had.

Hughes followed Murdoch's advice and had the soldiers' vote

'submerged' in the state figures. The soldiers had in fact voted for conscription by 72,339 to 58,894, hardly the ringing call from the trenches that Hughes had been hoping for, but the raw figures are misleading. Murdoch claimed that the voting on the western front was three-to-one against conscription. The votes of men on transports and in camps, plus those of the Light Horse in the Middle East and the 3rd Division in England, probably tipped the balance in favour of conscription.

We will never know for sure why the soldiers' vote turned out as it did, but two observations may hold clues. Sergeant Ted Rule wrote:

> The result was remarkable. All the troops in the back area, the butchers, the bakers, and the candlestick makers, voted 'Yes' almost to a man. The boys who had to endure the mud and carry the burden voted 'No' in a most determined manner. I have never solved the riddle as to why these fellows, who worshipped at the feet of the goddess of self-sacrifice and who spurned the ground the cold-footers walked on, voted for allowing them to stay at home. The nearest I can get to a solution is that a catch-cry properly caught on: 'I would not bring my worst bloody enemy over here to go through this.' Man after man repeated this, word for word.

Newton Wanliss, the historian of the 14th Battalion, said the average Australian viewed national questions largely from a personal standpoint. The Australian troops had grievances, some genuine, some imaginary. They blamed the military and political chiefs – 'the heads', as they were known – for these. The men knew the heads wanted a 'Yes' vote, so they voted 'No'.

The soldiers voted and headed for the Somme. An onlooker saw the 1st Division going south. 'The men all looked very serious – sturdy and solid, but not the least buoyancy about them.' Gough and his repeated attacks on narrow fronts had knocked the lightness out of them. We will never know why these men voted as they were said to have done. But we can say this: they knew about the war that had brought on the referendum; to that extent their vote was at least informed.

THE DEBATE AT home, less well informed, raged up to polling day. Hughes now made another bad mistake. Munro-Ferguson, the Governor-General, was in Sydney the day before the poll. Around midnight Hughes telephoned him at Admiralty House in Kirribilli. Three Cabinet ministers had just resigned, including the Treasurer, Hughes said. Hughes had ordered that male voters who appeared to be aged between twenty-one and thirty-five should be asked at the booths whether they were single and, if so, whether they had reported to the military authorities. The three ministers felt the Prime Minister was meddling with the democratic process. The regulation was withdrawn after the three ministers resigned.

Munro-Ferguson crossed Sydney Harbour to find Hughes hunched in a taxi at Circular Quay. Hughes knew the resignations would influence voting. 'The poor little man asked for advice and sympathy,' the Governor-General wrote. Hughes said he 'had not a brain wave left'. Munro-Ferguson suggested that Hughes censor the announcement of the resignations. Hughes left to do so, only to find that news was already out. The Great Fixer was tired and very much alone. In his final address he asked the voters to 'save the empire'.

THE PEOPLE VOTED 'No' and the empire did not fall apart, just the Australian Labor Party, shot in both legs, so to speak, at Pozières. To succeed, the referendum proposal had to be approved by a majority of the people and a majority of States. The votes came out like this:

	Yes	No	Result
New South Wales	356,805	474,544	No
Victoria	353,930	328,216	Yes
Queensland	144,200	158,051	No
South Australia	87,924	119,236	No
Western Australia	94,069	40,884	Yes
Tasmania	48,493	37,833	Yes
Federal Territory	2,136	1,269	Yes
	1,087,557	1,160,033	No

Enlistments fell to just 2617 in December. Hughes' recruiting problem was worse then ever. Munro-Ferguson wrote to Bonar Law, the Colonial Secretary: 'For the moment the anarchist and most ignorant section of society has shown itself more powerful than all the rest, and that in a community which is in the main the most irresponsible, self-confident and inexperienced in the Empire, or even perhaps outside of it.'

THE FEDERAL LABOR caucus met on November 14. The air was blue with tobacco smoke and heavy with recrimination. Two more of Hughes' Cabinet had resigned that day. He now had only four ministers left, which meant he didn't really have a government. He knew what was coming. A Queensland member put the motion: the Prime Minister no longer possessed the confidence of the party. Two amendments were offered. Hughes suddenly rose from his chair, picked up his papers and said: 'Let all who support me, follow me.' Hughes had sacked the party before it could sack him. Twenty-three of the sixty-five Labor parliamentarians, including George Pearce, the Defence Minister, followed him. Those left expelled Hughes from the leadership and elected Frank Tudor to replace him.

Hughes knew that the Liberals would want to join with him. He handed his resignation to Munro-Ferguson and asked to be recommissioned. The Governor-General, after seeking assurances from the Liberals, gave Hughes his job back. Early the following year Hughes' Labor rump merged with the Liberals to form the National Party.

Two months later, in May, 1917, Australia went to the polls. Hughes and his National Party won effortlessly. The Australian people still believed in the war and indeed in Hughes; they just didn't believe in conscription.

18

Last gasp

Haig planned to make a tremendous push above the Somme on September 15. Happily for them, the three exhausted Australian divisions were resting around Ypres at this time. Haig was going to attack on the front that now stretched beyond Pozières, Delville Wood and Ginchy. This salient, won at frightful cost to both sides, pointed north-east, towards the villages of Courcelette, Flers and Gueudecourt and, beyond them, to the market town of Bapaume. Haig was thinking of breakthrough again, as he had on July 1. Tanks were to be used for the first time in this offensive. Once the infantry and tanks had broken through three lines of German defences, five divisions of cavalry would pass through the gap.

Rawlinson's 4th Army had most of the front for September 15. Gough's army was to the north; it would be pushing out of the Pozières salient created by the Australians. The Canadians would be going for Courcelette, with help from tanks. In front of Rawlinson lay three lines of German trenches; the first of these had been the third line on July 1 when Haig launched the Somme offensive. It seemed the Germans never stopped digging: lose one, dig another, and don't spare the concrete.

Rawlinson wanted to attack these three lines step by step. Haig, characteristically, wanted to burst through to the third line in one rush. Rawlinson, characteristically, gave way. Haig was ready to embrace the tanks but he still hadn't learned much about artillery. The British didn't have enough guns or shells to attack three lines of trenches in one attack. As Robin Prior and Trevor Wilson wrote in *Command on the Western Front*, Haig was running the risk of achieving nothing by trying to achieve everything.

The bombardment opened on September 12 as rain threatened. Three days later the long-suffering infantry hopped over. A pilot flying overhead wrote: 'When we climbed up to the lines, we found the whole front seemingly covered with a layer of dirty cotton-wool – the smoking shell-bursts. Across this were dark lanes, drawn as it might be by a child's stubby finger in dirty snow. Here no shells were falling. Through these lanes lumbered the Tanks.'

There were forty-nine of them, Mark Is, on that long front. They lurched forward in shell-free corridors, about 100-yards wide, to protect them from the creeping barrage. This meant that the Germans within the corridors could man their machine guns without fear of being shelled.

GENERAL FERDINAND FOCH, commander of the French Northern Army Group, arrived at GHQ the day the new British offensive opened and asked to speak to Haig privately. Foch said Lloyd George had recently visited him. Lloyd George wanted to know why the British had incurred so many casualties on the Somme, then asked Foch for his opinion of the British generals. Lloyd George said nothing critical of Haig, but 'did not speak with confidence of the other British generals as a whole'. Haig wrote in his diary: 'Unless I had been told of this conversation personally by Gen. Foch, I would not have believed that a British Minister could have been so ungentlemanly as to go to a foreigner and put such questions regarding his own subordinates.' Lloyd George shortly after put similar questions to Sir Henry Wilson, then commanding a corps on the Somme. Wilson would have enjoyed this. He was so famous as an intriguer that it was said he fell into a state of sexual excitement whenever he saw a politician.

Lloyd George was a frustrated man: he couldn't understand what was happening on the Somme, or where the campaign was going. Haig had five armies, more than fifty divisions, under his command – English, Scots, Welsh, Canadians, Australians, Indians, New Zealanders – but he didn't want to say too much about what he was doing with them, least of all to people he would regard as 'uninstructed'. As Lloyd George's biographer John Grigg put it, the minister was trying to discover facts that he couldn't obtain from Robertson, whom he saw as Haig's man. The military leaders' idea of gentlemanliness implied 'a conspiracy against the public, whose interests it was [Lloyd George's] duty to serve'. Lloyd George, Grigg concluded, could be criticised for tactlessness but not for acting unpatriotically.

HAIG'S NEW OFFENSIVE opened reasonably well. On Gough's front, to the north, the Canadian infantry and six tanks enlarged the Pozières–Mouquet Farm salient to include the little village of Courcelette. The tanks struggled to keep up with the barrage and two broke down. They nevertheless comforted the Canadians and bewildered the Germans, who had to endure the bombardment, then the sight of khaki figures advancing to kill them, and, finally, the spectacle of creaking iron ships lurching across a sea of craters. Who was inside them? What was that smoke coming out? Poison gas? Some Germans pulled on their gas masks when they saw the exhaust smoke.

On the right of Rawlinson's front, on a line northwards from Combles to Ginchy, corridors in the barrage had been left for fifteen tanks. Only two turned up. The German machine gunners in the corridors, untouched by shells, cut down the infantry. The three British divisions here ran up 12,000 casualties, including more than 400 officers.

Rawlinson's centre, in front of Delville Wood and Longueval – three divisions, including the New Zealanders – made unusually strong gains, taking the village of Flers and ground beyond. The twelve tanks here (five didn't turn up) did just what they were supposed to do: crushed the wire, smashed machine-gun posts and unnerved the Germans. This was the big success of the day.

At the northern end of Rawlinson's front three divisions captured the village of Martinpuich and, at last, High Wood. The little salient won on July 1 had been pushed out by six square miles to take in Courcelette, Martinpuich, all of High Wood and Flers. After two-and-a-half months Haig was finally closing on Bapaume. The victories, however, carried a fearful price. Prior and Wilson estimate the day's casualties at around 29,000, or about half the total on July 1. And while the British had taken 4000 yards of the second line of trenches around Flers, the wire around the third line was still intact. Rawlinson couldn't call up reserves because he didn't have any. Most of the tanks had either broken down or been shot up. Rawlinson didn't have the means to keep the momentum going.

HAIG WAS IMPRESSED with the tanks, or what he heard about them. Hardly any of his information was first hand: that was one of the biggest flaws in his style of command. Some of the tanks had 'done marvels', Haig wrote. The men closer to the front weren't so sure. Only thirty-six of the forty-nine tanks had reached their departure points on time; less than a dozen helped to capture German positions.

Too much had been asked of them in their first outing. The crews suffered in their Wellsian coffins, which reeked of petrol and cordite. The crews were often burned and cut about the face by ricocheting pieces of red-hot metal known as 'bullet splash'. They often could not hear each other and communicated by mimicry. They felt cut off from the world. If the portholes at the front needed to be closed, the crew had to peer through holes the size of a threepence.

Patrick Wright in *Tank* tells the story of Basil Henriques, who may have commanded the first tank to fire in action. The tank's periscope was soon shot off and a front flap broke. Bullets and splinters of metal ricocheted around inside. The driver and gunner were hit. Henriques climbed out, bloodied by splinter wounds to his legs, face and eyes. He said one tank officer went mad and shot his engine in an endeavour to make it go faster. Another, overcome by a sense of failure, shot himself.

Churchill had been one of the enthusiasts who had brought the tank into being. He was dismayed that Britain's 'tremendous secret' had been disclosed to the enemy 'for the mere petty purpose of taking a few ruined villages'.

TEN DAYS BEFORE the battle of September 15, Raymond Asquith, the eldest son of the British Prime Minister and a lieutenant in the Guards Division, was summoned by his brigadier. Raymond's father was visiting France. Raymond was to meet him at a crossroads. He rode to the map reference, near Fricourt, and waited. The Prime Minister arrived with an entourage from GHQ. The party was inspecting captured dugouts when German shells began falling. 'The PM was not discomposed by this,' Raymond wrote, 'but the GHQ chauffeur to whom I had handed over my horse to hold, flung the reins into the air and himself flat on his belly in the mud. It was funny enough.'

Raymond was shot in the chest in the attack of September 15. He lit a cigarette while on the ground so that his men would not realise how badly wounded he was. He died on the stretcher taking him to the dressing station.

Also attacking with the Guards that day was Harold Macmillan, a future prime minister. He fell with bullet fragments in his pelvis. He lay in a shell hole and read from a pocket edition of Aeschylus's *Prometheus*.

HAIG DIDN'T HAVE the reserves to build on his successes of September 15. The following day Rawlinson called for an advance along the entire line. All his battered divisions could manage were sporadic attacks. Then the rains came. The big attacks were postponed and the Somme went back to attrition.

Rawlinson launched a new attack on September 25 after the rain cleared. This time he was going for only one line of trenches, the German third position. The artillery was thus able to dump a ferocious bombardment on the Germans, much heavier than that of September 15, and the attack succeeded. The British took the villages of Morval and Lesboeufs and large parts of the third line. Gueudecourt fell the next day. Combles fell to the south. Gough's army finally took Thiepval, a July 1 objective, on September 26.

The salient into the German lines was deeper again, but the Germans had now dug a fourth line of trenches between Thilloy and Le Transloy, a fifth in front of Bapaume, and a sixth behind that. The cavalry would not be passing through.

THE AUSTRALIAN 5TH Division, reinforced after its losses at Fromelles, would be the first Australian contingent to arrive at the new Somme frontline near Gueudecourt. The 1st, 2nd and 4th divisions would follow it south. These latter were still hurting from Pozières. Many of the Australians felt that they had been asked to do more there than the British, which wasn't true. Haig was very even-handed when it came to wearing out divisions. Some of the Australians were suffering from the invisible wounds of shell-shock. And some felt disenchanted with Birdwood for allowing them to be used in nineteen advances on narrow fronts in six weeks. The general, it was now obvious, had a problem. He had a moral responsibility to the Australian Government and a formal responsibility to the British army.

Haig decided on another grand advance, all along the British line, before the 5th Division came up. Rawlinson's 4th Army was to attack the line of trenches in front of Bapaume, running south from Thilloy to Le Transloy. Rawlinson gained more ground on the left of his line, near the village of Le Sars. Then the rain started, eight days of it. The churned-up battlefield became a bog. Rawlinson didn't want to move in such weather; he also knew Haig, who lived in a crater-free landscape, wanted to attack all winter. Rawlinson tried an attack on October 7. It failed after four days.

The 4th Army had pushed over a ridge and descended into a valley. It was a poor place for winter quarters and, worse, the Germans around Bapaume looked down on it. Rawlinson attacked again five days later when the rain eased briefly. Another failure. Rawlinson tried again six days later. Failure again. The front west of Bapaume seemed to be back to stalemate. There had been only three fine days in the first twenty days of October. A dozen horses were needed to move a relatively light eighteen-pounder field gun. Ammunition was being dragged on sleds made from sheets of corrugated iron. Haig tried to ignore the weather. He had to push on because the French to his south wanted to keep the offensive going. He also wanted to keep going for his own reasons. He needed more to show for his long Somme campaign. A conference would soon be called at Chantilly to discuss strategies for 1917. Haig longed to take along a success.

Rawlinson wanted to get beyond the valley before winter came. He attacked the Transloy Line three more times late in October, and failed each time. The ground behind his front was so muddy that all supplies had to come along a single road from Longueval to Flers. Lord John Gort, then a young staff officer (he became Chief of the Imperial General Staff in 1937), visited the front and told Haig the men were living on cold food and standing up to their knees in mud. Many had trench foot, a fungal infection caused by dampness that sometimes led to gangrene.

Haig ordered another attack on the Transloy Line for early November. Lord Cavan, whose corps was to carry it out, told Rawlinson the attack had practically no chance of success. His men were exhausted from dragging themselves through the mud. Rawlinson said the attack had to go ahead. Cavan insisted that Rawlinson look at the front trenches himself. Rawlinson went forward and, according to Cavan, agreed that attack was impossible. Rawlinson apparently convinced Haig that operations to help the French should be limited to raids and artillery shelling. Then Haig spoke to Foch and changed his mind: the attack had to go ahead. Here was the triumph of politics over commonsense. The corps commander, who knew the ground, said the attack had no chance;

the army commander, who had looked at the ground, agreed with him; and the commander-in-chief, who hadn't seen the ground, ordered the attack to go ahead. It failed with 2000 casualties, including 819 from the newly arrived 2nd Australian Division, which was not part of Cavan's force but attacking nearby.

LLOYD GEORGE IN mid-October came to see Haig and attempted to explain his side of the conversation with Foch about the capabilities of British generals. Haig said he interrupted him, saying he had never paid the smallest attention to it. Lloyd George complained that the War Office fed him only what it thought was suitable for him to know. Haig said he thought this was wrong; he would mention it to Robertson. Part of the trouble, of course, was that Haig told Robertson only what he thought it suitable for *him* to know.

Haig in mid-November reminded Gough that the Chantilly conference was about to open. 'The British position will doubtless be much stronger (as memories are short) if I could appear there on the top of the capture of Beaumont Hamel for instance and 3,000 German prisoners.' Next day Gough's army took Beaumont Hamel.

Haig had something to take to Chantilly. Three days later he called off the British offensive on the Somme. The Australians were stuck in the valley in front of Bapaume and winter was coming.

19

The terrible winter

Pompey Elliott came to the Somme with the 5th Division. He had just returned from leave in Britain, where he had visited relatives and bought himself a new uniform, which was pointless. Elliott always looked a shambles; the look came naturally to him. Once he had been arrested in London for impersonating an officer.

The other two brigades of the 5th Division went into the front-line. Elliott's 15th Brigade stayed three miles back in reserve. Elliott walked to the front and floundered around in the mud. For his next trip there Elliott rode Darkie, his black gelding. The return journey took six hours. 'My poor old horse was quite knocked up floundering through shell holes up to the knees in mud and water. Once he fell with me and I thought I'd never get him up again for the mud was like glue and he simply couldn't lift himself at all.'

Two days later Elliott's brigade took over a section of the front in drenching rain. This time they, and the other Australian divisions following, would be under Rawlinson rather than Gough. The trenches were wretched, Elliott wrote, full of mud that lapped over one's boots. There were no sanitary arrangements. Dead Englishmen lay everywhere.

Sergeant Jimmy Downing, from Elliott's brigade, trudged to the front through High Wood, which had been as much a hellhole as Pozières. He saw a Scot and a German lying beside the communications trench, each impaled on the other's bayonet. At the firing line Downing found himself buried to the waist in slush. Rain, and the odd German shell, fell from a grey sky.

> The dead lay everywhere. The deeper one dug, the more bodies one exhumed. Hands and faces protruded from the slimy, toppling walls of trenches. Knees, shoulders and buttocks poked from the foul morass, as many as the pebbles of a brook. Here had been a heavy slaughter of English lads four days before . . . There were also German dead, but it was hard to tell them from the rest, for khaki is grey when soaked and muddy. Our clothes, our very underclothing, were ponderous with the weight of half an inch of mud on the outer surface, and nearly as much on the inner. Casualties were heavy in the sixty hours we were in that place . . . There was no hot food and no prospect of it. We drank shell hole water, as it was too cold for the corpses to rot . . .

Elliott set up his headquarters in a German dugout and sniffled with a cold. He would visit the frontline before breakfast and return soaked through, then go to bed until his clothes dried in front of a fire. He didn't see how men could be asked to attack in this: they couldn't even walk. Nor could they stay in the frontline for long. Elliott's men were soon pulled out. In came the 7th Brigade of the 2nd Division, commanded by John Paton.

Downing said some of the 5th Division men took twenty-four hours to cover the three miles to the back area. 'There was a foot of slush on the changing surface of the clay. The sound of the wrenching of our boots from its grip was like the tearing of sheets of cloth.' Feet swelled and some turned black with trench foot. Downing and his mates rested for a few days, cleaned themselves as best they could, then returned to the front.

These men had voted on conscription a fortnight earlier. Elliott knew many had voted 'No' and understood why. They didn't want to force others into such 'dreadful suffering'. Now Elliott discovered the homeland had voted against conscription. 'I cannot understand it,' he wrote. 'I suppose it was the Catholics that were against England as usual, together with all the cold-footers and wasters . . . I hope we will never hear anything again about the loyalty of the Irish. They are a lovely lot.'

THE 1ST AUSTRALIAN Division came into the line on the right of the 5th on October 30. Two companies and three bombing parties from the 1st were to attack a sharp salient in the German lines. Machine guns were to be set up to cover the attacking Australians. Owen Howell-Price, the twenty-six-year-old commander of the 3rd Battalion, came up to supervise the placement of the guns in the parapet and fell, shot in the head. He was too straight-backed and serious to be popular – he perhaps felt he needed to prove something to older men – but none questioned his courage.

Howell-Price died from his wound. One account has him dying instantly on the parapet, shot in the brain. A Red Cross report has him lingering for more than a day and quotes the officer commanding the 36th Casualty Clearing Station.

> He came in suffering from a bad gunshot wound in the neck. He was unconscious most of the time that he was here and he died 24 hours after admission. Mr Dexter the Sen. Chaplain for the Australian forces happened to be in the same unit and did all he could for him as he was an old friend. He thought he recognised him once and just pressed his hand, but Col. Price never spoke I think . . .

Owen's brother, Philip, a captain, was leading one of the attacking companies. The mud was so deep that Philip's men could not keep up with the creeping barrage. On reaching the German wire they were met with grenades and rifle fire. 'This,' Howell-Price wrote, 'was the turning point . . . our men hesitated and were lost.' Some ran back to the Australian lines. Howell-Price tried a second attack. This failed too. The rest of the night was spent bringing in wounded. Casualties ran to 208.

This was on November 5. The bigger Australian attack that day was to be against a German salient called the Maze by Paton's 2nd Brigade. One battalion became lost in the dark and reached the front only minutes before the assault was to begin. Some of these men were so tired from floundering in the mud that they sat down and wept. The front trench had become too deep because of the need to toss mud over the parapet. Hundreds of scaling ladders were sent up so that the Australians could actually get out of their trenches. The ladders arrived late. Horses were taken from the field ambulances to drag the ladders up on sleds. This wore out the horses, which should have been available to bring out the wounded.

John Paton, the brigade commander, was wounded as he stood on the parapet trying to reorganise his battalions. A gale blew at sixty miles an hour. Then there was a mix-up about the creeping barrage. The infantrymen were supposed to hop over at 9.10 am, giving them three minutes to reach the barrage. Then the guns would lift their fire fifty yards every minute, leading the men up to the German line. Someone made an error in writing the orders: the infantrymen were told to hop over at 9.13.

They were thus too far behind the barrage. They saw Germans climbing out on to the parapet to fire their Mausers. Captain John Nix, the Townsville journalist, was soon hit. He, like Owen Howell-Price, had been heroic at Pozières, where he had been shot through the hand. Now he lay dead in the mud. Some Australians made the German front trench. Their rifles were clogged with mud and wouldn't fire, so they tossed bombs and, when these ran out, picked up German stick grenades and threw them. By nightfall it was apparent that only a handful of Australians were still in the German lines. The position was lost a few days later. There had thus been no gain from the attack – and 819 casualties.

Rawlinson ordered the attack to be repeated but November 7 produced half-an-inch of rain and another gale. The new attack was postponed to the 9th and then the 14th. All the time the battlefield became more of a bog.

BEAN WROTE THAT the interlude between the first attack and the second, on November 14, was 'the most trying period ever experienced by the AIF on any front'.

Here were the Australians, about four miles past Pozières, in a valley beyond the ridge that ran through Pozières, High Wood, Delville Wood and Ginchy. They were within sight of Bapaume, which was supposed to have been taken a few days after the Somme battle opened on July 1. Behind them, for seven or eight miles, lay the ruins of Thiepval, La Boisselle, Contalmaison, Pozières, Longueval, Delville Wood, High Wood, Ginchy, Flers and Gueudecourt. Behind them lay a sea of craters that had ruined the natural drainage of the downland and roads that had been washed away. If civilisation were to be defined as a town that still had houses standing, the nearest civilisation was at Albert, nine miles back. Anyone who was with the British or Australian troops, standing knee-deep in slush and shivering in their mud-caked greatcoats, knew that the Somme battle could go no further.

Seven or eight miles would be the extent of the gain, seven or eight miles that a French farm worker once might have walked in an easy afternoon. Soldiers now took a day to walk the two miles from Delville Wood to the front. The Germans had fought with a stubbornness that was astonishing, but they had not stopped Haig; the weather had.

In some places, the German and British troops walked about their parapets in sight of one another. Both sides were more interested in draining their trenches than in shooting each other. Haig, Rawlinson and Gough had no notion of what the front was like, which is why, for a few days more, they persisted with their fantasies. The ground was so soft that high-explosive shells speared deep into the bog before exploding. They splattered the landscape with slurry but produced no dust cloud to screen the infantry. The Australians gave up using the communications trenches to approach the front. They dragged themselves along sled tracks. Sleds now brought up the supplies and took out the wounded and ill. The wounded lay out in the weather for up to twelve hours without blankets. Sometimes three horses were needed to drag out one man.

Men pulled out of the sucking clay often left their boots and trousers behind. Rescuers of an officer accidentally broke his back.

Troops stayed in the frontline for just forty-eight hours at a time. They tried to escape the weather by cutting nooks in the trench walls but these soon caved in because of the seepage. No open fires were allowed and there was hardly any kerosene for primuses. Even in the back areas there was hardly any firewood. The only commodity that occasionally arrived hot was tea. This came in fuel tins and smelled so strongly of petrol that men said that after drinking it they feared to light a cigarette.

Disease broke out. Some men suffered shivering fits. Others collapsed from exhaustion. Trench foot became endemic. The 4th Army staff issued a memorandum saying the disease was 'merely a matter of discipline' and listing ways of preventing it. Another staff officer's delusion: there was no way feet could be kept dry.

AUSTRALIANS FROM THE 2nd Division went for the trenches around the Maze again on November 14. Some had fought in the previous attack. A senior officer said they looked 'pretty cheap'. Three battalions went over at 6.45 am. The battalion on the right broke into the German lines but was thrown out. It was ordered to attack again. Most of the centre battalion also failed. It too was ordered back. The battalion on the left took the German line. The Germans had left just about everything except themselves behind. The Australians fought with German Mausers, which allowed them to give their .303 rifle ammunition to their Lewis gunners, drank cold German coffee, warmed it with German alcohol, and hung on through the first night, thanks mainly to the firepower of their Lewis guns. The Germans counter-attacked on the afternoon of the 16th. The Australians fired two red rockets and one white – the SOS signal. It wasn't picked up in the Australian line. Two officers fell shot. The Australians lost heart and broke back towards their lines. The trench was lost, which meant the attack had failed everywhere and the 2nd Division had lost another 901 men.

The morale of the Australians was as low as it had been in the war. Bean said it was almost unknown for Australians to desert to the enemy, but in this winter there were 'one or two' cases of young Australians walking over to the German lines.

IN MILITARY TERMS the battle of the Somme was over, pulled up by wind and rain after going several weeks longer than it should have. In another sense the battle refuses to go away. You are reminded of this whenever you walk into a cemetery on the Somme and read an entry in the registry. The grandchildren, the words tell you, have brought the great-grandchildren to see *his* grave, the man they never saw, the man who, high on idealism, volunteered with his pals and chums and died on the chalk downs in 1916, an innocent abroad. There may be a photograph of him, enclosed in clear plastic and wrapped lightly around his headstone, or a wreath bought locally, or just a poppy. The Somme lives on because of the scale of the casualties and what these did to families and towns across the British empire.

Disputes still go on about estimates of casualties. We know with some certainty that the British and dominion casualties were about 420,000 and the French around 200,000. German casualties are harder to estimate. Edmonds, the British official historian, put them as high as 660,000 to 680,000. Others thought they were around 400,000. Lloyd George and Churchill contended after the war that British casualties were up to twice as heavy as those of the Germans. The German official history ventured 500,000 casualties, but the Germans didn't count wounded who were likely to recover 'within a reasonable time'.

Was it worth it? Haig was trying for a breakthrough on July 1 and September 15. In between those dates, and after September 15, he was trying to wear out the German army. In truth Haig's battle was about improvisation: it started as one thing and became another, and afterwards Haig's defenders said it was always about the second thing. Their hero was not trying to be Napoleon at Austerlitz but Ulysses S. Grant in Virginia. It was all about attrition, they insisted.

Haig could not have stopped, even if he had wanted to. He had to keep faith with the French. And he did relieve the pressure on Verdun and sap the spirit of the Kaiser's army, though not as much as he thought. The people in Britain and Australia were told of a procession of successes. Victories always look grander when presented on small-scale maps that make the six miles from Albert to Courcelette look like sixty. But that's what the Somme was: a succession of minor and grinding victories that forced the Germans off the ridges of their choice. The cost of them: that is the matter for judgement.

The Somme will always be an emotional argument. Some of the best spirits of a generation, hundreds of men like Raymond Asquith and Alec Raws, died on that soft downland. The New Army, raised on love of country, was offered up in sacrifice there. Much of the hope and optimism of the British people died there. After the Somme the war was less of a crusade and more of a burden. The battle had been very much like Haig himself. There was nothing particularly clever about it. It was about duty and sacrifice and holding one's nerve, about doing the same thing every day until, eventually, the other side gave way. It was about character rather than inspiration.

The battle also offered hints of how, one day, the trench stalemate might be broken. The Lewis gun had been important throughout. The tank had been launched as a weapon. Much more important were the lessons about artillery. When the guns were dispersed widely, as on the first day, most of the infantry failed. If, however, the fire was concentrated on a narrower front and the shells were mostly high explosive, the infantry could succeed. As the Somme battle went on the creeping barrage became more common. This forced the Germans to remain underground until the foot soldiers were just about upon them. High-explosive shells and a creeping barrage: these were ways the stalemate might be broken. The Somme also made the gunners think more about counter-battery fire. It was not enough to hit the enemy's front trenches; a way had to be found to hit their artillery pieces miles behind the lines, so as to give the advancing infantry extra protection. Aerial spotting was useful here – indeed this, rather than engaging in dogfights – was the main job of the Royal Flying Corps, but better methods were being investigated, such as measuring the distance of a German gun by tracking its sound with a microphone. Haig had not discovered as much as he might have about artillery: it was a foreign language and he learned only enough to get by. Others had learned a great deal.

HAIG ARRIVED AT Chantilly, the home of the French Derby, on November 15, a fine clear morning that reflected his mood. Also present were Joffre, Robertson and delegates from the armies of Belgium, Italy, Russia, Rumania, Serbia and Japan. At the same time the political representatives of the allies, including Asquith and Lloyd George, were meeting twenty-five miles away in Paris.

The Chantilly conference decided that the allies would resume offensives in the first fortnight of February, 1917. The generals and the politicians then came together. Here it became obvious that Lloyd George, the 'easterner', was at odds with Haig and Joffre on strategy. Lloyd George truly did think the war could be won from the east; he didn't believe in, nor like, Haig; and he was appalled by the Somme casualties and didn't want them repeated in 1917. Lloyd George wrote that he left the conference feeling that 'nothing more would be done except to repeat the old fatuous tactics of hammering away with human flesh and sinews at the strongest fortresses of the enemy'.

A little over a fortnight later Haig received a letter from Robertson: 'We are in a great political muddle here, and goodness knows what will happen. The P.M. has not kept his team in hand. They have now revolted.'

Next day, December 6, Haig received a telegram from the War Office: 'Asquith resigned. Bonar Law [the Conservative leader] trying to form Government.'

Then another arrived: 'Bonar Law failed to form Government. Lloyd George, Asquith and Balfour are to form National Government.'

Haig had other things on his mind.

This morning the A.G. brought me Court Martial proceedings on an officer charged with desertion and sentenced by the Court to be shot. After careful consideration, I confirmed the proceedings. This is the first sentence of death on an officer to be put into execution since I became C. in C. Such a crime is more serious in the case of an officer than of a man, and also it is highly important that all ranks should realise that the law is the same for an officer as a private.

UNLIKE AUSTRALIA'S LABOR Party, Herbert Asquith was not a casualty of the Somme, although he would have been less vulnerable if the campaign had gone better. Asquith was a victim of the way he was. Like Lloyd George, he was a self-made man, a brilliant student at Oxford and a successful barrister. By the time of the Somme he had been prime minister for almost nine years, and mostly he had been a good one, limiting the powers of the House of Lords, introducing old-age pensions, health and unemployment insurance and more progressive income taxes. As the years passed he took on the air of the distant statesman. He could be leaden and indecisive; this was obvious during the crises over Gallipoli in 1915, which, along with the munitions scandal in France, eventually forced him to form a coalition government with the Conservatives.

What had become clear was that Asquith, now sixty-four and ten years older than Lloyd George, was not made to be a wartime leader. Unlike Lloyd George (and Churchill in a later war), he could not find the words and the music. People expect theatre from their leaders in wartime: it diverts them from looking too hard at facts and makes sacrifice seem more bearable. All along Asquith had been too bland, while Lloyd George hummed with passion and mesmerised his audiences. Asquith admitted privately that it was not his way 'to carry round the fiery cross'.

Asquith's removal was a very British coup, complete with meddling press proprietors (notably Northcliffe and the future Lord Beaverbrook), planted news stories, clandestine meetings at the Hyde Park Hotel, whispers and arched eyebrows at dinner parties and lunches at country houses, exchanges of polite letters, hints of resignation, treachery dressed up as high-mindedness and high-mindedness mistaken for treachery. Lloyd George had not set out to topple Asquith as prime minister; he simply sought to put himself in charge of the war effort, which, some would say, was the same thing. Lloyd George wanted to chair a committee, with perhaps three to five members and independent of the Cabinet, to control the day-to-day conduct of the war.

Bonar Law and the Conservatives liked the idea. Asquith felt he was being made an 'irresponsible spectator', and he was. Lloyd George resigned, then Asquith. Bonar Law let it be known he didn't want the prime ministership. Lloyd George said he didn't want it either; all he wanted was to run the War Council and 'get rid of the Asquith incubus'. The King eventually asked Lloyd George to form a government.

Lord Derby became War Minister. He was in thrall to Haig and Robertson.

MONASH'S 3RD DIVISION had finally left for France after training for four months on Salisbury Plain. The troops took over muddy trenches in Flanders as France slipped into its coldest winter for decades. Monash, ever practical, had bought a pair of chamois underpants in London. He had also been working on his fifty-one-year-old body. He landed on Gallipoli with the figure of a middle-aged businessman in good flesh. Now, by dieting and exercise, he had shed forty-two pounds and trimmed his waistline by seven-and-a-half inches. The loss of weight left him with more lines on his face, an almost leathery look.

He had trained his division with a thoroughness that marked him as different from Birdwood and Godley and indeed most of the generals on the western front. He believed in preparation. On Salisbury Plain he gave three talks to his senior officers. He stressed that officers had to be loyal to each other. A senior officer needed to know he would receive the loyalty of his juniors even if they thought what he was doing was wrong. 'That is the only kind of loyalty that is worth a damn, or counts at all.' Officers should not be overwhelmed by death and bloodshed. 'You must get yourselves into a callous state of mind. A commander who worries is not worth a damn . . . Hypnotise yourself into a state of complete indifference as to losses . . . you have got to carry on.' Monash was neither cold nor callous. He simply knew what had to be done in war.

George V came to inspect the division, riding a black Australian waler he had bought in India. Monash was susceptible to flattery and in awe of the mighty. He wrote an effusive letter home. He had spent two-and-a-half hours with the King, who was 'chatty and breezy and merry all the time'. The King said he didn't think he had inspected a finer division. 'Splendid, splendid!' he said. The Australians cheered the King on his way to the railway station and raised their hats aloft on bayonets. The King dismounted at the station, gave his horse a lump of sugar and told Monash: 'Don't forget to come and see me.' Rain pelted down on Monash as he rode back to camp. He didn't mind. He knew he had made an impression.

Monash set up his headquarters in France in a château at Steenwerck with electric light and hot water. He had control of five miles of front and a back area that included the ruined town of Armentières. The country was so waterlogged that neither side could have attacked, even if they had wanted to. Monash came down with chilblains.

Haig arrived to inspect the division in pouring rain. The possibility is that the King had told him about Monash. Haig, Monash wrote, looked grey and old. 'On parting he put his arm around my shoulder (as I rode beside him) and with much feeling and warmth he said: "You have a very fine division. I wish you all sorts of good luck, old man."' Haig wrote in his diary: 'The men looked splendid and marched past in excellent style. M. Gen. Monash seems a clever Australian of Jewish type. I believe an Auctioneer in civil life.' (Haig had confused him with Arthur Currie, the Canadian general.)

The Australians from the other four divisions were still down on the Somme. They thought the 3rd Division had been pampered. One day it might actually do some fighting. They referred to Monash's men as 'the Neutrals' or 'the Deep Thinkers'. They were cold but they had not lost their wit.

GENERAL ROBERT NIVELLE, now commanding the French forces at Verdun, the other charnel house of 1916, had in October retaken Fort Douaumont. The attack was well thought out. Nivelle dropped a tremendous barrage on and around the fort. The Germans fled to shell holes outside. The attack was on a narrow front, but it was a victory, and these were rare enough, and because it was at Verdun it had symbolism as well. Nivelle was the coming man and he now began selling something the politicians found irresistible. He said he had discovered the secret. He knew how to break the trench stalemate.

In mid-December he took over from Joffre as the French commander-in-chief. Joffre had been tough and unflappable and now he was made Marshal of France, the first since 1870, as compensation for being bundled off to an advisory job that didn't matter. He looked grandfatherly. Nivelle, charming and eloquent, had charisma and freshness. He was sixty-one and looked younger.

Nivelle's plan was essentially about repeating the Fort Douaumont tactics on a big scale. There would be a massive artillery bombardment, as at the fort, except this one might be on a front of twenty miles. This would cause *rupture* [his word]. The infantry would then go forward behind a creeping barrage, smashing through three lines of German defences in one rush that might last forty-eight hours. The infantry would use *violence* and *brutality* – as though these things were new – and quickly break through into open country. There would be no attrition, no wearing out. From this distance it is easy to spot flaws in Nivelle's scheme. It is also possible to understand why he charmed the politicians. He was offering hope and Joffre and Haig were offering attrition.

ONE MILLION GERMAN soldiers were dead by the end of 1916. Over their bodies the Kaiser had extended his empire to take in Polish Russia, most of Belgium, much of northern France, Serbia and, most recently, Rumania. Holding on to these gains would mean more Verduns, more Sommes. The complete victories laid out in the Schlieffen Plan were no longer possible. The battle of Jutland meant the blockade of Germany would continue. Civilian life in Germany had become miserable. Malnutrition was common. Austria-Hungary was suffering worse and had been a weak ally, forever in need of stiffening up. Franz Josef, the emperor, had died late in 1916. Karl I, his successor, was looking for a negotiated peace.

Bethmann-Hollweg, the German Chancellor, had been thinking about the same thing. He had been trying privately to persuade Woodrow Wilson, the United States President, to negotiate a peace. Bethmann worried that if the war went on, Hindenburg and Ludendorff would opt for unrestricted submarine warfare to try to make Britain and France suffer as Germany was. This, Bethmann felt, would bring the United States into the war.

In mid-December he spoke about a negotiated peace in the Reichstag, Germany's farcical nod towards democracy. President Wilson asked each side what terms they would settle on. Germany offered no concessions. The allies demanded that Germany and Austria-Hungary give up all their conquests, and a little more as well. And they were unhappy with Wilson's holier-than-thou tone, which came naturally to him. Didn't he realise the Germans were the aggressors, criminals who threatened liberal democracy? Neither side was ready for peace talks. The war would get worse.

Ludendorff was now urging unrestricted submarine warfare to hurt Britain, which still had a huge army of conscripts to put into the war. Bethmann felt he had some say in this since submarine warfare bore on foreign policy, but the Reichstag now passed a motion that defined his place. The Chancellor, the motion said, was responsible to the Reichstag for political decisions relating to the war. But in making decisions he must rely on the view of the Supreme Command. The Reichstag would support a 'ruthless' submarine campaign if the military wanted it. Hindenburg and Ludendorff were running the country.

Their submarine campaign was scheduled to start on February 1, 1917. Neutral countries would be told the day before that all ships travelling to or from Britain and France would be sunk on sight. Hindenburg and Ludendorff also told the Kaiser that Bethmann had to go. He had too many qualms.

CYRIL LAWRENCE, NOW a lieutenant in the engineers of the 1st Australian Division, told his mother that the first thing he heard on Christmas Day was a driver swearing at his horse. The horses were up to their bellies in frozen mud and their long coats were a mass of congealed mud. Lawrence washed and shaved in water from a shell hole and sat down to a Christmas lunch of soup, asparagus with melted butter, roast beef, roast chicken, onions and carrots, then plum pudding and custard with rum sauce – 'a splendiferous affair'. The officers even managed to find a tablecloth.

Soon after Lawrence learned that his father had died. He wrote to his sister that he had become 'sort of reconciled' to death. The previous day he had seen two men carrying a stretcher. The figure on it was completely covered by a blanket.

The bearers were snorting and blowing, in mud up to their knees.

'Heavy going, isn't it,' Lawrence said.

'Oh, no, sir,' one of them said, 'only 'alf of 'im 'ere. A shell copped him and bust 'im and now 'es lost half hisself. Anyhow, we couldn't find the rest of 'im so we brought this bit in.'

PART TWO: 1917

I saw him dead so white and rigid and still and his loved ones left behind him. And we have buried him so far from home amongst strangers to him.

— Pompey Elliott at Polygon Wood

20

'Don't believe a single word of it'

General Nivelle journeyed to London in mid-January to explain his formula for winning the war. He was like a man peddling the patent medicine that is guaranteed to cure arthritis. Lloyd George, still feeling the sharp stabs of the Somme, lunged at the bottle. At the same time the British and Australian troops in the valley between Gueudecourt and Bapaume stood in their trenches and shivered. They were supposed to carry out small wearing-down operations but the mud made these impossible. For both sides the important thing was to stay warm.

Lieutenant Cyril Lawrence, behind the front at Mametz, acquired the sort of batman every officer needed in such conditions. 'Gets quite cross if I do anything at all,' Lawrence wrote to his mother. 'Thieves anything he can lay his hands on or carry if he thinks I may want it. Yesterday on three different occasions he walked in with 3 stoves which he had taken out of other huts. Of course, he was immediately followed by their irate owners. Majors, Captns. and God knows what.' Lawrence's man shrugged off abuse. When a major demanded the return of his stove the batman calmly asked if he could keep the chimney. The snows came on the night of January 17. One day was the coldest in France for twenty-three years.

Lawrence said the cooks took to the meat with an axe. Pickles, cheese and whisky all froze. The temperature dropped to twenty degrees below freezing. Lawrence had to use a candle to thaw the ink in his fountain pen before he could start writing.

Corporal Thomas told his mother he had tied bags around his boots to prevent him from slipping. 'Gad it is awful, too awful, frostbite is very common & cases of frozen to death innumerable . . . why we should be put in the trenches in mid-winter beats most of us.' There was a brazier nearby but, even with two blankets and a greatcoat, he couldn't sleep because of the cold. 'I want nothing but to get away from this awful carnage & waste of splendid lives . . . the whole business is a bad bargain from General down to the private.'

A sergeant in the 4th Division said that no water was carted to the frontline; it was hard enough sending up rations on the backs of mules. The men simply melted ice that had been broken up with an axe. One shell hole, the sergeant said, contained 'lovely clear water' beneath eight inches of ice. The men used it to make tea. After several days one of them noticed a pair of boots in the hole and, on investigation, that these were attached to a body.

Captain Gordon Maxfield, the accountant from Longwood, told his father he had had a 'rotten time' in the trenches in early January. They were more like drains, he said. Then he was given a temporary staff job. 'I now swank round with the General, live in beautiful châteaux and have two horses instead of one – in case one gets tired I suppose.' Next month he was sent back to the trenches. 'Crikey, it is cold – such cold as I never dreamt of.' The mud, instead of being thigh-deep, was now hard. He pitied the horses. They had no shelter at night when there was often twenty-two degrees of frost. As an aside, Maxfield told his father that Bean was the most 'coldly accurate' of the war correspondents. 'Moreover he *sees* what he writes about. He crawled over me in a narrow trench in Pozières orchard, trying to find the 5th Brigade.'

Captain Allan Leane of the 'Joan of Arc' battalion told his mother that he was sitting almost on the top of a brazier in a hut four miles behind the front. It had been snowing for the best part of four days 'and the whole country looks sweet, the ugly scars are for a little while covered & beyond the Boom of our own Heavies & the Crump of Fritz's exploding it would not appear as though a war were raging at all.'

Private David Whinfield of the 5th Division had just arrived at the front after training on Salisbury Plain. While there he had met a boy of fourteen-and-a-half among a new batch of reinforcements. Whinfield's trip across the Channel took less than two hours. 'They say we did 24 miles an hour, went like buggery.' Now, in late January, he was heading for the frontline. The duckboards were a terror, he wrote in his diary. They were all frozen up; one could not obtain a grip. One man had three heavy falls. The temperature dropped to seventeen degrees below freezing during the night. Rations at the front were issued at 8 am. 'Each man gets a quarter small loaf of bread, two tins of butter, one and a half tins of jam and three tins of cheese. And tea supplied for each meal with a 3" × 2" slice of ham for breakfast and a pint of stew for tea. Not forgetting the issue of rum at 9.' The rum mattered: more than anything it warmed the men up.

The generals wanted to keep niggling at the Germans through the winter. Birdwood suggested a series of minor operations along the Australian front. One was an attack on Stormy Trench, in front of Gueudecourt.

WHEN HAIG AND Joffre met at Chantilly in November, 1916, they had agreed to resume their attacks in mid-February and to broaden the Somme battlefield to the north and south. Then Joffre was sacked and Nivelle rejected the Chantilly plan. He would make 'one tremendous effort' in the French sector on the River Aisne. This, he thought, would win the war. The British contribution would be a subsidiary attack in Arras. Nivelle also wanted to put the offensive back from February to April. Haig went along with all of this on the condition that, should the Nivelle offensive fail, the French would support his own scheme to attack in Flanders and clear the Belgian ports. Nivelle readily agreed to this. The Flanders scheme was an irrelevancy: the Germans would no longer be able to hang on in Belgium after he had crushed them on the Aisne.

Lloyd George in mid-January invited Nivelle to London to address the War Cabinet. Robertson and Haig were also invited. Lloyd George first offered some blunt thoughts to Robertson and Haig in private and thereby reminded them that the polite age of Asquith was over. According to Haig, the Prime Minister said the French army was better than Haig's and able to gain ground at less cost of life. Lloyd George said that 'much of our losses on the Somme was wasted, and that the country would not stand any more of that sort of thing.' He said that, to win, 'we must attack on a soft front, and we could not find that on the western front'. Haig told Lloyd George that the general opinion in the British army was that French infantrymen lacked 'discipline and thoroughness'. Here was Haig at his most pompous, obsessed with form rather than substance. The truth was that French infantry tactics were often more sophisticated than those of the British; this had been clear on the first day of the Somme. Here was the formal start of the running scrap between the three men that John Grigg, Lloyd George's biographer, called a grave weakness at the heart of government.

The scrap was, most obviously, about strategy. Robertson and Haig believed the war could only be won on the western front. Lloyd George had since 1915 been searching for soft fronts elsewhere: Gallipoli, Salonika, the Middle East and, most recently, Italy.

Less obviously, the feud was about personalities. Robertson and Haig couldn't quite accept that they were the servants of a civilian who had the cheek – and Lloyd George had lots of that – to meddle in military affairs. Robertson and Lloyd George came from the lower reaches of the social stratum, yet Robertson, who could be gruff and prissy, disapproved of Lloyd George. The Prime Minister had never forgotten where he came from; Robertson had become the defender of a class to which he had never belonged. Robertson was the government's principal military adviser yet his first loyalty was not to his Prime Minister but to the patrician Haig. Haig had never approved of Lloyd George: he wasn't a gentleman. Haig's loyalty was to God and George V, with whom he conducted an improper correspondence. Lloyd George, it should be said, didn't help himself. He was not comfortable with soldiers, or at least with generals. He had never allowed them to know him. He had not visited the army in France as often as he should have when he was War Minister. And he was wrong about strategy: the war was not going to be won from Palestine or the Balkans.

One can only wonder at how things might have gone if Robertson and Haig had been articulate. Both could write sharp and clear reports. Both were hopeless at conversation: they could not present a case, let alone coax and persuade. They should have been able to explain to Lloyd George why his ideas on strategy were wrong.

ROBERT NIVELLE WAS better than articulate. He was a salesman who could invest a word such as *rupture* with magical properties, as though no general had thought about the tactics of breakthrough before him. The solution was so simple and others had walked straight past it. And of course he was selling something Lloyd George was likely to buy: a big offensive on the western front – but with the French doing most of the fighting. This was even more attractive than a big offensive on the Italian front with the Italians doing most of the fighting. Nivelle charmed the War Cabinet with his fluent English, his sureness and energy. He failed to charm Robertson and Haig, who knew there was more to breakthrough than a string of catchwords. They did not demur, however. This may have been due to courtesy, and perhaps also to their inability to find the right words.

These two went along with the War Cabinet's endorsement of Nivelle's scheme. Lloyd George went to unusual lengths to bind them into what would be called the Nivelle offensive. He instructed Robertson to tell Haig by letter that Cabinet expected the agreement with Nivelle to be carried out 'both in the letter and in the spirit'. Haig wrote in his diary that he thought the War Cabinet's conclusions 'hastily considered'.

Haig, now back in France, had George Bernard Shaw to lunch –

'an interesting man of original views'. Shortly after Major-General Frederick Maurice, the director of military operations at the War Office, arrived. Maurice told Haig he had been an admirer of Lloyd George; now he distrusted him. The Prime Minister was 'sketchy'; he didn't go into things thoroughly. 'It is, indeed, a calamity for the country to have such a man at the head of affairs in this time of great crisis. We can only try and make the best of him.'

CAPTAIN MAXFIELD WAS right to call Bean the most 'coldly accurate' of the war journalists. Bean later became an equally accurate historian. If he said seven men were running north along a trench and that one of them was a prospector from Norseman with a cleft palate, the reader could be sure that Bean had verified this from two or three sources and perhaps even gone to the spot and taken a compass reading. When it came to high-ranking officers, however, Bean would occasionally omit things and play favourites. So it was with his brief account in the official history of how generals McCay and Legge lost their field commands during the winter of 1917. Bean teased a little. He wrote that 'certain officers after prolonged trial were held to lack, or to have lost, some quality essential for command at the front. This was believed to be the case with Generals Legge of the 2nd Division and McCay of the 5th.' Then he danced away.

The reality was that McCay didn't know as much as he thought he did; that he was cranky and officious, more like a schoolmaster than a leader of soldiers; that for most of his military life he had quarrelled with superiors and subordinates; that he inspired little affection, either from his troops or his staff officers; that his performance at Fromelles had been poor, before, during and after the battle. McCay was also thought to be physically ill. And indeed he had been unlucky in his three major enterprises, the victim of a miscarried plan at the Gallipoli landing, of Hunter-Weston at Krithia and Haking at Fromelles.

Legge went into Pozières with much experience in administration and little in the field, which meant he was bound to be unlucky too. He was a victim of the Australian Government's insistence that, if possible, its divisions should be commanded by Australians. Perhaps Birdwood and White should have done more to protect Legge from Gough at Pozières. Some said Legge was in poor health by the time of the Somme winter; Legge himself said he had not been ill for one day in France.

McCay went to England to take charge of the depots around Salisbury, his ambition undimmed. Legge returned to Australia to become Inspector-General. His eldest son died in France as a private.

At around the same time as McCay and Legge departed, Vaughan Cox, the Anglo-Indian general, lost command of the 4th Division. This had nothing to do with his performance and everything to do with the Australian Government's wish to replace Englishmen with Australians.

So, suddenly, while the war had been reduced to ritual shelling, three divisions needed commanders. One trouble with the Australian Government's policy was that, at this point in the war, there were not enough Australians with sufficient experience to fill the vacancies. Thus Legge's 2nd Division went to Nevill Smyth, the Englishman and Victoria Cross winner who had led the 1st Australian Brigade to victory at Lone Pine. The 4th Division went to the Sydney-born William Holmes, who had been a citizen-soldier as a ten-year-old. Talbot Hobbs, who arrived in Australia from London as a three-year-old, took command of McCay's 5th Division. Hobbs, an artilleryman, had been a prominent architect in Perth. He had commanded the 1st Division artillery at Gallipoli, which gave him little chance to show his talents because he never had enough guns. Hobbs was an outstanding and thoughtful soldier with lots of good sense. He was short and slightly built, with what seemed like a nervous manner. He was often seen in the front trenches and the men warmed to him as they had never done to McCay.

HOLMES' FIRST TASK as commander of the 4th Division was to assault Stormy Trench, about 100 yards in front of the Australian line. The objective had no particular significance; the attack was simply to keep pressure on the Germans. Holmes sent in the 15th Battalion on February 1. The Queenslanders and Tasmanians took the trench easily enough but were thrown out by German counter-attacks and ran up 144 casualties. Holmes then sent in the 13th Battalion, which included Harry Murray's company.

Lieutenant-Colonel James Durrant, a permanent army officer from Glenelg, South Australia, commanded the 13th. The preparations he now made were an example of how attacks, even minor ones, should have been conducted on the western front, and usually weren't. He took an interest in the artillery plan: he didn't want his men exposed to German machine-gun fire in the snow and ice of no-man's land. He sent his company commanders out to scout no-man's land. Murray had a fine eye for the lie of country. When he returned he knew exactly where the wire was and had worked out the quickest route back. Durrant knew that his troops would be counter-attacked in Stormy Trench, just as the 15th had been. He loaded his men with bombs. The specialist bombers each carried twenty and infantrymen stuffed their greatcoat pockets with them, so that they clunked against their thighs. Harry Murray's company alone, some 140 men, carried more than 2000 grenades, including some that could be fired by a blank cartridge in rifles. The men were told to wrap sandbags around their boots so that the Germans would not hear them assembling. Lewis guns were rubbed with kerosene to keep them from freezing. The men were given a rum ration before the assault to warm them up.

Eight men of the 13th who were due to take leave in London volunteered to stay behind for the attack. A lieutenant in Murray's company who was in bed with dysentery announced that he was taking part. Murray had come down with influenza. A doctor, Major Roy Winn, attended him, found he had a temperature of 103 degrees and decided to send him out of the line. According to Winn, the conversation went like this:

Murray: You can cut that out. I'm not going away.
Winn: Not going? You'll get pneumonia if you don't. In fact I'm not too certain you haven't got it already.

Murray: Pneumonia or not, I'm not going to hospital. I'm going to take
Stormy Trench tomorrow.
Winn: Don't be silly. You're not fit.
Murray: I tell you I'm going to take Stormy Trench; and what's more let
me tell you, I'm going to keep it.

MURRAY, SHIVERING WITH fever, went for Stormy Trench on the night
of February 4. His company was on the right of the attack. Here,
paraphrased, is his account of what happened.

The night was one of austere beauty. A mantle of frozen snow
flooded by rich moonlight hid the scars of previous battles. The
men, many of them reinforcements who had never been under fire
before, lay on the snow, waiting. A whisper came back to Murray:
could they smoke? Many would not see the sunrise; a cigarette
would be a comfort. Yes, they could smoke, but one cigarette had
to be lit from another, lest the flare of a match be spotted. Three
minutes before the Australian barrage opened up the order 'Smokes
out' was whispered along the line. Men looked at their rifles and
fingered pockets that were bulging with grenades.

The artillery opened up. The horizon leapt into quick stabbing
flashes. The rush of the shells overhead made the men jump. Now
they edged forward. No fire from the German trench. The barrage
had been accurate. It was better to crawl. If one stood upright the
shells shrieking overhead seemed too close. The barrage lifted
exactly on time. The Australians rushed Stormy Trench.

The Germans sheltering in the bottom surrendered. The bombers
swung down the trench to the right, rushing traverse after traverse.
Lance-Corporal Roy Withers peered into a dugout and called on
the occupants to surrender. A shot rang out. Withers had a bullet
hole in his ear and was now very angry. He pulled the pins on two
Mills bombs, shouted 'Split that, and that, you -------s', and threw
them into the dugout. There was a yell below as the grenades went
off, then silence. There had been eight Germans down there. Seven
died outright. The eighth, an officer, staggered up. His body was
shattered; all that animated him was his spirit. He growled from the

spouting wound that had been his mouth. Murray thought he had never heard anything more terrible than that growl, which he took to be a surrender. The Australians tried to help the German. Murray felt it would have been a kindness to have shot him. The German died shortly afterwards.

The Australians built a bomb-stop across the trench and prepared for a counter-attack. They were no longer cold and there had been few casualties. Then the counter-attack came: artillery and mortar fire, then German bombers. Some Australians went beyond Stormy Trench, looking for the German bombers. Corporal Malcolm Robertson had been twice buried. Shell splinters had cut his face. But he kept firing rifle grenades, sitting with his rifle between his knees, the stock on the ground, checking his angle of sight of each shot.

The Australians' casualties were now heavy. The German bombers retreated, which allowed their artillery to start up again. The trench sides were torn away in frozen boulders of black earth. It was hard to find temporary havens for the wounded. The men became terribly thirsty. The water in their canteens had frozen. Some used pocket knives to chip lumps of ice out of their bottles.

The artillery fire suddenly stopped and the German bombers returned. The Australians sent up an SOS flare and their artillery replied. But the German bombers kept coming back. When they left the German artillery started up again. Those Australians not killed were knocked off their feet and buried. Then the German bombers came back again. Corporal Robertson, despite the wounds to his face, kept firing his rifle grenades and cheered on the bomb-throwers. Roy Withers, now wounded in the knee, hobbled along the trench, throwing grenades as fast as he could pull the pins. When that counter-attack ended the company was down to forty men, enough perhaps to repel one more bombing attack. But none came.

In daylight the Australians looked around and saw that the neat trench they had captured, six-foot deep and four-feet wide, was now just a depression strewn with boulders of frozen earth. Murray counted sixty-one dead Germans and twenty dead Australians in a short stretch of the trench. The Australians were still trying to prise ice out of their water bottles. A fresh company relieved Murray's men, who now discovered they had no cigarettes. A tarpaulin muster was organised, each man throwing whatever coins he could spare onto a tarpaulin. Two men were then sent to the canteen, which was just behind the front, for cigarettes.

THAT IS PRETTY much how Murray told the story in *Reveille*. All the descriptions are his. Murray left out certain things.

He didn't mention that he was close to pneumonia as he crawled out across no-man's land. He didn't mention that during one of the bomb fights he jumped out of Stormy Trench to charge six Germans, shooting three and capturing the others. Or that he carried at least three wounded Australians to safety, that bullets had torn holes in his uniform, that his hand was lacerated. And of course he didn't say, would never say, that he inspired his men by example.

Colonel Durrant recommended Murray, Withers and Robertson for the Victoria Cross. Five weeks later came the news that the award had been approved for Murray. Withers and Robertson received the Distinguished Conduct Medal. The following month Murray wrote to an old comrade, Cyril Longmore, to tell him of the death of a mutual friend, then added: 'My getting the VC was all rot and I'm seriously annoyed about it. I hate people booming a chap that is in no way entitled to it, and for god's sake, if you see anymore about me in the press don't believe a single word of it.'

After the war Colonel Durrant said: 'Harry Murray was not recommended for his VC because of one action. He was recommended because he gave more than brawn; he gave brains over a sustained period of twenty-four hours.'

RAIN RETURNED TO the Australian front in mid-February. The snow melted, mists and fogs rolled in and the battlefield became a bog again. It also become unusually quiet. The German artillery was hardly firing. Nor were its machine-gun posts. The Australians didn't think much about this. The Germans were always *there*, a few hundred yards ahead of you. That was one of the truths of the war.

On February 24 a British corps reported that the Germans had abandoned their front trenches. The Australian divisions were told to probe forward. They found the same thing. The Germans had gone. The idea seemed beyond imagination. Next day Haig wrote in his diary: 'Important developments have been taking place . . . The enemy had fallen back on a front of 18,000 yards . . .'

THREE DAYS EARLIER Haig had made another entry that didn't seem particularly important. Lloyd George wanted to hold a meeting, perhaps in Calais, about the problems with the French railways. Robertson was coming over for it. Aristide Briand, the French Prime Minister, and Nivelle would also attend. Haig and Nivelle had already agreed on what needed to be done about the railways. If Haig thought it strange that two prime ministers needed to go to Calais to talk about rolling stock, he didn't say so.

YOU DRIVE INTO Gueudecourt along a sunken road and on to what was once the Australian winter line. It is high summer but you know at once that this would be a cruel place in winter. It is open and exposed: no woods, no hedgerows; depressions here and there offer the only shelter. Friesian cows crop the short grass, withered by the sun but still light green. A Frenchman points towards the old front. Corporal Adolf Hitler, he tells us, was stationed over there in October, 1916. You look to where Stormy Trench once was. Nothing to see, just a fallowed field and a lone tree. There is an old trench practically at our feet. Its floor has been steadily filling up with red-tinged earth and pine needles; it is now only three-feet deep. But we should spare it more than a glance. It was an Australian trench. And it is the last scar from the Somme winter of 1917.

21

The plague bacillus

Haig must have assumed that military strategy would be raised at some point during the Calais conference that was supposed to be about railways. Nivelle was about to begin an offensive that, he claimed, would win the war. Someone would surely want to say something about it. What Haig didn't foresee was an ambush.

Thirteen days before the Calais conference Lloyd George interrupted a conversation between Maurice Hankey, the secretary to the War Cabinet, and the French liaison officer at the War Office. It turned out more than an interruption. The Prime Minister loitered with intent for two hours. He had a point to make. And he wanted that point relayed to Paris. Lloyd George told the Frenchman that the War Cabinet had 'complete confidence' in Nivelle. He was 'the only man who is capable of bringing the operations to a successful conclusion this year'. The Prime Minister said he was trying to bring his colleagues around to this view, but did not count on doing so – unless Nivelle and the French Government took a strong line on the subject. Lloyd George was prepared to subordinate Haig to Nivelle and he wanted the liaison officer to pass on the news to Paris, which he of course did.

The War Cabinet met ten days later. Robertson usually attended such meetings. Hankey telephoned him to say there was no need to attend this one. Robertson didn't go. The meeting gave Lloyd George authority at Calais to seek 'such measures as might appear best calculated . . . to ensure unity of command'. It is not clear whether all members of the War Cabinet took this to mean that Haig would be subordinated to Nivelle. The King was not told of the ambush that awaited Haig. Nor were the dominions, even though Lloyd George's scheme meant that Nivelle would have control of Australian, Canadian and New Zealand troops.

The conference that wasn't really about railways opened at the Hotel of the Gare Maritime after lunch on February 26 and after Lloyd George and Briand had met privately for half-an-hour. The initial discussion was about railways, but it lasted only about an hour. Then Lloyd George broke in and suggested that the railway specialists withdraw elsewhere so that the more important question of military plans could be settled at once.

Lloyd George asked Nivelle to explain his plan again, which was strange because everyone knew the details. Nivelle finished and Lloyd George appeared to become impatient. He turned to Briand and, according to Haig, said: 'Tell him to keep nothing back . . . as to his disagreements with Marshal Haig.' There had been no differences of significance. Nivelle, as one historian pointed out, had failed to take his cue. Lloyd George now suggested that the French draw up their proposals for a system of command before dinner so that he, Robertson and Haig could discuss it after dinner. Lloyd George didn't appear at dinner; he said he was ill. Haig dined with Nivelle and said he had 'quite a cheery talk' with him.

Robertson read the French proposals in his room. They had obviously been drafted several days before. Haig's army, some sixty-odd British and dominion divisions, would be put under Nivelle's command. Haig would be responsible for administrative matters, and not much more. An observer said Robertson's face turned to mahogany and his eyes became perfectly round. His eyebrows slanted outwards 'like a forest of bayonets held at the charge'. He looked as though he was about to have a fit. 'Get 'Aig,' he shouted.

Haig arrived. He was appalled, but there was a serenity about him, as though he was above such grubbiness. Robertson dealt with the frocks in London: he would have to sort this out. Hankey, as secretary to the War Cabinet, must have had a rough idea of what was going to unfold, but he too was said to be surprised when he saw the precise wording of the French proposals. Later in the night, he upset Robertson and Haig further by telling them that the Prime Minister did not have full authority from the War Cabinet for what he was doing.

Before that, Robertson and Haig had gone to Lloyd George's room. The way Haig tells it, there was a discussion. The way Hankey tells it, there was a row, and one is inclined to believe him. Hankey said Lloyd George was 'extremely brutal' to Haig. Haig said his troops would not serve under a Frenchman. The Prime Minister replied that he knew the British private soldier and there were people he criticised much more than Nivelle.

Robertson and Haig left and talked some more. According to Haig's diary, they decided they must resign rather than agree to the scheme. 'And so we went to bed, thoroughly disgusted with our Government and the Politicians.'

Only Haig slept the sleep of the good. Robertson didn't sleep at all. Lloyd George slept poorly. Hankey sat up and worked on a compromise. He was fortyish and wore a languid air, a soldier with a keen and subtle mind that he was careful not to flaunt. The scheme he devised became the basis for a new proposal the next day. The subordination of the British army would last only for the duration of the Nivelle offensive. Haig would have a right of appeal to his own government if he thought Nivelle's orders put his troops at unnecessary risk. And Haig would retain control of operations in his own sector. Robertson and Haig agreed to the scheme, although, if anything, their contempt for the politicians had been heightened by the compromise. Hankey and Robertson had saved Haig, who didn't seem as grateful as he might have been. The *coup de théâtre* scripted by Lloyd George and Briand had failed, mostly because of their clumsiness.

There *was* a case for a unified command on the western front and the highest position obviously had to go to a Frenchman. France was where the war was; she had 112 divisions in the field, compared with Britain's sixty-two. John Grigg, Lloyd George's biographer, points out that the scheme Lloyd George took to Calais was twice flawed. An allied supremo couldn't be responsible to one of the national governments, as Nivelle was. He had to be an allied officer responsible to an allied war council. And, second, Nivelle was the wrong man. Political difficulties had already started to overwhelm him.

And now they worsened. In mid-March the Briand Government fell. Alexandre Ribot became Premier and Paul Painlevé, a brilliant mathematician, took over as War Minister. Painlevé didn't like Nivelle's sums. He wanted to remove him and cancel his offensive but couldn't find a way. Nivelle's only champion now was far away in London. Lloyd George had to believe in Nivelle. He had gambled on him in London and doubled his bets at Calais.

Nivelle had another problem that he refused to see. The German withdrawal on the Somme and elsewhere to a new defensive position – the Hindenburg Line, as the allies called it – had changed the battlefield. And now too there were doubts about the eastern ally. A revolution had begun in Russia. The Tsar had abdicated. The allies had not seen the Hindenburg Line being thrown up amid the mists and snows of winter. Neither side had foreseen the Russian Revolution.

IMMEDIATELY THE CALAIS conference ended Haig wrote to his King, who also happened to be Tsar Nicholas II's cousin. The letter was not only improper but also rather clever. Haig said, in effect, that he had been ambushed at Calais. 'I think, as the actual document stands, no great difficulty should occur in carrying on just as I have been doing, *provided* there is not something behind it. It is for this reason I have written so fully, in order that Your Majesty may be watchful, and prevent any steps being taken which will result in our Army being broken up and incorporated in French Corps.' Haig said that throughout his dealings he had never offered to resign, but it was possible that the War Cabinet might want to replace him with someone more in their confidence. If this was so, the change should be made quickly. 'At this great crisis in our History, my sole object is to serve my King and Country ... I leave myself to Your Majesty's hands to decide what is best for me to do at this juncture.'

If Haig was trying to alarm the King, he succeeded. The King's private secretary wrote to thank him for his 'secret letter'. He must not think of resignation. That would be disastrous for His Majesty's army. 'Such a step would never have His Majesty's consent, nor does he believe that it is one entertained for a moment by his Government ... I am to say from His Majesty you are not to worry: you may be certain that he will do his utmost to protect your interests, and he begs you to continue to work on the most amicable and open terms with General Nivelle, and he feels all will come right.'

Constitutional monarchy takes many forms.

LATE IN OCTOBER, 1916, British airmen had noticed fresh earth thrown up around the villages of Quéant and Bullecourt. The Germans looked to be digging a trench and this was strange. The villages were about fourteen miles behind the front in Arras. Next month a Russian prisoner who had escaped to the French lines said that 2000 of his countrymen were being forced to build concrete dugouts, protected by wire, near St Quentin, thirty miles south of Bullecourt and behind the Somme front. Here were the first clues that the Hindenburg Line was being built, but allied intelligence officers did not connect the two events. There is no reason why they should have.

Only on February 25, 1917, the day after Australian troops had discovered the Germans had deserted their trenches, were the British able to plot the course of the new German defences. But they could only do so for their own sector. The French, to the south, didn't know where the Hindenburg Line ended.

In fact it ran for seventy miles to the Chemin des Dames ridge, where Nivelle intended to conduct his war-winning offensive in

The line at the end of the Somme battle

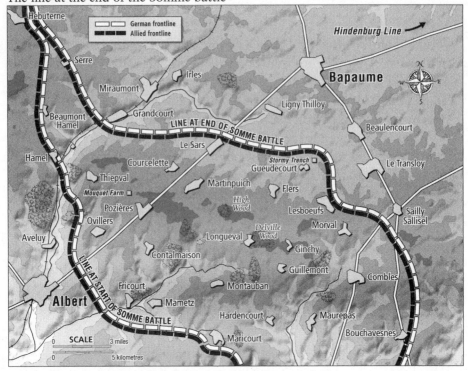

The pursuit to the Hindenburg Line

April. The Germans were to pull back fifteen to twenty-five miles along the length of it. The withdrawal was codenamed 'Alberich', after the cruel dwarf of German mythology, and his spirit dominated the orders. More than 100,000 French civilians were sent to Germany and Belgium as the Germans turned the country between the old frontline and the new into a wasteland. They wrecked houses, smashed crockery and seared upholstered chairs with hot irons. They fouled wells with horse manure and cut down fruit trees. These orders so offended Crown Prince Rupprecht of Bavaria, the commander on the Hindenburg Line front, that he considered resigning. He also thought the vandalism would give the Germans a bad name. Throughout the war the Germans had handed propaganda weapons, loaded and cocked, to the allies: the murder of Belgian civilians in 1914, the sinking of the *Lusitania*, the execution of Edith Cavell – now this.

The orders came from Ludendorff. He deplored the destruction, he said, 'but it could not be helped'. In ordering the withdrawal he was saying Germany could fight only on the defensive on the western front during 1917. He was outnumbered there by about 190 divisions to 154. He was hoping that German sailors could win the war with submarines, and do so before the United States was drawn in. He had not thought about a revolution in Russia. Such talk had been around for decades.

The Hindenburg Line was about economy: it eliminated two big salients bulging into the allied line, shortened the front by twenty-five miles and thus freed up thirteen to fourteen divisions. The new line was stronger than the old one. The Germans had turned the techniques of mass production to trench-building. The woodwork was of the same design throughout. So were the concrete dugouts beneath the parapet. The barbed wire hung from corkscrew pickets in three belts and shone new and blue in the sun. The line was 8000-yards deep in places.

Now it was ready. Ludendorff knew the allies would attack after the thaw. But where? Then Germans came upon an order, carried by a French prisoner, concerning a great French attack to be carried out on the River Aisne. Nivelle had already given up surprise.

BRITISH TROOPS WALKED into the villages of Miraumont and Pys on February 24. A few miles away the three Australian divisions left at the front (the 4th Division had been pulled out) were at once ordered out into the fog to occupy the ground the Germans had left. This meant advances of 1200 yards, maybe more if no Germans were found. Queenslanders, apprehensive about what they might find, leapt into a German trench near the Maze – and put up a black cat that bounded away at the sight of them. Not a single German. Australian lighthorsemen trotted up to the front. They and their shaggy mounts were going to do what cavalry used to do: ride out as a screen for the advancing infantry.

The Australian infantrymen were like convicts emerging from a prison hulk. The routines of confinement were no more: it was exhilarating and baffling. Somewhere up ahead there would be green fields and trees and birds and some day soon the sun would shine. Lieutenant Cyril Lawrence wrote that the horses went 'mad with delight' when they reached open country. 'After all those months of standing knee and more than often belly deep in half-frozen slush, they were crazy and tore round everywhere over the little hills and valleys just like lambs at play.'

Captain Ellis, the historian of the 5th Division, said that the end of trench warfare produced a 'spiritual thrill'. Ellis said the men had 'grown insensibly' into the habits of stalemate. Individual enterprise had fallen away. The infantry had grown used to fixed trench positions, the artillery to fixed battery positions. A colonel in the 1st Division found one of his Lewis-gun posts allowing retreating Germans to walk about with impunity 600 yards away. The men thought they were 'too far away' to fire at.

The generals didn't share the elation of their men. They saw the cleverness of Ludendorff's move. They knew it could undermine the logic of Haig's coming offensive in Arras, which, in turn, was to be the prelude to Nivelle's offensive on the Aisne.

The Germans were retiring in stages, holding up the allies here and there with bursts of machine-gun fire, then scurrying off. They had a timetable but the allies didn't yet know what it was. Where were the Germans going to stop? At the Hindenburg Line itself, or at some spot short of it? The orders to the Australians were to advance cautiously and not to get too far ahead of their artillery.

By late February the Australians had passed Le Barque, the village where Hitler had been stationed the previous year. Now they were in green country in front of Bapaume, the market town with ramparts and moat. They came on booby traps in the empty trenches but most of them were obvious: objects that might be picked up wired to a hidden grenade, loose floorboards hooked up to a mine. March 11 produced the first glorious spring day. The men's spirits rose.

Six days later, on St Patrick's Day, they were in Bapaume. The Germans had fought like fanatics for holes in the ground at Mouquet Farm and dozens of other killing grounds on the Somme. Now they had abandoned a big town without a fight, leaving just a few skirmishers behind. Plumes of white and grey smoke rose from burning houses. Men of the 5th Division simply walked into the town.

Private Eric West, a student at Roseworthy Agricultural College in South Australia before the war, was repairing the road outside Bapaume with rubble taken from the ruined villages to the west. Earlier he had walked through those villages. He came to country strewn with dead, he wrote to his father. 'In places they lie around in dozens. No doubt most are months old. The cold frosty weather preserves them pretty well. It is very interesting but *very* pathetic and gruesome. Here is a testament near a dead man. I open it and see on the first page: "To dear Jack, from Mable." Here is another man, a prayer book is beside him; I look for the man's name in it, but the first page is torn out. Evidently it has been used for identification purposes.'

West walked into Bapaume. 'It had been knocked about far worse than Albert. I don't believe there is one house intact . . . After the Germans had retired, three snipers were left here . . . They sniped a number of men before they were caught. I think they wanted to surrender at the end but were not allowed.'

Private David Whinfield dozed most of his first day near Bapaume. The next day, the 18th, he moved off with full pack as part of Pompey Elliott's force to pursue the Germans. He walked through the village of Bancourt, just east of Bapaume. 'No building is a quarter sound,' he wrote in his diary. 'Explosives have been used. It was not spoiled by shellfire. Trees have been cut down, fruit trees too and just let lay there. Vandalism. A road crossing nearby had a mine exploded in it. The hole was twenty feet across.' But Whinfield was happy. It was a nice spring day and he had heard a lark singing.

THE FIRST RUSSIAN revolution didn't happen because a firebrand climbed on to a platform and spoke words that exploded in people's minds. That would come later. The first revolution grew out of the combination of a shortage of bread in Petrograd, the capital, and a burst of winter sunshine. The shortage of bread in early March was just one symptom of how the war was hurting Russia; prices had increased fourfold since the war began and misery was everywhere. Then, around March 8 (February 23 on the Julian calendar that the Russians were using then), a weak winter sun glinted on the snow. The kinder weather allowed open-air demonstrations. These led to strikes and the burning of the law courts and police stations. In short there was civil unrest – no more. Petrograd (formerly St Petersburg) was home to a large garrison of soldiers. They were expected to reassert the Tsar's authority. Instead most of them joined in the demonstrations. And, at this point, a protest became a revolution, almost by accident, and with an element missing. The people wanted to get rid of the Tsar but there was no consensus on who or what should replace him. The British ambassador's daughter overheard a conversation between two soldiers.

'What we want is a republic,' said one.

'Yes,' said the other. 'A republic, but we must have a good Tsar at the head of it!'

Russia had suffered fearfully from the war. By now there were more than five million dead and wounded. But there was another figure that better explained the low morale of the army. Around two million Russians had become prisoners of war. The mass surrenders had nothing to do with the bravery or otherwise of the soldiers. They had everything to do with bad leadership and the fact that the average Russian soldier was poorly equipped and clothed, tired, cold, hungry and inured to failure. He also knew that his family was suffering back home, from soaring prices and black marketeering, shortages of food and fuel and the heartlessness of the tsarist system.

Nicholas was a dull and simple man who believed that God had appointed him and there was nothing more to say. The Enlightenment, French republicanism, constitutional monarchy, American democracy: these were for other men and other places. Nicholas was distant from his people and distrustful of intellectuals on the grounds that they might be smarter than him, which they invariably were. He resisted all attempts at liberal reform. In his heart and his head he was a medievalist, yet he lacked the willpower, the sureness, to be the man he wanted to be. Alexandra, his German-born wife and mother of their five children, had the mental toughness he lacked. She is credited with turning him against his military commander, Grand Duke Nicholas, whom he dismissed in 1915. The Tsar himself now became the commander-in-chief and moved to general headquarters at Moghilev, behind the Polish front, where he presided over a succession of defeats and became more isolated from the mood of the capital. The contempt for him went beyond the new proletariat to much of educated society, as well as conservatives and traditionalists. Most of the generals believed he should go.

He was at Moghilev when the riots broke out in Petrograd and tried to return, but his train was stopped about 100 miles south of the capital. There, on March 15, he abdicated in favour of his son, a twelve-year-old haemophiliac, who, ever so fleetingly, became Tsar Alexis II. That night, having been told that his son's condition was incurable, Nicholas changed his mind. He would abdicate in favour of his brother Mikhail. Mikhail became Tsar for about as long as young Alexis before deciding that he too wanted to abdicate. The 300-year-old rule of the Romanovs was over.

It had all happened too abruptly. Nicholas had been succeeded not by a man or an idea but by a vacuum. There was no suggestion, however, that Russia would pull out of the war. The President of the Duma, Russia's pathetic attempt at a parliament, told the British military attaché: 'My dear Knox, you must be easy . . . Russia is a big country, and we can wage war and manage a revolution at the same time.'

The competitors for power were the Duma and the Petrograd Soviet, the committees of factory workers, soldiers and middle-class intellectuals. Among the political groups the Petrograd Soviet claimed to represent were the Bolsheviks. They alone wanted to pull out of the war, but they were a minority and two of their most prominent leaders, Lenin and Leon Trotsky, were in exile. The Duma set up a provisional government and pledged to keep Russia in the war. The Soviet passed its famous Order No. 1, telling the military to obey only the orders of the Soviet. The army was broken in spirit before the revolution; now it was being torn apart.

This was not obvious in the west, which had been taken by surprise. Lloyd George welcomed the revolution publicly – the Tsar's medieval ways had long embarrassed his British and French allies – but privately feared that Russia was not ready for its lurch towards republicanism. Ludendorff saw an opportunity. What he had to do was to find a way to take Russia out of the war. Then he could transfer whole armies to the western front and go on the offensive. A brother-exile burst into Lenin's study in Zurich to tell him of the revolution. Lenin denounced the provisional government's decision to stay in the war and coined the slogan: 'All power to the Soviets.'

Alexander Helphand (real name Israel Parvus), a revolutionary from Odessa now living in Germany, was a conspirator of genius and a man of lurid contradictions. He managed to combine Bolshevism with war profiteering. He was a friend of Lenin and trusted by prominent Germans. Helphand was fiftyish, fat, balding and persuasive. In mid-March he came to Ludendorff with a scheme that would change the world.

Russia could be taken out of the war, he explained, not with howitzers but by shipping a single man there to do what came naturally to him. With Lenin in Petrograd, Helphand argued, the

Bolsheviks would unseat the provisional government and take Russia out of the war. Ludendorff arranged for a sealed train to take Lenin and other exiled revolutionaries from Switzerland across Germany and on, finally, to Finland Station in Petrograd. Churchill wrote in one of his memorable passages: 'The German leaders turned upon Russia the most grisly of all weapons. They tranported Lenin in a sealed truck like a plague bacillus from Switzerland into Russia.'

Unlike Tsar Nicholas, Lenin was the true autocrat, sure of himself, cold and ruthless, a logician of revolution who was never going to worry about the means if the right end was in sight. The liberals and ditherers in the provisional government didn't stand much of a chance against such a force. So here he was, on April 16, at Finland Station with his vaulting forehead and withering glare. The revolution had its firebrand.

WALTER ADCOCK OF the 2nd Australian Division was resting in the village of Favreuil, near Bapaume. He and others were sheltering in a house that still had beds, mirrors, tables and chairs. It was 'cosy looking' and brought on nostalgia. 'It is a long, long time since I have heard the voice of a child, and it seems ever so long since I have heard the voice of a woman. Men, men, men, from daylight to sunset . . .' That night Adcock drew a picture of soldiers at rest. Two were shelling boiled eggs. One was daydreaming. One man was cleaning out an old sandbag so that he could use it to carry rations. Another was enjoying a dixie-lid of rice he had scrounged. Several men were playing poker on the floor by the light of a half-inch of candle. Two idiots – 'we have quite a lot in the army' – were wrestling and swearing in another corner. Another soldier was catching insects – the men called them 'chats' – that had burrowed into his shirt. Next to him a young man was reading the Bible. Another was scraping mud from his boots with a bayonet.

These homely scenes were about to end. Private Adcock's brigade, the 6th, commanded by Gellibrand, would be one of two columns sent out to pursue the Germans to the Hindenburg Line, six to eight miles away. Pompey Elliott would command the other column. Elliott was excited: this was like the military history he had read as a young man.

HAIG WANTED THESE two columns, and those from the British divisions, to push forward cautiously. His main concern was his Arras offensive, due to open in a fortnight as the overture to Nivelle's offensive. Haig didn't want distractions and he didn't want to lose men he might need in Arras. Gough, who again had the Australians as part of his 5th Army, decided to chase the Germans with small columns that would be combinations of infantry, cavalry and field artillery. The main body would not be following. This pleased Elliott and Gellibrand, both unconventional soldiers who ached to be free of staff officers bearing sheaves of paper. General White, the staff officer's staff officer, tried to limit their independence by imposing daily limits on their advances. Both brigadiers, he thought, 'required holding'.

The interlude of open warfare began on the night of March 17. Elliott headed east along the line of the Roman road that ran on from Bapaume to Cambrai; Gellibrand, on his left, pushed northeast. The country fell in gentle valleys towards the Hindenburg Line. There were a dozen villages and hamlets ahead but hardly a fence or a farmhouse. Bright green grass peeped through the last straggles of winter snow. The allied cavalry and infantry actually *manoeuvred*. This hadn't happened since 1914.

But, as George Wieck, Elliott's brigade-major, noted, the mindset of the trenches lingered. The men were nervous about moving in the open – 'even one distant rifle shot would send a whole platoon to ground.' It was all so different. On its first day out Elliott's column advanced some four miles, took a village and a fortified farmhouse, and incurred casualties of eight. At Fromelles the same brigade had run up close to 1700 casualties in a night trying to advance 400 yards. Elliott was affronted by what the Germans had done. He told his sister-in-law: 'They've even bashed the poor kiddies' toys to pieces and burned them and chopped down all the fruit trees and put poison or nightsoil into the water.'

Elliott took three more villages but was worried by flanking fire from Bertincourt on his right, which was outside his zone of command. Next day he took that village anyway, and two more. Birdwood was angry that Elliott had ventured into British territory to take Bertincourt. White told Elliott he would have to curb his 'Napoleonic ideas'. White later said Elliott had cut an 'amusing figure' during the advance: he thought he was J.E.B. Stuart (the fabled cavalryman from the American Civil War), and that 'the whole German army was retiring before him'. Elliott was told to halt his advance.

Then the Germans counter-attacked one of the villages that Elliott had taken. Now Elliott was angry. 'Counter-attack me, would they?' he shouted. 'I'll teach them.' He paced and swore. 'I'll teach the bastards to attack me.' He decided to assault the next two villages on his list. George Wieck reminded him that he had been told not to attack any more villages. 'I don't care if I hang for it,' Elliott said. Wieck felt that Hobbs, the new divisional commander, at least had to be told that his orders were being ignored. He drafted a message for divisional headquarters and took it to Elliott. Elliott read it, thought about it for a moment, then said: 'Send it.' Hobbs refused to countenance the attacks.

A few days later Elliott wrote to his wife: 'The old Bosche cannot fight very well in the open, and my boys have found it out and are eager for the job . . . It is just the fun of the world.'

The 'old Bosches' were in truth fighting a delaying action, holding up the advance here and there, fighting briefly then running. The old war, they knew, would be resumed at the Hindenburg Line.

GELLIBRAND'S COLUMN, TO the north of Elliott, swept through the villages just as quickly. The Germans seemed to be falling back on Lagnicourt, about a mile-and-a-half in front of the Hindenburg Line. Gellibrand made a lunge towards Noreuil, probably the most important village after Lagnicourt, and was repulsed with more than 300 casualties. Like Elliott, Gellibrand wanted to chase the

Germans hard. Like Elliott, Gellibrand now came to be seen as a hothead by Birdwood.

Gellibrand's brigade was withdrawn, to be replaced by the 7th, also from the 2nd Division. The new brigade was to go for Lagnicourt. On the day the brigade took over the men were enthralled by a dogfight between nine aircraft. The planes were only a few hundred feet up and, as one Australian put it, it was like watching magpies fighting. One of the German planes crash-landed. The pilot began to run down the valley and the Australians shot him. As he lay wounded, he told them he was Prince Frederick Charles of Prussia. Lighthorsemen galloped up. They and the infantrymen took the prince's gloves, cap and goggles as souvenirs. A major arrived and the prince asked him to ensure that 'these Australians' did not maltreat him. From his hospital bed a few days later the prince thanked the Australians for their kindness and 'good sportsmanship'. He too was 'a sport', he said. Then he died.

The 7th Brigade took Lagnicourt at a cost of 377 casualties. Captain Percy Cherry, a young Tasmanian orchardist, captured a fortified farm on the edge of the village, then slogged up the muddy main street where he was fired upon from stables. He rushed the stable yard and the Germans surrendered. He moved on and found the main resistance was coming from a big crater spotted with white chalk. He and his men overwhelmed the Germans there, then pushed on to the far side of the village. Cherry already held the Military Cross. He was awarded the Victoria Cross for Lagnicourt but would never know of it. A shell-burst killed him after the village was won.

The 4th Division now came in to replace the 2nd. Glasgow's 13th Brigade took Noreuil with 600 casualties. Among the dead was Lieutenant William Hoggarth, a civil engineer from Adelaide, who had been the first Australian to break into Mouquet Farm. As he fell mortally wounded he shouted to those who tried to help him: 'Go on! Go on!' The villages were falling but the cost was rising.

Doignies and Louverval were the two villages Elliott had wanted to take as reprisals for the insult the Germans had offered him. Another brigade from the 5th Division now took them. Another

484 Australian casualties. At Louverval the Australians cut off twenty Germans who waved a white cloth in surrender. All but two were shot.

It was now April 3. There were just three more villages left between the Australians and the Hindenburg Line, which could be glimpsed up ahead, great heaps of chalk-shot spoil and barbed wire that shone blue-grey in the sun.

THE DAY AFTER the Australians threw the Germans out of Doignies and Louverval, senators in the United States prepared to vote on whether their country should go to war with Germany. It almost seemed as if the Germans wanted to drag President Woodrow Wilson into the conflict. Wilson had never wanted to be part of it. He was above such vulgarities. The war-makers were the kings and intriguers of Old Europe; he was the voice of the New World, the face of perhaps the truest democracy the world had known, a land of European immigrants, a good many of whom came from Germany. Wilson was prissy and proper. He had none of the warmth of Lloyd George or the wit of Billy Hughes. He seemed to care about humanity, but in the abstract. He believed in the nobility of ideas, that nations could organise themselves to avoid war.

The Germans had contrived to make Wilson's neutrality untenable. First, there had been the resumption of unrestricted submarine warfare. The United States was not at war with the Kaiser – yet the Germans were sinking American ships on sight. The second event that brought America into the war was a cable sent by Arthur Zimmermann, the German Foreign Minister. He proposed to Mexico that, should America be drawn into the war by the submarine campaign, Mexico should declare war on the United States. Zimmermann dangled the prospect of Mexico recovering Texas, New Mexico and Arizona. This was absurd as an idea; it became a disaster when the cable was intercepted and published in the United States. Isolationists became interventionists overnight. Two days later the United States declared war on Germany.

Within a month there had been two tremendous changes in the

war, but neither was quite what it seemed. The allies assumed that, despite the revolution, Russia would stay in the fight. And, at least on the battlefield, the American declaration didn't mean much for 1917. It was certainly no reason for the allies to alter their plans. The United States hadn't prepared for war. Its army numbered little more than 100,000. It had few modern weapons, such as how-itzers, tanks, mortars, rifle grenades or aircraft. It would send a division and two brigades of marines to France almost immediately, but this was a gesture. The true significance of America's entry was the number of troops it could supply in 1918 and beyond. Wilson had introduced selective conscription. From its population of 100 million the United States could supply at least two million con-scripts by 1918.

Here was the real change in the war, a matter of future arith-metic. The Germans now had to win, or negotiate a peace, before mid-1918. After that they would be outnumbered on the western front and starving at home.

ON THE DAY that the United States declared war Hooky Walker's 1st Division returned to the line to take the three villages that stood between the Australians and the Hindenburg Line. The villages fell, one by one and over several days, but at a cost of 649 Australian casualties. Three 1st Division men – Captain James Newland, Sergeant John Whittle and Private Thomas Kenny – won the Vic-toria Cross here.

The Australians were now within a mile of the Hindenburg Line. The war of movement, all three weeks of it, was over. Now it was back to one side grinding against the other from fixed trench lines. On their way from Bapaume to this spot the Australians had seen signs pointing to a little village on the other side of the Hindenburg Line. It's name – Bullecourt – meant nothing.

22

Bloody fiasco

They told Private Eric West, the student from South Australia, to dump his blanket and overcoat and anything else he didn't need. His battalion was going to storm the Hindenburg Line. It was April 9 and cold, a sharp cold that stung the nose and said snow was coming. Just up ahead, behind the heaps of spoil and the wire and pickets, lay two villages that had once sat up in a little valley but were now smoking and trembling and falling down under artillery fire. West knew the name of the village on the left well enough, but he didn't name it in the letter he wrote to his father.

> We took our capes, 24 hours rations and our rations for the morrow and, of course, any other ration we liked to take that we had. Also, our water bottles full of water. The riflemen had to carry 150 rounds of ammunition and 100 more rounds in bandoliers and two bombs. The grenadiers were issued with a bucket (that is a bag) of 15 bombs. We also had to carry our rifles and 50 rounds of ammunition . . . We all (I think the machine gunners included) had to carry 6 empty sand bags and a spade.

The men could return to their dugouts but they had to be ready to assemble at a moment's notice. They were called out at 3 am on

First Bullecourt

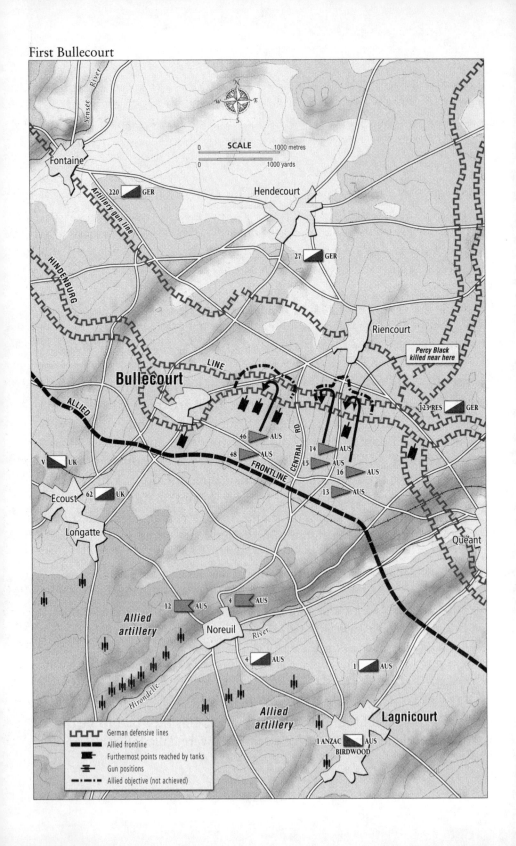

the 10th. A corporal told them they would be going over in two or three waves. West's battalion – the 48th, part of the 4th Division – would be in the second. Once the men had broken in, the corporal said, Indian cavalry would take over. There would be no artillery barrage. West went towards the jumping-off trench. Then he saw men in front coming back and he was told to return to his dugout. 'We learnt that the tanks that were to have been used hadn't succeeded in coming up, or something to that effect.'

West slept most of the next day. Towards evening the men were told to make the same preparations as the night before. This time the grenadiers were not issued with spades. This pleased West: his load would be lighter. In the night he heard the sound of engines and crawled out to see a tank. Three others followed at long intervals. West thought they were slightly different to the tanks he had seen on the Somme. They had no wheels at the back for steering. To turn the crew simply stopped the track on one side.

At 3 am the men were called out again. They were told German reinforcements had been seen moving up. The Germans had been warned by what had happened the previous night. 'Two tanks were to patrol the trenches we were to take,' West wrote, 'and two were to roll down the barbed wire. There were to be 12 tanks used in all.'

The men waited. Snow lay on the ground. 'At first we just knelt down, but as the fire became hotter, we gradually got down in a prone position and lay flat in spite of the cold. Machine-gun bullets kept whistling over our heads as we crouched lower.'

The attack began. German flares went up, red, green, all colours. West noticed they were using a new signal this time, a long stream of lights that moved upwards like a snake.

It was soon our turn to jump up and move forward. First we came to a sunken road in which was a trench. We halted here for the fraction of a minute, to get collected a bit, and then pushed on. We came to the first line trench where the 46th (I think) were and pushed on to the second. All the time men were falling right and left. A shell bursting would clear a space around the men dropping off like flies. Some would be actually blown up by the shells. Rifle fire and machine gun fire became hotter as we approached.

Then West felt 'a huge burning pain' in his stomach. He was in the battle that would be known as First Bullecourt.

BULLECOURT WAS THE name of the village on the left. West was on that side of the attack. Major Percy Black was on the right. Because of his rank, Black knew more about what was being asked of these men than did West. At a conference around midnight Black had said to his commanding officer: 'Well, goodbye, colonel. I mayn't come back, but we'll get the Hindenburg Line.' Earlier he had told his friend Harry Murray: 'Harry, this will be my last fight, but I'll have that bloody German trench before they get me.' Black seldom swore. Murray knew he was serious.

Some time before West had felt that 'huge burning pain', Black had led the West Australians of the 16th Battalion through one belt of wire, taken the first German trench, and gone on towards the second, where the wire seemed intact. Many of his men fell here. German bullets sparked off the wire and pickets. Someone thought they looked like a swarm of fireflies. German flares bathed the snow in red and green lights. Black found a gap in the wire and hurried his men through. He called to his runner and told him to take a message back to battalion headquarters at the railway embankment. 'Tell them the first objective is gained,' he said, 'and I am pushing on to the second.'

The miracle was that, given the way the attack came about, the Australians had come so far. It was around 5 am on April 11.

BULLECOURT CAME ABOUT, almost as an afterthought, because Haig had agreed to attack in Arras as a prelude to Robert Nivelle's offensive. The idea was to pin down the Germans there, so that they could not be rushed south, where Robert the Evangelist was going to win the war. Haig's 3rd Army, under General Edmund Allenby, would make the main thrust by driving from Arras towards Cambrai. To the north Henry Horne's 1st Army would send the Canadian Corps against Vimy Ridge and protect Allenby's left. To the south Gough's 5th Army, of which I Anzac Corps was part, would protect Allenby's right at Bullecourt.

The whole offensive, and it was a big one, was to help the French. Whatever may be said against Haig, he always accommodated his ally. He would have preferred to attack around Ypres, where there were two objectives of real value: the German rail junction at Roulers, and the ports of Zeebrugge and Ostend. Any offensive at Ypres needed to go in as soon as the winter mud had hardened, but Haig was stuck with Arras. Nivelle was running the war.

Haig, Allenby and Gough were all cavalrymen. Haig was indulgent of Gough and prickly towards Allenby, yet Allenby was clearly the more efficient and thoughtful soldier. He had already absorbed one of the great lessons of this war: the importance of careful preparations. Allenby was a man of contrasts. He was heavily built with a volcanic temper that earned him the nickname 'the Bull'. The story goes that he once abused an officer while inspecting trenches.

'Very good, sir,' the officer replied.

'I want none of your bloody approbation!' Allenby shot back.

Away from the army Allenby had a gentle humour and a warm spirit. He loved children, particularly his only son Michael. He also enjoyed sketching, natural history, flowers and music. He once stood for fifteen minutes in front of a 'really lovely carved church door' while humming the Emperor Concerto. Allenby wept and lapsed into despair when Michael, not yet twenty, was killed on the western front in 1917.

Allenby had Haig's sense of duty but didn't play at intrigues. Lloyd George liked him; so did Robertson. After the Arras battle Allenby was given command of the British forces in Egypt. Lloyd George told him to capture Jerusalem 'as a Christmas present for the British nation'. Allenby turned out to be a first-rate commander in Palestine. Some said this was because the war there was one of movement and that the Turks were less formidable than the Germans. Others said that Allenby had been liberated: from Haig and his court, its pettiness and protocols.

ALLENBY'S OFFENSIVE IN Arras began in sleet and rain on Easter Monday, April 9. Successes came early. This battle had been well planned. The British had learned much from the mistakes of the Somme. The concentration of artillery was the heaviest yet used on a British front. The gunners fired shells fitted with the '106' fuse, which exploded the shell the instant it grazed a hard surface. This made wire-cutting more certain. Fire-and-movement tactics were substituted for 'parade-ground' advances across no-man's land. Allenby used tunnels to feed troops directly into the frontline without exposing them to artillery. Tanks were sent out to take two strong points. And the Canadian Corps, already a splendid fighting force, stormed Vimy Ridge on the first day, its four divisions attacking in line. The ridge runs north to south for about seven miles, just north of the town of Arras. The Germans had taken it in September, 1914, and the French had tried repeatedly to take it back the following year, running up 150,000 casualties. The Canadians took it in a day with around 10,000 casualties and terrified the Germans with their ferocity. The battle went well elsewhere. Allenby's troops took 6000 prisoners and, on one front, plunged three-and-a-half miles into the German line, the deepest advance in a single day since trench warfare began.

But over the next two days the offensive lost momentum. Communications broke down as troops pushed far ahead of their divisional headquarters. The generals should have moved their headquarters forward but they were too used to the ways of trench warfare, where everything was always in the same place because the front was always in the same place. The Germans counter-attacked strongly and the battle came to be about 'bite and hold'. Cambrai seemed a long way away.

GOUGH STILL THOUGHT like a cavalryman. He looked back to the Duke of Wellington and didn't want to see Hiram Maxim and his chattering gun. His idea for Bullecourt had Australian and British infantrymen taking the village, as well as Riencourt and Hendecourt. He would then send Indian cavalry through to join up with Allenby's horse soldiers, who were supposed to be trotting down the Cambrai road, about three-and-a-half miles from Bullecourt.

Gough issued plans for the Bullecourt attack on April 5. Three days later General White, the chief-of-staff of I Anzac Corps, told him it would take eight days to cut the wire in front of the village. Gough simply didn't have enough artillery to do the job any faster. Next day Gough heard of the successes of Allenby and Horne on the first day of Arras. As the British official history (always temperate but often pointed) put it: 'It was galling [for Gough] to find himself helpless to aid in exploiting the great victory which appeared to be in prospect.'

Then, that afternoon, a tank battalion commander, Lieutenant-Colonel J. Hardress Lloyd, came to Gough with a scheme one of his officers had thought up. Gough had twelve tanks in his 5th Army. They were four miles behind the front and under the command of Major W. H. L. Watson.

Watson had worked out the scheme the night before. Like many tank men, he thought the new weapons had been misused. He felt they should be massed in front of the advancing infantry, not used in ones and twos. This was his idea for Bullecourt: a 'surprise concentration' of tanks massed in front of the infantry. The tanks would 'steal up' to the Hindenburg Line without a barrage and crush the wire. As they entered the line the barrage would come down on German positions further back. Under cover of this and the tanks, the infantry would 'sweep through'. Lloyd bought Watson's idea without demur, which is how the two now came to be explaining it to Gough.

'We want to break the Hindenburg Line with tanks, general,' Lloyd said. He briefly outlined Watson's scheme.

Gough embraced it as eagerly as Lloyd had. It didn't seem to bother him that he would be sending troops out without a barrage. He would attack at dawn the next morning, the 10th. He asked Watson when his tanks would need to move.

Watson was surprised. It had happened too fast. 'There were so many preparations to be made; but I replied my tanks should move at once . . . we drove at breakneck speed to the Château near, which was occupied by the Australian Corps, and were left by General Gough to work out the details with the Brigadier-General of the General Staff (General White).'

It *was* happening too fast. 'With two exceptions,' Watson wrote, 'my officers had neither experience nor skill.' When his tanks had been unloaded from a train near Bapaume the novice drivers had twice came close to flattening a railway building. Neither Lloyd nor Watson would be in the tanks attacking the Hindenburg Line. They were architects, not bricklayers.

Birdwood and White were sceptical, and not just because the Australians had never worked with tanks before. It all seemed too extemporary. And they were supposed to have orders written and men in position by dawn next day. Gough told them the tanks would smash the wire. Only then would the infantry be asked to advance. And, said Gough, there would be no attack unless Allenby's offensive was going so well that cavalry could pass through the Bullecourt front and begin chasing the Germans towards Cambrai.

White warmed to Lloyd and Watson. 'They were extraordinarily keen and gallant,' White told Bean that evening. They had said: 'Oh! We'll do that for you.' They were willing to take their tanks anywhere, White said, which was amusing because these two wouldn't actually be in them.

Birdwood remained doubtful. Anyway the first thing to do, he and White decided, was to send out patrols to see whether the Hindenburg Line was still occupied. Gough, on skimpy evidence, had suggested that it might not be.

Colonel Lloyd raced back to his headquarters to write orders for his tank company. These reached the tank crews at 6.30 pm and an hour-and-a-half later the tanks began to lurch towards the front amid sleet and snow.

Australian officers were also frantically writing orders for the 5700 infantrymen involved. General Holmes found out at 4 pm that his 4th Division was attacking Bullecourt with tanks at dawn. Troops had to be hurriedly brought forward from Noreuil and

Favreuil. The 4th and 12th brigades would be making the attack, the 4th on the right, and the 12th on the left. On the Australians' left would be the British 62nd Division, commanded by Major-General Walter Braithwaite, who, nearly two years earlier, had been much disliked as chief-of-staff to General Sir Ian Hamilton at Gallipoli, mainly because his chief interest seemed to be military etiquette.

Patrols went out to see if the Germans were still there. Captain Bert Jacka, now an intelligence officer, did the scouting for Brand's 4th Brigade on the right. He found the wire cut in some places and intact in others. And he found Germans everywhere: machine gunners firing from a forward sap, two parties mending breaks in the wire, a patrol sneaking across no-man's land. Jacka and the two officers with him felt that, without strong artillery support, the attack was doomed. Brand apparently passed on their views.

At 11 pm Birdwood telephoned Gough's chief-of-staff, Major-General Neill Malcolm. Birdwood had learned that Allenby's offensive was not going as well as it had been earlier in the day. Birdwood wondered whether a thrust towards Bullecourt was now justified, particularly as the German wire was still so strong. Why not wait for a day, when Allenby's progress would be better known? Malcolm broke off, presumably to talk to Gough. He returned to say that Gough said the operation had to go ahead. Haig wanted it to go ahead.

White appealed to Malcolm forty-five minutes later. He said patrols had found Germans all over Bullecourt. The arrangements were hasty and the tanks an unknown. Allenby's troops to the north had been driven back. This 'materially changed the situation and made a haphazard attack hard to justify', unless Gough's headquarters knew something the Anzac Corps didn't. Gough, through Malcolm, replied that the attack must go on. Gough said the failure of Allenby's right increased the need for the 5th Army to do something. The reason for the assault had thus changed completely.

Late into the night, as the wind howled and flurries of snow swept the jump-off positions, instructions were still being rushed to the infantry. The artillery would fire normally until 4.30 am, when the tanks would be lined up in front of the infantry. The artillery would then switch its fire to the flanks. The tanks would go forward and take the Hindenburg Line. The sound of them would be drowned out by Australian machine-gun fire. On reaching the German line they would display a green disc. This would be the signal for the infantry to come on across the open country.

Jacka went out again to lay tapes along the start line. He was almost finished when he saw two figures approaching from the German lines. If they saw the tapes and managed to return to their lines, all surprise would be lost. Jacka worked his way behind the Germans as they came close to the tapes.

'Halt!' Jacka shouted. The two Germans stopped but did not raise their hands. One carried a cane. He was obviously an officer. The other carried a rifle. They were five yards away. Jacka aimed his revolver. The hammer merely clicked. Either the chamber was empty or the round faulty. Jacka grabbed the officer, who dropped his cane. The other man dropped his rifle. Jacka began to herd them towards the Australian line. According to Sergeant Ted Rule, who was back in the Australian line, the German officer 'started to squeal and kick up a fuss'. Jacka hit him over the head with his revolver. Rule said 'the fellow calmed down and the pair of them were taken to our C.O. Here the Hun officer complained very bitterly of his treatment, but, when our colonel told him he was bloody lucky to be alive, he shut up.' Had the German lieutenant known the name and slightly violent record of his captor, he might have thought himself blessed.

By 4.15 am the infantrymen were lying out, waiting for the tanks. Not a sound. No tanks. The time for the attack was put back thirty minutes to 5 am. Dawn was close. When light came the Germans would see the khaki-clad figures lying in the snow. It turned out that the tanks hadn't even reached Noreuil. Major Watson was at 4th Division headquarters. The tanks had been held up by the snowstorm, he explained. They weren't lost, just going very slowly. The crews were exhausted. They would take another hour-and-a-half to reach the start point.

Holmes asked Watson if the tanks could attack in daylight. No, said Watson, the artillery would wipe them out. 'I think there is just time to get the boys back,' said Holmes, glancing at his watch. It was 5 am. It would be daylight in half-an-hour.

Colonel Ray Leane, the commander of the 48th Battalion, watched the men come back. 'Cold, and fed up, officers and privates casually withdrew like a crowd leaving a football match . . .' The men griped about what they began to call the 'dummy stunt'. It confirmed what they had long known: that the staff officers back there somewhere were muddlers. It was now 5.20 am. The Germans put down a barrage on the line of the ridge. Most of the Australians escaped it, but over on the left, in the 48th Battalion's sector, twenty-one were killed and wounded. Among the dead was Major Ben Leane, brother of the battalion commander. Ray searched among the dead for Ben, carried his body in and erected a rough cross over a grave that he dug himself.

Birdwood was delighted when the attack was called off. The British official history called the events of April 10 a 'fiasco'.

ONE HAS TO see the ground at Bullecourt to realise what was being asked of these men on that freezing morning in 1917. If you stand a few hundred yards east of Bullecourt, where the Hindenburg Line stood, you see a line of trees to the south, about 600 yards away, across a plain that rises so softly that a tractor driver would barely notice he was climbing. Beyond the trees the spire of Noreuil pricks the pale blue sky. Those trees, near an old railway line, were the Australian start lines. There is nothing now, nor was there in 1917, in the way of cover between them and where you are standing.

The men making that long dash were to be completely exposed to German fire, and it didn't matter too much that they were to start before dawn. Such an attack could only be justified if the German defences had been obliterated by artillery. This would have been difficult if Gough had possessed sufficient artillery, which he didn't. The prospect becomes worse as you mentally sketch in the rest of the German line.

The Australians were to attack into a re-entrant (an indentation in the German lines, the opposite of a salient) between Bullecourt and the village of Quéant, out of sight behind a low hill to the east. They would be running into a cul-de-sac. They would face machine-gun fire from the front, the right and the left.

But there was to be no barrage on the German frontline because Gough had clutched at the tank plan. The Australians at Bullecourt had never worked with tanks. The infantrymen and the tank crews needed to talk to each other, to find out what each could do. (Even today infantry and tank men are expected to 'marry up' before an attack.) The Australians would only see the tanks a few minutes before the attack began. There would be no chance to talk to the crews.

One senses that frontline soldiers knew the scheme was rotten with flaws. They fought battles on the ground; Gough, Birdwood and White fought them on maps and, when the line wasn't cut, telephones. One also senses that staff officers knew they should not have been cobbling up orders in such haste; they certainly knew the reason for the attack had changed. And one senses that Gough was determined to put himself and his army into the Arras battle, even if it meant clutching at half-thought-out schemes.

The attack had already been cancelled because the tank men had made appointments their machines could not keep. This should have been another warning. The British official historian had it right: it had been a fiasco. But a fiasco was better than a bloodbath and everyone had been given a reprieve. Birdwood could now argue that his doubts about the tanks had been justified. Gough could think more carefully about what he was doing.

At noon on the 10th the Australians slept in their dugouts or sat about cursing the 'heads'. The tank men threw tarpaulins over their machines. And Gough announced that the attack would go in around dawn on the following day. The plan would be the same.

GOUGH HAD THE instincts of a huntsman: squeeze the horse with the spurs, give him the reins and hope he clears the fence; don't think too much about what you are doing, lest you lose your nerve. Gough told the noon conference at his headquarters that Allenby would renew his attempt to break through the next day. Bullecourt would be attacked at 4.30 am on the 11th.

Birdwood and White argued against the plan. We don't know how vigorously. Birdwood said the non-arrival of the tanks the previous morning showed the risk of relying on them. He also said that, should they arrive on time, they still had to line up correctly. If they didn't, they would lead the infantry astray. Gough and the tank commander said they were sure at least three-quarters of the tanks would make it to the Hindenburg Line. Birdwood and White were unconvinced and kept raising doubts. Gough seemed to be losing his poise. Then he was called to the telephone. When he returned his tone was decisive again. He had been talking to Launcelot Kiggell, Haig's chief-of-staff. Kiggell had given him a directive from Haig: the attack must be made; it was very important; Haig set great store by it. Birdwood felt he could argue no more.

White felt Gough had been speaking to Kiggell but doubted whether the dispute had been referred to Haig. Long afterwards White said to Bean: 'I don't think I should have given way even then. I should have let him [Gough] send me back to England first – and I don't think we would have gone on with it.' Other ideas had begun to form in White's mind. Never again, he thought, should an Australian force be placed under external command unless the Australian commander had the right to appeal directly to the commander-in-chief, and also to the Australian Government.

The incident again drew attention to the curious position of Birdwood. He had affection for his Australians but he was also a serving British officer, and ambitious. He was formally accountable to Haig and Robertson and their political masters in London. And he was also, since 1915, administrative head of the AIF, which meant he was the representative of the Hughes Government in Melbourne. If there was a dispute, how did he reconcile these duties?

MINOR CHANGES WERE made to the attack plan. The infantry would go forward fifteen minutes after the tanks began their assault, regardless of the progress of the tanks. Six tanks would form up in front of each Australian brigade. The two tanks on each flank would turn outwards as they reached the German trenches. Four tanks on the left would turn towards Bullecourt village and lead the Australians in. Then six tanks would lead the British 62nd Division into Hendecourt. Finally four tanks would lead the Australians into Riencourt. Here was optimism of a high order. The previous day these tanks couldn't reach the start line. Now they were not only going to reach the German trenches but also wheel left and right with the lightness of horse cavalry.

There would be no creeping barrage to protect the infantry in the re-entrant. The routine shelling of Bullecourt would cease at 4.45 am, just as the tanks arrived at the Hindenburg Line. Infantry orders again went out in haste. Conferences were still going on at midnight. Troops in the reserve battalions tramped up in mud and snow from near Bapaume. Private Wilfred Gallwey, a new recruit, said that he became so tired during this march that he held his rifle by the sling and let the butt trail in the mud. 'Of what use would I be to fight tonight?'

SO HERE WERE the Australians out lying in the snow again, waiting for the tanks. The sound of the tanks' petrol engines was supposed to be drowned out by machine-gun fire, but scouts in front of the jump-off positions could hear the engines clearly. Jacka at 3.20 am guided the first tank to arrive to a position in front of the 4th Brigade. He asked the tank officer whether it could reach the Hindenburg Line in fifteen minutes, as the orders said. Impossible, said the lieutenant.

Jacka realised the infantry would reach the wire before the tanks arrived to break it down. He told two of the battalion commanders what the tank officer had told him. The battalion commanders telephoned to divisional headquarters, asking whether the tanks could go fifteen minutes earlier. No, they were told, it was too late to change the orders.

Two more tanks arrived and were lined up. A report came in that a fourth had broken down. The final two tanks for the 4th Brigade's front had almost reached the starting point. One became stuck in a bank; the other's engine broke down. One briefly opened fire on the Australians in the jump-off trenches.

At 4.30 am, zero hour, only three of the six tanks were in position. And the Germans had heard them. Shells were bursting around the tanks. At 4.30 the three tanks headed for the Hindenburg Line. Green flares soared up from the German trenches.

To the left, on the 12th Brigade's front, no tanks had arrived. By the time the infantry was supposed to go, one had turned up. The 46th and 48th battalions lay on the snow under a German barrage and waited. They could hear the tanks somewhere behind them. The first tank to arrive had opened fire on the 46th Battalion. The men yelled and cursed. A hatch opened. An officer's head appeared, and it spoke. What troops were these? He was told – rather roughly, one assumes – that they were Australians, and on the same side, actually. The officer alighted and apologised, then asked directions to where the Germans were. His tank now lumbered towards Bullecourt but appeared to be veering too far to the right. Shortly after one of the crew returned. A shell had hit the tank. The man believed he was the only survivor.

A second tank arrived at 5 am, when the first smudges of dawn were lighting the sky and the men could see about fifty yards. It broke down in front of the jumping-off position. Fire was now coming in on the two battalions from Bullecourt village on the left. The barrage had lifted off there. Every minute brought more light. The company commanders out in the snow asked battalion headquarters the obvious question: what should they do? Go, they were told. It was 5.15 am, half-an-hour after the 4th Brigade had gone. Private Eric West of the 48th Battalion headed for the Hindenburg Line.

WEST MADE THE first line of German trenches, which had been taken by the 46th, and was going for the second when the shell fragment hit him. It was a burning pain because the metal was hot. When

West fell he realised that his left arm was stiff and numb. He had been hit there too. He found a shell hole and lay on his back. A passing Australian pulled out West's field dressing and roughly bandaged him. West kept sipping away at his water bottle. Trench mortars or rifle grenades were dropping in front of him, spraying him with earth. He held his helmet in front of his face.

He lay there for an hour, then an Australian helped him into a sap that connected the first German line to the second. 'I was then told I should not drink any water and remembered it was dangerous to drink water with an abdominal wound, and also that I had already drunk half a bottle full. Someone discovered there were two holes in my abdomen, so put another bandage there.'

The shells kept falling. After a while the Australians realised they were being bombarded by their own artillery. Runners were sent back. 'The second came back and said the 46th had suffered heavily and were retreating, and the Germans were in their first line again and had cut us off.'

West thought he would be left behind. He got up and tried to walk. 'I was very stiff at first, but managed after a while.' He blundered along the sap, which was littered with dead. West and those around him decided all they could do was jump out and run for their lives.

'After getting about a chain, I was shot through the thigh . . . Our first line was along a railway embankment. By the time I reached it, I could hardly drag one foot after the other. I made my way to the dressing station and had my thigh bandaged.' Stretcher-bearers took West to another dressing station. 'Here our Doctor looked at my wounds and gave me my ticket and I was left outside for some time on a stretcher.' It began to snow.

PERCY BLACK WAS almost hit by a bus at Piccadilly Circus while on leave in London. When he reached the kerb he said he'd be glad to get back to France. 'A man's not safe here.' That was the style of his humour: dry and gentle. When a barrage was falling he would walk along the line, look down at a private cowering in a shell hole and say: 'Got a match, lad?' He inspired, but without bluster. He was a hard man: he probably had to be to survive on the West Australian goldfields. Harry Murray remembers Black fighting a well-known boxer there. Black was badly mauled early but the fight ended with Black's friends pulling him off the boxer to save the pug's life. Black was about the next day; the boxer was a month in hospital. Yet, Murray said, Black was 'as gentle as a Sister of Mercy'. His every instinct was that of a gentleman. His sense of justice was so strong he could see the other fellow's side before his own. 'Percy never went berserk and never sought death,' Murray said. Black 'had all the natural fear of the Unknown'; he just didn't let it show. He talked quietly, even in the worst of times.

Now he led the 16th Battalion out before dawn at Bullecourt. Behind him the 13th Battalion, in which Murray was a company commander, followed in support. Black had close to 700 yards to cover before he reached the German wire. He had gone about halfway when he came upon two tanks, both stopped. German flares, red, green and white, soared and fizzed over the snow. A German battery near Bullecourt village fired into the Australians from the left; another near Quéant hit them from the right. Machine-gun and rifle fire poured in from the front. Sparks flew off the wire and drummed on the tanks. Here was the madness of attacking into a re-entrant without artillery support. The tanks were supposed to have crushed the wire; in fact the infantry was ahead of them. The only thing the men could do was to try to struggle through the barbs while being shot at from three sides. 'Come on, boys,' Black shouted, 'bugger the tanks.'

Murray was 300 yards behind him. He yelled to his men to lie down as machine-gun fire swept over them. He saw the 16th being 'cut to pieces' in the wire.

Murray reached the wire. Dead and wounded from Black's battalion lay everywhere. Murray lost about thirty men to a German machine gun. 'How we got through the remaining wire, I don't know,' he wrote afterwards. 'A rifle bullet grazed the back of my neck, dropping me for a second. I was done! No, only a false alarm. Up again. The entanglement was just too high to straddle and so crossed and intertwisted that it formed an 8 ft mesh netting of barbed wire on which the enemy fire, converging from all points, sang a ceaseless death song.'

Lance-Corporal Bert Knowles was near Murray. 'Anywhere, where men were grouped together trying to penetrate the barbed wire, the machine-guns simply wiped out 50 per cent with a swish; but men lay on their sides and hacked at the wire with their bayonets. Some few had cutters; others tried to cross the top, leaping from one strand to another. Many slipped and became hopelessly entangled in the loosely bunched wire. Many were shot down halfway through, and hung up on the wire in various attitudes.'

Murray reached the first trench and its nests of dugouts and shafts. Black and the 16th had already taken it and headed for the second line, 170 yards ahead. Black had ordered sixty prisoners sent back. Forty-two made it; the rest were shot down by German fire.

Black found the wire uncut in front of the second line. Eventually he found an opening, pushed his men through and told his runner to take a message back. As he finished speaking he threw up his hands and dropped. Dead. Shot through the head.

There was no time to care. Death was everywhere here. When Murray came up they told him his best friend was dead. He didn't believe it at first. Then he saw Black's body. When news of Black's death reached Victoria, just after Anzac Day, the flag on a little schoolhouse outside Bacchus Marsh was lowered to half-mast. Black's body was never found. He is out there still, in the field in front of the pretty villages of Bullecourt and Riencourt, from where you can hear dogs barking and children playing.

AND THE WAR went on, though not for the tanks. They had been in this battle all right, and had the casualty figures to prove it. But they had not much influenced the course of it, apart from drawing some fire off the infantry. They had certainly not done what they were supposed to do.

Eleven tanks set out. By 10 am all were destroyed or disabled.

One – designated Tank Number 799, on the 4th Brigade's front – veered far to the right, towards the little hill that hides Quéant. The Germans peppered it with armour-piercing bullets. The tank caught fire and the commander was killed. The driver of a tank in the centre was decapitated. Most of the tanks became chambers of horrors: ricocheting bullets, flying splinters of metal, the smell of petrol and vomit and blood, noise and blindness. Of the 103 crewmen who went out, fifty-two were killed, wounded or missing.

Bean watched the battle from behind the embankment. When dawn came, he saw what looked like slugs crawling across the snow. A flash from the slug: the tank's six-pounder. Bean noted in his diary that the light that April morning was 'peculiar'. The snow on the ground made all objects look black. One couldn't tell the difference between German grey and Australian khaki.

THE POOR LIGHT produced a mistake that was to rival Gough's faith in the tanks. The Australians from both brigades had, despite frightful losses, fought their way to the second German line. It would have been foolish for them to have tried to go on further: there were not enough of them left. What they needed was artillery support to stop the Germans counter-attacking. Murray had effectively become the 4th Brigade leader in the frontline. At 7.20 am he first called for a barrage. Seventeen times his men fired the SOS signal: a green flare, followed by a red then another green. Not a shell came to help them.

There was a reason. At 5.35 am an Australian artillery observer reported seeing tanks in Bullecourt and Riencourt. Shortly after an observer said he could see Australian infantry in the two villages. The observers reported 'Bullecourt ours'. Now they could see Australians beyond both villages. Then they could see tanks moving on Hendecourt, which would have put them a mile inside the Hindenburg Line. All the reports were wrong.

Gough was delighted when they reached him at 7 am. It was time to bring up the cavalry. He ordered the 17th Lancers, Haig's old regiment, forward. Gough was going to do what he and Haig had wanted to do since the war began: pass cavalry through a gap. Except there was no gap.

MURRAY SENT A message back at 7.15 am. It arrived at 8.45. Murray reported that his brigade held the first objective and part of the second. The tanks were out of the fight. It was impossible to go further. He needed as many rifles, hand grenades, ammunition and white flares as could be sent. Major Black was dead. 'With artillery support we can keep the position till the cows come home.'

Before Murray's message arrived Bert Jacka had been prowling the back area of the battlefield. At 7.21 am he told General Brand, the commander of the 4th Brigade, that the tanks had failed completely: they weren't where the artillery observers were saying they were; they had never been there. Bean, who was nearby, wrote that the tanks could be seen motionless, and in most cases burning, all over the battlefield. The Australians here now knew the truth: they had to give their two brigades artillery support.

THE POSITION IN the frontline at this time was something like this. The four battalions of the 4th Brigade were in the two German trenches, but between one-quarter and one-third of them had already been killed or wounded, mostly around the first belt of wire. The men from all battalions looked to Murray for leadership: he was the best-known officer left. Several officers asked him if they should try to go on to Riencourt. No, said, Murray. They had no tanks to support them, their casualties were already high and they were short of ammunition. They had to fortify. They had to hang on.

The 12th Brigade was to their left. The two brigades had not quite linked up; there was a gap in the middle of the battlefield. There were also gaps between the front and rear battalions on the left. Only two battalions of the 12th Brigade had gone out: the 46th and the 48th. The 4th Brigade had been hit by fire from Quéant, to its right, the 12th by flanking fire from Bullecourt village, to its left. The 46th Battalion had reached the wire without help from tanks or artillery and taken the first trench. The 48th passed through them and went on for the second trench.

Lance-Corporal George Mitchell was a Lewis gunner in the 48th. He saw showers of sparks flying off the German wire, forty yards ahead. 'The ground was a carpet of dead and dying. On the wire were still forms, and others that squirmed violently.' Mitchell said he got the 'wind up' and thought of dropping into a shell hole. Then, he said, he thought of the strength and courage of his mates and went on.

Mitchell and the men from the 12th Brigade found the wire in front of the second trench mostly uncut. This is where Eric West was wounded. A South Australian farm hand said afterwards: 'We were being raked by machine-gun fire and shelled with shrapnel. Wounded and dead men were hanging in the wires all around me, and I noticed that the shell-holes were full of wounded.'

By the time the 48th Battalion took the second trench Allan Leane, nephew of Ray, was the only company commander left. He ordered his men to bomb to the right, towards the 4th Brigade. The 48th also tried to force its way to the left, towards Bullecourt village, but was held up by fire from a sunken road that radiated from a junction of six roads and tracks just in front of Riencourt. Back in the first German trench the 46th Battalion could make no progress to the right but extended its line to the left. Captain Frederick Boddington, a Queensland architect, is said to have himself killed eleven Germans as he pushed to the left and came close to the edge of Bullecourt village. Not long after Boddington was killed.

At 7 am the 4th and 12th brigades held an awkward and narrow front that was not joined up. They could hang on, tired and depleted as they were, if their artillery would only throw down a protective barrage just beyond the second trench. The brigadiers back at the railway embankment knew this well enough. But the generals further back again were still inclined to believe the reports that their men had gone on to Bullecourt and Riencourt.

THE HOLDING ON began. Murray remembered an incident that occurred about 9 am. A small party in his battalion had been assigned to fill in the German trench so that cavalry could cross. Only one member of this party survived to reach the trench. Men now came to Murray to complain that a man was filling in the trench and thus stopping them from getting along it. Murray found a youngster, working with pick and shovel, up on the parapet, completely exposed.

'What are you doing, lad?' Murray demanded.

The youngster stopped work, straightened himself up and told Murray he had orders from his colonel to fill in the trench.

'Get down at once,' Murray said. 'Don't fill that trench. We want it and you'll be killed if you stay there.'

The youngster grinned. He was uncertain. Should he obey the pre-attack orders or this captain with the neat little moustache? He decided to obey the captain.

Then Murray heard the 'sickeningly familiar thud' of a Mauser bullet hitting flesh and bone. 'He sounded a long shuddering "Ah-h-h",' Murray wrote nineteen years later, 'and toppled over, never speaking again.'

THE GERMANS MUST have wondered why they weren't being hit by artillery. They counter-attacked the 46th Battalion, the rear of the Australian left, after 7 am from Bullecourt village with bombs and a trench mortar. They also bombed the 46th from the gap between the two Australian brigades. The Australians were running out of bombs and ammunition. The 47th Battalion was drawn into the fight to carry up bombs. Around 9.30 Allan Leane counted his men in the front trench. There were about 227 of them holding a 600-yard front. About 750 had set out just over four hours ago. In the back trench, the 46th, even though it now included reinforcements from the 47th, was down to a little more than 100 men. There was now no way these men could join up with the 4th Brigade.

First Bullecourt, as this battle would be known, was like Lone Pine. The fighting was mostly with bombs and, occasionally, bayonets. As on the first day at Lone Pine, there was no continuous front but dozens of separate fights, many of them over stops hastily built into trenches. The Germans were in front of the Australians in the forward trench and also behind them. They were between the two Australian brigades. And they were still pouring in fire from the flanks of the re-entrant. First Bullecourt was about anarchy.

The 4th Brigade also fought off a series of counter-attacks. Wounded could not be got out. The Germans were still sweeping the plain between the front and the railway embankment with machine-gun fire. Two captured German medical orderlies tended the serious cases in the frontline. Thirty German prisoners were sent back towards the embankment, only to be shot down by their own side.

BY NOW BOTH brigadiers at Noreuil and the battalion commanders behind the embankment all wanted a protective barrage. The gunners refused, insisting that the infantry and tanks had gone past the Hindenburg Line and would thus be where the barrage would fall. Tempers rose. 'A most aggravating telephonic communication took place,' a man in Brand's headquarters wrote. The dispute was eventually referred to Birdwood at about 9.30 am. He supported the gunners.

Gough lived with the same hope. On his orders a squadron of the 17th Lancers had galloped up to the embankment. The Germans saw them and shelled them. Then they spotted the rest of the regiment massed further back and shelled it. A few horses were killed and many more ran about, big-eyed and terrified. The cavalry pulled back, but the horse culture lived on among men like Haig and Gough. One day there *would* be a gap. And then war would revert to its proper form.

Science had not taken over war entirely. Just before 10 am a pigeon brought a message from the 4th Brigade troops asking for bombs and ammunition. The message was timed at 7.10. Around the same time a message came in from the 12th Brigade. Its men also needed ammunition and water for their machine guns. They could see Germans massing at Riencourt.

By 11 am, General Holmes, the commander of the 4th Division, knew what the brigadiers and colonels closer to the front knew. He sent a telegram to Anzac Corps: 'Situation appears to be that we are in Hindenburg Line within our proper limits, but no more. Not in Bullecourt or Riencourt . . . Apparently no tank actually reached Hindenburg Line.' Holmes now wanted an artillery barrage.

AN HOUR EARLIER the Germans had begun a big counter-attack from the front and the flanks. The artillery could not have shelled the Germans on the flanks, even if it had wanted to: they were too close to the Australians. Fresh bomb fights broke out.

Captain David Dunworth was twice wounded and ended up a prisoner. Afterwards he told the story of Lieutenant Henry Eibel, a Queensland farmer who was a brother-officer in the 15th Battalion. When the bombing became furious Eibel paused, turned to a man and gave him his papers.

'Give these to Captain Dunworth and tell him I'm finished,' Eibel said.

'But you're not dead,' the man said.

'No,' said Eibel quietly, 'but I will be by the time you've delivered these.'

Eibel returned to the fight, and died.

Murray watched his men drop in dozens. 'Oh for that barrage!' he wrote long afterwards. A sergeant brought a message back that there was to be no barrage. Murray likened this to a death sentence. Men turned to him and said: 'What now?' The fighting became more desperate. The Germans with their plentiful supply of grenades were bombing the Australians out of bay after bay. A group of Australians put up a white flag. Murray ordered it shot down, but he knew the truth. All his men could do now was try to get back to the railway embankment. He wrote afterwards that he told the men they were entitled to surrender if they wanted to. The chances of escaping were almost nil. 'It was like expecting to run for hundreds of yards through a violent thunderstorm without being struck by any of the raindrops.' The men set off for the embankment. An officer with a smashed arm yelled: 'Every man for himself.'

Murray tore up copies of his code signals, trod them into the mud and started back. 'Now we turned for the last and most hopeless fight of the day; completely surrounded as we were, it looked as if it could only end one way, but, owing to the dust, haze and smoke, some of the German machine gunners mistook their own men for fleeing Australians and opened a murderous fire upon them, completely relieving the pressure on us and thus giving us time to get over the wire.'

Bert Knowles, who was in Murray's company, dived from shell hole to shell hole. He fell over climbing through the wire and lay still among the dead around him. Then he resumed his dash. Bullets droned past him and dug into the earth. He flopped into another shell hole. He thought he would have a spell there. 'I do not know what time it was then, but nothing had passed my lips since about 3 am. I had not even had time for a cigarette. My mouth was full of dust, and a taste of cordite and smoke of explosives. I ached all over through heaving bombs, dragging wounded men, and bags of dirt. My clothes were in rags and thighs and arms were scratched with barbed wire.'

Murray was struggling with the wire when he felt a bullet skim across his back. It broke the skin, nothing more. And now, now that he was almost safe, he succumbed to the strain. He was exhausted and unnerved and could go only a few yards at a time. A shell whined and left a crater ahead. Murray fell into it. He put out his hand and burned it on a hot fragment from the shell. The burn 'acted as a tonic, bucking me up a little bit'. His mind cleared.

He made the old frontline and began to trudge back towards Noreuil. All he wanted to do was sleep. His colonel gave him several nips of whisky. 'As a rule a little spirits affects me, but that night it had no more effect than water.' He met the quartermaster, who had brought up his horse. 'What a feeling of relief to sit back luxuriously while my neddy stepped smartly forward. I felt I could go to sleep and leave it all to him.'

The counting began. There were only seventeen unwounded survivors in Murray's company. The 4th Brigade had sent out four battalions and from these only nine officers had returned. No officers returned from the 15th Battalion from Queensland.

MUCH THE SAME had happened on the 12th Brigade's front, except that the men there hung on a little longer. Private William Evans of Penshurst, in Victoria's Western District, was cut off and taken prisoner. A German marched him along a trench where they met another German. The two lost interest in Evans. They stood on the fire-step and shot at the backs of the retreating Australians. Evans saw an Australian body at his feet. He stooped, pretending to tie a bootlace, and rummaged in the pockets of his dead comrade. He found what he was looking for: a grenade. He eased the pin out and gently placed the bomb between the feet of the two Germans, then slipped around the traverse of the trench. When the bomb exploded he jumped out and headed for the embankment.

The 48th were 150 yards ahead of the 46th. George Mitchell put down his Lewis gun, picked up a rifle and began a duel with a German bomb-thrower. He fired at him and missed. He worked the bolt to fire again. The magazine was empty. 'So I shook my fist in sheer rage, and the Fritz grinned amiably back at me.' Mitchell waited ten minutes or so. The German popped up again. Mitchell shot him through the head.

The 48th didn't realise that they were surrounded. Allan Leane wrote in his message book at 11.20 am that his position was 'as strong as it could be made'. Observers back at the embankment knew better. They could plot the German advance by the white puffs of German bombs. Then they saw men standing with their hands above their heads – Australians. Now they knew that the battle was lost. Colonel Leane called for an artillery barrage to protect the retreat. The artillerymen were now conceding that perhaps the Australians had not gone beyond the Hindenburg Line. At 11.45 am the gunners opened up on the 4th Brigade's front. The 4th by then was streaming back towards the embankment.

The 48th Battalion was still in the second German trench. Allan Leane tried to rally his men. Then he was wounded. And then, as

Eric West recounted in his letter to his father, the Australian barrage began to fall on the 48th. Now – it was about 12.25 pm – Leane decided to burn his codes and papers. An hour after the other battalions had left the 48th came out. Those who witnessed the 48th's retreat were astonished at what they saw. Bean saw them come towards him with 'studied nonchalance', walking, even though the German machine guns were still chattering, picking their way through the wire, carrying Lewis guns on their shoulders, arms around the walking wounded. 'Wherever Australians fought, that characteristic gait was noted by friend and enemy, but never did it furnish such a spectacle as here.' Many were killed or wounded as they returned. The wounded lay on the wire. The Germans shot those who were beyond recovery. These were acts of kindness rather than brutality. The 48th's officers came out last.

Allan Leane had recently become engaged to be married. He had written home that he felt 'the luckiest man alive'. He didn't come out. He was seen hopping towards the wire. He died a few weeks later in a German hospital. Ray Leane, whose tunic had been ripped off by a shell-burst, had thus lost his brother and nephew in the battle. Another of his relatives had been shot through the eye while trying to salvage a tank. The Joan of Arc battalion was no longer made of all Leanes.

George Mitchell wrote in his diary that he felt like weeping as he stepped over the wounded that had to be abandoned. 'They looked up at us but said nothing.' He tried to help a wounded man into a shell hole but the man shrieked with pain and he was too big to carry. Mitchell walked out alone, past blazing tanks and a wrecked aircraft. When he reached the old Australian line they told him Colonel Leane wanted to see him.

Leane had watched him walking back. 'I saw a tall non-com calmly striding down the hill with a Lewis gun on his shoulder. I was so impressed by his cool demeanour, despite the fact that he was under heavy shell and rifle fire, that I sent for him and congratulated him for his good work in sticking to his gun.' Leane promoted Mitchell to lieutenant. Mitchell also received the Distinguished Conduct Medal.

AN UNOFFICIAL TRUCE broke out about 2 pm. The Australian artillery was still firing when it was noticed that many of the Germans about the wire were medical orderlies. The Australians could see the white bandages they carried. The barrage was stopped. Australian parties went out. The Germans fired on the stretcher-bearers, then stopped when they saw the Red Cross flags. The Germans placed badly wounded men outside the wire where the Australians could pick them up. Snow began to fall about 6 pm. The Germans suddenly shouted: 'Finish hospital!' The truce was over. Neither side fired a shot during the night.

THE GERMANS HAD taken about 1170 prisoners, their biggest bag ever of Australians, and treated them well enough at the front. Once the prisoners reached Lille, however, other Germans set about punishing them. They were humiliated by being marched through the city's streets. Then they were crowded into dungeons in a fort. For eight days they were fed one slice of bread a day and ersatz coffee. The air was fetid. The men were given no blankets and slept on a damp stone floor. They were being treated so, an official explained, because the British had been making German prisoners work within range of German guns. They would be kept hungry, he said, given no beds and worked hard under shellfire. There would be no soap or towels or boots. He kept his word. The Australians were made to work under their own artillery fire for three months.

The Germans caught Bert Knowles. He had dozed off in the shell hole. Then he heard voices he could not understand. Germans. He and other Australians were taken to a house behind the lines. An officer looked into Knowles' diary and began yelling when he found pages torn out. Knowles understood only two of his words: 'Englander' and 'swine'.

THE CASUALTY FIGURES (which include those taken prisoner) were frightful. The six-and-a-half battalions went into the fight each about 750-strong. Murray's battalion lost 567 men, including twenty-one officers. Percy Black's battalion lost 636. The 4th Brigade's casualties came to 2339 of the 3000-odd troops it sent out. The 12th Brigade lost 950. Of these, 436 were in Eric West's 48th Battalion. Total casualties were thus 3289, which, in percentage terms, puts them on the same scale as Fromelles.

The 4th Division was pulled out of the line and rested in huts on the old Somme battlefield. As he left the battlefield Ted Rule saw Brand, his brigadier, and Colonel Peck, his battalion commander, 'sobbing like little schoolgirls'. A few days later Birdwood visited the 4th Brigade's huts.

Rule said that Birdwood had a standard 'bloodthirsty' speech. This usually began: 'Now, boys, I know you are all anxious to get back into the line and give the Huns another thrashing.' And it usually ended: 'Well, boys, I sincerely hope that you are all writing home to your mothers.' Birdwood delivered the standard speech, then gathered the men around him and started to unburden himself. This was a conversation, not a speech. Rule recalled parts of it: 'Boys, I can assure you that no-one regrets this disaster that has befallen your brigade more than I do . . . I can assure you that none of your own officers had anything to do with the arrangements for the stunt . . . We did our utmost to have the stunt put off until more suitable arrangements could be made.' Birdwood offered not a word of criticism of his superiors, 'but it was plain to me that he shrank from being contaminated by the bloody fiasco'.

The incident stirred Rule's imagination. 'Never before had I questioned the infallibility of those who held our lives in their hands . . . Now one recognised that, in spite of all the pomp and splendour of their rank, they were fallible flesh and blood; the same as we.'

THE HORSE AMBULANCE picked up Eric West, who we left lying in the snow with his three wounds. West said the horses were worn out. They took him some distance, then he was transferred to a motor ambulance, which was much smoother. The staff at the casualty-clearing station cut his clothes off. 'I was glad of this as I seemed to be lying in a sort of pool of water, and my feet were well nigh frozen as they had been for pretty well the last 24 hours.'

It was now the night of April 11. They put a blanket over him and carried him into the operating theatre. They laid him on a cold table. West objected and they put something under him.

> Picture one lying there; big, grim men standing around in white overalls looking at me menacingly. They paid first attention to the wound in my abdomen – started swabbing it. The pain was unbearable at the least touch. The operators put an instrument through the wound and told me I was very lucky. I could not see this. I had been cursing my luck for the last five minutes, but I did not start an argument over it. Someone then put a nosebag over me and let me inhale the beautiful fumes of chloroform and ether and I was told to count to ... then ...

When he awoke doctors and nurses kept telling him he was lucky. He was taken to another ward; another abdominal case was next to him. 'He was pretty bad, was not so lucky. An R. C. Padre came in to see him. He was not there next morning. One of the motor drivers was drunk that day. I learnt afterwards he drove rather recklessly and was arrested, as two abdominal cases he had on board died before morning.'

Several days later a doctor pulled out the plug in West's abdomen and he realised why everyone had told him he was lucky. The wounds in the abdomen were about three inches apart; each hole was about two-and-a-half inches by one-and-a-half inches; there were burn marks around the holes. But they were through-and-through wounds: the shell fragment had gone in one side and out the other. It was the same with his arm and the bullet wound to the thigh.

West recovered and took a Master of Science degree at the University of California. He became officer-in-charge of the CSIRO Division of Irrigation Research at Griffith, New South Wales. He had learned a little about irrigation in France. He told one of his sons that he was always bemused when officers ordered the men to bale water out of trenches. The scientist in him knew the floor of the trenches was below the ground water table.

THE BRITISH OFFICIAL history says of First Bullecourt: 'In the whole course of the War few attacks were ever carried out in such disadvantageous circumstances against such defences.'

At one level, that of the men on the ground – the Blacks, Murrays, Wests, Rules and Leanes – the attack had been an epic of great-heartedness. These men had broken the Hindenburg Line without artillery support and with modest help from the tanks. They had held two lines of German trenches for hours without artillery support. They had proved they had the discipline that counted: discipline under fire, discipline in adversity. And the unwounded had walked away with a mixture of nobility and cheek. War is often romanticised, mainly by leaving things out, and the abattoir is sometimes presented as an Arthurian jousting ground. First Bullecourt *was* an abattoir; but it also had moments that showed the human spirit at its most sublime. It remains curious that no Victoria Crosses were awarded afterwards. Murray received a second Distinguished Service Order and was promoted to temporary major. In his unpublished *Some Reminiscences* Murray said Birdwood told him that he would have received a second Victoria Cross had the battle been won.

At another level – that of the higher command, the world of the Haigs, Goughs, Birdwoods, Whites and countless staff officers – the battle should have been a thing of shame, a cause of sackings and censure. It might have been excusable in early 1915, but not in 1917.

Gough deserves most of the blame for First Bullecourt. Just as Fromelles probably would not have happened without Haking and his obsession, First Bullecourt could not have occurred without Gough and his bluster. Gough simply took a gamble with the tanks, the sort of risk other army commanders, such as Allenby and Herbert Plumer, would have spurned. When the tanks failed, nothing could save the Australians. Bean, a temperate man, assailed Gough in the Australian official history, which came out in 1933. Gough had conducted an 'experiment of extreme rashness'. He had tried with 'boyish eagerness' to deliver a death blow. He broke rules recognised even by platoon commanders. He attempted a deep penetration on a narrow front. He attacked into a re-entrant. He bought, on impulse, a scheme devised by an inexperienced officer of an experimental arm. After the tanks had failed on April 10 and confirmed the fears of his subordinates, he repeated the identical operation the next day. His judgement at Bullecourt was 'the plaything of an almost childish impetuosity'.

But it is too easy, and also unfair, to blame Gough alone. Birdwood couldn't seem to work out where his loyalties lay. He should have protested more strongly, as White should have. White was gracious enough to admit as much after the war. Birdwood glossed over First Bullecourt with two bland paragraphs in his autobiography *Khaki and Gown*.

And Bean glossed over the Australian mistakes at Bullecourt. No blame attaches to the brigadiers at Noreuil or the battalion commanders, who were under fire behind the railway embankment. Further back, however, the staff work was sloppy and the final plan too complicated, which in turn was one of the reasons the artillery performed so poorly. The gunners reported a series of false sightings, failed in their counter-battery work (the Germans reported that their gunners incurred only nine casualties) and, when they eventually began firing on the battlefield itself, managed to land shells among the 48th Battalion.

Communications broke down, as so often happened, shortly after the infantry went forward. For the next few hours there were at least four battles going on: the real one in the Hindenburg Line itself; the battle the brigadiers and colonels just behind the line *thought* was going on; the battle the artillery observers *thought* they were witnessing; and the one going on in Gough's mind as he sent cavalry into a gap that didn't exist.

A few hours after First Bullecourt ended Gough sent a message to the Australian division. He said he was 'satisfied that the effect upon the whole situation by the Anzac attack has been of great assistance'. Only he knows what he was trying to say.

BEAN IN 1930 sent the page proofs of his Bullecourt narrative to Edmonds, the British official historian. Edmonds passed them to

Gough for comment and the general reacted strangely. If he felt wronged, Gough needed to refute Bean's criticisms with forensic certainty, point by point. Instead his response was lame and rambling. He began by telling Edmonds: 'It is evident that the writer is animated by a strong personal dislike to myself, which causes me some pain, as I admired the Australians as soldiers and got on very well with those I met.' He said that at Bullecourt he was inspired with a determination to beat the Germans and win the war, which one would have thought was self-evident. He then admitted the attack was on too narrow a front. He was inclined to blame himself for attacking when he did, but he was trying to help Allenby. Gough concluded by saying that communications between his army and Allenby's were poor, and that Haig's headquarters was probably to blame for this. Kiggell, Haig's chief-of-staff, seldom visited the armies' headquarters. (Here Edmonds wrote in the margin: 'He [Kiggell] hardly ever left his office and did not visit the front until he was relieved of his post as CGS.') Gough said too much was done on the telephone.

Before Bean sent out his proofs Edmonds had written to Bean: 'I expect that I shall be in full accord with you over Bullecourt. I was at Gough's HQ at the time, and I remember that my opinion of him fell lower and lower. When the news of the Australians being cut off came he was furious and shouted over and over again, "They ought to have been supported," and began to look for scapegoats.'

Neill Malcolm, Gough's former chief-of-staff, also saw Bean's proofs. His response was as muted as Gough's. Bean, he said, would have been more sympathetic had he been at Haig's conferences. 'The only real mistake which can be seriously charged to Gough was, I think, his over-confidence in the tanks. The event proved him wrong, but the astonishing degree of success achieved by the 4th Aust. Divn. without them surely proves how great the result would have been had the tanks not failed us . . .'

In a note attached to Malcolm's comments Edmonds said the general opinion was that Gough and Malcolm were a bad combination. Gough needed a chief-of-staff who would restrain him. Both were too rash and headstrong. 'Both now have lucrative jobs in the City while many soldiers who did better service are living in poverty. Such is life.'

A month later Edmonds sent Bean a letter from Colonel D. K. Bernard, whom Edmonds described as 'one of the best officers in the Army'. He had been on the staff of the 4th Australian Division at Bullecourt and Edmonds had sent him Bean's proofs. Bernard replied: 'I read it with intense interest and it brought back vividly to my mind those tragic days of April 1917, when General Gough sent 4th Australian Division to what was really certain destruction.'

THERE IS LITTLE sign of destruction at Bullecourt today, not until you poke around. The three villages lie in strong cropping country, yellow-brown soil that, to the eye anyway, looks richer than the Somme. Wilting corn stalks sway seven-feet tall in the north wind. Big Friesians pick at the grass and stare with credulous eyes at passing cars. A crow circles overhead.

The villages belong to postcards: grey church spires, red and orange roofs, leafy glades, orchards, tomatoes blushing red in the vegetable plots, red-brick barns with lofts and old pig-sheds, dogs and ducks and cobblestones. And on all sides fields of wheat, barley, corn, sugar beet and vegetables. Driving a tractor here can still be dangerous. A farmer recently set off a phosgene-gas shell, inhaled the fumes and spent three days in hospital.

An Australian memorial, Peter Corlett's statue of an Australian soldier, rifle slung, his back lumpy with gear, stands on the Bullecourt–Riencourt road, *Rue des Australiens*. French and Australian flags flap in the wind. Gum trees have been planted near the statue and are doing poorly. The soil is too rich for them. Like the men in the ground here, the gum belongs to a harsher landscape.

This is roughly where the Hindenburg Line stood. Look to the south and you see the arena where dreams died for young men and bullets sparked off barbed wire. It is an open plain with barely an undulation. At the far end is a line of trees. They mark the line of the railway embankment, the Australian start line. That's where the colonels stood, wondering about the six-and-a-half battalions they had sent out. A spire peeps above the tree line. That's the village of Noreuil. The Australian artillery, for all the good it did, was in a valley between Noreuil and the tree line.

You walk along the Bullecourt–Riencourt road until you come to Six Cross Roads, which was on the German side of the front, facing the spot where the 48th Battalion was trying to hang on. German machine guns here shot down the Australians from the front. Look to the left and you see the gentle hill that hides Quéant. German machine guns fired into the Australians from there. Look to the right and you see Bullecourt. The Germans were firing from there too. Stand here long enough and First Bullecourt seems like madness.

And now you walk out into the re-entrant itself, a field of wheat stubble that crackles and crunches underfoot. Puffs of yellow dust rise with each footfall and you smell the dressing of blood and bone. It is hard to imagine how it looked on that day long ago when snow lay on the ground. An Australian sergeant taken prisoner passed close to where you are standing on his way to the German rear. He said the snow was broken by thousands of patches, black and red. The black patches were bodies, the red splashes of blood. He spoke of wounded men restlessly tossing and groaning.

Now you also start to notice the signs of destruction: a nose cone from a German shell, shrapnel balls, German bullets, sharp-pointed and rusted. On the hill that hides Quéant farmers found Tank Number 799 buried under topsoil. This was the tank that veered far to the right on the 4th Brigade's front. Pieces of the tank now lie in a farm barn. Here is a great rusting track and chain links as thick as one's thumb. Here is the six-pounder gun poking out of its sponson and, underneath, the rack for the shells. When you see a Mark I tank in a museum you are struck by its apparent blindness. There is no turret, nothing that says the iron creature can see. And that was the fate of 799. It blundered, like a blind and wounded animal, into the German lines, where it was surrounded, taunted, pulled down and killed.

Claude and Colette Durand, both formerly schoolteachers at Hendecourt, more than twenty years ago appealed for reminiscences from Australians who were at Bullecourt. They spread the handwritten letters on the kitchen table. A Tasmanian writes: 'The British Tank corps let us down badly & there was no co-operation between the Tanks and infantry.' A New South Welshman tells how he was wounded on the wire as a nineteen-year-old. When the retreat began two men grabbed an arm each and tried to drag him back. Both were killed by machine guns. Stretcher-bearers brought the man in near dusk. He thinks he may have been the last man picked up that day. They are all gone now, the Bullecourt men. We perhaps should have made more of them when they were alive.

WE RETURN TO the battlefield. A car pulls up. Two men alight.

'*Bonjour*,' we say in appalling French.

'Gidday,' one of them replies.

The men are Arthur and Clive West, sons of Eric West, come to look over the scene of their father's heroics long ago.

23

Mutiny

Robert Nivelle was so good at courting politicians that he almost qualified as a flirt. Yet he wasn't much of a politician himself. In selling his forthcoming offensive he had made a mistake. He had not only defined the terms by which his success should be judged; he had also defined them too narrowly. Talk of tactics and logistics tended to faze politicians. Victory, quick and neat: that was what they wanted to hear about. Nivelle had told them he knew things other generals didn't. He predicted that he would rupture the German lines in a day. He was the alchemist; he had the formula. Nivelle had set himself up: anything short of a quick breakthrough would be failure.

Haig and Robertson were clumsy at courting politicians. They patronised them, looked down on them as a lesser species. Both were inarticulate, secretive and narrow in their interests. Yet Haig would never have made the mistake Nivelle was now making. On the Somme the previous year he had not talked too loudly about breakthrough, even though that was what he was trying for. When the opening days brought failure and confusion, Haig and his apologists began to say the battle was about wearing down the Germans, and that would be their line for posterity.

By the time Nivelle's offensive began on April 16, five days after First Bullecourt, just about everything was against him. Prominent members of Ribot's new government, notably Painlevé, the War Minister, doubted the scheme would work and said so, causing Nivelle to offer his resignation. Painlevé and General Philippe Pétain preferred to wait for the Americans to come into the war. Nivelle's army commanders didn't believe in the offensive. They knew the Germans also had a new scheme and it was called defence in depth. The Germans had thickened their position on the Chemin des Dames ridge above the River Aisne with two extra lines of trenches. The defences ran back eleven miles and the strongest part of them was at the rear. Nivelle's plan called for the French to advance about four-and-a-half miles in eight hours. This would be a prodigious 'rupture' by the canons of the western front, but it would still leave the French infantrymen well short of the main German position, and exhausted too.

Nivelle had lost surprise. The Germans knew, in general terms, what was coming. Nivelle had allowed far too much loose talk. Moreover the Germans, as recounted earlier, had captured his plans with a French prisoner. The revolution had reduced the Russian army to a shambles: it could not help Nivelle with an attack in the east; it could not help itself. The Italians wanted to do something on their front but decided they couldn't.

All Nivelle had going for him was the enthusiasm of his rank-and-file troops and his own self-belief, and even that appeared to be faltering. Perhaps he simply didn't know how to escape from the trap he had built for himself.

THE ATTACK BEGAN at 6 am on the steep wooded ridge above the Aisne, in front of the line that ran from Soissons to Rheims, amid mist and icy rain that turned to sleet and snow. The rough weather made it hard to plot the course of the battle but some things were soon obvious. Nivelle's whole scheme depended on massed batteries keeping the Germans underground, but the German machine guns were firing and much of the wire was uncut. The barrage 'crept' too quickly for the infantrymen, who, as always, went forward bravely. Many of the tanks failed to reach the start line. Senegalese troops shivered in the sleet. Their hands were so cold they had trouble fixing their bayonets and their dark-brown faces turned grey. The casualty stations could not handle the procession of wounded. Lightly wounded Frenchmen pointed to the front and said 'C'est impossible.' The attack slowed, then stalled. The gains were negligible. The grand scheme had failed as quickly as it was supposed to have succeeded.

Nivelle had lost contact with reality weeks or months earlier; he wasn't going to re-embrace it now. He ordered fresh attacks. The deepest gain at the end of four days was about four miles. The French had taken about 20,000 prisoners. The frontline German divisions had run up unusually high casualties. But there had been no breakthrough, not a hint of it, and the war went on much as before, except that there were an extra 100,000 French casualties. The French soldiers were bewildered and, in some cases, broken in spirit. As Correlli Barnett wrote in *The Swordbearers*, Nivelle had aroused exaggerated hopes. French politicians were appalled. They didn't need to look for a scapegoat. Nivelle had nominated himself in advance.

He fell into depression and turned on his subordinates. When he told General Alfred Micheler he wasn't trying hard enough, Micheler replied: 'You wish to make me responsible for this mistake – me, who never ceased to warn you of it.' Haig treated Nivelle graciously. He didn't want the French offensive called off. This would give the Germans time to recover and perhaps interfere with his plans to attack at Ypres. But Nivelle now really had no say in what he was going to do. The politicians owned him the way a bank owned a defaulting mortgagor.

The Nivelle offensive petered out early in May. Frances Stevenson, Lloyd George's secretary and mistress, wrote in her diary: 'Nivelle has fallen into disgrace, & let D. [Lloyd George] down badly after the way D. had backed him up at the beginning of the year. Sir Douglas Haig has come out on top in this fight between the two Chiefs, & I fear D. will have to be very careful in future as to his backings of the French against the English.'

Nivelle was sacked shortly afterwards. He was eventually appointed commander-in-chief in North Africa. He had risen without trace; now he was going to disappear the same way.

Gough wrote in *The Fifth Army* that Nivelle had become 'the victim of his over-elaborate promises. I wonder what were the thoughts of Mr Lloyd George when he heard of the failure and fall of the military genius to whom he had endeavoured to hand over the British Army? But this disillusionment did not, unfortunately, induce Lloyd George to place more confidence in Haig or to work more loyally with him; nor had he the courage on the other hand to dismiss him.'

GENERAL PÉTAIN HAD been made Chief of the General Staff less than a fortnight after the Nivelle offensive began. No-one was quite sure what this meant. What his appointment was really about was the undermining of Nivelle. On May 15 Pétain replaced Nivelle as French commander-in-chief on the western front. Ferdinand Foch, a fiery soldier who had thought deeply about the psychology of war, became Chief of the General Staff. The signal Foch was said to have sent during the battle of the Marne in 1914 had already gone into military folklore: 'My centre is giving way, my right is falling back, situation excellent, I am attacking.'

Pétain was a realist with strong streaks of pessimism and kindness. Such people are not always the best leaders in war. Asquith had been too 'civilised': he could not declaim the bloody rhetoric of war with the naturalness of a Billy Hughes. Part of Churchill's genius as a war leader twenty-five years later was his skill at persuading people to ignore unpleasant facts. Pétain, a farmer's son, thought he had discovered the unpleasant facts about the Great War as early as 1914 and he didn't want to ignore them. He saw few chances for breakthrough. Pétain understood earlier than most that breakthrough could occur only if one had enough artillery to paralyse the German defenders. He had seen more of the war on the ground than Haig or Gough. He not only had sympathy for the common soldier: he thought he understood him, and probably did.

When he commanded at Verdun, during the worst of times, his heart lurched when he saw young men, high on enthusiasm, marching towards the furnace. And then he watched them coming out of the line. 'Their stares seemed to be fixed in a vision of unbelievable terror . . . they drooped beneath the weight of their horrifying memories. When I spoke to them, they could scarcely answer.'

Haig had a long talk to Pétain shortly after the Frenchman came to power. 'I found him businesslike, knowledgeable, and brief of speech,' Haig wrote in his diary. 'The latter is, I find, a rare quality in Frenchmen!' In truth they had little in common. Pétain believed in limited attacks on narrow fronts, not grand offensives like the one Haig was contemplating for Ypres. Pétain wanted to wait for the Americans. Haig wanted to be unrelenting.

At other times Pétain might have been an unsuitable candidate for his new post. If Haig and Gough believed too much in 'dash', Pétain didn't believe in it enough. He had an impressive presence but he lacked theatrics. He perhaps cared too much about the young men he sent out to die.

Yet he was right for this moment, just as he had been right for Verdun at its worst. All armies have a breaking point. Nivelle's offensive had turned the French army sour, just as the Tsar's blunders had turned Russian soldiers into deserters and revolutionaries. The Nivelle offensive had no sooner ended than mutinies broke out among the 2.8 million weary men of the French army.

'MUTINIES' IS THE noun most commonly used. It may not be quite the right word. It is hard to know what is. Unlike their Russian brothers, the French did not walk away from the front or murder their officers. The mutinies just happened naturally, in a regiment here and another there. They eventually spread to fifty-five divisions, half the army, yet no one person or political group was orchestrating them. They were more like strikes or demonstrations. They usually began when men were ordered back into the line. The men would refuse and many would get drunk on cheap wine. They might break windows, throw stones, jostle officers and hold meetings. A handful might head for the nearest railway station. There would be demands for more leave and better food. The *Internationale* would be sung. A red flag might be produced. Order would be restored. Then an identical incident would start in another regiment.

Pétain by late May was briefly looking at the possibility that the whole army would collapse. The French had 109 divisions on the western front, compared to Britain's sixty-two, which included the contingents from the dominions. If the French collapsed, Britain had no chance of holding off the Germans. France was much more war-weary than Britain, partly because it had lost nearly twice as many men.

Pétain knew what had set the mutinies off and he quickly told Painlevé, the War Minister. Nivelle, Pétain wrote, had aroused false hopes. His wild promises had been 'broadcast as far as the soldier in the ranks'. Then there had been the shambles after the opening day of Nivelle's offensive: troops marched here and there, attacks ordered and postponed, nerves tested and frayed, defeatist talk in the Paris press. But Pétain also knew he could not condone breaches of discipline. Armies were not democracies; they could not function if they were being subverted from within.

Pétain set out to do two things. He punished the ringleaders of the mutinies and restored discipline. And he tried to redress the men's grievances. Courts-martial were set up and eventually death sentences were passed on some 400 to 500 men. Around fifty sentences were carried out; some convicted men were sent to penal colonies. Pétain reformed the leave system. All were guaranteed seven days' leave every four months. Pétain told the War Ministry to build 400,000 bunks and ordered that mobile cookers be placed as close to the front as possible. He decreed that the wine ration be stopped the day before troops departed for the front. He implied, but did not say outright, that there would be no major offensives. He thus also implied that he was not Nivelle, who many soldiers now called 'the drinker of blood'. Pétain went around the divisions, talking to the men as well as the officers and fixing them with his calm blue eyes. He didn't try to charm the rankers or pretend he was one of them, but he left an impression of trust and concern.

And he averted a crisis. The British historian John Terraine wrote that the men felt they could trust Pétain with their lives. 'There was, in fact, a kind of unspoken compact between him and them: they would agree to obey; he would see to it that their obedience was not abused.'

By mid-July the mutinies had stopped, but the French army was not what it was. Patriotism was alive; it did not, however, run to big attacks, just stolid defence and an acceptance that the war would go on and so would life and both would mostly be miserable. For the rest of 1917 the British would have to do the attacking.

Haig might have been concerned about what support he could expect from the French for his Ypres campaign had he known how bad the mutinies were, but he didn't. The first reference to them in his diary is on June 7, when Pétain told him two divisions had refused to return to the front. Haig was still discovering details in November. He apparently told Lloyd George nothing of Pétain's troubles.

The most astonishing thing of all was this: the Germans didn't know the mutinies were going on, which perhaps says much about the Kaiser's intelligence arm. Had the Germans known, the shape of the war in 1917 might have been different.

WE DON'T KNOW whether General Otto von Moser, the German corps commander, was much like General Gough, but he now began organising an attack on the Australians that was straight from the script Gough had dashed off for First Bullecourt. It was April 13, two days after that battle. The 2nd Australian Division now held the front facing Bullecourt and Riencourt. The 1st Australian Division held a huge front, some seven-and-a-half miles, on the right of the 2nd, facing Quéant and several other villages behind the Hindenburg Line. Like Gough, Moser liked to ride his horse as often as possible. He had just returned from doing so on the 13th when his chief-of-staff told him that he was being sent a fresh division. Headquarters thought his front was about to be attacked, presumably by Walker's 1st Division. The chief-of-staff also offered the thought that the best plan would be to attack the Australians first.

Moser lunged at the idea like Gough reaching for a tank. He telephoned army headquarters and outlined his scheme. According to his memoirs, the answer came as 'swift as lightning'. Yes, he could carry it out. He would be given another two divisions to do so.

Moser worked frantically on a plan. The orders were only sent to divisional headquarters the following afternoon. The attack was to go in at 4 am the day after, April 15. The four divisions would go for the villages of Lagnicourt, Noreuil, Morchies, Boursies, Doignies, Demicourt and Hermies. Moser knew that the Australian artillery had batteries near Noreuil; he didn't know there were also batteries at Lagnicourt. His infantry would rush forward like storm-troopers, destroy artillery pieces, cause panic and confusion, then withdraw in darkness on the 15th.

The Australians were vulnerable. Gough had already decided that he was going to attack in the Bullecourt re-entrant again but he wanted the Germans to think the assault might come from anywhere. That's why he pushed the 1st Division's line out far to the right. Outposts of four to seven men held the long front there. In the valleys behind them lay the guns of the Australian artillery. No-one had given much thought to protecting them. The mentality of trench warfare lived on. Attacking infantry seldom made it to the other side's guns and history said that the Germans seldom attacked anyway.

Before dawn on April 15 the Australians in the outposts were astonished to see Germans advancing. The 1st Division was being attacked along the whole seven-and-a-half miles of its front by four German divisions. The battlefield fell into chaos. The Germans swarmed between the Australian outposts. Soon they were all around them and the Australians began to run out of ammunition. Lieutenant Charles Pope, a former London policeman, heard the Germans behind him. He sent a private back for more ammunition. After going 100 yards Private Gledhill, a farmer from Western Australia, ran into a line of Germans creeping forward. He skirted them, then ran into two Germans, who, as he put it, didn't bother him, just as he didn't bother them. Next he came upon a German lying down, who stood up and raised his arms. Gledhill swore at him and kept going. He reached company headquarters but could not get back with reinforcements and ammunition. 'Hang on', Pope shouted to his men. Then he was shot dead.

The light was still murky. Germans going forward passed Australians going backwards. They could hear, but not see, each other. The Germans broke the Australian line in front of Lagnicourt and captured several batteries. The gunners had not expected to be attacked by infantry. They had left most of their rifles back at the wagon lines near Bapaume. They were now told to remove the breech blocks and dial sights from their guns and retreat, which they did with some panic. The Germans were threatening other batteries near Noreuil. It was, as the British official historian observed, 'a very ugly situation'.

The Germans had broken through only at Lagnicourt. It was a big breach but the delaying actions fought by the outposts had bought time. Captain James Newland, a career-soldier from Launceston, Tasmania, set up a defensive post to the east of Lagnicourt. Battalion headquarters was not far behind him. Here cooks, batmen and other headquarters staff picked up rifles and joined the shooting war. The Germans had now pushed a salient one-and-a-half miles into the Australian lines around Lagnicourt.

Germans fired into Newland's party from the front and the rear and tried to set up a machine gun on a flank. Sergeant John Whittle ran out alone and not only killed the machine gunners but also brought back their gun. He, Newland and Pope were all later awarded the Victoria Cross.

It was not yet 8 am. The Germans hesitated when Australian reserves came up and began blazing away at them. Now *they* were being shot at from all sides. They had got into Lagnicourt easily enough but couldn't get out the other side. The counter-attacks intensified. The Germans began to break for home. Others surrendered. One handful of Australians, some of them unarmed, brought in 147 prisoners. When the Australians recovered the batteries the Germans had seized they found only five guns had been wrecked.

The Germans, it seemed, had spent much of their time foraging for food and souvenirs in the Australian dugouts.

The Australians re-occupied most of their old positions. General Moser's attack had failed. The Australians had suffered 1010 casualties, the Germans around 2300. Some of the German prisoners complained that they had been thrown into the assault at short notice and without a chance to look at the ground. Moser claimed the attack forced the enemy to bring up strong reserves. In truth it caused no movement of reserves and had no effect on the battle of Arras. Four thousand Australians in the front area had turned back 16,000 Germans. The only mistake the Australians had made was the failure to protect their guns.

PRIVATE ERIC PINCHES, a Queenslander, had rushed a German machine gun. Its crew surrendered and Pinches won the Distinguished Conduct Medal. He was wounded the following month in the battle that would become known as Second Bullecourt and died the next day. His name appears on the wall of the Australian National Memorial at Villers-Bretonneux. Many people want to see Private Pinches' name and even take a photograph of it. He was sixteen years old. He may have been the youngest Australian to die on the western front. There is no way of knowing for certain. It was a big war and many young men lied about their age.

PRIVATE BILLY WILLIAMS of the 2nd Australian Division was going to be in Second Bullecourt. This time Gough would use the 2nd Division. Williams first enlisted in New South Wales as a fourteen-year-old. He brought along forged papers and signatures. He was passed fit but, as he put it, sent home to his mother. 'When I was 15 years and 5 months,' he explained in 1980, 'I blackmailed my Mother with the threat that I would enlist under another name, and she would never know where I was because I knew I could pass the medical. She signed with much reluctance and with the remark that

Second Bullecourt

it would teach me a lesson, and that I would be glad to get back to home and Mother. There were many times when I wished just that . . .' The doctor who certified Williams as fit knew he was only fifteen. 'He delivered me into the world. But he was a "government man" by then.'

Preparations for Second Bullecourt were more thorough than for the first battle, although no-one seems to have given much thought to the obvious: why attack again in a re-entrant? Williams said the troops rehearsed the assault for several days behind the lines.

There were lines of white tapes laid out on the ground to represent the German front lines. Each line was referred to as OG (Old German) from No 1 to No 8. We were divided into 8 waves and each wave had an objective. The first wave moving forward under a protecting barrage were expected to take OG1, and then the second wave had to frog hop over No 1 wave and take OG2 and so on up to OG8. Most of us thought the rehearsal was farcical when the Light Horse were brought on to the scene at night rehearsals, and bore lighted torches in front of the moving troops. The moving torches represented covering barrage. I am sure that 'Fritz' *knew* our every move, because when the real thing started at 3 am May 3rd 1917, both barrages on each side opened up simultaneously. It was so thick that I wondered how a flea could come through it unscathed.

When the battle opened a lump of shrapnel tore into Williams' right shoulder blade and skidded off to lodge on a rib. He was sixteen years and seven months when they carried him out that day. When his war ended he was seventeen years and eight months, still too young to enlist.

THE REHEARSALS AND other elaborate preparations didn't mean that Gough had learned much from First Bullecourt. He had wanted to attack again on April 15, four days after the first assault had failed. Had this gone ahead, General Smyth's 2nd Division would have been rushed into the re-entrant as rudely as the 4th Division had. But Allenby's 3rd Army, to the north, was still too far back. Gough kept postponing the attack before finally settling on May 3, the day Allenby had set down for an advance on a fourteen-mile front, the widest attack ever tried by the British army in France. Bullecourt would be the right wing of this attack. Haig and Allenby were doing this to help Nivelle, who was resuming his doomed offensive to the south the next day. Haig thought Nivelle would almost certainly be sacked. With greater certainty he felt that the Nivelle offensive had already failed and would soon be called off. If so, there was little point in Allenby, with help from Gough, trying to reach Cambrai, because the French would not be surging up from the south to meet them.

Haig's big attack of May 3 would become another of the Great War's murderous gestures. It was, as the British official history notes, about holding the Germans to their ground and encouraging the French to keep their nerve. Haig's mind was elsewhere. Arras was not going to work. Ypres beckoned.

THE AUSTRALIANS WERE to attack over the same ground. This time John Gellibrand's 6th Brigade would be on the left and Brigadier-General Bob Smith's 5th Brigade on the right. This time Braithwaite's 62nd Division would attack at the same time as the Australians and try to drive deep into Bullecourt village. Ten tanks would help with the British attack; the Australians didn't want to see a tank on their front. Both divisions would advance 3000 yards in three stages. In the first the British would take Bullecourt and the Australians would retake the Hindenburg Line trenches in front of Riencourt. In the final stage the British would take Hendecourt and the Australians Riencourt.

This time the Australians would go in behind a creeping barrage and with ninety-six machine guns firing over their heads. The Anzac Corps heavy artillery had been reinforced with British guns from the north; its batteries had more than doubled to thirty-one. From mid-April the heavies reduced Hendecourt, Riencourt and Bullecourt to ruins, although the Germans could still shelter in cellars. Gunnery was all the time becoming more scientific. The order for the creeping barrage came as an elaborate map of which 300 copies were issued. But neither the staff at Anzac headquarters nor the gunners seem to have thought much of the German trenches in front of Quéant, which were largely untouched. These were only 1000 yards or so from the right flank of the Australians. True, there was a low hill between the Germans and the Australians, but the German machine gunners could still send grazing fire over the rise.

The rehearsals that Billy Williams wrote about took place near Favreuil on ground similar to the battlefield. Wire and tape were used to mark the German positions. Mounted men moved ahead of the troops to show where the creeping barrage would be landing. Aerial photographs of the German lines and the villages beyond were handed around. Gough and Birdwood turned up for a dawn rehearsal. Gellibrand noticed that bayonet scabbards made a loud flapping sound and ordered them tied down.

Zero hour was fixed for 3.45 am. This was a compromise. Gough had wanted the men to go at 4.20, when the first smudges of dawn were showing. The Australians wanted to go in the dark after the moon had set at 3.29. Braithwaite was worried that his British troops, who had never been in a major attack, would become lost in the dark.

The Australians from the two attacking brigades cast their votes for the federal election back home (which, as previously mentioned, resulted in a victory for Billy Hughes' new Nationalist Coalition) and returned to the frontline in the opening days of a glorious spring. Splashes of green appeared on bare fields, the few trees that had survived the shelling began budding and the sun cast a soft and golden glow. These men, had they not been hardened by Pozières, might have thought this a time for hope and regeneration.

BILLY WILLIAMS MAY well have been right when he wrote that ' "Fritz" *knew* our every move'. It is possible the Australians, without knowing it, had glimpsed the red-nosed aircraft of Manfred von Richthofen in the skies above Noreuil in the weeks before Second Bullecourt. The former cavalryman was swooping on

British reconnaissance aircraft from a field just behind Bullecourt. April had been his best month for kills. He now had fifty-two, which made him the most lethal German flyer of the war.

The day before Second Bullecourt opened a German aircraft crashed behind the Australian lines. Australians ran to the plane to find one flyer badly wounded and the other extremely voluble.

'What time is zero?' he asked a Queensland farmer.

'There's no zero,' the Australian replied. 'We're not thinking of attacking.'

'Oh, we know you are,' said the German. 'What time do you start?'

24

Gellibrand's martyrs

Brigade and battalion commanders had a problem that recurred with each fresh battle: where to place one's headquarters? If they set up too close to the front, there were two risks. The commander himself could be killed and, if one assumes he acquired his rank on merit, leadership would thus pass to a lesser talent. Second, if the dust and smoke were thick, the commander might be able to see only twenty yards. If, on the other hand, the brigadiers and colonels set up too far back, they had often to rely on scanty and conflicting information from runners, returning wounded, pilots flying over the battlefield and messages delivered by carrier pigeons (the telephone lines were almost always cut by shell-bursts). They would hear rumours and not know what to think about them. Sometimes their information would be hours out of date. In short they would have no 'feel' for the battlefield.

For Second Bullecourt, John Gellibrand, the commander of the 6th Brigade, set up his headquarters behind the railway embankment that looked across the plain to the three villages. He was a few hundred yards behind the jump-off tapes. Shells would almost certainly burst around him but he would have a reasonable view.

Brigadier-General Bob Smith, a tall red-faced Victorian and a close friend of Pompey Elliott, commanded the 5th Brigade, which would be on Gellibrand's right. Smith sited his post in Noreuil, more than a mile behind the jump-off point. This was a safer spot than Gellibrand's, but Smith would not see much of the battle and messages would take longer to reach him.

At the start of Second Bullecourt, Smith's brigade failed about as badly as any Australian formation ever failed on the western front. Afterwards it was said that Smith was too far back. He was. But this had little to do with the failure and is perhaps unfair to Smith. The blame lay with commanders further back than him and carrying more handsome badges of rank.

THE DAY BEFORE the battle began Lieutenant John Wright, who was acting as intelligence officer for the 17th Battalion, reconnoitred the ground where his battalion would be attacking. The 17th and 19th battalions were to lead Smith's assault. Wright found much of the wire uncut. The gunners took little notice of Wright's report. He also felt that his battalion would be a 'skyline target' for German machine gunners at Quéant. Wright explained what happened in a letter to Bean in 1937. 'I was told to shut up, that artillery would keep his nest of machine guns quiet. The artillery had no effect. The field of fire was perfect, the kind of thing a Machine Gunner dreams about.'

Wright next day directed the men into their positions on the jump-off tapes and returned to battalion headquarters at the embankment. The men hopped over on time at 3.45 am. They had to cover roughly 500 yards before they reached the first German trench. The Australian barrage opened up and the Germans replied. The first pricks of light began to appear in the inky sky. Communications broke down. Battalion headquarters, even though it was as close as it could be to the front, didn't know where the men were. Wright was sent forward to find out what was happening. He came upon men held up at the German wire, which looked ghastly because the bodies of Australians killed in First Bullecourt were still hanging on it. Wright knew at once why the attack had stalled. He saw spurts of earth thrown up by machine-gun fire from the right, from Quéant. Yesterday he had been told to shut up; today, just before dawn, he was being proved right. Then a bullet hit Wright in the abdomen and came out his left side.

Bob Smith's brigade was being cut to pieces. The men had bunched up when they neared the wire. They were now under fire from the front, from Bullecourt on the left and Quéant on the right. Many officers were hit. The men took cover in shell holes. The fire from the front became heavier. An Australian officer yelled 'Pull out'. Panic set in. Men began running back towards the embankment because they saw others running back. A small party had broken into the front German trench but were thrown out. Around 4.30 am some 400 men – unwounded, confused and without officers – were seen streaming back towards the jump-off line. Most said they did not know what had happened. Smith was told of this by telephone but did not report it to divisional headquarters. Gellibrand could see Smith's brigade coming back. He telephoned the news to divisional headquarters, which then asked Smith what was happening. Smith said some of his brigade had returned but he had ordered them forward again.

If he did issue this order, it was pointless. The moment had been lost. The right-hand side of the attack had become too hot, mainly because the planners at Anzac Corps had failed to hit Quéant hard with artillery. Smith had lost control on his front. He did not know how completely his attack had failed. But even if he had been alongside Gellibrand, the rout would still have occurred. The rout began at the wire, not the embankment.

GELLIBRAND APPEARS TO have planned better than Smith. Smith's greatest danger during the approach came from Quéant; Gellibrand's came from Bullecourt. Gellibrand ordered his machine gunners and mortar batteries to fire on Bullecourt. He seemed to sense the danger on his flank; Smith did not. Gellibrand also had two advantages denied to Smith. The artillery bombarded Bullecourt and neglected Quéant, and the terrain favoured Gellibrand's brigade. A road ran up the centre of the battlefield – the Australians called it Central Road – and its eastern bank protected Gellibrand's men from grazing fire from the Quéant machine guns.

Gellibrand was an unconventional soldier, especially when it came to form and dress. Before the battle began a staff officer from Braithwaite's British division, which was on Gellibrand's left, arrived at the Australian's dugout. He looked into the gloom to see a man rolled in a blanket on a table.

'Where shall I find the brigadier?' the Englishman asked.

The figure in the blanket turned in the direction of the voice. 'I'm he,' he said. 'What do you want?'

'I beg your pardon, sir, I want to speak to your brigade-major. Could you tell me where he is?'

'I keep him under here,' said Gellibrand, pointing under the table.

There lay Major Plant, like his commander snatching a rest before the battle.

All of Gellibrand's four battalions were from Victoria. The commander of the 24th had fallen sick. Captain Jack Lloyd, a twenty-three-year-old chemist from Melbourne, was suddenly a battalion commander. Captain Stanley Savige, four years older, was his adjutant. He had been a draper in Hawthorn, a practising Baptist and a scoutmaster. After nearly three years of war he was starting to wonder about his religious beliefs. He still believed in a supreme being but by the end of 1917 he was writing 'where He is or by what means we approach is beyond me'.

Savige wrote in 1933 that his battalion formed up in front of the embankment in the black early hours of May 3 amid 'chaos and confusion'. German shells were bursting among the men, who 'crowded like sheep in a pen'. But they kept their ground. 'What great fellows they were!'

Savige said the men were each carrying rations for two days and two water bottles. Two sandbags were wrapped around their legs and another two thrust through their shoulder straps. These were for rebuilding the German trenches. At the embankment each man collected extra ammunition and six Mills bombs. Some were given picks and shovels. Others carried boxes of ammunition, bombs and flares. A few carried rolls of expanding wire netting to throw over uncut German wire. Savige estimated the average load per man at more than 100 pounds.

He said the Germans became 'jumpy' before the Australian barrage opened up at 3.45 am. Flares went up from the German front trench, a searchlight stabbed into no-man's land and then shells began landing among the Australians. Nerves became strained, Savige said. When, fifteen minutes later, the Australians moved off it was almost a relief.

CAPTAIN GORDON MAXFIELD, the accountant from Longwood, was leading the fourth wave of Savige's battalion. Maxfield was to leapfrog through the front companies and take a position well beyond the two Hindenburg Line trenches and on the left of Riencourt. A few days earlier Maxfield had sent his parents studio photographs of himself taken in London. He didn't think them particularly good, but they would prove 'I am still in an undamaged condition and in possession of the full number of members'. The photographs show a twenty-seven-year-old with bright eyes and an open face unmarked by age. His hair is neatly parted and he has grown a crisp military moustache. The ribbon of the Military Cross sits above his left pocket and his Sam Browne belt shines.

He told his parents he had just finished supervising the troops' absentee voting in the federal election. Only about half the men bothered to vote. All seemed 'fed up' with Australian politics. Maxfield said the Anzac Day celebrations a few days earlier were more fun. He was judging the mule race and stood on a bully beef tin. The seventeen or eighteen animals and their flailing riders ran over him. 'I couldn't pick the winner & had the race re-run; the next effort was worse; you'd have split your sides – mine were really sore at the end of the day.'

THE 24TH BATTALION of Savige and Maxfield was soon in the first German trench, but the attack had not succeeded as well as

Gellibrand assumed it had. The 22nd Battalion was on the left and exposed to Bullecourt village. It was virtually wiped out by flanking fire. The 24th, followed by the 23rd, went on for the second German trench and stormed into it about 4.20 am. The battalions held it after terrible bomb fights but the success was uncertain. These men knew their flanks were 'in the air'. A look to the right told them Smith's brigade was not alongside them; indeed when they looked way back, they couldn't see it at all. If they looked to the left, they saw Germans where the 22nd should have been. They were alone. But they went on. Maxfield took part of his company 500 yards past the second Hindenburg trench to the second objective, a tramway line just west of the Six Cross Roads. According to the timetable Maxfield was to take this at 5.25 am. At 5.24 he sent up a flare saying he had done so. He also sent back a message saying that his flanks were exposed. 'Lobbed here absolutely on my own,' he said. This was pretty much the story of Gellibrand's brigade on this morning.

GELLIBRAND'S MEN LED from the front, like their leader. Lloyd and Savige, the relatively youthful commanders of the 24th Battalion, had gone forward an hour-and-a-half after the battle started and cheekily set up their headquarters in the second German trench. If they were perhaps too close, they would at least know what was happening.

Gellibrand took it upon himself to send the remnants of Smith's brigade back to the Hindenburg Line. He had to do so: how could his brigade go on to Riencourt without support on his right? Gellibrand ordered Captain Walter Gilchrist, a twenty-seven-year-old engineer, to round up Smith's men and take them back. He also sent in a company from the 7th Brigade, which was in reserve. No formation would be in reserve for long here. Second Bullecourt would suck in troops and divisions like a vortex. This was the start of the process.

Gilchrist and several others managed to round up 200 men from the 5th Brigade – others lying in shell holes refused to move – and lead them back towards the wire. No barrage protected them. German machine guns opened up. Dust flew and men fell. Gilchrist and a handful of others broke into the first German trench. He met an officer from Gellibrand's brigade who tried to explain how desperate things were. 'These men are all right,' Gilchrist said. 'All they want is a leader.' Gilchrist and others tried to clear the trench eastwards with bombs. They failed. They were too few.

On the 6th Brigade's front Maxfield kept looking to his left. He longed to see the British in Bullecourt, but Braithwaite's 62nd Division was in trouble too. Braithwaite's headquarters were well back from the front and for some hours he didn't know with certainty what was happening. While Gellibrand merely had to walk outside his dugout to know that the British attack had failed, Braithwaite listened to the usual nervous gossip. His men had taken Bullecourt; his men hadn't; the tank crews had been half-hearted; the infantry had let the tanks down. The truth emerged slowly. Braithwaite's centre brigade had fought its way through the village and its forward troops had taken a position on the left of Maxfield, but about 1000 yards from him and out of his sight. They stayed there, cut off, through the following night and were eventually killed or captured. Braithwaite's left brigade had reached the first German trench to be twice thrown out. His right brigade, the one nearest to Gellibrand's troops, also failed, although some men held on at the southern edge of the village.

Back on Smith's front Gilchrist held 200 yards of the 5th Brigade's objective in the first German trench. Most of those with Gilchrist didn't know who this inspirational figure was. He was bareheaded and wore a grey cardigan instead of a tunic; he hurled bombs and yelled to men in shell holes. And then Gilchrist was gone: no-one ever saw him again. Around 7 am the men he had been leading were driven back.

Gellibrand's men were on their own. Savige, now in the front-line, knew how perilous things were. 'We were 1,600 yards out, holding a 350-yard length of trench of the German main position with the enemy in the same trenches on either flanks.'

SOMETIME IN THE morning Gordon Maxfield lost the two lieutenants who had gone forward with him. One died trying to find
the 22nd Battalion on the left. The other was hit in the kidneys; he
knew he was dying and refused to let stretcher-bearers carry him
back. Then Maxfield was wounded. He handed over command to
a sergeant and tried to walk back to the Hindenburg Line. He was
killed on the way and his body lost. The circumstances of his death
are unclear. Some told the Red Cross he had been hit in the face;
others said a shell landed on him.

The Red Cross file also contains letters to and from Sister Jean
Simpson at the Second Australian Auxiliary Hospital at Southall. A
fortnight after the attack she wrote saying that Maxfield had been
reported wounded and missing. Was he on the Red Cross list of
prisoners of war? She wrote again late in June. She thanked the Red
Cross for the unofficial report of Maxfield's death. 'I myself have
had that same story from several 24th officers & his friends – it
seems to be the truth. I still wonder if he might possibly be a prisoner – would you let me know when the 3rd May prisoner list
comes through?' The Red Cross replied promptly. While he was still
officially 'wounded and missing', the Red Cross believed Maxfield
was dead and cited some of the eyewitness reports mentioned
above. In January, 1918, Sister Simpson received a two-sentence
letter saying that Gordon Maxfield was now officially listed as
killed. The nature of the relationship between her and Maxfield is
not apparent from the letters.

MAXFIELD'S MEN DRIBBLED back to the Hindenburg Line in twos and
threes. At one stage Maxfield had commanded about 100 in that
lonely outpost. Savige said only eighteen returned. So the second
objective was lost. The question now was whether what was left of
Gellibrand's brigade could hold on in the two German front
trenches. West Australians from the 7th Brigade were drawn into
the fight and bombed eastwards along the line of German trenches,
taking about 450 yards, or more than half of the 5th Brigade's
objective. Then they ran out of bombs and were driven all the way

back again. It was now late in the afternoon. The fighting had been furious. Savige wrote:

> . . . men fought until they dropped. Some badly wounded propped themselves into position and continued to fight. Before long we extended our foothold, and success rested on the knowledge that the small isolated groups, many without leaders, would fight on . . . One only remembers, from the blur of fighting, when one's head was dizzy, gallant men firing rifles until the barrels were hot and throwing bombs until their arms were numb . . . Time seemed to be lost. We appeared to have reached an eternity of day without night. On that day every man was a hero . . . Lloyd, as C.O., used a rifle as never before . . . Lieut. Reg Pickett . . . leader of a bomb party, still throwing bombs though shot through the right arm . . . And, above all, our brigadier, the beloved John Gellibrand, organising cooks, clerks, and batmen to rally to our assistance.

The carrying parties worked under shellfire, taking ammunition to the frontline and bringing back 1800 wounded in nine hours. Men from the 1st Australian Division were drawn in as carriers. The 28th Battalion, from the 7th Brigade, had already been drawn in to take the 5th Brigade's original objective. Three times these men bombed their way 500 yards eastwards along the Hindenburg Line. Three times they were turned back, the last at 8.40 pm, when dusk was settling in. Around this time men from the 5th Brigade's original attack were spotted emerging from shell holes and heading back towards the embankment.

The 6th Brigade was down to about 300 men holding some 500 yards of the Hindenburg Line. They had to hang on. They had been told that the British 7th Division, a more seasoned force than Braithwaite's 62nd, would now be attacking Bullecourt. They had also been told to retake the second objective that Maxfield had held. This was asking too much. Any advance would have to be made by fresh troops. The 1st Brigade of Hooky Walker's 1st Australian Division was now being drawn into the fight.

The Germans kept counter-attacking; they brought up a flamethrower. Sometime after dark the men of the 28th Battalion, on the right, heard a rumour that Gellibrand's brigade was pulling out. They began to retreat, except Captain Jack Roydhouse, a young schoolteacher. He refused to believe the rumour. He went over to the 6th Brigade's lines and, half in tears, told the men there that they were alone again. He would stay and fight with them.

The spirit of Gellibrand's men was extraordinary. They kept fighting. They could not spare men to act as stretcher-bearers. The wounded had to try to walk out. A corporal with a shell fragment in his knee carried another out. Savige told of one man whose entrails had spilled out. He lay smoking a cigarette. 'Give the bastards hell,' he told Savige. He later shot himself by placing a rifle between his feet.

Around 1 am on May 4 the relieving battalions from the 1st Division began to arrive. Two hours later Gellibrand's men were on their way back to the embankment. Then the Germans launched another counter-attack. The men of the 6th turned around and helped beat it off. Then they finally left. Along the sixteen miles of the British attack by the 3rd and 5th armies that day the only men who held the ground they won were the Canadians at Fresnoy, way over to the left, and the 6th Australian Brigade on the extreme right.

When the men of the 1st Division took over the trenches during the night they had no choice but to step on the bodies of men from the 6th Brigade. When daylight came they tried to avoid trampling on any body that carried the red-and-white diamond of the 24th Battalion.

25

Sorrow and honour

The Australian position, brave as it was, didn't make sense. It only made sense if the British could capture Bullecourt village on the left. If they couldn't, what was the point of a bridgehead 600-yards wide in the Hindenburg Line, with the Germans on both flanks and looped so far around that they could hit the Australians with diagonal fire from behind? Such a position would simply suck in more and more men. The village had to be taken.

Now, on May 4, the 1st Australian Division was in the line with orders to push it forward 1000 yards or more. Australian bodies lay everywhere: in trenches, slumped over parapets, in shell holes, hung up on wire. Gellibrand's brigade had run up 1600 casualties; it was now so small that it had been re-formed behind the railway embankment as a battalion. Its 24th Battalion had gone in 586-strong and lost around 350 – dead, wounded or missing. Its 22nd Battalion, with losses of 438, had been almost wiped out. Smith's brigade had lost more than 1500, an extraordinary figure considering that only a handful of its men had broken into the Hindenburg Line, and proof, one suspects, that it had been mauled by the machine guns on the Quéant flank.

The British 7th Division tried just before dawn on May 4 to take

Bullecourt and failed. Bean likened Bullecourt to Mouquet Farm, so ravaged by artillery that many of the trench lines were unrecognisable. The Germans were in deep dugouts so hard to find that other Germans bringing up food and ammunition had to search for entrances. The Germans no longer manned what was left of their trenches, not even at dawn. They merely posted sentries who would call the men from the dugouts if an attack seemed likely. The Germans were so hungry they were eating rations taken from British dead. They were also fighting as stubbornly as their comrades had at Mouquet Farm.

The 1st and 3rd battalions were now in the Australian line on the left. Their orders were to bomb west towards Bullecourt in the hope of joining up with the British. The 2nd Battalion was in on the right and the 4th was on its way to join them. These two were to bomb east and take the ground that Smith's brigade had failed to take. The two battalions on the left early in the afternoon fought their way towards Bullecourt and soon widened their front to 725 yards. The two battalions on the right took 400 yards of trench. The fighting was terrible. The German bombs – stick-grenades and the tiny egg-bombs – could be thrown further than the British Mills bombs, but the Mills was much more deadly. The Australians kept close to the Germans so that most of the stick and egg grenades went over their heads. Behind the leading wave of Australian bombers came parties of bomb-carriers and behind them came new bombers, ready to take over when the men at the front were killed, wounded or worn out. Other Australians fired Stokes mortars and rifle grenades along the line of the trench, over the heads of the leading wave. Lewis guns were used where possible. But it was mostly about bombs and grit, on both sides.

By late afternoon the Australians had almost doubled their front, yet this was still to little point unless Bullecourt village could be taken. Now the Germans opened a two-hour bombardment and casualties ran up quickly. The maw demanded more troops. The 11th and 12th battalions were brought up to take over on the right. The 5th Australian Division, at Albert, had already been told it might be needed.

THE REVEREND JOHN Howell-Price, vicar of St Silas's Anglican Church at Waterloo, Sydney, had wanted to enlist when war was declared in 1914. His sons told him they would remain behind if he attempted to do so. The reverend stayed behind and by late 1915 five of his sons were at the war. By the end of 1916 he had lost one, Owen, a lieutenant-colonel, shot through the head at Flers. Now, on May 4 at Bullecourt, he lost another. Lieutenant Richmond Howell-Price, a twenty-year-old, was wounded as his 1st Battalion pushed westwards towards Bullecourt. He died later in the day. Richmond was awarded the Military Cross three days after his death. He lies in a little cemetery near a copse behind Noreuil.

THE NEXT DAY, May 5, the British 7th Division tried to push patrols into Bullecourt. The fire was too hot. The divisional commander decided he needed a full artillery preparation before he could attack again. This, he said, would take three days to organise and carry out. His corps commander gave him two days, which meant the Australians would be alone on their 1100-yard front until May 7.

On the left the Australians repulsed three German counter-attacks from Bullecourt. On the right the 11th and 12th battalions took over and tried to bomb eastwards along the wrecked trenches. The Germans dropped a barrage on them. Men were buried all along the lines as trench walls caved in. One corporal dug out three men, then was buried himself. One of his men rescued him and the corporal dug out another six. Some said this barrage was as cruel as any at Pozières. The senior officer on the right received an order from battalion head-quarters to keep bombing to the east. This might have seemed sensible back at the embankment; it made no sense at the front. There, Major A. H. Darnell, a Gallipoli veteran, knew he had only about 200 unwounded men. That was all that remained of the two battalions that had just come into the line. He called a meeting of the remaining officers. All thought the Germans were about to counter-attack; it would be foolish for the Australians, the few of them left, to try to advance at the same time. Darnell refused to obey the order. His colonel insisted the attack go ahead. Darnell stood firm.

WHILE DARNELL WAS showing the sort of resolve the leaders of the Anzac Corps sometimes lacked, the 5th Australian Division, resting near Albert, was holding a horse show in balmy spring weather. Harness was oiled and buckles polished, manes tidied and tails thinned. Driver J. C. Sutherland had the best travelling kitchen and pair of horses. Corporal T. A. Buckingham won the woodchop. Earlier the men had celebrated Anzac Day with dinners and much carousing. They were in good heart. They didn't know that their general had already been told they would probably be needed at Bullecourt. Two days later a brigade of them was on the train to Bapaume.

MAY 6, THE fourth day of Second Bullecourt, began with a German barrage landing on the remnants of the 11th and 12th battalions. More men buried. More dead. The 10th battalion came up as reinforcements. The Germans counter-attacked from the east, along the line of the trenches. The long nozzles of their flamethrowers blazed and hissed in the gloom before dawn. Clouds of oil smoke hung in the air. The squads with the flamethrowers came along the line of the trench; their comrades tossed bombs from craters along both sides of it. The Australians fell back to the Central Road. The 400-yard gain had been lost.

Corporal George Howell, a builder from Enfield, New South Wales, was on the other side of Central Road, holding a post for the 1st Battalion. He jumped up into the open and ran alongside the trench the Germans had just taken back, throwing bombs. The Germans began to fall back and the exhausted men of the 11th and 12th battalions chased them with bombs and Lewis guns. The Australians took back the 400 yards they had lost. Corporal Howell later received the Victoria Cross.

That night Charles Bean, as he nearly always did, wrote in the tiny grey pages of his diary. Sometimes he wrote in pencil, sometimes in ink. Occasionally he would lapse into shorthand for a word or a sentence. Tonight he wrote:

The Army [Gough's 5th] seem to be doing nothing in particular to help us out. At present there is an almost endless vista of Bdes put in to hold this impossible position. The 7th Divn *is* going for Bullecourt again tonight – I believe ... They have crumped Bullecourt a lot today White says ... White is very angry with the way in which Gough has messed up this corps. It is very hard luck that the First Divn sld be dragged in like this just when it was coming out. Birdwood was saying today he might offer the Army to take Bullec't with our 5th Divn if they w'dnt do anything. He could guarantee the 5th Divn doing it.

NEXT DAY, THE fifth of the battle, the British again went for Bullecourt. They were trying only for the south-eastern corner. The idea was to link up with the Australians' exposed left flank. A fresh Australian battalion, the 9th, was sent in there. It was to bomb towards Bullecourt shortly after the British attack began.

The British went in under a full moon and behind a creeping barrage. Some fourteen minutes later, just before 4 am, the Australians climbed the barricade they had erected in the German trench and began to fight their way towards the village. At 5.15 am the Australians saw, standing on the parapet ahead, amid smoke and dust, Captain M. L. Gordon, of the Gordon Highlanders. Gordon and his men had been fighting their way along the eastern edge of the village when he heard the distinctive sound of Mills bombs. He knew the Australians must be close. Not long after Gordon was killed. The fighting here went on for hours. The Germans counter-attacked with a flamethrower, then dumped shells on their lost positions, but the Australians and the Scots held on. The Australians' left flank was finally connected to something, and it was something to believe in. Australians and Scots always seemed to find things to admire in each other.

Fresh troops were needed. In the dark the 2nd Brigade of the 1st Division took over the bloody earth on the left. The British next day would try to take the rest of Bullecourt; the Australians would try to push on and meet them at the north-eastern corner of the village.

NEXT DAY, THE sixth day of the battle, the British at 11 am tried to strengthen their hold on Bullecourt. They took parts of the Red Patch (as it was designated on the maps) on the south-western corner of the village, only to be pushed out of most of it. Rain had made the battlefield muddy. The Australians captured another 150 yards of German trench along the eastern edge of Bullecourt.

Sergeant Percy Lay, a drover from Ballan, Victoria, was there. He was wounded that night while firing a rifle grenade. The cartridge failed to propel the live grenade off the rifle. Lay held the rifle high in the air and the bomb blew it to pieces. A fragment of metal landed in his hand. The Germans kept counter-attacking. Lieutenant William Donovan Joynt was near Lay. 'During a respite at night,' Joynt wrote, 'when we could hear the Germans assembling for a further attack, apparently very much against their will, Lay, unarmed, suddenly hopped out of the trench, disappeared into the darkness, and in a few minutes reappeared at the double with (six) Fritzies in front of him, belting the hide off them with his tin hat as his sole weapon.' For this, and for fighting on while wounded, Lay received the Military Medal.

Walter Hill had been in the line several days with the 1st Division. In 1980, when he was eighty-five, he wrote about his time there. He remembered being buried up to his neck when trench walls caved in and seeing shell-shocked men wandering aimlessly – and something else. Pioneers had dug a communications trench to the front along the line of Central Road.

> Here I witnessed the most tragic episode of my service. A corporal was working to deepen the section of trench his men occupied, throwing the earth out to where several corpses of soldiers killed the night before [lay]. Noticing the colour patch on one corpse, he remarked, 'That is my brother's battalion.' As he crawled to it, he turned the corpse to discover with terrible grief that he had been throwing the earth on his dead brother.

THE 1ST DIVISION came out and the 5th Division went in. Up came Simon Fraser, the forty-year-old farmer from Victoria's Western

District, now a lieutenant, who had told of the stricken Australian at Fromelles calling to him: 'Don't forget me, cobber.'

Up came Sergeant Jimmy Downing, who had also been at Fromelles. He later remembered the journey to the embankment. Scraps of bodies poked from the earth. The land was bare, except for tree stumps, curled and broken railway lines and houses reduced to a shattered chimney or a broken wall. Downing watched 1st Division men coming out 'dull-eyed, shambling, half-crazed'.

Field guns flashed behind Downing; the sky ahead was lit with the flare and flicker of German artillery. He passed a British soldier lying on the ground. His hair was bloody and Downing could see the red skull beneath. The fingers of one hand had been smashed to a pulp. His legs were broken and his puttees were twisted and bloody. 'Keep to the left,' the Tommy said between moans, 'keep to the left, they want you there, boys, keep to the left.'

Downing reached the front. 'A man with both eyeballs hanging like poached eggs on his cheeks was sitting at the bottom of the trench groaning.' A man babbled on the parapet. The German barrage became heavier. Downing heard the sound of German bombs. And then he saw the grey mass of Germans rise out of the ground. He and the others fired until their rifles became hot. The attack was beaten off.

And up to the front came Lieutenant Rupert 'Mick' Moon. He had filled one of the many vacancies for officers in the 15th Brigade after the slaughter at Fromelles. Moon was twenty-four, a bank clerk, less than five foot six inches tall and slightly built. He looked more like a boy than a man. Blue eyes gazed out of a gentle and intelligent face. Moon liked horses and served on Gallipoli as a dismounted trooper. He transferred to the infantry and was commissioned in the field in France.

He hadn't liked the freezing winter of 1916–17. 'A terrible time, sheer misery,' he said when he was ninety-one. 'The shell fire, the dominance of the German air force, the appalling conditions, rain and mud made life very, very difficult, but we were very young and it didn't do us any harm.'

He left us with none of his thoughts as he neared the front at

Bullecourt that day (indeed he never talked publicly about the day), but we know what others were thinking about him. Pompey Elliott, his brigadier, doubted if Moon would make a good officer. The extroverted Elliott thought Moon too timid. Major George Wieck, Elliott's senior staff officer, mentioned to Bean that Moon had been marked down as an 'unsuitable' leader. Moon, however, told Bean long after the war that this was not so, that he had had the confidence of Elliott and Lieutenant-Colonel Charles Denehy, his battalion commander. Two days after Moon arrived at the Bullecourt front Denehy called him and other officers in to talk about an attack early the next day. 'You've got the tough one, Mickey,' he told Moon.

THE ARRAS BATTLE was petering out. Haig was more interested in planning a big offensive at Ypres. Bullecourt was kept going. It was the only breach in the Hindenburg Line and it led nowhere, but it had to be kept going because otherwise there would be little to show for the Arras offensive. It also had to be kept going to lull the Germans into thinking the battle there wasn't over. If they thought it was, they would begin to guess at the site for Haig's next big battle and would surely come up with Ypres.

So the British 7th Division was ordered to try to capture the rest of Bullecourt in the early hours of May 12. One battalion of Elliott's brigade – the 58th, that of Denehy, Fraser and Moon – was to assist by attacking westward along the two German trenches. It would join up with the British at the crossroads above the north-eastern corner of the village. Moon's party would storm a concrete machine-gun post that sat between the two German trenches. Another party, under Lieutenant Norman Pelton, would climb over the bomb-stop in the second German trench and push the Germans back to the crossroads and capture a large dugout. Then a third party, under Lieutenant Jimmy Topp, would capture the German dugouts beyond the crossroad. After taking the machine-gun nest Moon was to help with the other two attacks.

Moon took the nest after a bomb fight but was hit in the face.

He and his men went on to help with the fight for the second objective. Here Moon received a second wound, this time to the shoulder, that spun him around and left him dazed. The Germans broke. Moon followed them. Moon and his men trapped the Germans in dugouts and took 184 prisoners. By now Moon had received a third wound, to the foot. Blood and sweat dripping from his face, he sat down among his men and said: 'I've got three cracks and not one of them good enough for Blighty.' (A 'Blighty' was slang for a wound that warranted a man being sent to England.)

Moon worked to strengthen the new Australian position. Then he received a fourth wound. A bullet smashed his jaw and twelve teeth. This one was a Blighty. Moon bound up his face and continued to work on building up the position. Only when he was satisfied that this was being done correctly did he agree to leave the front. The Australians and the British eventually met, as they were supposed to, at the crossroads.

Moon received the Victoria Cross. Pelton and Topp, the leaders of the other two parties, were killed. It was Topp's thirty-seventh birthday. Killed too was Simon Fraser.

ELLIOT'S BRIGADE CAME out of the line the following night, relieved by British troops. The only Australians in the frontline now were on the right of the Central Road. The British 7th Division was shortly after relieved by the 58th Division, which meant the two battles for Bullecourt had used up three British divisions and four Australian. The front was approaching a stalemate. The British and Australians couldn't push on and the Germans couldn't recover their lost trenches.

The Germans eventually gave up. They blew up their dugouts and pulled back. Late in May the Anzac Corps left Bullecourt.

THE BRITISH OFFICIAL historian concludes his account of Second Bullecourt with a coy sentence: 'The Battle of Bullecourt is instructive as well as terrible to contemplate.' It is easy to see how it was terrible. Allied casualties for the second battle ran to more than 14,000: 7482 Australians and some 6800 British. But how was the battle instructive?

Charles Bean in the Australian official history was quick to criticise Gough for twice attacking into a re-entrant, the first time impulsively. He said that Bullecourt, more than any other battle, 'shook the confidence of Australian soldiers in the capacity of the British command; the errors, especially on April 10th and 11th, were obvious to almost everyone'. He described some of the tactics as 'impossible'. And there Bean left it.

He returned to Second Bullecourt in his 1957 book *Two Men I Knew*, a memoir about the generals Bridges and White, but gave it only eleven lines. He called the battle a success, 'though this fell far short of Gough's objectives which, so far as Australian experience went, had up to this stage in the war been tragically inflated.' Elsewhere Bean wrote of White: 'He was the greatest man I have known. In no other was genius so quickly and so clearly evident.'

Gough's 1931 book *The Fifth Army* is no help either. Gough merely said that on the first day the Australians succeeded and the British division didn't, mainly because its men were inexperienced and lost direction. There is no mention of tactics.

In 1990 the Australian historian Eric Andrews questioned Bean's account of Second Bullecourt. He conceded that Gough – and Haig – were to blame for the folly of attacking into a re-entrant, but said Bean ignored failures in Australian staff work and failed to analyse the Anzac Corps' artillery work. 'It is like a historian writing of the Vietnam war and ignoring the use of helicopters.' Andrews argued that the artillery plan underestimated the threat from Quéant and that this allowed German machine gunners to knock Smith's brigade out of the fight in the first hour. He said Bean failed to mention that Gellibrand resigned command of the 6th Brigade a month after Second Bullecourt (he took up a training post in England) because he was unhappy with the staff work of Smyth's 2nd Division. Andrews concluded that the Australian staff work was 'incompetent'. White, he said, 'appears a poor operations commander and an incompetent tactician'.

Andrews said Bean was too much concerned with telling the story of infantrymen, whom he admired, and often became lost in a fog of detail that confused and deterred readers. Bean didn't provide enough analysis of the artillery plans or the Australian staff work. And he hero-worshipped White. He took White's criticisms of Gough at face value and didn't realise that White and Birdwood were excusing themselves. Andrews wondered whether Bean 'hesitated to look too closely at the battle, lest he be obliged to condemn his hero. It was all so much easier to attack Gough, and revert at the end of the long account to righteous indignation against the British High Command.'

Andrews' criticism is persuasive.

JEAN LETAILLE, A farmer and former mayor of Bullecourt, has created a private museum, perhaps the finest on the old western front, under the whitewashed walls of what were once his wheat sheds. Here is a rusting *minenwerfer*, the German mortar so feared by allied soldiers. Barbed wire, in all its varieties, lies everywhere. The prongs are three times longer than those used for cattle fences and also thicker and closer together. Here are tobacco tins: Gold Flake Honey Dew (a gold tin), Craven 'A' (red), Capstan (light blue). Here are wire-cutters: long, short, British, German, wooden handled, cantilevered. There is a German sniper's breastplate, not much different to the armour Ned Kelly fashioned from the mouldboards of ploughs. And here is a saw used for surgical amputations.

Doves coo, bees hover over the flowerbeds and the whiff of blood-and-bone fertiliser is heavy in the air. Bullecourt is as tranquil as it was before 1914. The war is gone. The tunnels and trenches and dugouts have been filled in and ploughed over and the corn stands seven-feet high. And war hasn't gone. The ploughs still bring its debris. And the war hasn't gone, because people here remember.

You can find the spot where Moon won his Victoria Cross. It's in the yellow stubble in front of the Australian memorial on the sunken road between Bullecourt and Riencourt. Walk out there and you'll find shrapnel balls and nose cones. The chances are that you'll also see a hawk circling high overhead and a swarm of white butterflies. War and peace, death and life. And you think of the words of Jimmy Downing: 'Bullecourt represents for Australians a greater sum of sorrow and of honour than any other place in the world.'

26

Roses with carmine petals

The captured trenches at Bullecourt were built into the British lines and the place reverted to the norms of trench warfare. Bodies were buried, sentries posted and cookers brought up behind the front. Each side lobbed the odd shell on the other and riflemen blazed away at shadows in the night and longed for the rum ration. By June the Bullecourt front was like any other quiet sector. Yes, it was a rupture in the Hindenburg Line, but it led nowhere. The last days of this battle had been about bluff. Bullecourt became a 'local objective', not, as it had once been, a step in a journey of break-through. When Second Bullecourt was only two days old Haig was saying he wanted to keep the Germans in doubt about where he would start his next offensive. He wasn't much interested in what was happening at Bullecourt. His mind was fixed on the Ypres salient and the high ground that curled around it.

Haig, with justification, believed that his British empire army was the only robust arm of the allied coalition. The Italians were badly led and inclined to muddling, the Russians were in turmoil after the revolution, the French seemed incapable of mounting an offensive (Haig didn't yet know the extent of the mutinies), and the Americans hadn't arrived. Haig, moreover, had little confidence in

Third Ypres: the battlefield

Steenstraat
Bixschoott
Langemarck
Poelcappelle
Pilckem
Passchendaele
Boesinghe
Hill 29
St Julien
Gravenstafel
Ysers – Ypres Canal
Steenbreek
River
Broodseinde
Roulers
Wieltje
Frezenberg
Poperinghe
Ypres
Westhoek
Hooge
Becelaere
Observatory Ridge
Gheluvelt
Mount Sorrel
Hill 60
Ypres–Comines
St Eloi
Roozebeek
Canal
River
Wytschaete
Oosttaverne
Wambeke
River
Spanbroekmolen
Messines
Doyne
River
River
Comines
Lys
Warneton
St Yves
Ploegsteert Wood

SCALE

| 0 | | 4000 metres |
| 0 | | 4000 yards |

his own navy, which was clamouring for the Belgian ports to be cleared by the army. Many thought the navy was too cautious, that it wanted to win the war without fighting. Haig called Jellicoe, the First Sea Lord, an 'old woman'.

Lloyd George, also with some justification, didn't believe in Haig. He refused the field-marshal (Haig had been promoted earlier in the year) substantial reinforcements for his Ypres campaign. Lloyd George had ideas that the war could be won from Italy; he also placed an absurd importance on the capture of Jerusalem. Still, one has to be careful in trying to characterise Lloyd George's attitude. He was not *against* the battle that would be designated Third Ypres. He didn't like the idea; he didn't like Haig or the prospect of another Somme-like casualty list. But, when it came to grand strategy, he lacked the confidence to overrule Haig and Robertson (who, it should be said, didn't believe in the Ypres offensive as ardently as Haig). Lloyd George simply wasn't *for* Ypres.

Haig lacked the Prime Minister's quickness of mind; he was stiff-necked and dull. But he was full of resolve in a way the Prime Minister was not. Haig didn't lapse into the self-doubts that bothered men of sharper intelligence. And, most of the time, Haig, the amateur politician, seemed to best Lloyd George, the amateur strategist, not through brilliance but with a tactic he understood well: attrition. Haig prevailed by stubbornness, by force of character rather than force of intellect. He was always in front of you, saying in awkward and often incomplete sentences exactly what he had said yesterday. Lloyd George kept changing his mind and Haig kept saying the same things. Haig had a plan and he challenged you to come up with a better one. And now he was stronger because he had been right about Nivelle and Lloyd George had been wrong. If the Prime Minister was brighter, Haig was doughtier. He didn't, as some have suggested, think of trying to bring Lloyd George down. If he could avoid it, he didn't think about Lloyd George at all. The Prime Minister lived in a world he didn't understand and didn't much want to.

So Third Ypres – or Passchendaele as it later came to be known in folklore and nightmares – came about because Haig and the hand-wringers at the Admiralty wanted it. It came about after attempts at breakthrough elsewhere – on the Somme, along the Chemin des Dames and at Arras – had failed. It came about because it was one of the few options left and had definite and worthy objectives that were not present in the Somme campaign. It came about because the War Cabinet wasn't sure what to do. Above all it came about because Lloyd George, while he seldom felt comfortable about it, lacked the resolve to say no to it.

The low ridges that Haig wanted to capture at Ypres were roughly in the shape of a sickle that swept around the ruined city. As a first step he would use sixteen divisions and lots of artillery to capture a ridge and a village on the handle of the sickle. The village was called Messines.

Sir Herbert Plumer would attack Messines with his 2nd Army. Plumer, as requested, wrote a scheme for the first stage of the push to the coast. It was a step-by-step plan, careful and typical of Plumer. Haig thought it too careful. He wanted to see bold arrows on a map, to hear the word 'hurrosch'. Plumer always seemed to come up with a scheme that was a few thousand yards short of Haig's idea of glory. Haig eventually decided that Gough should take over the main offensive after Messines: Gough, who didn't take staff work too seriously, who had neither the organisational skills of Plumer nor his even disposition, who didn't know the salient well, who had just blundered at Bullecourt and was almost certainly Haig's least competent army commander.

The coming of Gough meant there would have to be a gap of seven weeks between Messines and the offensive towards the coast. The Germans would have time to work out what was happening.

JOHN MONASH HAD set up his headquarters in a château north of Armentières. He hung photographs of his garden at Toorak on the walls. Part of him was thrilled by his elevation to command of a division – he had always craved recognition – but another part was homesick. On March 7 General Godley told Monash his 3rd Division would be part of the attack on Messines. The New

Zealanders would also take part. Both divisions were in Godley's II Anzac Corps. Monash at once began working on a scheme that became more and more intricate. He called it 'Magnum Opus'.

He interrupted this to take leave on the Riviera, where he panted up donkey tracks to old villages 'past beautiful villas all smothered in flowering creepers, and later through olive forests and lemon groves'. He watched fishermen and took the tram to Monte Carlo where he enjoyed a performance of *The Barber of Seville* at the opera house. His eyes missed nothing. The villagers in the mountains looked 'just as if they had stepped out of a picture, the men with thick stockings, plush corduroy breeches, blue kummerbund and sash, Garibaldi shirts, and Tyrolean hat, the women with bulging skirts, aprons, and flat chacot, all carrying great loads on their heads – like Arab women'.

Back at the château he worked on Magnum Opus and on April 15 showed it to his three brigadiers and told them to discuss it with their battalion commanders. He then began working on specific tasks for platoons and even sections. Monash wanted to know where the man from the YMCA was going to set up his coffee stall. Soon 'Magnum Opus' was six-inches thick. 'Wonderful detail but not his job', Major-General Charles 'Tim' Harington, Plumer's chief-of-staff, said.

Monash wrote to John Gibson, his partner in a reinforced concrete business in Melbourne. He needed to tell Gibson that there was no prospect of him returning home to help with the business.

Any attempt to desert my post is unthinkable . . . even if I could have had my discharge for the asking, and this is most assuredly not the case, every dictate of honour and proprietary prevents my even contemplating such a thing. For myself I am very heartily sick of the whole war business. Its horror, its ghastly inefficiency, its unspeakable cruelty and misery have always appalled me, but there is nothing to do but to set one's teeth and stick it out as long as one can.

Monash kept refining his plan. He had been in several badly planned attacks at Gallipoli under Godley, who was a lazy commander there and no better here. Godley's genius, if he possessed any, lay in distancing himself from failures. This time Monash was doing the work Godley couldn't do. It was a set-piece and Monash had time to get everything right. Bean wrote in the official history: 'His Jewish blood gave him an outstanding capacity for tirelessly careful organization.' Bean had interesting ideas about genetics.

Haig came to inspect the division. During the preparations a Jewish officer was thrown from his horse. Haig seemed distant and unimpressed during his visit, although he wrote afterwards that Monash was a 'most thorough and capable commander'. The mood in the 3rd Division officers' mess that evening was subdued. Monash rose to read the weather report.

'A heavy dew fell this morning,' he began.

LIEUTENANT PHILLIP SCHULER, known to his friends as Peter, was in Monash's divisional train, looking after baggage and food supplies, and it seemed odd that he should be there. He was about to turn twenty-eight, tall, olive-skinned and handsome. Everyone seemed to like him. His father, Frederick, had come to Australia from Germany as a child and was editor of the *Age*; his mother, Deborah, was blind as a result of a fall down stairs. Phillip had started a law degree and failed, mainly, it seems, because of his busy social life. Phillip joined the *Age* and quickly proved that he was a natural writer. He liked books and plays and dining out and was the youngest member of the Savage Club, then a meeting place for Bohemians.

Schuler left with the first convoy of Australian troops in 1914 as the *Age* correspondent. Sir Ian Hamilton thought him a 'delightful personality'. Schuler wrote a series of articles about the scandalous treatment of the wounded taken off Anzac Cove after the landing.

What did they come back to? The best attention and comfort that medical skill could provide? No! The bare iron decks of the transports where they had been living for the last three weeks. To medical comforts? No! To the old grey blankets they had just discarded and the decks. To milk and soft food for those unable to take the iron rations and bully beef? No, to their ordinary rations.

He reported that wounded had been left untreated aboard a hospital ship in Alexandria because the medical staff ashore had gone to the races. Schuler's reports were not only accurate; they were foremost among the few critical pieces published while the Gallipoli campaign was actually going on.

Schuler's photographs from Lone Pine were haunting and remain the best-known images of Gallipoli. He returned to Australia to write, in 'fever heat', the book *Australia in Arms*, the first long account of the Gallipoli campaign. Monash read the proofs of the book on Salisbury Plain. He thought the manuscript more accurate than Hamilton's dispatches.

Schuler had tended his credentials as a journalist and writer and they were better than those of just about anyone else in the country. He might, one would have thought, have been given accreditation to cover the war on the western front. Instead he enlisted, and not as an officer, as he could have been easily enough, but as a driver. He was sent to Monash's 3rd Division. Why did he swap the relative ease of life as a war correspondent for that of the lowliest soldier? And there was another mystery. He had met a 'beautiful and gifted' woman in Cairo, a widow with two children. According to Roy Bridges, a colleague of Schuler's at the *Age*, they were engaged.

Schuler had been promoted to lieutenant by the time Monash was planning for Messines. He wrote to Bridges just before the battle opened. The letter ended: 'Keep on remembering.'

HERBERT PLUMER, SIXTY at the time of Messines, an old Etonian and an infantryman, was an English gentleman in the best sense of the word. A staff officer once suggested to him that a certain person was too much of a gentleman to handle the job for which he was being touted. Plumer screwed his eyeglass into his eye, looked at the staff officer, smiled, and said: 'Can you be too much of a gentleman?' It

Messines: the attack, June 7, 1917

Legend:
- ●●●●●●● Allied first objective
- —x—x— Allied second objective
- —●—●— Allied third objective

Ypres

Observatory Ridge

23 UK

X UK

47 UK

Hill 60
204 GER
Mount Sorrel GER

The Caterpillars

Battle Wood

Canal

The Bluff

Spoil Bank

41 UK

St Eloi

Hollebeke

35 GER

204 GER

19 UK

Vierstraat

Bois Quarante

Martens Farm

Damm Wood

Denys Wood

Rose Wood

River

Roozebeek

IX UK

Hollandscheschuur Farm

GERMAN SECOND LINE

Bug Wood

Comines

LINE

7 GER

Vandamme Farm

Grand Bois

Hospice

Oosttaverne

Petit Bois

16 UK

Wytschaete

Torreken Farm

Wambeke

Wambeke

River

FRONTLINE FIRST

2 GER

GERMAN THIRD LINE

Spanbroekmolen

1 GD RES GER

Huns Farm

Delporte Farm

Gapaard

36 UK

3 BAV GER

Messines

2 GER

WARNETON

25 UK

13 AUS

Bethleem Farm

3 BAV GER

12 AUS

Wulverghem

40 NZ AUS

Petite Douve Farm

Doyne

River

4 BAV GER

37 AUS

Warneton

4 AUS

38 AUS

II ANZAC GODLEY

3 AUS

35 AUS

39 AUS

Hill 20

La Passe Ville

Hill 63

Heavy gas shelling here

33 AUS

St Yves

Deulemont

Lys

N
W E
S

SCALE
0 _____ 2000 metres
0 _____ 2000 yards

Ploegsteert Wood

Ploegsteert

ALLIED GERMAN

is often said that, because of his looks, Plumer was the inspiration for David Low's cartoon character Colonel Blimp. He wasn't, but he could have been. Philip Gibbs, the English war correspondent, described him thus: 'In appearance he was almost a caricature of an old-time British General, with his ruddy, pippin-cheeked face, with white hair and a fierce little white moustache, and blue, watery eyes, and a little pot-belly and short legs.' His men called him 'Daddy' and his friends called him 'Plum', and he was almost certainly the best of the British army commanders. Plumer was thorough and measured in everything he did and he understood the nature of the war and the primacy of artillery. He didn't see cavalry galloping through gaps; he worried about casualties. Haig thought Plumer sound but perhaps lacking the 'real offensive spirit'.

Plumer had been in charge of the Ypres front since the spring of 1915 and, as the British historian John Terraine put it, he and Harington, his chief-of-staff, had created an atmosphere that was unique. John Charteris, Haig's head of intelligence, wrote: 'Plumer and Harington are a wonderful combination, much the most popular, as a team, of any of the Army Commanders. They are the most even-tempered pair of warriors in the whole war or any other war. The troops love them . . . Nobody knows where Plumer ends and Harington begins.' Philip Gibbs said of Harington: 'For the first time, in his presence and over his maps, I saw that, after all, there was such a thing as the science of war, and that it was not always a fetish of elementary ideas raised to the nth degree of pomposity, as I had been led to believe by contact with other generals and staff officers.'

Despite the long casualty lists from the battles of 1915, from the Somme and from Arras, many of the allied generals were starting to understand how to fight the first war of the industrial age. They knew artillery pieces had to be concentrated, so that barrages were heavy enough to keep the Germans away from their machine guns. They accepted the need for creeping barrages. More thought was being given to knocking out German artillery pieces – counter-battery work. Gunners were experimenting with flash-spotting and sound-ranging as ways of locating the German batteries. The machine-gun barrage was becoming more common. More time was

being spent on preparation. Aircraft were becoming more important as artillery techniques became more sophisticated. The British
had twice as many planes in the Messines area than the Germans.
The realisation had come: it took more than 'character' to break
into the enemy's trenches.

Plumer brought all these ideas into his plan to capture Messines.
He had two extra advantages. This was a set-piece battle with limited objectives and he had plenty of time to plan it. And he had a
weapon that had never been used on this scale in the war before.
Since 1915 his men had been tunnelling under the German lines.
The Germans didn't know it but they were sitting on close to one
million pounds of explosives.

British, Canadian and Australian tunnellers had pushed more
than twenty galleries out under the German lines. Several were
more than 2000-feet long. Most were between fifty and 100 feet
below the surface. The shafts had been sunk well behind the British
lines. The signposts said they were 'deep wells' and the spoil that
came up, a distinctive blue clay, had to be hidden so that German
airmen would not spot it.

The clay, similar to that which was excavated to build the
London underground railway, was difficult to mine with mechanical diggers. Men with spades and picks did most of the work. One
would lie on his back on a plank and would use both feet to drive
a spade into the face. Another man would gather the clay into a
sandbag and a third would drag this back to the trolley rails.

More than 173 miles of new railways had been laid behind the
lines. For the first time light railways carried ammunition right up
to some of the heavy batteries. And Plumer had lots of batteries.
Here was another change. Artillerymen now related the number of
guns to the length of trench to be attacked. Plumer had 2200 guns
for his ten-mile front, 756 of them heavies. He had twice as many
guns as the Germans. A year earlier, on the first day of the Somme
offensive, and on a wider front, the British used only 1400 guns, of
which fewer than 400 were heavy or medium.

The business of killing was being reduced to a mathematical
formula.

PRIVATE GEORGE DAVIES, a signaller, came up to the front with Monash's 3rd Division. Davies didn't like war, scientific or otherwise. He was an ardent Methodist and often preached at church services and helped with burials. The men seemed to like him, but he wrote early in 1917 that their swearing, drunkenness and general immorality horrified him. He was an acute observer of small but telling incidents. He recalled that the day before Messines opened a soldier who had never been in a big attack before asked him the simple question: 'Do you take your overcoat?'

The same day Davies wrote to Willie, his adopted brother in Australia. If he lived through the battle, he told Willie, he would do 'all I can to crush any military tendencies in my nation'. He would 'uphold the very highest and best socialism' and try to make his life more like Christ's. But Davies had a premonition of death. He told Willie he was leaving him his war diary and his books. 'All my Poet's works are yours . . . I hope you will read them as they will make your life beautiful and sweet.' He also left Willie his bicycle.

Then he wrote to his mother. 'If I live I shall stand by red-hot socialists and peace cranks to stop any further wars after this one, but while I am at it I will fight like only one facing death can fight.' Davies survived the opening of the battle. He was killed when it was five days old.

Lieutenant Walde Fisher, a law student and tutor, also came up with Monash's division. He survived. He wrote a highly readable diary for the months preceding Messines. One day on the Armentières front he and his men could not get a drain to run. A man went down to find the obstruction. 'That's the silly ------ who blocked it,' he exclaimed. 'That' was the decaying body of an officer of the Sherwood Foresters. Fisher noted in May: 'One of our chaps got 29 wounds yesterday, and was as bright and cheerful as ever. The M.O. asked him: "Well, and what have you got?" "Everything," he answered, "except the bloody nose cap." He may pull through, Casey is his name.'

Captain Bob Grieve, a twenty-seven-year-old commercial traveller from the Melbourne suburb of Brighton, heard the sounds of the nightingale and the cuckoo for the first time while waiting in

Ploegsteert Wood for the battle to start. He wrote that on the night of June 6 he and his men shook hands all around and started for the front and the attack. They hadn't gone far before they realised the Germans were firing gas shells. They could smell the gas and the shells made a distinctive *pop* as they exploded. The men pulled on their masks, immediately became half blind and almost suffocated because their lungs were heaving from the long walk through the barrage carrying ammunition and tools. Grieve said it was pitiful to see horses and mules gasping for breath.

Lieutenant William Palstra, a twenty-five-year-old accountant from the Melbourne suburb of Surrey Hills, had stared at a plane flying overhead while he was training on Salisbury Plain. He decided at that moment that he wanted to be a pilot. Soon after he began sending off applications to join the flying corps. But here he was at Messines, leading a platoon in Monash's division up to the start line. Then the gas came. 'Have to wear box respirators,' he wrote. 'The remainder of the march . . . was one long drawn-out hell.' Some men, he said, were gassed when their masks slipped. The hours that followed were worse than anything that happened in the three days of fighting that were to follow. 'The night was fairly dark, one's gas mask glasses were continually becoming fogged with perspiration, one tripped over obstacles – barbed wire and groaning men.' The gas took half Palstra's platoon. The other half arrived at the start line, stripped off all their equipment and lay exhausted on the duckboards.

FIVE DAYS BEFORE Messines opened Harry Murray, walking his easy walk and wearing a slouch hat, received the Victoria Cross from George V in Hyde Park. A friend 'smartened him up a bit' before the ceremony. Murray was never one for spit and polish. Sometimes he wore his leather officer's belt, known as a Sam Browne, with the buckle in the wrong place. The King spoke with Murray at length. Though he would have hated the thought, Murray was becoming famous. He had now won the Victoria Cross, two Distinguished Service Orders and the Distinguished Conduct Medal. Murray wrote that the King did not pin the medal on. It was hung on hooks that had been attached to Murray's uniform beforehand. An official who took himself rather seriously told Murray the hooks had to be returned after the ceremony. 'Evidently he had heard of Ned Kelly,' Murray wrote.

He took a trip to Scotland, then returned to France. His 4th Division was the reserve division for the battle of Messines.

AT BULLECOURT THE Australians had been half the attacking force. Here they were a small part of a bigger and better-planned assault. Plumer was using nine divisions from three corps for his initial attack. Monash's division was the southern flank of the whole attack; it would go for the lower shoulder of Messines ridge. Above it the New Zealand Division would take Messines village. The British 25th Division, loaned to Godley, would attack further north between Messines and Wytschaete village. The long-suffering Australian 4th Division, reinforced after Bullecourt, started out in reserve but was told shortly before the attack that it would be in action on the afternoon of the first day. Monash would attack with two brigades up, the 9th and the 10th. The 11th was in reserve.

Plumer had at first planned to take only the German frontline. This was 1500 yards away, in the valley in front of the ridge itself. Haig persuaded Plumer to go through the frontline and take Messines and Wytschaete on the first morning. In the afternoon the troops were to head down the reverse slope of the ridge and capture the German intermediate position known as the Oosttaverne Line, an advance of 3000 yards. Four-and-a-half German divisions held the ridge, which was dotted with concrete pillboxes. In other circumstances the German position might have been formidable. But this time the British artillery had done its job well; this time the bombardment bore a sensible relationship to what the infantry was being asked to do.

Wire-cutting had begun on May 21. By zero hour – 3.10 am on June 7 – most of the wire had been pulverised. So had the two villages and most of the German trenches. Many of the German guns had been knocked out by counter-battery fire. Only the pillboxes remained. The Germans were addled by the fury of the bombardments. One wrote: 'All the trenches are completely smashed in . . . we are forced out into the open without any protection.' And then there were the mines.

Nineteen of these went off over forty-five seconds at 3.10 am. It was the largest man-made explosion in history. One hundred and thirty miles away Londoners heard it as a distant roar. Fifteen miles to the east German soldiers in Lille ran in panic, fearing an earthquake. Buildings swayed and window glass fell into the streets. Perhaps 10,000 Germans died as the mines went up, some of them simply atomised. The earth trembled, a wave of hot air ran up the ridge and beyond, black clouds of smoke and dust rolled over the German rear positions and blotted out the light of the sinking moon, craters hundreds of feet wide opened up and the sky rained clods of Flemish clay. The Germans who survived were half-mad and mostly wanted to surrender. Philip Gibbs watched the spectacle.

> The most diabolical splendour I have ever seen. Out of the dark ridges of Messines and Wytschaete and that ill-famed Hill 60 there gushed out and up enormous volumes of scarlet flame from the exploding mines and of earth and smoke all lighted up by the flame spilling over into mountains of fierce colour, so that the countryside was illuminated by red light.

Bob Grieve watched a big mine go up on the Australian front. The earth rose like a huge mushroom, he wrote. 'Debris of all description rained down with dull thuds for quite a time, then all was over.'

A German witness saw 'nineteen gigantic roses with carmine petals' rise slowly and majestically out of the ground. After the explosions the Germans on the rise leading to the villages sent up white and green flares. They were asking for artillery support. But the British gunners had already hit the German batteries with gas shells and high explosives. By the time the German counter-barrage began falling on the assembly areas, most of the British and dominion troops had left. In no-man's land they encountered dazed Germans and hardly any machine-gun fire. They crossed the cratered valley and begun to push up the hill with dust swirling in front of them and their own barrage shrieking overhead. No British battle of the war had begun with such promise.

Lieutenant Palstra watched a mine on his right go up 'like a volcano, the earth coming down like a hailstorm for minutes afterwards'. Palstra and his men followed the creeping barrage. 'The moment we entered his wire the Hun abandoned his guns and left his trenches in a solid line. Our men stood in that wire and shot them down . . .' Palstra found mineral water and cigars in the pillboxes and handed them out among his men. So many senior officers were killed or wounded that Palstra ended up commanding his battalion for two days. Afterwards he was awarded the Military Cross. But he still wanted to be a pilot.

THE AUSTRALIANS WERE unlucky. The gas shells that fell among them as they made their approach march through Ploegsteert Wood caused at least 500 casualties before the formal battle began. Some gas-affected men retched and collapsed and others fell asleep on reaching the assembly trenches, but the Australians had still managed to arrive before zero hour.

Charles Bean was heading towards Ploegsteert Wood with Malcolm Ross, the official New Zealand correspondent, and a photographer when they smelled gas. 'Pretty strong,' Bean scribbled in his tiny grey notebook. 'We put our helmet nozzles in mouths . . . As we went up thro wood . . . gas shells began to fall fast – pot, pot, pot all around. We stopped and put on [gas] helmets – photographer tore his off presently – we were going too fast. I made him put it on once again. We tried them off presently but Ross was sick at once. We got up without accident – trenches were pretty well steeped in gas.'

Bean waited for the mines to go off. He kept making notes: 'Men have had their breakfast . . . Moon bright . . . Red of dawn over Messines . . . Our bombt begins . . . Mine after mine.'

THE PASSCHENDAELE CAMPAIGN, of which Messines was the start, has produced a considerable literature, much of it about sacrifice and sadness, mud and muddling. This is right enough: there is an analogy of sorts, as we will see, between Passchendaele and the Passion of Christ. For clarity of analysis, however, nothing matches Robin Prior and Trevor Wilson's *Passchendaele: The Untold Story.* The authors divide the Messines attack into four phases: the capture of the German frontline; the taking of the crest of the ridge, including the two villages; the consolidation of the positions won; and, finally, the bit Haig had added on, the advance to the Oosttaverne Line. The first three phases went well.

After the mines sent crimson fire into the sky some 80,000 British and dominion troops headed for the ridge, dust clouds from the mines rearing in front of them. Sometimes the dust was so thick that compasses had to be used. Never had German troops seemed so demoralised. Bean reported that on Monash's front the Australians found a few Germans cowering in the front trench. Many had fled, leaving behind a trail of abandoned rifles, ammunition, cigars and scraps of food. And many quickly surrendered. An Australian lieutenant said the Germans attempted to embrace their captors. 'I have never seen men so demoralised,' he said.

To the north the 36th (Ulster) Division, which had fought so bravely on the opening day of the Somme offensive, went over the parapet after the Spanbroekmolen mine, the second biggest of the nineteen, went off. They met no opposition. The Germans there were either dead or out of their minds. Lumps of blue clay the size of farm carts lay around the mine craters.

All along the line the German front trenches were taken in the thirty-five minutes laid down by the barrage timetable. Casualties were light, astonishingly so for an operation of this sort, as though the history of the Great War was being defied, which it was.

The New Zealanders went for Messines village, where machine guns were still chattering. The Germans had turned the village into a fortress. Just about every cellar had become a dugout and five concrete blockhouses had been erected. The Germans here wanted to fight. But the New Zealanders, showing that same doggedness that had marked their time at Gallipoli, methodically took the village, flushing out the Germans with smoke bombs. They captured the commandant and his staff in a dugout below what had been an orphanage. Wytschaete village, also fortified, fell to two Irish battalions.

The second objective had been taken, not as easily as the first, but easily enough by the standards of this war. The violence and accuracy of the barrage had smothered German attempts at counter-attack. The British and dominion troops owned the ridge from north to south. Beyond the edge of the plateau they could see lush country to the east: hedgerows, untorn grass, trees with leaves on them and, far away, the steeple of Menin. Battalions slated for the afternoon advance to the Oosttaverne Line began to assemble and move up. In the case of the Australians this meant parts of General Holmes' 4th Division and Captain Grieve's battalion of Monash's division.

Bean and others have left us with sketches of the scene in the early morning. Cavalrymen on the crest north of Messines. A sky crowded with British aircraft. Dozens of British observation balloons, like huge grubs, as one officer put it, searching for artillery targets. Maori pioneers below Messines digging in the Flemish clay. Dust plumes from shell-bursts up on the plateau. Tanks grumbling and groaning. New battalions lining up on flags marked with their colours. Artillery teams trotting back to the music of tinkling chains.

And there was something else about this battle, something one could not see. It was eight hours old and this time, this once, the generals running it had not lost control. They knew what was happening and, for once, what was happening was what was supposed to happen.

Grieve came up for the afternoon attack, past dead Germans and ruined farmhouses and unbroken pillboxes. He reached Betlhéem Farm, south-east of Messines village, and found Australians from the morning attack digging in. 'Digging away for all they were worth they yet found time for a smoke and a joke and when we arrived it was more like a picnic than a battle.' Grieve and the 4th Division men who had come up to the north of him were to go for the Oosttaverne Line.

THE FINAL PHASE of the battle plan didn't go as easily as the first three. The advance on the Oosttaverne Line began at 3.10 pm. The allied gunners began dropping shells into their own infantry. Tanks came up to help the 4th Division in its attack. One can only wonder what these Australians thought, particularly when one broke down before the assault started. The last time they had been 'helped' by tanks was at First Bullecourt.

The Australians were attacking north and south of a road they called Huns' Walk and came under machine-gun fire, some of it from pillboxes. The Hindenburg Line did not extend to the Messines–Ypres sector, but the German defences there were exceptionally deep and dotted with pillboxes, which were, in part, a response to waterlogged ground. Some had loopholes for machine guns; others were simply shelters. Squat and lumpy, they could survive just about anything other than a direct hit. The Germans in these concrete forts could fire away until their ammunition ran out, or until the allied troops got behind them. When grenades started coming through the loopholes the Germans usually wanted to surrender, and this was thought a little too neat. As Bean wrote: 'When they [the Australians] have been racked with machine-gun fire, the routing out of enemy groups from behind several feet of concrete is almost inevitably the signal for a butchery at least of the first few who emerge, and sometimes even the helplessly wounded may not be spared. It is idle for the readers to cry shame upon such incidents, unless he cries out upon the whole system of war.'

Germans in a pillbox near Huns' Walk were firing into 4th Division men. Lewis gunners fired into the loophole until the German gun fell silent. Private Wilfred Gallwey wrote in his diary that the Australians went to the door at the rear of the pillbox and found the gun crew huddled inside, some wounded, some dead. The Australians fired point-blank into the huddle. 'There was a noise as though pigs were being killed. They squealed and made guttural noises which gave way to groans after which all was silent.' The bodies were thrown in a heap outside and lay there for days.

Grieve came under fire from another pillbox. He lost half his men and all his officers. He decided to attack the pillbox alone with a bag of bombs. He would throw one, then dive into a shell hole, all the time working closer. He landed a bomb close to the loophole – he had been a good left-arm bowler with the Brighton cricket club – and the machine gunners ceased firing. This allowed him to rush forward and drop two grenades inside. Silence. Grieve went to the back door and found the crew lying dead or wounded.

The survivors of Grieve's company went on to capture a large batch of prisoners. Then a sniper in a tree shot Grieve in the right shoulder. A Lewis gunner fired a whole magazine into the tree and the sniper 'dropped like a stone'. Grieve kept pushing his men forward to the Oosttaverne Line, but he was losing too much blood and decided to walk back to the casualty-clearing station.

The 4th Division battalions on Grieve's left also took heavy casualties as they approached the Oosttaverne Line. Bean described the Australians as 'maddened'. The Germans were 'panic-stricken': they had the Australians in front of them and the British barrage crashing down behind them. Many quickly surrendered with cries of 'Mercy!' Some clutched at the Australians' knees. The Australians came on a farmhouse flying a flag that said it was a German aid post. An Australian officer beckoned to the thirty Germans inside to come out. As they did so, the officer was shot through the shoulder. The Australians behind him closed in, thinking the shot had come from the farmhouse. The officer, though in pain, stopped them shooting thirty unwounded Germans.

By darkness Plumer's troops had taken the Oosttaverne Line except for two small sections, one on the British front to the north and another where the Anzac line joined that of the British corps above it. No British attack in the war had succeeded so well on the first day.

GRIEVE ARRIVED AT the casualty-clearing station. The staff was busy with cases that Grieve considered more serious than his, so he left and had something to eat with two stretcher-bearers he knew. He then went to battalion headquarters, explained what had happened at the front and made suggestions about the next day's fighting. He walked another 1000 yards to a dressing station and had his shoulder bandaged. 'I was covered in dirt and mud – my tunic saturated with blood so I must have presented a pretty picture. I was that tired that I could have laid down alongside the road and gone to sleep.'

Grieve was sent to hospital in England, spent some months there, then rejoined his battalion, only to fall ill and be invalided home. He married a nurse, May Bowman, who had looked after him during his illness. He won the Victoria Cross for his day at Messines.

HAIG WROTE UP his diary for the day:

> Soon after 4 pm I visited General Plumer at his H. Qrs. at Cassel, and congratulated him on his success. The old man deserves the highest praise for he has patiently defended the Ypres Salient for two-and-a-half years, and he well knows that pressure has been brought to bear on me in order to remove him from the Command of Second Army . . . The operations today are probably the most successful I have yet undertaken.

Bean tried to write up his diary: 'More c-attacks, I'm afraid. Too dead sleepy, what with gas & fatigue of this morning's work, I can scarcely write sense – keep on dropping asleep.'

And there his notes ended.

27

The road to Passchendaele

As dusk approached on that first day at Messines the generals and artillery officers in the back areas briefly lost control of the battle on the Australian front. They didn't know where their own infantrymen were on the reverse slope that Captain Grieve had helped capture. They began dropping shells on them. These fell so heavily, and killed and wounded so many, that the infantrymen had to pull back. Wounded lay everywhere amid hot shell fragments. Some of the wounded begged their comrades not to leave them; one man asked to be shot. But the Australians retreated and more died as they tried to run back through the barrage.

Around this time Major Consett Riddell, an engineer in the 4th Division, had to supervise the digging of a trench at the new front-line. Riddell, thirty years old, held degrees in mining engineering and science from Melbourne University and had been wounded on Gallipoli and in France. He sent home elaborately crafted drawings of trench systems and tunnels. Now at Messines he decided to go some hundreds of yards ahead of where his engineers were about to start work. He wanted to look back at the lie of the land, to see what the Germans would see. Then he would know where to site the trench. When he returned a barrage was falling where he had left his men. There was no sign of them. Riddell searched for them for about an hour before being knocked unconscious by a lump of earth or brick. He woke up at dusk, and eventually found his men. By dawn they had almost completed the new trench and its screen of wire.

Riddell walked back through Messines with his runner. Near a wrecked house they saw a board that read '*Ortskommandant*' (town commander). They went inside and filled two sandbags with maps and papers and also took two hurricane lamps. They headed for divisional headquarters, each with a sack over his shoulder and a lantern and, as Riddell put it, looking pretty disreputable. They ran into a colonel who greeted Riddell as 'Bill Sikes', the robber and murderer in *Oliver Twist*. Riddell pulled out a handful of maps. 'Almost the first one we looked at had the whole detail of the German battery positions . . .'

The runner was sent straight to artillery headquarters with the map. Riddell had to go forward with the colonel and spent the whole day showing him over the front. At 9 pm Riddell ate his first meal in thirty-six hours. 'So ended one of my busy days.' Riddell was awarded the Distinguished Service Order for his work. He received a letter of congratulations from his father, and replied:

> You know that for a long time I have been very sorry that you were disap-pointed because I was never any good at games, I could not play any game at all. I could see that you and your old school friends expected more. When the War started I made up my mind to make up by length of service what I could not hope for in brilliance, so that you would not have any fur-ther cause to think that in this biggest of all games I was also a failure. It is this thought that has mainly kept me going.

THE BIG BATTLE at Messines had been virtually won on the first day, indeed in that first hour when the mines went off and the barrage rolled across the German lines. And it had been won in the weeks before because of the finicky planning of Plumer and Harington, and of artillerymen who had glimpsed the formula for success and, to a lesser extent, the skills of divisional commanders such as Monash. The Australian wrote a short letter to his wife on the night of the first day. It was typical of him in that he sometimes measured his own success, and his own importance, with numbers. His casualties were about 2000, he told Vic. His division captured eleven field guns, fifty machine guns and lots of trench mortars and munitions. 'I fired from first to last over £1,000,000 worth of ammunition . . .'

The battle went on another week. The British and dominion troops strengthened their front positions. The Germans counter-attacked, mostly without much heart, and eventually began to pull back. The allied staff work wasn't always as thorough as on the first day. The gunners didn't seem to know where their front troops were and kept hitting them. And the fighting was often as cruel as anything that had happened at Mouquet Farm and the two Bullecourts.

Joseph Trotman was a young sergeant in the 4th Australian Division. A shell hit him on the fourth day of the battle, the day his battalion was due to come out. 'He sent some H. E. over & luckily I was the only one hit. We had a muster & roll call before this & only 170 answered it so you can guess it's pretty rough.' It wasn't so rough early in the battle. Trotman said the Australians lay down and shot the Germans as they ran – 'it was like knocking rabbits.' Trotman captured a group of prisoners by himself. 'They didn't want any forcing to come when I had a revolver in one hand & a couple of Bombs in the other. Some of the beggars were only youngsters about 17 to 18.' Trotman's wound healed and he rejoined his battalion the following month, on his twentieth birthday.

Lieutenant Walde Fisher, whom we left watching the preliminary bombardment, wrote in his diary for June 12 that he had been through a terrible time. He and his company had been under a heavy barrage all day and all night. There were no proper trenches, just shallow ditches. 'Men were blown up and killed all along – it was impossible to describe the scene.' By morning Fisher and two others were the only officers left in two companies. Fisher's own company was down to fifty-eight men. They were still trapped there the next day. 'The stench from the dead was dreadful – many were in pieces and could not be identified – while the dead and unburied enemy in front of us added to the nauseous horror . . . What has been doing in the rest of the line we know not, though we hear rumours of great deeds . . .' Two days later he was out of the line, 'but many of us are yet sick from gas and "dennerite" fumes – it brings on a condition akin to bronchitis, most annoying.'

Lieutenant George Carson, from Monash's division, wrote home a few days after he came out of the fight:

> I've been knocked over by a shell covered by another and dug out disputed the point with four Fritzies and hung on to a position for 32 hours with one man only and four dead stinking Huns. We could not get Food sent up the shelling was damnable and eventually the four Napoo Huns were so objectionable that we had to *cut* them up bit by bit and throw them as far away from us as possible.

BEAN KEPT SCRIBBLING notes as the battle petered out. On June 11 he noticed a small detachment of cavalry going towards Huns' Walk. 'Fancy cavalry!' They were supposed to establish outposts beyond the front. 'Pure eyewash,' Bean declared.

Godley was unpopular as a corps commander, Bean wrote. One day he changed an order four times after the men had started out. Holmes, commander of the 4th Division, and other senior officers told Bean they were longing to be back under Birdwood. Bean said Godley 'never strikes me as being in the least sincere'. Godley sent Bean a message saying that he was going to review the 3rd Division, which was now back from the front. What he was really saying, Bean felt, was: 'Come and report my speech.'

Bean felt the 3rd Division was 'finding its feet'. The only trouble was that some of the commanding officers 'are a bit shy of fire in some cases & Monash is not the man to keep them up to it'. Bean didn't approve of Monash. It shows in his diaries and notes and in the official history and it is tiresome. Monash had already shown at Messines that he was better at planning a battle than Birdwood or

White or any of the other divisional commanders. But Bean, with perhaps a touch of malice, had identified the one defect in Monash's leadership. It was not Monash's way to go briefly to the frontline and see what was really happening. Holmes went to the front at least twice during Messines.

Bean by now had heard a little about the French mutinies. 'The French don't seem to have the stick of other troops,' he wrote, which overlooked the fact that the French had suffered worse casualties than other allied troops. 'The Russian relaxation of army discipline – voluntary salutes etc – has not affected our men in the least. I suppose Australian salutes are mostly voluntary as it is.' But desertions among the Australians had increased. 'There is a fair amount of feeling amongst Australian officers that one or two of the worst cases ought to be shot. The same sort of thing started in the Canadian Force . . . Two men were shot & it stopped.'

WE DON'T KNOW what Phillip Schuler, the journalist turned soldier, did during the battle of Messines. Bean simply tells us in one of his oblique footnotes that Schuler 'won much credit for his gallantry'. A fortnight after Messines opened Schuler was guiding an expert on cooking arrangements around the back area when a shell landed. Schuler was carried to the casualty-clearing station at Trois Arbres near Steenwerck, just over the border in France, with wounds to his left arm, face, throat and right leg.

Lieutenant-Colonel Richard Dowse was a staff officer in the 4th Division and a friend of Schuler's. He drove to Trois Arbres to see Schuler. 'His head was all bandaged up,' Dowse wrote, 'but he had use of one eye & when he saw me remarked "Dick, well I ask you", a favourite saying of his. He knew he was for it & gave me a few messages and instructions before I left. He died about an hour later . . .'

Dowse wrote to Sir Ian Hamilton in London. 'Your letter . . . has made me feel very bad,' Hamilton's reply began. 'From the first moment I met Phillip Schuler I was attracted by his personality and instinctively made friends with him . . . I am quite upset myself to think that a man who had such a future before him; who possessed such a delightful personality and who would certainly have made a name for himself by his writings in the future has prematurely dropped out. I must write to his father by this Mail.'

Frederick Schuler became withdrawn on hearing the news. He had been pilloried for his German origins; now the war had taken his only son. He sought consolation in reading, art and music. Eventually he received Phillip's personal effects. They included a Bible, a watch (damaged), a gold ring, a pair of spurs, a fountain pen, two erasers, a dictionary, a riding crop, an ashtray and three pairs of socks.

Schuler had attended Melbourne Grammar, which ran an obituary that included a tribute from Bean. 'All his friends knew him for the brilliantly handsome, bright, attractive, generous youngster that he was.' Bean said Schuler wrote only what he saw. 'His [reports] were true, and only those who know what oceans of false stuff have been poured out on to the world in this war can appreciate what that means.' Bean spoke of 'a boy of delicate, almost fastidious tastes, fond of flowers, scrupulously neat, even under conditions of discomfort'.

The 'beautiful and gifted' woman who was said to be Schuler's fiancée placed a tablet to Phillip's memory in a Cairo church.

A LITTLE MORE than a week after Schuler's death General William Holmes, the citizen-soldier who commanded the 4th Division, died in similar circumstances. He was showing a group of politicians, including William Holman, the Premier of New South Wales, around the Messines battlefield. The party was well behind the front. A shell burst. Holmes alone was hit, in the chest and lungs. He died while being carried to a dressing station. He was the most senior Australian officer killed on the western front. He lies near Schuler in Trois Arbres cemetery.

THE DAY BEFORE Holmes died the Russians began an offensive on their southern front against Austria-Hungary. It was folly, but one can see how it came about. Russia was in no state to mount an offensive anywhere. Bean had been worrying about the odd desertion among Australian troops. Some two million Russians had deserted in March and April. The revolution was half-complete. The Tsar was gone and few were sorry, but Russia didn't know what it wanted to become. The authority of the provisional government was forever being challenged, chiefly by the soviets that claimed to represent the workers and soldiers. Lenin was waiting to strike; he knew exactly what sort of country Russia should become.

Alexander Kerensky, the Minister for War and the dominant figure in the provisional government, thought a victory would lend authority to the government. Hence the offensive on the Austrian front. It went reasonably for several days. Then came mutinies and mass desertions. The Germans and Austrians drove the Russians back. The broken army became a rabble. It was finished, and this had implications for the offensive Haig and Gough were planning for Ypres. It wasn't immediately obvious in the west, but the balance of the war had changed again. American troops had begun to land in France on June 25. Before they would be in the field Russia would be out of the war.

HAIG WAS RIGHT: Messines had been his most successful operation, even if the credit belonged with Plumer and Harington. The battle had mostly gone as it was supposed to go; the Germans could no longer watch the British preparing for the new Ypres offensive from Messines ridge. The British and dominion casualties came in at about 26,000, half of them on the Anzac front. The New Zealand Division lost about 5000 men, Monash's 3rd Division 4100 and Holmes' 4th Division 2700. Most of the casualties came after the frontline and the two villages had been taken.

There were obvious lessons from Messines. The mines had broken German morale but they couldn't be used on that scale in future battles. The artillery plan could. It had shown that trenches could be captured, quickly and with relatively light casualties, if firepower was concentrated and ammunition plentiful. The counter-battery work had been good. The machine-gun barrages had worked. The wire had been cut. The attack had also shown the importance of superiority in the air. And it had not been too ambitious: Plumer had gone for a bite-and-hold operation that was achievable rather than a dramatic attempt at breakthrough that was not. Did Haig and Gough realise what had happened at Messines? Did Lloyd George?

HAIG WAS TELLING Lloyd George and others that German morale was crumbling. It wasn't, not in the frontline anyway. Charteris, the head of intelligence, tended to tell Haig what he thought the field-marshal wanted to hear. Ludendorff, for his part, was saying before Messines that the German submarine campaign had been so successful that Britain could stay in the war only another three months. Then she would run out of food. This wasn't true either. Lloyd George had encouraged the ever-timid naval leaders to introduce a convoy system for merchant shipping. German submariners at once found fewer easy targets.

Hindenburg and Ludendorff had other problems. Austria-Hungary was searching for a peace formula. Turkey was war-weary. The Reichstag had begun to split into factions. Socialists and communists were more vocal now that the Tsar had been thrown out. The struggle between labour and capital had taken on a new edge: workers sensed their power and rulers worried for theirs. Bismark's idea of government was breaking down. It depended on a strong monarch or a strong chancellor. Germany had neither. Kaiser Wilhelm was not made for adversity. Bethmann, the Chancellor, was close to a nervous collapse. Neither the Reichstag nor the monarch nor the military leaders much believed in him.

Bethmann late in June received a Papal envoy. Pope Benedict XV had offered to broker a peace. Bethmann rashly talked about Germany giving up Belgium. He had wandered down a cul-de-sac. Hindenburg and Ludendorff didn't want this sort of negotiated peace; neither did Britain or France. The Reichstag now came up with a peace resolution. Hindenburg and Ludendorff were appalled, but they also saw a chance to rid themselves of Bethmann. They told the Kaiser they could not work with the Chancellor. Bethmann resigned in mid-July before the dispute could be arbitrated. Georg Michaelis, a little-known bureaucrat, became Chancellor. Bethmann had lost his job; the Kaiser had lost authority. Hindenburg and Ludendorff had increased theirs. Germany edged closer to a military dictatorship.

HAIG COULD ONLY assume that he would receive Cabinet approval for his Ypres adventure. Planning went ahead. Gough and Neill Malcolm, his chief-of-staff, set up headquarters north of Poperinghe. Before they had worked out a final plan they had already handed the Germans an advantage. Haig's insistence that Gough, rather than Plumer, lead the main attack meant there would be a gap of six-to-seven weeks between Messines and the opening of Third Ypres. The German defences at Ypres were formidable before Messines; now Ludendorff, sensing what was coming, ordered them strengthened. As a result the British in some places faced seven lines of defences that stood seven-miles deep. The British might break into the front trenches easily enough (these were in fact breastworks because of the high water table), but they would keep meeting fresh German troops as they moved deeper into what the Germans called their 'battle zones'. Dotted between the lines were hundreds of concrete pillboxes covered with earth and turf. Regiments marked down as counter-attackers waited behind the third line. Most of the German heavy guns were out of sight behind the Gheluvelt Plateau and the Passchendaele Ridge. As Prior and Wilson say in *Passchendaele*: 'Haig, in short, had arranged matters in a way which proved greatly to his enemy's advantage.'

Gough decided to attack on a front of about eight miles, from around Steenstraat, north of Ypres, to Kleine Zillebeke in the south. The thrust of the offensive would be roughly north-east. The vital ground Gough had to take were the ridges to the east that led on to Broodseinde and Passchendaele. Gough had French troops above him on his left and Plumer's 2nd Army below him on the right.

He didn't have to think too much about his preliminary bombardment: it would have to be long and terrific because of the depth of the German defences. Gough tried to be typically cavalier in plotting his first-day advance. He would try for 4000 to 5000 yards, to take a line from Langemarck in the north to Polygon Wood in the south, in four phases. This would carry him beyond Pilckem Ridge in the north and well on to the Gheluvelt Plateau in the south. One suspects that Plumer or Rawlinson, had they been in charge, would have gone for a first-day advance of about 2000 yards. This would have allowed the artillery fire to be concentrated.

Gough didn't have enough artillery to advance 5000 yards. He and Haig were forgetting the lessons of Messines, if indeed they had ever recognised them. Gough would have about 1400 field guns and some 750 heavy pieces. He would also have support from French artillery in the north and Plumer's army to the south. He had more guns than Plumer had at Messines. But he didn't have Plumer's mines, and he had further to go. His troops would be going beyond the range of the field guns. There would be no creeping barrage for the infantry going for the farthest objectives. And Gough's intelligence staff had decided there were 205 German batteries opposite him. In truth the figure was nearer to 400.

Gough planned to use nine infantry divisions, some 100,000 men, on the first day, the same number that Plumer had employed at Messines. No Australian divisions would be taking part: most were having a long rest.

HAIG CONTINUED HIS wearing-out campaign against the frocks. The doubters in the War Cabinet included Lloyd George, Bonar Law and Lord Milner. Jan Christian Smuts, the South African statesman, and Lord Curzon were in favour of the Passchendaele offensive – but vaguely. Robertson, the chief military adviser to the Cabinet, was a doubter in private: he thought Haig had underestimated Germany's ability to fight on. Still, he was always going to back a gentleman-soldier against a clutch of politicians.

There was 'trouble in the land', Robertson told Haig by letter in mid-June. The War Cabinet wanted to 'get at facts'. Robertson warned Haig that Lloyd George wanted to settle the war from Italy – 'today the railway people have been asked for figures regarding the rapid transfer of 12 [British] divisions and 300 heavy guns to Italy! They will never go while I am CIGS but all that will come later.' Then he told Haig how to negotiate. 'Don't argue that you can finish the war this year or that the German is already beaten. Argue that your plan is the best plan – as it is – that no other would even be *safe* let alone decisive, and then leave them to reject your advice and mine. They dare not do that.'

Haig went to London to argue his case. He wrote in his diary that Lloyd George wanted to do little or nothing, except support Italy with guns and gunners. Haig told the War Cabinet that Germany was within six months of running out of reserves, so long as the fighting continued at its present intensity. He wanted more men and guns. Jellicoe, the First Sea Lord, told the Cabinet that Germany's submarine campaign meant that Britain could not stay in the war in 1918. 'We cannot go on,' he said. This claim probably helped Haig's case for the Passchendaele campaign, yet one senses that Haig dismissed it for the panicky outburst it was. It has long been part of the mythology of the Great War to cast Britain's army leaders as butchers and buffoons; one day someone may look at the fretful men who had charge of the Royal Navy.

Lord Derby, the War Minister, came to see Haig in London. He pulled a slip of paper with notes written on it out of his pocket. He then made a speech offering Haig a peerage. Haig thanked him and said no. A peerage, he said, would force him to live beyond his means.

Haig returned to France. King George came across and made him a Knight of the Thistle. Queen Mary dined at Haig's headquarters, the first woman to do so. A few days later Raymond Poincaré, the French President, came to lunch. Haig wrote a typical judgement: 'He is a worthy little man, extremely self-satisfied I think, and rather unsympathetic and cold, a regular lawyer in fact.'

Haig was at it again a few days later when General John Pershing, the commander of the American Expeditionary Force, and several of his officers, including an aide-de-camp, came to dinner. Haig was struck by Pershing's 'quiet gentlemanly bearing – so unusual for an American'. The aide-de-camp, a Captain Patton, was 'a fire-eater, and longs for the fray'. This was the young George Smith Patton who would do much fire-eating in another world war.

On July 19, when Gough was only twelve days away from launching his first attack at Ypres, Robertson told Haig that Cabinet still hadn't approved the offensive but probably would in the next few days. Haig made the reasonable comment that Cabinet didn't understand how the army prepared for a battle. A few days later the approval came, but with a condition and a concession.

The condition was that if the first phase of Third Ypres failed to succeed, the offensive would be called off and troops sent to Italy. Haig did not have authority to run another Somme campaign. He described the idea of sending troops to Italy as 'the act of a lunatic'. One indeed has to wonder whether this prospect made Haig push even harder for Ypres: did he feel he had to tie up his troops before Lloyd George grabbed them for a half-thought-out adventure in Italy? Lloyd George also longed to capture Jerusalem, which would make an uplifting tale for vicars to deliver in their Sunday sermons but had almost nothing to do with winning the war.

The concession granted to Haig was that he would be consulted before any decision was made to halt the offensive. This raised questions. Who would define 'success'? And how would it be measured? Lloyd George and his Cabinet – and the same had been true of Asquith's administration – didn't really want to know too much about tactics and detail. Otherwise they would have wanted to know more about Messines and why it worked. They simply longed for a big victory.

WE ARE CLIMBING the Wytschaete–Messines ridge when a young pheasant hen, fawn and short-tailed and confused, trots frantically beside the road, veering this way and that before darting into the underbrush. 'Climbing' is too lofty a verb. The ridge doesn't seem high, mainly because it isn't, just a bump on a soggy plain, but high enough for one to see just about everything to the south and west. You know, as soon as you reach the crest, why it had to be taken before Haig could begin his Passchendaele campaign.

Two German pillboxes stand sullenly in the New Zealand Memorial at Messines. The concrete walls are more than two-feet thick and reinforced with looped iron rods now rusty and spiky. From here the Germans could see the villages of Wulvergem and Neuve-Eglise on the plain to the west and, to the south, Ploegsteert Wood, where the Australians were gassed. Beyond the wood you can see deep into France. Philip Gibbs, the journalist, stood near here a few days after Messines opened. He looked back at the old British lines and saw every detail laid out like a relief map brightly coloured. 'My God,' said a British officer standing nearby, 'it's a wonder they allowed us to live at all!'

From this spot you also realise the importance of the mines and the massed artillery. The New Zealanders advanced across an exposed plain that in other circumstances would have given the Germans a clear field of fire. But on that morning long ago the plain was about mushroom clouds and shivering earth, dead Germans and half-crazed Germans. The rim of Spanbroekmolen crater is overgrown with tangles of blackberries and weeds. The green-stained water with its beds of lilies stretches for several hundred feet. All around are fields of corn and small herds of fat grey cattle, low-slung brick piggeries and, near Ploegsteert Wood, fields of hops. A family is out harvesting potatoes. Red poppies burn brightly amid the withered plants.

> *In Flanders fields the poppies blow*
> *Between the crosses, row on row . . .*
>   *If ye break faith with us who die*
> *We shall not sleep, though poppies grow*
>   *In Flanders fields.*

A tractor, clanking and rolling like a tramp steamer in a swell, works through wheat stubble under a big grey sky near Trois Arbres cemetery. The discs throw up a cloud of brown-red dust beyond which one can glimpse the spire of Steenwerck. A grave lies in the shadow of a crab-apple tree. Here, a long way from home, is Phillip Schuler.

On the outskirts of Wytschaete a contractor works a backhoe to dig a trench for an electrical cable. The trench is ten-feet long and perhaps six-feet deep. So far it has produced thirty-one shrapnel canisters from British eighteen-pounders, the base of a toffee-apple mortar and hundreds of rusty tendrils of barbed wire. The likelihood is that the contractor has strayed into a shell hole that had been filled with debris in the nineteen-twenties. There was human 'debris' too back then. A local man tells us his father could remember seeing children playing soccer with human skulls.

28

And the rains came

Hubert Gough settled into La Lovie, a large and ugly château north of Poperinghe and about ten miles behind the front, and began to plan his Ypres offensive. Plumer at Messines had captured the handle of the sickle of ridges that curved around Ypres and glowered down on it. Gough now had to strike at the blade, at Pilckem Ridge to the north of the town (average height about sixty feet) and at the Gheluvelt Plateau (average height roughly 150 feet) along the Menin Road to the east. Above the Menin Road were gloomy woods with names such as Château, Sanctuary, Glencorse and Inverness and, deeper in, Polygon. The woods had been flayed by artillery fire: stumps of trees now stood without leaves, branches or bark. North of Polygon Wood, high on the ridge, lay the little village of Passchendaele, just a dot on the map with nothing to suggest that the very word would one day command instant recognition as a synonym for Gothic tales of sacrifice. The evidence suggests that Gough worked harder at his planning than he had on any of his earlier campaigns, and that he was a little awed by what he did not know about the salient; but at heart he was never going to be comfortable, as Plumer and Monash were, with maps, artillery fire plans, conferences and the sheer tedium of preparation. Much of his life had been about theatrical gestures.

He had been prominent in the Curragh 'mutiny' of 1914, even though he was then the commander of a cavalry brigade and thus far from being the most senior officer caught up in the Asquith Government's attempt to impose the Irish Home Rule Act on Ulster. Here he stepped up to play the martyr and got away with it. Earlier, in the Boer War, he had stepped up to play the man of action and got away with this too. He took his men forward without having made a reconnaissance and ran into a large party of Boers. Many of his men were killed and Gough was briefly captured. Before that, after passing through Eton and Sandhurst, he had been sent to India and was naturally attracted to the sport of pig-sticking. At his first outing he managed to break his horse's neck. Later, riding in a steeplechase in England, Gough fell so heavily that he lay unconscious for several days. If it is true to say he had little fear for his own safety, it is also fair to say he didn't have much concern for the lives of the men who served under him. To Gough, war most of the time seemed like a steeplechase.

The plans he drew up for Third Ypres could not be described as rash, although he was trying to go too far on the first day. Other factors, however, were against him, and over these he had no control. One was the place itself. Another was the weather. And a third may have been the fact that his patron, Haig, needed to present his political masters with a win, lest he lose troops and guns to a weird scheme to win the war from Italy.

West Flanders had frustrated armies since Roman times. The mud sucked the boots off soldiers and broke the spirit of horses. The louring skies, the mists and fogs, turned men sour. The Duke of Marlborough, Churchill's ancestor, reported that ordinary soldiers 'swore terribly in Flanders'. The Somme is rolling downland; the Ypres landscape is flat, apart from the Messines–Passchendaele ridge. The chalky topsoils of the Somme are deep and absorb moisture. They can become boggy, as the Australians discovered in the winter of 1916, but only after heavy rain. The topsoils in the Ypres salient are shallower. Beneath them lies clay that feels like plasticine in the hand. The water table is within a few feet of the surface. And now there was a problem that armies had never encountered before: shell holes. These filled with putrid water and wrecked the system of drains that had been built up over hundreds of years. The more shells Gough fired at the Germans, the harder he made it for his own troops to get across the ground. And Gough had to fire lots of shells. This was not like the Somme: there were no main lines of trenches on which the artillery could concentrate. Whole areas had to be obliterated in the hope of hitting a pillbox or fortified farm. Defence in depth took the symmetry out of battlefield maps.

Heavy rain began to fall at about 4 pm on July 31, the opening day of Gough's offensive, and after some four million artillery rounds had been fired into the reclaimed swamp during the preliminary bombardment. Next day *The Times* reported a 'great Allied attack' and an advance of two miles. A photograph taken on the same day tells a truer story. Seven stretcher-bearers stand trapped in a sea of mud that looks like porridge. Two of the bearers have mud up to their knees. The seven are trying to carry in one wounded man.

GOUGH'S DIVISIONS ATTACKED at 3.50 am on July 31 when the first lights of dawn should have been streaking the sky. Low clouds, heavy with rain, blotted out the sun. The infantry set off in the dark.

The French were to secure the northern flank of the attack. By the standards of the western front, they did brilliantly. They pushed forward 2500 yards with relative ease and light casualties. There was a reason for this: the French had used more artillery per yard of trench to be attacked than they had ever used before. They were much better at war than Haig acknowledged.

The Earl of Cavan's corps, below the French, also did well on Pilckem Ridge and reached the western bank of the Steenbeek River, an advance of 3000 yards. This was 1000 yards short of the final objective.

Gough used two corps in the centre. They were going for St Julien and Gravenstafel with the support of twenty-four tanks. The further they went, the harder the advance became. Many pillboxes were still intact and firing. Formations became ragged after troops had to be left behind to fight their way into pillboxes and other fortifications. And the covering barrage became lighter as the men neared their distant objectives. A lieutenant in the Royal Scots told of seeing one of his men hit by a huge shell fragment that cut him in half. The top half of him fell into the mud; his legs and the kilt bobbing around them kept running for a few strides. A few men came close to Gravenstafel, which meant they were only two miles or so from Passchendaele village, which lay on the high ridge to the right. The rain came after noon. Some of the troops in the centre had pushed 4000 yards into the German lines. Their divisional commanders didn't know where they were, which meant that artillery fire could not be directed accurately. And now the Germans were counter-attacking. The British were forced to give up St Julien. German shells were coming in from the British right flank, from batteries behind the Gheluvelt Plateau.

The Gheluvelt Plateau: this was the vital ground the British had to take, and here the assault by General Claud Jacob's corps failed. The ground was much harder than on the flats: dark woods and mud everywhere. British counter-battery fire was poor: German guns poured fire on the advancing troops. Jacob's men took the German frontline and clawed their way about 1000 yards forward. That was all they could do.

British soldiers learned much this day. There were so many ways of killing a man in the Great War, but here was something new. Wounded men lay in shell holes – and drowned. They lay out there because it sometimes took six stretcher-bearers an hour to carry one wounded man 100 yards. When they did deposit a man at a clearing station doctors and orderlies often had to cut off his mud-stiffened clothes with scissors. Men with relatively minor wounds had arms or legs amputated because they had lain in the mud too long. Unwounded soldiers discovered that the mud had no bottom, that if they struggled too violently against it, they would only sink deeper. Officers in the frontline learned not to pull out maps to check their position. The maps either disintegrated or turned into a soggy pulp.

The poet and critic Edmund Blunden was in the attack on the first day. He saw a storm 'creeping on miserably with grey vapour of rain over the whole field'. At battalion headquarters he saw a man with a wound to the back propped up in a doorway. 'I'm cold, cold,' the man moaned again and again. A doctor looked at him, turned to Blunden and shook his head. Blunden went on to company headquarters, which turned out to be a waterproof sheet stretched over a shell hole that was filling with water. Blunden began to lose his temper the next day, which was 'dismal, noisy and horrid with sudden death'. He found himself threatening to arrest a sergeant-major for saying uncharitable things about the headquarters staff. Blunden wrote of a 'stricken landscape'.

By nightfall on the first day Gough's army had captured some eighteen square miles, including the higher ground around Pilckem Ridge. Against that he had taken little of the high ground on Gheluvelt Ridge. Gough had run up close to 27,000 casualties, a frightening figure for an opening day that had fallen well short of complete success. The German losses were thought to be roughly the same. It had been better, much better, than the first day of the Somme; but, as on that day, there was no hint of break-through. And the rain kept coming.

HAIG DIDN'T SEE things so bleakly. As on the first day of the Somme, he was living with his fantasies. Part of his diary reads: 'I sent Alan Fletcher [his senior aide-de-camp] and Colonel Ryan [his medical officer] round the Casualty Clearing Stations. They report many slight cases, mostly shell fire. Wounded are very cheery indeed.' One may only presume that Fletcher and Ryan saw men who had not had their jaws shot away, or that the pair decided to tell Haig what they thought he wanted to hear.

Haig also wrote that he had told Gough to continue with the

original plan – 'the next advance will be made as soon as possible, *but only after adequate bombardment and after dominating the hostile Artillery*'.

Next day Haig wrote of a 'terrible day of rain'.

AFTER THAT FIRST day Gough still had so much to do. He had already lost so many men and exhausted so many others that it became inevitable that dominion troops would be drawn in. The 1st, 2nd and 5th Australian divisions were enjoying a long rest near Amiens. Monash's 3rd Division was still around Messines and the 4th, which had been so wretchedly misused and been in more fighting than any of the other Australian formations during 1917, was trying to re-build its numbers and morale.

Its strength was still about 2000 men below that of the other Australian divisions. Brigadier-General Charles Rosenthal, the architect and musician who had been wounded three times, took temporary charge of the 4th after General Holmes' death. A fortnight later Major-General Ewen Sinclair-MacLagan, an Englishman and career-soldier who first came to Australia in 1901, took command. He had led the covering force, the first brigade ashore, at the Gallipoli landing. He has often been criticised for misreading the battle there on the first day. The criticism, while accurate enough, is probably unjust: the landing was all about confusion and mad terrain. Sinclair-MacLagan was unlucky enough to be in charge of the first hours of it, and anyone who follows his footsteps on that morning soon understands why he became confused.

The 4th Division had had several short breaks in Flanders while the 1st, 2nd and 5th divisions enjoyed long breaks around Amiens and Albert. Harry Murray's battalion of the 4th Division spent its first spell in old trenches inhabited by lice and rats that had grown fat on old corpses. The earth there smelled of death. The battalion historian wrote: 'It was a medical miracle that whole divisions were not exterminated by such conditions.' Later the men spent a few weeks in a Flemish village, where they bought eggs, potatoes and plonk (*vin blanc*). Murray sometimes had temporary command of the battalion. As an administrator, he was generally thought to be a very good frontline soldier.

The three divisions near Amiens held tournaments and sports days and enjoyed the summer sun and the sight of green fields unmarked by shells. Some found themselves in an Arcadian spot with two clear streams where fish could be seen swimming lazily. Needles were bent over the flame of candles to make fishhooks; flies and frogs were caught as bait. The fish wouldn't bite. One of the men explained that he used to shoot fish in Queensland. Out came a rifle. The catch was considerable. Next day men turned up with rifles, revolvers and grenades. Eventually an order was issued: the bombing of streams by Australians must cease.

Australian gunners had already been sent north to help with Gough's preliminary bombardment. They set up on the muddy flats, in view of the Germans on the heights, and suffered their worst casualties so far in the war. The Germans sent lots of shells into the back areas, hitting roads, railways, assembly points and mule trains. They could see all the preparations for a great battle. Edmund Blunden wrote that from Poperinghe to Ypres 'the place was like a circus ground on the eve of a benefit'. The Australian gunners were also shelled with a new poison, mustard gas, which contained a blister agent. The box respirator still protected a soldier's eyes and throat but mustard gas brought up fierce blisters on any exposed skin, and particularly on the thinner parts of it. As a Scots soldier noted: 'In these circumstances the kilt is not an ideal garment.'

Australian infantrymen began arriving in the salient five days before Gough's offensive began. Bean wrote that it was at about this time that the Australians and New Zealanders came to be known as 'Diggers'. Why the word caught on is not entirely clear. All soldiers in this war were diggers. The most industrious were the Germans, probably because they regarded their lines as permanent. The Australians liked their nickname, unlike the English, who often seemed uncertain about 'Tommy', with its connotation of big-hearted lads from the working classes.

The 4th Division had been moved back to Birdwood's I Anzac Corps. This pleased the men. They were less pleased about being sent to the slaughter grounds again without having had as long a rest as the three divisions from I Anzac Corps. The men of one 4th Division battalion made what Bean called 'audible protests' upon being told the news at a parade.

Lieutenant Lawrence of the 1st Division engineers came up behind the front before Gough's offensive opened. He told his sister the biggest battle the world had ever seen was just starting. The gunfire was terrific and could be heard in London. 'You read of "drum fire" and that is just what it is like. From a distance of ten miles behind the line it sounds just like thousands of big drums being bashed simultaneously.'

Next day, in a letter to his mother, his engineer's brain was estimating probabilities. 'It has rained for two days solidly now and I am afraid it will spoil our offensive. You see it is so difficult to move guns etc and even men over ground torn to pieces by artillery fire and then soaked with rain. It just becomes a sea of mud.'

IT RAINED FOR five days after that. Then it stopped for a day, August 7. Next day it started again. It rained for the rest of the month, bar two days, a little more than five inches in all, nearly twice the August average. This would have made Flanders muddy and bleak in a normal summer. But every day in August, 1917, tens of thousands of men were struggling back and forth through the mud, and thousands of horses and mules were floundering in it, sometimes up to their bellies, sometimes being unharnessed and shot where they lay; guns were being dragged through it, sometimes at the rate of forty yards an hour; and all the time both sides were firing more shells, creating more holes that would fill with putrid water in less than an hour.

Gough at first wanted to go on. He proposed attacks on limited objectives, then abandoned them when the weather rendered them impossible. Haig wanted to go on too – he needed to show gains to prevent some of his divisions and guns being sent to Italy – but he urged patience on Gough and (as noted in the underlined text in his diary, quoted in italics above) wanted him to ensure that his artillery bombardment was adequate.

Gough finally attacked towards the Gheluvelt Plateau on August 10. The troops took no ground on the right of their attack and a few hundred yards on the left. The cost was another 2200 casualties.

Next, just short of a week later and after another series of downpours, Gough decided to attack again on all of his fronts. In the north his men took Langemarck. In the centre they mostly failed. Two Irish divisions attacked here. One was the 36th (Ulster) Division that had fought so well on the first day of the battle of the Somme. Both divisions were exhausted before the attack. They went forward slowly, dragging one leg out of the mud, then the other. German shells fell among them and the casualties ran higher and higher; Gough's gunners could not seem to find the opposing batteries. Haig's diary entry for August 17 said that Gough was unhappy with the work of the two Irish divisions. 'They seem to have gone forward but failed to keep what they had won . . . The men are Irish and apparently did not like the enemy's shelling, so Gough said.' As Prior and Wilson say in their *Passchendaele*, comment on this seems superfluous, but one is irresistible. That Haig could allow such a remark to pass gives another hint of the sweep of his prejudices. He was comfortable with proper English gentlemen, particularly those who said they wanted to 'help' him; he was suspicious of the English lower classes, the French, colonials, Catholics, lawyers, Americans – and, now, Irishmen who slogged through the mud and died for him.

On the right the attack on Gheluvelt Plateau failed again. Some troops reached the edge of Polygon Wood but were thrown out. Gough had run up another 15,000 casualties. Those who were not casualties were exhausted. Gough didn't seem to understand about exhaustion, as he had demonstrated at Mouquet Farm and Bullecourt. Haig seemed to better understand what was going on. The commanders were in too great a hurry, he wrote in his diary, adding two exclamation marks. The artillery had not been given enough time to do its job (one exclamation mark).

Gough turned cranky at La Lovie Château. The troops had let him down. They couldn't seem to hold on to ground they gained. He told his corps commanders on August 17 that it might be necessary to court-martial some 'glaring instances'. He also thought frontline divisions were being relieved too quickly. He then gave his approval to a series of attacks on narrow fronts, most of which, happily, never happened.

Another attack towards the Gheluvelt Plateau failed badly. And now the rain became heavier: about an inch-and-a-half fell in the four days to August 29. Gough's forces were worn down. They could do no more, yet the general was still planning new attacks. According to one officer present, Colonel C. D. Baker-Carr of the Tank Corps, Gough was inclined to begin his conferences at La Lovie with something like this: 'Gentlemen, I have just come from an interview with the Commander-in-Chief and he tells me that everything points to a complete breakdown of the enemy morale and that one more hard thrust will crumple up his defences.' It is doubtful if Gough really believed this. One suspects that by mid-August he was finding it all too difficult and wished to be somewhere else. In his *The Fifth Army*, published in 1931, three years after Haig's death, Gough wrote that by the middle of August he had been so concerned about the waterlogged ground and the 'fearful strain' it had put on troops that he had urged Haig to abandon the attack. Haig had insisted it had to go on.

Prince Rupprecht, the commander of the German troops opposite, noted in his diary that British prisoners seemed uncharacteristically down. They were critical of their officers and the staffs and more inclined to surrender than they had been before. Haig's headquarters was now starting to say – shades of the Somme – that the offensive was not about breaking through to the Channel ports; it was about wearing out the Germans. The trouble here was that Haig was wearing out his own troops faster than he was wearing out the Germans.

The officers planning these attacks at La Lovie and elsewhere seemed to have little idea of how bad the ground was. Men, however brave or determined they might have been, simply couldn't get through it. Baker-Carr recounts how he delivered a lecture on tanks at Haig's headquarters and afterwards said that the fighting, especially as it concerned tanks, was 'as dead as mutton' and had been since August 1. Brigadier-General John Davidson, Haig's director of operations, asked Baker-Carr to come to his office. Baker-Carr found Davidson with his head in his hands.

'I am very upset by what you said at lunch, Baker,' Davidson began. 'If it had been some junior officer, it wouldn't have mattered so much, but a man of your knowledge and experience had no right to speak as you did.'

'You asked me how things really were and I told you frankly.'

'But what you say is impossible,' Davidson replied.

'It isn't. Nobody has any idea of the conditions up there.'

'But they can't be as bad as you make out.'

'Have you been there yourself?'

'No.'

'Has anyone in [the operations staff] been there?'

'No.'

'Well, then, if you don't believe me, it would be as well to send someone up to find out.'

HAIG LATE IN August decided to change the areas of command. The biggest problem was the higher ground on the Gheluvelt Plateau. Plumer, Haig decided, should take over this front. Gough would remain in charge of the northern fronts. Gough seemed relieved and continued with pointless attacks in his sector. He didn't seem to understand what was happening out in the sea of mud, or that he was turning good men sour by pushing them too hard, or that infantrymen could only succeed if artillery could protect them. Less than a fortnight into September, Haig became worried that Gough's subordinates were not telling him [Gough] the truth about what was possible. This may have been true. The deeper problem, however, was Gough himself. He had been promoted quickly in the first two years of the war. It is possible that he knew less about the *nature* of the contest than captains and majors and colonels, many of them citizen-soldiers, who had spent years nearer to the frontlines.

Plumer, meanwhile, decided he would take the Gheluvelt Plateau methodically, in a series of steps, one small advance of perhaps

1500 yards followed by another. Among his troops would be I Anzac Corps.

LLOYD GEORGE HAD allowed Haig's offensive because he lacked the nerve to say no and because he didn't have a better idea. Gough was now on his way to running up more than 60,000 casualties in his first month, yet Lloyd George still baulked at calling off the campaign.

Haig, as usual, was telling the frocks as little as possible. When the battle was three days old Robertson wrote a letter to Kiggell, Haig's chief-of-staff, that may fairly be described as pathetic. Robertson told Kiggell he knew Haig was very busy. 'Not unnaturally the Cabinet ask me my opinion every morning and it is rather difficult for me to say much as I have nothing to rely upon but the Communiqué and the slight additions you occasionally send to me . . .' Ministers had asked him for an opinion that morning. 'All I want is some interesting information that I can properly give to these people, to which I think you will agree they are entitled.'

A few days later Robertson wrote to Haig. The Italian front on the Isonzo River was teasing Lloyd George again, Robertson said. Lloyd George was 'a real bad 'un. The other members of the War Cabinet seem afraid of him. Milner is a tired, dyspeptic old man. Curzon a gas-bag. Bonar Law equals Bonar Law. Smuts has good instinct but lacks knowledge.'

HAIG WENT TO London early in September and Lloyd George told him that Russia was finished as a war ally. Neither seemed to realise how serious this was, if only because it would allow Germany to transfer divisions from the east to the western front. Kerensky was now Prime Minister in Russia, but his provisional government was failing. The Left was on the rise: the Bolshevik Party could marshal only 30,000 members at the time of the Tsar's abdication; now it had close to 200,000. The Bolsheviks campaigned on a simple slogan: 'Peace, Land and Bread'. If they won the power struggle, they would obviously try to strike a peace treaty with Germany.

Churchill, now back in Cabinet as Minister for Munitions, visited Haig in France a few days later. Haig said Churchill admitted that he and Lloyd George were doubtful about being able to beat the Germans on the western front. 'I have no doubt that Winston means to do his utmost . . . to provide the army with all it requires, but at the same time he can hardly help meddling in the larger questions of strategy and tactics; for the solution of the latter he has had no real training, and his agile mind only makes him a danger because he can persuade Lloyd George to adopt and carry out the most idiotic policy.'

Battle of the Menin Road, September 20, 1917

White House
Rose Farm
Poelcappelle
Delta Farm
Langemarck

1 FR ANTHOINE
Steenbeck

Quebec Farm
51 UK
Hubner Farm

Pilckem
XIV UK
River

58 UK
London Ridge
Bellevue

XVIII UK
St Julien
Hannebeek
St Julien Spur
Gravenstafel

Pilckem Ridge

Abraham Heights
River

Gallipoli Farm
Aisne Farm
Iberian Farm

53 UK
Zonnebeke Marsh
Hill 40
Broodseinde

V UK
Potsdam Farm
Zonnebeke

5 UK
GOUGH
9 UK
Draught House

Ypres–Roulers Railway
Zillebeke Lake
Westhoek

MENIN
ROAD
I ANZAC
2 AUS
Glencorse Wood
Polygon Wood

Ypres
1 AUS
Black Watch Corner
Cameron House

Hooge
Zillebeke Lake
Sanctuary Wood
23 UK
Inverness Copse

Gheluvelt

X UK
41 UK
Tower Hamlets

Shrewsbury Wood

2 UK
PLUMER
39 UK

Battle Wood
IX UK

19 UK

SCALE
0   1000 metres
0   1000 yards

29

The Menin Road

September came, the last three weeks of the fourth summer of the war that – despite what Haig was saying – seemed without end. Gough no longer made bold attacks, merely a niggle here and a parry there. These weeks were like a brief waking in a nightmare. The rain stopped, the sun rose in a golden orb each morning over Passchendaele Ridge and by noon the air was warm and balmy. Birds could be heard singing, hope amid the ruins. Here and there a blackened stump of a tree put out a single green leaf in a show of defiance. The ground mostly dried up and the sun baked a thin crust on it, so that wagon wheels sometimes produced puffs of dust. The shell holes still stank but the water in them had retreated to shallow puddles. The British soldiers who had fought in August knew this was all a tease; the newly arrived Australians didn't think the place too bad. It was certainly good weather for flying. Soldiers on both sides stood and watched specks spitting at each other in the skies. Manfred von Richthofen was up there in his red Fokker; so too was Hermann Goering, a twenty-four-year-old who had grown up near Nuremberg, a city that one day would have another significance for him. Some Germans during the first week of September thought that the British had abandoned their offensive.

They were wrong: lack of resolution had never been one of Haig's vices. Nevertheless the nature of his offensive had changed. By mid-September it was six weeks old. Like the Somme, it had started out as one thing and become another. It was no longer, in the first instance, about taking the Belgian ports. It was about taking the heights, the Gheluvelt Plateau, all 150 feet of it. It was not now so much about Gough, who would still command on the northern front, as about Plumer, who would be careful and limit his advances to a distance where his artillery could protect his infantry. Plumer didn't see the Belgian ports or cavalry galloping through gaps, just the little ridges and pillboxes that had to be taken on either side of the Menin Road. He saw artillery ladder maps and just 1500 yards ahead: that was how far he intended to advance in a day, no more. Third Ypres now had the characteristics of a grinding match.

Two days before Plumer began what would be called the battle of the Menin Road, Bonar Law, the Conservative leader, wrote to Lloyd George, who was in Wales and unwell. Bonar Law said he had told Robertson that he [Bonar Law] had lost all hope of Haig's offensive succeeding. He believed that Robertson agreed with him. Bonar Law felt that Haig could renew his attack any time. Therefore it was time for Cabinet to decide whether the offensive be allowed to continue.

PLUMER'S SCHEME, WHICH the Prime Minister and Bonar Law knew little of, was rather like his plan for Messines, except that he brought even more artillery to the battle. This time he had nearly 1300 guns for a frontage of less than 5000 yards. Plumer came up with a creeping barrage that was particularly sophisticated. His forces would go for Nonne Boschen, Glencorse Wood and part of Polygon Wood on the north side of the road, and Inverness Copse and Tower Hamlets on the south side. Plumer would use two Australian divisions, the 1st and the 2nd, north of the road and three British divisions on the southern side. Gough would be attacking towards Gravenstafel at the same time with four divisions, but Plumer was the main player. Plumer's attack would go in at 5.40 am on September 20. The preliminary bombardment began a week earlier. The fine weather continued. Then, just after dark on the night before the attack, drizzle began to fall, followed by heavier rain. The ground turned greasy and began to cut up. As one chronicler of the battle put it, Gough had become neurotic about rain, which at least proved he was learning something. He telephoned Plumer, wanting to call the assault off. Plumer hesitated and consulted. He decided to go ahead. Plumer was not only a better tactician than Gough; he was also luckier. The rain stopped just after midnight.

MAJOR FRED TUBB came from the congregation of the little Anglican church set beneath granite hills at Longwood in Victoria. He was relatively short, a little over five feet five inches, a farmer with strong expressive eyes and a neat moustache. He was a natural leader, an extrovert who loved sports – particularly football, horse-riding, foot-running and shooting – and every night wrote in a tiny diary. Lady Clementine Waring looked after him at her convalescent home in England in 1915 when he was recovering from the wounds he received at Lone Pine. 'I can see him now,' she said afterwards, 'his whole personality radiating vitality and energy.' When the award of the Victoria Cross was announced Tubb lost his ebullience. Lady Waring organised a reception. Tubb was confused and overwhelmed. 'Finally in a broken voice,' Lady Waring said, 'he murmured a few incoherent words of thanks, and espying my small two-seater car nearby, leaped in with an imploring "For God's sake get me out of this!" and whirled off through the gates.'

Tubb was invalided back to Australia early in 1916 because an appendicectomy had left him with an incision hernia. He eventually persuaded a military board to pass him fit to return to the 7th Battalion in France. His brother, Frank, was a captain in the same battalion. Menin Road was to be Fred's first big battle after Lone Pine.

Tubb's battalion was billeted in farmhouses around Bailleul, just over the border in French Flanders. Women, boys and old men were doing the ploughing and harvesting. The Australians helped one of the farmers bring in his wheat crop. Tubb's hernia was obviously bothering him. He won his heat of a foot race at a sports day but wrote that 'the race knocked me out'. The next day he was 'unwell' and on the following day he stayed in bed. He got up to go to Poperinghe to look over a model of the ground over which the Australians would attack above Menin Road.

The battalion left for the front on September 13. The night before Tubb wrote: 'Am handing this [the tiny diary] to Frank tonight. I must not take it into the line with me. I hope to enter up my future doings on this when we come out.'

CAPTAIN A. M. McGRIGOR, an English officer, was an aide-de-camp to Birdwood, whom he referred to in his diary, and with affection, as 'the Little Man'. He liked the way Birdwood responded to the sensibilities of the Australians he commanded. McGrigor said that if the men were not wearing greatcoats at church parades in winter, Birdwood would also appear coatless. McGrigor, like Tubb, went to see the model of the battlefield at Poperinghe. It covered two to three acres, McGrigor said. The scale was one in fifty for the flat country but the ridges were exaggerated – 'one could see clearly all the Bosche trenches, outposts and woods.'

The day before McGrigor had watched an Australian brigade practising an attack with a creeping barrage.

> Very interesting it was too, but it did bring home to one how appallingly mechanical everything is now, and how every man must conform to and advance with the barrage. Initiation and dash must to a certain extent be fettered as every forward movement is worked out so carefully and mathematically and must not be exceeded or the objective fail to be reached, otherwise the effect of the carefully thought out barrage is lost and the attack is possibly beaten off or an entire failure.

McGrigor, in two sentences, had caught the essence of the new tactics that were evolving, though not yet generally accepted. They were ideas that had been born out of failures that had been called Loos and Fromelles, the first day of the Somme and First Bullecourt. Prior and Wilson contend in *Passchendaele* that McGrigor's remarks highlight the difference between Gough's opening offensive at Third Ypres and what Plumer was now trying to do above Menin Road and beyond. Gough had tried to advance 4000 yards on the first day, not because this was the effective range of his artillery but because he wanted to place his troops within striking distance of Passchendaele Ridge. Plumer, the authors say, had not set his eyes on some desired geographical objective. 'He calculated the distance over which his artillery could provide a safe passage for his advancing infantry.'

Menin Road would be won or lost on the effectiveness of the artillery. Artillery would conquer and infantry would occupy.

THE ATTACK OF September 20 – Plumer in the south, Gough in the north – involved eleven divisions on a front of eight miles. The 1st and 2nd Australian divisions were roughly in the centre. Two Australian divisions were attacking side by side for the first time. They liked this and also the fact that they had a Scottish division on their immediate left. The Australians were assaulting a position different to anything they had tackled before. There were no formal lines of trenches, just outposts and pillboxes and machine-gun nests that went on and on without apparent pattern. But there was a pattern. The Germans here were happy enough to let the enemy enter their front positions; their true strong points were much further back. And between the lightly held front and these strong points the Germans could counter-attack a confused enemy. The British artillery barrage would thus not fall, as it had at Second Bullecourt and Pozières, as a line of shell-bursts parallel to the Australian jump-off positions. This time there had to be a storm of shellfire at least 1000-yards deep. The gunners had to try to obliterate everything. And of course they couldn't. It would be impossible to score direct hits on every pillbox. Plumer had an artillery piece for every five yards of front; the ratio for Gough's attack of July 31 had been one-to-six. Plumer would fire 3.5 million shells during the preliminary bombardment and throughout the first day. The Australians had never gone out behind such a ferocious barrage.

When the Australians arrived at the front the ridge looked dry and yellow and the broken walls of farmhouses stood up like headstones. Then, during the dark before the attack, the rains came and in an hour the clay first became greasy, then gummy and noisome. The Australians were to take their ground in three advances. The first would take them to the Red Line. They would pause there, then go on to the Blue Line. After waiting there for two hours they would go on to the final objective, the Green Line. This is where the counter-attacks were expected to come. Fresh battalions, Tubb's 8th among them, would leapfrog through the lines to take and hold the final objective. Also marked down for the Green Line was the 17th Battalion. This contained three brothers, the Seabrooks, aged twenty-one to twenty-five, from the Sydney suburb of Five Dock.

Many of the Australians were wet from the waist down and carrying several pounds of mud on each boot as they assembled for the jump-off. Then a German barrage came down on half of the 1st Division. The casualties were severe. One battalion lost all its company commanders and half its officers. This was in the hour before the British barrage opened up at 5.40 am. The Australians set off, most of them lighting the cigarettes they had been denied in the assembly areas. Zero hour had been set at 5.40 because at this time it would be possible for the men to see 200 yards. The smoke from their own barrage meant they couldn't see fifty yards. But it didn't matter: mostly the Germans were too dazed and demoralised to resist strongly. Dozens of isolated fights broke out around pillboxes that had survived the barrage. These sometimes ended with Germans waving white handkerchiefs or bandages and trying to surrender and Australians wanting to kill them as they blundered out of the bunkers. The Australians usually had time to rifle through the bunkers for souvenirs before going on.

Joe Maxwell, a knockabout sergeant-major with a dry sense of humour, an ear for the vernacular and a taste for booze, set off with the 2nd Division. A shell fell behind Maxwell, knocking him down.

'I crawled a few yards, scraped the mud from my eyes, and peered down into the terrified face of a German whose right arm hung a mangled red mass by his side.' Through chattering teeth the German said '*Kamerad*'. Maxwell reached the German front positions.

And among that wilderness of broken timber and shattered concrete squirmed live Germans the colour of mud in which they wallowed – live men who had lost the power to think. Their eyes were glassy, and had lost all expression. They were sunk in faces that were ashen grey, drawn and paralysed by the terror of the storm that had burst over them. There they wandered without arms, mere husks of the men they were, for all practical purposes, men who were temporarily dead.

Maxwell received the Distinguished Conduct Medal for his part in Menin Road and was commissioned as a lieutenant. He had been fined twenty pounds for brawling in London. Fifteen pounds of this was now refunded and the DCM carried a grant of twenty pounds, so, as Maxwell put it, 'I came out on the right side of the ledger.'

Private Walter Bradby of the 1st Division had enjoyed his four months away from the front, particularily when he downed his fourth glass of *vin blanc* at the *estaminet* that displayed a sign: 'English spoken. Australian understood.' Bradby was following the creeping barrage when a man about twenty-five yards ahead fell. He asked Bradby for a cigarette. Bradby recognised him as a man who had lived near him at Ballarat. Arch Sneddon had been hit in the back by shell fragments. Bradby said he seemed cheerful enough. Sneddon died at a dressing station.

Bradby saw British troops capture a pillbox on lower ground to his right. One German began pushing and jostling his captors. Two British troops bayoneted him. Up ahead Bradby could see a wood – almost certainly Polygon – 'that seemed to have survived three cyclones and two tornadoes'. Bradby and half-a-dozen men reached their objective and started digging a trench. A small shell landed among them. Bradby and the others arose and began brushing earth from their eyes and ears. Bradby noticed that an older man named Malone – Bradby was only twenty and Malone looked to be thirty-five or older – was fumbling. He told Bradby he couldn't see. A hand was passed to and fro in front of Malone's open eyes. He didn't blink. Then someone noticed a tiny hole in his left temple. Bradby was told to lead him to a dressing station.

They came on Paddy Morgan and other stretcher-bearers clustered around a stretcher on which a wounded Australian lay. Three German prisoners were standing docilely nearby. A fourth German stood apart.

It transpired that he could speak English, and Paddy was pleading with him, cajoling him, threatening him to take hold of the fourth arm of the stretcher – all to no avail. The German, standing at attention and drawing himself up to his full height, stated that as an officer he would not help to carry the stretcher. This went on for a while until Paddy, losing patience, took a few paces forward and, drawing a revolver (which he had no right to be carrying), shot the German officer.

Bradby deposited Malone at the dressing station. Months later he heard that Malone had recovered his sight.

Sergeant Percy Lay, whom we last met at Second Bullecourt, wrote in his diary that his battalion took hundreds of prisoners who never attempted to fight – 'we could have got to Berlin as Fritz was absolutely disorganised . . . It was very amusing to see the way our chaps went into the battle. It looked more like a race meeting than a battle. A good few got caught by our own barrage by being too eager to get forward.' Lay's diary rather understated what he had done. His platoon commander had been hit during the assembly. Lay led the platoon on to the final objective. For this the drover from Ballan received the Distinguished Conduct Medal. It was his third decoration for bravery in just over a year. He was also made a lieutenant.

Captain Stanley Calderwood of the 2nd Division came upon a three-roomed pillbox flying a Red Cross flag and bristling with two machine guns. He wrote in his diary: 'All the tenants received permanent eviction notices . . .' He also recalled a redheaded sergeant rounding up prisoners and decorating himself with their watches and chains.

THE PILLBOXES HERE caused a series of brutal incidents. Troops from the 2nd Division rushed a line of concrete shelters. Some Germans inside wanted to surrender and others didn't, a common point of confusion. One came out with his hands up. Another fired between the first man's legs and wounded an Australian sergeant.

'Get out of the way, sergeant,' a Lewis gunner yelled. 'I'll see to the bastards.' He fired three or four bursts into the entrance and killed or wounded most of those inside.

While the 1st Division was making for its first objective Lieutenant Ivon Murdoch (a brother of Keith) was passing a pill-box that he assumed the battalions in front of him had dealt with. A bomb suddenly went off at his feet. Murdoch told his men to fire at the loophole. Another lieutenant worked around to the entrance of the pillbox and took nine prisoners. Murdoch's men were unaware these men had surrendered and shot them all.

Around the same time a machine gunner on the roof of a pillbox checked the advance of the 11th Battalion. The battalion was inter-mingled with the 10th, commanded by an eccentric Englishman, Lieutenant-Colonel Maurice Wilder-Neligan. He sent a lieutenant and his platoon to take the pillbox. The lieutenant was within a few yards of the pillbox when a German shot him in the head. Wilder-Neligan said the men 'went mad'. Germans tried to surrender and Australians pelted them with bombs. Eventually they allowed a German officer and forty men to go to the rear. Wilder-Neligan was an unusual commander. While his men were resting – some of them puffing on German cigars – before going on to the final objective, they received the latest copies of two Fleet Street dailies, the *Mail* and the *Mirror*. Wilder-Neligan had arranged to have them brought up to the front.

Another group of 1st Division men were resting before going on to the final objective when they came under fire from a pillbox. Captain Fred Moore ran towards the pillbox to be shot and killed by a German, who, it was later said, had already surrendered. The Australians killed this German and others. Officers intervened and stopped them killing the whole garrison.

Lieutenant Donovan Joynt of the 8th Battalion told of what was probably the worst such incident for the day. He came on troops shooting at a loophole in the upper storey of a pillbox from which fire was coming. The Germans in the lower storey surrendered. The Australians relaxed as the Germans emerged. Then a shot from the upper storey killed an Australian. The Germans there were apparently unaware of the surrender of their comrades below. The Australians began bayoneting their prisoners. One went to bayonet a German, only to realise that, in his fury, he had forgotten to fix his bayonet to his rifle. The German begged for mercy. The Australian fixed his bayonet and killed him.

Bean wrote in the official history that such incidents are inevitable in war, which is true enough, and that 'any blame for them lies with those who make wars, not with those who fight them'. Perhaps. One also thinks of a line from Frederic Manning, an Australian who served with an English regiment. In *The Middle Parts of Fortune*, one of the most stylish pieces of writing to come out of the Great War, Manning wrote: 'A man might rave against war; but war, from among its myriad faces, could always turn towards him one, which was his own.'

BEFORE LEAVING FOR the front Fred Tubb told the senior men in his company that Menin Road would be his last battle. There is nothing to suggest he had a premonition of death; more likely he had realised that he could not go on soldiering with a hernia.

Tubb took his company through to its final objective and seized a cluster of nine pillboxes south of Polygon Wood. These should have been 250 yards short of the British barrage, but shells began falling on Tubb's men. Tubb hastily wrote out a field message saying that the barrage was falling short.

What happened next is not clear. One story has Tubb the extrovert dancing with delight on top of a pillbox, where he was wounded by a sniper's bullet. While being carried off on a stretcher he was wounded again by a shell-burst. The casualty form says he was 'dead on admission'. The cause of death was 'G.S.W. [gunshot wound] Back penetrating abdomen'.

All three Seabrook brothers died at Menin Road. All had enlisted in August, 1916, two of them on the same day. William (known as Keith), a lieutenant and the youngest at twenty-one, lingered until the next day. He appears to have been hit while moving up to the assembly positions. His batman, who did not go up with him, said Keith was pale and anxious before leaving for the firing line but his handshake was spontaneous and affectionate. The other two brothers were both privates, Theo, twenty-four, and George, twenty-five. They died during the attack. Several eyewitnesses told the Red Cross the same shell killed both brothers. These accounts, however, are scrappy and inconclusive. The bodies of Theo and George were lost, although one of them may have been buried where he fell.

Private William Tooney, a thirty-seven-year-old railway worker from the Sydney suburb of Redfern, was particularly annoyed about being wounded at Menin Road. He had been hit in the right leg. He had to crawl to the dressing station because the stretcher-bearers had been killed or wounded. A few months earlier he had been wounded in the same leg at Bullecourt and spent twelve weeks in hospital. But he had larger concerns. His wife had died after he left for France and their two small children were with relatives. Lying in a London hospital and watching the 'cruel' German air raids, he longed for fresh photographs of his children. He wrote to his daughter, Edna, after she had sent him a postcard. The card showed 'you are thinking of poor daddy, and I want you to think of your mother too although she is dead . . . all I want now is for the war to finish, when I can come home to you & Bim [his nickname for his son, William] and look after you both.' Tooney did come home late in 1918, discharged as medically unfit. He died less than a year later from mustard gas poisoning.

Major Donald Coutts, a doctor with the 2nd Division, came up to the front the night before the attack. He had to dodge German shells on the way to his aid post, a tiny concrete structure only five-feet high. Outside stood a small sandbagged shelter for dressing the wounded. Coutts said the stretcher-bearers were demoralised by the shelling and the mud. 'Some of them didn't seem to understand when you spoke to them.' His first casualty was a self-inflicted wound: the man had all but blown off his right hand.

Captain McGrigor, Birdwood's aide, went to a hospital after the Menin Road battle.

One Australian whom the General spoke to, hit in both legs, the shoulder and the head, was as cheery as though nothing was the matter with him. It was an extraordinary and sad sight to see the fellows lying there, our fellows and Bosches side by side waiting to have their wounds dressed, no discrimination being shown between friend and foe. Went into the operating theatre where six men were being operated on at once, poor devils.

BEAN IN THE official history called Menin Road a 'complete success', better than Messines. In one sense Menin Road was something to celebrate. Plumer had advanced his army an average of 1250 yards. The planning had been thorough. The artillery diagrams were starting to look like the doodles of Albert Einstein, who, incidentally, was writing new theories of physics at Berlin University and saw the war as a form of insanity. The barrages had been tremendous, even if some of the counter-battery work had failed. The standing barrage prevented the usual counter-attacks and befuddled the Germans. The infantrymen mostly reached their objectives on time. Communications had not broken down; the generals never lost control. Plumer looked impressive; so did his tactics.

In another sense Menin Road played into the hands of Lloyd George and other doubters. The British generals didn't seem to realise that the casualties were frightful for the amount of ground gained. Haig was wearing out his own troops faster than he was wearing out the Germans. If Plumer's tactics were the right ones, then the price of victory was going to be outrageous. The 20,000-plus casualties at Menin Road bought a gain of about five-and-a-half square miles.

This was more than double the ratio of casualties to ground gained on July 31, the first day of Gough's offensive that quickly bogged down in the mud. German losses at Menin Road were thought to be about the same as Plumer's, or slightly less.

The Anzac push in the centre had succeeded better than any Australian attack so far in the war: it had literally gone by the clock, one step after another. But the Australians had still lost 5000 men dead or wounded. This was the equivalent of one-third of a division, or two months' voluntary enlistments back in Australia. These losses had been incurred in roughly the same time span as the failed attack at Fromelles in 1916. And while Menin Road was a success, it was hardly going to win the war, or even open the way to the Belgian ports. This was the thought that seemed to be running around in Lloyd George's mind.

HAIG SAW MENIN Road as a great victory. He doesn't appear to have gone near the front since Third Ypres opened, yet he felt even more certain that German morale was breaking down. His confidence was up. He would now take all the Passchendaele Ridge, step by step. The next step would be Polygon Wood in a few days. After Menin Road, Lord Bertie, the British ambassador to France, wrote in his diary: 'We have done a good offensive which is much appreciated. But will it lead to anything really important?'

This is how Lloyd George saw things. He didn't believe the story that Haig and Charteris were pushing. He saw Third Ypres as another of Haig's grinding matches, another unending list of casualties. On July 31 Haig was going to take the Belgian ports. Now, seven weeks later, Haig and the military trade union were selling an advance of 1250 yards on the outskirts of Ypres as a triumph. Lloyd George was still looking elsewhere – Italy, Mesopotamia, southern Turkey – and Robertson was wearing himself out trying to deflect him back to the western front.

Lloyd George went to see Haig in France around the time of Menin Road. He wrote afterwards: 'I found there an atmosphere of unmistakable exaltation. It was not put on. Haig was not an actor.

He was radiant . . . the politicians had tried to thwart his purpose. His own commanders had timidly tried to deflect him from his great achievement. He magnanimously forgave us all.'

Haig and his staff told the Prime Minister how poor the German prisoners looked. This was proof that Germany was running out of good fighting men. Lloyd George said he would like to see some of these prisoners. The story goes that someone on Haig's staff telephoned Gough's headquarters and said all able-bodied Germans were to be removed from the cage. Lloyd George was driven to the 5th Army compound. He thought the German prisoners were a 'weedy lot . . . deplorably inferior to the manly specimens I had seen in early stages of the War'.

Gough was sitting in his office at La Lovie Château. He looked out the window and saw the Prime Minister walking past with Charteris.

> I was struck by the discourtesy of the Prime Minister in actually visiting the Headquarters of one of his Army Commanders and not coming in to him . . . It was an amazing attitude for a man in his position . . . He had never met me, and it would have been an opportunity of at least seeing for himself what manner of man I was, and of exchanging some ideas . . . It was in fact his duty to do so. I have since understood that he blamed me for this Ypres battle and for its long continuation . . . I merely received my orders from the Field Marshal . . . even so, the responsibility was not entirely his [Haig's] – the Cabinet must certainly have known the situation also and consented to these operations.

If there is an arrogant tone to Gough's prose, there is also some truth in what he was saying. Cabinet had consented. It had not exercised its right to call off the operation. Lloyd George should have talked to Gough. Here was the whole trouble. Lloyd George didn't like the military brass and wanted as little to do with them as possible; the military brass didn't like Lloyd George and patronised him.

The Prime Minister went home unconvinced that Third Ypres was achieving much. Haig and Plumer went on with planning the battle that would be called Polygon Wood.

CLAUDE AND COLETTE Durand, retired schoolteachers from Hendecourt, the little village within walking distance of the old Bullecourt battlefield, have driven north, past fields of hops and herds of sleek Friesians, to lay a wreath on an Australian grave in a small cemetery near Ypres. The family of the Australian soldier are all too old to fly across the world to visit the grave. They asked the Durands to lay the wreath for them. It was important that the soldier be remembered. The Great War is gone and past; and it is still with us.

Fred Tubb lies in the ground here at Lijssenthoek Military Cemetery near a pink rose bush; Keith Seabrook lies nearby. Staff Nurse N. Spindler of the Imperial Military Nursing Service is also buried here. She was twenty-six. The inscription on her headstone says: 'A noble type of good heroic womanhood.' This is one of the largest British graveyards, simply because it was close to four hospitals. Poplars, willows, pines, maples and oaks rise among the graves. More than 1100 Australians lie here. Behind the cemetery is the cutting for an old light railway line that ran towards Ypres, and beyond that a large farm shed where one can still read soldiers' graffiti from the Great War. Once this area was alive with roistering soldiers, hospitals, huts, tents and horse lines. Now it slumbers in the summer sun. It is quiet, except for the birds. That is the predominant sound of these hundreds of cemeteries all over northern France and Belgium: birdsong. Men die in their hundreds of thousands, usually to the shrieking sounds of shells, and afterwards birds sing over their graves.

Captain Fred Moore, whose death led to the killing of German prisoners at a pillbox above Menin Road, lies in Menin Road South Military Cemetery. He was twenty-two. Nearby is the headstone of a twenty-three-year-old Englishman from the King's Royal Rifle Corps. The inscription reads:

NO MORNING DAWNS
NO NIGHT BEGINS
BUT WHAT WE THINK OF YOU
OUR BOY.

Gough was attacking in front of Langemarck at the same time as the Australians fought the battle of Menin Road. Langemarck has a German cemetery that assaults the senses, simply because it is so different. The British and French cemeteries have a pastoral elegance. They are sad places – they cannot be otherwise – but the light shines in and one is drawn to the cliché that these men are at peace, even if, in the case of the Anzacs and the Canadians, they are far from the sights and sounds of their youth. The German cemetery at Langemarck is Gothic and gloomy: it belongs to the forest rather than the plain, to the dark side of the heart. It speaks of pain and misery; it does not allow for redemption or peace of mind. Somehow it does not even allow for pity: it is working too hard at being spooky. The oaks are set so closely together that the light cannot shine in, even in summer. Birds do not sing here.

Many of the students, the carefree young volunteers of 1914 who died in 'the Massacre of the Innocents', lie in the mass grave that is the first thing you see as you enter the cemetery. Some 24,000 Germans are underneath, in a tomb that measures perhaps twenty-five yards by fifteen. Red begonias and rhododendrons frame the grave and beyond it is a trapdoor. Any bodies found on the nearby battlefields and identified as German go through this. At the far end of the cemetery stand the black statues of four men, just standing there, life-sized, ghosts in a forest who somehow seem to be saying that, here anyway, men still wander in purgatory.

A Belgian tells us that when he was fifteen he worked at Langemarck as a telegram boy. He says he always pedalled faster when he passed within sight of those four men, particularly if it was a grey day.

At Longwood, in north-eastern Victoria, the birdsongs are different, the music of magpies and the screeching of cockatoos. St Andrew's Anglican Church, a token gesture to God in the Great Australian Nothingness, is a small white weatherboard with a corrugated iron roof and a lean-to at one end in which the priest can change, taking his white surplice from a hook and his Bible from a battered tin trunk. Outside a grey bell is mounted on an iron post; it still sounds every Sunday and seven or eight worshippers turn up.

Inside the church is bright and friendly: white walls, a tiny organ, bar radiators on the walls, homemade cushions on white pews. The hard light from outside streams in through windows stained yellow and pink. The Tubb family once sat in the second and third rows on the left. Above these pews is a list of golden names on varnished wood: the Victoria Cross winners Tubb and Leslie Maygar, the Military Cross winners Frank Tubb and Gordon Maxfield, and dozens of other locals who went off to the Great War.

Across the highway is the Tubb family home, which was originally built as a hotel. It is two-storeyed, Georgian in style, European rather than Australian, so it's probably right that Fred's father, who was fascinated by Napoleon, called it St Helena, an island in a sea of yellow grass. Ten children were born in this house; the nearest doctor was at Seymour, twenty-five miles away.

Near the old Melbourne-to-Sydney road a small cairn rises out of the bleached grass, a simple column that honours the district's three Victoria Cross winners (the third being Alex Burton of Euroa). This is where Fred Tubb farmed and where his nephew, also Fred Tubb, still farms. The Great War is gone and past, and it is still with us.

Battle of Polygon Wood, September 26, 1917

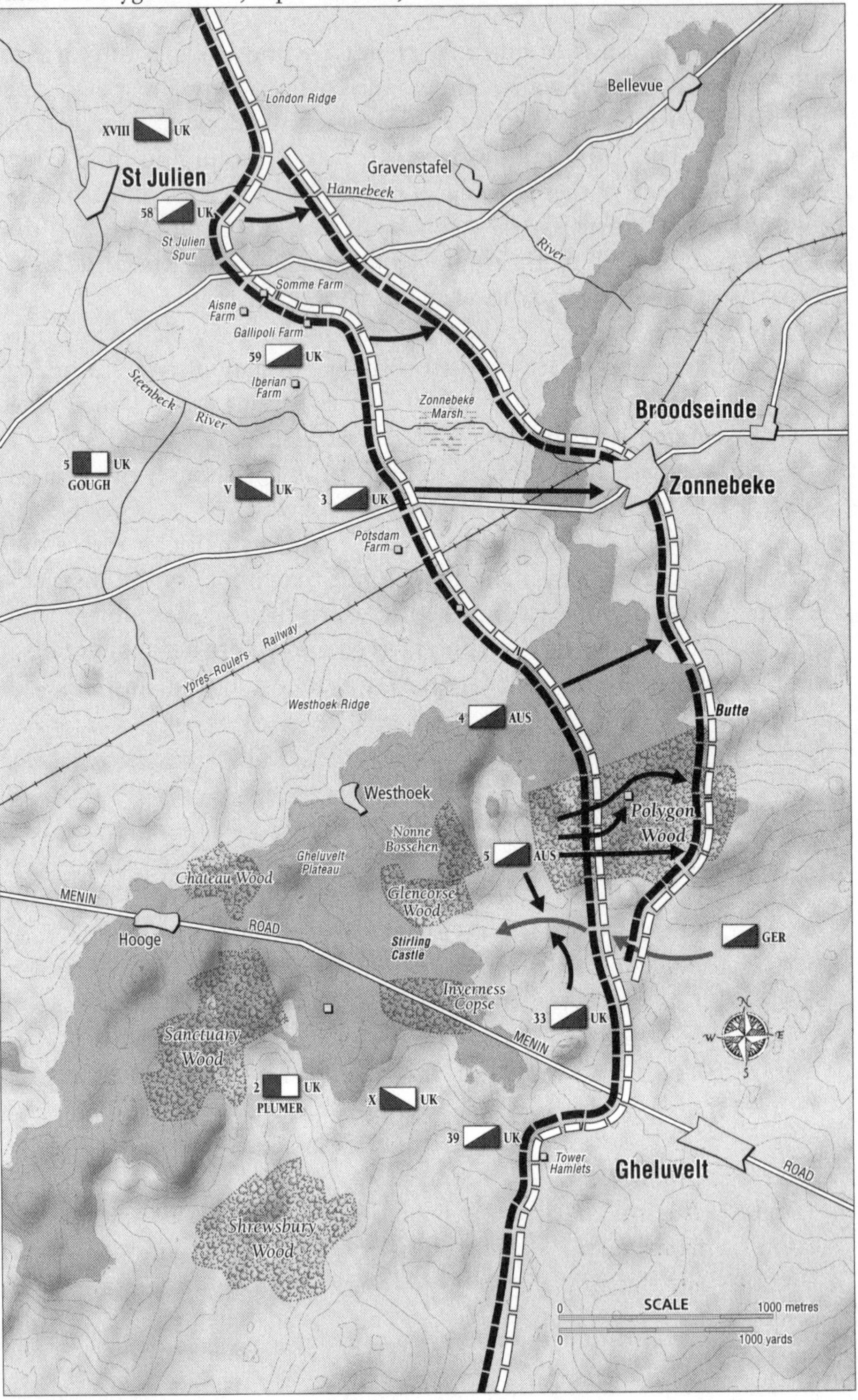

30

Two brothers

The 1st and 2nd Australian divisions left the front and the 4th and 5th came up for what would be called the battle of Polygon Wood. The wood today is mostly pines with a heavy undergrowth of ferns and tangles of blackberries. Lumps of reinforced concrete from German pillboxes are still there and a few straggly trenches, now almost filled in by erosion and pine needles, wander through the trees. This is the typical European forest, gloomy and mysterious. It was not like this in 1917. The trees, most of them about twenty years old, had been stripped of their foliage by shells; from a distance they looked like the black pickets upon which both sides strung barbed wire. There was still some knee-high undergrowth and the ground was a mess of craters and old trench lines, but one could see well enough to notice a mound up ahead, perhaps thirty-feet high. This was the Butte. Belgian artillerymen had practised here in the days of cannons and solid shot; the mound had been a stop-butt. In front of the Butte, now destroyed by artillery, lay an oval track that had been a racecourse.

Some Australians came up to the wood by marching cross-country from bivouacs south of Ypres. Others, like Corporal William Gamble, a machine gunner in the 5th Division, came down the Menin Road. Gamble had been enjoying his rest, playing poker, at which he usually won because he believed he had mastered the art of bluffing, and walking into Poperinghe for a meal: two eggs, bread, butter and coffee. Now he marched through Ypres and out along the Menin Road and its debris: horses and mules bloated in death, broken-down ambulances and abandoned wagons, discarded rifles and bicycles, and dead men lying in absurd postures on the edge of craters, like other things that had been thrown away. It was Gamble's first time at the front. The dead were 'not a very helpful sight'.

Sergeant Jimmy Downing had a hellish trip to the front. He went across country from a bivouac south of Ypres. The final approach was at night. Downing lit up with a waterproof sheet over his head so that German airman could not see the glow from the cigarette. The German barrage caught his battalion.

> There was a crash close by, a red flame, flying sparks. Another – and two men were seen in the flash, toppling stiffly sideways, one to the right, one to the left: the one with a forearm partly raised, the other lifted a little from the ground, with legs and arms spread-eagled wide – all seen in an instant – then a second of darkness, then shells, big shells, flashing and crashing all around . . . A sergeant ran around his platoon. Then the top of his skull was lifted from his forehead by a bullet, as on a hinge, and his body fell on two crouching men, washing them with his blood and brains.

He had arrived at Polygon Wood. The real battle hadn't started but already Downing's 57th Battalion was 'a few handfuls of black-faced men wearily digging'.

Two brothers came up to the front. We know one of them. Brigadier-General Pompey Elliott, commander of the 15th Brigade, was cranky and inspirational, hard and soft, rough with men and gentle with women and children, ambitious yet tactless, intelligent but unsubtle, cocksure and insecure. George, his younger brother, had spent most of his life having fun. He liked a drink and, better still, four or five. Pompey was a teetotaller. George was a brilliant student but at Melbourne University, where he was studying medicine, carousing and football distracted him. George played for Fitzroy and University in the Victorian Football League and was chosen for the State side. Pompey had a sense of purpose, took himself seriously and liked giving orders; George muddled along, enjoying himself. He took a decade to qualify as a doctor and this had nothing to do with lack of academic ability. And here he was now, a captain on the western front, the medical officer of the 56th Battalion, also part of the 5th Division, but in a different brigade to Pompey's. George carried a photograph of his daughter, Jacquelyn, born in 1916. Everyone seemed to like him: he was an officer and a doctor but he wasn't stuffy.

Ross McMullin, in his biography *Pompey Elliott*, tells of an incident at a divisional tournament a few months before Polygon Wood. Pompey was in serious conversation with several high-ranking officers. George had enjoyed several rounds of drinks. He spotted his brother, walked up behind him, thumped him on the back and greeted him warmly with: 'Hello, Pompey, how are you?'

Pompey whirled around with 'a look of thunder' that softened as he recognised his brother. An onlooker reported: 'He tried, however, to cool the "doc's" ardour by a sign which drew attention to the quality of the little gathering.'

George said: 'I don't care a damn who you're talking to with all those ribbons on your chest, you should be glad to see your little brother.' Pompey was; he just wished for a little more decorum. George visited Pompey about six weeks later and relieved him of twenty pounds: he was going on leave and needed spending money.

Now they came up to the front for Polygon Wood. Pompey set up his headquarters in a mine crater at Hooge, several miles behind the front. George went on to Château Wood, behind the 14th Brigade's jump-off point. Hooge and Château Wood were both under shellfire.

HAIG HAD SEEN the vision again: the Belgian ports. No matter that they were twenty-five miles to the north and that he had already run up more than 80,000 casualties to gain 1000 yards here and

1000 yards there. The myth about Haig is that he lacked imagination. Yet here he was dreaming of breakthrough again: up the ridge, step by step, to Passchendaele village, then a lunge towards the Belgian coast. He had glimpsed the denouement. And Charteris, his sorcerer, was priming the fantasy by feeding Haig tales about the collapse of enemy morale and exaggerating the extent of German casualties. Haig's imagination only ran down certain roads, however. He apparently didn't think much about the weather. October, only four days away at the time of Polygon Wood, usually brought about three inches of rain to Ypres. That would be enough to turn the battlefield into a swamp again.

The front for Menin Road was 14,500 yards; for Polygon Wood it would be 8500. The ratio of artillery to the yardage of front being attacked would be about the same as at Menin Road. To the north Gough would go for Zonnebeke village, or what was left of it. In the centre the 4th and 5th Australian divisions would take the rest of Polygon Wood. To the south of the wood the British 33rd Division would come up alongside the Australians. Or at least this was the plan.

THE DAY BEFORE the set-piece was due to begin the Germans, who had clearly not been reading Charteris's intelligence reports, counter-attacked just after dawn on the front of the 33rd Division, firing a tremendous barrage: high explosive, shrapnel and gas. Some said afterwards the bombardment was the most intense ever fired by the Germans to support an attack by a single division. It fell not only on the British division but also on Elliott's 58th Battalion, waiting for the next morning's attack on Polygon Wood. German infantrymen drove 700 yards into the British lines and exposed Elliott's right flank.

Elliott, meanwhile, was being shelled at his headquarters two miles back at Hooge crater. Talbot Hobbs, the divisional commander, tried to drive down the Menin Road to Elliott's post. 'Dumps were going up in all directions,' he wrote in his diary. 'Motor lorries and cars burning along the Rd, broken down wagons, dead men and horses.' Hobbs came to within 200 yards of Elliott's post, then decided to go back, and perhaps saved his life. Three minutes after he turned back a lorry loaded with ammunition blew up. It was just in front of where Hobbs had been stopped. Those who had to stay on the road watched with astonishment as two Australian official photographers – Frank Hurley and Hubert Wilkins – stood up and clicked their cameras as tails of earth erupted on either side of the road.

Elliott's plans for the following morning were being wrecked. He sent up part of the 60th Battalion to help the 58th. Later in the morning he sent up the rest of the battalion and its commander, Colonel Norman Marshall, a public schoolboy who had been amateur middleweight boxing champion of Victoria and was also an intrepid cross-country horseman, particularly after he had downed a few drinks on a moonlit night. Marshall steadied the men but the two Australian battalions were being chopped up under the barrage and the British troops on their right still had not regained their old frontline. Late in the afternoon Elliott threw in his 57th Battalion, which brought Jimmy Downing into the madness.

Private David Whinfield had gone up with the 60th. 'We passed many killed. Tommies and Scotties in useless shelters, were devilish scared.' The German heavy guns were firing at the rate of four shells a second, he wrote in his diary afterwards. 'It was more than men could stand.' Downing's battalion was shelled all night. Many men were buried two or three times.

As darkness came Elliott knew he was in trouble. Three of his four battalions had been shot up before the attack, his right flank was still exposed, many of his supply dumps had been blown up and the British commander on his right didn't know where his troops were. Elliott also knew he would have trouble trying to assemble what was left of his battalions for the assault. Many of the officers who were to act as guides had been killed or wounded. About 8 pm Elliott told Hobbs that he didn't want to attack. Hobbs talked to Birdwood. Both decided the 15th Brigade's assault had to go ahead. The 15th was only a small part of a big attack but its objectives – the wood itself, which opened the way to Broodseinde and Passchendaele Ridge – were probably the most important on the whole front.

Hobbs accepted that Elliott now had only one battalion that was in proper fighting shape, the 59th. The scheme for the assault by Hobbs' division had two brigades attacking, Elliott's 15th and the 14th. The 8th Brigade was in reserve. Elliott was now given two battalions from the 8th. They would go on to the final objective, the Blue Line. The 59th would take the first objective, the Red Line. Elliott's other three battalions would be used for carrying and support.

GEORGE ELLIOTT WAS in the 14th Brigade, which had had an easier time than his brother's brigade. He was in Château Wood, a few hundred yards ahead of his brother's post, waiting in the dark with the headquarters staff of his battalion. Soon the barrage would begin and George and the others would move up closer to the front-line troops. Then a shell crashed down among them. A fragment smashed into the back of George's skull. He lost consciousness.

THE BRITISH BARRAGE opened just before daybreak on September 26, a misty morning a few days into autumn. Sinclair-MacLagan's 4th Division was north of the 5th Division, going for the northern edge of Polygon Wood and a spur beyond. The historian of one of the 4th's battalions wrote that the British barrage 'was the acme of perfection – a gigantic thunderstorm of bursting steel hurled out of the lips of thousands of guns . . . So close overhead was it that the warm air caused by the friction of the shells could be distinctly felt.' Bean said that the barrage was the most perfect that ever protected Australian troops. It seemed to break out with a single crash and produced a wall of dust and smoke that appeared to be solid and rolled ahead of the Australians, as someone said, like a Gippsland bushfire. Officers had to use compasses to keep direction. Jimmy Downing said the sky behind him flamed like the Aurora Borealis. The barrage moved across the German lines like the shuttle on a loom, combing the country with intersecting teeth that passed and repassed. And the machine

The Ypres battlefield after the Passchendaele campaign. British troops wash in a shell hole that is also the grave for at least seven soldiers. *[IWM Q11562]*

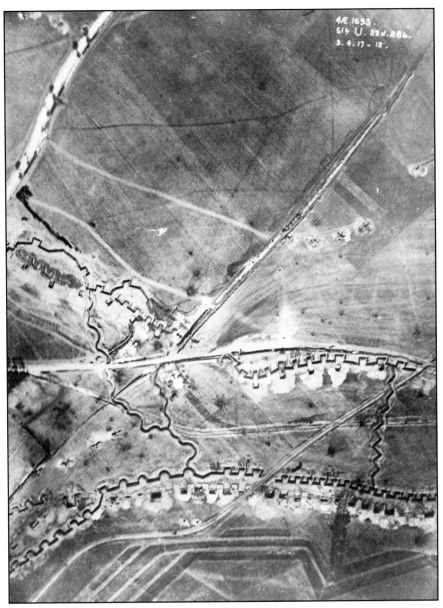

The formidable defences of the Hindenburg Line east of Bullecourt village,
photographed from the air a week before the first Australian attack
in 1917. The notched lines are the two Hindenburg trenches. German
batteries can be seen behind the second line on the right of the photograph.
The grey bands in the foreground are uncut wire. *[AWM A01121]*

Harry Murray, from Evandale, Tasmania, became the most decorated infantry soldier in the British empire armies of the Great War. He won the Distinguished Conduct Medal on Gallipoli, the Distinguished Service Order at Mouquet Farm in 1916, the Victoria Cross at Stormy Trench in 1917 and a second DSO at Bullecourt later in the same year. The French awarded him the *Croix de Guerre*. No cult developed around Murray, a modest and reflective man. After the war he bought a grazing property in outback Queensland and told Charles Bean he was teaching his sheep to march in fours. [AWM P02939.053]

Percy Black, born at Bacchus Marsh, Victoria, was Harry Murray's best friend. Both were working in Western Australia when war broke out, Murray as a sleeper-cutter and Black as a prospector. Black died on the uncut wire at First Bullecourt. By then he had won the Distinguished Service Order, the Distinguished Conduct Medal and the *Croix de Guerre*. Murray said Black was 'the bravest man in the AIF'. When a barrage was falling Black would walk along the line, look down at a private cowering in a trench or shell hole and say: 'Got a match, lad?' [AWM J00369]

Australians holding the first line of Hindenburg trenches during Second Bullecourt. Nearest the camera is Lieutenant William Donovan Joynt, who won the Victoria Cross the following year. *[AWM E00439]*

The debris of war: the railway embankment that ran parallel to the Hindenburg Line at Bullecourt. Both Australian attacks began from here. *[AWM E1408]*

A crippled Mark I tank, the type used at First Bullecourt. The Great War was all about new technology – submarines, machine guns, quick-firing artillery, aircraft – but these, and other relatively new inventions, pre-dated the conflict. The tank was conceived during the war, as a means of crushing wire and crossing trenches. The Mark I weighed thirty-one tons and had a top speed of 3.7 miles per hour. [AWM P00826.001]

Rupert 'Mick' Moon, winner of the Victoria Cross at Second Bullecourt, where a bullet smashed his jaw and twelve teeth.
[AWM A02592]

General Sir Herbert Plumer, the British army commander who planned the set-piece at Messines. [IWM Q23665]

Phillip Schuler, who wrote so well of Gallipoli as a journalist and died in Flanders as a soldier. [AWM G01560]

No figure has polarised the chroniclers of the Great War so well as Field-Marshal Sir Douglas Haig, the British commander-in-chief on the western front. His admirers say he had great gifts as a commander; his detractors say he was a butcher and a muddler. His admirers say he was bright and his detractors insist he was dull. He stood far back from the war, more like a king than a general, but never lost his nerve. *[IWM Q23659]*

Lloyd George, one of the great British prime ministers of the twentieth
century, cut a dramatic figure with his wayward hair, dreamy eyes
and inspirational words. He understood the rhetoric of war, but was
intimidated by Haig, whom he despised. Lloyd George never believed in
Haig's Passchendaele campaign, yet would not overrule him. *[IWM Q70208]*

The ruined Cloth Hall at Ypres, 1917. Only soldiers and rats lived here. Most Australians who passed through the town on their way to the war thought it so ruined by shellfire that it could never be restored. But it was. Ypres today is one of the most beautiful and hospitable places along the old line of trenches that stretched south and east to Verdun. *[AWM E1230]*

Dead and wounded
Australians and Germans
in the railway cutting on
Broodseinde Ridge during
the battle for Passchendaele
village. [AWM E03864]

Fred Tubb won the Victoria
Cross at Lone Pine on
Gallipoli. He was one
of several distinguished
soldiers who sprang from
the congregation of a little
wooden Anglican church
among gums at Longwood
in Victoria's north-east.
Tubb was killed in the battle
of Menin Road. [AWM H06786]

Australian troops in craters on the edge of Polygon Wood – except the wood has been obliterated by artillery fire. *[AWM E00971]*

The Seabrook brothers from Five Dock, Sydney: Theo (left), William (centre) and George. All were killed in the battle of Menin Road. Several Red Cross reports have Theo and George being killed by the same shell. *[AWM H05568]*

The way to the war, paved with bad intentions. Menin Road, near Idiot Corner, late in the Passchendaele campaign. *[AWM E01197]*

Jarvis Fuller (top), from Moonambel in Victoria's west, his brother Roy and four of their sisters. Jarvis 'disappeared' in the fighting at Broodseinde. Roy, who was in the same battle, months later discovered that his brother had been buried by another battalion. *[Valma Harris]*

Eight brothers from the Handcock family of Myrrhee, near Wangaratta, went to the Great War. Jack (top row, centre) was killed on Gallipoli. Frank (top row, right) lost a leg at Broodseinde. Charles (bottom row, second from right) died from pneumonia a day before the war ended. *[Colin Handcock]*

Frank Hurley, one of the official Australian photographers, was a master of composition. All of his work bears a signature: you know it is a Hurley before you read the credit line. Here he captures Australian artillerymen crossing the flooded Ypres battlefield in late October. *[AWM E01220]*

The Bulletin

Registered at the General Post Office, Sydney, N.S.W., Australia, for Transmission by Post as a Newspaper.

Vol. 38.—No. 1929.   THURSDAY, FEBRUARY 1, 1917.   Price 6d.

THE PEACEMAKER.

WOODROW WILSON: "Come, come, kiss and be friends!"

President Woodrow Wilson, the idealist from the New World, fancied himself as the peacemaker in 1917. But many in France, Britain and Australia thought he was too indulgent of the Germans. Norman Lindsay's 'Hun', as always, wears a helmet several sizes too small; 'Belgium', as always, has been ravished. [PBL]

Billy Hughes, the Australian Prime Minister, twice failed to introduce conscription at home. Here he addresses troops in France late in the war. As Australia went to war in 1914, Andrew Fisher, the Labor leader, said Australia would support Britain to the last man and the last shilling. When Hughes, who succeeded Fisher as prime minister, turned up behind the lines in France in 1916, soldiers joked that Fisher indeed had sent the last man. Hughes had great affection for the Australian soldier. *[AWM E02651]*

Keith Murdoch (right) played journalist and courtier from London for the last three years of the war. He wrote for a string of newspapers in Australia while also acting as Hughes' agent and emissary.
[AWM E02650]

An Australian infantryman uses his .303 rifle to ease the weight of his pack during a halt in the pursuit of the Germans to the Hindenburg Line early in 1917. Charles Bean said Australian troops were always easy to recognise from a distance because of their 'easy attitudes'. Australian and New Zealand troops only began referring to themselves as 'Diggers' late in 1917. *[AWM E00227]*

guns: they were fired as barrages now as part of the new tactics. Downing thought they sounded like the leitmotif from a piece by Wagner. North of Downing a captain in the 14th Brigade led his battalion forward, a cigarette in his mouth and a map in his hand. Germans emerged from pillboxes offering souvenirs.

Sinclair Hunt, a schoolteacher from Croydon, New South Wales, shortly to be promoted to lieutenant, had come up with the 14th Brigade. A shell fell among Hunt's men while they were in the support trenches. One of the six men hit was a 'platoon favourite'. Hunt wrote that the man's wounds were terrible, though bleeding little. 'Great lumps had been chopped out by the pieces of shell and one leg was smashed. He bore up like a true man, would insist on seeing every wound as we hastily dressed it and quietly weighed up his chances of life, which as he said didn't look over bright.' He moaned as four men lifted him onto a stretcher, then thanked everyone for helping him. He died two days later.

Before the barrage, Hunt wrote, a man would rise here or there to tighten his belt or stretch a cramped limb. Then the guns opened up and Hunt was on his way. When he had gone seventy-five yards he saw his first Germans, 'chewed up by the barrage'. When he had gone 100 yards he saw scared-looking German prisoners hurrying back with their hands up. They seemed to know the way better than their guides. He passed the Butte. Australians swarmed all over it, flushing out Germans. He went on. The casualties were light and mostly caused by Australian shells dropping short. One landed a foot behind Hunt's heels but failed to explode. The moment the barrage lifted off a pillbox the Australians would be all over it, looking for flues or ventilator shafts, then dropping bombs down them. Mostly, Hunt said, the Germans didn't want to fight; many hadn't bothered to fix bayonets to their rifles.

Everything had gone well here. The brigade took its objectives easily enough. The barrage had been 'perfect'. The men were in good spirits. Few had the heart to kill the shell-shocked Germans. Hunt said there were rules. 'If Fritz fights, he gets fight with interest, but the moment he throws up his hands then fight finishes, for to kill an unarmed and defenceless man is as abhorrent . . . as to kick a man when he is down.' But there were also exceptions to the rules, 'when men wrought to a pitch of momentary insanity by the terrific strain of a barrage endured for hours perhaps, or by the loss of mates killed at their sides, act as they would never do in saner moments.'

Hunt watched the souvenir-hunters. As soon as the Germans emerged from a pillbox they would be roughly searched. Watches, pouches, cigarette cases, revolvers and field glasses were the most common trophies.

Corporal Gamble, back with the machine-gun barrage, saw his first German prisoners. Back in Australia he had seen drawings of cruel-looking Prussians in spiked helmets threatening women and children. These prisoners wore the 'coal scuttle' helmets that had come into use the previous year. They didn't impress him, 'dressed as they were in sloppy fitting tunics and helmets that looked for all the world like upturned chambers on their heads'.

The 4th Division brigades took their second objective after a short fight but German snipers became busy. Captain Harold Wanliss fell dead here, shot in the heart, throat and side. He was buried where he fell. Wanliss, dark-haired and well liked, had gone out on a trench raid in French Flanders during 1916 to be shot in the mouth in no-man's land. Bleeding freely, he went on to the German trench and directed the raid from the parapet. On the way back to the Australian line he tried to carry a wounded man but did not have the strength to free him from the wire. Wanliss was then hit by shrapnel and fainted from loss of blood. Three sergeants carried him through the mud to safety. Wanliss received the Distinguished Service Order, a high honour for a twenty-four-year-old lieutenant.

He was a farmer who, like the Elliott brothers, had been dux of Ballarat College; he had also been dux of Hawkesbury Agricultural College and had travelled in Europe with his father, a Ballarat solicitor, before the war. He was a high-minded young man, full of ideas about what Australia might become after the war. His comrades caroused in *estaminets* and he read and studied. That had always been his way. Around the time war broke out he had broken his leg in a riding accident and couldn't enlist. While his leg knitted he studied the history and theory of war. After Wanliss's death his battalion commander wrote: 'Many brave men – many good men have I met . . . but he was the king of them all.' Bert Jacka, who was in the same battalion, said: 'A hero and a man.'

It had been generally accepted that Wanliss would go into politics after the war. Some, including Monash – and perhaps also Bean – appeared to see him as a future prime minister. The historian Bill Gammage wrote of Wanliss: 'His death demonstrates that Australia's World War I losses cannot be measured simply by numbers.'

ELLIOTT'S BRIGADE, BOLSTERED by the 29th and 31st battalions from the reserve brigade, also took its objectives, but it was a day of desperation and confusion because the British division on the right had not caught up and the flank was still open. Elliott's line was often bent back to the right because of flanking fire. Battalions became intermixed. At one point a lieutenant in Elliott's brigade found himself in charge of troops from four Australian battalions, plus a few lost Royal Welch Fusiliers. The 15th Brigade seems to have struck more resistance from pillboxes than the brigades north of it.

Early in the advance Lieutenant John Turnour, a theology student from Bendigo, positioned his men in an arc in front of a pillbox. Then he stood up and charged. He ran on, even though he was hit time and again by machine-gun bullets, and eventually fell in front of the loophole. But he had distracted the Germans and his men took the pillbox.

Private Patrick Bugden was caught up in several fights around pillboxes. After rushing one of them he noticed three Germans leading an Australian corporal away as a prisoner of war. He shot one of the Germans, bayoneted the other two and rescued his comrade. Five times during the battle he went out under fire to rescue wounded men. Then he was killed. He was never to know that he had won the Victoria Cross.

The 59th Battalion took the Red Line on time at about 6.45 am. There was, however, still no sign of the British troops who were supposed to be on their right. At this stage the two battalions that had been loaned to Elliott were supposed to go through the 59th and press on to the Blue Line. Their commanders were wary of doing so with their right flank unprotected. Elliott, back at Hooge, was becoming testy, and more so when he heard that the 14th Brigade had already reached its final objective. 'Push on,' he told the commanders of the two battalions. Two hours passed and Elliott had heard nothing. It was time for one of his theatrical gestures. He sent a message up: the two battalions were to get moving or he would place a 15th Brigade man in charge of them.

The commander of the British 33rd Division, which should have been on the Australians' right, was also becoming frustrated. He threw in the 2nd Royal Welch Fusiliers, the battalion of Robert Graves and Siegfried Sassoon. The battalion was sent forward in the afternoon through ground already taken by Elliott's brigade rather than on its own front. The Welch Fusiliers were shelled on their way forward and held up when they went for German positions just south of Elliott's open flank. They eventually fell back through the Australian lines. British and Australian officers stopped the rout. German airmen flew low over the front, strafing with machine guns. The Australians shot down one of the aircraft, an event so dramatic and unusual that it figured in many soldiers' diaries.

The British divisional commander again told his troops to push on to the Blue Line. Elliott, meanwhile, told Colonel Marshall to try to take some of the British objectives on the right. Around midnight Marshall took a strong point on the British front, but back at Hooge it wasn't clear what blockhouse had been captured or precisely where it was. Marshall himself wasn't entirely sure where he was.

Elliott decided to go to the front himself at dawn, even though Hobbs' chief-of-staff advised him against this. Ross McMullin recounts in *Pompey Elliott* that on his way forward Elliott came upon an unwounded 15th Brigade officer in what he considered 'suspicious circumstances'.

'Your men are up their fighting for their lives – what are you doing?' Elliott demanded, and we may presume that he spoke in a very loud voice. Typically again, Elliott decided he might have to shoot this man, then, just as typically, allowed himself to be talked out of it.

Elliott reached the frontline about 8 am. His men were pleased, though not surprised, to see him. The Welch Fusiliers were astounded. One wrote: 'It was the only time during the whole of the war that I saw a brigadier with the first line of attacking troops.' Another said it was 'rare for anyone who combines authority and nous to be on the spot'. Elliott wrote to his wife a few days later: 'I never saw such a scene of confusion, men of all regiments mixed up all over the place, dead of all regiments lay aside the enemy everywhere.'

Elliott told Marshall to consolidate the position around the strong point he had taken. He told the commander of one of the battalions he had been loaned to push on to the Blue Line. He urged the Welch Fusiliers officers to reorganise their men. And then he left.

That day the Australians took all their objectives here. Marshall ended up holding 250 yards on what should have been the British front. The Welch Fusiliers went forward, superbly, Marshall said. The battle was won. Elliott had prevailed. Force of character had a little to do with it.

AT 3 PM ON the day before Elliott had been told that his brother had been badly wounded.

> They brought the news to me when I was tied to my office directing the fight and I could not go to him though they said he was dying. [George had lingered for several hours but never regained consciousness.] I hope never to have such an experience again. The effort to concentrate my thoughts on the task of defeating the enemy as the messages came through revealing each move and the changing phases of the battle to me seemed as time went on to turn me into stone and half the time I was like a man sleepwalking, yet I do not think I made a single error that I would not have made at [training] manoeuvres under similar circumstances.

While Polygon Wood was going on Elliott also discovered that his legal partner back in Melbourne had run up heavy debts. Elliott could be liable for them and the figure could run to thousands of pounds.

He went to see his brother's body. He cut off the shoulder straps with the captain's stars as a memento for his sister-in-law. Field ambulance men later gave him George's watch and cigarette case.

Poor old Geordie, I saw him dead so white and rigid and still and his loved ones left behind him. And we have buried him so far from home amongst strangers to him. I am so glad I was able to bring his body back from the shell torn zone to a little cemetery where the grass was smooth and green and we fired the volley over his head and laid him in the grave with the Union Jack flying over him and our great guns still roaring in the distance. Poor Lyn [George's wife] and poor little darling Jacquelyn. You must tell our bairnies to love them both well.

The children, Elliott told his wife, need to be told what happened, that 'the Germans hit poor old Uncle Geordie with a shell and he died and has gone away to heaven . . . then Dida's own soldiers got up and they chased those nasty old Germans back for a long way through the bush that is called woods here and they caught and killed such a lot of them and those that weren't killed . . . have been sent away to jail again.'

Not long after Jack Campbell, Elliott's brother-in-law, was killed north of Polygon Wood, dying instantly from a bullet that entered under his left eye. Jack's mother lived with Elliott's family. News of the death of her only son and of George is thought to have caused her to suffer a stroke from which she never truly recovered. The European war was doing terrible things to Australian families. And Billy Hughes was again thinking about conscription.

JIMMY DOWNING WON the Military Medal for Polygon Wood. On the morning of the second day, when the barrage eased, Downing and those around him still alive realised that they were hungry. They took food and water from the dead, saying: 'Pardon, brother, you don't need it.' In the afternoon Downing noticed a carrying party of sixteen men coming up. The non-commissioned officer in charge placed eight men in one trench and seven in another while he went on to reconnoitre. He returned to the eight to find them all dead, 'chopped into lumps like butcher's meat'. He went to the other seven. They were dead too. Downing said the NCO threw his steel helmet far away and sat down. 'His body seemed shrunken. "This is the finish, the finish," he whispered from cracked and blackened lips.'

Downing left the front. 'We were a pathetic band, with dirty faces and stubbly beards. All were hysterical in varying degrees.'

Sinclair Hunt came out too. He wrote that fear gripped hardest when men were coming out. Having survived, they didn't want to be hit on the way out. 'Men tended to hurry away, until some puffing hero declares he won't run another step for every Fritz in creation and the pace slackens.' Weary men limped along the roads, stopping to take a cup of coffee at a YMCA stall. Then they slept and slept. Hunt was happy enough: he had survived Polygon Wood. He was killed the following year.

LIKE MENIN ROAD, Polygon Wood was a success. The objective had been gained along the five-mile front. Another three-and-a-half square miles had been won. And, as with Menin Road, the cost had been close to outrageous. There was something perverse about this. The British had spent most of the first three years losing battles, not because of their infantrymen but because the artillery support was poor. Now they were winning battles because they had discovered how to use artillery. They had forced the Germans to revise their tactics and strengthen their frontlines because the ferocity of British barrages stopped German counter-attackers getting through. The trouble now was that the cost of winning was too high and the pace of advance too slow. Haig wouldn't have enough men left to take the Belgian ports, although he didn't yet seem to see this, or that he had little prospect of threatening the coast before the autumn rains came. There was another trouble that Haig failed to identify. The advances were so shallow that German artillery pieces were not being captured. This virtually ensured that the next shallow advance would be costly.

The casualties along the whole front for Polygon Wood came in at around 15,400. This was a much higher rate, in terms of the ground captured, than for Menin Road. The Australian losses amounted to around 5400: about 1700 in the 4th Division and more than 3700 in the 5th. Elliott's brigade had suffered worst: 1204 dead, wounded or missing.

In a week, in two short and 'successful' battles, the Australians had lost 10,000 men to advance the allied line in Belgium a few thousand yards.

EARLY IN OCTOBER Haig held a conference with Plumer, Gough and others. He wrote in his diary that night: 'I pointed out how favourable the situation was . . . Charteris emphasised the deterioration of German Divisions in numbers, morale and all-round efficiency.' Haig thought that by October 10 he might be able to do away with bite-and-hold operations and begin a rolling advance on the railhead at Roulers. This would of course involve cavalry. One gains the impression from Haig's diary entry that Plumer and Gough were less enthusiastic than Haig, but they went along, as they always did. Dissent – open dissent, anyway – was a stranger at Haig's court.

A few days earlier A. G. Gardiner, editor of the *Daily News*, had visited Haig's court. 'Gardiner says [Lloyd George] never reads anything or thinks seriously. How unfortunate the country seems to be to have such an unreliable man at the head of affairs in this crisis. I thought Gardiner much above the usual newspaper man who visits France.'

THE 4TH AND 5th Australian divisions came out of Polygon Wood and the 1st and 2nd divisions, plus Monash's 3rd and the New Zealanders, now came up for the next step in the journey towards Passchendaele village. For the first time four Anzac divisions would be attacking in a line. They would call this battle Broodseinde.

31

They rob while they fight

John Monash took eleven days' leave in London after Messines, celebrated his fifty-second birthday, went to four stage shows as well as a performance of *Aida*, and watched a German air raid from his hotel at Piccadilly. The raid seemed nothing much to him – he was used to the thunder and lights of the western front – but it bothered Londoners, who had been listening for Gotha bombers since the first raid in May. One raid on Folkestone had killed twenty-five children. Monash also caught up with Lizzie Bentwitch, who had been friends with him and Vic, his wife, in Melbourne in the 1890s. She had moved to London around 1900 after collecting an inheritance. Sometime in 1917 she and Monash became lovers.

Monash returned to France and eventually took his division to rest at Boulogne on the coast, to sunshine and sports days. Vic had sent him a list of questions and he tried to reply to them in a letter late in July. Yes, the washing of socks in forward areas was done in bulk: the men didn't get their own socks back from the pool, even if they had been knitted by wives or sweethearts. No, he didn't know what they told the relatives of men shot for desertion or cowardice. 'Probably the truth.' Monash said the Australian Government's refusal to allow the death penalty was bad for

Battle of Broodseinde, October 4, 1917

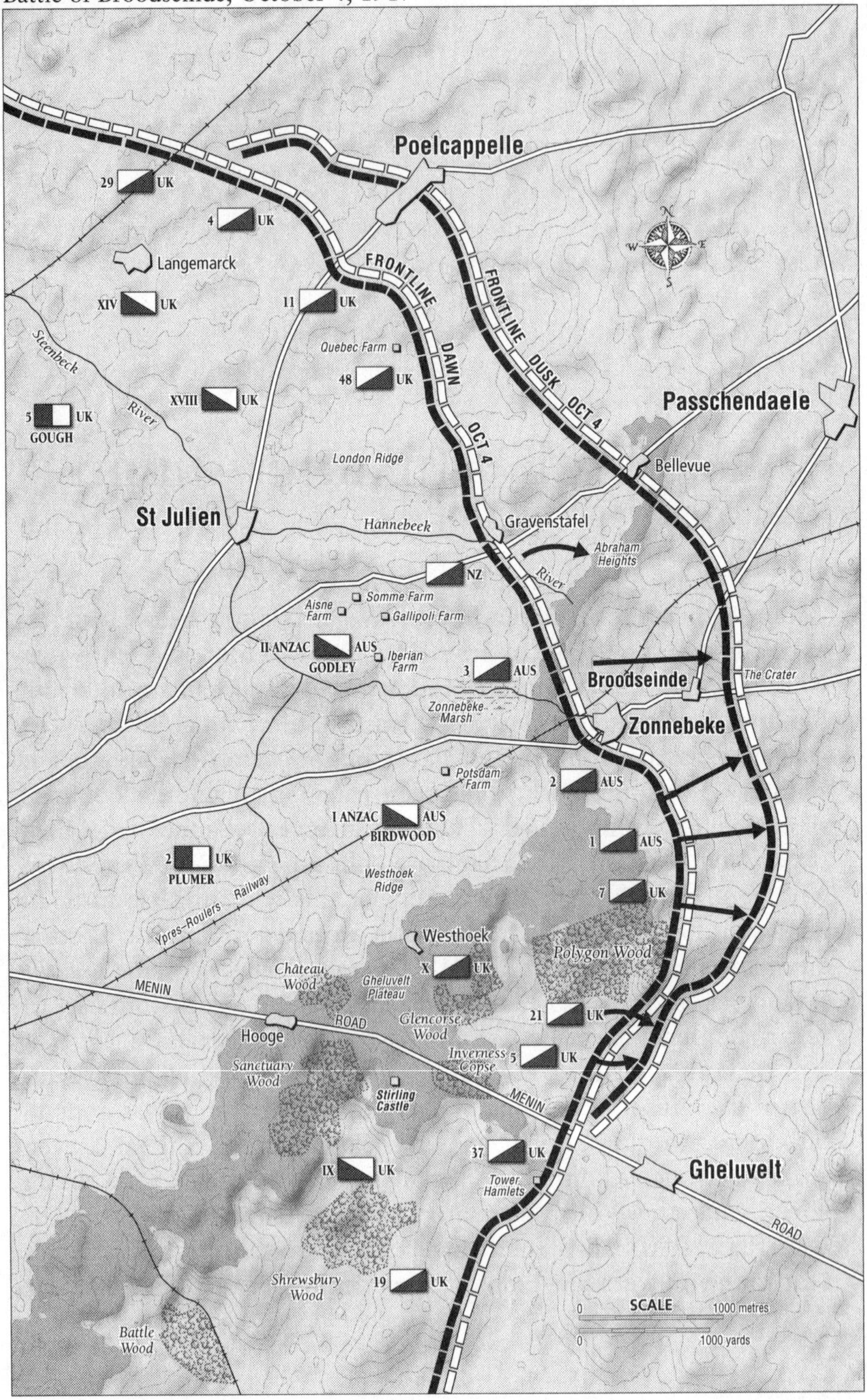

discipline. He had recently acted as corps commander during Godley's absence. He had confirmed six death sentences on 4th Division men 'but they have had to be commuted to ten years' penal servitude'.

By late September the division was preparing to go up for Broodseinde. Monash dined at Haig's headquarters with the field-marshal and two of his staff. After each course the mess stewards left and the doors were locked from the inside. The concern for security was misplaced. Haig was on a romantic flight. He was rapidly wearing the Germans down, he said. It was only a question of time and weather. Monash, with no first-hand experience of the Belgian front, appears to have believed this. Then he left for the ancient town of Ypres to obtain some experience. He set up in the ramparts near the Menin Gate.

Bean's reporting of Messines had irritated Monash. It was 'the apotheosis of banality. Not only is the language silly tosh, but his facts are, for the most part, quite wrong.' The second charge is unfair: Bean was always careful with facts. But he also tended to write like a solicitor, loading up sentences with caveats and parentheses that sucked the sap out of them, and sometimes the clarity as well. Monash, the writer, owned a sharp eye and a relaxed style, and now, in a letter to Vic, he turned it on Ypres.

It had once been one of the great cloth-weaving towns of Europe, with a moat on three sides, backed by massive walls and ramparts. The Cloth Hall, built in the thirteenth century, was at once intimidating in all its Gothic greyness and fussiness, and quaint, friendly almost, like something from a fairytale. Before the Great War shepherds had grazed fat sheep within sight of the spire. Then the German artillery set upon the town and its people fled west along the road to Poperinghe pushing handcarts and wheelbarrows. Only soldiers and rats lived in the ruins of Ypres now. Yet it mattered more than it ever had in its glory days. If it fell, the Germans could fall upon the Channel ports. From a British viewpoint it was the most important town in the Great War.

Monash told Vic: 'For three years it has been dying a lingering death, and now there is nothing left of its fine streets, its great square, its cathedral, the historic Cloth Hall, its avenues, and boulevards of fine mansions, its hospitals, its town hall, or its straggling suburbs, but a charred collection of pitiable ruins – a scene of utter collapse and desolation.' The Germans were still shelling the town 'and every day a few more of the gaunt, spectral pillars, which once were fine historic buildings, are toppled over and crumbled into dust'. The traffic between Poperinghe and Ypres was 'simply incredible'. Monash likened it to Elizabeth Street, Melbourne, after the last race on Melbourne Cup Day.

Here comes a body of fighting troops, tin-hatted and fully equipped . . . There follows a string of perhaps one hundred heavy motor lorries . . . a limousine motor car with some divisional staff officer; a string of regimental horse- and mule-drawn vehicles . . . some motor ambulance wagons; more heavy motor lorries, a long string of remount horses, marching in twos . . . a great 12-inch howitzer, dragged by two steam traction engines; more infantry . . . more motor lorries, a long stream of Chinese coolies, smart and of magnificent stature . . . dispatch riders on motor bikes . . . a battery of artillery, all fully horsed and clattering and jingling . . . motor wagons bringing forward broken stone and road-making materials . . . a Royal Flying Corps car carrying parts of aeroplanes to forward hangars; more ambulances; and so on and on and on in a never-ending stream.

Monash's headquarters in the ramparts were safe enough. The walls were so thick that they deflected the heaviest shells, but Monash said he felt as though he was living in a mine. 'It is cold and dank and overrun by rats and mice, and altogether smelly and disagreeable . . .'

It was October 1. This was not like Messines. Monash had just a few days to finalise plans for his division's part in Broodseinde, which was due to open on October 4.

TWO BROTHERS CAME up for Broodseinde. Monash may have seen them tramping the roads as part of that endless stream of traffic. They were privates and it was the lot of privates to tramp roads and for the webbing straps to rub against their shoulders. Jarvis Fuller was in the 7th Battalion of the 1st Division; Roy Fuller was in the 2nd Division. They had both been marked down in England as reinforcements for the 7th Battalion. Then both fell sick: Jarvis with bronchitis, Roy with pneumonia. Jarvis recovered first and was sent to France. Roy took longer; by the time he left hospital he was told that he would have to go to the 2nd Division. The brothers were close. They had gone joy-riding on the trams of Durban on the voyage over and Roy had entertained their mates on the ship by playing a tin whistle. The separation hurt. Jarvis twice went searching for Roy's battalion in France. They had not met by September 29 but both were going to Broodseinde. They might meet there.

Jarvis was the younger at twenty-two. Tall, thin, blue-eyed and with a thick mane of hair, he had the look of an ascetic, a school-teacher perhaps. In truth he was easy-going and worked in a rope factory in Footscray after growing up in the hot and dusty sheep country of Moonambel in Victoria's west. It was the spectacles – winkers, he called them – that gave him that studious look. He had worn them since he was at least twelve and had been initially rejected by the army because of his poor eyesight. He told his sister, Ruby, that he was in 'bonzer nick' in France. He wasn't wearing his glasses – 'I honestly believe my eyes have improved, [but] perhaps you had better not tell mother as she may think I'm foolish.' He worried about Les Darcy, the middleweight boxer, who was being hounded in Australia because he had not joined up. Jarvis liked the fights: he felt 'wowsers' were pursuing Darcy. Jarvis was 'having the best time since I left Ausy', although French showerheads amused him. 'They're exactly the size of a penny with five holes. The stream nearly knocks you over.' He wished Roy could be with him.

Five days before Broodseinde opened he wrote to another sister, Pearl. 'I feel in bonzer health and I'm going strong like Johnnie Walker. I reckon the war will be over before the winter sets in, we have had a marvellous run of successes, but you won't see it in the papers, but it's true.'

Major Philip Howell-Price also came up for Broodseinde. He didn't have to be there. His brother Owen had been killed near Flers the previous year. Richmond, another brother, had died at Bullecourt. Philip, twenty-three and twice decorated, had been wounded at Lone Pine and Second Bullecourt. Birdwood, conscious that Philip had lost two brothers and anxious to save his life, had seconded him to the staff of the 1st Division.

Philip wrote home from Flanders late in September. The weather was beautiful, he said. 'Some old men (I mean *old men* mind you) are still living round about and it really cuts one to the heart to see them doing hard manual labour . . . Can't . . . believe that I am going to be spared by God to return to my home.'

Philip didn't tell his parents that, upon hearing that his old battalion was going to Broodseinde, he had begged to be sent back to it. Birdwood eventually let him go.

Charles Bean came up in the night, along with Keith Murdoch and another journalist, to watch the attack from the ridge behind the Australian lines. Bean knew this was the most important of Plumer's step-by-step advances. The two Australian corps were the centrepiece of the assault. They would be going for Broodseinde Ridge with its string of observation posts. From here, Bean wrote years afterwards, the Germans could look down on the British salient as if it were a spread-out map. The narrow ridge led north to the village of Passchendaele and the red ruins of its church. Gough would be going for the village of Poelcappelle. This opened the way to Passchendaele from the east. Hardly anyone in Britain or Australia had heard of Passchendaele village before 1914; now it was taking on an absurd significance, as though it were Rome or Jerusalem.

Bean began to follow the duckboards up to the front. The sky was grey and drizzling. White flares floated lazily above the German lines. Bean thought they looked like fishes' eyes. Then, about 5.20 am, forty minutes before the attack was due to begin, the Germans sent up a yellow flare, then another and another until there were sheaves of them. 'About seven minutes later, or less,' Bean wrote in his notebook, 'the German barrage came down, battery by battery. By 5.30 it was really heavy – *crump, crump, crump, crump, crump,* like empty biscuit-tins banging down into the valley ahead . . .' Bean thought the Anzac attack had been discovered. It hadn't. What he couldn't know was that the Germans were about to attack Zonnebeke, on the Australian front. This assault had been set down for 6 am on October 4, the very time at which Plumer would be attacking from the opposite direction. Bean was watching the preliminary bombardment for the German attack.

Most of the German barrage fell on the 1st and 2nd divisions. They, like Bean, thought their attack had been discovered. Bean estimated that about one-seventh of the attacking force of the 1st and 2nd divisions were killed or wounded here. Some twenty officers were killed, including Philip Howell-Price. The third brother had fallen.

Private Paul Johanessen wrote to his parents:

> We were formed up on the tapes by about midnight, and lay in shell holes in the rain till about a quarter to five and Fritz put down a terrific barrage on us for a quarter of an hour. It was awful, I will never forget it. It was just one continual crash of bursting shells and the screams of wounded and dying men. Well just as their barrage lifted ours came down, and over we went. We both attacked . . . in 'No Mans Land', but they had a stomach full and threw down their arms. They were dazed by the suddenness of our attack. We got our objectives by about eight o'clock and were digging in when I got hit in the ribs . . . I was sent to the base hospital but the wound soon healed up.

Percy Lay, newly promoted to lieutenant, wrote in his diary that the losses from the German barrage were so heavy that the men were pleased when the attack began and they could move. As usual they lit cigarettes as soon as they set off. The ground was wet; the Australian shells falling in front of them threw up steam rather than dust. Lay wrote: 'We met Fritz attacking and then we had some great fighting and beat him badly. When he saw us coming he turned and got.'

The Australians had gone 100 yards or so, slipping and sliding as they tried to catch up with their barrage, when they saw figures carrying fixed bayonets ahead. Were they Australians or Germans? Then the figures opened fire and fled. The Australians now realised that the Germans were attacking at the same time as they were.

Private Frank Handcock didn't make the first objective, the Red Line. He came from a farming family from Myrrhee, south of Wangaratta, in north-eastern Victoria. Eight Handcock brothers had gone off to the war. Jack, the first to enlist, was killed at the Gallipoli landing. Enlistments at Wangaratta were reported almost like cattle sales in 1916. The *Wangaratta Chronicle* reported a busy day at the recruiting office in February, 1916. 'The accepted included some exceptionally fine men. One stood 6ft 1in in his socks, weighed 13 [stone] 7 [lbs] and measured 40in normal round the chest. Two others stood 6ft ½in, and another 6ft . . .'

Frank Handcock, a farm labourer, had enlisted as a nineteen-year-old. A few months after leaving Australia he had been wounded in the right leg at Mouquet Farm. They patched him up in England and sent him back, but his leg hadn't healed and he apparently had difficulty marching. Because of his weak leg he was sent out into no-man's land as a sniper before the Broodseinde attack. He thus missed the carnage of the German barrage but still ended up wounded. It was the right leg again and the upper right arm.

His sergeant asked: 'Are you all right, Frank?' Handcock had lost much blood. He was lapsing in and out of consciousness. The sergeant thought Frank would almost certainly die. He called for stretcher-bearers and moved on for the Red Line. The bearers must have assumed Frank was dead. They didn't collect him.

Two Germans came along. The evidence suggests they may have been dazed and muddled by the British barrage. They heard Handcock groaning, picked him up and started carrying him towards their lines as a prisoner.

DONOVAN JOYNT OF the 8th Battalion rushed towards the crest of Broodseinde Ridge, the Red Line position, with his men. Their blood was up. They were charging. Joynt's sergeant was shouting something to him. The sound of the barrage blotted out his words.

'What is it you want?' Joynt shouted. 'What is it?'

And the sergeant shouted back: 'One minute of this is worth a lifetime of ordinary life, isn't it, sir!'

The Australians reached the Red Line between 6.45 and 7.20 am. They were supposed to wait there until 8.10. In some places, however, they could neither wait nor rest.

Lay and his men, who were near Joynt, came under shellfire. At first they thought their own shells were dropping short. Then someone observed the flash of a field gun up ahead. The Germans were firing 'whizz-bangs' at them over open sights. There were in fact two seventy-seven-millimetre field guns, plus machine guns and a pillbox, up ahead. The Australians went for them as their Lewis gunners tried to keep the Germans' heads down. Lay and others crept so close that German bombs were bursting behind them. The pillbox was an artillery headquarters. The way Bean tells the story, a white flag appeared from a trapdoor, but 'most of its defenders were shot down'.

THERE WERE LOTS of German prisoners this day, 5000 of them along the whole front, a huge bag by the standards of the western front and another reason for Haig and others to see Broodseinde as a grander victory than it was. Percy Lay told the story of the attack on the German field guns in more detail than Bean. 'About six of us had some fun,' he wrote in his diary. 'We got a bit ahead of the others. At first we got 35 prisoners out of three strong posts then we had a good chase after a Headquarters' staff.' The staff men escaped but Lay captured all their papers and sent them back. They were 'important' papers, he later heard. 'We then started on a machine gun position and shot the crews of the two guns with the exception of one man and we made him turn his gun on his own men but *our* people thought we were Huns and opened fire on us.

So we had to shoot the Hun and get the guns back.' Lay, while a sergeant, had won the Military Medal and the Distinguished Conduct Medal. Now, at Broodseinde and as a lieutenant, he was to be awarded the Military Cross.

Charles Carrington, the young English officer we last met on the Somme, attacked with the English division immediately north of the New Zealanders. Later in the day he was sharing a tin of hot food when an intelligence officer told him a story about himself, the commanding officer, and a wounded German. The German was squirming, the intelligence officer said, done for. The kindest thing to do was to shoot him. 'You'd best shoot the poor fellow,' the CO told his runner. The runner unslung his rifle, fingered the trigger, but couldn't squeeze it. The CO then told the intelligence officer to shoot the German. He couldn't do it either. The CO drew his revolver, 'looked fierce' and walked up to the German, who knew exactly what was happening. The CO couldn't shoot either. They left the German there. As the intelligence officer said, he probably died in the mud that night.

Lieutenant William Palstra, from Monash's division, had come up through Ypres, 'a grand monument to the desolation of war . . . Not one stone in this once large and prosperous city is undamaged or in its place. The streets are tracks among huge mounds of brick dust.' Now he was behind the lines at Broodseinde, watching hundreds of German prisoners come out. As they 'got near our lads the astonished Hun found about half a dozen hands in his pockets looking for souvenirs'.

Bean came upon a captured German officer later in the day. The German, a career-soldier, had lost much blood from a wound to the arm. The Australians had cut off his shoulder straps as souvenirs. They had also repeatedly brought him cups of tea.

'Your men are funny,' the German said. 'They rob while they fight.'

THE AUSTRALIANS TOOK the final objective, the Blue Line, over the crest of the ridge, and could have pushed on further. Allied troops had not trodden this ground since May, 1915. The Australians came upon the decomposing bodies, identifiable by scraps of uniform, of British troops killed here in either 1914 or 1915. And to the south-east they could see where the war wasn't: copses and hedgerows, cows grazing and smoke drifting lazily from farmhouse chimneys.

The Australians were astonished at what the Germans had been able to see from here. 'As we gazed back over the country,' one battalion historian noted, 'we could see plainly the movements of our own units . . . Guns, transport, and men were all exposed to the splendid observation from this position. It was a prize worth having . . .'

But, again, the price was high. Broodseinde looked a better victory from the relative serenity of Haig's and Plumer's headquarters.

THE GREAT VICTORY had cost 20,000 casualties along the British line. This for an average advance of about 1000 yards. But Passchendaele was in sight, so long as the weather held. Something close to elation seemed to pass through Haig's headquarters. Broodseinde rather proved what everyone who hadn't visited the frontline was saying: the spirit of the German army had been broken. Hurley and Wilkins, the Australian photographers, knew what the front was like. They were just behind it at Broodseinde. 'Every 20 paces or less lay a body,' Hurley said. 'Some frightfully mutilated, without legs, arms and heads and half-covered in mud and slime. I could not help thinking that Wilkins and I, trudging along this inferno and soaked to the skin, talking and living beings, might not be the next moment one of these things – Gee – it puts the wind up one at times.'

There was elation in the Australian divisions too, even among some of the men in the frontline, and it was understandable. They had been misused at Fromelles, Pozières, Mouquet Farm and Bullecourt. Now, under Plumer, they had been winning, quickly and decisively. Plumer looked better than Gough because he set objectives that were modest but achievable. What everyone seemed to be ignoring, however, was the scale of casualties. The three quick victories on the ridges east of Ypres had so far cost Haig's forces 56,000 men.

The three Australian divisions lost another 6432 men at Broodseinde. The casualties were heaviest in the 1st and 2nd divisions. These two had been caught lying under the German barrage.

AT FIRST PRIVATE Jarvis Fuller appeared to have disappeared on the battlefield. Roy, his brother, had been working to the north as a stretcher-bearer with the 2nd Division. He saw Jarvis' battalion from the 1st Division coming out. Had any of them seen his brother? A sergeant told Roy that Jarvis had been wounded and taken to an aid post. But there was no record of Jarvis being admitted to a clearing station or a hospital. He was listed as missing. Two months later Roy wrote home, saying one should not give up hope. Ten days later he reported that he still had no news of 'our Dear Brother'. Christmas came and went; Roy said he didn't enjoy it as the others had. Thoughts of 'Dear Brother Jarvis' and what might have happened to him filled his mind. He said he even found it hard to write letters.

A few months later Roy heard of a 2nd Division officer who claimed to have buried Jarvis. Roy went in search of him. Eventually Lieutenant A. G. Taylor wrote to Jarvis' mother: 'Madam, Your son Private Fuller J. B. did not belong to our Battalion, but I discovered his body a few minutes after he was killed, and we buried him . . . Your boy . . . had died nobly, doing his duty. My men made a cross, which now marks the spot where his body lies . . . His personal effects were returned to his Battalion.'

The effects sent to his mother comprised a purse, four coins, two religious books, a wallet, cards and a letter. There was no mention of the spectacles he had learned to live without.

Philip Howell-Price's body was never found. He simply disappeared in the barrage before the hop-over. The Reverend John Howell-Price and his wife Isabel had now lost three sons, who, between them, had won two Distinguished Service Orders and three Military Crosses. But they were still dead.

We left Private Frank Handcock, badly wounded in the leg and arm, being carried off as a prisoner by two Germans who had been bewildered by the British barrage. They were so muddled they took Handcock to the Australian lines, where they collapsed and became prisoners themselves. Handcock was sent to a hospital in England. Surgeons amputated his leg above the knee. He returned to the paddocks of Myrrhee but died in his thirties as a result of his wounds.

BEAN CALLED BROODSEINDE an 'overwhelming blow'. The German official history referred to it as 'the black day of October 4'. Plumer is said to have referred to it as the greatest victory since the Marne. Bean said that English war correspondents at the front felt it was Britain's most complete success on the western front. General Godley, the English commander of II Anzac Corps, wanted to push on about noon on the day of the battle. Godley didn't care too much for the finer points of tactics – such things smacked of intellectualism – but he had always been good at telling troops to push on. Birdwood and Plumer promptly scotched his scheme.

Charteris, Haig's head of intelligence, was also having a rush of blood. In 1932 Harington, Plumer's chief-of-staff, wrote to Edmonds, the British official historian, after reading the proofs of Bean's account of Broodseinde. Harington said that Haig and Charteris arrived at Plumer's headquarters. Charteris, Harington wrote, came into his room and said: 'Now we have them, get up the Cavalry, now we have them on the run. Push on, push on etc.' Harington wrote that he told Charteris 'in no uncertain terms of what I thought of him for urging the C-in-C to rush us wildly without preparation & lose the lives of the bulk of the men who had just done so well. It would have been madness & my old Chief was not going to be bluffed. It would have been sheer murder . . .'

WHAT DID LLOYD George think about all this success? Between the battles of Menin Road and Polygon Wood the Prime Minister and Robertson had attended a conference with their French allies at

Boulogne. Haig was not present. Lloyd George agreed to a French request that the British take over more of the line. This was his way of saying he didn't believe in Haig's Passchendaele campaign; it may even have been a way of trying to end it. If Lloyd George was right to doubt Haig's chances of achieving a worthwhile success in Flanders, the Prime Minister was still wrong – hopelessly so – in his thoughts about where the war might be won. He wanted Robertson to transfer five or six divisions from the western front to Allenby in Egypt. The idea was bizarre. Robertson resisted it.

Haig became angry upon learning, just before Broodseinde opened, that he was to take over more of the line in France. What annoyed him most was that Lloyd George and Robertson had agreed to the proposal without consulting him. 'R[obertson] comes badly out of this,' he wrote in his diary.

Lloyd George decided a week after the victory at Broodseinde to seek second opinions about the western front strategy. He sought these from Sir John French and Sir Henry Wilson. French had failed on the western front and knew little about modern artillery. Sir Henry Wilson was the best-known intriguer in the British army; hardly anyone trusted him. The politics of Britain's war were becoming nastier. Robertson stood in the most exposed position. Haig niggled at him from one side and the Prime Minister from the other.

ONE THING HITS you at once as you walk along Broodseinde Ridge: the Germans could see just about everything in the British salient below. The spire of the Cloth Hall, risen from the ashes, soars above the plain; it is all laid out, the salient, just as Bean said, like a spread-out map.

Tyne Cot Cemetery lies on the ridge, on ground captured by Monash's division in 1917. German blockhouses lie among the graves. This is the largest British Commonwealth war cemetery in the world: nearly 12,000 graves, 8366 of them with no names. Look further up the hill and you can see the spire of Passchendaele, so close, just the other side of a ploughed field that in 1917 was a sea of craters, all full of slimy water.

Down the ridge from Tyne Cot, hemmed in on all sides by the dark pines of Polygon Wood, is Buttes New British Cemetery, perhaps the most dramatic graveyard on the western front. The rebuilt artillery butt-stop is at one end, topped by a memorial to the 5th Australian Division that looks out over a vast lawn where the white-grey headstones stand up like soldiers on parade. Most of the Australian graves have no name. Silver birches are scattered among them and roses sway in the soft breeze. Jarvis Fuller rests here, next to a red rose, far from the dust clouds of Moonambel, but not forgotten: someone has left a poppy on the grave.

Geese graze the bank of the moat at the Menin Gate, near where Monash had his headquarters. Ducks, undercarriages down, glide in to land on the green-brown water. A fisherman casts a line as the crowd gathers for the playing of the Last Post under the archway of the Menin Gate memorial to the missing. The names of the 54,000 British and dominion soldiers who disappeared in the salient rise on panels reaching towards the sky and bugles ring out in the gloaming. More than any other town along the line of the old western front, Ypres has a heart. It remembers the Great War like no other place, and on every night of the year.

32

The way of the Cross

John Monash wrote to his wife three days after Broodseinde. 'Great happenings are possible in the very near future,' he reported. The Germans were 'terribly disorganised'. The day before Monash had told his brother-in-law that the Germans were 'staggering'. Twelve days later he was writing that Australians were being 'sacrificed in hair-brained [sic] ventures'.

Twelve days and Monash's mood had changed utterly. But in that time his division had been in the battle for Passchendaele village. In those twelve days the rains had come, day after day. The downpours not only changed the landscape, returning it to lakes and bog holes, but also the conduct of the British commanders. Until the coming of the rain Haig, acting not altogether in character, and Plumer, acting entirely in character, had been careful investors. They contented themselves with shallow advances that could be guaranteed by artillery. Now they became gamblers, betting that the wet ground would not impede them too much, that their heavy guns would not sink in the mud each time they were fired and that their field pieces could actually be dragged forward.

Bean had seen more of the ground than most of the generals. He later wrote that the campaign, in these days before the lunges at

Passchendaele, took on the trappings of a classical tragedy. The cast, one has to say, might have appealed to Homer or Tolstoy. There was Haig, desperate for a victory that he could hurl back at his detractors in London. And Plumer, being carried along not, as he usually was, by his own good sense, but by the mood of bravado coming out of Haig's headquarters. And Gough, the former fire-brand, now unsure of himself. And Charteris, lurking in shadows just off stage and whispering stories of how the Germans were on the lip of moral collapse. And Monash, a mere divisional commander, who was hearing one story from the staff officers in the châteaux to the west and another from his men in the mud to the east. And Birdwood, the administrative head of the AIF, who would dissent, but carefully. In London there was Robertson, who didn't much believe in Third Ypres but thought that supporting it was better than siding with a huddle of dithering politicians. And there were the dithering politicians themselves, who wanted to tut-tut about Third Ypres but would not monitor it, would not look at the detail. There was Lloyd George who had the power to call off the campaign but didn't. And back in Australia there was Billy Hughes, unaware that his Australians were being sacrificed at a faster rate than at any time in the war, and thinking about conscription again.

HAIG BROUGHT UP the cavalry after the victory at Broodseinde. We should not blame him for still seeing cavalry as the arm of mobile warfare. We can blame him for failing to accept what military leaders had known for thousands of years, that horses are useless in bogs. And the battlefield was a bog again. This was the trouble: Haig and Plumer and the staff officers who buzzed around them didn't know what the battlefield was like.

There had been drizzle on the day after Broodseinde, showers on the day after that, squalls on the day after that and torrential rain on the 8th. The meteorologists now said things would worsen: a storm was blowing in from Ireland. The troops in the field were exhausted from working on roads and light railways, and simply from dragging one clay-caked leg after another. Guns could not be moved.

Gunners could not find stable platforms for the heavies. Clay had to be scraped off shells before they could be loaded. Men and mules drowned when they strayed from the duckboards. Spotter aircraft could not fly.

Haig had to decide whether to close down the campaign. He knew by now that his dream of taking the Belgian coast was dead, at least for 1917. But Passchendaele village still mesmerised him. If he took that, he could at least say that he had thrown the Germans off the ridges. According to Edmonds, the British official historian, Haig called a conference after the squalls on the 7th. Edmonds says Gough and Plumer wanted to end the campaign. If this is true, there is no written evidence of it. And the anecdotal evidence suggests the opposite. Gough doesn't mention the conference in his memoirs. Harington, Plumer's chief-of-staff, told war correspondents at a briefing the next day that while the flats were wet, the crest of the ridge was 'as dry as a bone'. Bean, who was at the briefing, wrote in his diary:

I believe the official attitude is that Passchendaele Ridge is so important that tomorrow's attack is worth making whether it succeeds or fails . . . I suspect that they are making a great, bloody experiment – a huge gamble . . . I feel, and most of the correspondents feel, awfully anxious – terribly anxious – about tomorrow. They don't know the fight there was for the last ridge, these major generals back there . . . They don't realise how much desperately hard it will be to fight down such opposition in the mud, rifles choked, LGs [Lewis Guns] out of action, men tired and slow – a new division like the 66th amongst them! Every step means dragging one foot out of the mud . . . I shall be very surprised if this fight succeeds. They are banking on their knowledge of the German troops demoralisation . . . They don't realise how very strong our morale had to be to get through the last three fights.

Anyway, regardless of who said what at the conference on the 7th, Haig was always going to prevail and his army commanders were always going to defer. That was how GHQ worked. And Haig wanted to go on. One might have thought that he would have felt the need to look at the state of the ground for himself. One can only wonder at his lack of curiosity. Passchendaele village, it was decided, would be taken in two steps, the first on October 9, the second on the 12th.

THE FIRST STEP came to be known as the battle of Poelcappelle, after the secondary objective, a village on Gough's front. Godley's II Anzac Corps, which had been loaned two British divisions, the 49th and the 66th, would make the main thrust. The two British divisions would be doing the attacking. Birdwood's I Anzac Corps would be on their right, the 2nd Australian Division guarding the flank of the 66th. The attack was to go in at 5.20 am. It was still raining at midnight. Birdwood favoured a postponement but apparently did not ask for one, perhaps because he had the lesser task in the operation. Godley had the main task; it wasn't his way to protest.

The 66th Division had only recently arrived in France. The approach to the front was hellish for the new soldiers. The duckboards were slippery and in some places shattered or submerged. Men fell into shell holes and the water there was so rank that some vomited upon being pulled out. After five hours they had covered a mile. It was midnight and they had another mile-and-a-half to go to reach the tapes (which, incidentally, had been fitted with aluminium discs to prevent them sinking in the slime). They were not going to make the tapes by zero hour. The plan had called for them to be at the start line by midnight so that they might rest for five hours before attacking.

The 49th, the other British division under Godley's control, made the tapes on time but the men were worn out, covered with slime and white-faced from the cold. An English war correspondent who saw them said they looked like men who had been buried alive and dug up again.

The artillerymen who were to supply the barrage had to leave guns behind bogged. One pair of Australian six-inch howitzers was fifteen times derailed from the light railway. Mules carried the ammunition forward. Their trip from the wagon-lines to the batteries had taken around an hour in the dry weather; now it took seventeen. Mules were shot where they lay bogged. The gunners worked to exhaustion. The barrage they eventually put down was so light that infantrymen often could not pick up the line of it.

The infantrymen went out into the swamp below Passchendaele village. Some made progress; most didn't. Germans untouched by the barrage sniped at them with rifles. Men following the bed of a tiny stream towards Passchendaele found themselves waist-deep in water. Others came upon wire uncut by the barrage. This was nothing like the three step-by-step attacks that preceded it. They went to a timetable and the results seemed predestined; this was chaos.

The Australian 2nd Division on the flank of the two hapless British divisions put in two brigades, the 5th and the 6th. The 5th had been in reserve at Broodseinde and could field some 2000 men. The 6th had not only fought at Broodseinde; afterwards, as the rain tumbled down, the men had been used to lay cables and extend duckboards. These men had slept in water-filled shell holes. They had no greatcoats, just capes. Hundreds collapsed with exhaustion; others came down with trench foot. The 6th Brigade could field only about 600 men for the battle. The two brigades went out into the bog, did better than most, and ran up 1253 casualties.

The attack failed just about everywhere. Plumer's run of successes had ended. His formula rested on the inspired use of artillery. It was worthless once the ground became so wet that guns could not be dragged forward and wire remained uncut. Nor could it work if infantrymen were exhausted before they even crossed the start tapes.

But unreality had now set in. For what would be called the first battle of Passchendaele, set down for October 12, three days after Poelcappelle, the infantrymen were to advance up to 2500 yards, much further than they had been asked to go in the three successful battles. In truth the 3rd Australian Division and the New Zealand Division would have to go further if they were to push beyond Passchendaele village. Haig, Plumer and Godley had all misread what had happened in the battle of Poelcappelle. Plumer told Haig that the line had been pushed forward, thus making the capture of Passchendaele easier. Haig, in turn, refused to be downcast about the weather. His diary entries suggest he had no notion of how bad the ground was, how ineffective his artillery had become or even where the frontline lay. On the night after Poelcappelle he wrote in his diary: 'The results were very successful.'

Events were not going his way in London either. He received a note from Robertson on the day Passchendaele began. Lloyd George was 'out for my blood', Robertson said. The Prime Minister's conduct was 'intolerable'. Matters might come to a head. 'I rather hope so. I am sick of this d----d life.'

All this – the mud on the battlefield, the tension in London – seemed to wash over Haig like a passing breeze. It was as if he only saw what he wanted to see. He met Raymond Poincaré, the French President, briefly on October 11. Poincaré asked him when operations would stop. The question offended Haig, who told him his only thought was to attack. In his diary that night Haig called the President a 'humbug'.

In London the chief of intelligence at the War Office, Brigadier-General George Macdonogh, a career-officer of sharp intellect, had been questioning whether German morale really was collapsing. Haig wrote in his diary: 'I cannot think why the War Office Intelligence Dept. gives such a wrong picture of the situation except that Gen Macdonagh (DMI) is a Roman Catholic and is (perhaps unconsciously) influenced by information which doubtless reaches him from tainted (i.e. catholic) sources.'

Charteris, meanwhile, suddenly gave up hope. His Pauline conversion came when he visited the front on the day of Poelcappelle. There was no chance of complete success in the salient this year, he wrote in his diary the next day. All he could see now was 'the awfulness of it all'. But he didn't say this to Haig.

When men from Monash's division came up to relieve the 66th Division on October 10 the Englishmen were unsure where their front lay. Lieutenant Walde Fisher, a university tutor, went forward to scout, picking his way among the dead. He came upon fifty English soldiers sheltering in a pillbox. 'Never have I seen men so broken or demoralised,' he wrote. Wounded lay everywhere, groaning and moaning. And the rain kept falling.

The next day, the eve of the battle, Monash's men finally worked out what had happened. The English division had hardly pushed forward at all. This meant the Australians would have to advance close to 3000 yards the next day, more than had ever been attempted in Plumer's set-pieces over dry ground. It also meant their barrage had to be brought back 350 yards and that they would have to hurry forward at a pace never attempted during Plumer's attacks in dry weather. The evidence suggests that Godley and Monash didn't know precisely where the front was on the eve of the battle or how bad things were on the ground. Monash told his wife afterwards that he sought, and was denied, a postponement of twenty-four hours. What he perhaps should have done is gone to the front himself rather than sitting in his headquarters trying to make sense of the conflicting reports of junior officers floundering around in the mud.

HAIG TALKED TO the war correspondents before the battle opened. Bean said Charteris sat alongside the commander-in-chief in a drawing room with gilt Louis XVI chairs and a fine view over the French plain towards Hazebrouck and St Omer. '[Haig] sat down with us around him. He is a gauche, nervous man in drawing room functions, but here he had something to say & he was at his best. He rubbed his hands, a sign of nervousness, I thought; but he spoke straight enough.'

One of the journalists asked about the mud. Could this be mentioned in press reports without cheering the Germans? Haig said the best thing was to tell the truth, from which Bean concluded that the field-marshal had not been much consulted in censorship matters. 'It was simply the mud which defeated us on Tuesday [the battle of Poelcappelle],' Haig said. 'The men did splendidly to get through it as they did; but the Flanders mud, as you know, is not a new invention. It has a name in history – it has defeated other armies before this one and it is tremendously difficult to make even as much headway against it as the troops did . . . I certainly think you should explain the difficulty of the mud.'

Bean stayed behind to ask Haig about a minor matter. Haig told Bean the Australian army had some very capable commanders. He singled out Monash – 'a very solid man'. This caused Bean to fall into politicking. He knew Haig was thinking of forming an Australian corps with Monash in command and Birdwood as administrative head. It would be a great pity to change Birdwood's position, Bean said. Australians trusted him; he had won himself a great place with them.

Haig agreed but said Australia should have a corps commander and a complete corps staff. 'Yes, sir,' said Bean, 'you know, we look upon General White as the greatest soldier we have by a long way . . .' It is not clear whom *we* constituted in this case. The average Australian soldier didn't know White. The men didn't mention him in their letters home, as they did Birdwood, Hooky Walker and Pompey Elliott. Bean idolised White, like a boy in awe of his headmaster. He saw Monash as an upstart who didn't play by the school rules. He wrote in his diary after this meeting that Monash, if appointed, would go along with Haig and GHQ. Haig would be glad to be rid of the 'independence' of Birdwood and White. Here one has to wonder about the word *independence*. Was independence apparent when the 5th Division was handed over for ritual slaughter at Fromelles, or at the two Bullecourts?

Bean wrote that Haig impressed him more than he ever had before. He was 'slow but very clean; quite different from Charteris'. Haig had earlier been asked about the morale of the German army and, according to Bean, had 'referred over his shoulder to Charteris; as though Charteris keeps that portion of his brain & he completely relies upon him'.

SISTER ELSIE GRANT had served at an Australian casualty-clearing station near Ypres during Gough's waterlogged offensive in August. The hospital had been shelled for the third time. 'Those brutal Germans deliberately shell our hospital with all our poor helpless boys but really God was good to us. We had four killed but it was just miraculous that there were not dozens killed.' Grant and the other sisters were sent by car back to a town in France (probably St Omer). Her brother Allan, a grazier from Queensland and now a lieutenant in Monash's division, had arrived in the same town about two hours before Elsie. He was waiting when she arrived. 'We all embraced him & the dear left at 5 am next morning.' Allan didn't know it then, but he was on his way to Broodseinde and then the first battle of Passchendaele.

Elsie said in her letter that she wanted 'ever so badly' to come home 'but I really can't bring myself to leave Allan behind. That is the principal reason I don't come.'

CROWN PRINCE RUPPRECHT of Bavaria, the German commander opposite Plumer and Gough, also kept a diary. On the day the first battle of Passchendaele opened he wrote: 'Most gratifying – rain: our most effective ally.'

Gough had watched the rain pour down the previous afternoon. His army would be attacking around Poelcappelle simultaneously with Plumer's at Passchendaele. Gough telephoned Plumer and said the attack should be postponed. Plumer consulted his corps commanders and said, No, it should go ahead. Gough had become the pragmatist and Plumer the romantic.

The plan was for the 3rd Division to attack Passchendaele Ridge and go 400 yards further to the last of three objectives, the Green Line. One of its battalions was carrying an Australian flag – 'specially worked' – that would be raised above the village. Haig had told Monash that once the flag was flying the news would be immediately cabled to Australia. The New Zealand Division, north of the Australians, was going for Bellevue Spur on the eastern side of the village. To reach this they had to follow the valley of a stream, the Ravebeek, which was hopelessly flooded. One brigade of the 4th Australian Division would protect the right flank of the 3rd Division.

The two attacking brigades of the 3rd Division spent the night of October 10 on the flat country just east of Ypres. The men lay down on wet ground, huddled under bits of timber and sheets of iron. Next night they began the march to the front. They were shelled with gas soon after they moved off, then the rain came, showers around 1.30 am, heavy rain around 3.30. It was a black night and the men moved in single file, each man clutching the webbing of the man in front.

Bean was writing in a hut near Poperinghe, listening to the patter of rain and the scratching of branches on the roof from a tree being tossed about in the wind. He slept in his clothes for about three-quarters of an hour, then drank some warm cocoa before leaving for the front about 3 am with Keith Murdoch. The misty rain seemed endless and the night was black. The rain became heavier at Ypres. Bean and Murdoch decided to wait for daylight at Monash's headquarters. They left the car standing up to its axles in water. 'Zero hour was to be at 5.25 am,' Bean wrote. 'The Meteor[ology] report was through by 9 the night before – so the battle could have been stopped. Of course now it was far too late.'

Lieutenant William Palstra of the 3rd Division had been sent forward to find a spot for battalion headquarters and a regimental aid post. The road from Ypres to Zonnebeke astonished him – 'a hopeless tangle . . . shelled more or less continuously'. It was one long traffic jam and he found it easier to walk in the mud 100 yards off the road. The road was crowded with three-ton lorries, packhorses, ambulances, motorcycles and lines of wounded and prisoners. Every now and then a German shell would fall among this struggling mass. 'There would be momentary confusion, and then the wreckage would be pulled to the side of the road, the shell hole filled with anything available – I saw one hole being filled with eighteen-pounder ammunition – and movement at a snail's pace would recommence.'

Private John Hardie, a machine gunner in Monash's division, headed for the front on the night of the 11th and stumbled into a bombardment of high-explosive and gas shells. 'I don't think I shall ever forget that night even to my dying day,' he wrote home. 'Every little track was congested with troops going up . . . We were slipping and sliding all over the place and falling into shell holes and to make matters worse we were losing men every few yards. Well, we got to our hopping off place . . . wet to the skin and dead beat.' The German guns opened up. 'Battalion after battalion got practically cut to pieces and I don't know how our team got through but several of them had their clothes torn with bits of shell. I got a small splinter in the hand. We only got about five hundred yards when we were held up.'

The British barrage was feeble by the standards of the three successful battles. The artillerymen couldn't drag enough guns forward. Sometimes twenty-six horses were harnessed to try to bring one gun up. The platforms of the guns that were firing quivered and sunk in the mud. There are stories of guns sinking up to their muzzles. Warheads would often bury themselves so deeply in the mud before exploding that all they threw up were fountains of brown water and slime. The New Zealanders had a worse front than the Australians because of the flooding of the Ravebeek and the uncut wire in front of them. The New Zealand artillery commander reported on the day before the battle that his guns might be unable to support the infantry properly. No-one, it seems, took any notice of him. Bean had left Ypres to watch the barrage through his telescope. Casual shelling, he called it. One battalion history said the men made no effort to conform to the barrage. 'There was really nothing to conform to.'

Here was a throwback to the way attacks used to be carried out in the Great War. Why Plumer allowed this to happen is still mostly a mystery. If he is entitled to the credit for the mechanical brilliance of Messines, Menin Road, Polygon Wood and Broodseinde, he must also take much of the blame for First Passchendaele.

THIS TIME THE infantrymen didn't light up cigarettes and go forward briskly, hugging the screen of their barrage. They came under machine-gun fire from the moment they left the tapes. They had to slither from shell hole to shell hole. They sunk up to their waists. Rifles clogged. Casualties ran up quickly. Eight or more bearers were needed to carry one man out, which meant most of the wounded lay in the slime.

The New Zealand Division set off with no hope. Bean later wrote that no infantry in the world could have crossed the Ravebeek mud, smashed through the uncut wire and assaulted the pillboxes on Bellevue Spur. The right brigade of New Zealanders barely edged past the start line. Machine guns tore through those who made the first belt of wire.

The slaughter of the New Zealanders left the Australians, immediately south of them, open to flanking fire. The Australian brigade alongside the New Zealanders was held up by machine-gun fire near the first objective, about 1000 yards in. The other of Monash's brigades pushed on towards the second objective. Captain Clarence Jeffries, a young mining surveyor from Wallsend, New South Wales, rushed a pillbox near the highest point of the ridge with about a dozen men, capturing twenty-five Germans and their two machine guns. When Jeffries' brigade went for the second objective the barrage was so thin that he and other officers could not be sure where it was. Then another machine gun opened up. Jeffries and a small party rushed it. The post was taken but Jeffries was killed. He received the Victoria Cross. To Jeffries' left, Major Lyndhurst Giblin, a fruit grower from Hobart, was trying to work out where the barrage was. He lived and became Ritchie Professor of Economics at Melbourne University.

About twenty Australians had pushed into Passchendaele. They went straight to the church and found no Germans there. Neither was there any sign of other Australians working their way up. The patrol withdrew. Around this time the senior officer of the right-hand Australian brigade looked about him. Fire was coming from his front and he was losing men every minute. Looking to his left, he knew that the other Australian brigade was well behind him. He sent a note back: 'What am I to do?'

It was pointless asking those at the rear. Monash, at Ypres, had no notion of what was happening. He merely thought he did. For most of the morning, partly on the basis of reports of what prisoners and wounded Australians had said, he thought his division may have taken the village. Around 11 am he heard that the New Zealand attack had failed. After noon the truth came rushing to meet him. His left brigade, alongside the New Zealanders, was held up; the casualties were heavy. His right brigade had reached the second objective but both its flanks were exposed.

Lieutenant-Colonel Leslie Morshead, a schoolteacher who a quarter of a century later would command an Australian division at Tobruk and El Alamein, sent back a message before noon. 'Things are bloody, very bloody.'

LIEUTENANT PALSTRA SAID there were two big problems at the front: getting supplies up and getting wounded out. The ground was so soggy that stretcher-bearers could do only two trips a day from the frontline to the clearing stations. 'In the vicinity of my own battalion regimental aid post, which had been established first in a pillbox and later, as the battalion advanced, in a shell hole, there were many dead, the majority of whom, according to the regimental medical officer, had died from exposure and not primarily from their injuries. It seemed that any man whose wounds prevented him from making his own way to the rear had but a very poor chance of pulling through.'

There is no way of knowing how many men simply drowned. Soldiers' letters and diaries repeatedly refer to men trapped in mud and crying out for help.

The battle had been lost before it began. It was formally lost on the afternoon of that first day. The two Australian attacking brigades began to fall back on their start lines. There was nothing else they could do. They lacked the artillery support to go on. They were exposed on their left because the New Zealanders had been asked to cross ground that was impassable.

Across the front British losses for the day were 13,000. Gains were negligible. Monash's division had lost 3200, the New Zealanders 3000, the 4th Australian Division, in support, 1000.

ABOUT A FORTNIGHT after Passchendaele, Sister Elsie Grant received a letter from a sergeant who served with her brother Allan. Lieutenant Grant had been killed during First Passchendaele. In the tradition of such letters Sergeant Carey said Allan had died a 'grand & noble death fighting for his God, King, Country & dear ones'. In the same tradition the sergeant did not say how Grant died or the nature of his wound. There was a postscript: 'I have enclosed . . . a five-pound note which he left in his wallet.'

THE DAY AFTER the battle, Lieutenant Fisher wrote, the Australians, back in their old frontline, were 'utterly done'. His battalion was down to ninety men; there were twenty-three left in his company. Men were dropping with tiredness. The ground was thick with dead and wounded, some of them Englishmen still out in the weather after the battle of Poelcappelle.

> Our men gave all their food and water away, but that was all they could do. That night my two runners were killed as they sat beside me, and casualties were numerous again. He blew me out of my shell hole thrice, so I shifted to an abandoned pillbox. There were twenty-four wounded men inside, two dead Huns on the floor and six outside, in various stages of decomposition. The stench was dreadful . . . When day broke I looked over the position. Over forty dead lay within twenty yards of where I stood, and the whole valley was full of them.

Sergeant Watkins was kept busy looking after the wounded. 'During the afternoon of the 13th an Armistice was arranged between us and the Germans so as to give both parties a chance of getting in the wounded. It only lasted a few hours. Our fellows brought in several wounded Tommies, who had been wounded and living in shell holes for four days.' Watkins' brigade was relieved at 7 pm. He was exhausted, they all were, and they had to walk four or fives miles back to their camp. Watkins fell into a deep hole and lost his rifle and helmet. Two men pulled him out by extending their rifles for him to grab. When he reached 'civilisation' he was given hot cocoa.

One of the most vivid accounts of Passchendaele comes from a medical officer – surname unknown – with an English division on the left of the New Zealanders. The man may have been an Australian and he was probably with the British 18th Division. He was dressing wounded in a shell hole when he felt something red-hot shoot through his neck. He didn't remember much for a while. Then he heard one of his medical staff saying: 'Are you dead, sir? Are you dead?' A sergeant ripped open the medical officer's tunic. 'It's all right, 'e ain't dead,' he announced. 'Bit of blood about, but it's gone right through.'

It had, a clean in-and-out wound. The medical officer told his parents that 'for a while all the nerve was knocked out of me and I broke down and sobbed like a confounded baby, for every man seemed to be killed or wounded – Officers, NCOs and men. All the fellows I knew and liked, Pater, men I had been through other shows with.'

The doctor had a good pull on a flask of whisky. After two hours in the shell hole he went back to dressing the wounded. They were crying out: 'Water, for Gawd's sake water.' The doctor said he found a new respect for the Germans. 'Several times we found ourselves working in places surrounded by shell holes full of Huns but none fired at us. Many pointed to where wounded were lying – Hun snipers pointed to where their victims were . . . I have never experienced anything like it before . . .'

He had another pull of whisky and a piece of bread for lunch, then went back to the wounded. He couldn't bandage any more: his arm was too stiff. There were no other doctors or stretcher-bearers left. All had been killed. 'To those [wounded] in great pain and [with] no chance of living, I gave enough morphia to put them out peacefully and it was pitiful to hear their thanks with white faces twisted into a smile "Thanks Doc – I'm not afraid but this damn pain gets you down", or a message to someone at home they would never see again . . .'

The doctor eventually found his way to a dressing station and thence to hospitals in France and England. He told his parents: 'I am not very keen about going out again just yet, as my nerves are really pretty rotten, and I still have rather bad nights, when I go over all that awful show again, and I see all those fellows die, and get wounded again every time, but it is passing off.'

PASSCHENDAELE WAS A failure, a wild throw. Yet four days after the battle Lloyd George sent Haig a telegram congratulating him on his achievements in Flanders since July 31. Haig and his men, the Prime Minister said, had shown 'skill, courage and pertinacity'; they had 'filled the enemy with alarm'. The Prime Minister told the field-marshal he wanted to renew his 'assurance of confidence in your leadership'. Why Lloyd George did this is unclear. He hadn't congratulated Haig on his march from Messines to Broodseinde; he congratulated him after a blunder, which suggests the Prime Minister still wasn't looking at the detail of the campaign. It was right for him to laud the bravery of the soldiers – this part of the telegram was obviously sincere – but why did he say that he believed in Haig? Nothing had changed in Lloyd George's mind. He still thought Haig was a dull man running a charnel house. And he had never believed in the Flanders campaign.

Haig was astonished. He copied the contents of the telegram into his diary and then penned a few sentences of his own that ended with exclamation marks. Dull he may have been, but he knew at once this was not what it seemed to be.

GENERAL ARTHUR CURRIE, the citizen-soldier who someone said looked like a company cook, had a few weeks earlier shown the sort of independence that the career-soldiers Birdwood and White never quite managed. The Anzacs and many of the British divisions were exhausted. The Canadians were to be brought into the Ypres campaign as fresh troops. Currie, the corps commander, a real estate agent before the war, at once said they didn't want to serve under Gough. Currie thought him inept, and that was the polite version. Haig put the Canadians under Plumer.

Every Canadian, Currie wrote afterwards, hated to go to Passchendaele. 'I carried my protest to the extreme limit . . . which I believe would have resulted in my being sent home had I been other than the Canadian Corps Commander. I pointed out what the casualties were bound to be, and asked if a success would justify the sacrifice. I was ordered to go and make the attack.' According to one of Currie's biographers, Haig gave Currie no reason for continuing the campaign on the wet and stinking ground. He simply said that Passchendaele had to be taken and 'some day I will tell you why'.

Currie won the concession he wanted. He needed time, at least a fortnight, to prepare. He wanted to give his men the artillery protection that the Anzac and British troops had been denied. He set engineers to work at stabilising gun platforms, improving roads and drainage channels, constructing light railways and laying telephone lines. Currie decided that instead of trying to take the village in one bound, he would creep up on it in three steps, each of about 500 yards. He brought his troops into the frontline early so that, unlike the Anzacs, they would not go into the attack exhausted from an approach march through mud. And, all through, Currie went back and forth to the front in the rain, looking for himself, finding out for himself, talking to gunners, infantrymen, engineers and medical staff, insisting that this be changed and that be fixed. This was what gave him a style all of his own among the Great War generals. He was not only careful in his planning; he had to *see* the ground. Maps were not enough. Pencils always travelled over maps more easily than men.

Lieutenant Fisher of the 3rd Australian Division knew all about the ground. He and his men pulled back 1000 yards as the Canadians came up. 'Here we stayed four days, and got shelled to hell, but no-one minds that – a shell drops alongside, and one merely calls it a bastard, curses the Hun, and wipes off the mud. Anyhow we are out now and I don't mind much. Only I'd like to have a talk with some war correspondents – liars they are.' The reaction to his spell at Passchendaele was still to come, he wrote. 'I'm rather frightened of it – I feel about eighty years old now . . .' Fisher survived the German bombardment of the back areas with mustard gas, only to be killed five months later.

THE CANADIANS ATTACKED on October 26 and took their first 500 yards, but at a terrible cost: 3300 casualties. Two Australian battalions fought on the right flank of the Canadians. This was the end of the Australian infantry's part in the struggle for Passchendaele.

On the evening after this first Canadian battle Lloyd George ordered Hair to send two divisions to Italy at once, with the ominous rider that this was a preliminary measure. The Italians had collapsed at Caporetto on the Isonzo front, where six German divisions had reinforced the Austrians. Those Italians who hadn't surrendered were in frantic retreat. There was a fear in London that Italy could fall out of the war.

The day before Currie's attack a young German lieutenant commanding a force of 200-odd had taken 3600 Italian prisoners around Caporetto. He took another 5400 prisoners in the next few days and won the *Pour le Mérite*, Germany's highest award for bravery. His name was Erwin Rommel.

The day after Currie's first attack one of Italy's most outspoken newspaper editors called for more patriotism. People had to forget about liberty, he wrote. The watchword now was 'discipline', which some of his countrymen might have found bemusing, since discipline in the Italian army was cruel, worse arguably than in the Russian army, and this, in turn, was a prime reason why the Italian army had performed so poorly. The editor, barrel-chested and with a great jaw that he thrust forward, had been wounded on the Isonzo front earlier in the year. He was sharp-witted, but had been a bully since childhood. His name was Benito Mussolini.

Italy suffered massive casualties at Caporetto, hundreds of thousands at a time, most of them prisoners of war.

CURRIE TOOK HIS second step on October 30. Again the Canadians gained their 500 yards. They were on the edge of the village. Conditions were frightful. Pigeons became so caked in mud that they couldn't fly.

The Canadians were to go for the village on November 6. Two days before this Lieutenant-Colonel C. E. L. Lyne, a British artillery officer, wrote: 'Dante would never have condemned lost souls to wander in so terrible a purgatory . . . How weirdly it recalls some half formed horror of childish nightmare, one would flee, but whither? – one would cry aloud but there comes no blessed awakening.' Gas at night was the crowning horror. Lyne would risk only three men to a field gun at the same time because of the gas. 'I've got a throat like raw beef and a voice like a crow . . . Great days these.'

Ludendorff was not at Passchendaele but he understood it well enough. In his autobiography he said it was worse than Verdun. 'It was no longer life at all. It was mere unspeakable suffering.'

The Canadians attacked again and took the village after about three hours. They bayoneted Germans in the main street and among the ruins, which were littered with the body parts of Germans hit by shellfire. The church was the only building that was recognisable. The Canadians attacked again on November 10 during a rainstorm, took a little more ground and a few days later were pulled out.

They had run up 12,400 casualties. The Canadian official historian wrote: 'It is not too much to compare the Canadian troops struggling forward, the pangs of hell wracking their bodies, up the Ridge, their dying eyes set upon the summit, with a Man who once crept another hill, with agony in soul and body, to redeem the world and give Passchendaele its glorious name.'

Haig showed no signs of elation. He did much the same things every day, such as tapping the barometer after dressing, whether the news was good or bad. 'Today was a very important success,' he wrote in his diary after the Canadians took the village. As he often did, he got his own casualty figures wrong. As always, his estimate was on the low side. Anyway Haig had no cause for elation, and he knew it. The capture of this village, six-and-a-half miles from the Menin Gate, had not changed the strategic balance on the western front. It was a trifling substitute for what the offensive had once been about, the capture of the Belgian ports. In the days after the Canadian sacrifice Haig began to realise something else. The ground around the village was going to be hard to hold. It constituted a little bump of a salient within the much larger Ypres salient. The Germans could fire into it from three sides.

But Haig's mind was drifting elsewhere. He was set on one more operatic gesture before the year ended. He was looking to a stretch of the Hindenburg Line south-east of Arras, near Cambrai.

THE STORY GOES – there seems to be no verification of it – that after the final Canadian attack Launcelot Kiggell, Haig's chief-of-staff, went to look at the front. He became upset as his staff car rocked through the mud and began to weep. 'Good God,' he is supposed to have said, 'did we really send men to fight in that?'

The man next to him knew the front well. 'It's worse further on up,' he replied.

JUST AFTER PASSCHENDAELE fell Lloyd George delivered an energetic speech in Paris in which he called for the establishment of a body to advise on overall allied strategy. Two lines in this speech were loaded with shrapnel; the fuse was set to explode over the heads of Haig and Robertson. 'We have won great victories,' the Prime Minister said. 'When I look at the appalling casualty lists I sometimes wish it had not been necessary to win so many.'

Lloyd George at this time didn't know the butcher's bill for Third Ypres. We still don't know precise figures. Edmonds, Britain's official historian, put the British and dominion casualties from July 31 at around 240,000. He hinted that the German casualties might be 400,000. Prior and Wilson in *Passchendaele* estimate British and dominion casualties for Messines and Third Ypres at 275,000, including 70,000 killed. They estimate German losses at Third Ypres at just short of 200,000.

The French, Russian and Italian armies had all broken under pressure. Whatever the final casualty figure, the wonder of the Passchendaele campaign is that it failed to break the spirit of the British and dominion armies. Morale certainly suffered among Australian troops and it was easy enough to measure this. Court-martial charges against Australians for being absent without leave and for desertion peaked in October, 1917. After Third Ypres the rate of imprisonment of Australian troops stood at more than eight times that of the British home army.

If the total British and dominion losses at Third Ypres are still a matter for argument, we know the Australian figures with some precision. The Australians suffered 55,000 casualties for the year, 38,000 of them in Belgium. A crisis was approaching: there simply weren't enough reinforcements to make up the losses. During September and October, when the Australians had fought their way from Menin Road Ridge to the edge of Passchendaele, enlistments at home had totalled only 5221. A few days before Passchendaele closed down Billy Hughes announced that there would be a second referendum on conscription.

PASSCHENDAELE TODAY IS larger and prettier than it was before the Great War. Back then it was just another crossroads village with a pious name and a church of white stone and red brick. Now it is a word loaded up with symbolism, like Gettysburg or Stalingrad. The war is just beneath the surface. A farmer near here owned a small field that, as he put it, refused to grow anything. One year he set the plough a little deeper than usual. Up came 630 German hand grenades.

One grave at Poelcappelle British Cemetery beckons to visitors. The headstone says that here lies 6322 Private J. Condon of the Royal Irish Regiment. He was killed here in 1915, as were thousands of others. Private Condon was different: he was fourteen.

Ypres used to be about cloth and God. Now it is a plangent town – bells always seem to be ringing somewhere – that each day receives throngs of British pilgrims. They stand in their hundreds at the Menin Gate to hear the Last Post played by buglers with white gloves.

Sometimes the Last Post seems more affecting when the crowd is small. An elderly Belgian woman comes to the ceremony tonight, walking slowly, a collapsible chair in one hand, a walking stick in the other. She sits just inside the eastern end of the arch and wears a beatific smile. Behind her, framed by the farther arch, the spire of

511

the Cloth Hall spears towards clouds bruised with rain. She left here as a child with her parents when the Great War came and grew up in Derbyshire. She was present when the Menin Gate memorial opened in 1927. The townsfolk tell you that sometimes on a cold winter's night, when few come out for the service, her voice can be heard at the end saying: 'We will remember them.'

33

False dawn

Lieutenant-Colonel John Fuller, now in his late thirties and the chief-of-staff of the Tank Corps, owned one of the brightest minds in Haig's army. Fuller early in 1917 had begun to envision a form of breakthrough involving masses of tanks with strong air and artillery support and infantry brought forward in motor lorries, an idea that one day would be embraced by the Germans (who didn't have any tanks in 1917) and called *blitzkrieg*.

Fuller didn't think much of Haig. Forty years after the war Fuller, by then well known as an author of incisive books on military tactics, wrote that Haig was 'stubborn and intolerant, in speech inarticulate, in argument dumb'. But Fuller said that Haig, unlike most cavalrymen, had studied war and 'this was to be his undoing, because he was so unimaginative that he could not see that the tactics of the past were as dead as mutton . . . Thus, in spite of fire, wire and mire, cavalry figured in all his battles, and to the detriment of the other arms, because they and their enormous forage trains blocked communications.'

Fuller in June, 1917, sent a paper to Haig's headquarters saying that the country in front of the old textile town of Cambrai was ideal for an attack by tanks. The ground was not badly cratered and rolled about gently. Fuller thought tanks had been misused on the Somme and at Bullecourt, where they had been doled out to infantry formations in 'penny packets'. He thought they should be used *en masse*: hundreds of tanks on a front of four or five miles, a weapon of surprise and terror. Fuller didn't see Cambrai as a major offensive so much as a raid, big and brief, that would panic the Germans.

Brigadier-General Hugh Elles, the commander of the Tank Corps, liked the idea. Kiggell, Haig's chief-of-staff, didn't, and it was put aside. Fuller put up the scheme again in August, by which time tanks had been proved of little value in the bogs of Ypres. Now the scheme had another supporter, General Sir Julian Byng, whose 3rd Army occupied the front facing the Hindenburg Line at Cambrai. But Byng had enlarged the scheme. He was thinking of breakthrough and of cavalry galloping through the gap opened by the tanks. Haig was now interested, even though he was in the middle stages of Third Ypres. Breakthrough and cavalry always made his heart leap. Byng was told in mid-October to start planning the attack for November 20.

This was an astonishing decision. Haig had lost the equivalent of ten to twelve divisions at Third Ypres. The two armies he had used there were worn out and couldn't be used elsewhere. Third Ypres had failed in the terms under which Haig had sold it to Lloyd George. Haig knew that Lloyd George saw Third Ypres as butchery and waste and was more disenchanted with him than he had ever been. Haig didn't tell Lloyd George he was planning a new offensive at Cambrai. He didn't tell Robertson until October 20 and Robertson, staunch as ever, didn't tell the frocks. Worst of all Haig didn't think about reserves for Cambrai. He had a manpower crisis, as it was called, because of his losses at Third Ypres. So even if Byng initially succeeded at Cambrai, Haig could send him no troops to widen and exploit the breach.

Byng had 474 tanks, the new Mark IVs with improved armour plating, seven infantry divisions for the initial attack and others in reserve and five divisions of cavalry. The tanks would break through the Hindenburg Line, supported by infantry, and take the high ground in front of Cambrai, which lay seven miles behind the German frontline. Then the cavalry would gallop through and surround Cambrai before pushing on north and east. Elles, Fuller and the other tank men had thought carefully about what they were going to do. They came up with the first sophisticated plan for ironclads. Most of them were designated fighting tanks, but around fifty would act as supply vehicles dragging sleds, thirty-odd would carry chains and hooks for tearing out the German wire and several were equipped with wireless so that they could pass messages to the rear and to aircraft. The leading tanks would carry rolls of timber. These would be dropped into the German front trenches, which were ten-feet wide, to make bridges over which the tanks could cross.

The tank men were different. General Elles announced on the eve of the battle that he would personally lead the attack in a tank called *Hilda*. It would carry the brown, red and green flag of the Tank Corps.

There was to be no preliminary bombardment, which would have told the Germans an attack was coming. The British artillery opened up only ten minutes before the tanks began to roll. Cambrai was going to be that rare thing: a surprise.

And it was. The Hindenburg Line was captured in the first ninety minutes. The tanks tore up the wire so that the cavalry might push through. Hundreds of Germans trudged into captivity. Prince Rupprecht, in charge of this section of the front as well as Flanders, asked Ludendorff for reinforcements. The British pushed on. By 11.30 am, five hours after zero, they had taken much of the second line on a six-mile front. The bag of prisoners now ran to thousands. *Hilda* eventually broke down in the German wire. Elles was undismayed. He had already proved what tanks could do and how they should be used. He began the walk back to his headquarters. He expected to see cavalry trotting up at any moment.

The commander of the cavalry corps, a more cautious spirit than Elles, had set up his headquarters six miles behind the front and wasn't sure what was happening there. Two of his divisions were even further back. By mid-afternoon the tanks and infantry were five miles in on a six-mile front but the cavalry was slow in coming up, and then had to return because there was no water for the horses. It has been claimed this was something close to a tragedy. It probably wasn't: horses are fine targets for machine guns. The tragedy was that Byng didn't have enough *infantry* to exploit the early gains.

The British press hailed Cambrai as a great victory. The Bishop of London ordered that the bells of St Paul's Cathedral be rung. Soon bells were ringing across the British Isles, as though the war-winning blow had been struck. It was the first time bells had been rung for a victory.

The attack began to stall on the second day. Many tanks had been hit or had broken down. Rain came. Byng's troops were held at several places, notably at Bourlon Ridge, which overlooked the British position. The Germans were bringing up fresh divisions. It was a familiar tale from the Great War: success followed by a loss of momentum. Haig could have called off the battle at this point. He decided to go on. Cambrai became another slogging match, with this difference: the Germans had reserves and Haig didn't. After a week Haig wanted to call the battle off. The Germans didn't. They counter-attacked on November 30 with fresh divisions. The British now had only sixty-three tanks to support the infantry. When Cambrai ended in snow and rain on December 7 the British still held part of the Hindenburg Line but had lost part of their own frontline to the south. Cambrai was another stalemate. British casualties had been only 4000 on that brilliantly successful first day. Now they were 45,000; the German figure was about the same.

Haig's biographer, John Terraine, wrote that Cambrai was the low point of Haig's career. 'It weakened his prestige and position at a time when he needed every support he could get.' In another familiar tale from the Great War the public's hopes had been raised then lowered. It might have been better if those bells had not been rung. Cambrai had never been winnable because Haig never had the means to win it.

LLOYD GEORGE WAS vexed anew, for three obvious reasons. He had been given no advance notice of the battle; this was Haig at his most clumsy and high-handed, contemptuous not only of the Prime Minister but of the ways of democracy. Second, the attack had failed after the British people had been given false hope. And, third, Haig had presented the country with another long casualty list. But there was something else, something more subtle, that made Lloyd George even angrier.

Haig and Charteris had said all through the long days of Third Ypres that the German army was about to collapse. Yet the Germans were able to summon up a dozen divisions to deal with a crisis at Cambrai. And they could do this while also sending troops to Italy and to Riga on the eastern front. How could they do this if their army had been broken in spirit in Flanders?

Robertson conceded in a private letter to Plumer just after Cambrai ended that 'the diminution of German morale has been greatly overdone at general Headquarters'. Northcliffe, the press baron who owned *The Times* and the *Daily Mail*, had long been Haig's booster. Now, after Cambrai, he turned against him.

The political aftermath of Cambrai came close to farce. Robertson wrote to Haig, telling him Lloyd George was 'well on the warpath . . . His great argument is that you have for long said that the Germans are well on the downgrade in morale and numbers and that you advised attacking them though some 30 Divisions should come from Russia; and yet only a few Divisions have come, and you are hard put to hold your own!' The Prime Minister, Robertson said, believed Charteris had made mistakes about German numbers and morale.

Haig wrote back to say he understood Robertson had been having a 'terrible time' at Cabinet meetings. 'I gather that the PM is dissatisfied. If that means that I have lost his confidence, then in the interests of the cause let him replace me at once. But if he still wishes me to remain, then all carping criticism should cease, and I should be both supported and trusted.'

Haig appeased the politicians. He replaced 'Poor Charteris' as chief of intelligence, while denying that his work had been faulty and expressed surprise when Kiggell told him Charteris was much disliked among the armies and corps. Haig pretended to face up to the problem of Gough. He transferred Neill Malcolm, Gough's overweening chief-of-staff, to command of a division. He told Gough, for the first time, that it was common for divisional commanders to hope that they would not be sent to Gough's army. Gough feigned surprise at this news. Haig wrote in his diary that he hadn't told Gough this before because it might have affected his self-confidence.

Kiggell, Haig's chief-of-staff, was thought to be ill; he was certainly tired. Fuller described him as tall, gloomy and erudite. 'He was essentially a cloistered soldier; he never went near a battle, and – if correctly reported – only once visited a battlefield, and then long after the battle had been fought.' Major-General Herbert Lawrence, a tense-looking divisional commander, replaced Kiggell. Kiggell's deputy also went, as did the Quartermaster-General, the Engineer-in-Chief and the Director-General of Medical Services. This is sometimes referred to as a purge. It wasn't: Haig and the army commanders stayed. John Grigg, Lloyd George's biographer, wrote: 'Though [Haig] often insisted that he was responsible for his subordinates . . . he did not ultimately act on the principle. They went; he stayed. However much he may have believed in them, he believed in himself more.'

The politicians could play at farce too. Early in 1918 Lloyd George sent Smuts, the South African general who was in the War Cabinet, and Maurice Hankey, secretary to the War Cabinet, to France. They were to talk to lots of generals. Lloyd George apparently explained that he did not know many of the generals. The secret brief given to Smuts and Hankey was to find a replacement for Haig. They couldn't find a candidate. Here was Lloyd George leading a country in a long and terrible war that touched every aspect of life and had brought sadness across the land – and he didn't know enough about his own commanders to alight on a replacement for Haig.

WHILE THE FROCKS and the generals were teasing and appeasing, each side not quite bold enough to tell the other what it truly thought, Vladimir Lenin was playing rougher politics in Petrograd. Kerensky still headed the provisional government but his authority was shrinking. Lenin had established himself as leader of the Bolsheviks. He was ready to launch the 'real' revolution. The first was merely about getting rid of the Tsar. The second was about a Marxist state and world revolution.

On November 7 (October 25 on the old Russian calendar, hence the 'October Revolution') the Bolsheviks seized power in Petrograd, taking over railway stations, bridges, post offices and telephone exchanges, and the world changed forever. Lenin announced a three-month armistice with Germany.

Lenin eventually sent a delegation, headed by Leon Trotsky, to negotiate a peace settlement with the Germans at Brest-Litovsk, the Polish fortress town. Talks began on November 22, two days after Cambrai opened. Lenin deliberately prolonged the negotiations. He needed to buy as much time as he could. He hoped German troops might join in his world revolution. He also knew that he had to take Russia out of the war. There was more to this than ideology: he suspected he would have to fight a civil war at home. But the Germans tired of his delaying tactics. In February, 1918, fifty German divisions went back to invading Russia, which was now even easier than before. Lenin and Trotsky suddenly wanted to negotiate again.

Hindenburg and Ludendorff were now running foreign policy as well as the war. They dictated the terms of the treaty and these were cruel. Hindenburg and Ludendorff were making a gigantic land grab. Russia lost Finland, the Ukraine, Lithuania, Poland Courland and Livonia, about one-third of her people, much of her best farmland and most of her coal and iron mines. Russia also had to pay reparations.

Russia's collapse had fearful implications for her former allies. Germany would be able to transfer dozens of divisions to France and Belgium. And indeed this eventually happened, but Germany could move only part of her army in the east. The new empire of Hindenburg and Ludendorff, much bigger than Germany itself, had to be garrisoned. Fifty divisions, some one million troops, had to stay behind to protect the spoils of war. Had Germany been less greedy in the east, she might have been able to send twenty-five divisions to the west at a time when the French army was still recovering from its mutinies and the British army was short of men after the carnage of Passchendaele and Cambrai.

Germany was as artless as ever at Brest-Litovsk, all Prussian thumbs and arrogance. In the words of one historian, the Brest-Litovsk treaty 'flashed the brutality of German greed to the world. This was to be the fate of Belgium, France, Britain and Italy should Germany win the war.'

A WEEK AFTER Lenin, a cold man, came to power in Petrograd, Georges Clemenceau, a man of fiery passions and a radical of a different stripe, became Premier of France. Like Lenin, he came to the post by default: Painlevé had resigned after being defeated in the Chamber. Clemenceau was seventy-six and still bursting with the fire and patriotism that during his noisy career in journalism had earned him the sobriquet '*Le Tigre*'. (Clemenceau wrote the famous headline *J'Accuse* for Emile Zola's open letter on the Dreyfus case.)

Lloyd George had first met Clemenceau nine years earlier. He remembered 'a short, broad-shouldered and full-chested man, with an aggressive and rather truculent countenance, illuminated by a pair of brilliant and fierce eyes set deeply under overhanging eyebrows. The size and hardness of the head struck me . . .' Clemenceau and Lloyd George had argued on this occasion. Years later Lloyd George discovered Clemenceau's 'real fascination: his wit, his playfulness, the hypnotic interest of his arresting and compelling personality'.

Clemenceau was two people: the amiable companion who loved literature and the simplicities of rustic life, and a hard man with a dictatorial streak. Churchill witnessed Clemenceau's first speech to the Chamber as Premier in 1917. Clemenceau spoke without notes and in short sentences. 'He looked like a wild animal pacing to and fro behind bars, growling and glaring . . . France had resolved to unbar the cage and let her tiger loose upon all foes . . . With snarls and growls, the ferocious, aged, dauntless beast of prey went into action.'

Clemenceau reduced his platform to three words. 'Home policy? I wage war! Foreign policy? I wage war!' He was the man for his times, as Churchill would be twenty-three years later.

34

The Australian Corps

B illy Hughes was trying to be a man for his times too. But what were the times saying in Australia? It had all seemed so simple during the federal election of 1914. Support for Australia's part in the war had been bi-partisan. Few had envisioned the age of the howitzer and casualty lists that every day filled columns in the newspapers. The political conversation had turned nasty during Hughes' conscription referendum in 1916. Fissures had opened up in a society that had mostly been united about the big issues since Federation. The arrival of the Nationalist Government – a coalition of former Labor men, such as Hughes and Pearce, and the conservatives – had ensured that the fissures widened.

Not that Australians had lost faith in the crusade against the Kaiser: the election of the Hughes Nationalist Government in May, 1917, had rather proved that. But there were now tensions between Catholics and Protestants, between those who believed in conscription and those who thought Australia had contributed enough, and between those who thought Billy Hughes a patriot and those who thought him Judas, the man who betrayed his class. It may also have been true that the rhetoric of the conscription campaign and the issues that had been dragged into the public arena were now working against voluntary recruiting, which had fallen away badly after the referendum. A wounded officer who had served at Gallipoli and in France urged university students to enlist. As Stanley Bruce he would become Prime Minister of Australia. An engine-driver from Bathurst, a good trade unionist, was shocked at the way strikes were being suppressed in the interests of the war effort. As Ben Chifley he too would become Prime Minister. The crusade had become muddled. The clarity of 1914 had gone.

There was another problem, though many people in 1917 were unaware of the extent of it. People trying to make judgements about the war didn't know with any accuracy what had been happening at the front. Newspapers were their main source of information and the papers were omitting so much that their reports were often misleading. The allies had won so many 'victories' yet the frontline had advanced only a mile here and a mile there. Censorship is inevitable in war and no-one should be surprised by it, but in the Great War some journalists and editors seemed too comfortable with it.

So here was Hughes, on November 12 at Bendigo, trying again to introduce conscription by referendum. In theory he didn't need a referendum: he had a majority in both Houses of Parliament. In practice he had no choice: he had pledged that conscription would not be introduced without another referendum. And a new poll would only be called if 'the tide of battle turned against the Allies'. Hughes was even more devious this time. This is the question people were to be asked on December 20: 'Are you in favour of the proposal of the Commonwealth Government for reinforcing the Australian Imperial Forces oversea?' No mention of conscription, and an assumption that the voters knew what the proposal was. But both sides played at deviousness. Daniel Mannix, now Archbishop of Melbourne, was Hughes' most obvious opponent in the coming debate. Mannix, who inevitably appeared in his clerical robes, was to claim during the campaign that when he spoke about conscription he 'did not speak as a priest or as an archbishop, but simply as an honest, straight and loyal citizen of Australia'.

HUGHES WASN'T GOING to the people again simply because he believed the 'tide of battle' had turned against the allies, although he was clearly worried about the defeat at Caporetto and anarchy in Russia. He was most likely unaware of how badly Third Ypres had run down British and dominion troop numbers and how little it had achieved. Hughes was first of all going to the people because he needed an army large enough to give him a loud voice at any peace conference. He had been worrying about troop numbers long before Caporetto or Lenin's coup. He may also have thought that Australia would now be more receptive to conscription.

Hughes had tried to stimulate voluntary enlistments after the first referendum failed. Recruiting committees were set up in all States. Public meetings were held, so many that handbooks were written for speakers. One handbook, *The Speaker's Companion*, included 'Sister Susie's Creed'. Sister Susie said: 'I refuse to establish propinquity or to flirt with any male who cannot produce statutory evidence of ineligibility for active service. If there are not enough soldiers to go round I will cheerfully die an old maid . . .' Here was something new: no uniform, no propinquity. Speakers, sometimes wounded soldiers, occasionally women, turned up at theatres, cinemas, town halls, sporting events and even beaches. Women tried to shame perceived shirkers. The big daily newspapers still supported conscription. The *Bulletin* ran savage cartoons against 'cold footers'. Church of England clergymen preached in favour of compulsion. And none of this produced the numbers required.

Enlistments had peaked during the Gallipoli campaign of 1915. July of that year produced 36,575 recruits and August 25,714. These figures were never approached again. In June, 1917, when the Australians took 7000 casualties at Messines, enlistments were only 3679. In September and October, when the Australians ran up tens of thousands of casualties between Menin Road and the edge of Passchendaele, enlistments were 2460 and 2761 respectively.

Hughes at Bendigo was careful to talk about 'compulsory reinforcements' rather than 'conscription'. The system of voluntary enlistment would continue, he said, but Australia needed to supply 7000 men a month. If enlistments failed to reach this figure, compulsory reinforcements would be called up by ballot to make up the deficit. The ballot would be taken among single men only, between the ages of twenty and forty-four, including widowers and divorcees without dependent children. The list of exemptions included judges, magistrates and clergymen. 'Those of you who have relatives in the trenches cannot heed their cry unmoved,' Hughes said. 'If they hungered, would you not send them food? If they were sick, would you not succour them? Their need is reinforcements. They need rest, they need help. The only way you can help the boys at the front is to send them more men . . .'

Then he soared on a rhetorical flight. It was the hour for Australians to *prove* their mettle. The heavens were *dark* with portents of evil. Russia was *torn* by anarchy. Italy was *reeling*. The spirit of disintegration *threatened* to divide the allies. It was an hour when men of weaker fibre would *quail*. Now was the time for Australians to draw themselves *erect*. 'I tell you plainly that the Government must have this power. It cannot govern the country without it, and will not attempt to do so.'

Mannix's style was lighter, simpler and more twentieth century. 'The wealthy classes would be very glad to send the last man,' he told a meeting a few weeks after Hughes had opened the campaign, 'but they have no notion of giving the last shilling, nor even the first.' The capitalists would not pay for the war. 'You know that these people have a remarkable facility for passing these obligations on.'

KEITH MURDOCH KNEW about the new referendum before it was announced. Hughes had been cabling him. Murdoch had become the Prime Minister's main agent in London. Matters that should have gone through the High Commissioner, Andrew Fisher, and the Colonial Office went instead to Murdoch, by coded cables from Hughes that were marked 'secret' or 'most secret'. Murdoch in turn went to Lloyd George, Haig, Birdwood and others as Hughes' representative. How Murdoch reconciled this double life – journalist one moment, emissary the next, observer today and player tomorrow – has never been explained. Most journalists sought out government secrets and contrived ways to publish them; Murdoch kept government secrets and fed his readers platitudes.

Murdoch had worked for Hughes during the Australian federal election earlier in the year. Hughes had wanted Murdoch to arrange for troops to be 'canvassed' about the election. Birdwood told Murdoch that Haig would not permit this, but then suggested other ways of sending political messages to the troops. Shortly after Murdoch cabled Hughes saying he need 1000 pounds immediately to cover expenses.

Six days before his Bendigo speech Hughes told Murdoch that another referendum was likely. 'Anzac vote vital to success. Will you get committee together and explain position most confidentially: ask them take steps immediately make all preparations for very vigorous campaign. Everything is to be kept very quiet until public announcement . . . Feel confident can rely on committee which did such splendid work recent election to spare no effort secure same large majority of Anzac votes . . . Secrecy vital.' (The 'committee' was a small group of Australian civilians in London, of which Murdoch was the luminary. All members were pro-Hughes and pro-conscription.)

Murdoch cabled back a few days later saying that Haig had promised to rest the Australian troops a month before the vote. The divisions had come away from Passchendaele badly under strength. There had been talk at the front of turning the 4th Division into a 'depot' division, providing reinforcements for the other four. Murdoch now made an astonishing suggestion to Hughes. Break up a division (presumably the 4th), he cabled. 'This would have striking effect public opinion of Force and in Australia providing War Office permitted fact to become widely known.'

THE *AUSTRALIAN WORKER* called the scheme Hughes announced at Bendigo 'a game of chance viler than any played in the hells of Monte Carlo'. It was a lottery. 'Lives are to be drawn for on Tattersall principles; souls are to be made the subjects of a hideous sweep. The equivalents of eligible males are to be tossed into a hat or something; then someone – Death, who knows? – plunges in a hand, and all who are drawn are doomed to be the victims of bloody war.'

Nellie Melba, the soprano and socialite, sent a message to the women of Australia, encouraging them to vote for Hughes' scheme. 'I tried to make it strong,' she wrote to Hughes, 'because *entre nous* very few Australian women use their brains.'

Some called for Mannix to be deported. Mannix called Hughes 'the little Tsar' and said, with justification, that the Prime Minister was not putting a 'straight question' to the people. Hughes and Mannix were portrayed as the main players (which probably over-states Mannix's part), and there was something fantastic about this that was lost in the flurries of argument. Hughes was a Welshman who had been born in London and had come to Australia in his early twenties. Though an Australian nationalist, he also had a fondness for his old world that now loaded him up with baubles and praise. Mannix was an Irishman who came to Australia in his late forties. He still had loyalties both to Ireland and ideas of Irish independence. Yet both these men purported to speak for Australia.

Hughes stumped up and down the country, bursting with nerv-ous energy that exhausted his secretaries. The campaign was noisier and nastier than the one before. It was not so much about the real-ities of the western front as perceptions of patriotism. Both sides exaggerated.

At Warwick, on Queensland's Darling Downs, someone threw two eggs at Hughes. One hit his hat. A scuffle began and accounts of this vary spectacularly. One has Hughes emerging with bleeding knuckles.

In Sydney, according to the *Bulletin*, an army medical officer was addressing a referendum meeting when an anti-conscriptionist shouted: 'Did *youse* ever do any fightin?'

The officer lifted his head and said: 'I didn't even know the little man had even enlisted.'

The interjector couldn't understand why the crowd burst into laughter.

LIEUTENANT CYRIL LAWRENCE was still behind the Passchendaele front a week before Hughes' speech at Bendigo. In letters home the previous month he said he had been stuck in mud up to his thighs for an hour. Eight men, he said, took seven hours to carry a wounded officer about 2000 yards. In his letter of November 5 he worried about where the war was going. 'We can't go on forever like this and the old Hun, drat him, is nothing like finished yet.' Both sides were losing their 'very best manhood' while the slackers remained behind. People were talking about the new world after the war. Lawrence felt the shirkers would inherit it.

Early next month he was preparing to vote. 'Will I vote – will I what! . . . The whole area is posted up with great sheets just like an election at home. They promise us all sorts of things – "more rest" is the best we can see, but it is an empty promise and everyone knows it.'

Other soldiers were less worried about shirkers. Sapper Frank Heerey, a miner from Tasmania whose family had fled the Irish famine, wrote a typically laconic diary entry: 'Another cold day. In aft voted NO on conscription question. Fluff & I had a spread for tea. On duty till 8.30 pm, wrote letters.'

HUGHES LOST THE referendum. He knew he had lost before midnight on polling night. It was worse than last time. The 'No' majority more than doubled to 166,588 and this time Victoria also voted 'No'. The only States that voted 'Yes' were Western Australia (by a large majority) and Tasmania (narrowly). Sectarian issues had been present throughout the campaign, but there was more to the 'No' majority than the dissent of some, though certainly not all, Irish Catholics. People of all persuasions, from the Left and from the Right, were uncomfortable with Hughes' scheme and perhaps also with his divisive style. The electorate had again shown its subtle colours. It was still for the war; it still didn't believe in conscription.

Hughes had said over and over during the campaign that he could not govern without conscription. Early in the New Year he tendered his resignation to Munro-Ferguson, the Governor-General. Who could Munro-Ferguson turn to? Frank Tudor, the Labor leader, lacked the numbers in Parliament. So did Sir John Forrest, the explorer and former West Australian Premier who wanted the prime ministership. Munro-Ferguson was thus justified in making a decision that doubtless pleased him. He reappointed Hughes.

THE SOLDIERS HAD again voted for conscription, this time by a majority of 9879. Bean felt that a majority of troops at the front voted 'No'. Private Roy Brewer of the 2nd Division wrote to his parents a few months after the referendum. 'Well father you asked me some time ago what I thought of the referendum. Well I was against it, and I think the majority of our Battalion were against it. I would not vote to pitch a man over here against his will.' Private Brewer, a winner of the Military Medal, was killed later in the year.

The *Bulletin* ran a letter from a soldier in a 'sloppy trench'. 'We've just heard the result of the Referendum. Lord knows what's going to happen now! I suppose we'll just have to keep on splitting up until there's not enough left to split, and then turn it in. Some wag said they'd only need two ships to take the Australians home – one for the staff and the other for the identification discs.'

Pompey Elliott had gone to England after Polygon Wood. Gas had blistered his face and the pain prevented him sleeping. He stopped shaving – the razor was spreading the infection – and his beard came out blotched with grey. He was just short of forty years old. Other things were wrong. He missed his wife and children, whom he had last seen in 1914. 'Tell me all about the wee people,' he wrote home, 'tell me everything about their hair and cheeks and chins . . . I can never hear enough of them.' He was only hard-bitten on the outside.

On his return to France in December it was apparent that something else was wrong. 'Yet sometimes I feel that I have reached the limit of my strength and that I cannot stand the strain much longer . . . I am always tired and sometimes my head aches . . . and my nerves seem all raw and aching.' He was also worrying about the financial troubles of his law firm and what they might cost him.

Elliott had the symptoms of what these days would probably be called depression. And the rejection of conscription made all seem worse. Mannix's pronouncements had infuriated him. It was as though Elliott's own country had abandoned him, a sentiment he wrote to a friend and which ended up being published in the *Argus*.

Major Consett Riddell felt abandoned too. He said he lay in bed thinking: 'What am I fighting for?' Not for France, Italy, Belgium or Russia, he decided. They had nothing to do with him.

> I even wonder now if it is for my own country Australia which evidently does not want my help, and the only thing left is for some vague ideals about small nations and the fact that I could never have held my head again if I had not come. This is all a very small thing but takes the heart out of one terribly, I wanted to think I was fighting for Australia and now I can't . . . The result is that first one division and then another must be broken up to provide men to fill the gaps in the others, and probably my division the 4th will be the first to go . . .

THE 4TH DIVISION wasn't broken up, but it nearly was. The offer to disband it led, almost by chance, to the formation in November of the Australian Corps, all five divisions in one corps under Birdwood. No longer would the divisions be swapped between Birdwood's I Anzac and Godley's II Anzac. Godley was gone from the Australians' lives, and this was no loss. And no longer would the Australians serve alongside the New Zealand Division, which had been part of II Anzac. This was a loss. There were no better troops on the western front than the New Zealanders.

Murdoch, as Hughes' agent, did much to bring the Australian Corps into being. If Murdoch liked to play the kingmaker, he was also an Australian nationalist. On July 12, 1917, he cabled Hughes, first mentioning attempts to sell Australian flour in the United States – he was handling that too – then this:

> Re troops, urgently ask your immediate consideration following important representations behalf whole AIF FRANCE. Officers men have very strong

Australian feelings prize highly distinctive Australian identity find that Australian comradeship valuable moral support. Moreover several recent battles they lost heavily owing weakness failure support of British troops. Third Division never assimilated rest AIF, because separated and under Godley, who notoriously anti-Australian. Separation prevents enforcement Australian democratic policy by Monash. Very strong desire exists expressed insistently through all Divisions that they be brought together as soon as possible . . . Officers men strenuously dislike GHQ policy regarding all as merely British troops refusing recognise Australian nationality even omitting them from communiqués. Leading officers also consider Australia should have Liaison Officers War Office. At present important decisions affecting Australian Government public and national future taken without our recognisance by people responsible to quite another public.

Much of what Murdoch said was true. Haig and others at GHQ couldn't see the Australians as allies fighting alongside them; they saw them as another arm of the British army, like the Irish and the Scots. GHQ wanted the Australians to conform, to adopt English forms and bring in the death penalty for desertion. Haig in his diary entries never seemed to accept that these volunteers had made an exceptional sacrifice. Haig was five hours from Charing Cross Station, from his wife, Doris, and their children. Some of the Australians had not been home for three years. They were months away from Australia, and they would only be sent home if they were seriously wounded or so ill as to be of no further use. Haig simply assumed it was their *duty* to be there – for him – and that they came from a colony, rather than a new nation with aspirations of its own. Communiqués often referred to Australians, Canadians and New Zealanders as 'British' troops. Haig didn't much understand Australians. A few months into 1918 he told his wife the Australians had been put in convalescent camps of their own 'because they were giving so much trouble when along with our men and put such revolutionary ideas into their heads'.

Hughes told the British authorities that all Australian troops should be grouped together under Birdwood. The staff officers should be Australians. Murdoch spoke to Haig. The field-marshal, he said, thought a corps of five divisions would be unwieldy. Murdoch felt that Haig favoured Monash as the corps commander. Murdoch told Hughes that White would be more acceptable than Monash. He also belittled Monash in a letter to Hughes.

Birdwood and White now put up a proposal that was prompted by their need for reinforcements. The 4th Division should be used as a depot division. There would be only four fighting divisions in the new corps. Haig on November 1 accepted the idea. The Australian Corps was a reality. Haig also agreed that no British officers would in future be appointed to Australian staffs. British officers still serving with the Australians would be gradually taken back into the British army, including the divisional commanders Walker and Smyth. Monash said goodbye to Godley. 'I served him loyally and faithfully for nearly three years and he has done nothing for me that he could not help doing.'

Birdwood didn't really want to break up the 4th Division. It was regarded as the depot division for just a few weeks, then used as a fighting force again to plug holes in the British line. Hughes and Murdoch thus had what they had wanted all along: five divisions under Birdwood.

But Birdwood's numbers were too low. The 3rd Division was down to about 8500 men, the 4th to roughly 9700. The Australians had been sent to the now quiet Messines sector. The troops played football, wearing guernseys in the colours of their brigades and battalions. One battalion started a newspaper and a debating society. And the wounded men came back, along with whatever reinforcements could be found in England, swelling most of the divisions by several thousand men. But what the corps needed was fresh men, not just those who had been wounded or whose nerves had been undone by years of fighting. As Bean put it, the Australian Corps was feeding upon itself.

PART THREE: 1918

Do you think Fitzroy'll beat Carlton on Saturday?
– One Australian to another during a lull in the
battle for Hamel.

35

Ludendorff's gamble

Mons, the old cloth-weaving town now well behind the Belgian front, was where the war began for the tiny British Expeditionary Force of 1914. The retreat to the downlands of the Somme and the sticky flats of Ypres began here. British hopes that the war would be short ended here. Now, in November, 1917, as the Australians prepared to move into the quiet Messines sector after the agonies of Passchendaele, Ludendorff came to Mons to work up his plans for 1918. Hindenburg, his superior, stayed home. Hindenburg and Ludendorff had an interesting working relationship. Ludendorff did most of the work. Hindenburg took any credit that was going, read novels and attended to his image as a national hero. Hindenburg was serene; Ludendorff often became ratty. Those close to him had long ago learned to identify the symptoms. The chins trembled like jelly, the face flushed red and, at dinner, Ludendorff screwed pieces of bread into tight balls with his fingers.

The Kaiser did not go to Mons either. He was not running the country; people merely thought he was. Wilhelm still swaggered about with a chest heavy with medals; in private he was no longer sure of himself. He had never recovered from the failure of the Schlieffen Plan in 1914, which had been Germany's only

537

comprehensive scheme for winning the war. Hindenburg and Ludendorff were running the country, which meant that Ludendorff was, and this was a risk, because Ludendorff knew little of diplomacy or economics. Ludendorff's main concern was Germany's military reputation. At this time he probably didn't believe Germany could win in the west. He certainly believed that if Germany could take ground in the next few months, it would be in a stronger negotiating position in any peace talks.

If Ludendorff didn't much understand human nature or grand strategy, he was a good tactician. He knew that 1918 was going to be about numbers. In the short term the numbers were with him. The war against Russia had been won. Dozens of German divisions were being moved to the west. In the long term the numbers were against Ludendorff. The Americans were coming, if slowly. Perhaps one million would land in France in 1918; there would be several more million behind them. All Germany could expect in the way of reinforcements was the annual intake of youths reaching military age. Ludendorff had already decided that he would go on the offensive in the west. What he had to decide at Mons was where.

The western front had hardly changed in 1917, despite all the killing. The British had made small gains, about five miles in each case, at Arras and Passchendaele. They had done most of the attacking; the French army was still recovering from its mutinies. The big changes in the war had been elsewhere. Russia was out and Rumania was beaten. Italy was faltering after Caporetto. But Germany's allies were not doing well either. The army of Austria-Hungary had needed rescuing since the first week of the war. In Palestine the Ottoman army was on the run from Allenby but, despite what Lloyd George thought, what happened there didn't matter much. And Germany had troubles at home. The blockade was hurting more every month. People were starving and freezing in the cities; infant mortality was rising and strikes were becoming more common now that the Bolsheviks had come to power in Russia. Unrestricted submarine warfare, Germany's answer to the blockade, had failed; indeed it had brought the United States into the conflict. This was the number that was running around in Ludendorff's head, one million Americans, fresh and keen.

For the moment Ludendorff had numerical superiority on the western front. If he was to go on the offensive, he had to do so as soon as the ground dried in the early spring. Towards the end of the fight for Passchendaele Ridge the Germans had been outnumbered on the western front by about 175 divisions to 150. By March 20, 1918, the start of the northern spring, the Germans, having brought troops back from the east and from Italy, would outnumber the allies by about 190 divisions to 170. And the allied figure was misleading. It included American divisions that were unready to be thrown into the line and two Portuguese divisions that were low in numbers and lower again in spirit.

Haig's fifty-seven divisions included the ten from the dominions: five from Australia, four from Canada and one from New Zealand. All of these had taken heavy casualties at Passchendaele. Haig's forty-seven divisions from the British Isles were well under strength. It had been another shocking year for casualties: Haig's armies had lost about 850,000 men. The Australians had lost 55,000, which was equivalent to about half the number of troops they kept in the frontline.

HAIG STILL WANTED to attack in 1918, just as soon as the ground dried. Early in January he attended a meeting of the War Cabinet. 'All were most friendly to me,' he wrote. He told the Cabinet that the next four months would be 'the critical period' of the war. He thought the Germans might attack. The best defence, he believed, would be to continue his offensive in Flanders.

But he couldn't. He didn't have the numbers and he wasn't going to get them. Cabinet wasn't nearly as 'friendly' as he assumed. Lloyd George believed in him even less after the false dawn at Cambrai. The Prime Minister lacked the nerve to sack Haig or to dictate strategy to him; instead he was trying a new tactic, characteristically sly. From late in 1917 he had denied Haig reinforcements from England. Lloyd George might have given

Haig reasonable reinforcements – on the condition that Haig stand on the defensive until more American troops arrived and the numbers swung back in the allies' favour. But that would have required a confrontation, a spelling out of responsibilities. Instead Lloyd George simply turned off the tap. Churchill, back as Minister for Munitions, had been appalled by the slaughters on the Somme and during Passchendaele, yet he now urged Lloyd George to send reinforcements to Haig, simply so that he might *defend* the line he held. And that line had grown longer: Lloyd George had agreed to a French request for the British to take over another twenty-five miles of front at the southern end of their line.

At the start of 1918 there were more than 640,000 troops in England who were fit for immediate service in France. Haig, typically, wanted them all, but 150,000 would have restored his divisions to reasonable strength. Lloyd George kept them home. He was also plotting to remove Robertson. Haig, always implacable, somehow intimidated the Prime Minister; Robertson, his nerves frayed, didn't.

AFTER PASSCHENDAELE THE Australians were in and out of the line in Flanders and northern France. There were gas attacks and bombing raids from the air. Mostly, though, both sides drew breath as snow lay on the ground. Many Australians wondered when they were going home. Private Walter Adcock received a letter from home after Christmas and began thinking about his 'real home'. 'I felt I had made a horrible mistake by coming to this hell on earth,' he wrote. 'It is impossible for me to ever be the same, physically, after all this gas . . . my pals say this is another Hundred Years' War.' He cheered himself up by taking up golf, fashioning a club from a branch and using a bully beef tin as a ball. Others played football in the mud. The 24th Battalion played another Victorian battalion behind the front at Messines and lost for the first time in fifty-two games. Betting was involved.

Before Christmas the Gallipoli veterans sewed a brass 'A' (for Anzac) on their unit colour patches. Lieutentant Cyril Lawrence found himself in a French village and couldn't adapt. 'It is too quiet, after the awful roar of the guns, to sleep.' Early in the New Year he was awarded the Military Cross for his work at Broodseinde. The much-decorated Lieutenant Percy Lay had been a drover. He was astonished by market day in a French village behind Armentières. 'It was the funniest collection of cows, calves, pigs, fowls and people that I think I have ever seen.'

John Monash was resting behind Messines. He did some pencil sketching, read a volume of O. Henry's stories and took leave in London, where he enjoyed strolling about in a grey tweed suit. 'It was quite pleasant to be jostled and edged into the gutter by crowds of young second lieutenants and Tommies.' On New Year's Day he found he had been made a Knight Commander of the Bath and wrote a 'monstrously egotistical' letter to his wife, Vic. He might, he speculated, become vice-chancellor or chancellor of Melbourne University. He might even be made Governor of Victoria. Vic had written to him: 'My darling. Best love wonderful man. What a genius you are. Jewish community gone mad, off their heads. KCB!!! I don't think that I have anything left to wish for as a title and to dine at Government House were both my greatest ambitions.'

Around this time Private Paul Johanessen was in the line at Warneton, near Armentières, 'and it rained very hard so we were swamped out and so was Fritz. There we were sitting on the parapet all day talking to the Squids and swapping cigarettes.'

Lieutenant Joe Maxwell was on patrol in no-man's land at Ploegsteert Wood just before Christmas. 'Three Nuns', the name of the English pipe tobacco, was the password that night. As Maxwell came within the Australian wire he heard the nervous challenge of the sentry.

'Three Nuns,' Maxwell shouted back. A bullet fizzed past his ear.

'You stupid cow!' Maxwell yelled. 'Didn't you hear me answer "Three Nuns"?'

'I'm sorry, sir,' the sentry stuttered. 'I thought you said "Three Huns".'

Maxwell trudged through snow to attend midnight Mass in a French village. It was the first time he had entered a church since leaving Australia. Over the boom of the distant guns the old priest spoke on the text 'God so loved the world that He gave His only begotten Son'. Maxwell's mind wandered off. He thought of the Seabrook brothers who had been killed by the same shell a few months earlier. 'It seemed almost a travesty on commonsense to reflect on the love of man for man at Christmas with the most civilised nations of the earth using every means that the human brain could devise to tear one another limb from limb.'

The Christmas of 1917 was bleaker for civilians than the one before. The price of meat in Britain had been fixed back in September. Many foodstuffs were rationed. Sugar cards appeared in the New Year. In Germany, Caroline Cooper, the Adelaide woman living in Leipzig, wrote that people were drinking tea made of elder flowers and strawberry leaves. An elephant at the Leipzig zoo was fading for lack of food. It was killed and sold as elephant steaks at a well-known hotel. In Paris people brought along their own sugar and milk when going out for a meal.

In Australia, Archbishop Mannix spent Christmas at the Victorian seaside resort of Lorne. The *Bulletin* reported him 'dipping his toes in the ocean so kindly kept free of submarines by the brutal British'.

IN DENYING HAIG reinforcements, Lloyd George was playing at something he little understood, military strategy. In making his plans at Mons, Ludendorff was straying into fields he didn't understand at all, foreign affairs and the human condition. The idea behind his coming offensive, he later explained, was to 'make the enemy inclined to peace by fighting'. Did he really think that one German victory would bring Clemenceau and Lloyd George scurrying to a peace conference? Both knew why they were fighting, and it was not to have Germany bully its way into ownership of large tracts of France and Belgium. Tactics were Ludendorff's *metier*. As his wife was to write: 'Ludendorff never possessed any knowledge of human nature.'

Hindenburg saw a different virtue in the spring offensive. His thinking was as muddled as Ludendorff's. Hindenburg thought a victory would lift morale at home, raise the people above their 'sullen brooding'. Hindenburg didn't know much about people either. Those in Berlin and Munich were supposed to look at their sickly children, their cold hearths, the turnips on the dinner table, the photograph of the dead son on the mantelpiece, and take heart that Hindenburg had made a lunge for Paris or the Channel ports. Hindenburg and Ludendorff, one suspects, thought a victory would create a momentum of its own. There didn't seem to be much more to their strategy than that.

When it came to tactics Ludendorff was much cleverer. Unlike Haig at the Somme and Passchendaele, he knew how he would break through. The problem was where to strike, and Ludendorff didn't find all of the answers at Mons. Ludendorff rejected Verdun as a battleground. Even if the Germans succeeded there, the British forces to the north would be largely untouched, the blockade would continue and Britain and the United States would still constitute a formidable alliance. No, Ludendorff decided, 'we must beat the British'. If he did that, he could then turn on Paris.

Ludendorff decided late in January on a scheme called 'Michael'. The Germans would attack on a long front between St Quentin in the south and Arras in the north, across the old Somme battlefield. The original idea was not, as some thought, to go for Amiens and then on to the coast. Having broken through, the Germans would turn right and push the British north, presumably all the way to the Channel ports. It was rather like Haig's plan for the Somme in 1916 in reverse. But the German attack was much more ambitious: the front was to be about fifty miles, around three times longer than Haig's of 1916. Ludendorff was going to direct the battle himself. He set up an advanced headquarters behind Cambrai. He wanted to be where he could easily reach the front by car. The attack would open on March 21.

Ludendorff told the Kaiser in mid-February: 'We must not imagine that this offensive will be like those in Galicia or Italy; it will be an immense struggle that will begin at one point, continue at another, and take a long time; it is difficult, but it will be victorious . . .'

Ludendorff named the spring offensive on all fronts *Die Kaiserschlacht*, 'the Kaiser's battle'.

Wilhelm must have been impressed. The day before the battle began he turned up with his entourage at Ludendorff's headquarters.

WHEN IT CAME to the evolution of tactics, the Germans were less hidebound than the British and more trusting of the good sense of their lower ranks. Three men were to greatly influence the style of the German attack.

One was General Oskar von Hutier, a Prussian who had been fighting on the eastern front and was credited as the first to use infiltration tactics, or, as the German army called them, 'Hutier tactics'. At Riga, the last big offensive in the war against Russia, Hutier had fought what was seen as the template for 'breakthrough' battles.

His artillery adviser at Riga had been Georg Bruchmüller, a middle-aged colonel who had been brought back from the retired list and was spoken of as a genius when it came to organising firepower. It was said that troops went forward with more confidence when it was known that Bruchmüller had devised the fire plan. Now Bruchmüller was on the western front, alongside Hutier again, with the greatest array of artillery in history, more than 6400 guns, or four times as many as the British used on the opening day of the Somme. Bruchmüller believed in surprise bombardments, short and terrible, with no registration of targets beforehand. He used combinations of shells that he had thought out carefully and was a strong believer in gas. For the *Kaiserschlacht* he would use a combination of high explosive and phosgene gas during the preliminary bombardment. For his counter-battery fire he would use four gas shells to every one of high explosive. Bruchmüller also wanted his bombardment to reach deep into the British lines, to assembly areas and crossroads. The idea was to create chaos behind the front. Like Napoleon, Bruchmüller understood the terror effect of artillery fire. He wanted to create the conditions for infantrymen to break through and keep going, all the time coming on a confused enemy peering at them through the mad lens of a gas mask. But Bruchmüller's 'genius' and his surprise bombardment of only five hours would not, of itself, carry the infantry deep into the enemy positions. Not, that is, if the Germans used the same techniques of attack, rigid and almost bureaucratic, that the British had been employing for most of the past three years. Which brings us to our third man of influence in the planning of the *Kaiserschlacht*.

Captain Hermann Geyer, a Bavarian, had written a manual titled *The Attack in Position Warfare*. Geyer stressed that infantry was not to be given a fixed objective. Nor did it need to go forward in straight lines that looked good on the pin-pocked maps back at headquarters. There was no demand for a continuous frontline. Geyer was about infiltration, dozens of spears stabbing into the British lines, some deeper than others, but all pushing relentlessly forward. Everything was fluid. These tactics, or variations on them, had been tested at Riga and Cambrai.

The infantrymen of the first wave, the storm troops, were simply told to go forward as far and as fast as they could behind a creeping barrage. They were not to worry about their flanks: if these were 'in the air', it didn't matter. If the storm troops hit points of strong resistance, they were to go around them. The crucial thing was that they kept rushing forward, all the way to the British artillery lines. This was about momentum. Once the battle opened the decisions would be made not by staff officers but by colonels and captains on the ground.

Normal infantry regiments would follow the storm troops and bring up heavier armaments: mortars, machine guns and field artillery pieces. These 'battle groups' would knock out the British strong points left by the storm troops. Behind the battle groups would come another wave of conventional infantry. Here was the genesis of a form of warfare that would eventually become known as *blitzkrieg*, with one element missing. The Germans would use only nine tanks, five of them captured British machines and four that had been knocked up by a German factory. Tanks didn't impress Ludendorff.

The Germans would attack with three armies: seventy divisions, some one million men. To the north was General Otto von Below's 17th Army. Below, a Prussian, had fought on the eastern front and in the Balkans. He had led an Austro–German army to victory at Caporetto. He was going for Bapaume, which had been Haig's original objective in the first Somme battle. South of him was General Georg von der Marwitz's 2nd Army. Marwitz, a Prussian cavalryman, had also fought on the eastern front, returning to the west late in 1916. His greatest success had been the counter-attack at Cambrai. He was going for Péronne.

Below and Marwitz were under the control of Prince Rupprecht's army group. Once they had reached Bapaume and Péronne respectively they were to turn right and push the British north. Their rear would be protected by von Hutier's 18th Army, which was to smash through the British lines in front of St Quentin and take the town of Ham, then become a flank guard for the two northern armies. Hutier was attacking the softest part of the British line. He was under the control of the army group commanded by Crown Prince Wilhelm, the Kaiser's son. The split command for the offensive suited Ludendorff: he could assume overall command. It also suited the Kaiser: if there was glory to be had, 'Little Willie' gave the Hohenzollerns a stake in it.

LLOYD GEORGE HAD a constituency. If he moved in rarified circles and played power games with the patricians, he was still very much a man of the people. He understood them and they warmed to him. Haig had a constituency too, narrow but powerful. It included the King, much of the military establishment, several Cabinet members (notably Lord Derby, the War Minister) and sundry newspaper proprietors, editors and war correspondents.

'Wully' Robertson, the Chief of the Imperial General Staff, didn't have a constituency. He had come from the same place in society as Lloyd George. He was the ranker who had become a general, but, unlike the Prime Minister, he had forgotten where he came from and was not altogether accepted for what he wanted to be. Haig sometimes treated him like an errand boy. Robertson was stuck between

Lloyd George and Haig and pushed and shoved by both. Lloyd George didn't like his gruffness, his disdain for politicians and 'civilians'. Haig, one suspects, had been disappointed by Robertson's qualified enthusiasm for the Passchendaele campaign. Robertson was an easy man to topple and Lloyd George had been manoeuvring for months to do so. The Supreme War Council gave him this opportunity.

The council had been set up the previous November after the Italian debacle at Caporetto and sounded grander than it was. It sat at Versailles and consisted of representatives of Britain, France, the United States and Italy. The idea was to try to bring some unity to the allied war effort, but the council had no executive power. Part of its appeal to Lloyd George was that it gave him a source of advice independent of Robertson and Haig. General Sir Henry Wilson, who had all the social skills Haig and Robertson lacked, was Britain's military representative on the council.

In January, 1918, the Supreme War Council suggested the creation of an allied reserve for the western and Italian fronts. A council committee, chaired by France's General Ferdinand Foch, would say where and when the reserve would be used. As Haig noted, this made Foch something of a generalissimo; the council suddenly had executive powers. Haig and Robertson were offended by the idea of handing over British troops to Foch and the council, but Haig was less troubled than Robertson. He knew he could truthfully say he didn't have any reserves to hand over, as could his French equivalent, Pétain. Robertson's anger was obvious to all at Versailles.

The rift between Robertson and Lloyd George widened when the pair returned to London. Both drifted towards paranoia. Robertson saw the British army falling into the arms of 'foreigners'. The Prime Minister saw a conspiracy. His political enemies, using Robertson as their point man, were trying to overthrow his government and set up something close to a military dictatorship – or at least that's the way he told it in his memoirs. There is no evidence of such a plot – nothing. Lloyd George was in an unusually strong position. There was no obvious alternative prime minister. Haig, though not nearly as 'straight' as he claimed to be, accepted the constitutional principle that he was responsible to the elected leaders.

Lloyd George decided to replace Robertson with Wilson. It would be a simple swap: Robertson would replace Wilson at the Supreme War Council. Lloyd George summoned Haig from France and told him what he intended to do. Haig did not speak up for Robertson. Haig went to see Robertson and told him 'it was his *duty* to go to Versailles or anywhere else if the Government wished it'. Haig next went to Buckingham Palace, where he told the King to insist on Robertson going to Versailles. Haig then returned to France. Robertson had been faithful to Haig, and Haig had deserted him. That was Haig's way. He believed in himself most of all. Comrades were expendable. Loyalty was supposed to flow to him, not the other way. He didn't see himself as selfish: it was simply that he was a man of destiny and others weren't.

Robertson kept fighting and had to be sacked. Wilson took over. He would not see Haig as Robertson had. A few months later Wilson would write in his diary: 'I have never seen him [Haig] so stupid and unaccommodating. He is a remarkably stupid, narrow, prejudiced, insular person.'

Derby had offered his resignation during the Robertson affair 'out of loyalty to the men with whom he had worked at the War Office'. Derby was forever making such gestures. He too was loyal to Haig but the field-marshal didn't take him seriously. A few weeks earlier Haig had written to his wife from France: 'D. is a very weak-minded fellow I am afraid, and, like the feather pillow, bears the marks of the last person who has sat on him!'

THE AUSTRALIANS MOVED from rest areas to garrisoning the front-line in February and March. The front was mostly quiet but the Germans seemed to be sending over more gas shells. In early February one battalion near Warneton suffered six or seven bombardments of mustard gas, one of them lasting fourteen hours. More than 260 men, one-third of the battalion's strength, became casualties. Others coughed for days but stayed at the front.

Corporal Arthur Thomas was with a party laying cables by moonlight in March when he heard the shriek of shells. Two sniffs and Thomas knew it was mustard gas. He pulled on his mask. 'We have a lot of new men & they completely lost their heads . . .' Some tore their masks off 'so I had to risk everything & yell out orders & help the poor excited humanity about me, of course I got a gut full but I didn't give a damn . . .' He led the gasping men back to a hospital, where they were given a drink of ammonia, which was supposed to help. Two of the men died – 'weak hearts, you see'. In the old days, he wrote home, warriors fought each other like men, unaided by 'loathsome sneaks who work in laboratories. GAS! GAS! GAS! How I hate it . . .'

Thomas came to thinking about himself in the same letter: '. . . here I am forty years old on May 12th & still going strong & I haven't nursed myself at all, tis a damn shame that I am childless . . .'

The Australians began to hear rumours of a coming German attack. Private Whinfield, a stretcher-bearer, stayed out late dining in February and was marked absent without leave, but 'we didn't lose any sleep . . . Our Lieut. Alladyce got the crime wiped out.' Next day he wrote in his diary: 'The big German offensive is supposed to be imminent now.' The men talked about it in the hut that night. Two said that as soon as the offensive began they would bolt to the rear. Another declared the Australians came to do a job and must do it and said he'd shoot anyone who left his mates. Whinfield said nothing but thought 'lowly' of the two who wanted to bolt.

Lieutenant Joe Maxwell had heard whispers of German divisions and guns being moved to the west. German prisoners shook their heads knowingly and said: 'Wait 'till the spring offensive.' Harry Murray would have heard the same rumours. On March 7 the timber-getter was made a lieutenant-colonel and given command of the 4th Division's machine-gun battalion.

HAIG HAD BEEN attacking for all of the two years he had commanded on the western front. He hadn't thought too much about defence; now, returning to France after the Robertson affair, he had to. He knew the Germans were about to attack him.

Haig held 126 miles of front with around fifty-seven divisions.

The first priority of those divisions was to protect the Channel ports. Pétain held the rest of the front to Switzerland with around ninety-eight divisions. The first priority of these was to protect Paris. The British frontline, unlike that of the Germans, had not evolved with thoughts of defence in mind. In places the line was where it was simply because that was where an offensive had finished. Bullecourt and Passchendaele village were good examples of this. As the winter went on, and the German threat became more real, the British began to think about defence in depth.

They decided that the existing frontline would become an outpost line. They called it the 'forward zone', and it was there to hold up the advancing Germans. At a certain point the troops here could fall back. The main defences, called the 'battle zone', were 2000 to 3000 yards back, on ground more suited to defence. There were no fall-back provisions here: the battle zones, up to 3000-yards deep, had to be held. There was nothing much behind them, just camps, ammunition and stores dumps and, ultimately, the sea. There was supposed to be a third zone, called the corps line, but there wasn't time to do much work on this. Gough commanded the southernmost army and had much the largest front, more than forty miles. Haig gave him a dispensation: he could fall back beyond his battle zone until French and British reserves arrived to help him.

Haig's dispositions reflected his first priority, the Channel ports. From north to south they looked like this:

	Divisions	Length of front in miles
2nd Army	12	23
1st Army	14	33
3rd Army	14	28
5th Army	12+	42

The 2nd Army stood in front of the ports of Boulogne and Calais. The 1st Army front stretched south almost to Arras. Well behind it, near the coast, lay Haig's headquarters at Montreuil. The two armies that were to take the brunt of the *Kaiserschlacht*, General

Byng's 3rd and Gough's 5th, between them held seventy miles of front. Their twenty-six divisions were to be attacked by more than seventy German divisions. Byng, with twenty-eight miles of front, was reasonably placed, but Gough's forces were spread too thinly. The British had to be thin somewhere. The thinking went something like this: the front above Arras was roughly fifty miles from the coast and the ports that supplied Haig; the front at La Fere, close to Gough's southernmost point, was ninety miles from the sea. Haig couldn't lose the Channel ports, his link to home. Nor could he allow the Germans to break through around Arras: this would split his forces into two. If there was to be a soft spot, it had to be Gough's army in the south. Behind it, and also behind Byng's 3rd Army, lay the devastated Somme battlefield of 1916. And beyond that lay the important railhead at Amiens.

Gough didn't have time to build proper defences. His second line, the battle zone, was incomplete. His frontline was a series of outposts, manned in some cases by less than a dozen men. Just behind the front, before the battle zone, stood a series of forts built on ground suited to defence. But they were too far apart to be able to support each other, which meant storm troops could slip between them. Ludendorff's men made their preparations by night; Gough's men frantically dug holes in the ground by day.

Haig had responded to his shortage of men by proposing that the number of his divisions be reduced. If he could do away with fifteen divisions and spread their troops around his force, the divisions remaining would be roughly up to strength. There was an element of mischief in the proposal. What were the French going to say if their ally was suddenly fielding forty-two divisions instead of fifty-seven? The War Office eventually told Haig to keep all his divisions intact but to reduce the number of battalions in each. A British division normally contained three brigades, each of four battalions. Now, in most cases, each brigade would contain only three battalions. (The order did not apply to dominion divisions.) The reorganisation was complete by early March. Some thought Haig should disband his cavalry divisions and use them as infantry. Haig thought this heresy.

THE AMERICANS WERE not going to be much help. They now had seven divisions in France and these were huge by the standards of Britain and France, up to 28,000 men in each. But only one was ready to fight, and General Pershing, the commander of the American Expeditionary Force, didn't want to lend out formations piecemeal to Haig and Pétain. He wanted the Americans to fight as an independent entity. If this was mostly a matter of national pride, it was also wise. Haig seemed to think the English-speaking world owed him troops and that he, better than their own commanders, best knew how to use them.

They called the Americans 'doughboys' and no-one quite knew why. The Americans were like the Australians before Gallipoli and the New Army men before the Somme, full of cheer and hope, brows unfurrowed, bright-cheeked and wearing uniforms untainted by the dust of Verdun or the mud of Passchendaele. They had little in the way of equipment. Their government bought field guns from the French and .303 rifles from the British.

British instructors began to train the Americans behind the lines. The cult of the bayonet, like the spirit of cavalry, would not die. An eighteen-year-old doughboy recalled his instructions from a Cockney: 'He would calmly advise the Yanks to shove a bayonet only a "hinch" into a man's throat, two "hinches" into his kidneys, or a couple of "hinches" into his "art". If you git the blade too deep in 'is ribs, you will 'ave difficulty in gittin' it out, and the next Boche will git you.' Another instructor offered this advice: 'If the blighter's down – stick 'im. If he puts 'is 'ands hup – stick 'im. If 'e turns 'is back – stick 'im.'

PRIVATE LYALL HOWARD of the 3rd Australian Division's pioneer battalion was in London on leave in March. He wrote in his tiny diary: 'Met Dad at WC Club at night while air raid on London.' This was a long essay for Howard. His diary, smaller than his hand, is a series of laconic entries and understatements: 'Inoculated again', 'First day in trenches', 'Shoved in old barn'. When his best friend was killed he would write: 'Will wounded and dies.'

Seven months before the London meeting with his father Howard had written two words: 'Slightly gassed.' He was sent to the casualty-clearing station at Trois Arbres (where Phillip Schuler had died), then spent two-and-a-half months in hospitals and convalescent homes. Bronchitis and skin rashes would trouble him for the rest of his life.

Howard, an apprentice engineer at a sugar factory in northern New South Wales, had enlisted as a nineteen-year-old in 1916 after previously being rejected for being too short. His father, Walter, was in his early forties. Lyall was the eldest of Walter's nine children. Walter, a private in the 5th Division, was training in England and would not go to France for several months. Walter had enlisted after the two conscription referendums had failed. He may have lied about his age.

LUDENDORFF PUT HIS faith in Bruchmüller, the artilleryman, and Geyer, the infantry tactician; Haig put his faith in the Old Testament. In late February he wrote to Lady Haig, who was heavily pregnant: 'I must say that I feel quite confident, and so do my troops. Personally, I feel in the words of 2nd Chronicles, XX Chap., that it is "God's battle" and I am not dismayed by the numbers of the enemy.' In the same letter he said the Canadian soldiers were smart and clean, much more so than the Australians. 'I put this down to Birdwood, who, instead of facing the problem, has gone in for the easier way of saying everything is perfect and making himself as popular as possible.'

In London in mid-March the field-marshal saw Lloyd George and Bonar Law. He said they tried to make him say the Germans would not attack. He said he told them the Germans seemed 'drunk with their success in Russia and the Middle East'; they might attempt anything. 'In any case we must be prepared to meet *a very strong attack indeed on a 50 mile front, and for this drafts are urgently required.*'

Back in France a few days later Haig saw reports on the interrogation of prisoners. These said the Germans were planning to attack around March 20 or 21.

Lady Haig had delivered a son, their first, a few days before the field-marshal had returned to France. Haig was fifty-six. For once his reserve fell away. He embraced the doctor and kissed him on both cheeks. 'Like a damned foreigner!' the doctor said.

Haig now wrote to Lady Haig from France. The enemy was rather threatening. It might be better for him to delay coming over to see her for a week. He would come on the 29th. The cook was making soup for her; he would send it over by King's Messenger. He lapsed into fantasy. 'Everyone is in good spirits and only anxious that the enemy should attack.' Then back to reality. 'And if he did attack on Saturday [March 21], and I was in England, it might lead to "talk".'

Haig was forty miles behind the front, fawned on by an entourage of staff officers. They were the 'everyone' who was in 'good spirits'. For what he knew about the mood of the men at the front Haig might just as well have been in London.

ROBERT GRAVES, THE poet and novelist, wrote that the world of trench stalemate was a sausage machine. It was fed with live men, churned out corpses and remained firmly screwed in place. As Ludendorff prepared to launch Operation Michael on March 21, he was thinking of nothing less than the unscrewing of the sausage machine. He was going to restore movement to the battlefield. There would still be killing, just as much as before, maybe more, but if he had his way, the sausage machine would become a mobile abattoir.

36

Bruchmüller's orchestra

Winston Churchill, now Minister for Munitions but not quite forgiven for Gallipoli, happened to be in France when Operation Michael opened at 4.40 on the foggy morning of March 21. All his adult life Churchill had been a man of Bohemian habits. He napped when others worked. He worked at 1 am when others slept. If the ideas and words kept coming, he went on until dawn, sipping at brandy as his sentences, crisp and clean, marched into the night. On the night of March 20 he was staying with his old friend Henry Tudor, a divisional commander in Gough's army, in the ruins of Nurlu, ten miles north of Péronne.

Churchill awakened a little after 4 am. He lay musing for perhaps half-an-hour. Then he heard Ludendorff's 6600 guns, the heaviest barrage in the history of warfare.

> . . . the silence was broken by six or seven very loud and very heavy explosions several miles away . . . And then, exactly as a pianist runs his hands across the keyboard from treble to bass, there rose in less than one minute the most tremendous cannonade I shall ever hear . . . through the chinks in the carefully papered window the flame of the bombardment lit like flickering firelight my tiny cabin.

The German advance, March, 1918

North Sea

HOLLAND

GREAT BRITAIN

Strait of Dover

Ostend
Bruges
Antwerp
Nieuport
Dunkirk
Calais
Dixmude
Ghent
Demer River
4 GER
ARMIN
Roulers
Maastricht
2 BEL
ALBERT
Ypres
Passchendaele
Brussels
St Omer
2 UK
PLUMER
Liège
Boulogne
Hazebrouck
Lille
Mense River
Neuve
Chapelle
6 GER
QUAST
GER
RUPPRECHT
1 UK
HORNE
Loos
Vimy
Mons
BELGIUM
GHQ
HAIG
Arras
17 GER
O. BELOW
Maubeuge
Bastogne
Abbeville
Doullens
Cambrai
Le Cateau
Dieppe
3 UK
BYNG
Bapaume
Albert
Somme River
2 GER
MARWITZ
Neufchâteau
Ardennes Forest
Amiens
Péronne
18 GER
HUTIER
GER
CROWN PRINCE
Sedan
Meuse R.
Villers-
Bretonneux
St Quentin
5 UK
GOUGH
7 GER
BOEHN
1 GER
F. BELOW
Argonne Forest
Rouen
Compiègne
Soissons
3 GER
EINEM
5 GER
GALLWITZ
Reims
Verdun
6 FR
DUCHESNE
5 FR
MICHELER
Troyon
Paris
Château
Thierry
Epernay
Chalons
4 FR
GOURAUD
2 FR
HIRSCHAUER
St Gond Marshes
FRANCE
Seine River
Oise River
River

German frontline
Allied frontline
German gains
March 21–April 4

SCALE
0   30 miles
0   50 kilometres

N
W   E
S

Churchill went outside. 'This is *it*,' Tudor said. He had ordered all his batteries to open up. Churchill could see the frontline for miles.

> It swept around us in a wide curve of red leaping flame stretching to the north far along the front of the Third Army, as well as of the Fifth Army on the south, and quite unending in either direction. There were still two hours to daylight, and the enormous explosions of the shells upon our trenches seemed almost to touch each other, with hardly an interval in space or time. Among the bursting shells there rose at intervals, but almost continually, the much larger flames of exploding magazines. The weight and intensity of the bombardment surpassed anything which anyone had ever known before.

Daylight came. Mushroom-headed clouds rose above exploding British dumps. At 10 am Churchill left for Péronne. Tudor held his frontline, then had to retreat when the divisions either side of him gave way.

HAIG WAS NOT a man of Bohemian habits. Bohemians were foreigners and not to be trusted. Haig's life was built around order. Most of the time his daily timetable was as rigid as *Field Service Regulations*. At 8.25 each morning Haig's bedroom door opened at his château outside Montreuil and he walked downstairs. In the hall he would stop in front of the barometer and tap it. He then walked for four minutes in the garden before returning for breakfast at exactly 8.30. At 9 he went to his study and worked for two to two-and-a-half hours. Lunch was at 1 pm. If he visited an army or corps headquarters by car, he would arrange for a groom to bring up his horse so that he could ride the last three or four miles back to the château. If he didn't leave Montreuil for the day, he rode in the afternoon, accompanied by an escort from the 17th Lancers. On the return journey he would walk the last three miles back to the château. He would then bathe, do his physical exercises and change into slacks, working at his desk until dinner at 8 pm.

He then returned to his room and worked until 10.45, when he always rang the bell for his private secretary, Sir Philip Sassoon. When Sassoon appeared Haig always said: 'Philip – not in bed yet?'

Haig's diary for March 21 begins: 'Before 8 am General Lawrence came to my room while I was dressing to tell me that the German attack had begun.' More than three hours after Churchill, Haig had discovered that the Germans had launched a massive assault. His staff must have known about the attack shortly after it began. They must have realised it was nothing less than a crisis. But no-one woke up 'the Chief'.

Haig came to the event three hours late, and the rest of his diary entry suggests he never came close to understanding what had happened on the battlefield that day.

AUSTRALIAN CORPS HEADQUARTERS first heard of the German attack at 9.59 am. White was in charge. Birdwood was on leave in England; Monash, who would normally take over in Birdwood's absence, was on leave on the Riviera and reading George Bernard Shaw. White was apparently told that GHQ considered the situation 'satisfactory', which squares with Haig's diary entries. Communiqués published in Britain took the same line. Bean said the public realised only with difficulty that the great battle of the war had begun. What was happening became clear to English newspaper readers in the next few days when they recognised the names of villages. Weren't they the villages 'we' had taken in 1916 and early 1917? Weren't they well behind 'our' frontline?

Birdwood returned by aircraft. This was thought adventurous: generals and politicians (with the exception of that irrepressible adventurer Churchill) invariably crossed by sea. Monash arrived back on March 25 after a thirty-two-hour journey. His division had first been told to move to Ypres, then ordered the other way, towards the Somme. Sinclair-MacLagan's 4th Division was also sent south. The 5th Division was sent south to near Doullens, before marching to Corbie on the River Somme. All the Australians were talking about the electrifying news from the south. The

Germans were within five miles of Pozières. Many Australians thought Pozières their cruellest battle. They could not conceive that the Germans might now take it back.

Bridadier-General Walter McNicoll, who commanded Monash's 10th Brigade, called his officers around him before the move south and pulled out a map. According to a battalion historian, he told the officers that Gough's army had been driven back and was retreating everywhere, that the British and French armies were in danger of being separated and that a long-range gun was shelling Paris. McNicoll told them that they would be in the battle of their lives 'as the fate of the war now hung in the balance'.

GENERAL GOUGH CLEARLY didn't think the fate of the war hung in the balance when he was awakened by the drumfire of artillery some time after 4.40 on the morning of March 21. He was at his headquarters at Nesle, about fifteen miles behind the front. He wrote afterwards that the barrage was 'so sustained and steady that it at once gave me the impression of some crushing, smashing power'. Gough was told that his entire front was being hit. That was the serious part: the *whole* front. It meant he could not move divisions from quiet spots to places where the Germans were threatening to break through. There were no quiet spots and all his reserves were forward.

What did Gough do? He went back to sleep for another hour, arose, had breakfast, then began to deal with the worst crisis of his military life. Four days earlier, when just about every private in his army knew the Germans were about to attack, Gough had taken the Sunday off and ridden one of his horses to victory in a showjumping competition.

There were two reserve divisions under Haig's control behind Gough's front. Gough rang GHQ and was immediately given them. He spoke to General Davidson, the head of the Operations Section. The possibility is that Gough did not talk directly to Haig at any time throughout the day or night. Haig seldom used the telephone himself. According to Charteris, his long-time chief of intelligence,

Haig believed that 'conversations were inaccurate and liable to be distorted over the telephone, and that the agency of a third person using the telephone on his behalf ensured greater care and accuracy'. This may have been a windy way of saying that the field-marshal was often inarticulate.

Gough told Davidson he needed more than two divisions. He wanted help from the two armies at the northern end of the line that were not being attacked. Davidson said five divisions were being sent south, but the first four would go to Byng. Gough could not expect any help from the north for three days. The implication was clear enough. GHQ had to protect the Channel ports; Gough was in the wrong place. That night Gough spoke to General Lawrence, Haig's chief-of-staff. Gough wrote afterwards that Lawrence 'did not seem to grasp the seriousness of the situation' and thought the Germans 'would not come on again the next day'.

BRUCHMÜLLER HAD ARRANGED his barrage like the conductor of a huge orchestra. Instead of woodwinds, brass, percussion and strings, he had heavies, mortars, field guns and the German staple, the 5.9-inch howitzer; he had high explosive, shrapnel and gas, lots of gas: chlorine, phosgene, lachrymatory and mustard. Sometimes Bruchmüller played fortissimo and sometimes diminuendo, back and forth across the British line, from a front trench to a canteen in the back areas, and even as far as Péronne, more than ten miles behind the front. The gas shells exploded with a *pop* and the high explosive with a roar. The howitzers lifted off the front positions, then, just when the stunned Tommies thought they had received a respite, returned again. In the crescendo, the last five minutes before the German infantry began its advance, all the howitzers fired on the front trenches. It was a complex score and there were limits to what it could do. It was to last only five hours and was spread over a fifty-mile front. The one thing it did achieve was to cause confusion deep into the British lines, and the fog made everything worse. British infantrymen couldn't see the units on their flanks and this sometimes led to panic. Telephone cables were soon cut, even though they had been buried six feet in the earth. Men didn't know what was happening fifty yards from them.

A private who had been in a tent in the battle zone with sixteen others told Martin Middlebrook, author of *The Kaiser's Battle*, that the men had difficulty getting dressed when the bombardment began. They grabbed at their trousers, then found that they had one leg in theirs and the other in someone else's. Another private told Middlebrook that no-one could stand shelling for longer than three hours before going sleepy and numb. 'The first to be affected were the young ones who'd just come out. They would go to one of the older ones – older in service, that is – and maybe even cuddle up to him and start crying. An old soldier could be a great comfort to a young one.'

The German infantry, mostly storm troops, crossed no-man's land at 9.40 am and met little resistance. Except in the Flesquières Salient opposite Cambrai, which the Germans intended to pinch off rather than attack head on, the British front fell everywhere within an hour-and-a-half of the infantry assault. Here was something new in the Great War: an attack that was instantly successful on a front of fifty miles. And this one did not stall. The Germans surged on, leaving pockets of resistance here and there, and all the time causing confusion. They came out of the mist, spectres in dull grey that were suddenly on the flank of some battered British outpost then behind another one. The Germans put up partridges as they went forward.

The Germans followed their barrage and reached the British battle zone, the main defence, well before noon. Lieutenant-General Ivor Maxse's corps put up a strong fight opposite St Quentin but in many places the battle zone had been completely overrun by late afternoon. The Germans had broken right through on the fronts of three of Byng's divisions to the north. On Gough's front they had burst through the battle zone in front of Péronne. The southern end of Gough's line, which ended at the Oise River, was a disaster: the battle zone had been completely lost on the front of his four southernmost divisions. Some Germans paused for booty, food and alcohol first of all, and also boots and leather jerkins. A German artillery officer whose horse had been killed picked up an English thoroughbred that stood beside its dead rider.

British counter-attackers tried to go forward as wounded and unhinged comrades tried to fall back. Lieutenant-Colonel J. H. Dimmer commanded a battalion in one of Maxse's divisions. Dimmer had won the Victoria Cross at Ypres in 1914. He had grown up in the old British army and was loath to abandon its traditions. He decided he would lead a counter-attack himself – mounted. A junior officer suggested Dimmer dismount once he came under German fire. Dimmer refused and rode on with his groom riding alongside him. The watching troops couldn't believe what they were seeing: Don Quixote and his faithful servant tilting at machine guns. The Germans shot them down. Dimmer's horse bolted back through the British lines.

Mostly, though, the British troops were retreating. Men worried that they had no support on their flanks and pulled back. A chain reaction began all along the front. Some of the forts on Gough's front held on after they were surrounded. There were 168 men in the Manchester Hill redoubt, on a small hill on the St Quentin front, when the Germans surrounded it. The men were from a battalion that had originally been the 1st Manchester Pals. Their commander was Lieutenant-Colonel Wilfrith Elstob, a burly schoolmaster who had joined up as a private.

When the fog began to lift on March 21 the Manchesters could see Germans streaming past the fort, ignoring it. They were following their orders: keep going; leave the points of resistance to the troops following. Then the Manchesters saw British troops coming towards them in a column. They were prisoners from the battle zone.

The Germans attacked the fort at 3 pm. Elstob refused a call to surrender. Elstob told brigade headquarters the Germans were in the redoubt but the Manchesters would fight 'to the last'. He began to throw grenades and was shot. His adjutant tried to pull Elstob back into the trench. The adjutant was shot too. Both died and the Manchesters soon after surrendered. Elstob received a posthumous Victoria Cross.

Most of the forts were overrun or surrendered; the few that held out surrendered the next day. There were so many surrenders. At the end of the day the Germans had bagged their biggest haul of British prisoners in the Great War, 21,000. Many were taken to St Quentin where they were marched around the square for photographs that would appear in the German press. Crown Prince Wilhelm, the commander on the southern front and the eldest of the Kaiser's five sons, came forward to see the prisoners. 'He spoke to us in good English,' a British prisoner said, 'and congratulated us on putting up such a good show and on our excellent rapid fire.' The Crown Prince was pleased with himself. He was the lesser commander in Operation Michael but the biggest successes had come on his front, against the southern portion of Gough's line.

Gough went around his four corps commanders in the afternoon. He then made a decision that was out of character: he ordered his southern divisions to pull back even further to a better defensive position. Haig approved the decision.

On the night of March 21 the two generals did not know the extent of the crisis that was upon them, although they were looking at it from different vantage points. Gough knew his army could be pushed back much further; he may have been worried that he could be separated from the French to his south. Haig knew Gough was in trouble but also that the Channel ports were not yet under threat. The Channel ports were more important than Gough.

It had been the heaviest day's fighting ever on the western front. It was the day infantry tactics changed. The Germans had taken ninety-eight square miles: nineteen from Byng and nearly eighty from Gough. Included in this area were the ruins of forty-six villages. In the Somme battle of 1916 the British and French had also gained ninety-eight square miles – but it had taken them four-and-a-half months to do so and cost them around 600,000 casualties. And, because of Gough's decision to pull his southern divisions back and Byng's decision to abandon the Flesquières salient, the Germans were about to gain another forty square miles, another eleven villages, without any serious fighting.

There are no official figures for the first day's casualties.

Middlebrook estimates German losses at 10,851 dead, 28,778 wounded and 300 prisoners, a total of 39,929. And for the British: killed 7512, wounded 10,000, prisoners 21,000, a total of 38,512. These figures, though roughly equal in total, favoured the Germans. The British had lost 28,512 men as dead and prisoners. These men were out of the war. The comparable figure for the Germans was 11,151.

ERNST JUNGER HAD joined the German army straight from school. After the war he would write the best-selling memoir *The Storm of Steel*. On the first day of Operation Michael he was leading a company. He went forward into the fog, having first taken a long swig of whisky. He came upon a wounded British soldier. Junger pointed his revolver at the man's temple. The man pulled a photograph of a woman and children from his breast pocket. Junger lowered his revolver. He could not kill a man in front of his family.

37

The generalissimo

The Germans rolled westwards, pausing here and there to drink French wine and to disport themselves in top hats looted from shops. And Gough's army fought gamely here and there but mostly became a shambles. To the north Byng's army was also pushed back but held itself together rather better than Gough's. Byng had less front to defend and better positions to fall back upon. Haig, moreover, was more sympathetic to his troubles because Byng was nearer to the Channel ports. Haig remained confident, as was his way, and also because for the first few days of the offensive he didn't much know what was happening. Lloyd George in London also took several days to realise the extent of the emergency; when he did he held his nerve well. Pétain, the French commander, lived under a cloud of gloom that grew blacker each day. It did not help that on March 23 the Germans began shelling Paris with an eight-inch gun firing from seventy-five miles away. Plumer handed over to Haig the 3rd, 4th and 5th Australian divisions and the New Zealand Division.

These would be the chief reinforcements sent south. They headed for the Somme and gradually took up a line that started at Hébuterne, north of Albert, and ended near a town on the red-brown downland south of the Somme. The town had flourished on the spinning of wool but most of its citizens, apart from a few old people, had now fled. It had a church with a red tower, several elegant châteaux and a textile factory. From the gentle rises outside the town one could see the spire of the cathedral at Amiens, about ten miles away. The town was Villers-Bretonneux.

AS THE GERMANS pressed forward on the second day Haig wrote in his diary that 'our men are in great spirits. All speak of the wonderful targets they had to fire at yesterday.' The rest of the entry seemed to be at odds with this bravado. Haig had sent a message to Pétain, telling him that Gough was falling back behind the Somme, except at Péronne. Could Pétain relieve Gough's army up to Péronne? This was a long stretch of front and Pétain was worried that the Germans were about to strike in the Champagne, where the frontline ran nearest to Paris. He nevertheless offered help. General Marie Fayolle would bring up French reserves and take command of Gough's army and the supporting French divisions.

Next day the Germans crossed the Somme at Ham. Fayolle's troops were rushed in piecemeal. The Germans pushed them back too. The commander on the spot told Pétain that he needed another six divisions. Haig drove to Villers-Bretonneux to see Gough, whose old headquarters at Nesle, fifteen miles behind the front on the first day, was about to be overrun. Haig said he was surprised to learn that Gough's troops were now behind the Somme. 'On the first day they had to wear gas masks all day which is very fatiguing, but I cannot make out why the 5th Army has gone so far back without making some kind of a stand.' The truth was Gough didn't have any prepared positions to fall back on. Haig then saw Pétain and asked him to put another twenty divisions in near Amiens to prevent the French and British armies being separated. Pétain said he would try but that he also expected to be attacked in the Champagne. He was obviously torn between trying to help Haig and his fears for Paris. The long-range shelling of the capital so excited the Kaiser that he insisted on announcing it himself. He sensed a great victory and shortly afterwards decorated Hindenburg with the Iron Cross with Golden Rays. Hindenburg wrote to his wife: 'What is the use of all these decorations?'

Horse racing went on at Moonee Valley in Melbourne on this Saturday and those present had no way of knowing that Pozières, which had been won with 23,000 Australian casualties, was about to be overrun. The racebook said: 'After [a certain race] there will be an interval of 15 minutes for recruiting speeches. During that time the bookmakers will not call the odds.'

HAIG WAS DRIFTING in the market. The next day, March 24, was one of the critical moments of the Great War. The Germans kept coming. They were now close to Bapaume and the old Somme battlefield. A gap opened north of the Somme between Gough and Byng's armies. In the evening Clemenceau dined with Pétain. They discussed moving ministries and their staffs from Paris to Tours. Pétain's fears were starting to overwhelm him. At 11 pm he arrived at Haig's advanced headquarters on the southern outskirts of Amiens.

The way Haig tells it, Pétain was 'very much upset, almost unbalanced and most anxious'. Haig told Pétain of his plans to bring reserves, including four Anzac divisions, south to help Byng. He again asked Pétain to concentrate as many French divisions as possible in front of Amiens. Pétain said he expected to be attacked in Champagne at any moment. He did not think the main German blow had yet been delivered. He said he had told General Fayolle that if the Germans continued to advance on Amiens, he [Fayolle] was to fall back southwards to cover Paris. This would separate the French and British armies.

Haig wrote in his diary: 'I at once asked Pétain if he meant to abandon my right flank. He nodded assent and added "it is the only thing possible, if the enemy compelled the Allies to fall back still further".' Haig assumed Pétain had orders to cover Paris at all costs.

And now Haig finally realised he had a crisis. He had taken over extra front on the understanding that the French would help him if there was a big attack. He was being told the arrangement was off.

He had operated all along on the understanding that the French and British armies should not be separated. This arrangement also seemed to be off. Haig's army was in peril. It was possible Britain and France could lose the war. Pétain's defeatism had to be checked.

Haig hurried back to Montreuil, arriving at 3 am. He telegraphed Wilson, the new Chief of the Imperial General Staff, asking him and Lord Derby, the War Minister, to come to France immediately. They should arrange that 'General Foch or some other determined General who would fight, should be given supreme control of the operations in France'.

Haig had long opposed the idea of a generalissimo. Now, to save the cause, he was prepared to give up much of his own independence. He had made the decision quickly and calmly. He was sure it was the right one. It was one of his best moments.

NEXT DAY, THE 25th, the Germans pushed across the old Somme battlefield. Another day or so at this rate and their frontline would be back where it was before July 1, 1916. During the night a Saxon division that had fought against the Australians at Pozières crossed the River Ancre between Albert and Hébuterne. The Australian 3rd and 4th divisions were assembling as a reserve between Arras and Doullens. The New Zealanders were already being rushed into the battle nearby at Auchonvillers. The Anzac divisions ran into rare confusion. The British army had not been in a rout like this since the retreat from Mons. Great columns were shuffling west: artillery pieces, wagonloads of wounded, walking wounded, stragglers. Communications had broken down days ago, mainly because brigade and battalion headquarters were constantly being shifted west. As often happens there was probably more panic in the back areas than in the frontline.

LLOYD GEORGE WASN'T going to send Lord Derby across to Haig: the War Minister was too easily manipulated. Instead he sent Lord Milner, a member of the War Cabinet, to accompany Wilson. The allies met the next day, the 26th, at Doullens, fifteen miles north of Amiens.

There were in fact three meetings. First, Haig met his army commanders, Horne, Plumer and Byng. Gough was not present. True, he was now officially under Fayolle and he had more troubles than the other three commanders, but one would still have expected him to be there. It was as though he and his front had already been written off. Haig explained what had to be done. Amiens had to be held and all reserves had to go to Byng.

The army commanders stayed for the second meeting, which was joined by Milner and Wilson. Wilson was confused: he loved politicking but this was happening too quickly. Milner's mind was as clear as ever. He wanted to know what Haig intended to do; Clemenceau, whom Milner had already spoken to, was worried that Haig was about to fall back on the Channel ports. No, said Haig, he wanted a 'fighting' French general in supreme command so that together they could save Amiens.

The main meeting began at noon. Raymond Poincaré, the President, Clemenceau, Foch and Pétain appeared for France. Milner, Wilson and Haig were there for Britain. Haig looked tired, probably because his routine had been disturbed by two late nights. Haig thought Pétain looked terrible. 'He had the appearance of a Commander who was in a funk and has lost his nerve.'

Haig spoke first. He said his objective now was to defend Amiens and hold on north of the Somme on Byng's front. When Haig mentioned Gough's army, Pétain said it was 'broken'. Pétain said he wanted to defend Amiens too, but it would be hard to move French divisions up. He refused to give guarantees. Pétain had lost faith. Foch hadn't: the allies should fight in front of Amiens – 'we must not retire a single inch.' Clemenceau proposed a formal scheme: Foch would co-ordinate the British and French armies in the defence of Amiens. Haig thought the proposal 'worthless': he wanted Foch to be able to overrule Pétain. Haig proposed that Foch should co-ordinate all the allied armies on the western front. This was adopted. There was finally a unified command – of sorts. Ludendorff had brought about something he never intended.

Foch's appointment was defined more precisely the following

month when Pershing and the Americans became party to the contract. The agreement gave all national commanders-in-chief the right of appeal to their own governments if they believed Foch was putting their forces in peril. Foch would work with a small staff of about twenty officers. His writ was limited. How it ran would depend on the power of his personality.

Foch and Clemenceau tended to grate against each other. After the Doullens conference, Clemenceau is supposed to have said to Foch: 'Well, you've got the job you so much wanted.' To which Foch is said to have replied: 'A fine gift. You give me a lost battle and tell me to win it.'

Haig returned to Montreuil and went riding. Wilson saw him and thought he looked ten years younger. Foch immediately began to impose his personality. After leaving Doullens he ran into Gough further south and spoke brusquely to him, appearing to question Gough's courage. Haig said Foch had spoken 'most impertinently'. Yet it was also evident that Haig was moving away from his protégé and thought that he had made mistakes over the last five days. According to Wilson, he and Milner that evening talked to Haig about removing Gough. Wilson said he told Haig he could have General Rawlinson (now the British military representative on the Supreme War Council in Versailles) as a replacement and that Haig agreed to this. Haig did not mention this in his diary but said that he defended Gough. 'He had never lost his head, was always cheery and fought hard.'

ONE ANECDOTE SOMETIMES tells more about an event than boxes of official documents. Brigadier-General Henry Sandilands commanded a brigade in Gough's army. He was on leave when the Germans attacked. He was ordered back and arrived in Amiens around midnight on March 25. He walked for almost an hour trying to find someone who could tell him what was going on and where his division, the 35th, was. Eventually he found the officers' club. He was told his division might be near Maricourt, a few miles south of Pozières.

Next morning – the 26th, the day of the Doullens conference – he still couldn't discover what was happening. Then he heard that Gough's headquarters was in a suburb of Amiens. He induced the manager of the officers' club to run him there in a Ford van. He found an unpretentious villa and 'great confusion'. Sandilands came upon some junior officers that he knew. He also noticed an officer sitting on a chair with his mouth wide open. A doctor was prodding at his teeth. Sandilands didn't pay much attention to the officer.

'Feeling rather cheerful myself, I said to the assembled company: "What on earth are you all running away for like this?" My remark was received in dull silence, and to my horror the officer with his mouth open sprang up and said: "What the hell are you doing here?" This was no less a person than General Gough, with whom, like most people, I had had one or two encounters.'

Sandilands said he was trying to find his brigade and hastily left the room. No-one at the villa knew where the 35th Division was; they didn't even know what corps it was in at that moment. Sandilands hung about outside the gate to the headquarters 'waiting for something to turn up'.

About 11 am a limousine arrived. Out stepped Lord Milner and Wilson. They were on the way to the Doullens conference. Wilson knew Sandilands. He asked him if it was safe to drive through Amiens. Sandilands said it was. He assumed the pair was looking for Gough's headquarters. The general was inside the villa, he told Wilson.

Wilson replied: 'Oh, he is here is he? Well, good morning.' Wilson and Milner climbed back into the car and drove off. Sandilands said he thought: 'That's the end of Gough.'

About noon a staff officer told Sandilands that the 35th Division was in General Walter Congreve's corps. Congreve's headquarters was ten miles east at Vadencourt, near Albert. Sandilands was to go there at once. But, sorry, there was no car. Well how was he to get there? No-one knew.

Sandilands fell back on the manager of the officers' club and his Ford. He arrived at Congreve's headquarters a few hours later. Congreve had won the Victoria Cross in South Africa. Sandilands had never met him and was shocked at his appearance. 'He struck me as being absolutely down and out and incapable of any clear thinking.

He was evidently suffering from want of sleep and both mental and physical fatigue.' Congreve told Sandilands to go to his division and tell its commander, Major-General George Franks, to pull back. He must not fight because there were no troops to send to him.

Sandilands arrived at the 35th Division headquarters and delivered the message to Franks. The general said he had just received a message from corps headquarters to go forward eight miles to near Bray. The division had retreated from there that morning. Sandilands said the order had to be a mistake. Only half-an-hour ago he had been told the 35th was to pull back. No, said Franks, he had now been told to return to Bray.

Franks said: 'As an infantry officer do you think it possible that men who have been fighting a rearguard action and retiring for about eight miles could now turn round and advance again towards the position they were originally holding in the morning?'

'No,' said Sandilands, 'it would be madness to attempt it and I should refuse to do it.'

'That is what I have done,' Franks said. What he did not say was that, for doing so, he had just been relieved of his command.

Sandilands now left to find his brigade, which was supposed to be near the village of Buire. He arrived there about 6 pm after passing groups of senior officers along the road 'just standing about in a hopeless sort of way, doing nothing'. No sign of his brigade. He eventually found it after dark. While his men ate and slept Sandilands scouted to see if any other troops were about. He found the remnants of the 21st Division and stragglers from many others.

Sandilands found a defensive position for his men and fought off four weak attacks during the next two days. Such was the way of things near the frontline on the day that Foch became generalissimo.

NEXT DAY, THE 27th, the Germans kept coming, but their momentum began to slow. The direction of the attack was now pointing south-west, towards Amiens, rather than north-west towards Arras and the Channel ports, as Ludendorff had intended. The Germans were threatening Montdidier in the south, having advanced thirty miles in a week. In the centre they were within seven or eight miles of Villers-Bretonneux. They would be able to bombard Amiens with ease from there. In the north, where the two Australian divisions were coming into the battle, the Germans had entered Dernancourt. They were in nearby Albert too. British artillerymen fired on the basilica to deny the Germans use of the tower for observation. The Hanging Virgin fell but the war didn't end.

Long before they entered Albert the German infantrymen had discovered that British soldiers were better fed and clothed than they were. The Germans stopped to eat, drink and grab items of clothing. The novelist and poet Rudolf Binding, a German staff officer, was astonished by what he saw in Albert. Some of his countrymen were rounding up cows. Others were carrying hens and bottles of wine. Some had looted a stationer's shop and were making off with writing paper and coloured notebooks. Some were wearing top hats. Others were drunk. A lieutenant emerged from a cellar. 'I cannot get my men out of this cellar without bloodshed,' he said.

ON THE EIGHTH day of the battle Hubert de la Poer Gough became its most famous casualty. He lost his job, not his life, his honour, not his limbs, cut down by multiple wounds inflicted over a week. Lloyd George and others in London saw the British retreat as a shambles and a humiliation; it demanded a scapegoat, preferably one high up the chain of command. Gough's first wound came when he returned to his headquarters about 5 pm. As he tells it in his *The Fifth Army*: 'Here I found General Ruggles-Brise, Haig's military secretary, and not having an idea what he had come about, I sat him down to some tea. He then asked to see me alone and told me as nicely as he could that the Chief thought that I and my Staff must be very tired, so he had decided to put in Rawlinson and the Staff of the Fourth Army to take command. I was very surprised, and I suppose I was very hurt, but beyond saying "All right", I only asked when Rawlinson would be coming to take over.'

Haig had Gough to dinner the following night. He told him he wanted him and his staff out of the line so that they could reconnoitre the Somme valley from Amiens to the sea, in case the British had to fight there.

A few days later Haig was at a conference to define more precisely Foch's powers as generalissimo. Here Gough received his second wound. Lloyd George told Haig it was not enough for Gough to be out of the line: he must be sent home. Haig wrote: 'To this I said I could not condemn an officer unheard, and that if L.G. wishes him suspended he must send me an order to that effect. L.G. seems a "cur" and when I am with him I cannot resist a feeling of distrust of him and of his intentions.' Next day the order came in writing from Lord Derby. Gough was sent home on half-pay. Haig told Gough: 'You will have every chance to defend yourself, Hubert. There will be a court of enquiry.' Gough, according to his account in *The Fifth Army* told Haig: 'Don't worry about me', and left.

Several months later Haig wrote to his wife:

> As regards Gough, I am sorry that he is talking stupidly, but I don't think it would be any use writing to him. Some of his friends are advising him to keep quiet. I am doing all I can to help him, but, as a matter of fact, some orders he issued and things he did were stupid – and anything of the nature of an enquiry would not do him any good. In my report, of course, I will give him every credit for being in a very difficult situation, and will stick up for him as I have hitherto done.

It was typical of Haig. Loyalty ran so far: in the end everyone was expendable but himself. It seems perverse that Gough was sent home in disgrace for losing a battle he could never have won.

Gough had been failing and bungling and cobbling up attacks for close to two years. He had been promoted far beyond his ability – by Haig. His ideas on tactics were old-fashioned. He lacked the analytical powers of men like Monash and Currie. He had none of the charm of Birdwood or the grace of Plumer. He inspired no affection. Politicians didn't like him: Lloyd George had wanted him removed in 1917. His luck always seemed to be bad, mainly because he didn't do enough preliminary work to give good luck a chance. He might have been sacked for First Bullecourt or August at Ypres. Instead he was dismissed for something that would have confounded a better general.

Haig is supposed to have told one of Gough's staff officers that public opinion at home demanded a scapegoat 'and the only possible ones were Hubert and me. I was conceited enough to think that the army could not spare me.'

LUDENDORFF SUFFERED TOO. His youngest stepson, a pilot, was shot down and killed over the battlefield. Ludendorff asked that a search be made for his stepson's aircraft. It was found late the following month. A grave was nearby. Ludendorff sent the lieutenant who discovered the wreckage a personal note and a photograph of himself as a mark of gratitude.

ON THE 28TH, the day that Gough was relieved, the Germans made small gains north of the Somme but pressed on strongly south of the river. Ludendorff's plan to capture Arras and drive north was being compromised every day. The German infantrymen were following the path of least resistance, and that was south-west. They were now only a mile or so from Villers-Bretonneux.

The 4th Australian Division had come into the battle north of the river at Dernancourt, near Albert. The front here was fluid and uncertain, more so because the Germans were slowing down. They had been diverted by beer and top hats; they were also tired.

A railway line ran north–south past Dernancourt. Immediately east of the line was the River Ancre, fast-flowing and sparkling, and then Dernancourt. The Germans were in the village. The Australians were on the western side of the railway line, peering into a misty dawn. Sergeant Stan McDougall, a Tasmanian blacksmith, was behind the railway embankment. His job was to watch a level crossing. Just after dawn McDougall heard the sound of bayonet scabbards slapping on thighs. He knew the Germans were coming, even though he couldn't see them. McDougall ran to summon help and brought back seven men. He picked up a Lewis gun and began firing it from the hip, pouring fire into Germans trying to cross the embankment, killing eight. Fifty-odd Germans had crossed the embankment and were threatening the Australian flank. McDougall opened up on them. The barrel casing of the Lewis gun became so hot it blistered his left hand. A sergeant contrived to support the gun while McDougall squeezed the trigger with his good hand. The Australians took about thirty prisoners.

McDougall's citation for the Victoria Cross said his actions 'saved the line'. Seven days later McDougall was at Dernancourt when the Germans attacked again. He took a Lewis gun out into no-man's land. When German fire damaged the gun he crawled back 300 yards to find another one. Then he led a counter-attack. This time he won the Military Medal.

Lieutenant John Barton of the 5th Australian Division passed columns of refugees as he approached the front west of Albert. Beds, tables and chairs swayed on overloaded carts. Men and children trudged beside them. There were few women. Most, Barton wrote, had stayed in their homes until the last. They would have a little bundle ready. If the Germans appeared, they would pick it up and flee. The refugees greeted the Australians with 'Tres bon Australie'. And the Australians replied: 'Cheer up, Froggie.'

In the village of Acheux the Australians came on a woman 'living rough'. The kitchen furniture had gone with her husband and children. She had her bundle of luggage in a towel tied up at the four corners so that she could thrust a stick into it and sling it over her shoulder. She ended up cooking for the Australian officers.

A week later Major Donald Coutts, the doctor with the 2nd Division, arrived in the nearby village of Millencourt. The villagers had obviously left in a hurry, leaving clothing, plates, cutlery, food and wine behind. Private Roy Brewer, from the same division, also came on a village (he didn't name it) where the French had left everything behind. The Australians found a cow wandering. They shot her and ate steak and chipped potatoes for three days. The 24th Battalion from the 2nd Division arrived at Millencourt in the first week of April. The men had no clean underwear and made use of women's underclothing left behind. They also took to wearing silk hats and frock coats. An order was eventually issued prohibiting the wearing of civilian clothes.

MARCH 29, THE ninth day of the battle, brought a pause. Ludendorff tried to reorganise his forces. He decided to move five divisions to the south. His armies there would next day push west, towards Amiens, and south to herd the French away from the British. Everything was slowing down in the north; the artillery was struggling to catch up with the infantry. Ludendorff's armies there had advanced twenty miles, the last half of this over the old Somme battlefield. In the south, however, the Germans had now pushed back the right of what remained of Gough's army south of Villers-Bretonneux. The 9th Australian Infantry Brigade, part of the 3rd Division and commanded by Monash's friend Charles Rosenthal, had been guarding bridges on the Somme near Corbie. Now it was rushed to Cachy, south-west of Villers-Bretonneux and in front of Amiens.

THE GERMAN ATTACK on the 30th, the tenth day of the offensive, mostly failed. Just north of Villers-Bretonneux sits the pretty little village of Le Hamel. On the 30th the Germans, according to one of their histories, could hear roosters crowing in Hamel. 'We'll have you in the pot tomorrow,' one soldier announced. Not to be. The Germans were repulsed there and at Villers-Bretonneux, a few miles south. Just south of Villers-Bretonneux is Hangard Wood. The Germans took ground in front of this, which was close to Rosenthal's new position at Cachy.

ON THE ELEVENTH day Ludendorff's attack paused again. The French at the southern end of the line below Amiens now believed the Germans had gone about as far as they could. Yet Amiens tempted Ludendorff. He was so close: if he broke through at Villers-Bretonneux he was almost there, even though his artillery was lagging.

38

Stragglers and heroes

The spring grass was peeping through on the Somme, sappy and irrepressible, as if to say that whatever men and machines did, the earth abideth forever. The last days of March and the first days of April were strange times on the British front. Not since 1914 had the war been so errant, so confused. The era of trench stalemate, its certainties and rituals, had passed. The frontline now changed by the hour. In many places there was no such thing, just lines of outposts. In the morning they were here and in the evening they were there; they were hardly ever where the generals thought they were. Haig's army had prided itself on its orderliness. In the last days of March many of the divisions that faced Ludendorff's onslaught lived in chaos and listened to rumours.

Formations south of the river were hopelessly mixed up. Gough's 5th Army – what was left of it – had become Rawlinson's 4th Army. Enterprising officers would cobble up scratch 'divisions' from labour companies, lost infantrymen, railway workers, walking wounded, the odd American and passing cavalrymen carrying lances. The cavalrymen were full of boyish ardour: they hadn't much been in the war before and it still seemed like an adventure. Among the infantrymen, who knew it wasn't an adventure, straggling had become common. Confusion always breeds stragglers and few aspects of war are more confusing than a retreat.

The Australian divisions were on the move, tramping down the line that began at Hébuterne, north of Albert, and stretched south, through Dernancourt and Morlancourt, and on to Corbie, on the river, and then south again, to Villers-Bretonneux. Strange incidents were taking place. The townspeople of Villers-Bretonneux had left hurriedly, leaving much wine and champagne behind. The Australians who arrived there in the last days of March used the champagne to wash down their hot meal in the evening. Some may also have used it for shaving and washing. A British divisional general came upon Australians carrying lumpy sacks that, one assumes, were also clinking. Much like a housemaster at one of the better public schools, he slashed at them with his oak stick, causing red and white wine to cascade down the Australians' backs. The Australians 'resented' this high-handedness. Several of their officers arrived in time to ease the tension.

Pompey Elliott had brought his brigade south to the pretty town of Corbie, on the Somme. Elliott had always done a nice line in high-handedness. The looting of French houses appalled him. When a British captain was caught with a mess cart loaded with champagne Elliott posted a written ultimatum. The next officer caught looting would be summarily hanged in the Corbie market square and his body left swinging there as a deterrent. Elliott had read too much about the Duke of Wellington's campaign in Spain, but the looting stopped. Elliott was to wonder later in the year why he was passed over for a divisional command.

Sergeant Frank Wormald came to Corbie with a detachment of 5th Division's artillery.

The French had got out. They left everything, the shops, the pubs, the farms . . . Hens, talk about hens for dinner. They were laid on for a while. Booze, talk about booze, you could get all the champagne you wanted . . . Our wagon lines was at Bonnay [two miles north of Corbie] . . . We'd send a wagon into Corbie every night for booze and tucker and all that sort of thing. Don't think that we living on booze – we wasn't. You can't fight a war like that and have booze.

A group of cooks went into Corbie one night.

They took off their clothes and dressed up as gentlemen – claw-hammer coat, white shirts, spats and the bloody lot . . . then they got on to the champagne and they couldn't find the place where they'd left their clothes again, so they had to come home – in this bell-topper hat, claw-hammer coat and dress suit. It was a bit funny dressed like that in the frontline.

VILLERS-BRETONNEUX IN early April was just about the most important town in the war. It offered the Germans the best approach to Amiens. The town lay on a low plateau that looked down on the spire of the great cathedral at Amiens, ten miles away. A railway line and a Roman road both ran west to east through Villers-Bretonneux. About a mile north-east of the town the plateau rose to a point called Hill 104. From here one not only had a better view of Amiens but also to the lazy loops of the Somme to the north, to Corbie and Sailly le-Sec on the river itself and to the little village of Hamel to the east. Hill 104 would be the Germans' best observation point. Even if they didn't take Amiens, they could destroy its railway yards by artillery fire directed from here. South of Villers-Bretonneux a poplar-lined road led to the village of Hangard. Three woods rose out of the springing crops on the plain here: Monument (near a large farm of the same name), Hangard and Lancer. About three miles to the east lay the villages of Marcelcave and Aubercourt. The frontline in the last days of March was roughly halfway between these villages and Villers-Bretonneux. And it was to here that the Australians from Monash's 3rd Division came on March 30.

The 9th Brigade, commanded by Charles Rosenthal, had been sent south the previous night and placed under the command of a British division. Rosenthal was a cavalier leader – he liked to be

First Villers-Bretonneux, April 4–5, 1918

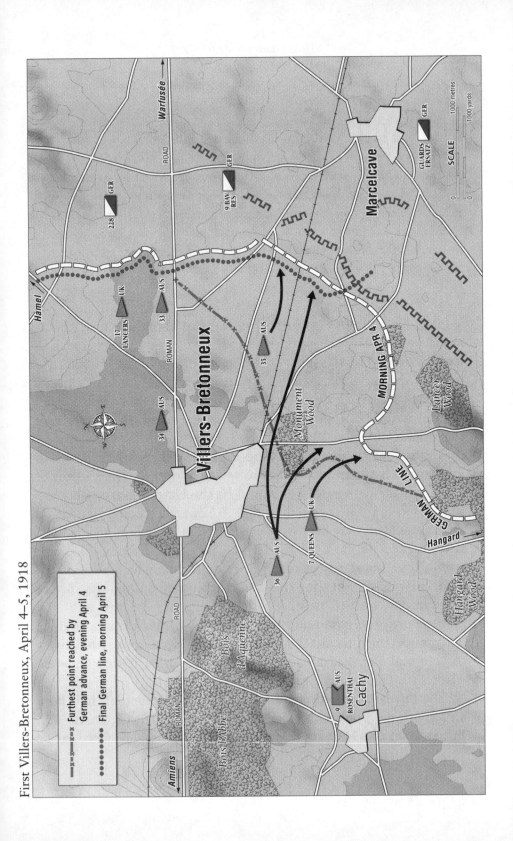

Warlusée

ROAD

228 GER

9 BAV RES GER

Hamel

17 LANCERS UK

33 AUS

ROMAN

34 AUS

Villers-Bretonneux

35 AUS

Monument Wood

MORNING APR 4

Lancer Wood

GERMAN LINE

Marcelcave

GUARDS ERSATZ GER

SCALE

0   1000 metres
0   1000 yards

Amiens

ROAD

ROMAN

Bois l'Abbé

Bois d'Aquenne

36 AUS

7 QUEENS UK

Hangard

Hangard Wood

9 AUS ROSENTHAL

Cachy

Furthest point reached by
German advance, evening April 4

Final German line, morning April 5

near the shooting – but the British general insisted that he place his headquarters well behind Villers-Bretonneux. Rosenthal's four battalions were the 33rd, 34th, 35th and 36th. Leslie Morshead, a twenty-eight-year-old schoolteacher, commanded the 33rd. He was short, dapper and punctilious; it bothered him that rankers sometimes had the cheek to address officers while smoking. He was also a fine soldier; he had proved that from the moment he waded ashore on Gallipoli.

Rosenthal told Morshead he was to counter-attack to the east, towards Marcelcave and Aubercourt. Morshead was supposed to hold a front of 2700 yards with a battalion that, at around 500 men, was only at half strength anyway. And he was to have no artillery support. Morshead and his men set off across the open plain in drizzly rain that turned the red-brown soils greasy. A cavalry regiment, the 12th Lancers, came up to help on the northern flank. The cavalry and the Australians advanced south of Villers-Bretonneux towards Hangard and Lancer woods.

Morshead rode with the cavalry, pleased to be alongside a famous regiment. At Lancer Wood, Morshead wrote afterwards, he came upon British troops 'uselessly entrenched in queer places, and large bodies of stragglers'. The troops were all pulling out, even though there was no hint of an attack. Morshead told the English officers he was about to launch a counter-attack and asked them to put their men back in the line. The British infantrymen turned around, but reluctantly. Stragglers were still leaving and no-one stopped them.

At 5 pm Morshead's battalion, which was still back in Hangard Wood, began its attack. The men advanced quickly, despite the heavy ground, towards Aubercourt. The Germans could see them clearly and put up a heavy fire; there was no artillery barrage to keep them underground. The Australians fell thickly. Nowhere was the objective reached and the line, now down to about 300 men, was strung out over a mile.

A young cavalry officer who was with Morshead begged him to allow the Lancers to charge. 'Oh, let's have a go at them, sir,' he said. Morshead admired the sentiment but said no. The cavalrymen, as was their custom, pulled out at dark. Morshead thanked them warmly.

Rain was still falling. Rifles and Lewis guns became clogged and maps turned to pulp. At dawn Morshead's troops were pulled out and replaced by British troops. The objective had not been reached but the Germans had been checked.

THE NEWLY ARRIVED Australians and cavalry were supposed to be reserved for counter-attacks like Morshead's, but some of the British divisions were down to 2000 men. So now another of Rosenthal's battalions, the 35th, was on the night on March 30 told to take over the whole sector of a British division, some 2800 yards, on the southern front at Villers-Bretonneux.

The Australians went out in the dark. Captain Gilbert Coghill led the right company, which was near the railway line. He came upon five junior British officers crouched in a dugout in the embankment. They said that their men were 'out there', pointing to the plain to the south-east, but Coghill's men found no line of posts. The Australians had to dig in before dawn. Most had dropped their entrenching tools while trudging through the mud. They dug with their hands.

Coghill was still there four days later, on April 3, when German aircraft swooped low over the Australian frontline. The men sensed the Germans were about to attack. Coghill's batman was a resourceful man who had scrounged well in Villers-Bretonneux. Next morning he had just served Coghill a breakfast of chicken and champagne when the Germans began shelling the frontline. The bombardment lasted an hour. Visibility was poor and light rain was falling. As the shell-smoke cleared the Australians saw grey figures up ahead. The Germans were going for Villers-Bretonneux. Richthofen and his 'flying circus' were in the air.

Coghill told his men they were not to fire until he raised his arm. He didn't want the Germans to take cover. He stood on the embankment so that all his men could see him and repeated his order. 'All right,' said one of his lieutenants, 'but Christ couldn't make me stand up there.' When the Germans were forty yards away Coghill raised his arm, in which he held a map-case. Straight away he was shot in the arm. The Germans broke under the fire of the Lewis guns. Their officers rounded them up and sent them forward again. Each time Coghill allowed the Germans to come close before opening fire.

The Germans turned south to attack the British troops on Coghill's southern flank. After the first assault the 7th Buffs, a famous British regiment, began to retreat. Coghill ran across to them and promised covering fire from his Lewis guns if the Buffs would return. They did. Coghill ran the 500 yards back to his own position as machine-gun bullets played around him. When he was almost back to the Australian line he looked around. The Buffs had left again.

North of the Roman road, where the 35th Battalion's other flank lay, a newly arrived British division broke. Now both Australian flanks were open. The northern end of the line began to fall back, then the centre. Coghill, at the southern end, tried to hold on. His men were now being shot at from behind. They pulled back gradually towards the support position, lest they be cut off. Coghill was hit again, this time in the knee. He waited until his company was in the support trenches before going to the aid post.

Morshead's depleted 33rd Battalion was sent up to help the 35th. By 9.30 am the new Australian line was reasonably strong, but the British line to the north was being rolled back. The village of Hamel seemed likely to fall.

The British 14th Division held the line north of the Roman road, past Hamel and on to the Somme. The division had performed poorly on the first day of Operation Michael and its commander had been sacked. According to Haig's diary, his successor 'went off his head with the strain'. The division, under its third commander in a fortnight, now couldn't hold the line north of the Roman road. Some of its troops seem to have simply fled. Men from Monash's division on the river saw Germans creeping into Hamel. Monash wrote home: 'These Tommy divisions are the absolute limit, and not worth the money it costs to put them into uniform . . . bad troops, bad staffs, bad commanders.'

Elliott was told that as soon as his brigade could be relieved it was to cross the river and help the cavalrymen who were doing what the 14th Division was supposed to be doing. One of Elliott's officers was already south of the river. With the help of cavalrymen he rounded up about 500 British stragglers. Many were without rifles. They said they had been told to dump them.

At noon Hill 104, behind the front where the 14th Division had been routed and offering the best view of Amiens, was in danger of falling.

IN THE AFTERNOON the two remaining battalions of Rosenthal's brigade, the 34th and the 36th, were thrown into the battle to hold Villers-Bretonneux. The 33rd and the 35th still held the frontline just south of the Roman road. The 35th was on the southern end of the line and many of the men were so tired they were starting to fall asleep. Then, about 4 pm, they saw the British line to the south of them retreating. And now the Australian line became a shambles. A lieutenant at the southern end ordered his men to fall back and form a defensive flank. The Australians to the north thought the whole battalion was pulling back and a rout began. Two officers tried to steady the troops and failed. They ended up standing in the line alone, watching the Germans advancing towards Villers-Bretonneux. Much of the 33rd Battalion to the north also fell back as part of the chain reaction.

Colonel Henry Goddard, the commander of the 35th Battalion, was also in charge of the 9th Brigade's forward headquarters. His post was in Villers-Bretonneux. Around 5 pm he discovered that his two front battalions had fallen back in disorder. His headquarters was suddenly the most forward Australian position. Panic now broke out here as well. Goddard ordered the 36th Battalion, which was south of the town, to counter-attack.

AROUND 4 PM CHARLES Bean was walking towards Villers-Bretonneux in the drizzle with Hubert Wilkins, the polar explorer who had become an official photographer. British troops were straggling back towards them without rifles. The pair soon realised 'that the whole countryside was retiring'.

A soldier asked them: 'Which is the road to Amiens?'

Bean and Wilkins asked two youngsters why they were retreating. 'Too many Germans,' they replied.

Bean noted that the German artillery had lengthened its range. Shells were falling on the back areas behind him. 'It seemed to me,' Bean wrote in his diary, 'that he knew he had a broken crowd in front of him, and was turning his guns on to their retreat.'

Bean and Wilkins came on their first Australian stragglers, men from the 35th and 33rd, half-a-mile west of Villers-Bretonneux. Unlike the British they had their rifles, but they were still stragglers. One said the Germans were probably in Villers-Bretonneux by now.

Bean and Wilkins turned north towards the Somme, about three miles away. Near Corbie they met Pompey Elliott and told him what they had seen 'so that if Villers-Bretonneux were taken he would not be caught in the flank'. Bean wrote in his diary: 'I thought Villers-Bretonneux had gone, though I didn't say so.'

COLONEL JOHN MILNE ran much of the way to his 36th Battalion to arrange the counter-attack ordered by Goddard. His men were south of the town, near Monument Farm. Milne arrived breathless and began issuing orders. The battalion would counter-attack due east towards Monument Farm and the wood of the same name just past it. One company commander asked: 'How far shall we go?'

'Go 'till you're stopped,' Milne said. He walked along the lines of men shedding their overcoats and other gear they wouldn't need in the counter-attack. 'Goodbye, boys,' said Milne. 'It's neck or nothing.'

The men set off at a jogtrot. Soon they saw Germans pouring out of Monument Wood. The Germans saw them and returned to the wood and opened fire. Some sheltered behind haystacks near the farm. The Australians fell thickly, particularly officers, but they began to push the Germans back. When it was over Milne's men had advanced a mile at the northern end of their front and half-a-mile at the southern end.

As they began digging in a man arrived and told them to pull back. He was wearing an officer's tunic and a private's cap. The lance-corporal in charge had been warned by his superiors about German tricks. He asked the man for his papers. He had none, so the lance-corporal shot him dead. No evidence was ever found to suggest that the dead man was a German.

On the other side of the railway line a company of the 35th had also gone forward strongly. The captain in charge jumped into a shell hole occupied by three Germans. He hit one over the head with the man's coal-scuttle helmet and strangled a second. The third German escaped. Further north again, Morshead's 33rd Battalion was falling back in some disorder when the 17th Lancers cantered up. The Australians turned back towards the enemy. According to Morshead, the sight of the cavalrymen – all their panoply, the drawn sabres and lances – inspired the Australians.

Villers-Bretonneux had been saved, for now, but the Germans had edged closer and Rosenthal's brigade had lost 665 men. The counter-attack by Milne's 36th Battalion had made the difference. Rosenthal, frustrated at being forced to stay so far behind the fighting, came forward after hearing of the straggling. He reached the frontline in the dark and ordered it moved forward slightly to better ground. More Australians were coming: brigades from the 2nd and 5th divisions had begun to cross the Somme. Soon Australians would hold most of the front.

NEXT DAY, APRIL 5, Bean and Wilkins went to Villers-Bretonneux. 'It was a shocking sight – every house seemed to have been hit,' Bean said. At the villa that had been Goddard's headquarters the roof of the dining room was all over the floor. The kitchen door had been blown forward, hitting Morshead on the back of the head. A fortnight later Morshead was in a cellar when gas shells landed. He was blinded for three weeks and in hospital for two months.

Also on April 5 the 4th Australian Division fought a fierce

battle at Dernancourt, about ten miles north of Villers-Bretonneux and on the other side of the river. The Germans here were also going for Amiens. Two Australian brigades held off two-and-a-half German divisions. Ray Leane's 48th Battalion again fought magnificently. The Germans buried two Australian bodies at one of the 48th Battalion's posts. They marked them with rough crosses, on which they wrote with an indelible pencil: 'Here lies a brave English warrior.'

A German war correspondent wrote after the battle that 'the Australians and Canadians are much the best troops that the English have'.

LUDENDORFF'S OPERATION MICHAEL virtually ended the day after this first battle for Villers-Bretonneux. Some of the Germans had advanced forty miles; they were tired and it was becoming difficult to supply them. Ludendorff was cranky and looking for someone to blame. The Germans had made the biggest breakthrough since trench warfare began. In fifteen days they had captured more than 1000 square miles and some 75,000 British prisoners, panicked the governments in Paris and London and caused the sacking of Gough. And yet the offensive had to be judged a failure. Ludendorff had been trying to capture Arras as a prelude to driving the British to the sea. He had never come near to achieving these objectives. Once the battle had begun he had settled on capturing Amiens and separating the British and French armies. He had failed here too, on the plain just east of Villers-Bretonneux. Instead he had managed to unite the British and French armies under Foch. He had broken Gough's 5th Army but not Byng's 3rd. He had captured dozens of towns and villages, yet none had strategic or symbolic value. Bapaume and Albert were not the same as Ypres and Arras.

Some of Ludendorff's tactics – Bruchmüller's barrages, the ever-moving storm troops – were inspired, but, as Correlli Barnett wrote in *The Swordbearers*, battles are not displays of virtuosity. 'They are the means to the end of strategy, and Michael was therefore a titanic failure.'

And there was the matter of casualties. The British and French had lost about 240,000 men, the Germans at least 250,000. The grotesque arithmetic here went like this: the allies had a supply of replacements – more than 120,000 Americans were arriving each month – and the Germans did not. Yet Ludendorff was a gambler: another throw might do it. He decided to attack the British again, this time in Flanders.

39

Backs to the wall

The 1st Division was the last of the Australian formations to leave Flanders for the Somme. Lieutenant Donovan Joynt of the 8th Battalion stepped on to a train on the night of April 5 and next morning was washing his hands and face in the Somme before moving into billets in a village. 'Terrible stories were told by the French people of the disgraceful behaviour of the English troops during the retreat – for such it appears to be,' he wrote in his diary. 'The newspapers make out that it was a withdrawal, but panic and a disgusting stampede appears to be nearer the mark. "English no *bon*" was heard everywhere we went.' Lieutenant Cyril Lawrence also came down with the 1st Division. 'The people of Amiens nearly wept with joy when they saw us,' he wrote home.

A week later Joynt and Lawrence were on trains going north again. There was a new crisis. The Germans had launched an offensive in Flanders. Hazebrouck, near the Belgian border, was being threatened much as Amiens was in the south. Hazebrouck, like Amiens, was a critical rail centre. Half the food and munitions for the Ypres front came through its yards. Behind the town, stretching to the coast, were depots, dumps, training camps and railway

591

systems. And behind them were the ports of Dunkirk, Calais and Boulogne. If Hazebrouk fell, the ports were at risk.

Lawrence had been three days and two nights without sleep by the time he reached the line west of Hazebrouck. The French had fled their thatched farmhouses, leaving behind wine, flour, potatoes and coal, as well as cows, fowls, pigs and rabbits. Clothes were strewn about. Lawrence observed that French girls owned fine underwear. Joynt watched crowds of refugees heading west as villages burned in the distance. Photographs taken at the time show plough horses pulling farm carts piled high with household goods; alongside the carts are women in broad-brimmed hats and stout boots carrying round bundles that appear to be tied up with tablecloths or towels. The locals were familiar with the Australians, who had been in the sector before. Among the refugees was a village watchmaker who was carrying away his stock. He handed out watches to the Australians as they passed.

Joynt was told that his battalion was to take up a position in front of the Nieppe Forest, east of Hazebrouck.

THE FRONT AT Fromelles had changed little since more than 2000 Australians had been killed there in a single night in 1916. The bones of the dead lay out in no-man's land, clinging to scraps of uniform that shivered in the wind. General Haking was still the corps commander here. Two Portuguese divisions held the front and they were close to mutiny.

Fromelles was where Ludendorff attacked on the morning of April 9. Crown Prince Rupprecht knew the Portuguese front was soft. The two Portuguese divisions were 6000 men under strength. The soldiers were unhappy. They didn't know why they were in the war; they said they had nothing against the Germans, and they wanted more leave. One battalion had mutinied. Haking said the Portuguese were 'bait' for the Germans. He wanted them out of the line. Before this could happen the Germans attacked. This was 'Operation George', a plan that Ludendorff had rejected for Operation Michael on the Somme, but it was not to be carried out in the expansive style of the original scheme. George became 'Georgette', as if to announce that Ludendorff was now making it up as he went, which he was. Georgette was still a big offensive: it had a front of about twenty miles and twelve attack divisions; the objectives were Hazebrouck and the Channel ports.

The Portuguese broke quickly under the barrage that came shrieking out of the fog. One German history said prisoners began to arrive before the German infantry went over. Most Portuguese fled, not just from the frontline but through the back areas as well. Some stole the bicycles of a British cyclists' battalion. The Germans had soon penetrated three miles on a ten-mile front. Armentières fell. Further north Messines, the site of Plumer's triumph in the previous year, was also overrun on the second day. Georgette worried Haig more than Michael. It threatened his lines of communication; worse, he was just about out of reserves. Whatever reinforcements he could scrape up for the battle, including the Australian division, would still leave him outnumbered almost two-to-one. Haig appealed to Foch to take over part of the British line. Foch declined. Haig said the Frenchman was 'most selfish and obstinate'.

On the third day of the battle, with the Germans pressing in on Hazebrouck and the British command still trying to find out where its forward divisions were and what they were doing, Haig wrote an appeal to all British forces in France. The last paragraph read:

> There is no other course open to us but to fight it out! Every position must be held to the last man: there must be no retirement. With our backs to the wall, and believing in the justice of our cause each one of us must fight on to the end. The safety of our Homes and the Freedom of mankind alike depend upon the conduct of each one of us at this critical moment.

These were emotional words from a man of such reserve. One historian called it 'un-English'; another wondered where the wall actually was. Joynt received a copy of Haig's message as he took his troops forward to near the village of Vieux Berguin. He didn't read it to the men. He didn't think they needed to be inspired.

The 29th Division was one of four British divisions at the front he was now approaching. The 29th had been a crack regular division and the Australians had looked on it with awe on Gallipoli. The Lancashire Fusiliers, part of the 29th, had won six Victoria Crosses during the landings near Cape Helles. The Fusiliers had been around, in one guise or another, since 1688. Their battle honours included Culloden, Saratoga, the war of 1812, the Peninsular War, the Crimea, the Indian Mutiny, Omdurman and the Boer War. The 29th Division had suffered frightful casualties on Gallipoli, on the first day of the Somme and at Passchendaele. So many of its stalwarts were dead. Its composition had changed so many times that it was no longer what it used to be.

JOYNT HAD MARCHED through the night to positions near Vieux Berguin where the Australians had been ordered to dig in. They were supposed to be the support line for the British divisions in front of them but everyone knew the Australian posts would become the new frontline as the British troops fell back.

Joynt chose a thatched farmhouse for his company headquarters. It had more than a dozen rooms and most of the furnishings had been left behind, including a gramophone. Joynt went off to inspect his forward positions. The front was rolling towards him; he could hear machine guns in the distance. About twenty men from the Guards Brigade were retreating through the village. Joynt said 'Good day' to the officer. He didn't reply. His men looked 'done'.

As Joynt returned to the farmhouse he heard a gramophone playing. Men in frock coats and top hats and 'women' in Parisian gowns were dancing on the lawn. His men had raided madame and monsieur's wardrobes. Joynt laughed at the absurdity of it all. The Germans were just down the road. He shouted 'Stand to'. His Lewis gunners went to their posts in dresses. Soon they were firing at grey figures in Vieux Berguin as stragglers from four British divisions arrived at the Australian line. Some began digging in forward of the Australians; some kept going, and others simply stood around. A battery of British artillery galloped past shouting the now familiar cry that the Germans were coming. An Australian shouted back: 'Mind you don't get drowned in the Channel.'

A colonel from the 29th Division stumbled into one of Joynt's posts. 'Boy,' he said to an Australian lieutenant, 'is this your post?'

'Yes, sir,' said the lieutenant.

'Well, give me a rifle – I'm one of your men.'

The colonel told the Australian he was disgusted with his men, who turned out to be the 1st Lancashire Fusiliers. They had retreated without orders. This was the first time in the history of the regiment that such a thing had happened. The colonel kept muttering. Suddenly he jumped up. 'My boy,' he announced, 'you can report that the 1st Lancashire Fusiliers held the village to the last man.' And he went back to the village to round up what men he could and fight. The Australians cheered him as he set off. All night fighting could be heard in the village.

Joynt could now see the Germans forming up in their hundreds in the village square, preparing to attack. Their artillery spotters were in the church steeple. The Germans were 'cheeky', showing themselves openly, as if they believed all resistance had broken down. Joynt's men shot down a company of them marching in column of fours along the road leading from the village.

Next day the Germans began shelling Joynt's farmhouse, where he had about twenty-five of his own men and another eighty, including one officer, from the 29th Division. Joynt eventually sent the 29th Division men to the rear. 'Their officer was very apologetic over the conduct of his Division and alluded to Gallipoli and how well it had done there fighting with the Australians.'

The Germans wiped out Joynt's advanced post on the right, enfilading it from a two-storey brick factory. The battle had begun.

IT WENT ON for days. The British and Australian troops held on in front of Hazebrouck. Georgette never developed the momentum of Michael down on the Somme. On the fifth day Crown Prince Rupprecht received a signed order from the Kaiser telling him to advance. 'But what help are all orders to attack,' Rupprecht wrote in his diary, 'when the troops are no longer able to attack?' After four or five days the Germans were struggling to keep going. Still, they took Bailleul, north of the Australian positions, and Wytschaete, on the old Messines battlefield. Plumer decided to pull back his frontline at Ypres. Passchendaele Ridge and other ground won so expensively the previous year reverted to the Germans. When the Germans took Mount Kemmel, west of Messines, from a French division Haig wrote in his diary: 'What Allies to fight with!' The Canadians were also annoying Haig. General Horne, the 1st Army commander, told Haig that Currie had 'a swollen head'. He didn't want his troops used piecemeal but only as a corps. This caused Haig to make favourable comment on the Australians, who had been 'used by Divisions and are now spread out from Albert to Amiens and one is in front of Hazebrouck'.

THE GERMANS COULD not break the Australian line at Hazebrouck. Lieutenant Lawrence and his men were caught up in the battle and also, as he put it, 'living like lords' on what had been left behind at the farmhouses. 'Bacon and *eggs*, lunch cold roast fowl, roast pork, mashed potatoes and whatever other delicacies that the farm offers, generally good home made jam. Dinner. Roast fowl, suckling pig, rabbit . . .' Lawrence was also drinking Moët and Chandon.

He had heard of the retreat from Passchendaele. 'If this is true it will be a great shock to our boys. First of all Bapaume and the Somme then Fleurbaix [opposite Fromelles] and Estaires (our first home in France), Messines and now Passchendaele and the Ypres salient. When we think what our boys with other colonials did at all those places, and then to think that they have *retired* from them.'

In his next letter, to his mother, he said the Germans had recently made thirteen attacks on his front. The Australian machine gunners 'piled them up and piled them up'. A boy from the farm where he was living had returned to retrieve a pair of boots for his mother, who had none. 'Gee, it makes a fellow thankful that this war is not in Australia, and yet our homes out there do not mean one hundredth of what these homes mean to people here. They live in the one home for centuries and even the grown-ups often have never been into the nearest big town generally not more than six or seven miles away anywhere.'

Lieutenant Joynt held his little front too. Several days before his company was relieved he needed to send a runner to one of his posts. A stretcher-bearer called Parfrey volunteered and set off. Joynt then decided to go up himself.

> On the way I saw Parfrey returning and could see he had something to tell me as he signalled me. I made towards him, he stopped running and opened his mouth to speak and then suddenly collapsed with the words on his lips unspoken. I dropped alongside him to find the blood gushing from a bullet hole in his neck. I tried to stop the flow of blood but found the bullet had made a hole the size of an apple in his throat and that it was hopeless trying to block the flow of blood without choking him, the gash was too big, so leaving him I crawled out the remainder of the distance . . .

It was a life of absurd contrasts. Joynt returned to the farmhouse and eventually fell asleep in a feathered bed with snow-white sheets. He played the gramophone whenever the Germans shelled. There were only five records and the Australians played them over and over, 'pretty French dance tunes, mostly Quadrilles'.

Joynt carried the gramophone out in his pack when he was relieved; his bugler carried the funnel. Joynt called the British captain who replaced him a 'great dud'. Joynt didn't think the officer had ever been in the frontline before but 'he knew everything'. As the two stood talking a cook passed carrying a dixie of potatoes and walked to a hedge where he drained off the water. The Englishman was appalled. Why hadn't Joynt constructed proper grease traps as laid down in the Manual of Field Training – Cooking Arrangements for Bivouac Camps?

Joynt took his gramophone and left. Hazebrouck held.

The second great German offensive was failing. As with Michael, the Germans had gained much ground but little of strategic importance. And, because two bulging salients had been created, their front was now much longer. But Ludendorff was going to try again for Amiens, which meant he had to try again for Villers-Bretonneux.

40

'Into the bastards, boys'

Anzac troops by early April held most of the Somme front. In the north the 4th Brigade of the 4th Division and the New Zealanders were at Hébuterne. Below them two brigades of the 2nd Division held the front south of Albert. Further south two brigades of Monash's 3rd Division held the line to Corbie on the Somme. Two brigades of the 5th Division, including that of Pompey Elliott, had crossed the river and were spread out south towards Villers-Bretonneux. Other Australian brigades were in Villers-Bretonneux and south of it.

Foch and Haig were worried about the small German salient that poked into the allied line at Hangard Wood, about two miles south of Villers-Bretonneux. The line needed to be straightened and this looked easy enough on a staff officer's map. The 5th Brigade from the 2nd Division was given the task.

We last met Captain Clarence Wallach at Pozières in 1916, where he won the Military Cross after being in charge of Blancmange Trench, so named because, as a result of German shelling, it changed shape every time he visited it. He was to lead one of the attacking companies at Hangard Wood. Wallach came from Bondi, New South Wales. Five of his brothers had also enlisted. All had attended

Second Villers-Bretonneux, April 25, 1918

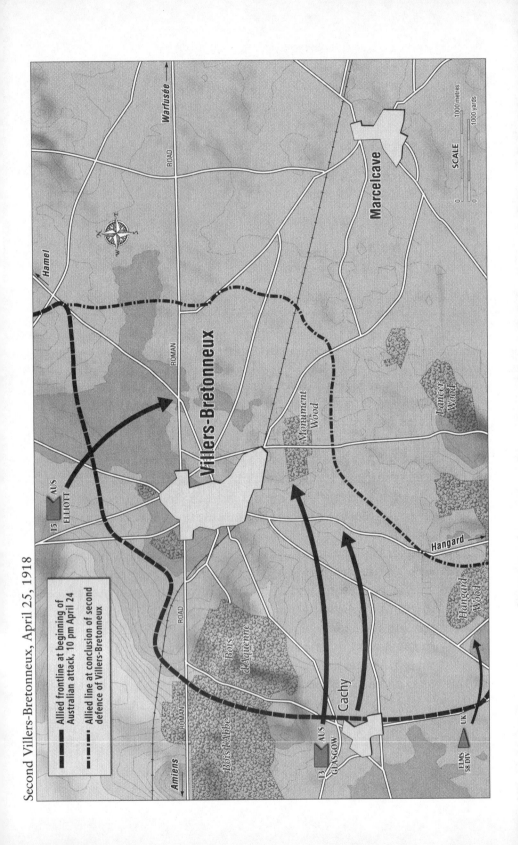

Allied frontline at beginning of
Australian attack, 10 pm April 24

Allied line at conclusion of second
defence of Villers-Bretonneux

Sydney Grammar. One brother, Neville, had been twice wounded. He too was a captain and had won the Military Cross. Clarence was tall with long legs, an open face and strong blue eyes. He had played rugby for Eastern Suburbs and for Australia in 1913–14. On Gallipoli he wrote a diary notable for its matter-of-fact style. Hardly anything bothered him. 'Nothing of note, two skittled by shrapnel' was a typical entry.

Lieutenant Percy Storkey, a twenty-six-year-old law student, was Wallach's second-in-command at Hangard. He had migrated from New Zealand to Sydney in 1911 after being dux of Napier High School. Storkey had already been twice wounded. The attack, supported by a barrage, was to go in at 4.55 am on April 7. Rain had fallen in the evening and the night was cold. Storkey fell asleep. He awakened to find that the attack had begun. The rest of the company, including Wallach, was seventy-five yards ahead of him. This lapse may have saved his life.

Something had gone wrong on Wallach's front. No barrage came down on the Germans ahead of him. Wallach waited a minute in hope, then set off across the 400 yards of open country towards the wood. German machine gunners, untouched by shells, opened up. By the time the company reached the edge of the wood one man in four had been hit. Wallach fell with wounds to both knees. Storkey took command.

He pushed into the undergrowth with eleven men, trying to get behind the German machine guns he could hear chattering on his right. The Australians came to a clearing. There, with their backs to them and only twenty yards away, were close to 100 Germans firing at Wallach's company out on the open plain.

One of Storkey's party yelled. The Germans looked around. Storkey shouted as if he had a battalion behind him. The Australians charged. The Germans in the nearest trench raised their hands. Those behind hesitated. They could have quickly turned a machine gun on its tripod and wiped out the dozen Australians. But Storkey's manner bothered them. What if there were hundreds of men behind him?

Storkey called on them to surrender. The Germans hesitated.

Storkey shot three with his revolver, which then jammed. His men rolled grenades into the trenches then shied away to avoid the blasts. Thirty Germans died. The other fifty-three surrendered.

Storkey's men pushed on towards the company's objective, where they were supposed to dig in. But where? The scrub near the objective was so thick that a man entrenched there couldn't see more than a few feet. And about 400 yards ahead Germans could be seen on higher ground. It was pointless to entrench in a valley with Germans above them. Someone had made an error in selecting the objective. Storkey ordered his men to return to the start line.

Storkey found his battalion commander and told him the objective was impossible to hold. Go back and hold it, he was told. Storkey said he hardly had any men left. He would not take them back. He would go himself, if ordered, but only after he had explained the impossibility of the objective to his brigadier. Storkey's fifty-three prisoners appeared under escort on a nearby slope as the argument continued. According to Bean, this saved an 'awkward situation'. Storkey eventually saw his brigadier. He was not ordered back.

Wallach had a compound fracture of his left leg. Gas gangrene had set in and doctors amputated the limb. Wallach's temperature soared to 105 degrees. He was given a blood transfusion, a relatively new technique at the front, to try to save the other leg, but eventually it had to come off too. Wallach began to weaken: the shock was too great. He died on April 22, aged twenty-eight.

Neville, his brother, also a good rugby player, died a little over a week later at Villers-Bretonneux. A shell burst at his company headquarters, sending a splinter through his head as the officers were sitting down to tea. Neville was twenty-one. The men made a 'beautiful cross' from a piece of furniture and erected it over his grave. The family never received the effects of Clarence and Neville. The ship taking them back to Australia was torpedoed.

Storkey survived the war, resumed his law studies, and eventually became a judge. For his day at Hangard Wood he won the Victoria Cross.

WHILE CLARENCE WALLACH lay dying Captain Manfred von Richthofen, the man Ludendorff had said was worth three divisions, was hunting over the Somme in his Fokker triplane with other members of his 'circus'. The Australian and British troops stared up at the dull-red planes. Here was another hint that the Germans were going to try for Amiens again. There had been stronger signs.

On April 16 and 17 the Germans had sent over tens of thousands of gas shells on the Villers-Bretonneux front: mustard, 'sneezing gas' and phosgene. The Australians had pulled on their masks but the gas still got to them. Thin-skin areas, under the arms and around the crotch, became inflamed and the men's eyes began to stream. The casualties ran to about 650. The shelling was obviously a prelude to an infantry attack. German guns were registering on the roads around Villers-Bretonneux. And the men on the ground kept seeing the red planes of Richthofen's circus.

Rawlinson reorganised his front. The Australian Corps had been holding the line from Albert to the River Luce, a few miles south of Villers-Bretonneux. Now the Australian line would stop at Hill 104, on the northern side of the town. The British III Corps, under Lieutenant-General Richard Butler, formerly of Haig's staff, would defend the town. The 8th Division, heavy with inexperienced reinforcements, took over the ground in front of Villers-Bretonneux.

POMPEY ELLIOTT'S 15TH Brigade had been holding part of the front north of the town. It was now in reserve. Elliott was convinced the Germans would go for Villers-Bretonneux again; he wasn't impressed that British troops had taken over its defence. He had briefly lived in 'a most glorious house' near Corbie. It had a billiards room, a rare collection of butterflies, exquisite furniture, a conservatory and a Cootamundra wattle in bloom. Elliott got about in a French car that had been abandoned. This was not 'looting': Elliott knew this because he wrote the rules about such things.

Elliott was full of bluster in these days. Haig's headquarters had become concerned about rumour-mongering among British troops and the risk that this could lead to panic. GHQ said anyone spreading rumours was to be taken to the nearest commanding officer. Elliott issued an edict of his own. Anyone caught peddling rumours was to be treated as an enemy agent and court-martialled. If a battalion was in action and no satisfactory explanation was forthcoming from an accused man, he was to be summarily shot. Like Elliott's threat of public hangings, the order was illegal and spoke to the infantile side of Elliott's character. In other matters his judgement was better. He had been at the frontline almost continuously for three years. He knew a lot about this war. From what he had seen and heard he didn't believe the British 8th Division could hold Villers-Bretonneux.

RICHTHOFEN AWOKE NEAR Cappy, a village below one of the southerly loops of the Somme, on the morning of April 21. He was happy. All his life he had enjoyed hunting and killing: boar, deer, elk, rabbits, bison, birds (including three pet ducks belonging to his grandmother) and, more recently, allied planes and their crews. He had made his eightieth 'kill' the day before. Toasts had been drunk. 'Eighty – that is really a decent number,' Richtohofen is supposed to have said. The German public lionised him: he was a superman from Nietzsche. He had shot down more planes than any pilot in the Great War. And in three days he was going on leave. He would shoot pigs in the Black Forest.

Richthofen was twenty-five and handsome in the style of a Prussian aristocrat: slim with finely chiselled features, blond hair and a cold stare. Each time he shot down a plane he ordered an inscribed silver cup from a jeweller in Berlin. He liked to display trophies, be they antlers or silver cups that represented men.

Richthofen breakfasted and stepped out into the cold east wind. A military band, sent over to celebrate the eightieth kill, was performing. Richthofen said the music was too loud and walked towards the hangars, stopping to play with a pup on the way. He climbed into his Fokker and flew west, along the Somme valley and towards the allied lines above Villers-Bretonneux.

On the same morning Captain Roy Brown, a Canadian flyer and a year younger than Richthofen, awoke about twenty miles to the west, near Bertangles Château, the headquarters of the Australian Corps. Brown had a stomach ailment; it was so bad he had been living on brandy and milk for a month. He was also worn out and unnerved by fourteen months of flying and killing. He should have been in a hospital. Instead he would fly his Sopwith Camel twice a day, then go to bed after dosing himself with brandy and milk. Brown had been credited with at least nine kills and awarded the Distinguished Service Cross. He was a modest man who did not keep trophies. Some of the kills had been awarded to him only because others had reported them.

Brown climbed out of bed and flew east. His squadron and Richthofen's flying circus met near Cérisy, just below the Somme on the German side of the line. A dogfight began. It was a little before 11 am.

Richthofen, much like a lion that has spotted an antelope with a limp, chased an inexperienced Canadian pilot, Lieutenant Wilfred May, who lost altitude and scooted for home along the Somme valley. Roy Brown tried to save his comrade by chasing Richthofen and firing at him from behind and from the left before breaking off. May and Richthofen flew towards the Morlancourt Ridge on the northern bank of the river, where the Australians had set up anti-aircraft batteries.

May zigzagged and flew low along the valley before easing his stick back to climb over the Morlancourt Ridge. Australian ground forces had opened up on Richthofen. Down in the valley Sergeant Cedric Popkin fired bursts from a Vickers machine gun. Up on the ridge two gunners, Bob Buie and Snowy Evans, blazed away with Lewis guns. Richthofen usually played percentages. He was breaking his own rules by flying low over enemy ground. The trophy had become everything.

May flew on for Bertangles. Richthofen suddenly banked to the right above the ridge. He turned towards the German lines, giving Popkin a second shot at him and at a closer range. Other Australians were also firing. Richthofen's engine roared, as if to announce that something was wrong. The red Fokker rose abruptly, swung to the right, then sank like a game bird hit by shotgun pellets. It came down in a field above the valley, near the brickworks on the Bray–Corbie road.

The Australians rushed the plane. Richthofen was dead. A single bullet had hit him under the right armpit and come out near his left nipple. The bullet was lying loose in his clothing. Someone took it and it was never seen again. Sydney Leigh, a young Victorian transport driver, was driving along the road when he saw 'the red aeroplane lying in a paddock'. Soldiers were swarming around it, taking souvenirs. Leigh acquired part of the propeller and it became a family heirloom.

Who killed the Red Baron? Roy Brown initially received the credit. Medical theorists have since said that a man with a chest wound similar to Richthofen's would have had only about twenty seconds to live. If so, this rules out Brown, who had broken off the chase long before Richthofen's plane turned and sank. The probability is that Richthofen was killed by ground fire.

The Red Baron was buried with military honours at Bertangles. Brown was said to be nauseated at the sight of Richthofen's body. Australians fired volleys over the grave. Messages and photographs of the grave were dropped over the German lines the next day. Less than three months later the Richthofen squadron had a new commander. His name was Hermann Goering.

No journalist at the Great War was more conscientious than Charles Bean. He was at Villers-Bretonneux, now being held by the 8th Division. The 8th, Bean said, had been a good British division. What he now saw dismayed him. The scale of casualties the 8th had sustained had changed its character. During Operation Michael the division had lost nearly 5000 men, half its infantry strength, including 250 officers. England was now sending over eighteen-year-olds as reinforcements. Bean saw them arriving as Operation Michael ended. 'For two days companies of infantry have been passing us on the roads – companies of children, English children; pink faced, round cheeked children, flushed under the weight of their unaccustomed packs, with their steel helmets on the back of their heads and the strap hanging loosely on their rounded baby chins.' The 8th Division was now thick with these 'children'. One may only wonder why General Rawlinson moved the more seasoned Australian troops out of the town.

The Germans began shelling the Villers-Bretonneux positions at 4.45 am on April 24. Many of the shells were mustard gas. It was not yet dawn and a mist was rolling in. The barrage was particularly heavy.

Pompey Elliott was at Blangy-Tronville, a few miles west of Villers-Bretonneux. He had for days been working on a plan of counter-attack and soon after the German barrage began he issued provisional orders for it. He did not yet have permission for the enveloping manoeuvre he had in mind; he didn't even know what was happening at Villers-Bretonneux.

The British front positions were outposts rather than continuous trenches. The men who had survived the barrage could see less than 100 yards because of the mist and smoke. An English officer wrote that the German machine-gun fire seemed unusually accurate. When the fire ceased he peeped over the parapet and discovered why. An 'enormous and terrifying iron pillbox' was coming straight for him. The Germans were using a handful of tanks they had recently built and it is easy to understand the officer's horror. These tanks were bigger, squarer and uglier than the British models, lumbering forts that carried a crew of eighteen. The English officer crouched as the tank, wheezing and heaving, passed over his trench. He then stood up and fired at the water jacket of one of its machine guns. That was the only thing he could see that looked vulnerable.

The tanks caused panic, more so because they came out of the mist. The British line broke and the Germans claim to have taken more than 2000 prisoners. The town fell. Foch, as generalissimo, told Rawlinson to get it back. Major-General Heneker, the commander of the 8th Division, tried several counter-attacks. None worked.

POMPEY ELLIOT WAS becoming cranky. He had a plan and he wanted to use it. The reports he was receiving were inconclusive but they all hinted at a German breakthrough. Australians holding the line near Hill 104 could see Germans emerging from Villers-Bretonneux and pushing north. Elliott rang Talbot Hobbs, his divisional commander. He had devised a counter-attack, he told Hobbs. Could he launch it? According to Elliott, Hobbs said yes. In truth Hobbs said much more. He said Elliott could only operate on the 8th Division's front if he received an urgent request from the British to do so. Meanwhile he could move his brigade forward to bring it alongside the other Australians at Hill 104. And he had to keep Hobbs informed of whatever he was doing.

Elliott at once issued an order to his 59th and 60th battalions. They were to begin an enveloping movement on the northern side of Villers-Bretonneux. The order included this sentence. 'All British troops to be rallied and re-formed, as our troops march through them, by selected officers, and on any hesitation to be shot.' Here was another hint of megalomania, written down so that the world could see it. Elliott was close to his fortieth birthday and one step from command of a division; yet every now and then he behaved like a teenager who had become fevered from reading too much about Cromwell and Marlborough. A copy of the order went to Hobbs' headquarters. Hobbs told Elliott to remove the sentence. Elliott couldn't understand what he had done wrong, and still couldn't a month later.

Hobbs had been trying to obtain information from Heneker, who had lost touch with his troops. Then Hobbs heard that Heneker was about to counter-attack. Hobbs told Elliott to wait. Small groups of British stragglers were arriving at the 15th Brigade's lines. Elliott, mounted on Darkie, drew his revolver and threatened to shoot British gunners who wanted to pull back to the Somme. They decided to stay.

Noon passed. Heneker muddled, as did Butler, his corps commander. Elliott waited and, one suspects, swore a lot. Rawlinson, meanwhile, had ordered Glasgow's 13th Brigade, on the Somme near Corbie, to march south eight miles and help with the recapture of Villers-Bretonneux. Heneker still seemed to be suggesting his own men could carry out the counter-attack. Rawlinson became more insistent that the town be retaken. He had now decided that the reinforcements in the 8th Division were children – his word – who had been shaken by their first bombardment. Heneker telephoned corps headquarters and said he couldn't organise a counter-attack because 'we don't know where we are and where enemy is'. In truth he probably hadn't known these things since early in the morning.

The generals talked through the afternoon and eventually came up with a scheme. There would be a night attack. Elliott's brigade would attack on the northern side of the town, pushing east then turning south to the Roman road. Glasgow's brigade would attack south of the town, then turn north to meet Elliott's men and envelop the Germans. Two of Heneker's battalions would then clear the town. Both Australian brigades would be loaned to Heneker. If this latter decision made little sense, it was the way things were done. Haig's army was not a meritocracy; few armies ever are.

Glasgow was tough-minded and practical. He needed to know more about this night attack he was to make over ground he had not seen. He went to Heneker's headquarters on the Somme flats. Glasgow wanted to work out a safe starting point, which meant he needed to know where the British troops were. Heneker pointed to spots west of Villers-Bretonneux. But he said the positions kept changing. 'I can't be sure of it,' he admitted. Glasgow said he could easily find out where the troops were. 'I'll go up there myself and come back and see you.' Glasgow went forward and satisfied himself that the British lines south-west of the village would hold. On the way back he saw his own men marching south, helmets cocked, cigarettes dangling.

A dispute now arose about where Glasgow should start his attack. Heneker said it had to start from the village of Cachy, because 'the corps commander says the attack is to be made from Cachy'. Glasgow said he wanted it to start further north, between Cachy and Villers-Bretonneux. Heneker deferred to him. Glasgow said he wanted to start the attack at 10.30 pm. Heneker said it had to start at 8 pm, only a few minutes past sunset, because the corps commander 'wished it done' at that time. 'If it was God Almighty who gave the order, we couldn't do it in daylight,' Glasgow said. Heneker referred the question to Butler, then successively asked Glasgow whether 8.30, 9 or 9.30 would suit him. Glasgow eventually conceded half-an-hour. The attack would go in at 10 pm.

Bean thought the night attacks would fail. Before going to sleep he wrote in his diary: 'One cannot help thinking of our magnificent 13th Bde going over – as they may be doing now. I don't believe they have a chance . . .'

Private David Whinfield, a stretcher-bearer in Elliott's brigade, scribbled in his diary:

Such a day – I never want to see any more like it. Suspense specially deadly suspense like this has not one redeeming feature about it. Since 10 last night we have been rigged up all ready and to march off to support and now it is to counter attack for some ground lost by the Tommies this morning. We were moving off at 10 last night, 4 am, 9 am, 1 pm, 5 and now 7. It is a terrible time. How will men hang on at this awful cruelty. Nerves are being shredded. Men's future strength is being heavily drawn from. My nerve is weak.

SERGEANT JIMMY DOWNING set off with one of Elliott's battalions, the 57th. The 59th and 60th battalions were leading the northern attack, with Downing's battalion following the 59th, which was on the right and closest to the town. 'There were houses burning in the town, throwing a sinister light on the scene,' Downing wrote. 'It was past midnight. Men muttered: "It's Anzac Day," smiling to each other, enlivened by the omen.'

The men blundered into wire and took their bearings from the burning town on their right. A machine gun opened up ahead. A captain in the 59th Battalion gave the order to charge and a great swelling noise rose over the battlefield. All the men were yelling, shouting, howling, cheering. A shout went up: 'Into the bastards, boys.' The roar was so loud that Glasgow's brigade heard it on the other side of the town. Downing said the men rushed straight at the machine-gun posts, rather than trying to take them in the flank. The Germans fought bravely, even continuing to fire machine guns when transfixed by bayonets.

The Australians 'killed and killed', Downing wrote. 'Bayonets passed with ease through grey-clad bodies and were withdrawn with a sucking noise.'

> Some found chances in the slaughter to light cigarettes, then continued the killing. Then, as they looked for more victims, there were cries of "There they go, there they go!" and over heaps of big dead Germans they sprang in pursuit . . . One saw running forms in the dark, and the flashes of rifles, then the evil pyre in the town flared and showed to their killers the white faces of Germans lurking in shell holes, or flinging away their arms and trying to escape, only to be stabbed or shot down as they ran . . . It was impossible to take prisoners. Men could not be spared to take them to the rear . . .

These are Downing's recollections as published in 1920 in *To the Last Ridge*. He was more explicit in a letter written to a friend four days after the attack.

> We made a long line and advanced. A petrol shell landed on an outlying building & set it aflame. We were seen. A tornado of machine-gun & rifle fire burst on the land. Some four men were smacked. That was the stark end of it. We all went fighting mad and did a thing almost unprecedented in war. There was a yell of rage and we *charged* – charged like hell hounds – like a pack of wolves . . . Then we were among them. We were Beserk, every one of us . . . There was no quarter. I remember bayoneting one Hun, a square fair solid fellow, and one old score was paid off. The bayonet passed right through his heart with surprising ease . . . One came to a machine-gun post which kept firing at us till we were on it & then surrendered. It was no use, this man said: 'How many of you are there? Oh six. Then share that among you' and he dropped a bomb among them. 'Now you've got your issue' . . . I saw Hun running away. I shot one *dead*. The rest disappeared in the gloom. The killing went on. I was mad. There was

blood all over my rifle & bayonet & hands and all. Dawn broke & we started sniping & got many more Huns . . . We were sick of killing . . . We had avenged Fleurbaix [as the battle of Fromelles was then called]. I wouldn't have missed it for anything. We settled many an old score. They were Prussian Guardsmen, too . . .

Downing dug in around dawn. He and the two companies of the 57th were near the Roman road east of the town. Two other companies of the 57th had been kept back as a flank guard. Now they pushed into the town. British troops were moving in from the west and Glasgow's men from the south. Some of Elliott's men arrived at a château on the edge of Villers-Bretonneux. They found a billiards table inside and began to play while bullets smacked through the window above their heads. They sniped back between shots. One man pounded out ragtime on a grand piano.

GLASGOW ATTACKED SOUTH of the town. There had been no time for a reconnaissance. Clouds blotted out the moon and the night became unusually black. The men had to reach Monument Wood, due east of their starting point, by 11 pm. The front formations were to push on speedily, leaving pockets of Germans to be mopped up by the second line. Billy Harburn, a captain in the 51st Battalion, told his men: 'The Monument is your goal and nothing is to stop you getting there. Kill every bloody German you see, we don't want any prisoners, and God bless you.'

His battalion, mostly West Australians, held the left flank of the attack and it was immediately in trouble. German machine gunners opened up from a wood to the left. Many of Harburn's men fell; there was a risk that the attack here would be held up.

Lieutenant Clifford Sadlier, a twenty-five-year-old commercial traveller from Western Australia, commanded a platoon in Harburn's company. Sergeant Charlie Stokes, a horse driver from Western Australia, was in the platoon next to Sadlier's. Stokes crept up to Sadlier and asked him what he was going to do.

'Carry out the order – go straight to our objective,' Sadlier said.

'You can't do it,' Stokes replied, 'you'll all be killed.'

'Well, what can we do?'

'Collect your bombers and go into the wood and bomb those guns out,' said Stokes.

Sadlier decided to leave the line with his platoon, turn left and attack the wood. Sadlier and Stokes, who had grabbed a bag of bombs, led the rush, firing around bushes and trees. At the first machine-gun post they came upon a German who held up one hand in surrender and with the other shot Sadlier through the thigh. Sadlier shot him with a revolver, then kept going, dragging his leg.

The scene in the wood must have seemed Dantean: the Australians blundering in the dark, bright needles of tracer bullets streaming towards them, the crump of bombs, shouts and sighs, death and confusion. Sadlier attacked a post alone. He killed the crew of four with a revolver. He was wounded again and couldn't go on. Stokes went from post to post and ran out of bombs. He met a corporal who had picked up some German stick-bombs. He used two of these to wipe out another German post, then went on and knocked out another two.

The crisis was over. All the posts – there were at least six of them – had been taken. The flank was safe. Sadlier and Stokes were both recommended for the Victoria Cross. Sadlier received it; Stokes was given the Distinguished Conduct Medal. It is hard to understand, on the known facts, how this distinction was made.

The line went forward again. Shots rang out in front. 'Bomb the bastards,' someone yelled. Bombs were thrown. The 'bastards' turned out to be remnants of two British battalions. They knew nothing about a counter-attack. They thought the Germans had got behind them.

Glasgow's men next ran into a line of wire in their approach to Monument Wood. The German fire on the other side of the wire became heavier. A machine gun to the left was firing along the line of the wire. Sergeant Stokes eventually knocked out this gun too.

Before he had done so, the gun had left dozens of Australians dead or wounded on the wire. Captain Harburn and another company commander alongside him decided to blow their whistles and rush the wire. Many were hit as they tried to find gaps. German flares and the fires of Villers-Bretonneux lit up the battlefield. A corporal said it was just like daylight.

Those who got through the wire rushed the German machine-gun posts. Harburn's company, much depleted, came on a group of Germans who put up their hands. 'No prisoners,' said Harburn. Afterwards he said: 'I did not know what to do with them.'

Glasgow's men finished a mile short of their objective in places, which meant they were about 1500 yards behind Elliott's brigade on the other side of the town, but they had done enough. They had pushed the German line back a mile. If the pincers had not quite closed, the Germans in the town were close to being cut off, especially since Elliott's men held the Roman road leading east.

IN THE MISTY dawn two battalions from Heneker's division and two companies from Elliott's brigade began clearing the town and the wood behind, taking a large haul of prisoners. Next day the two Australian brigades finally linked up on the eastern side of the town, although Monument Wood still had not been taken. Glasgow's brigade, which had been given the harder task, had incurred 1009 casualties. But for the bravery of Sadlier and Stokes, the figure would have been much higher. Elliott's brigade lost 455 men.

The victory found many fathers. Haig said he 'felt very pleased at the quiet methodical way' General Butler arranged the counter-attack. The war of movement had left Haig even more remote from what went on at the front. Birdwood came to congratulate Elliott. Elliott said that the general 'really tried to be nice to me . . . but he rather looked as if I had made him swallow a bit of green apple. I wore my old Australian jacket and looked as disreputable as I could too. It's a joke on these spick and span soldiers to show them that Australians have a few brains sometimes.'

Heneker didn't bother to congratulate the two Australian brigadiers who had made him look better than he was. He was himself claiming credit for the operation. The headquarters of Butler's

III Corps announced in an official document that 'the brilliant idea of the III Corps for the recapture of Villers-Bretonneux was ably carried out by the 8th Division, assisted by the 13th and 15th Australian Infantry Brigades'. According to Captain Ellis, the chronicler of the 5th Australian Division, the pomposity of this claim sent a flicker of amusement through the Australian brigades.

Elliott was furious with the British commanders: he felt that he should have been named as author. Here was another grievance he could carry for the rest of his life. The list was becoming rather long. Hobbs, the commander of the 5th Division, wrote in his diary:

> Our people have had very trying experience with British people under whose control they have temporarily been. III Corps in an order issued claim credit for the admirable planning of the night operation . . . I really planned it, but I felt I should never get the credit of it. My experience of higher British command this last 4 weeks has not been very inspiring . . . and the conduct of some of the troops through the ignorance, neglect and I am almost tempted to say – but I won't, I'll say nervousness of their officers – has had a very depressing effect on me and I expect many of my officers and men.

Brigadier-General G. W. St G. Grogan commanded one of Heneker's brigades at Villers-Bretonneux and a month later won the Victoria Cross. Writing in *Reveille* in 1936 he said: '[Villers-Bretonneux] will ever be remembered for perhaps the greatest individual feat of the war – the successful counter-attack by night across unknown and difficult ground, at a few hours notice, by the Australian soldier.' Grogan had witnessed the start of Glasgow's attack. He recalled that one Australian officer used very simple words: 'Boys, you know what you have to do. Get on with it.'

PRIVATE WHINFIELD, THE stretcher-bearer who had written 'My nerve is weak' before the battle began, received the Military Medal for bravery. With typical modesty he doesn't mention in his diary the incident that won him the decoration. Villers-Bretonneux didn't leave him with the warm glow it bestowed on others. 'I can't rhapsodise over last night's very successful counter-attack,' he wrote on April 25, 'others who feel different may.' He had carried out wounded under shellfire – 'a heavy strain on the nervous system'. And then things got worse.

Next day his diary entry began:

> Harry Bramley killed. I've suffered a severe loss this morning my best friend who came over with me, been near and with me ever since got killed instantly at about 4 this morning. I was out with a wounded Fritz at the time. Such a straight goer, such a reliable fine man. And now he is gone from me. I feel for his people, for his May. I wonder why such good men suffer. This is the third of my best mates I've lately lost. Catto, Ryan and Harry. I am going to try to see him.

And he did. 'Cliff Adams, Stan Newell, Jim O'Brien and I went and got Harry's body and gave it a Christian burial in a cemetery on the road midway between Corbie and Villers-Bretonneux.'

A few days later Whinfield was out of the line. 'No work or drill today. Had a bath the first for 8 weeks.'

Charlie Stokes had three children at the time of his exploit with Sadlier. A fourth, Gwen, was born after the war. Stokes was later to tell her that he had wept the morning after at Villers-Bretonneux when he saw what he had done to other human beings.

BUTLER AND HENEKER and their staff officers could cling to their delusions about what happened at Villers-Bretonneux; the present-day residents have no doubt about who recaptured their town. The school carries the words 'N'oublions jamais L'Australie' – 'Never forget Australia'. The school stands on Rue de Victoria, which runs into Rue de Melbourne, and has a fine museum. Here is a photograph of Billy Hughes and Charles Bean together on the Somme in 1918. Bean looks fresh and clean cut in his captain's uniform. Hughes is all hard bones covered with crinkly leather. You are reminded of a comment once made of him: 'Too deaf to listen, too loud to ignore, too small to hit.'

On the northern outskirts of the town stand the ruins of a château, owned by a local factory-owner and destroyed by shellfire in 1918. Scars show on its red bricks. It must have been stately in its day; now it somehow seems magnificent, deserted and shot to pieces, but still standing and showing its wounds to the world. One wonders if this is the château where the Australians played billiards and ragtime. The position is right.

The Australian National Memorial stands high on a hill north of the town. From its tower you look over a patchwork quilt: the yellow of stubble, the green of sugar beet, the brown of fallow. Charolais cattle, sleek and heavy, graze in the summer sun and brown-red clouds swirl behind tractors scratching at the stubble. Through the haze one can just make out the spire of Amiens cathedral and, near it, a rival built long after the Great War, a grey industrial building that would have surely beckoned to King Kong. From this hill the Germans could have shelled Amiens to ash.

A few miles away, on the other side of the Somme, on the road from Corbie to Bray, near the old brickworks, corn is ready for harvest in the field where Richthofen died. The Morlancourt Ridge is on your left and the picture-book valley of the Somme on your right. There is no traffic on the road. All is quiet. And the place speaks to you. You can see a red triplane coming up the valley to the left of Hamel; you can hear the chatter of machine guns and the shouts of men on the ground. And then a car comes along the road to Bray and the triplane is gone.

THREE DAYS AFTER the counter-attack at Villers-Bretonneux a young man with a haunted face died of tuberculosis in a prison hospital in the Bohemian town of Theresienstadt. He was Gavrilo Princip, the Bosnian Serb who as a nineteen-year-old had shot Franz Ferdinand in Sarajevo. Princip was a nobody, a conspirator but no intellectual. Yet with two shots from a Browning revolver he had started perhaps the most terrible chain-reaction in history.

Dr Jan Levit, a military surgeon, attended Princip during his final days. Levit in 1942 found himself back at Theresienstadt – as a prisoner. Theresienstadt was now a concentration camp for Jews. Levit was sent to Auschwitz and killed. The author of the racial laws that deemed him unfit to live was in 1918 a corporal on the western front.

41

The press gang

Charles Bean first met Brudenell White in Melbourne in September, 1914, and liked him at once. White had fair hair, a high forehead, a Roman nose, pinky-white skin, twinkling blue eyes and two kind lines around a mouth that broke into a wide smile. Everyone remarked about the eyes and the smile: the eyes were piercing, the smile avuncular. White was a man of Victorian courtesy and charm. Even at thirty-seven he had an air of paternalism. He didn't swear; he cared about manners and disapproved of showiness; he believed in duty and modesty. His handwriting was extraordinarily neat and he had a gift for clear English. He had an even better gift for organisation, sorting out problems with quiet persistence rather than bluster. He believed passionately in the British empire and its values. He was suspicious of democracy: to him it smacked too much of rule by the mob. 'From his first word,' Bean wrote, 'I felt he was my friend.' After Gallipoli the affection grew to something approaching idolatry. Bean saw White as a genius – his word – and perhaps also as the man he, Bean, would have liked to have been.

And now, on May 16, 1918, almost four years later, Birdwood had called Bean aside to tell him in confidence that Monash would

shortly take command of the Australian Corps. Birdwood was leaving to command the 5th Army, which was being re-formed. He was
taking White with him as his chief-of-staff, which made sense
because White was good at the things Birdwood wasn't, notably
administration. Birdwood had in fact been holding two jobs: he
was the field commander of the Australians on the western front;
and he also had administrative control over all of the AIF, be it in
Palestine, at AIF headquarters in Horseferry Road in London or the
depots on Salisbury Plain. He was proposing to go to the 5th Army
but also to retain the administrative post, General Officer
Commanding (GOC) of the AIF.

Bean was so upset by what Birdwood told him that he appears
to have fallen into a panic. Monash was a showman, too pushy, too
ambitious, not Bean's sort of chap – never had been. He was a
'lucid thinker' and a 'wonderful organiser' but he lacked 'the physical audacity [whatever that meant] that Australian troops were
thought to require in their leaders'. He might not be able to resist
the callings of personal ambition. He might not stand up to an insistent superior or the strain of a disaster in the field. But it was the
loss of White that bothered Bean most. White was 'brilliant' and
'noble', the obvious choice to command the Australian Corps. Bean
not only believed all this was true: he thought many others in the
AIF felt the same.

The next night he 'blurted out' the news to Will Dyson, the fine
cartoonist who had become the official war artist, and Hubert
Wilkins, the official photographer, at the Australian correspondents' headquarters at Querrieu, near Amiens. Afterwards Bean
wrote in his diary:

> There was immediately a great consternation . . . We had been talking of
> the relative merits of White who does not advertise and Monash who does
> . . . Dyson's tendencies are all towards White's attitude – 'Do your work
> well – if the world wants you it will see that it has you' . . . Dyson thinks
> it a weakness, but he takes it better than the advertising strength which
> insists on thinking or insinuating itself into the front rank. He says: 'Yes –
> Monash *will* get there – he must get there all the time on account of the

qualities of his race; the Jew will *always* get there. I'm not sure that because of that very quality Monash is not more likely to help win this war than White, but the manner of winning it makes the victory in the long run scarcely worth the winning.'

This all seems strange. Did Dyson truly believe that winning the war was somehow shabby if a man he and his friends disliked happened to command the Australian Corps? And did Dyson really talk in such a stilted way in conversation with two friends?

The three decided that they would fight for White because they knew he would not fight for himself. They decided that Birdwood should go, that White should be given the field command and Monash the administrative post (which would possibly see him promoted to full general).

Bean cabled Senator George Pearce, the Defence Minister, in Melbourne, telling him that White, 'universally considered greatest Australian soldier', should not leave the corps. Then Bean and Dyson left for London to see Keith Murdoch. Murdoch knew about politics in a way they didn't; he would know what to do.

ERIC EDGERTON OF the 2nd Division had seen some of Dyson's sketches. He wrote in his diary early in 1918 that they were 'very fine and typical of what the men actually look like in France'. Edgerton, big-framed and boyish, was in his third year of war and about to turn twenty-one. His life had moved at frantic speed since he had left Wesley College, Melbourne. He had enlisted as a student and risen from private to lieutenant; he had twice won the Military Medal for bravery; he had seen the horrors of Lone Pine and Pozières. Yet everyone spoke of his sunny nature. Now he was at the Amiens front, on the northern side of the Somme. 'The villages around here are pitiful to see,' he wrote just after his birthday. 'If a few Australian towns were levelled in the same manner and the inhabitants had to leave all their possessions the general attitude of the Australian public to the war would alter . . .'

Edgerton was in action at Ville-sur-Ancre the day after Bean left to see Murdoch in London. He led five of his men into the village, rushed the German line, shot five Germans himself, then captured a machine-gun post. Edgerton had shown 'brilliant leadership', his battalion commander wrote in recommending him for the Victoria Cross. Edgerton received the Distinguished Service Order.

LUDENDORFF'S TWO BIG offensives had faltered and died. The cost on both sides had been terrible. British casualties for the forty-odd days after the opening of Operation Michael on March 21 came in at 236,300, nearly as high as for the Passchendaele offensive, which had lasted sixty-five days longer. The figure was worse than it looked: it included 70,000 men taken prisoner, which meant they were out of the war just as surely as the dead. The French had lost some 90,000, which brought the allied casualties to around 326,000. The Germans appear to have lost slightly more than this. And Germany, unlike the allies, was running out of men.

Yet Ludendorff and Hindenburg – in theory his superior – were still living with the delusion of total victory when they should have been thinking about how to negotiate a peace while they still held large tracts of France, Belgium and Russia. They were also delusional about conditions at home. More people were being drawn to Bolshevism. More were questioning the divine rights of Kaiser Wilhelm and asking where he was leading them. They didn't know that he wasn't leading them, that on most matters he had abdicated to Hindenburg and Ludendorff. Worst of all, Operation Michael had raised expectations at home; now it had petered out and so had the expectations. The war would go on without the prospect of a decision; children would grow up cold and hungry.

Robert Asprey wrote in *The German High Command at War* that Hindenburg and Ludendorff probably believed that the tide of defeat could be reversed.

Had they talked to ordinary people, perhaps they would have gained a more realistic notion of civil and military morale. They did not talk to ordinary people. They talked to people as pig-headed, blind, and greedy as themselves: industrialists, conservative politicians, bankers and economists who lied about production capabilities and fiscal soundness; to army group and army commanders and their chiefs of staff who lied about ground gained and enemy killed and the state or morale of their men; to navy admirals who had guaranteed that not one American soldier would land in France and who fatuously continued to claim that the crippled submarine offensive would any day force Britain from the war . . .

Ludendorff became more of a gambler. Now he came up with Plan Blucher. He would attack the French on the Chemin des Dames on May 27. The Germans surged across the Aisne and reached the Marne; soon they were only sixty-or-so miles from Paris, where the mood became panicky. Two American divisions were thrown in on the Marne and fought well. French troops retreating through an American position told a marine officer that his men should retreat too. 'Retreat? Hell,' said Captain Lloyd Williams, 'we just got here.'

Ludendorff called off Blucher on June 3. Further gains there seemed improbable and his infantrymen had outrun their supply columns and artillery. Again, Ludendorff had taken large amounts of ground and caused affright. But, again, the blow was not decisive. And Ludendorff had lost another 100,000 men. It was not enough to say the allies had lost about the same number. The allies could replace their losses; Ludendorff couldn't.

WHEN BEAN, DYSON and Murdoch met in London in mid-May they were trying for nothing less than to overturn a Cabinet decision. Birdwood had told Monash on May 12 that he had recommended him to the Australian Government for command of the corps. The only other contenders, Birdwood thought, were White and Hobbs, but Monash was the obvious first choice. Haig agreed with Birdwood. White, ever gracious, told Birdwood that Monash should have the job: he was an 'abler man'. The Australian Government approved the recommendation on May 18 (the day Bean and Dyson travelled to London) in the absence of Billy Hughes, who was sailing to England via North America.

Birdwood telephoned Monash and told him he had the job and promotion to lieutenant-general.

Monash's chest swelled, as it was inclined to at such times. He wrote to Vic, his wife, that his corps was two-and-a-half times the size of the respective armies of Wellington and Napoleon at Waterloo. He had also worked out that his artillery was 100 times more powerful than Wellington's. A few weeks later he mentioned that he was now driven about in a Rolls-Royce. By then he had moved into Bertangles Château, north of Amiens. It had an imposing façade of about 300 feet, Monash told Vic. Monash, as Birdwood later noted without rancour, liked to put all his goods on the counter.

Bean and Dyson apparently had to convince Murdoch that White should take over the corps. Bean says in the official history that the two of them *swung* Murdoch; in *Two Men I Knew* he says they *persuaded* him. After the meeting Murdoch cabled Hughes in the United States. Bean said that Murdoch's cable exaggerated the intriguers' case, then added that Murdoch was doubtless misled by himself (Bean) and Dyson, 'who believed that their views represented those widely held in the AIF'. Murdoch's cable claimed that White was 'immensely superior in operations strategy and more likely inspire all divisions whereas Monash's great ability certainly lies in administrative work'. Murdoch suggested the appointments be made 'temporary'.

Hughes cabled Pearce in Melbourne urging that the appointments be held over until he reached London. Birdwood suddenly heard from the Army Council in London that his appointment to the 5th Army was temporary.

Murdoch, reverting to his other job as a journalist, tried to send a story to the Sydney *Sun* saying that there was a 'strong unanimous view' that Birdwood should not retain administrative command of the AIF, that White was likely to become corps commander and Monash GOC. The censor refused to pass the story.

THE DRAMA HAD now lurched towards farce. Consider, first, the behaviour of Hughes. He had twice divided Australia with campaigns for conscription. In doing so he had said, in effect: 'Trust me. I know what is going on at the war.' Yet he knew so little about what was going on that he relied on Murdoch to tell him who was fit to command the AIF. One might have expected the Prime Minister to have thoughts of his own on who should command his army.

Second, consider the position of Murdoch. He was playing courtier and journalist at the same time. Elected by no-one, apparently accountable to no-one, he was as powerful as anyone in the Cabinet in Melbourne. He had just managed, with one cable to Hughes and a word here and there around London, to have Birdwood's new command changed to 'temporary'. And he had his facts wrong.

There was no groundswell for White. It was misleading and, worse, an irrelevance, to claim that Monash lacked operational skills, and to imply that White possessed these qualities in larger measure. White had never held a field command during the war. Pompey Elliott was all about daring and dash, yet he was quick to realise that such qualities were not the most important credential for a corps commander in modern war. After the war Elliott would describe himself as an 'efficient foreman', a lawyer who instinctively looked to the past for enlightenment and precedents. Monash, the scientist and engineer, Elliott contended, had seen the future; he was 'the designer of the new'.

Finally, consider the emotional journey that Bean was on. Everything he had done in the last few days was out of character. He had always been careful, as journalists should be, to be an observer rather than a player. He was a conscientious reporter, always checking to ensure that he had his facts right, no matter how minor the skirmish. And here he was, plotting and intriguing and counting numbers, not because he wanted to be a player but because he sincerely believed he was working to stop a 'tragic mistake'. Bean thought all of the AIF adored White as he did. He likened him to Victor Trumper, the Australian batsman who had been called 'the perfection of grace.' In truth most Australian soldiers knew less about White than they did about Monash.

Monash was a modern man and this seemed to offend Bean. White, on the other hand, seemed to embody the values Bean had embraced as a public schoolboy in England. Monash had intellectual qualities – he was the true Renaissance man – that should have appealed to Bean, but they didn't. Monash saw war as a vast engineering undertaking. Mastery of detail was more important than heroics. Realism was better than romanticism, clarity better than bluster. It was true that Monash didn't get out among the frontline troops the way Birdwood did, and he probably should have done so more often, but 'Birdie' was a poor planner, and preparation was more important than gladhanding. What seems to have offended Bean most – and this is only apparent from reading his diaries and notes – was Monash's vanity, his need to 'advertise' and seek the baubles of conventional success.

Colonel Thomas Dodds, Birdwood's deputy adjutant general, ended up telling Bean he was an 'irresponsible pressman', which was sad because Bean was a man who put accuracy above all else. Bean, in turn, told Dodds that Monash had worked for Birdwood's job 'by all sorts of clever well hidden subterranean channels'. Bean decades later scribbled in the margin of his diary: 'I do not now believe this to be true.' The likelihood is that in later life Bean regretted his part in the plot.

Murdoch luxuriated in intrigues. Power interested him more than words. Manipulating people was his *metier* and he was good at it. Having cabled Hughes and caused confusion, he set about widening his front. Soon the dispute became even more confused. Was it, as Bean wanted it to be, about the respective merits of White and Monash as corps commander? Or was it about whether Birdwood should hold the job of administrative head of the AIF while also commanding the 5th Army? Everything now became muddled and nasty.

Birdwood realised what Murdoch was doing and wrote to Munro-Ferguson, the Governor-General, and other supporters. Murdoch, he said, was trying to be the 'Australian Northcliffe'. Murdoch wrote to Monash to offer his 'hearty congratulations'. Monash wrote to Vic, saying: 'I profoundly distrust this man.' Monash then wrote to Billy

Hughes, suggesting he come to France and disputing Murdoch's claim to be the spokesman of the AIF.

Bean wrote to White:

> You know and I know and Gen. Birdwood knows and everyone knows, that our men are not so safe under Gen. Monash as under you. You know that no-one will safeguard them against a reckless waste – or useless waste – of life in impracticable or unnecessary stunts, or will get so much effect out of them in a good stunt – as you can or would.

Murdoch wrote to Monash again. Professor Geoffrey Serle, Monash's biographer, called this letter an 'explicit bribe'. Murdoch said that people had encouraged Monash 'to regard me with suspicion and even with hostility, just as on occasions some have whispered and lied to me about you'. In fact he valued Monash's 'extraordinary ability' and had always admired him as a soldier. 'It takes two to make a friendship, of course, but please let me assure you that you have my personal esteem as one young Australian towards a much abler and wiser compatriot.' Murdoch admitted he had recommended White for corps commander. He thought Monash's 'genius' lay in the 'higher sphere' of administration and policy. The job of GOC was important. Monash might become a full general if he took it. Murdoch reminded Monash that his cables went to 250 newspapers.

Monash sent a diplomatic reply. Then he began to write to Birdwood about Murdoch. 'It is a poor compliment, both for him to imagine that to dangle before me a prospect of promotion would induce me to change my declared views, and for him to disclose that he thinks I would be a suitable appointee to serve his ulterior ends.' Monash didn't send this letter.

Bean came to see Monash. Bean wrote in his diary afterwards:

> Monash is a man of very ordinary ideals – lower than ordinary I should say. He cannot inspire this force with a high chivalrous patriotic spirit – with his people in charge it would be full of the desire to look and show well – that is the highest. There is no question where the interest of the

Australian nation lies. It lies in making White one of its great men and makers.

Hughes arrived in London on June 15. He was the man both sides had to convince. Birdwood attended a reception for Hughes in London. The general was becoming unusually feisty. He had already written to Murdoch: 'I dare say you will beat me, but, I warn you, I shall make a hard fight before I die.' Andrew Fisher, the Australian High Commissioner, spoke disdainfully of Monash. Birdwood rebuked him. Murdoch asked Birdwood whether Monash really was fit to be corps commander. 'Of course,' Birdwood snapped, 'he can do it much more ably than I.' White wouldn't accept the corps commander's job if it were offered, Birdwood said. To do so would be to suggest that he had been intriguing with Murdoch. Birdwood told Hughes that he had complete confidence in Monash and that Rawlinson and Plumer also believed in him. Hobbs wrote to Pearce in Melbourne to say that the AIF respected Monash as a 'fighting leader'. Bean wrote a note to Hughes setting out the case for White. Rawlinson said Murdoch was 'a mischievous and persistent villain'. Bean wrote to White again. One has the feeling that Bean was embarrassing White. Monash told Vic that he had trumps to play. They were called Haig and Rawlinson.

Hughes came to France on July 1 with Joseph Cook, the Deputy Prime Minister, and Murdoch. The timing was poor, although Hughes didn't know this. Monash was planning a set-piece battle north-east of Villers-Bretonneux for three days hence. Hughes eventually told Monash that he wanted to postpone the questions of who should command what. Monash told Hughes that he would regard his removal as corps commander as a humiliation. He would not voluntarily give up the command. Hughes tried to soothe him.

Three Australian divisional commanders saw Hughes. All were for Monash. Hughes' confusion grew; he became more crotchety than usual. He called Murdoch aside and told him he had met no-one who agreed with his [Murdoch's] views. Here was the pith of the matter. It had been there since May 16 when Bean, Dyson and

Wilkins sat down at Querrieu. There had never been strong feeling against Monash; there had never been a push for White. Everything had proceeded from false premises.

White's embarrassment grew. He wrote to Monash to say that 'if the conspirators in this matter do happen to be General White's friends, they are not acting at the suggestion or with the approval of General White'. White in mid-July rebuked Murdoch for impropriety and meddling. Murdoch took little notice: he didn't take White as seriously as Bean.

Hughes eventually decided that Monash could have either job – corps commander or GOC. When it became apparent Monash wanted to stay with the troops, Hughes offered the GOC job as a full-time post to Birdwood, thinking he would be unwilling to resign his 5th Army command. It was now mid-August. Birdwood spoke to Haig, who told him to take the job but on the basis that he be loaned to the British army until November 30. This was apparently agreed to. The dispute was over. Nothing had changed. Monash commanded in the field; Birdwood retained the powers of GOC while also commanding the 5th Army.

JOHN GELLIBRAND, THE brigadier who in dress often looked scruffier than his men, in 1915 described Pompey Elliott as 'gallant and despotic'. He also said he was 'bull-headed and ultra-Victorian'. Gellibrand was now given command of Monash's 3rd Division and Elliott was outraged.

The corps was being 'Australianised'. Thomas Glasgow took over the 1st Division from the Englishman Hooky Walker. Nevill Smyth gave up the 2nd Division to 'Rosie' Rosenthal, the architect who sometimes walked up to twenty miles on his brigade front and had been three times wounded and once gassed. The Australian Corps was now a true citizens' army, commanded by an engineer who also had degrees in law and arts and who entrusted his divisions to a Queensland grazier (Glasgow), two architects (Hobbs and Rosenthal), and a Tasmanian orchardist who had once served in the British army (Gellibrand). Sinclair-MacLagan, a career soldier born in Scotland, still commanded the 4th Division. He had first served in the Australian forces in 1901 and was apparently considered sufficiently 'Australian'.

Elliott felt he had been superseded. He hadn't: appointments to divisional commands were by selection, not seniority. Elliott had never been in contention, although he didn't yet know this. He wrote to White, incensed that Gellibrand had been chosen ahead of him, and more so because Gellibrand was a 'British officer'. Elliott hinted that he might appeal to Pearce, the Defence Minister. Elliott wrote in heat; White demolished him with cool prose. Gellibrand, White pointed out, was an Australian.

> Then as to yourself why all this great assertion? Do you think anyone doubts your courage? No-one in the AIF, I assure you. Or yr ability? It is well known; but – you mar it by not keeping your judgement under complete control – your letter is absolute evidence. Finally you actually threaten me with political influence. You have obviously written hurriedly and I am not therefore going to regard yr letter as written. But let me say this: if the decision rested with me I should send you off to Australia without the least hesitation if calmly and deliberately you repeated yr assertion to seek political aid . . .

White saw Elliott and they argued. White said Elliott 'suffered from lack of control of judgement'. He offered a string of examples, including Elliott's threat to hang looters at Corbie. Elliott withdrew his letter but his anger grew. Ross McMullin, Elliott's biographer, wrote that the 'supersession' was the greatest personal disappointment of Elliott's life. The grievance never left him.

BEAN AND MURDOCH had failed in their intrigue. Bean admitted his errors and reported the affair at length in the official history. In *Two Men I Knew* he wrote: 'So much for our high-intentioned but ill-judged intervention. That it resulted in no harm whatever was probably due to the magnanimity of both White and Monash.' No harm whatever? While Monash was being undermined by Bean and

Murdoch, while Billy Hughes was trying to discover things he should have known, the new commander of the Australian Corps had been trying to plan a battle for the little village of Le Hamel, three-and-half miles north-east of Villers-Bretonneux. Nine days before the battle was supposed to open Monash wrote to Vic: 'It is a great nuisance to have to fight a pogrom of this nature in the midst of all one's other anxieties.' Geoffrey Serle wrote in *John Monash* that Australia's higher commanders were distracted during some of the most vital days of the war. 'It is perhaps the outstanding case of sheer irresponsibility by pressmen in Australian history.'

Battle of Hamel, July 4, 1918

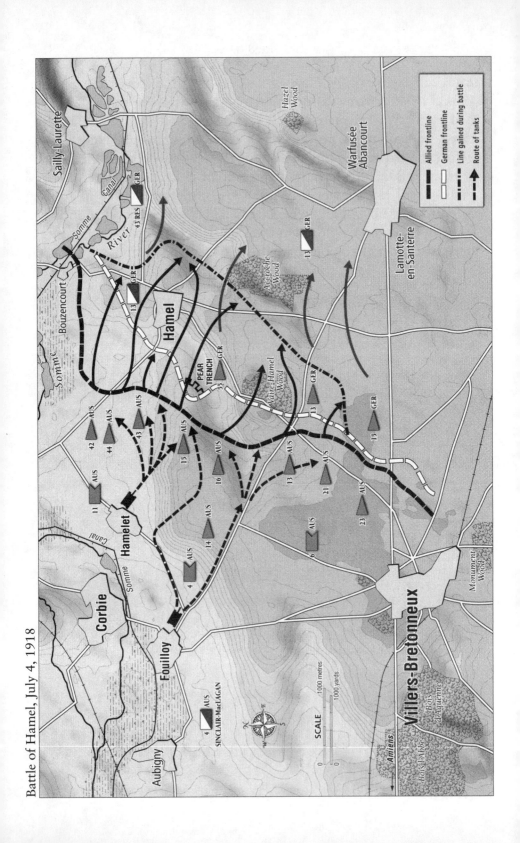

42

Ninety-three minutes

Bertangles Château, built in 1730, takes its elegance from the simplicity of its lines and the refusal of its architect to show off. The façade stretches for more than 80 yards in white-grey stone topped with a slate roof. It sits at the end of a long gravel drive and is flanked by glades of trees. Beyond them are double-storeyed barns, grain sheds and coach houses. One barn has a small clock tower, presumably to inform the farm labourers that they still had another two hours to work. A tractor with lugged iron wheels lies rusting in a patch of weeds. The main gates are topped by iron filigree, lots of delicate loops and curls. A blacksmith at Corbie hammered them out in the eighteenth century. He also made the gates near the choir stalls in the Amiens cathedral and the similarity of the work is uncanny.

Bertangles sits there with cold dignity, locked away like a museum piece behind glass. You have to imagine how it might have looked when it was Monash's headquarters: an Australian flag flapping in the breeze; dispatch riders waiting alongside their motorcycles and pulling on cigarettes; a groom holding officers' horses with hogged manes; staff officers tapping their leggings with canes, rather like red-tabbed prefects; corporals carrying sheaves of papers and looking deferential.

When Monash received his knighthood he fantasised about becoming governor of Victoria. That was before he came here. Here, perhaps, his ambitions widened. The governor's residence in Melbourne could fairly be described as homely in comparison to this. Here, in June, 1918, Monash cut off plugs of pipe tobacco – Capstan, full strength, brown label – and planned the attack on Le Hamel while also trying to finesse the intriguers Murdoch and Bean.

Hamel was between Villers-Bretonneux and the Somme. The Germans' front here bulged into the allied line. Monash, with the blessing of Haig and Rawlinson, was planning to take it with a tank attack.

NEAR VILLERS-BRETONNEUX on June 7, 1918, Private Henry Gibb died when a shell burst at his feet. An eyewitness told the Red Cross: 'He was so badly damaged that I would not tell his people. The parts of his body were gathered up and buried . . . A mate of mine took H. J. Gibb's son who is in the Artillery, to see the grave.'

Gibb's headstone at Villers-Bretonneux carries the words 'Peace after Strife' and lists him as being forty-five years old. His wife, Agnes, in supplying details for the roll of honour at the Australian War Memorial, said his age was sixty-three. Henry Gibb is probably the oldest Australian to have died during the Great War.

THE SPIRIT OF the Australian troops was better than it should have been. By a perverse turn, one reason for this may have been the fact that recruiting had dried up at home. The Australian Corps had a higher proportion of experienced men than Haig's armies, which were heavy with eighteen-year-olds. Natural leaders had emerged among the Australians and their authority came from who they were rather than badges of rank. Men who had enlisted as privates were now captains. Men who had been reckless at Pozières had learned to be careful and had survived and learned more. The Australians in late April came up with a tactic they called 'peaceful penetration'. The noun was right enough; the adjective was absurd. Some called the tactic more sensible names, such as 'nibbling' and 'winkling'. Whatever it was, it worked. The Australians practised it on the Villers-Bretonneux front south of the Somme, around Morlancourt in the triangle between the Ancre and Somme rivers, and in front of Hazebrouck in French Flanders. The British divisions at this time were mostly content to hold their lines.

Peaceful penetration was about changing the line without the fanfare of a set-piece. It was about sniping, harassment, shelling with gas, the snatching of prisoners and playing on the Germans' nerves. It was a new form of the trench raid, but this time the raiders did not withdraw after doing as much damage as possible in the shortest amount of time. The Australians tried to hold the positions they had raided and often did. So the German line was pushed back fifty yards here and seventy-five there, night after night. Peaceful penetration was a way of saying that no new status quo should be allowed to develop, that the war had to be kept fluid. Monash, while still commanding the 3rd Division, forced the Germans back about a mile at Morlancourt with a succession of raids. He had always liked to take prisoners, whom he would sometimes interview in German. They were now sufficiently demoralised to want to talk freely, he wrote. Here was another big change in the war: the morale of the German army was finally in decline. This was one reason peaceful penetration worked so well.

The 1st Australian Division at Hazebrouck worked hard at nibbling. Late in June, on a warm summer's day, Corporal Phillip Davey, a twenty-one-year-old horse driver from South Australia, a Gallipoli veteran who had won the Military Medal, went out on a raid near Merris. Davey's platoon came under fire from a machine gun and the platoon commander was killed. Davey twice went out alone with bombs, wiped out the gun crew, then turned the machine gun on the Germans. He was wounded in the back, legs and abdomen. His wounds were so bad that he was eventually invalided home. He received the Victoria Cross.

Four of Davey's brothers had enlisted. According to a *Bulletin* article in 1918, one of them was under fifteen when he joined up.

Two of the brothers, as well as Phillip, had won the Military Medal. One of these, Claude, had been killed at Bullecourt in 1917.

PEACEFUL PENETRATION, AND the information it produced about German morale, was one factor that led to the Australian attack at Hamel, which was to be led by Sinclair-MacLagan, commander of the 4th Division. Another was the availability of the new Mark V tanks. The Australians had been leery of tanks since First Bullecourt, where the Mark I had been used. The Mark V was faster – it could manage all of 4.6 miles per hour – and needed only one driver rather than three or four. It also had a reverse gear, could turn on the move, and generally was more reliable than the Mark I. And another factor that led to Hamel was that the allied commanders, having withstood Ludendorff's lunges, wanted to change the tempo. Foch, Haig, Rawlinson and Monash (whose corps was part of Rawlinson's 4th Army) all wanted to go on the offensive. The bulge at Hamel was a likely place to start.

Monash, Sinclair-MacLagan, and Gellibrand, the new commander of the 3rd Division, had considered a conventional infantry and artillery assault there in June. Monash put the scheme aside. Then the new tanks arrived. Monash was interested again. So was Rawlinson. It is unclear which of them came up with the idea of a tank attack. Both claimed credit and both may have been right.

Brigadier-General Hugh Elles, the commander of the Tank Corps, knew that the 4th Division men didn't trust tanks. He invited Monash and his chief-of-staff, Tom Blamey, to come and see the new Mark Vs. Monash talked to Brigadier-General Courage of the 5th Tank Brigade. Courage's idea was for a tank attack in three waves; the infantry would take any strong points that managed to hold out. There would be no creeping barrage but smoke shells would be used to screen the tanks from German observers on the Morlancourt heights on the other side of the river. Monash drew up a scheme. The artillery, he decided, would fire combinations of smoke and gas shells in the days before the attack. Then, on the morning of the assault – eventually set down for July 4 – the gas would be omitted. Monash hoped that the Germans, having been thus conditioned, would still pull on their gas masks and be disoriented while trying to fight off the attack.

To others in the Australian camp the memories of First Bullecourt in 1917 were still raw. Blamey, Sinclair-MacLagan and Brigadier-General Walter Coxen, the AIF artillery commander, thought the Courage–Monash plan too much of an experiment. They wanted a creeping barrage to protect the infantry. Monash and Rawlinson deferred to them. Monash was given extra artillery for the attack.

The battle plan that was taking shape was an eternity away from the rough schemes that sent thousands to their deaths in 1916. It accepted that, to succeed, attackers needed artillery superiority. With the extra artillery pieces loaned to him by British divisions, Monash outgunned the Germans at Hamel. Sound-ranging, flash-spotting and improvements in aerial photography meant that the allied gunners had a good idea of where the German guns were. There was no need for ranging shots before the main barrage; the opening shots would land just about right. Rawlinson and Monash were using all the technology they could to protect the infantry. The sixty tanks would crush wire, attack machine-gun posts and carry supplies. Aircraft would fly low to drown out the noise of the tanks; other planes would drop ammunition by parachute.

And the planners had thought well about where they were going to attack. Hamel, the village and the two woods south of it, were not particularly strong positions. The morale of the 2500 German infantrymen there was known to be poor. Their trench lines were shallow. This battle would be about using overwhelming force to crush a weak spot. It was an example of how to shorten the odds in one's favour.

THERE WERE AMERICANS on this front. They were supposed to be training alongside the British and Australian troops rather than fighting. Lieutenant Ted Rule of the 4th Division, a man of some wit, looked them over and pronounced: 'These Yanks view things just the same as we do, and their general trend of ideas was very sensible indeed.' The Australians were predominately Anglo-Celts; Rule could see among the Americans 'all the nations under the sun'. He enjoyed eavesdropping on American rollcalls and listening to the Italian and Polish surnames that he could not pronounce.

Lieutenant Eric Edgerton wrote in his diary: 'There is a great feeling of comradeship between the Colonials, Scotch and Americans – who, of course, are going to win the war! I suppose they wonder what we have been doing the last three years. Perhaps a little scrapping will quieten them down a bit. They are full of fight and enthusiasm, just like our old boys . . .'

Bean too was overcome by nostalgia. He saw athletic-looking and fresh-faced men wearing canvas gaiters and Puritan hats. 'The swing of them . . . the independent look upon their faces' – these reminded him of the old Australian 1st Division before Gallipoli, of men still, in a certain sense, innocent.

Rawlinson thought the Americans could learn much by being part of Hamel. Would Monash like to include them in his force? Monash asked for eight companies, about 2000 men. The American commanders on the spot agreed.

MONASH BROUGHT HIS engineer's mind to the final details of the plan. He sent the attacking brigades off to look at the tanks. The Australians watched the monsters (they were close to nine-feet tall) pirouetting to crush mock trenches, clambered over them, went for joy rides, even drove them. Each tank was given a pet name by the infantry company with which it was to serve. Infantry commanders talked and argued with tank men, who, in turn, dined in the infantry messes.

If there was one thing that set Monash apart from all other commanders on the western front, it was his conferences. They were just that: discussions where differences of opinion could be aired and resolved, rather than a harangue by the commanding officer. Monash drew up an agenda of 118 items for his first conference on June 28. Two days later he held a larger one. All the arms were represented: infantrymen, machine gunners, gunners, tank officers, airmen. Aerial maps were passed around. This time the agenda ran to 133 items and the conference lasted four-and-a-half hours. It is doubtful if any attack during the Great War had been planned with such care.

AND THEN, TWO days before the battle was to start, Billy Hughes turned up with Joseph Cook, the Deputy Prime Minister, and Keith Murdoch, none of whom knew that a battle was about to open. Hughes was still trying to work out who should be commanding his army. The timing of the visit could hardly have been more inconvenient, Monash told Birdwood. But he had to see Hughes, if only to tell him he would not voluntarily give up his command. Hughes wanted to talk to the troops and Monash had to tell him they would be attacking Hamel in two days. Hughes didn't want to talk about command of the corps; Monash had to raise the question himself.

Private Walter Adcock of the 2nd Division was part of a group that was marched four miles to listen to Hughes and Cook. All manner of threats were flying about during the march, Adcock wrote. 'The troops were going to count them out, and goodness knows what else.' As Hughes stepped forward there was a mumble from the lines but no interjections. Hughes started by saying he was there to thank them on behalf of the Australian people. 'It sounded so funny to me that he should say the people of Australia, when we are people of Australia ourselves,' Adcock wrote. 'However, it touched a very tender spot in the hearts of a good number of our boys. The very word "Australian" tingled in their veins.' The mood of the men changed. Words about home had softened them. On the march back they sang patriotic songs. Billy Hughes wasn't so bad.

While Cook was speaking at one gathering Hughes lay full-length on the ground, looking into the faces of the soldiers and chewing on a stalk of grass. One observer wrote that he 'seemed wrapped up in the men, and was gazing into their faces all the time'.

Hughes was becoming confused: the senior officers he met

mostly told him they were happy to serve under Monash. According to Bean's diary, Hughes confronted Murdoch and wanted to know the names of the anti-Monash group. Murdoch had no answer. Bean quoted Hughes as saying: 'Well, I haven't met a single one of them that thinks as you do.'

MONASH SUDDENLY HAD a more urgent problem. On July 3, as the men were moving up to the front, half the American contingent, 1000 men, was withdrawn. Pershing had only just discovered that his troops were involved. He didn't think his men were sufficiently trained and Haig, playing at diplomacy, ordered them out. Around 4 pm Rawlinson told Monash that *all* the Americans would have to be withdrawn. Monash asked Rawlinson to meet him at the village of Bussy-les-Daours, just north of the Somme, where Sinclair-MacLagan had set up his headquarters.

Monash was using only ten battalions for the assault; it was no small thing to lose 2000 men just as the battle was to begin and after he had planned every detail with such care. According to his account, he told Rawlinson it was too late to withdraw the second lot of Americans. If they were pulled out, he was prepared to cancel the attack. Unless he was ordered to abandon the battle, he intended to use the 1000 Americans. And any order to cancel the attack had to arrive by 6.30 pm. After that it would be too late to call it off.

Monash told the war correspondents that Rawlinson had said: 'Do you want me to run the risk of being sent back to England? Do you mean it is worth that?'

'Yes I do,' Monash said he had replied. 'It is more important to keep the confidence of the Americans and Australians in each other than to preserve even an army commander.'

Rawlinson finally got a message to Haig around 7 pm. Haig agreed that the battle had to go ahead and that the four American companies could not be withdrawn. The only detailed account of this incident comes from Monash, but it rather mocks Bean's assertion that Monash would not stand up to his superiors.

Zero hour was 3.10 am. Monash went to bed early. Coxen, the artillery commander was up well before zero hour. He looked out the window at Bertangles Château and saw a man slowly pacing up and down the gravel drive. It was Monash. Every now and then he would pause and look at his watch. The thunder of the guns opening up rolled across Bertangles. Monash stopped, looked to the south-east, then went inside to his office. Around 5 am he sketched the head of Hughes' chauffeur, a Frenchman. 'I find this occupation keeps my nerves cool and steady,' he wrote to Vic. He enclosed the sketch.

MONASH HAD TIMED the battle to last ninety minutes. He got that wrong: it lasted ninety-three.

He used brigades from three different divisions, all under the temporary command of Sinclair-MacLagan. In the centre, and with the hardest task, was the 4th Brigade from Sinclair-MacLagan's 4th Division. This was the same brigade that had suffered so badly from the failure of the tanks at Bullecourt. The word 'tank' became a form of obscenity in the brigade after that, yet here the men were, ready to believe again. The 4th Brigade was going for Pear Trench, which poked out in the centre of the battlefield, and Vaire and Hamel woods.

To the north, the 11th Brigade from the 3rd Division was going for Hamel village and beyond. To the south the 6th Brigade from the 2nd Division was covering the flank almost as far as the Roman road that ran eastwards from Villers-Bretonneux.

Before midnight some of the infantrymen had been given a second hot meal for the night, the tanks had begun to assemble behind the front and men were out in no-man's land removing the Australian wire and laying the starting tapes. The night was black and quiet. The Australians were given sips of rum to warm them up, then they and the Americans lay out in the wheat crop, which was waist high in places, and waited. A 3.02 am the Australian artillery began the harassing fire it had been sending over for the last fortnight.

Aircraft bombed the German positions to drown out the noise of the tanks. Then the main barrage opened up. It mostly fell just right. Shells from the field guns landed 200 yards in front of the waiting infantry. The smaller howitzers and heavies probed deeper into the German lines and massed machine guns poured fire in from the flanks. The infantrymen rose out of the crop, lit their cigarettes, slung their rifles and walked towards the barrage. The Americans, fighting in their first battle and full of derring-do, often pushed too close to the barrage and some were hit by the Australian artillery.

The 4th Brigade approached Pear Trench through the smoke. The tanks had not caught up with the infantry here and the artillery had failed to cut the wire. Machine-gun fire came from the parapets of white chalk ahead. Private Harry Dalziel, a railway fireman from north Queensland, was the second member of a Lewis-gun team. He helped his partner load a fresh drum then rushed a machine-gun post alone with a revolver, shooting two Germans and sparing a boy who had fought bravely. Part of Dalziel's trigger finger was shot away. He was bleeding badly and sent to the rear but decided to return to the fight. He was again ordered to the rear. Again he disobeyed orders, helping to bring up ammunition dropped by an aircraft. While doing this he was shot in the head. It was a terrible wound: his skull was smashed and his brain exposed. Dalziel lived to receive the Victoria Cross.

The Australians stormed into Pear Trench and chaos. One German kept firing his machine gun until the Australians reached him. Some of the Germans held up their hands; others behind them kept throwing bombs. The Australians saw this as double-dealing. It wasn't: it was just the way of war. Bean wrote that the Australians killed 'right and left' here.

To the south another battalion of the 4th Brigade approached Vaire and Hamel woods. A machine gun opened up. Lance-Corporal Thomas Axford, a brewery worker from Kalgoorlie who had been wounded in 1916 and 1917, rushed forward, threw his bombs at the Germans, then jumped into the trench with a rifle and bayonet. He killed ten Germans and captured six. Axford too received the Victoria Cross. Many of the Germans here were wearing gas masks. Monash's ploy had worked.

To the north the 11th Brigade went for Hamel village, which was on fire. The men could see the village blazing in front of them and Germans outlined against the glare. They took it with relative ease. Prisoners came blundering up from cellars. Bean wrote that the attitude of the men was noticeably carefree. An officer heard his men yarning as they dug in near the village. 'Do you think Fitzroy'll beat Carlton on Saturday?' one man asked.

On the southern front the barrage for the 6th Brigade was said to be perfect. The infantry and their tanks advanced steadily behind the smokescreen. Everything went as it was supposed to, and this didn't happen often.

Daylight came and the tanks were able to do more in the better light. They waddled (this was the verb many of the Australians used) up to machine-gun posts and opened fire at close range. Sometimes they ran over the posts, crushing everything – and everyone – underneath. Then they would reverse and run over it again.

THE 4TH BRIGADE in the centre of the attack had missed some German posts as it passed through. Ted Rule's battalion was digging a support trench about 500 yards behind the front when bullets began fizzing past him. Rule and his men, with help from a tank, went forward to attack the post. A white rag appeared. Rule and five others walked towards the trench, expecting a surrender. The Germans opened fire on them. The tank returned to help and the Australians took the trench. Rule came on two dugouts.

> When I yelled out to the occupants, out came two hands with a loaf of black bread in each, and presently a pair of terrified eyes took a glimpse at me. They must have been reassured by my look, because the Huns came out at once, and, when I sized them up, all thoughts of revenge vanished. We could not kill children, and these looked to be barely that. If any of us had been asked how old they were, most of us would have said between fourteen and fifteen . . . We knew these babes had not worked the white flag on us – they were too terrified for that, and, with a boot to help them along, they ran with their hands above their heads back to our lines.

More Germans came out to surrender, one or two at a time. Rule wrote:

> What a harvest for our boys! Talk about 'ratting' . . . as each Hun advanced with his hands above his head several of our lads would dive at him, and, before the astonished Hun knew what was happening, hands were in every pocket, and he was fleeced of everything but his name and his clothes . . . a new reinforcement was working like a cat on a tin roof, pulling cigars out of a Hun's pocket. In a ferocious manner I asked him if he was not aware of the order that all loot had to be handed over to an officer to be sent back to headquarters. He meekly handed them over. I smoked cigars all day, and the rest of the platoon tormented the life out of the youngster for falling to the joke.

Rule's battalion was relieved after forty-eight hours and went back to rest north of the Somme. Word went around that 'four ladies of easy virtue' were visiting a nearby village and would be 'at home' to their friends. 'The ladies handed out refreshments for all they were worth, until some brass hats bundled them out of town.'

RULE'S PLATOON HAD received supplies of ammunition from the air on that first morning; they then used them to shoot at German planes. The ammunition-droppers came in at 1000 feet or below and dropped two brown parachutes, each carrying a box of ammunition. Some 111,000 rounds were dropped this way. The technique was not new: the Germans had twice used it earlier in the year. The great innovation of the battle was the use of four 'carrier' tanks to bring up supplies. Here is what a single tank delivered in one load: 134 coils of barbed wire, 450 pickets on which to hang the wire, forty-five sheets of corrugated iron, fifty petrol tins filled with water, 150 mortar bombs, 10,000 rounds of small-arms ammunition and twenty boxes of grenades. The four tanks delivered supplies that once would have required fatigue parties totalling 1200 men, some of whom would inevitably have been killed or wounded as they crossed no-man's land.

If First Bullecourt was the debacle of the tank, this was the triumph. Only three of the sixty at Hamel failed to reach their objective; all but five were back behind the frontline by midmorning. Casualties among the tank crews numbered just thirteen.

By 4.45 am the Australians watching from the heights on the other side of the river could see tanks all over the battlefield and beyond Hamel village. Bean wrote that they could also see infantrymen 'standing in those unmistakable easy attitudes that marked the Digger in every fight'. A tank could be seen to slide forward, then back, then forward again, like a housewife's flat iron. It was rubbing out a German shelter.

In the dawn light the battle was already over. Lieutenant Eric Edgerton summed it up with a single sentence: 'Never have I seen such brilliant co-operation of all arms of the service, and with such excellent result.' Hamel was not a big battle but Monash (to use his own analogy) had scored the orchestra for infantry, artillery, tanks and air power better than anyone had ever done before. He had also proved that he was the right man to lead the Australian Corps and that he understood modern warfare better than Birdwood, White, Hughes, Murdoch, Dyson or Bean.

John Fuller, the Tank Corps staff officer who had planned Cambrai, later called Hamel 'the perfect battle'. Monash in his 1920 book *The Australian Victories in France in 1918* suggested that Hamel awakened the offensive spirit among the allies. This was an exaggeration. Before Hamel the French had made three strong attacks to the south of Rawlinson's army. One of these involved twice as many tanks as Monash had used at Hamel.

The three attacking brigades at Hamel had run up 947 casualties, a low figure by the canons of the Great War; the Americans had lost 176. Some 1600 prisoners were in the cages. A senior Australian officer called them 'the poorest lot I have seen'.

CLEMENCEAU, THE FRENCH Prime Minister, was at a meeting of the Supreme War Council at Versailles when word arrived of the victory at Hamel. Clemenceau began to tell his secretary to send a note of congratulations, as Lloyd George, Hughes and others had done. Then he changed his mind: he would go and see these Australians himself. Clemenceau liked to be out among the troops. The following Sunday he arrived at the 4th Division's headquarters at Bussy-les-Daours.

Hubert Wilkins, the Australian official photographer, was there to capture him in colour. Three days earlier Wilkins had been cut on the face and chin and shot in the right arm at Hamel. His work at Bussy shows Clemenceau in a brown three-piece suit, bow tie and floppy hat. His moustache is white and droopy, his girth ample and he leans on a walking stick. He looks all of his seventy-seven years – and also indomitable, in much the same way as Churchill would nearly a quarter of a century later.

Rawlinson, Monash, Sinclair-MacLagan and Bean, as well as men from the three attacking brigades, were there to meet him. They formed a circle around him. Clemenceau spoke in English:

> We knew that you would fight a real fight, but we did not know that from the very beginning you would astonish the whole continent . . . I shall go back tomorrow and say to my countrymen: 'I have seen the Australians. I have looked in their faces. I know that these men . . . will fight alongside of us again until the cause for which we are all fighting is safe for us and for our children.'

Clemenceau panted as he spoke, partly from asthma and partly from emotion. Sinclair-MacLagan led the Australians in three cheers for France.

HAIG THOUGHT HORSES were for cavalry; Australians knew what horses were really for: betting. A few weeks after Hamel the Australians staged a race meeting at Allonville, a few miles north-west of Bussy. Some 11,000 men attended – generals, privates, Australians, Canadians, Englishmen, Frenchmen – and one woman, identity unknown. There were a dozen bookmakers and a totalisator, a clerk of the course decked out in hunting pink and a judge's box. The betting was furious on the Gallipoli Hurdle and the Pozières Stakes. Much *vin blanc* was drunk in lieu of beer. Major A. W. Hyman of the 4th Division was clerk of the scales. He borrowed a butcher's scale for weighing the 'jockeys'. Two officers were killed in a fall in the first race. 'Fortunately', Hyman wrote, 'we were able to keep the fact from the crowd.'

German balloons to the east overlooked the race meeting but not a shell was fired. Two months earlier at Allonville a German shell had burst in a barn where 4th Division men were sleeping. The shell killed thirteen and wounded fifty-six. It was said to be the most costly shell-burst in the history of the AIF. Ted Rule went to help. A man with both legs cut off said to his rescuers: 'I'm all right – get the badly wounded boys out.'

THE WAR NEVER quite reached Bussy-les-Daours, so most of the houses in the present-day village, one of the most beautiful in the Somme country, were there when Clemenceau met the Australians in 1918. Friesian cows now graze in a bright green meadow alongside the Hallue River, where the Australian horse lines were in 1918. A mile or so to the south-east the downland suddenly drops and there, spread out below, is the Somme plain, a panorama of ponds, lagoons and marshland stretching away to the south for about a mile-and-a-half. The only sound is the honking of ducks. Australian pioneers rested above this flood plain in 1918. One suspects they shot the odd duck.

Clemenceau spoke to the Australians at Bussy Château, which is now empty. If it is no Bertangles, it is handsome enough: more than 200 years old, white-grey stone, slate roof, eight chimneys, six dormer windows. A London plane tree, as old as the château and one of the most dramatic trees on the Somme, soars above brambles, unkempt lawns and entrance gates mottled with rust. Once this place rang with the words of Clemenceau and the cheers of soldiers from the other end of the Earth. There are no echoes today, just the quacking of ducks in a backyard across the road.

Battle of Amiens, August 8, 1918

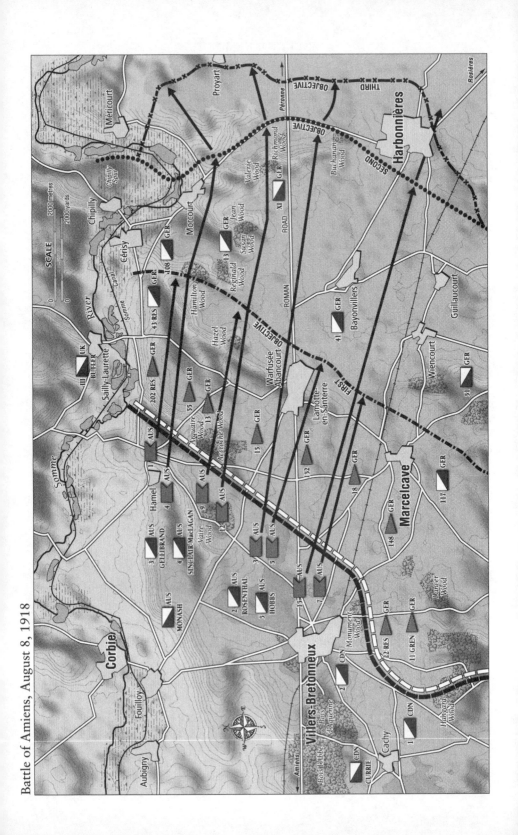

43

A very 'British' victory

After Hamel the allied commanders began to crystallise their ideas for a big counter-attack on the Amiens front. Foch, Haig and Rawlinson were thinking of nothing less than a second battle of the Somme, except this time the main front would be south of the river. What happened at Hamel might have made them more comfortable with their scheme, but it didn't cause it. The Australian tactic of peaceful penetration was probably more influential than Hamel. A staff officer wrote in the 4th Army's diary that the Australians had gained 'a mastery over the enemy such as has probably not been gained by our troops in any previous period of the War'. Peaceful penetration resumed on both sides of the river after Hamel and the message from the raiding parties was the same as before: the Germans' morale was low; their trenches were mostly shallow; there seemed no plan to fortify the new frontline. Here was an opportunity. Why couldn't the tactics of Hamel be repeated in a battle ten times bigger?

If there was a single event that emboldened the allied commanders, it was the counter-attack by General Charles Mangin's French armies on the Marne and towards Soissons on July 18, a fortnight after Hamel. The German salient there was bulging so close to the capital that Parisians could hear the guns and see the glow of artillery explosions at night. Mangin attacked with twenty-three divisions, four of them American, and close to 500 tanks, many of them the new two-man Renaults with rotating turrets. The Germans lost badly. Ludendorff had planned to attack Haig in Flanders. He now abandoned the idea: Foch and Mangin had forced his armies on to the defensive and thrown him into a tizz. If there was a tipping point in the Great War, Mangin's victory on the Marne was probably it.

But the genesis of what would become the battle of Amiens went back further, to at least mid-May, when Foch asked Haig to think about an Anglo-French offensive south of the river. Haig's response was to earmark the Australian and Canadian corps for the offensive. The scheme was put aside when Ludendorff attacked towards Paris, then revived after Hamel. Rawlinson sent his preliminary battle plan to Haig on July 17. He would attack with eleven divisions, including all of the Australian and Canadian corps, on a front of 19,000 yards, from Morlancourt, on the northern bank of the Somme, to Demuin, south-east of Hangard Wood.

Rawlinson had run the first battle of the Somme; the offensive he was now planning would be nothing like that. The Age of Reason had arrived. The belief that German trenches could be taken by an act of faith, by force of character, was in decline. Artillery tactics were now seen as the determinant of success or failure. It is probable that the men on the ground – battery commanders, colonels of machine-gun battalions, captains of infantry – had absorbed more about modern war than the Haigs and Rawlinsons. In a sense Haig and Rawlinson were less in control of the war than they were in 1916. Power had devolved downwards, to doers rather than overlords. Corps commanders, experts on tanks and artillery and aircraft: these men were all more important than they had been in 1916.

The belief at the first battle of the Somme was that all the artillery had to do was hit the enemy's front trenches. Now there was the concept of firepower, a formula of guns and shells and firing patterns that meant infantry could take trenches without fearful losses. Accurate counter-battery fire, creeping barrages, smoke barrages and tanks now protected the foot soldiers. Now the German wire was mostly cut, thanks to the graze fuse. The infantry itself had more firepower: battalions had fewer men but seven times as many Lewis guns as in 1916. Men such as Monash saw an 'orchestral composition' of artillery, infantry, tanks and air power. As Monash put it: 'Every individual unit must make its entry precisely at the proper moment, and play its phrase in the general harmony.'

There were other big differences. The Somme battlefield south of the river in 1918 was nothing like that north of the river two years earlier. The German fortifications of 1916 were fearsome: line after line, mile after mile, lots of concrete and timber, caverns and strong points, networks of communications trenches, and all of this set on high ground. It was formed up as if it was meant to be permanent, which it was. In 1918 the position of the German frontline had been mostly determined by chance, by where Operation Michael had finally petered out. The front trenches were often no more than rifle pits. The Germans still had their fortifications, but at the Hindenburg Line, twenty miles behind them.

In 1916 morale was high in both the German and British armies. Now, for the first time in the war, German morale was falling. The temper of Haig's home armies had also declined, mainly because of Operation Michael, but Australians and Canadians dominated Rawlinson's attacking force and their spirits were strong. And anyway, as Prior and Wilson point out in *Command on the Western Front*, this battle was not going to be about morale; it was going to be about firepower. Before a shot had been fired the British gunners had discovered the location of ninety-five per cent of the German batteries facing them. Science was in the ascendancy.

The date for the attack was set: August 8.

FOUR DAYS BEFORE this Adolf Hitler, the dispatch runner, received the Iron Cross, First Class, a decoration seldom given to corporals. He had been wounded in 1916 and spent almost two months in a hospital near Berlin. The mood of pessimism at home shocked him.

He noticed, or so he wrote years later in *Mein Kampf*, that most of the clerks were Jews and that few Jews were at the front. (In truth the number of Jews killed fighting for Germany was disproportionately high.)

Hitler returned to the front and served at Vimy, Ypres and Alsace, then on the Marne in 1918, where he won his Iron Cross, First Class. The story was later put around that he received this for single-handedly capturing fifteen Frenchmen. In fact he appears to have been decorated for delivering a message to the front after the telephones failed. The officer who recommended Hitler was Hugo Gutmann. He had to argue strongly before the decoration was approved. Leutnant Gutmann was a Jew.

RAWLINSON'S SCHEME CALLED for a deep and fast advance in three stages. In the first stage the infantrymen would go past the German frontline for another 1000 to 2500 yards. This would bring them to the inner Amiens defence line built by the French in 1916. Four divisions would do this work: one British on the northern bank of the river, two Australian in the centre and south of the river, and one Canadian below them. Four divisions (again one British, two Australian and one Canadian) would then leapfrog through them to capture the second objective, 3000 yards beyond the first. Here the men would halt before going on to the third objective, the old outer Amiens defence line, about 1000 yards ahead. Extra Canadian divisions would be brought in to secure the southern flank of the attack.

Then the plan was amended. Foch wanted a French attack south of the Canadians and Haig agreed to this. Lieutenant-Colonel Fuller of the Tank Corps came up with a strange pairing: cavalry with Whippet tanks. The two were to attack alongside each other to prevent the Germans withdrawing their guns. The three-man Whippet, at fourteen tons, was half the weight of the Mark V and could supposedly reach eight miles an hour. The horses could of course go much faster than that, but they had no armour plating.

Mostly, however, the battle plan was much like Monash's for

Hamel: the use of artillery, tanks and aircraft to protect the infantry, smoke barrages, a creeping barrage with up to forty lifts, meticulous planning, realistic objectives. Monash again held two conferences, the second one lasting four hours. Again he tried to think of everything. He ordered that one officer in each battalion be delegated to ensure that the men rested the day before the battle – 'no football, no wandering, but sleep.'

So whose plan was it in the end? Foch, Haig and Rawlinson can all claim a part in thinking up the idea. Rawlinson and Archibald Montgomery-Massingberd, his chief-of-staff, are entitled to most of the credit for the tactical plan, particularly on the Canadian front. The Canadians arrived late and didn't know the ground, which was more difficult than on the Australian front. Rawlinson's staff did much of the work for them. Fuller could take credit for the use of tanks on a massive scale. Monash's contribution was twofold: at Hamel he had demonstrated how to interlock four arms of warfare; and he was the chief architect of the plan for the Australian front.

The question of authorship arises because Monash for years afterwards believed he had caused the offensive to come about, as well as the form it took. White said in 1935 that Rawlinson, a subtle man, might have encouraged Monash to think that the overall plan was his [Monash's]. White said that Montgomery-Massingberd had told him that the British high command was 'deadly anxious not to do anything which might offend the Australian Corps or antagonise Monash, or Hughes, who at that time was a cloud on the horizon, on the subject of the employment of Australian troops'.

HUGHES HAD BEEN told in the political salons of London and elsewhere that the war would go on until at least 1919. Wilson, the Chief of the Imperial General Staff, thought it would still be going in 1920 and so did many others. All the Australian divisions in France were under strength. Enlistments at home had become a trickle. If the war went on until 1920 Hughes' force might be reduced to a rump. This would leave him with a weaker voice at any peace conference, and all along Hughes' strategy had been to ensure that Australia spoke with a loud rasping voice – rather like his own, actually – when the time came to share the spoils and punish the losers. Hughes wanted to be consulted before the Australian Corps was committed to any attack likely to involve high casualties. He was not consulted before Amiens.

The 'colonial' prime ministers were restive; Passchendaele had been the trigger. Sir Robert Borden, the Canadian Prime Minister, had arrived in London before Hughes. At a meeting with Lloyd George and others in mid-June he said that the British force's failures were 'largely due to lack of foresight and preparation, and to defects in the organisation and leadership of our forces'. Commanders should be appointed on merit, he said. The Canadian force was well organised 'under officers of whom only a small proportion were professional soldiers'. He mentioned that in the British army no 'civilian soldiers' had been given fighting commands above brigade level. This was equivalent to 'a wholesale scrapping of the brains of a nation in its struggle for existence'. Lloyd George was not the least offended by this criticism of his high command.

Hughes arrived in London and said he agreed with Borden. But he had a larger complaint: he hadn't been told enough about what was happening on the western front. He wanted to be assured that men were not being 'wasted for want of proper leadership and strategy'. Hughes said at a later meeting of the Committee of Prime Ministers that if Australia had been consulted, he would have opposed Passchendaele.

ONE MATTER TROUBLED Monash right up to zero hour. The boundaries for the Australian Corps were the Villers-Bretonneux railway line in the south and the river in the north. This was mostly good ground: a broad plain with gentle swells and valleys, much of it under crops. At the northern end, along the southern bank of the river, the ground was rougher and broken by gullies. Monash had wanted at least one of his brigades on the other side of the Somme.

The river looped to the south at the village of Chipilly, creating a peninsula of high ground called the Chipilly Spur. The Germans held this and it would give them a clear shot at the Australians on the other side of the river. The British III Corps under General Richard Butler was to take Chipilly Spur and other positions on the north bank while the Australians and Canadians poured out across the plain. Small ravines and woods broke the ground the British had to take; it was nothing like as kind as that in the centre of the Australian attack. And this was the same III Corps, led by the same General Butler, that had performed so poorly at Villers-Bretonneux. Butler was frazzled and the Germans had mauled his divisions during the two days before August 8. Monash didn't believe in Butler or his men.

THE AUSTRALIANS MARCHED to the start lines. This was going to be different to the attacks they had been in during 1916 and the first half of 1917 and they knew it. Monash had tried to think of everything. As Bean wrote, the men knew that whatever might lie in front, all was right behind them.

The Australians were attacking on a front of 7500 yards. Zero hour was 4.20 am. The 2nd and 3rd divisions were to go 3000 yards to take the first objective, called the Green Line. The village of Warfusée lay within this advance. The 4th and 5th divisions were to pass through at 8.20 and take the second objective, 3000 to 5000 yards east. This would take them through the villages of Cérisy and Morcourt, both in the north and close to Chipilly Spur, and also Bayonvillers to the south. There would be no creeping barrage for this second stage. The infantry would stop at the Red Line. The same two divisions would then go on a short distance to the final objective, the Blue Line. This would involve taking the village of Harbonnières in the south and pushing to the edges of Méricourt and Proyart in the north. The 1st Division, brought down from Hazebrouck, would be in reserve.

Monash had asked to be woken before 4 am on August 8. He paced up and down on the gravel outside Bertangles with a staff officer. Inside, other staff officers were laying out coloured pencils to record the tracks of men and tanks. Monash kept looking at his watch. Around 4.15 he and the staff officer began to count off the minutes. Then they heard the drumfire.

Monash slowly climbed the steps and headed for his office. Tom Blamey, his chief-of-staff, was sitting with his feet up, smoking a cigar. 'Sir,' he said, 'I have nothing to do, so we can wait while they count thousands of prisoners.'

THERE *WAS* SOMETHING different about the prelude to this battle. It wasn't just Blamey puffing on a cigar; the men marching up to the white tapes east of Villers-Bretonneux couldn't afford his cocksureness – they had to fight with rifles rather than coloured pencils – but they were confident that this attack was going to work, that all had been done right at Bertangles. Some cheered when the Australian barrage opened up. The throaty sounds of the tank engines and the drone of aircraft above gave them hope. The Canadians were on their right, another cause for hope. The Canadians were good shock troops.

It was as though the 'great adventure' that had been spoken of back home had finally arrived. There would be a war of movement, the way war used to be before late 1914. Not only would the infantry go forward but the artillery too, the horse teams trotting between the lines of infantry. The infantry would not go 150 yards and try to hold a trench. It would go for miles and miles, past villages and factories, through woods, up rises and along shallow valleys, past the enemy's artillery lines. It had never been like this before in the Great War.

The Australians left their tapes and plunged into a thick mist. Major Donald Coutts, the doctor with the 2nd Division, wrote that he couldn't see ten yards; Private Whinfield, who had been swimming in the Somme the previous day, said he couldn't see five. Soon after the start two Germans came running into Coutts' aid post 'looking for someone to surrender to'. Then a party of 150 prisoners came up and sat on the parapet. Australians crowded around them, going through their pockets. The counter-battery fire was so good that hardly any German guns replied to the Australian barrage. Whinfield said that the German artillery fire was like 'an inch to a chain'. Bean followed the advance and likened it to a day's shooting in the English countryside. Infantry scouts were out in front of the tanks and the main body of foot soldiers. These scouts were the 'beaters': they put up the Germans and those behind dealt with them.

All over the battlefield Germans raised their hands to surrender. On the southern front Lieutenant Alfred Gaby, who had worked on the family farm in Tasmania before going off to become a labourer in Western Australia, single-handedly attacked machine-gun posts armed only with a revolver. He came back with fifty prisoners. For this, he won the Victoria Cross, except he was never to know it. Three days later a sniper killed him.

The Germans sometimes simply sat in shallow trenches and waited to surrender. Australians on the northern front thought they might have to fight hard for Accroche Wood; instead, most of the Germans gave up without firing a shot. A German officer taken prisoner near here escaped from his escort, only to be recaptured. The officer said after the war that he was then 'gone through' by a 'horde of drunken Australians'. He escaped again to be caught again and 'gone through' a third time. Other Germans were more accepting. They would throw up their hands on seeing the approaching tanks and wait to be robbed. Some had their watches ready before the troops arrived.

Lieutenant John Barton and a sergeant watched a German prisoner limp by. He was tall and handsome but looked to be about forty and carried one of his boots. 'Good day, Fritz,' said the sergeant. To which the German replied in perfect English: 'I am going to England.' Barton said the German looked pleased.

Major Consett Riddell, the engineer, saw parties of fifty and sixty prisoners straggling back carrying white flags. They wanted to surrender to someone but Riddell said the drivers and others in the back area were too busy – 'so we merely directed them back along the road where someone would be sure to take charge of them, and they would probably get a job of road-mending for a few hours.' Later in the day he found a copy of *Hamlet* in a German sausage factory that had been set up in the field. He wrote home: 'Somehow it is hard to imagine anyone but a German sitting down to a close literary study of Shakespeare among surroundings that would outclass the worst that Footscray [a Melbourne industrial suburb] can do.'

Much later in the battle Gunner James Armitage came on a wounded German croaking: 'Not shoot, not kill me.' One of his legs was almost blown off. 'The dope we gave him eased his pain a bit,' Armitage wrote, 'and among other things he gratefully forced on me was a 2nd class order of Iron Cross.'

This time the attackers captured not only machine guns but also field guns and small howitzers, whole batteries at a time. Some German gunners fired over open sights, depressing the muzzles to the horizontal, using howitzers like giant shotguns; others simply sat on the trails on their guns and waited to surrender.

The village of Warfusée fell easily enough. Most of the Australians reached their first objective by 7 am. The casualties among the eleven attacking battalions were well under 1000.

AT 8.20 AM the two fresh divisions were passing through on their way to the second objective. The mist suddenly lifted. Bean said this happened so quickly that it was like a curtain rising. And the panorama was revealed, one that had never been seen on the British front before. There, in sunlight, was the plain in front of Villers-Bretonneux with its little valleys running back to the Somme. Larks rose singing from the crops. It is possible to reconstruct this scene from photographs and the letters and diaries of soldiers who were on the higher ground.

Near the frontline Australians from the first two attacking divisions are standing around in their loose-fitting tunics, looking far too casual to be in a war. A few are digging defensive positions. Most are smoking and yarning. A few are inspecting their 'souvenirs'. Rifles are slung. The Lewis gunners rest their weapons

Gassed, blinded and bewildered: the morning after a gas attack, near Villers-Bretonneux, late May, 1918. Australians, some blinded, at an aid post after being hit by 18,000 gas shells, many of them mustard, in the previous two days. Mustard gas caused blindness (usually temporary), swelling of the eyes and eyelids, vomiting, and burns and blisters to the skin. By 1915 the German, French and British armies were all using gas as a weapon of terror. About three per cent of gas casualties turned out fatal, but the figure is misleading. Many who had been gassed returned home with chronic bronchitis and skins rashes and died young. *[AWM E04851]*

Fresh from the frontline, troops from the 5th Division playing football in mid-September, 1918. [AWM E03356]

A typical scene inside the courtyard of a French farm being used as a billet for Australians in 1918. The men are clustered around a field cooker. The fowls are in some danger should their owner look the wrong way.
[AWM E02297]

Sir William Birdwood, a British cavalryman who always looked neat on a horse, had charge of the Australian forces throughout the war, although he handed over the field command to John Monash in 1918. He had affection for Australians and understood the way they thought. Birdwood was no tactician or organiser. His gift lay in building morale. He would pop up just behind the frontline to shake hands with privates from Bendigo or Dubbo. They mostly decided he 'wasn't a bad sort of cove'.
[AWM E00537]

Brudenell White, Australian born, was Birdwood's chief-of-staff. He was good at the things Birdwood was not: organisation and staff work.
[AWM G01329]

Sir John Monash, the son of Jewish immigrants and a Renaissance man of commanding intellect, led the Australian Corps to a string of victories in 1918. Monash was a 'modern' man who understood war in the industrial age. It was probably to his advantage that he did not come from the military establishment. He proved himself a master of the set-piece at Hamel and of the fast-moving battle at Mont St Quentin. Few Australians have better claims to greatness. [AWM E02350]

Bertangles Château today. This was Monash's headquarters when he took over the Australian Corps. Before the battles of Hamel and Amiens, Monash paced the gravel drive, waiting for the thunder of the artillery barrage. *[Denise Carlyon]*

Arthur Currie, the citizen-soldier who commanded the Canadian Corps. His figure might have been unsoldierly but, like Monash, he was one of the great generals of the war. Currie liked to visit the front to see the battlefield first hand. He has perhaps never received the acclaim he deserves. *[AWM H06979]*

Handsome, yes, but with a cold stare. Baron Manfred von Richthofen,
the German air ace, liked shooting things: boar, deer, elk, rabbits, birds
(including three pet ducks belonging to his grandmother) and allied aircraft
– eighty of them. He was killed, probably by Australian ground fire, in
the Somme valley in April, 1918, and buried near Bertangles Château.
Hermann Goering took over Richthofen's 'flying circus'. *[AWM A04803]*

An Australian platoon, now reduced to just seventeen men, resting during the battle of Amiens. By now the Australian fighting numbers were low – there were virtually no new recruits – but the men left were hard and experienced. *[AWM E02790]*

Georges Clemenceau, the French Prime Minister, with Major-General Sinclair-MacLagan, commander of the 4th Australian Division, after the battle of Hamel.
[AWM E02527]

Marshal Ferdinand Foch of France: no man imposed his personality on the war as robustly as Foch. *[AWM H09473]*

The Great War was all about artillery. More than half the deaths may have been caused by shellfire; bayonets caused about one per cent. The barrel of this German gun, captured during the Amiens battle, is now on display outside the Australian War Memorial, Canberra. *[AWM P01887.001]*

Kamerad: Germans surrendering to Australians several miles west of the Hindenburg Line in September, 1918. *[AWM E03274]*

A FIGHTING FAMILY OF BONDI

SIX WALLACH BROTHERS.

(1) Gunner A. Wallach, enlisted on his 17th birthday, and left for the front last May. (2) Cpl. H. Wallach, left Australia in September, 1916. (3) Lieut. A. Wallach, expects to leave for the front shortly. (4) Lieut. C. Wallach, left for the front in June, 1915; was four months in Gallipoli, and was one of the last to leave the peninsula; he served afterwards in France, where he won the Military Cross. (5) Lieut. N. Wallach, left Sydney as a private in February, 1915, served through the Gallipoli campaign, and later in France, where he has been wounded. (6) Pte. R. Wallach, saw service in New Guinea, Gallipoli, and France; he is at present recovering from wounds.

The Wallach family of Bondi sent six sons to the war. All had attended Sydney Grammar. Clarence (No. 4 in this *Sunday Times* photograph) played rugby for Australia; he was killed at Villers-Bretonneux in 1918. Neville (No. 5), also a good rugby player, was killed near the same spot a little more than a week later. *[State Library of New South Wales]*

An Australian searches a German prisoner for 'souvenirs' in late 1918. High on the list of desirables were watches, shoulder straps, binoculars and Luger pistols. A German officer captured at Broodseinde in 1917 said: 'Your men are funny. They rob while they fight.' He was then given a cup of tea. [AWM E03919]

Charles Bean explains the Mont St Quentin battlefield to Billy Hughes.
[AWM E03292]

Lieutenant Joe Maxwell, VC.
[AWM P03390.001]

Private Robert Mactier, VC. [AWM H06787A]

Lieutenant William Donovan Joynt, VC.
[AWM P02939.034]

Lieutenant Eric Edgerton. [Ian Clarke]

Lieutenant Cyril Lawrence.
[AWM P02226.001]

Kaiser Wilhelm (centre) with his army commanders Paul von Hindenburg
(left) and Erich Ludendorff. By 1918 Hindenburg and Ludendorff were
effectively running Germany, and Ludendorff was running Hindenburg.
[AWM H12326]

A château, wrecked by shellfire in 1918, shows its wounds to the world at
Villers-Bretonneux in 2003. *[Denise Carlyon]*

Harry Fletcher (left) and Austin Mahony (right). They lived in the same boarding house near Melbourne University before the war. They enlisted together and went to Gallipoli together. They both died at Montbrehain in October, 1918. Montbrehain was the last Australian infantry action of the war. *[AWM P03668.006]*

One of the most dramatic photographs from the Great War. Men of the British 46th Division listen to an address from their brigadier after crossing the St Quentin Canal near Riqueval bridge during the breaking of the Hindenburg Line. *[IWM Q9534]*

Adelaide Cemetery, Villers-Bretonneux, 1919. French children tend the graves of Australian soldiers. The long mourning has begun. *[AWM E05925]*

easily on their left shoulders, like wheat-lumpers. Among these men are great Mark V tanks, their caterpillar tracks rising several feet above the soldiers' heads. Columns of German prisoners, big-eyed and pale, are trudging westwards. Behind the two fresh Australian divisions come horse teams, their chains clinking, pulling field guns and wagons loaded with water and ammunition and stores. Further back squadrons of cavalry, saddles creaking, are trotting up, and with them Whippet tanks. The first of the Austin armoured cars has reached Warfusée. It has spoked wheels and looks like a touring car designed by a boilermaker. A line of observation balloons follows the cavalcade eastwards and, higher still, aircraft buzz and dart like rabid insects. Medical teams head towards the front and pioneers and engineers begin to mend roads and fill in trenches. The road from Villers-Bretonneux to Warfusée, empty yesterday, is packed with cars, lorries, horses, tanks, wagons, limbers and staff officers on horseback. The whole front is shifting forward – effortlessly, inexorably.

Lieutenant Barton gazed out over the panorama. 'As we watched during a halt young Bill Foulkes crowed: "The war is over."'

Consett Riddell told his father:

> It was all a most wonderful sight, tanks and infantry in the lead and not ten minutes behind them a solid stream of wagons and guns all moving slowly and steadily forward. Officers and men riding about over the paddocks and only an occasional shell to worry us, the Germans having become so accustomed to small advances of a thousand yards or a mile were completely nonplussed. I could not help laughing when I sat down on a bank to write progress reports and messages to headquarters. It was all so like peacetime soldiering.

Lieutenant Percy Lucas of the 5th Division watched a dogfight. 'Round and round they flew just above our heads, so low, in fact, that we could see the German pilot's moustache.' Lucas and his division were heading for the second objective. A German field gun began shooting at them over open sights. The Australians replied with Lewis guns and rifles. The Germans limbered up and galloped off down the road. 'We could not help admiring their courage,' Lucas said, 'and I, for one, hope they got safely through the war.'

Jimmy Downing was going forward with the same division. The Canadians were across the railway line on his right in rougher country. Downing watched them take the village of Marcelcave. Except for the fighting at dawn, he said, it was more like a picnic than a battle. 'There were few of the usual depressing concomitants of a major action – rain, tumbled waves of earth, enemy barrages, mutilation.'

Downing neared the final objective. 'We passed a derelict armoured train on a loop siding. It carried a huge gun . . . One of our planes landed in our midst. The machine was riddled with bullet holes. We gave the pilot goodday and went on. He nodded cheerfully and lit a cigarette.'

MONASH HAD BEEN right to question whether Butler's corps could take Chipilly Spur. During the second and third phases of the attack the Australians had to take Bayonvillers and Harbonnières in the south and Cérisy and Morcourt along the southerly loop of the Somme in the north. The men of the 4th Brigade took Cérisy but came under heavy fire, artillery and machine guns from Chipilly Spur as they headed for Morcourt. The Germans on the higher ground could see the Australians easily and were firing their artillery at close to point-blank range. From 9 am Monash had been receiving conflicting messages. The British were telling him that they had taken their objectives on Chipilly Spur; the Australians were saying that they were being shot up from the same place.

The Australians nevertheless managed to capture Morcourt. They found fresh grapes and eggs in an officers' mess, cigars, a pay office containing a case, which was blown open to disgorge 25,000 marks, and sixty horses. Captain John Geary, a miner from Meekatharra, Western Australia, took one of the horses for a gallop amid cheers. He dismounted and was killed by a bullet to the head.

During the final phase on the southern front a squadron of

cavalry attacked three trains standing near the village of Vauvillers. Two of the trains steamed away. The cavalrymen and the Australians behind them noticed a hump-backed truck in the third train. Several times it set off a cloud of tawny smoke. This was the 'huge gun' Downing had mentioned. It had an eleven-inch bore and had been shelling Amiens from 23,000 yards. A British plane bombed the third train as it tried to move off. The train stopped, its engine hissing steam. The cavalry galloped up and captured the gun and the crew. The gun, the grandest trophy of the battle, was named 'the Amiens gun'. Its barrel now stands in the grounds of the Australian War Memorial.

The armoured cars were raiding ahead of the infantry. Four headed for the village of Framerville. Two ran into a line of German transport wagons and machine-gunned the horses and drivers. The two cars next shot up three artillery limbers, killing the drivers and causing the horses to bolt. Then they poured fire into a lorry. Lieutenant E. J. Rollings, a Welsh policeman, came up with the other two armoured cars. Rollings found German staff papers, including plans of the Hindenburg Line defences, in a house that had apparently been used as an advanced corps headquarters. He stuffed the papers into sandbags and nailed a small Australian flag given to him by Monash above a door. Monash said in a letter home that his men found a box containing 100 Iron Crosses ready for issue. They came back wearing them 'all over their anatomy'.

The 5th Division took Harbonnières with help from the Tank Corps. A tank officer fixed an Australian flag, also given to him by Monash, on a house and the Australians placed another on the church. The Germans had obviously left abruptly: two saddled horses were found in a stable and hot food stood ready. Soon after, between 11 and 11.30 am, most of the 5th Division had reached the final objective. To the south the Canadians were coming up along-side them. The Germans were retreating everywhere, except on the wooded slopes of Chipilly.

Below Chipilly and south of the river the 16th Battalion of the 4th Brigade had to take their final objective, which was close to the village of Méricourt. Messages from Butler's III Corps were coming back saying that his troops were on their second objective. The Australians across the river knew these reports were wrong: they could see the puffs from German field guns firing at them from 1000 yards away. With help from tanks, and despite the fire from across the river, the 16th Battalion took its final objective. Casualties had been severe: the battalion ended up holding 2200 yards of front with around 300 men.

By early afternoon the Australian attack had succeeded right along the line. The men from the 2nd and 3rd divisions, who had taken the first objective, had been digging in. They were told to stop. There was no need for a fall-back position: the front was safe. This time the Germans were not going to counter-attack. The Canadians and French to the south were approaching their final objectives. The only failure had been at Chipilly Spur.

A few days later General Butler was temporarily relieved. The official story was that he was suffering from insomnia and taking prearranged sick leave. It was also true that Rawlinson didn't much believe in him, and hadn't before the battle began. Butler's replacement was General Godley, formerly of the old Anzac Corps. Godley was a mechanical soldier: he would do what he was told, sleep well, and not think too much.

AT LAST IT had come: a 'British' triumph on the western front, decisive and certain and done by the clock, and it seems churlish to mention that it was mostly carried out by Canadians and Australians, but that was the truth of it. Rawlinson's 4th Army had advanced eight miles and captured more than 12,000 prisoners and 400 guns. On the southern flank the French had taken 3300 prisoners and 300 guns. German casualties on Rawlinson's front were thought to be 27,000. Rawlinson's casualties were about 8800: 3500 Canadians, around 3000 Australians, 1700 British on the north side of the river, and 600 cavalrymen. The Canadians had taken more than 5000 prisoners and the Australians close to 8000. The dominion troops had also captured the bulk of the guns. John Terraine, Haig's biographer, wrote that at this time most British divisions were 'neither morally nor materially the equal of the dominion divisions . . . There was no lack of bravery, but skill and spirit were often wanting among these conscripts.'

Some German pilots flew for ten hours on August 8, going from one dogfight to another. Hermann Goering now commanded Richthofen's circus. Richthofen had been calculating; Goering was reckless. The circus lost so badly on August 8 that it had to be pulled out of the battle. It never recovered from this day.

Haig's communiqué and press reports presented August 8 as a 'British' victory, and this annoyed the Australians. Bean and Murdoch complained to White, now at the 5th Army with Birdwood. White told Bean 'the British had to have a success. It was all-important for their army to have a victory . . . and in order to do so he [Haig] had to make use of the only corps upon whom he could rely to do it; but the value of that victory was lost if it was made out as a victory for Canadian and Australian troops.' Bean kept complaining. White said Australia had to make sacrifices 'for the whole'. He told Bean that the British home army was 'in a very bad way'.

LUDENDORFF THOUGHT WORSE of his army: it had let him down; it was not worthy of him. He called August 8 *der schwarze Tag* – the black day – of the German army. It was no worse than his defeat by Mangin's armies on the Marne nearly three weeks earlier. What bothered Ludendorff about Amiens, however, was what it said about German morale.

> I was told of deeds of glorious valour [he wrote in *My War Memories*] but also of behaviour which, I openly confess, I should not have thought possible in the German Army; whole bodies of our men had surrendered to single troopers, or isolated squadrons. Retiring troops, meeting a fresh division going bravely into action, had shouted out things like 'Blackleg', and 'You're prolonging the war,' expressions that were to be heard again later.

Ludendorff is not a figure who attracts sympathy: it is hard to feel human feelings for a man who worked so hard to suppress human feelings from his own personality. Yet one can understand why he was now beginning to tip towards paranoia, and it wasn't just the failures of his armies. He was doing nearly all the work at the high end of the German command. In theory he had two superiors, the Kaiser and Hindenburg. Wilhelm had begun to sulk after the first battle of the Marne in 1914. He wanted victories; lesser beings were supposed to arrange them for him, and they hadn't. Hindenburg was Ludendorff's token superior. He enjoyed dressing up in uniforms, playing the father figure, reading and hunting. He was seldom flustered or worn down, partly because it was his nature to be so but also because he was happy to let Ludendorff do nearly all the work. Most of the time Hindenburg didn't know where his corps and divisions were.

Ludendorff decided the war had to be ended. Germany still held large tracts of France and Belgium; these were negotiating chips at a peace conference. But how should he try to hold on to them? By fighting on the present fronts? Or by retreating to the Hindenburg Line, where the fortifications were much stronger? And how long should he fight? When the Americans came into the war in large numbers he would lose his numerical advantage. And maybe this was an illusion anyway. The French and the British, exhausted and outnumbered as they were, were beating him without much help from the Americans.

HAIG DIDN'T BELIEVE in elation: that emotion was a little showy for an English gentleman. But he wrote in his diary that 'the situation had developed more favourably for us than I, optimist though I am, had dared to hope'. Three days after the opening of the Amiens battle Haig met the Australian divisional commanders at Villers-Bretonneux. According to Blamey, Haig spoke a few words of thanks, then said: 'You do not know what the Australians and Canadians have done for the British empire in these days.' He opened his mouth to continue but no words came. Blamey said tears rolled down Haig's cheeks. There was a 'dramatic pause', then the Australians filed out.

There is no reference to this in Monash's papers, but the Australians must have confused Haig. They had offended his ideas of soldierly behaviour since he first saw them. Yet he now had to concede, in private and discreetly, that these same men, along with the Canadians and New Zealanders, were the best shock troops he had.

The deeds of the Australians also caused Billy Hughes some confusion. Charles Harington, General Plumer's chief-of-staff, had been sent to the War Office in London as an assistant to Wilson. In 1932 he told Edmonds, the British official historian, that 'on Aug 8th 1918 I was at a Cabinet meeting with Henry Wilson when news came in of our 4th Army advance. Hughes, the Australian PM, was simply furious at [the Australians] being used. When later they succeeded we heard no more!'

THE NEXT DAY Pompey Elliott was shot in the left buttock. The wound was not serious and Elliott refused to go to the rear, even if the bullet had. Besides, he was busy trying to help the Canadians on his right. Events were not going as they were supposed to on the second day. The staff work had been close to brilliant the day before; today it was a series of muddles. Elliott was at the front because the 1st Division (which had been in reserve on the first day) was late in coming up to attack alongside the Canadians.

He was standing near a tank, talking to its crew, when the bullet hit him. According to Ross McMullin, Elliott's biographer, the general stood on a mound with his trousers around his ankles, looking out over the battlefield and dictating messages while lesser men fussed over his wound. Soldiers made ribald comments about the bovine dimensions of his hindquarters. One senior officer who had been fighting since Gallipoli said seeing Elliott 'with his tail-board down' was one of the sights of the war.

RAWLINSON HAD TO continue with the attack on August 9. For one thing Haig had told him before the battle opened that he wanted to go on towards the north–south line of the Somme below Péronne. For another Rawlinson knew from what had happened on August 8 that the Germans in front of him were panicky and disorganised. He didn't want to give them time to breathe. Neither did Foch or Haig.

But the second day was going to be harder. Rawlinson's staff was slow to issue orders. Orders began to go out after midnight on the 8th, which gave the divisional commanders little time to pass them on to their troops. And passing on messages was not as easy as on the first day, simply because the front had moved eight miles. This was also a problem for the artillery. Heavy guns could not be dragged forward quickly enough and the gunners were unsure where the new line of German batteries lay. On the first day Rawlinson had 500 tanks; only 145 were available for the second. The success of the first day had been built on the accurate counter-battery fire of the heavies and the use of tanks on a massive scale. Rawlinson didn't have the means or the time to mount an attack that had the surgical precision of the first day.

Rawlinson's order was for his troops to push forward about three miles in the centre towards the village of Chaulnes. This was to be done in three stages. It would take the Canadians and Australians through the villages of Framerville, Vauvillers, Rosières and Lihons. In the north Butler's III Corps was to take the ground above Chipilly that it had failed to take the day before. This would allow the northern flank of the Australian front to go forward. But from midnight on the 8th the confusion in Rawlinson's camp grew.

The Canadians were supposed to be reinforced by the British 32nd Division. This didn't happen and the Canadians had to redraw their plans of attack. The Australians along the Somme didn't know when Butler's III Corps was going to attack Chipilly. There were thirteen different starting times among the sixteen attacking brigades on Rawlinson's front. Five brigades had no artillery support and six had to go forward without tanks. August 9 was very much a shambles. Prior and Wilson say in *Command on the Western Front* that there was 'an appalling sense of *déjà vu*' about the day.

BECAUSE OF ADMINISTRATIVE muddles, the Canadians could not start before 11 am. The Australian 1st Division, because of other administrative muddles, could not reach the start line in time to pass the 5th Division front and head towards Lihons. By early afternoon the Canadians had advanced two miles to Rosières, a German railhead. North of them the Australians took Vauvillers.

Private Whinfield of the 5th Division was carrying out wounded. 'We took 150 prisoners,' he wrote in his diary. 'Later I saw over 200 dead Germans in this part. It is the way to win the war but it is a terrible thing. Walking through so many killed men was a sad sight. All were souvenired by the chaps.'

Two brigades of Whinfield's division had, in effect, completed the first phase of the attack the 1st Division was supposed to be making. The 1st Division men, who had already marched about ten miles to reach the front, finally began to pass through the 5th around 2 pm, heading for Lihons.

The 2nd Division, north of the 1st, was attacking towards Framerville. Here too there was great confusion. A colonel wore out two horses trying to find his battalion. Framerville was taken, along with 300 prisoners.

GENERAL BUTLER'S III Corps was becoming sorrier by the day. Butler was so short of men that he obtained permission to use three American battalions. Butler's staff was still sending out orders for the fresh attack at 2.20 on the morning of the 9th. The attack was supposed to begin at dawn; it was postponed until the afternoon because the Americans could not arrive in time. British troops eventually attacked Chipilly village around 5 pm. German machine gunners held them up about half a mile from their objective.

Australians watched this from across the river. Earlier that morning two Australian sergeants had crept across the bridge and gone through Chipilly looking for souvenirs. Now the two were ordered to take four men, cross the river again and see what was holding up the British attack. The six met up with the British attackers and led them into the village and across the high ground to the north. The British and Australians took 200 prisoners, of whom the six Australians claimed eighty.

To the north and higher up the peninsula American and British troops took Gressaire Wood. Most of the artillery fire that had hit the Australians on August 8 had come from here. The fighting on Chipilly Spur went late into the night. When it was done the British were still not quite abreast of the Australians across the river. By now Monash had talked Rawlinson into handing over the Chipilly front to him.

Despite the shambles, August 9 was another small triumph: Rawlinson had stolen three more miles from the Germans.

ON THE THIRD day of the battle, August 10, only fifty-seven tanks were available. Attacks went in with token artillery support. Rawlinson acquired one extra division and the Germans four. The Canadians managed to advance two miles on the southern front. The Australians pushed on towards Lihons without taking it. The Canadians and Australians were now in the Somme battlefields of 1916: old trenches and shell holes, brambles and thistles, lines of rusty wire. This terrain favoured the Germans. In the north an Australian brigade was sent across the Somme at night and attacked successfully eastward, taking the Etinehem spur above the next loop in the Somme after Chipilly and closing on Bray. Another Australian brigade simultaneously attacked along the southern bank of the river towards Méricourt and Proyart. This venture failed.

The character of the battle of Amiens had changed: it was now a grinding match and casualties were rising. If they were modest compared with the 1916 battle north of the river, they mattered greatly to the Australian Corps. Battalions had been at half strength before the battle opened and there was no hope of significant reinforcements. Men who had been fighting since Gallipoli or Pozières were being asked to finish off the war. Men who had been wounded or gassed were being sent back to fight again. Haig, Rawlinson, Monash and, in particular, Currie knew the battle was becoming too costly. Foch had been created a Marshal of France after his victory on the Marne in July. He loved to attack, to keep needling the Germans so that they had no time to think. He wanted to keep the Amiens battle going.

Foch met Haig on the 10th. Foch said he wanted Rawlinson to push on to Péronne and the line of the Somme below it. Haig wanted to open out the front to the north by sending Byng's 3rd Army over the old 1916 British battlefield towards Bapaume. Foch of course had no objection to this, but he still wanted to keep Rawlinson's attack going. Haig afterwards told Byng to prepare for a thrust towards Bapaume and Rawlinson that he must keep going.

THE GRINDING MATCH continued on the 11th. The Canadians gained ground on their right front and lost some on their left, alongside the Australians. The Australians took Méricourt on the Somme and the high ground at Lihons in the south. In the Australian centre the 2nd Division pushed towards Rainecourt.

Lieutenant Eric Edgerton was here. He had enlisted as an eighteen-year-old from school. He had been away three years. He had been decorated three times and recommended for the Victoria Cross. Late in July he wrote to his parents: 'The fields are covered with poppies, white marguerites, blue cornflowers and grass knee-deep. Nature had transformed the bitter winter battlefield . . . into a garden where the horrors of war have been overgrown by the grass.' He thanked his sister for sending him a pair of Wesley College socks to keep his feet warm. And now, on the night of August 11, having survived so much, he died.

He stepped out of a trench near Rainecourt and was talking to his men in the outposts when a bullet hit him in the chest. Edgerton died in a few seconds. He did not speak. The men laid him in the trench and folded his arms. Sid Horton, an orderly room sergeant, went to his burial. 'At 3.30 pm,' Horton wrote, 'we lowered the bodies into separate graves. I could not resist a last look at my dear friend, and I found him looking so peaceful and calm, and appeared to be simply asleep . . . We waited at the cemetery until nearly 5 pm but could see no sign of our chaplain.'

The chaplain had been sent to the wrong cemetery. He borrowed a horse and rode to the right one. Horton had left. The chaplain read the burial service alone and another shining youth went into the ground.

Twenty years later Horton recalled that he had been evacuated from Gallipoli with dysentery late in the campaign. 'Eric walked alongside the stretcher as I was carried to the boat, and the last thing I remember was him pressing an English ten-shilling note into my hand together with a string of figs. I learned months later that that was all the money he then had in the world.'

Major Coutts, the doctor with Edgerton's battalion, heard of Eric's death from the battalion commander. 'He seemed very upset about it,' Coutts wrote in his diary. Coutts had the day before walked into an abandoned German dressing station and found a very good violin.

THE DAY EDGERTON died was an important one in the war. The conflict had already broken the French, Russian and Italian armies. Now the German spirit was wilting. Hindenburg, Ludendorff, Prince Rupprecht and others high in the command knew it, and it frightened them. 'Drunken Bavarians' had shouted abuse at reserves coming up to the line. A few weeks later troop trains were seen bearing the words: 'Slaughter cattle for Wilhelm & Sons'.

The Kaiser met Hindenburg and Ludendorff on August 11. A heavy defeat had been suffered, Ludendorff said. Some of his divisions had lost the will to fight. The Kaiser suggested too much had been asked of the troops. Ludendorff denied this and offered to resign. It was not accepted. According to a major who was present the Kaiser then said: 'I see that we must strike a balance. We have nearly reached the limit of our powers of resistance. The war must be ended.'

On the same day Clemenceau suddenly arrived at Villers-Bretonneux, where he met Sir Henry Wilson, the Chief of the Imperial General Staff, Haig, Currie, Monash and his five divisional commanders, and senior officers from the Tank Corps, cavalry and air force. Foch came with Clemenceau. Clemenceau understood something Lloyd George did not: there were times when it mattered to be seen near the front shaking hands and saying thanks.

And on the same day Rawlinson, with Haig's blessing, virtually ended the battle of Amiens. He would try to launch a new set-piece battle on August 15.

Mont St Quentin, August 29– September 4, 1918

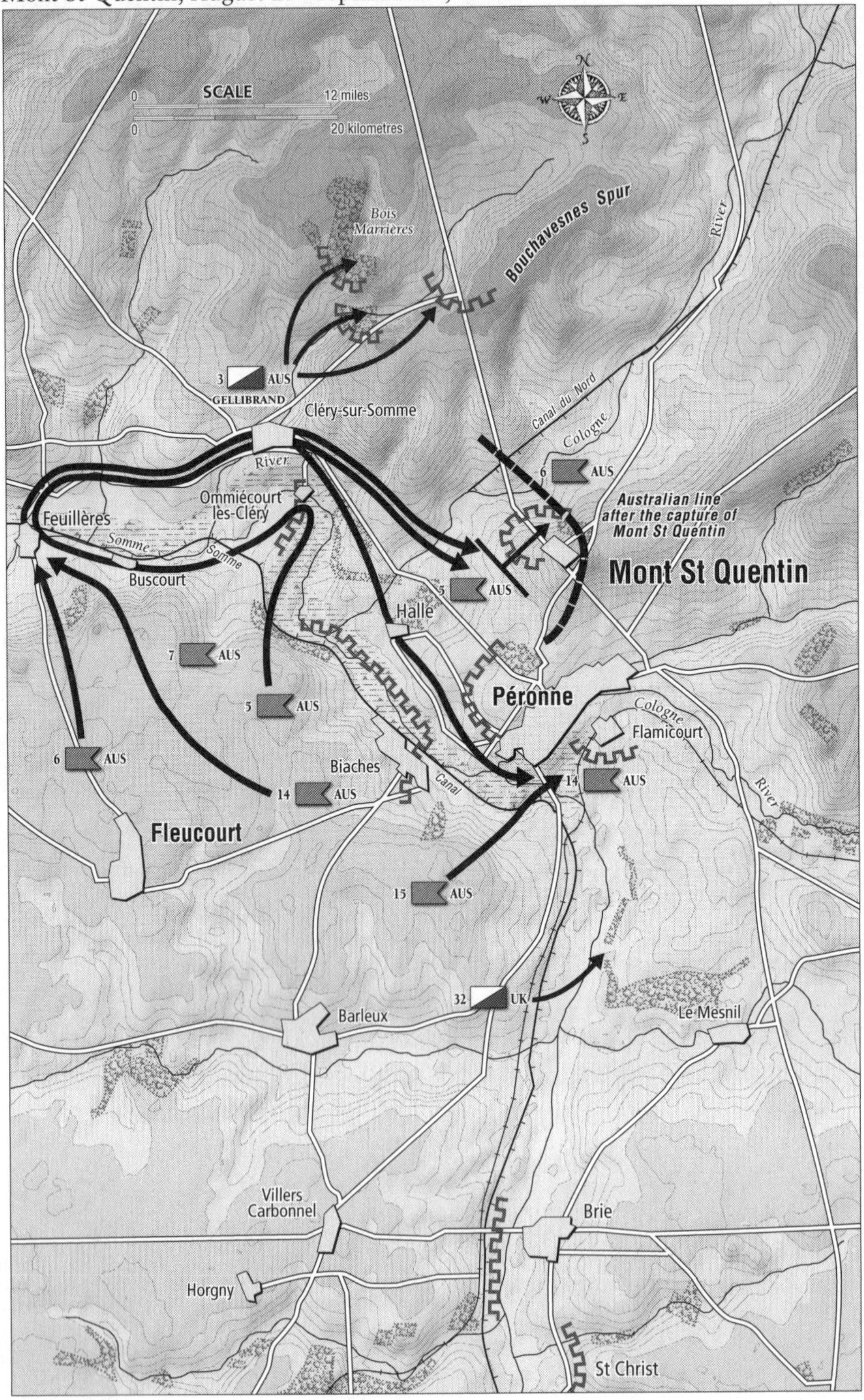

44

The bend in the river

The new set-piece battle Haig and Rawlinson were planning for August 15 never happened; it never could have. Rawlinson couldn't get his artillery ready by that date. Nor could he replace the tanks he had lost. And, besides, Arthur Currie, whose Canadians had the biggest part in the new attack, was against it. He didn't like what he had seen in the aerial photographs: the Germans were now in stronger positions protected by wire.

Rawlinson had to take Currie's dissent seriously (although in this case he probably agreed with it). Here was another change in the war. In 1916 the politicians saw men like Haig and Rawlinson as 'experts'. As with physicians, it was discourteous to question their wisdom. The slaughters on the Somme and at Passchendaele had changed all that. In 1918 a Haig or a Rawlinson could not afford to offend Lloyd George, or the dominion prime ministers Borden and Hughes, both of whom were now asking why so many of their countrymen were dead. Canada and Australia (and even New Zealand with its one division) mattered in a way they didn't in 1916. They owned the most experienced troops in Haig's armies. Haig looked at Currie's photographs and called off the attack.

Haig was reading the war better than he ever had. As Trevor

Wilson wrote in *The Myriad Faces of War*, Haig 'had at last divined the manner of proceeding on the western front'. He was no longer trying to win by knockout. He was going to win with a flurry of blows, limited and carefully crafted, so that, in sum, they would be mortal.

MONASH WAS MORE concerned with where his frontline would lie when winter came and the fighting had to stop. The river bothered him. He wanted to keep 'hustling' the Germans so that they could not use the north–south line of the Somme as a winter line of defence.

The Somme on Monash's front had two faces. One was the series of loops he had been following from west to east towards the old fortress town of Péronne. His corps was on both sides of the river here, slowly pushing east. At Péronne the river turned abruptly south and headed in a relatively straight line towards St Quentin. This was the face of the river that worried Monash. He was about eight miles short of it. If the Germans were given time, they could blow the bridges here, fortify their positions on the other side and perhaps hold off the pursuing armies until the spring, which would mean 1919. Monash had to find a way of driving the Germans beyond the natural fortress of the river before the snows came.

His force continued to nudge eastwards, overrunning strong points and woods. Monash used this interlude to give his divisions a few days away from the frontline. All had been fighting just about continuously for five months. The Australian casualties from the Amiens battle (to August 14) were about 5900. This was relatively light by the standards of previous years, but where were the replacements to come from? The corps was winning virtually every day – and killing off a little of itself each time.

Monash acquired the British 32nd Division to bolster his numbers and began planning a new advance for August 23. The Germans were now being pounded on an ever-widening front. South of the Amiens battlefield, the French attacked near Soissons, taking some 8000 prisoners on the first day. Byng on August 21 began what would be called the battle of Albert. His front extended north-east from Albert to beyond Bullecourt, just short of the Arras battlefield of 1917. The New Zealanders were in the centre, going for Bapaume. The attack began modestly on a hot summer's day but from the start it had momentum. Byng and Mangin's French forces to the south were closing the pincers. In the centre Rawlinson and Monash now went for Bray on the north bank of the Somme and Chuignes and other villages on the plain to the south. Haig's front stretched for thirty-five miles. He had never had a chance like this.

Churchill lunched with Haig on the day Byng's attack opened. Churchill promised immense quantities of shells, tanks and gas. Haig was astounded that Churchill's schemes were timed for completion by June, 1919. Haig told him Britain should be trying to win the war this autumn. Churchill replied that the general staff in London believed the decisive point of the war would come in July, 1919.

The following night Haig issued an order saying, in effect, that he thought the decisive point had already been reached. 'Risks which a month ago would have been criminal to incur ought now to be incurred as a duty. It is no longer necessary to advance step by step in regular lines.' Divisions were to go for their objectives and not worry too much about their flanks.

MONASH'S TROOPS WENT for Bray, Chuignes, Herleville and several other villages in stifling heat. The 1st Division had only a dozen-or-so tanks but their sweating crews wiped out line after line of machine-gun posts. When the infantrymen reached St Martin's Wood they had to wait for the tanks to catch up. They found a piano in a hut and a man from the 7th Battalion began playing. When, after about fifteen minutes, the men left the piano could be heard tinkling behind them.

Lieutenant Lawrence McCarthy, a farmer from Western Australia, was not in the main attack. He was in the 4th Division, which was holding the front south of the British 32nd Division, which was trying to take Herleville. The British were held up by German fire from an old 1916 trench system. McCarthy, who had landed at Gallipoli as a private, came up to help. He and Sergeant Frederick Robbins, a locomotive cleaner from South Australia, attacked the nearest machine-gun post, then fought their way down the old trench network. McCarthy may have killed as many as twenty Germans himself. He was at times out of touch with Robbins as he stormed along the trench line with revolver and bombs. He captured five machine guns and fifty-odd prisoners. His last lot of captives patted him on the back. But the more extraordinary thing was this: McCarthy, often alone, had captured about 500 yards of German front. Bean said that, next to Albert Jacka's 'charge' at Pozières in 1916, this was perhaps the most effective feat of individual fighting in the history of the AIF. McCarthy received the Victoria Cross and lived to return to Gallipoli for the fiftieth anniversary of the landing.

Lieutenant Donovan Joynt won the Victoria Cross on the same day. He was about two miles north of McCarthy. He was behind the front but could tell from the sound of firing that the advance had stalled. He said to his batman, Private Thomas Newman: 'Let's go and have a look.' The two found a 6th Battalion company sheltering in a sunken road. Machine-gun fire was coming from a wood to the left. Joynt told the men to advance in rushes of twenty-five yards at a time. This worked for a few hundred yards, then the attack stalled again. Joynt and Newman went forward to 'ginger them up'. They came upon a dead German officer and Joynt told Newman to search his body for papers. A German shell burst almost on top of Newman. Blood gushed from a wound in his throat. Joynt tried to bind the wound with a bandage. He couldn't tie it tight enough to staunch the blood without suffocating Newman. He propped him up against a bank and went on to the fighting. Newman lived.

Joynt found the men pinned down by fire from Plateau Wood. He took thirty men and began to make his way to the far side of the wood. His scheme was to rush it from there. As he worked around he came upon Lieutenant Les McGinn from his own battalion with twenty men, which meant Joynt now had a force of fifty.

The wood looked to be swarming with Germans. 'Let's rush the bloody place,' a redheaded Australian shouted. 'No,' Joynt yelled. He knew a charge would be suicidal. He decided to scout ahead with McGinn and three men. He was hoping to find an old sap that would lead him into the wood.

The five worked along an old communications trench. Suddenly a party of Germans came around a corner in the trench. Joynt raised his revolver and pointed it at the head of the first German to round the corner. The German dropped his rifle and raised his hands. Each German did the same thing as he came around the corner: it was as though they were surrendering in sequence. Soon there were twenty of them, covered by three Australians with bayonets. With an acute sense of what was important in this war, the three rankers began 'ratting' the Germans for watches. Joynt objected. The three said that if they didn't take the watches, others would. Joynt conceded the point. 'What about one for me?' he said. 'Take your pick, sir,' a man said, offering clasped hands full of watches.

Joynt abruptly realised how absurd the scene was. 'Twenty or more Huns all standing with their hands held high, with our diggers "ratting" them and McGinn and myself looking on with one Hun still on his knees.' Joynt started to laugh. So did McGinn. 'I suppose it was a sort of hysteria after the strain we had been through. We leaned against the wall of the trench and laughed and laughed – it was some time before we could stop.' Joynt sent the Germans back with an escort of two. He had found the spot from which to attack the wood.

The Germans there were surprised when the attack came from the east rather than the west. The Australians chased them, shouting. Joynt rounded up 100 prisoners. The wood had been cleared without a single Australian casualty.

Several days later Joynt was hit in the thigh by a shell fragment. His men used a piece of signal wire as a tourniquet. At the hospital a nurse told him he was going to England. Joynt begged the nurse not to move him; he was in too much pain. She told him the Channel crossing would take only two or three hours.

Joynt was laid out on the open deck of a hospital ship. The crossing took fifty hours as the ship dodged German submarines. Joynt lay in agony and unattended. An English medical orderly eventually came past. Joynt asked him to release the tourniquet because it was hurting so acutely. The orderly looked at Joynt's wound and turned away. 'It's too awful for me to look at,' he said. 'I can't bear to see it.'

Joynt lived to be ninety-seven.

HAIG'S WAR HAD never been so good. Each day his front shifted east-wards, and he didn't have to do too much to make this happen. The corps commanders were now largely running the tactical side of the war and Foch was writing the strategy. Each day the cages filled with prisoners. Each day brought a fresh nightmare for Ludendorff, not only in France but also on the lesser fronts in the Middle East, Macedonia and Italy; shortly he would seek psychiatric help. Each day life became harder for German civilians: the meat ration was down to four-and-a-half ounces a week; people were dying of hunger and those who weren't talked of revolution, be it Bolshevism or a constitutional monarchy. Each day Foch's spirits rose: this was his sort of war – attack, attack, attack, so that eventually your opponent seeks psychiatric help. Each day Pershing came closer to taking his independent American army of close to twenty divisions to war: a young colonel named George Marshall was helping to plan a big attack against the St Mihiel salient near Verdun.

Péronne, at the bend in the river, was now in sight on Rawlinson's front. Bapaume beckoned on Byng's front. Monash had done better than he had expected with his new attack. South of the river he had pushed three German divisions back another one-and-a-half miles. The British 32nd Division had taken Herleville. The 1st Division had taken Chuignes and was moving on Cappy. North of the river the 3rd Division took Bray.

Byng had retaken Albert; the New Zealanders were heading for Bapaume. The *Times* correspondent reported: 'These are great days

... The sweep of our advance is so rapid that no man can say where our advanced line as a whole may stand at any given moment, for every half-hour brings news that this or that village is in our hands, or that an airman has seen the khaki figures somewhere where we never dreamed that they had reached ...' The newspaper readers of Britain and Australia were not yet convinced these were great days. They had been misled before.

Lloyd George still thought Haig too optimistic. This time, however, Haig had spotted a genuine weakness. This time the evidence was there, staring sullenly from the prisoners' cages. Haig and Foch were as one: if you see a weakness, exploit it so ruthlessly that your opponent doesn't have time to think. Haig told General Henry Horne, commander of the 1st Army (which now included the Canadians as a spearhead), to prepare to attack north of Byng's army. This would extend Haig's offensive front to Arras and threaten the northern end of the Hindenburg system near Bullecourt. Haig also told Rawlinson to push on to Péronne.

Rawlinson wondered whether he had the means. He had been denied fresh divisions. Haig wanted these to go to Byng and Horne: their fronts were now considered more important. Rawlinson decided to 'ease down' his offensive and passed the news to Monash on August 25. Monash was bemused. He didn't want to lose momentum; he thought his Australian divisions, tired and under strength as they were, could drive the Germans back to Péronne. He disobeyed Rawlinson's instruction – but subtly. He passed on Rawlinson's order, and added a few of his own. Close touch would be kept with the Germans 'and advantage will be taken of any opportunity to seize the enemy's positions and to advance our line'. Rawlinson was even subtler. He knew what Monash was doing and didn't try to stop him.

MONASH PULLED THE 1st and 4th divisions out of the line for a rest. Gellibrand's 3rd Division continued to push eastwards on the north bank of the river and took Suzanne. Rosenthal's 2nd Division and Hobbs' 5th took over on the southern bank, where Cappy had fallen.

Engineers and pioneers began to repair the bridges on the east–west line of the Somme. This way the Australians would still be able to cross the river if the Germans blew the bridges below Péronne.

On August 27 Australian patrols found many German strong points abandoned. Without reference to Rawlinson, Monash ordered a general advance. The pursuit had begun. Day after day the villages fell on the southern front: Vermandovillers, Foucaucourt, Fontaine. And they fell on Gellibrand's northern front: Vaux, Curlu, Hem. Soon Gellibrand was threatening Cléry. Here the Somme began its sharp turn to the south and its topography began to change.

Along the stretch the Australians had been following the Somme had relatively sharp banks, but as the river started its curl southwards near Péronne its valley widened out; the slopes on both sides were gentle and exposed. The river was more than 1000-yards wide here. First came the Somme Canal, its banks lined with masonry. Then came a broad marsh, a series of channels meandering around little islands heavy with rushes. The channels were too deep to be waded. There were three main bridges on Monash's front between Péronne and St Christ, five miles to the south. The 'bridge' at Brie, in the centre, was in truth a causeway with eight separate bridges at intervals. The crossing at St Christ was similar and that at Péronne involved two bridges and reclaimed marshland.

Péronne itself was formidable. Vauban, the famous French military engineer of the seventeenth century, had designed the ramparts, which rose sixty feet above the river. The Cologne River joined the Somme here, which meant that the town had a moat around much of its perimeter.

By August 29 the Australians had driven the Germans out of the bend in the river. On the same day the New Zealand Division entered Bapaume. Further north Horne's 1st Army had begun what would be called the battle of the Scarpe in Arras. Another big breach had opened in the German line and Haig, who couldn't help himself, talked of putting cavalry through.

As they neared the bend in the river the Australians could see Mont St Quentin, about a mile north of Péronne and about 140 feet above it. It didn't look much, just a bump with a few trees on the summit, but it commanded Péronne and the land to the east that stretched away to the Hindenburg Line. North of Mont St Quentin the Germans had set up machine guns on the Bouchavesnes Spur, which looked down on Cléry and the bend in the river. Monash's divisions could not take Péronne, nor safely cross the river near the town, until they had taken Mont St Quentin and Bouchavesnes. The 2nd Prussian Guards, one of the best divisions in the German army, held both positions.

We don't know whether Lieutenant Cecil Healy stared across the river, as others did, to the ravaged hill. As he neared the river on August 29 he was wounded, then, while pointing to the position of the machine gun, hit again and killed. He was thirty-five and had given his occupation as commercial traveller and journalist of Darling Point and Darlinghurst, Sydney. At the Stockholm Olympics of 1912 he had won a gold medal with the Australian 4 × 200-metres freestyle relay team. He could have won another in the 100-metres freestyle but for an act of grace. The American team missed the semi-finals because of an error by its managers. Healy insisted they be swum again; it would be unsportsmanlike to do otherwise, he said. Healy finished second to an American in the final.

Monash didn't want to give the Germans time to reorganise or to wreck too many bridges. He wrote afterwards in *Australian Victories* that a plan had been 'vaguely forming' in his mind over the past fortnight. He would use the bridges he had ordered repaired on the east–west stretch of the river to cross troops and attack Mont St Quentin and Péronne in a looping movement from the north.

First, however, Monash tried the obvious. He would try to take Péronne and Mont St Quentin on the run by driving due east, as he had been doing for weeks. He would send the 2nd, 5th and 32nd divisions straight at the north–south line of the river. The 5th Division would try to cross at Brie, the 2nd at Halle. The 2nd would then go for Mont St Quentin.

The obvious didn't work. German machine gunners held up the advance; German engineers wrecked the bridges and causeways; and German gunners burst shells over the Australians. There was nowhere that the Australians could cross. Nor could the British 32nd Division cross at St Christ. Monash now turned to the plan that had been 'vaguely forming'. He would take Mont St Quentin from the north.

Monash explained his plan on the afternoon of the 29th. First, his three frontline divisions would sidestep to the left. The 32nd would take over the 5th's front. The 5th would take over the 2nd's line. And the 2nd Division would move north to the bend in the river at Ommiécourt, opposite Cléry. Second, Gellibrand's 3rd Division, on the other side of the river, would take Cléry, then push on to the German strong point on the Bouchavesnes Spur, north of Mont St Quentin. Gellibrand's clearing of the northern bank was the crucial element in this scheme. The 2nd Division was still going for Mont St Quentin, but there were now three routes open to it – in theory anyway. It could try to cross on its new front near Ommiécourt and Halle. If this was impossible, it could go south and cross with the 5th Division, which was now opposite Péronne. And, finally, if no crossing was possible here, the 2nd Division could march west, find a crossing near one of the villages Gellibrand had already secured, then march east again towards Mont St Quentin. If the 5th could not cross at Péronne, it was to follow the 2nd Division, then head for the heights on the eastern side of Péronne. As battle plans went in the Great War, this one was not only complex but also unusually flexible: power would devolve to brigade commanders, who would make their decisions on the run. Engineers worked through the night repairing bridges, including one at Feuillères, about two miles west of Ommiécourt and Cléry.

Rawlinson visited Monash on August 30, the day the operation began. Monash explained his scheme. Monash said Rawlinson was pleasantly satirical. 'And so you think you're going to take Mont St Quentin with three battalions!' Monash quotes him as saying (three battalions of the 5th Brigade had been earmarked for the final assault). 'What presumption! However, I don't think I ought to stop you! So go ahead and try! – and I wish you luck!'

WE NEED TO pause here to consider what was being asked of the men who were going to storm Mont St Quentin. Monash was all about boldness. This was right enough: he was winning and it was important to keep the rhythm going. But what of the men? Most had been in the fighting line for close to five months, except for a few rest days here and there. Many were exhausted from the approach to the bend in the river. Some on the northern bank of the river had not slept for eighty hours. The 2nd Division, on the opposite bank, was in slightly better shape; but, if it could not cross at Ommiécourt or Péronne, it would have to march west along the river to Feuillères, cross there, then march east for a few miles, then turn south and attack Mont St Quentin.

And there was the matter of numbers. When the Australians came to the western front, battalions comprised around 1000 men, with a fighting strength of about 900. Each of the battalions' four companies contained around 200 men. Most of the battalions were now down to a fighting strength of 300; companies were down to fifty and sometimes less. Which meant the arithmetic had changed: every casualty now had the same impact as three in mid-1916.

The 5th Brigade of Rosenthal's 2nd Division was ordered to take Mont St Quentin. One of its attacking battalions had been reduced to about 300 men; the other two each had fewer than 400. Nine hundred-odd men, tired and worn and without the protection of tanks, were supposed to take one of the toughest fortresses on the western front. Rawlinson was right to talk about presumption.

Private Robert Mactier of the 2nd Division, a farmer with a strong handsome face, one of ten children, wrote home to Tatura in Victoria's Goulburn Valley: 'Most of us are a dilapidated-looking lot, haven't had our clothes off for 60 days until last night.' That was in early May and Mactier had been in the line most of the time since. He had not been away from home as long as many of his comrades. He had come to 'Froggy land', as he called it, in

November, 1917 after enlisting as a twenty-six year old. In London he had gone to Rotten Row in Hyde Park – 'the place where the "heads" go for their morning ride. The nags they ride and the way most of them are ridden made us "smile",' he wrote in his diary. Around Christmas he was making for a 'comfort fund joint' in France for a cup of cocoa when he and his friend saw 'General Birdwood and his crowd' walking towards them. 'Of course we saluted him and he said: "How are you, boys? A happy New Year to you." "Thank you, the same to you," says we. So he's not a bad sort of a coon after all . . .'

Friends of Mactier called him 'Nuggety' or 'Little Mac' and said he was an uncomplaining soldier. Nothing seemed to bother him: the voice was always laconic. On being gassed he wrote: 'I got a bit of it . . . lost my voice for 3 weeks . . .' A week before Mont St Quentin he was pleased at being made a company runner – 'anything does me rather than "stand to" all night.'

Mactier was in the 6th Brigade, which would follow the 5th Brigade to Mont St Quentin.

IT SOON BECAME clear that Monash's plans for August 30 were too ambitious. Zero hour had been set for 5 am. Gellibrand's 3rd Division had the crucial task, the capture of Cléry. The 2nd Division had to get itself across the river. All this was to happen without tanks and with limited artillery support.

The 2nd Division soon found that it could not cross large numbers of men at Ommiécourt or other bridges to the south. The men of the 5th Brigade therefore headed for the bridge at Feuillères, crossed there and moved into trenches on the western outskirts of Cléry. The exhausted 3rd Division pushed on north of Cléry towards Bouchavesnes Spur but were held up by machine guns. The attack on Mont St Quentin was put off until the following day.

TWO BATTALIONS OF the 5th Brigade, the 17th and 20th, prepared to attack Mont St Quentin at 5 am on August 31. This sounds more impressive than it was. The two battalions were down to 550 fighting men between them. The 19th Battalion, perhaps 250-strong, was on their right flank. The 18th Battalion, also weak in numbers, was in reserve. All the men were worn out. Few of them in the hours before the jump-off thought they had much hope of taking Mont St Quentin. There was no hot evening meal for the two attacking battalions, although dry rations were brought up. Better still, at 3 am the rum arrived. Some managed to get themselves two issues.

The first blushes of dawn had appeared when the barrage opened up. The field pieces shelled the lower slopes and the heavies pulverised the summit. The infantrymen moved off towards the dawn sky and soon realised that the Germans had been taken by surprise. Right across the base of the hill they could be seen scurrying to higher ground. The Australians in places broke into a jog. When a group of Germans broke from the trenches ahead the Lewis gunners would throw themselves down and fire off a drum. Trenches were rushed with loud cheering, so that the few hundred Australians sounded like a few thousand. They came on Germans who had run until they were breathless and now simply wanted to surrender. On reaching Gottlieb Trench on the lower slopes the Australians sat down and lit cigarettes as the heavies continued to bombard the summit.

The 20th Battalion was on the left of the attack. Its men simply walked from Gottlieb Trench to their objective, the Bapaume road north of Mont St Quentin that led to the little village of Feuillaucourt. Three companies from the 17th Battalion now rushed at Mont St Quentin village. One observer described it as 'a regular old-fashioned charge'. A few Germans fired off token shots then ran away. The Australians took more prisoners, including a clutch of draughtsmen and their maps, as they worked their way through the ruins. A captain in the 17th sent a message back: 'Casualties slight, troops awfully bucked.'

By 8 am, before the sun had pierced the grey clouds, the Australians had taken one of the most feared German positions on the western front, as well as Feuillaucourt to the north and Halle to the south. They had sent back 700 prisoners, or more than their own number.

Lieutenant Joe Maxwell came up with the reserve battalion, the 18th, and met droves of prisoners being driven to the rear, among them a Prussian colonel. 'He wore his monocle and strode over the torn earth and shell holes with the poise and air of a stroller along the Strand. There was not a speck of dust on his bluish uniform and he swished in one hand a pair of fawn gloves. Across his shoulder was a pair of field glasses and he gazed on his captors with a super-cilious and disdainful air.' The Australians began robbing the colonel's servant of a toilet and manicure set.

The colonel strode to Maxwell and bellowed in English: 'Remember you are an officer, and I demand to be treated as a gentleman.'

'Well, this is where you get off, old man,' Maxwell said, reliev-ing him of his field glasses. Shortly after the colonel lost his riding breeches.

At 8 am Rosenthal, the commander of the 2nd Division, passed the news to Monash: '5 Bde report having captured Mt St Quentin from which the Australian flag now flies.' That night Rawlinson wrote in his diary: 'As . . . I was dressing this morning Archie [Montgomery-Massingberd, his chief-of-staff] rang up to say that the Australians had captured Mt St Quentin! . . . I was overjoyed. It is indeed a magnificent performance and no praise is too high for them.' Haig was impressed too but he was more interested in the 1st Army's attack at Arras, where the Canadians were on the verge of breaking through the Drocourt–Quéant switch line. This was more important than Mont St Quentin because it would force the Germans into a massive retreat. Edmonds, in the British official his-tory, called Mont St Quentin 'a magnificent feat of arms'.

It was. But it wasn't over.

THE 9TH AND 10th brigades of Gellibrand's 3rd Division had headed north-east towards the Bouchavesnes Spur forty-five min-utes after the attack on Mont St Quentin began. Their artillery support was thin and German machine gunners held up the 33rd Battalion in front of Road Wood. Private George Cartwright stood up and fired at the machine gunner. He kept walking forward, firing from the shoulder. He shot the machine gunner and then the two men who replaced him. He threw a bomb at the trench, rushed it and captured nine prisoners and the gun. The men of the 33rd stood up and cheered him. Cartwright was twenty-three, a labourer from northern New South Wales. A month after this day he was wounded and sent to a hospital where he was told he had won the Victoria Cross. Gellibrand's men had captured much of the spur by the time the 5th Brigade had taken Mont St Quentin.

THE AUSTRALIANS HAD never been in a battle that moved so fast as this one. It did not go by mathematical precision like August 8 at Amiens. It was like a bushfire: first the crisis was here and then it was there, and all the time there were logistical problems. It confirmed two things about Monash: he was as good at making quick decisions, at improvising, as he was at designing set-pieces; and he had the ruthlessness that generals need to have. By shortly after 8 am on August 31 he knew he had an improbable success, the capture of Mont St Quentin, and also a string of problems that could stop him from exploiting his gain. His men were so exhausted that they would flop down and fall asleep if given a chance. Gunners dropped off while riding their horses to new positions. Monash had to push the other two brigades of the 2nd Division as well as the 5th Division across the river. The two brigades from the 2nd were needed to reinforce the battered 5th Brigade on Mont St Quentin and take that front forward another half-mile. The 5th, now down to the numerical size of a battalion, was two miles in advance of the Australian front and exposed on both flanks. The 5th Division was needed to take Péronne. And it was also important that Gellibrand's worn-out 3rd Division took the rest of its objectives around Bouchavesnes Spur to protect the flank.

Monash telephoned Gellibrand at 8.35 am and told him he had to take the rest of Bouchavesnes Spur. 'Casualties no longer matter,' Monash told him.

The 6th Brigade of the 2nd Division crossed by pontoon bridge near Cléry at 11.30 am. One brigade of the 5th Division, the 14th, followed it across. Then the 7th Brigade of the 2nd Division crossed at two spots and Cléry became crowded with troops as German shells threw up geysers in the Somme marshes. Germans at Florina Trench near Halle held up the 6th Brigade's advance on Mont St Quentin. Another problem became apparent: the 5th Brigade was not quite where Rosenthal thought it was. The Germans had begun to counter-attack on Mont St Quentin and the two battalions on the summit didn't have the numbers to fight them off. A few hours after taking the village the Australians had to give it up and retreat down the hill.

Private Roy Brewer was on the hill. He had recently returned from leave in London. He wrote to his parents: 'There was a big day in London yesterday, the opening of Australia House, it is some place and I believe altogether it cost nearly a million pound. That would do me to have fourteen days leave on. My word Billy Hughes has been making some great speeches over here. He'll nearly work his way into a job over here I reckon.' Brewer fought bravely during the German counter-attacks. Mortar shells killed or wounded the men around him but Brewer, although slightly wounded and now alone, kept firing his Lewis gun. Then a shell hit him. He died five days later, unaware he had won the Military Medal.

Major Coutts of the 6th Brigade had set up his regimental aid post in a tunnel. 'We were kept going continuously all night . . . I had to amputate one man's arm at the shoulder, and another man's leg through the right thigh – I had to use a razor for this.'

THE GENERALS MADE their plans for the next day, September 1. The 6th Brigade would recapture Mont St Quentin. The 14th Brigade, the only 5th Division formation that had managed to cross the Somme, would attack towards Péronne. Gellibrand's 3rd Division would again try for its objective around Bouchavesnes Spur.

The 6th Brigade set off in drizzling rain. The 23rd Battalion couldn't advance because of machine-gun fire coming from Florina

Trench, about a mile south-west of Mont St Quentin. Private Robert Mactier, the company runner, was told to scout ahead. He set off alone with a revolver and several bombs. He rushed the first machine-gun post, killed the garrison of eight and threw the machine gun out of a trench. Mactier went on, through twenty Germans who held up their hands, to a second post and took that. Then he charged a third. What happened here is unclear; he may have taken this too. What we do know is that he was hit by fire from a fourth post. Forty Germans surrendered as a result of Mactier's one-man war. The 23rd Battalion could now begin its advance on Mont St Quentin.

An officer later told the Red Cross that Mactier was hit in the body and chest and lived only a few minutes. 'He tried to speak to me before he died but he was not intelligible . . . I have just got him recommended for the VC.' A clergyman told the Mactiers at Tatura that their son was dead. The family appears to have received no official news after this, even though Mactier's Victoria Cross was gazetted on December 14. Mactier's father in mid-January wrote to the Defence Department. He began: 'I write to try and find some information re our dear boy Robert Mactier No 6939.'

Six Victoria Crosses were awarded to Australians for September 1 at Mont St Quentin and Péronne. At Lone Pine in 1915 Australians won seven Victoria Crosses but these covered several days of fighting.

The 23rd and 24th battalions of the 6th Brigade made the fresh attack on Mont St Quentin, attacking over much the same ground as the 5th Brigade had the day before. The 24th was on the left and didn't receive its orders until 3 am on September 1. According to the battalion historian, Mont St Quentin dominated the ground in front of them and looked 'impregnable'. One of the battalion's companies was down to seventy men, yet it had a front of 400 yards. The front wave was to advance with a gap of sixteen yards between each man, which meant every casualty would open up a gap of thirty-two yards. The men smoked, told jokes and stared vacantly at the parapet, waiting for the officer to yell 'Over!'

The machine-gun fire from the hill was so intense that the men went forward in short rushes, going from one shell hole to another in the rain. Fire from a crater near the summit held up the attack for several hours. When the men were ordered to resume their advance they thought (the battalion historian wrote) it would be like throwing peas at a whale. They were outnumbered about ten-to-one. Yet they took the crater with hand-to-hand fighting. Some Germans bolted eastwards, discarding their equipment as they did so. Others, addled by the fire that had descended upon them, ran around in circles. By early afternoon the 6th Brigade had recaptured Mont St Quentin and pushed the line well east of the village. The casualties had been heavy, but the Germans were not going to get it back this time.

North of the hill Gellibrand once more attacked on the Bouchavesnes Spur. The 11th Brigade took 400 prisoners here but again failed to take its objectives.

South of Mont St Quentin the 14th Brigade of Hobbs' 5th Division attacked towards Péronne. Anvil Wood lay between their start line in the west and the town. Here a German field gun was firing point-blank at the Australians. Private William Currey, a wireworker from Leichhardt, Sydney, won the Victoria Cross by rushing forward with a Lewis gun, killing the crew and capturing the gun. Elsewhere in the wood the Australians captured 200 Germans in one group. The German battalion commander was astonished when he and his men were handed over to two privates for escort to the rear. The Australians crossed the moat and moved into Péronne, where the Germans chose to fight from cellars and houses rather than man the ramparts.

MONASH WANTED TO pause the next day, September 2. The battle for the bend in the river was close to being won. He had Mont St Quentin; Péronne and its suburbs would fall in the next few days. His men were worn out and some battalions were down to a few hundred men. He needed to replace the 6th Brigade with the 7th on Mont St Quentin and to move more of his artillery across the Somme. Commonsense said ease up for a day.

Alexander Godley had been a stranger to commonsense for most of his career as a Great War general. Godley's corps, part of Byng's army, now held the ground to the north of Monash. Godley had acquired a new division, the 74th, from Palestine and, as was his way, wanted to rush it into battle and drive eastwards. He asked Monash to protect his flank. Monash eventually agreed. There would be no pause.

So on September 2 the 7th Brigade passed through the 6th on Mont St Quentin and pushed eastwards, capturing several villages, 200 prisoners and ninety-three machine guns. Godley's new division, unused to heavy artillery fire, could not keep up. Monash kept the battle going in the south, where the rest of the 5th Division and most of his artillery crossed the river. Péronne fell.

This day the Germans were ordered to retreat all along the line from Arras to the Somme. The trigger for this was not the fall of Péronne but the breaking by the Canadians of the Drocourt–Quéant line, which ran into the Hindenburg Line in Arras. Ludendorff ordered his troops back to the Hindenburg Line. This amounted to a retreat of about twelve miles on Monash's front; all the gains of Operation Michael were to be given up.

'PÉRONNE TAKEN,' PRIVATE Lyall Howard of the 3rd Division pioneers wrote in his diary for September 3. It was a typical entry: no waste, no embroidery. A dozen words was a long diary entry. Howard had covered the period from March 30 to May 10, when the Ludendorff offensive was running, with just three words: 'Very warm corner.' His entry for August 30, when the battle for Mont St Quentin was starting was typically brief and dead-pan, yet affecting to anyone coming upon the diary almost ninety years later. 'Met Dad at Cléry,' it said. Lyall had enlisted as a nineteen-year-old early in 1916; Walter, his father, had joined up later as a forty-two-year-old father of nine. Lyall was working on the roads and bridges leading to Cléry. Walter, a private in the 5th Division, was moving up for the attack on Péronne. He was hit in the leg and abdomen a few days after meeting Lyall at Cléry. The pair met up again when

Walter was recovering in hospital. Family folklore has it that Walter was treated and saved by an American doctor.

Major Coutts had treated the wounded from Mont St Quentin. Now he walked up there, as if to discover why the place had become famous. 'There were machine guns everywhere and dead Huns lying round them . . . The battalion [he was attached to the 24th, which had helped recapture the hill] was a very small one now, and all the men were terribly knocked up, but in good spirits.' A few days later Coutts went fishing in the Somme, using the traditional Australian method: grenades exploded in a few feet of water. He was awarded the Distinguished Service Order for his days at Mont St Quentin.

MUCH OF THE credit for Mont St Quentin belongs to Monash. He improvised and delegated and demanded, modifying his scheme day by day without ever forgetting what he was trying to do and why. He had realised weeks earlier that he had to have troops on the northern side of the river. Gellibrand's push eastward along the northern bank had set up the victory. Monash had been ruthless. He knew this and why it had to be. If he showed pity for the tired men he was driving, he might lose. He had only three divisions in the fight and each had a distinct part: Rosenthal's 2nd at Mont St Quentin, Gellibrand's 3rd on the northern flank, Hobbs' 5th at Péronne. If one failed, the others probably would too. Monash had displayed what he would later call 'intellectual arrogance', which was his way of saying that a general had to believe in himself and, if necessary, be callous. He had long ago proved Bean and Murdoch wrong: he had talents unknown to the duo of Birdwood and White.

But Monash wasn't the hero of Mont St Quentin, and he was gracious enough to admit it. This battle belonged to soldiers rather than generals, corporals and privates who did astonishing things that are not easily explained. Monash's army was getting better as it wasted away. Mont St Quentin brought another 3000 casualties: battalions of 300 became battalions of 200. Yet the spirit of these men was extraordinary, and it comes through in their letters and diaries. Why it was so is not altogether clear. Logic would say that a few hundred men should not have taken a fortress like Mont St Quentin from a crack Prussian division. But they did. Mont St Quentin was probably the finest thing Australians did in the Great War.

ABOUT SIXTY MEN in Pompey Elliott's brigade went on strike just after the battle for Péronne. They had been told to chase Germans fleeing east. They refused, saying they were too tired and that they were being used too much because of deficiencies in the British divisions. Their colonel was so embarrassed he offered to resign. Elliott asked the men to write out their grievances, then spoke to them without bluster. There was some truth in their grievances, he said, but mutiny was the wrong response. He would leave for half-an-hour. If, on his return, the strikers refused to obey the order, he would send them to the rear. If they chose to obey it, he would speak on their behalf when the affair was investigated. The men decided to call off the strike and chase the Germans. Elliott was a man of many dimensions: this was an essay in tact and subtlety. Haig would not have understood what Elliott did.

Haig met a party of Australian editors and newspaper proprietors shortly after Mont St Quentin. They might have expected him to talk warmly about what the Australians had done there. Instead, to their surprise, he spoke sternly of the need to extend the death penalty to the Australian force. Many Australians had done things at the front that Haig had never managed in his brief and modest career as a fighting soldier. But the field-marshal didn't want to congratulate them so much as shoot the odd one in the interests of discipline.

FOCH WAS IN heartier form. Charles Repington of London's *Morning Post* interviewed him on September 3. Foch explained his strategy, which was not at all complicated, with vigorous hand gestures.

I attack them. Good! I say: 'Into battle!' Everyone goes into battle. Good! I don't let go of them, the Boches. So – they're not let off. Good! They don't know what to do. I do know. I don't have a plan. I watch what happens. Good! Something does happen. I exploit it. They're chased with a sword in their backs. Good! . . . In the end they'll be worn out. Good! We'll take prisoners and guns. Good! We'll chase them with the bayonet. Tic! [Foch lunges at an imaginary German.] We kill them. Toc! [He shoots at an imaginary German.] They're off balance. Germany is disillusioned . . .

LUDENDORFF WAS MUCH disillusioned. Sometimes he slept for only an hour. He had eyestrain from poring over maps with a magnifying glass. He abused his generals and broke down and wept. He ate hastily. In early September he was sufficiently concerned about himself to ask an old friend, Dr Hochheimer, a retired army doctor specialising in psychiatry, for help.

Hochheimer said he told Ludendorff that he had been neglecting his soul. 'He had only worked, worried, body and mind tensed, no relaxation, no fun, hastily eaten meals, he had not breathed correctly, had not laughed, had seen nothing of nature and art, heard nothing of the rustle of the forest and the ripple of brooks . . .' Hochheimer expected a tirade from Ludendorff. Instead the general asked him what he should do. Hochheimer told him to start breathing exercises, to take walks, sleep longer, rest his eyes and 'to sing German folksongs upon awakening'.

Within a few days Ludendorff became more amiable. Then he heard that Bulgaria, one of Germany's alleged 'props', was seeking a separate peace. He suffered a fit and foamed at the mouth before collapsing.

ANZAC COVE ON Gallipoli has atmospherics: tawny ridges rise out of a sea that displays all the colours of a peacock's tail. Gallipoli is part of Australian folklore; it is a place for pilgrimages. Mont St Quentin isn't like that. It doesn't have the atmospherics: a low hill rises out of the plain; the village, church and memorial to the 2nd Division lie near the summit, from where you look down on Péronne and the tree-lined river. Nor does Mont St Quentin have a place in the folklore; it is hardly spoken of. There is no sense to these things.

45

A very Australian mutiny

And so the new pursuit began. The Germans fell back on the Hindenburg Line: there was nowhere else for them to go. They were tired and ragged and the dream of conquest, which had flickered in March, was dead; the war was all about hanging on now. The Germans wrecked everything they could as they fell back. In daylight the sky to the east of the Australians was smudged with smoke. At night the burning villages gave off a pink glow.

The Australians' numbers were falling every day. They too were hanging on, but with a difference: if they and the rest of Haig's forces could hang on, they could win. The prospect had never been so close. Monash was wearing himself out. He had left the splendour of Bertangles, shifting his headquarters from one village to another along the Somme as the battle moved east. Photographs taken at this time show him looking thin and strained, folds of skin hanging on his face. His diary suggests he was suffering from nervous tremors. He impressed the English journalists who came to see him, partly, one suspects, because he was nothing like the British generals they were used to. Arthur Conan Doyle saw 'a rare compelling personality'. Arthur O'Connor of the *Weekly Despatch* summed him up as a strong man: intellectual, original, democratic and ruthless.

Monash knew he was pushing his men unreasonably. He also knew the Germans must not be given time to reorganise. He cared about the welfare of his men; and he cared, perhaps more, about winning. On September 4, when Rawlinson ordered him to chase the Germans beyond Péronne, Monash told Bean his troops weren't tired, just 'a little footsore'. Monash was too intelligent to believe this; but he could hardly tell Bean, who had never understood him, that the end justified the means. Bean wrote in his diary that there would be no more AIF before long.

Monash couldn't use the 2nd Division to chase the Germans: it had suffered too much on Mont St Quentin. He couldn't use the 1st and 4th divisions: he had earmarked these for the final approach to the Hindenburg Line itself. So he had to bring Gellibrand's worn-out 3rd Division back for the pursuit. He set off for the Hindenburg Line with three divisions: the 3rd, 5th and the British 32nd.

The men went out into rolling country. There were more than a dozen villages between them and the Hindenburg Line, and the Germans were busy razing them and setting up machine-gun posts to cover their withdrawal. The Hindenburg Line here ran north–south on either side of the St Quentin Canal, which ran through the village of Bellicourt and close to Bellenglise further south. The canal was obstacle enough: it ran in a cutting with almost vertical sides that plunged fifty feet or more; it wasn't particularly deep but it was thirty-five feet wide, with a muddy bottom and barbed wire on both banks. North of Bellicourt the canal ran into a tunnel, built in Napoleonic times, three-and-a-half miles long. Here, at least, tanks might be used and the foot soldiers would not have to swim. In one form or another the Hindenburg Line ran from Flanders to beyond Verdun. The fortifications in front of the Australians, the *Siegfried Stellung*, were the oldest and most intricate part of the line. Old British trenches infested with thistles lay just before the line. These had been the frontline before the March offensive.

Rawlinson and Monash were unsure where the Germans would stand: at the Hindenburg Line itself or at the old British trenches? Rawlinson laid down four objectives for the Australians as they tramped east. The third was the old British reserve line and the fourth the former British frontline. The troops took the first three objectives easily enough and without a formal plan beyond driving the Germans before them. Monash felt the old British frontline could only be taken by a set-piece. Rawlinson decided to attack it on September 18. His army had been reinforced by the arrival of IX Corps of three relatively fresh divisions commanded by General Braithwaite. Braithwaite would attack in the south, the Australians in the centre and III Corps, now again under the command of the muddling Butler, to the north. The 1st and 4th Australian divisions came up for the attack and the 3rd and 5th left for a rest.

Private Whinfield found himself 'resting' near Péronne. The men dug shelters into banks and used iron sheets discarded by the Germans to keep out the rain. Whinfield's battalion played Australian rules football against brigade headquarters 'and gave them a big trouncing'.

As RAWLINSON AND Monash were plotting their final approach to the *Siegfried Stellung*, a position of critical importance, General Pershing at last took his American Expeditionary Force to war at the St Mihiel salient, a position that hardly mattered. The salient jutted into the French line south of Verdun. Foch wanted to save the Americans for a big offensive he was planning through the Argonne Forest towards the German railhead at Mezières. Pershing insisted on attacking at St Mihiel first; he was looking for a morale booster, something that was distinctly American.

So, on September 12, seventeen months after the United States had declared war, Pershing sent in a dozen divisions at St Mihiel, supported by close to 1500 aircraft. Colonel William 'Billy' Mitchell commanded the aircraft. He suggested that aircraft would one day win wars. This outraged brother-officers who still wore spurs. What Pershing didn't know was that Ludendorff had already ordered the salient be given up to shorten his front and save men. The Germans fought like men who were leaving anyway. By the evening of the 13th St Mihiel was a huge success, at least in statistical terms. The Americans and the French divisions attached to them had wiped out the salient and taken 15,000 prisoners.

Two operatic figures fought here. Brigadier-General Douglas MacArthur was first in his brigade to clear the parapet. Major George S. Patton commanded a wedge of tanks. The two found themselves together during a bombardment. Patton recalled that neither was much interested in what the other said 'as we could not get our minds off the shells'. MacArthur said afterwards that Patton flinched, then looked annoyed with himself. 'Don't worry, major,' MacArthur claims to have said, 'you never hear the one that gets you.'

MONASH WAS GIVEN only eight tanks for the attack of September 18, which would be known as the battle of Epéhy, so he decided to build dummy ones from wooden frames covered with hessian. The engineers and pioneers competed to construct the most 'lifelike' model. The dummies were dragged out before dawn into positions where the Germans would have to see them. Monash's other innovation was to bring in the machine-gun battalions of the 3rd and 5th divisions, so that he had 256 Vickers guns firing a barrage 300 yards ahead of the advancing infantry. By now it had become clear that the Germans would stand on the old British frontline rather than retreat to the Hindenburg Line.

Monash's two attacking divisions each had a frontage of 3500 yards. They had to go about 5000 yards in three bounds. The first would take them to the old British frontline, the second to the old British outpost line and the third to the Hindenburg outpost line. The four attacking brigades averaged only 1500 men each, less than half their nominal strength. They set off in rain and fog under a creeping barrage. The machine-gun barrage was so ferocious that a captured German battalion commander said: 'The small-arms fire was absolutely too terrible for words. There was nothing we could do but to crouch down in our trenches and wait for you to come and take us.'

And take them they did. In the first phase the 16th Battalion of the 4th Division took 450 prisoners (which would have been more than its own number), sixty machine guns, several field guns and two anti-aircraft guns. On the 1st Division front an officer reported Germans running past him and asking 'Which way?' to the Australian rear. By 10 am the Australians were on their second objective. In the north the 1st Division pushed on easily to the final objective. The men looked down on the canal and its bridges, the entrance to the tunnel and Bellicourt village. The 4th Division came up south of them about an hour later. Rawlinson's other two corps – Butler's to the north and Braithwaite's to the south – failed to take their third objectives.

The Australians had taken 4300 prisoners for casualties of about 1260. This was a modest figure but, with the Australian formations so wasted, it amounted to the loss of a brigade. In his report to Haig, Rawlinson mentioned that German officers were saying their men no longer wanted to face Australians.

THREE DAYS LATER Butler's III Corps was still trying to come up alongside the Australian 1st Division. Butler asked Monash for help. General Glasgow had arranged for his tired men to be relieved; now he had to order them to attack again. Some in the 1st Battalion refused to move. They said they weren't getting a 'fair deal', that they 'were being put in to do other people's work', and that they were tired of British divisions failing on their flanks. One hundred and nineteen men disobeyed their officers and walked to the rear. All but one of them was later found guilty of desertion rather than mutiny, and sentenced to up to ten years' imprisonment. Monash failed to confirm the sentences and the men were eventually pardoned. This annoyed Glasgow, who had none of Monash's wiles.

But mutiny was coming. As Monash was planning his attack on the Hindenburg Line he had to order the disbandment of seven battalions: the 19th, 21st, 25th, 37th, 42nd, 54th and 60th. This was a rough blow. Men first of all identified with their battalion rather than their brigade or division. The battalion was like a large and vaguely feudal family, the source of traditions and inspirations.

Haig's headquarters and the Army Council in London had for months been urging the Australians to adopt three-battalion brigades. Monash had resisted. He knew what the breaking up of battalions would do to the morale of his force. He didn't think numbers mattered too much so long as each battalion had thirty Lewis guns. And, one suspects, he thought chasing the Germans to the Hindenburg Line more important than housekeeping.

Billy Hughes unwittingly forced him to adopt disbandment. Hughes had decided in August that the 1914 men in the AIF – there were about 6000 'originals' left – should be given two months' leave in Australia. But he couldn't find ships to take them home. Then in September, after much nagging and prodding, he found one. Birdwood, still the administrative head of the AIF, was told 800 men could go home at once. Monash was told on September 12, just as he was planning his attack on the Hindenburg outpost line. Most of the originals were in the 1st and 4th divisions, the two that were carrying out the coming attack. Monash resisted and Birdwood insisted. The men left. Monash had been prevaricating about disbanding battalions. Now, faced with the loss of another 5000-odd men, he accepted that the battalions that were badly depleted had to be broken up.

The moral case for sending the men home was just about incontestable. English, Irish, Scots, Welsh, French and German soldiers received home leave. The original Australians had been fighting since Gallipoli without seeing home, which was deemed to be too far away. Many had been wounded several times. Some looked ten years older than when they had left home: boyish curves had become hard angles. But the case for keeping them, more pragmatic than moral, was strong too. Battalions were down to 400 men or less; the originals were the most experienced men and, in many cases, the best. Monash needed every man he could find for the Hindenburg Line. This was the climactic point of the war. If the line was broken here, at its strongest point, the war could end in months.

Men, and officers too, in the formations marked for extinction held angry meetings. Feeling was particularly strong in the 37th Battalion of the 3rd Division commanded by Lieutenant-Colonel Charles Story, a good soldier. He protested to his brigadier, then went over his head to Gellibrand, Monash and Birdwood. For this he lost his command. His men decided that at their final parade they would obey every instruction except the last order, which would tell them to march off and join other battalions. They did just this a few days after the battle for the Hindenburg outposts. Walter McNicoll, their brigadier, spoke to them. The men still refused the final order. The officers were told to fall out. They did so – reluctantly, it was said. The sergeants then fell out, along with a corporal and a private. The others were told that they would be posted as absent without leave if they failed to join their new battalions by that afternoon.

Left to themselves, the men decided that the battalion would continue to be run along military lines. Men were chosen to carry out the officers' tasks; a corporal became the battalion commander. Food was obtained from sympathisers in other battalions. Rations tended to fall off wagons as they passed the 37th's camp. It was all very Australian, rather like shearers making a stand on principle at a hot shed in western Queensland.

The other battalions marked for disbandment did much the same things. Monash and Gellibrand talked with delegates from the 37th. Monash told them: 'I have done a thing unprecedented in military annals in holding an informal conference such as this, but I realise that the AIF is different from any other army in the world.' Men of the 25th told their brigadier that they wanted to be given the roughest task in the next battle. That way, the battalion would be wiped out, or it would leave such a mark that no-one would dare try to disband it.

Pompey Elliott intended to roll his 60th Battalion into the 59th. Most of the men of the 60th went on strike when Lieutenant-Colonel Scanlan tried to give orders to them. Private Whinfield was there. Elliott rode up, Whinfield wrote in his diary.

[Colonel Scanlan] ordered slope arms – none budged. He then demanded it again – none stirred. Then old Pompey on his big black neddy fell on us like an avalanche. Man he was mad. If he'd had his revolver a few would have been shot very likely. He picked out the Major, a captain, odd men,

701

then he stormed – detailed the law dealing with mutiny. Then he dealt with the necessity of being broken up. Then he pleaded.

According to Ross McMullin, Elliott's biographer, the brigadier at first thundered: 'This nonsense must cease at once.' If a large body of men mutinied, Elliott said, the ringleaders would be executed. He fell into hyperbole. If the identities of the ringleaders could not be determined, then probably one in every ten men would be shot. 'We've got bullets too,' one of the men said.

Elliott became conciliatory. It was no use blaming the AIF authorities, he said. Better to blame the politicians in Australia who had failed to provide reinforcements. Elliott would leave them for half-an-hour so that they could think about what to do.

When he returned the men still seemed likely to oppose the disbandment. 'It seems like deserting our dead,' some said. Elliott talked some more, quietly and sensibly. The 60th men could retain their colour patches, he said. The men agreed to disband. Thus was the power of Elliott when he spoke softly.

The other six battalions refused to disband. Elliott was furious upon learning, the day after he had talked the 60th around, that Monash had deferred the break-up of the other six. But Monash had shown much commonsense. He said privately that he wasn't going to let the men dictate to him; he would work out a way to disband the battalions in his own way and on his own terms. Mutiny was dramatic enough: he wasn't going to inflame it by responding the way generals were supposed to respond. And, anyway, planning the attack on the Hindenburg Line was more important.

There had been a mutiny, but there was a nobility to it. The men weren't refusing to fight; they simply wanted to do so in their old formations. None of the mutineers was punished.

MUTINY WAS SWIRLING around Kaiser Wilhelm too, except that he couldn't see it for what it was.

Since late 1915 France and Britain had kept a large force at the Macedonian port of Salonika. This pleased the easterners, who saw

Salonika as the gateway to Bulgaria, the Danube and the underbelly of Germany; but for years the 600,000 troops there had done little except come down with malaria. Now, reinforced by a large Greek force, the so-called 'Army of the East' was driving north into Bulgaria, which had come into war in 1915 for no grander reason than that it thought Germany might win. Prince Ferdinand, who styled himself as Tsar of Bulgaria, told his troops to die rather than retreat but they preferred to live. It was all over by late September when Bulgaria sought a separate armistice.

The Turks were just about beaten too. General Allenby in September attacked along the coastal plain of Palestine, heading for Syria. Allenby advanced so fast that Liman von Sanders, the victorious German commander on Gallipoli, had to flee his headquarters at Nazareth in his pyjamas. On October 1 Australian horsemen would enter Damascus.

On September 26 a huge force of Americans and French attacked in the Argonne Forest. This was always going to be a difficult front because of the rough terrain, but now Ludendorff was being tied down at the lower end of the western front. Captain Harry Truman commanded an artillery battery of 'wild Irish and German Catholics' in this battle. Bespectacled and with short-cropped hair, Truman knew how to curse. A runner who arrived breathless at Truman's battery said: 'I never heard a man cuss so well or intelligently, and I'd shoed a million mules.' Truman's father was a mule trader.

On September 27, towards the other end of the front, Haig sent his 1st and 3rd armies at Cambrai. By the following day they had penetrated six miles. Plumer's 2nd Army and the Belgians were preparing to push out from Ypres. That day Ludendorff is said to have 'lost his nerve'. He fell into a rage and blamed the Kaiser, the German people and politicians for Germany's setbacks. In the evening he calmed down and told Hindenburg there must be an immediate armistice. Hindenburg agreed. Ludendorff was presumably thinking that Germany could find a way to keep her Russian conquests in any peace deal. He still had fifty divisions protecting these spoils. This was one of the reasons he was short of men on the western front.

Next day the pair went to see the Kaiser and Paul von Hintze, the Foreign Minister. Ludendorff told the Kaiser the army was near to collapse. He said Bulgaria was lost and that Austria and Turkey would soon follow. Germany should seek a ceasefire and then begin negotiations on the basis of President Wilson's Fourteen Points, even though these called on her to give up all conquests in Russia, France and Belgium. Hintze thought Germany would do better if she presented a more democratic face. Someone thought more liberal, such as Prince Max of Baden, the Kaiser's cousin, should replace Count Georg von Hertling, the conservative Chancellor who never argued with the military. A parliamentary government should be cobbled up as quickly as possible. Hindenburg and Ludendorff, who had enjoyed the powers of dictators, should be answerable to the new chancellor. Kaiser Wilhelm accepted what he saw as a 'revolution from above'; it was preferable to anarchy from below.

Hindenburg and Ludendorff liked the idea. As one historian wrote: 'Having rigorously excluded Germany's civilian leaders from the waging of the war, Ludendorff and Hindenburg wanted to make them responsible for its loss.' Prince Max became chancellor.

Before this happened the Australians had attacked the Hindenburg Line.

46

An American tragedy

General Rawlinson didn't much believe in General Richard Butler; he had no reason to. The advance eastwards of Butler's III Corps, on the northern flank of the Australians, had been a series of stutters and failures, all the way from Villers-Bretonneux to the edge of the Hindenburg Line. Butler, a former deputy chief-of-staff to Haig, had been replaced temporarily after the Amiens battle. He appeared to have been suffering some form of nervous collapse. Now he was back. On September 16, two days before the attack on the Hindenburg outpost line, Rawlinson wrote in his diary: 'I am pretty sure the Aust & IX Corps will do their jobs but am not so confident about the III Corps . . . If they make a mess of this show I shall have to talk seriously to Butler for it will be his fault.' As Prior and Wilson write in their *Command on the Western Front*, here was an extraordinary confession. Rawlinson had not only foreseen failure but also identified its cause in advance. As we saw in the previous chapter, III Corps did 'make a mess' of the approach to the Hindenburg Line. This was to influence the attack on the main line in ways that no-one could have foreseen.

The Hindenburg Line, September 29–October 6, 1918

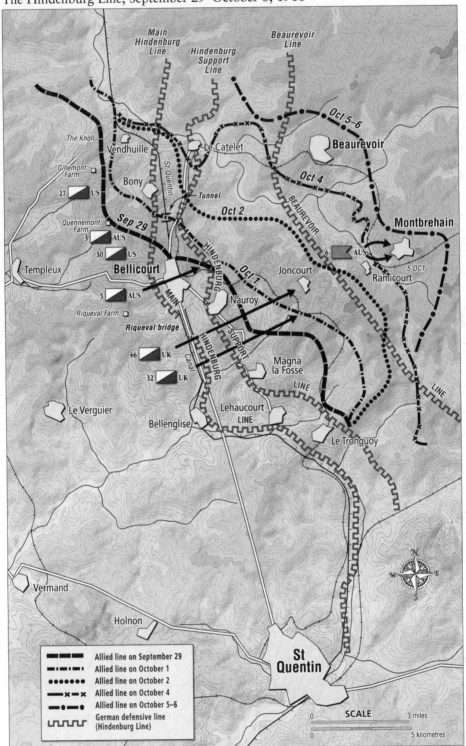

Legend:
- Allied line on September 29
- Allied line on October 1
- Allied line on October 2
- Allied line on October 4
- Allied line on October 5–6
- German defensive line (Hindenburg Line)

SCALE

0 — 3 miles

0 — 5 kilometres

Map labels: Main Hindenburg Line, Hindenburg Support Line, Beaurevoir Line, Oct 5–6, Beaurevoir, Oct 4, Le Catelet, Montbrehain, The Knoll, Vendhuille, Gillemont Farm, Bony, Tunnel, Oct 2, 27 US, Quennemont Farm, 3 AUS, 30 US, Sep 29, Templeux, Bellicourt, 5 AUS, Nauroy, Oct 1, Joncourt, 6 AUS, 5 OCT, Ramicourt, Riqueval Farm, MAIN, Riqueval bridge, SUPPORT, HINDENBURG, 46 UK, 32 UK, Canal, Magna la Fosse, LINE, LINE, Le Verguier, Bellenglise, Lehaucourt LINE, Le Tronquoy, Vermand, Holnon, St Quentin

A PILOT FLYING in the summer sky over the Hindenburg Line on Rawlinson's front would have seen row after row of German defences running north to south, each side of the canal. This was not like the German line east of Villers-Bretonneux at the time of the battle of Amiens. There was nothing improvised or accidental here: this was meant to be permanent, the final redoubt, heavy and Teutonic. It could not be reduced with a short barrage. And there could be no surprise. The Germans knew they were going to be attacked. They also knew that if they didn't hold the line, they would be on the run for Germany.

The pilot would have seen the canal, a tough enough obstacle in itself with its steep banks and dark belts of wire zigzagging each side of it. He would have seen the canal go into a tunnel just south of Bellicourt. The line of the tunnel itself was easy enough to pick up. The spoil from long ago lay banked above it, broken here and there by ventilation chimneys of grey brick. Five lines of trenches also marked the course of the tunnel. These defences along the canal and above the tunnel were the main Hindenburg Line.

Glancing to the east the pilot would have seen the reserve positions, about a mile behind the main line. These ran from the village of Le Catelet in the north, through Nauroy and on to Le Tronquoy in the south. More wire, more dugouts, more blockhouses. Two miles further east was the reserve line, known as the Beaurevoir Line because it was just west of the village of that name. South of Beaurevoir the pilot would have seen another little village, Montbrehain, out in open country.

Glancing west the pilot would have seen the new British front-line after the battle for the Hindenburg outposts. Its shape would have puzzled him. In the centre the Australian line had pushed past the Hindenburg outpost defences and was staring down the valley at the canal. But to the north the British line was up to 3000 yards behind the Australian line. Three strong German positions were intact here: the Knoll, Gillemont Farm and Quennemont Farm, all on high ground. This was the line held by Butler's III Corps. Butler had tried to straighten it after September 18 and failed. Butler eventually told Rawlinson that his troops were too exhausted to go on.

This left Monash with a problem. He had already begun to plan his assault on the main Hindenburg Line before the battle for the outposts. He reasoned that it would be best to attack across the 6000-yard line of the tunnel with his corps as the spearhead. The casualties would be too high if he tackled the canal itself. The tunnel was a land bridge: tanks could cross it and he would not have to worry about how to get thousands of infantrymen across water.

Monash's idea had been for the Australian Corps to sidestep to the north and take over the III Corps' front, which faced the line of the tunnel. Braithwaite's IX Corps would then shift north and occupy the old Australian position. Point three of Monash's plan said that it was based on the assumption that all the objectives of the attack on the Hindenburg outposts would be taken. This, as we know, hadn't happened on the III Corps' front. On September 24 III Corps was still more than 1000 yards behind the start line for the new battle. The creeping barrage that would take the men to the tunnel was also based on the assumption that the start line would be reasonably straight.

Monash had a second problem: his five divisions were at half-strength or worse. He sent the 1st and 4th divisions back and brought the 3rd and 5th divisions up for the new attack. He knew these two had only one big battle left in them. He told Rawlinson that he didn't have the means to keep the pressure on the Germans. Rawlinson said he might be able to borrow the 2nd American Corps: two big divisions untouched by war, some 50,000 men, fresh and eager. Would Monash be prepared to use them? Yes, said Monash. He now had four divisions – the two American formations plus his own 3rd and 5th – for the fight, and he could also call on the 2nd. He would use the American divisions, along with tanks, to attack over the tunnel. They would go 4000 yards, taking the main line and the reserve line. Then the two Australian divisions would pass through them and take the Beaurevoir Line, 4000 yards beyond. Butler's III Corps and Braithwaite's IX Corps would flood through the breach opened by the Americans and the Australians and turn left and right respectively, widening the front.

Monash's eagerness to take the Americans and send them out to fight almost at once says something about his flustered state of mind. Of course he had to take them, but he, a logician of war, seemed to make light of their newness, their lack of knowledge of weapons and logistics. This was not going to be like Hamel or Amiens; this was going to be more like a 1916 battle: infantry trying to advance on a heavily fortified and deep line from which the Germans were unlikely to flee. Monash seemed to think that the Americans could be 'taught' in a few days what his own troops had taken years to learn.

RAWLINSON MODIFIED MONASH'S plan for his attack, which was due to go in on September 29. Rawlinson's changes made sense. He thought the frontage of the assault, limited to the 6000 yards of the tunnel, too narrow. He ordered it widened to 10,000 yards so that there would be fewer casualties from flanking fire. This meant there would also have to be an attack south of the tunnel, across the water. Walter Braithwaite, the commander of IX Corps, wanted to send a division across the canal opposite Bellenglise, then pass another division through it. He selected the 46th (North Midland) Division, which had an indifferent reputation, to tackle the water. Rawlinson agreed to Braithwaite's plan. The engineers would have to find a way of getting the 46th across the water. They came up with rafts made from petrol tins, collapsible boats, ladders and lifebelts sent up from the leave-boats at Boulogne. Rawlinson also cut down the part of Butler's III Corps; it would do no more than guard the left flank of the Americans. Rawlinson was probably also saying that he didn't trust Butler to do anything harder.

Rawlinson and Monash could not use the artillery as they had at Amiens. The battle for the Hindenburg Line would be a throwback. There would have to be a long bombardment, which meant there could be no surprise, as there had been at Amiens. This time the gunners would have to smash trenches and dugouts and, on the 46th Division's front, the steep banks of the canal; they would also have to cut belt after belt of wire. And of course there would be a creeping barrage for the infantry. Here the problem caused by the failure of III Corps to take the outpost line again arose. Barrage maps had to be printed and distributed well before zero hour on September 29. Monash decided to assume that the ground Butler had failed to secure would be taken before September 29. He was gambling and didn't like it. 'It was contrary to the policy which had governed all my previous battle plans, in which *nothing* had been left to chance.'

THE POSITION ON what had been III Corps' front became even more complicated because of Monash's decision to sidestep his troops to the north. The III Corps front, which faced the tunnel, was now the Australians' front, except they weren't there. Monash had taken the chance to give his divisions a brief rest. The Americans now held the III Corps front. The 27th American Division held the northern end of the line and the 30th the southern end. And, despite the fresh attacks by Butler's men, this front was still 1000 yards short of Monash's proposed start line. Rawlinson decided the 27th Division would have to take the ground before the main attack on the 29th. He was asking the Americans to do what Butler couldn't do.

EARLY ON SEPTEMBER 27 three battalions of Americans set off in the fog and rain and behind a creeping barrage to capture the German strong points at Quennemont Farm, Gillemont Farm and the Knoll. Some reached the ridgeline that looked down on the line of the tunnel. Most didn't; most simply disappeared into the fog and for the rest of the day Monash and others wondered where they were. Some reports said the Americans had taken their objectives; others said they hadn't. British airmen couldn't be sure what line the Americans held. 'Situation very obscure all day,' Monash wrote in his diary.

It was still obscure the next day, except for one obvious conclusion: the attack had failed. It was years before the truth about that day emerged. The Americans had quickly become lost in the fog and smoke. They had gone out with only eighteen officers – many were apparently away at schools and courses – and seventeen of these had been killed or wounded. The Americans had fought bravely, but in the confusion had broken up into disconnected groups. Most of them didn't know where they were or what to do. The attack would have been difficult for experienced troops with forty-or-so officers. The New Yorkers had been tested too severely. Their casualties ran to more than 1500.

Monash now had a dilemma, and it played on his nerves during the afternoon of September 28, the day before the big attack. A pilot reported seeing Americans out near the outpost line. If, on the following day, Monash brought his creeping barrage back 1000 yards to protect the advancing Americans, their comrades lying wounded and cut off in no-man's land would be killed. If, on the other hand, he started the creeping barrage at the outpost line, the Americans would be unprotected by artillery for the first 1000 yards of their approach. He decided on the second option.

It was the sort of problem he hated, and not just because, as a matter of morality, there was no 'right' answer. So much of Monash's confidence and authority came from the thoroughness of his preparations. He tried to win battles before they were fought, to bring mathematical certainty to warfare, so that a battle unfolded in steps that seemed inevitable and unstoppable. And here he was walking around with all these doubts that in the past he had always been able to eliminate. He was improvising and hoping. The Americans from the 27th Division might be shot up badly crossing the first 1000 yards without artillery support; the whole attack might be compromised. Monash could not be sure what was going to happen. This not only offended him but also softened his confidence.

He asked Rawlinson to postpone the battle for a day in the hope that the Americans could push their line forward a little. No, said Rawlinson, the attack was timed to fit in with other big offensives all along the line from Flanders to Verdun.

Haig arrived at Monash's headquarters. Monash told him he was in a 'state of despair'. Haig told him it was 'not a serious matter'. The field-marshal was of course wrong, but larger pictures captivated him. The news from the Ypres and Cambrai fronts that day was good. To Haig, the problem was a small thing in a day of successes; to Monash, it was everything. Haig was like a country gentleman visiting his tenant farmers. He called on Major-General George Read, the commander of the American corps. 'He is a good, honest fellow,' Haig decided, 'but all this class of warfare is quite new to him, and he was genuinely very anxious. I did my best to cheer him up, and told him that the reality was much simpler than his imagination pictured it to his mind.'

LIEUTENANT WILL PALSTRA, the decorated infantryman from the 3rd Division, had wanted to be a pilot from the moment he saw an aircraft flying overhead while he was training in England in 1916. On the day that the American preliminary attack failed, he was flying over the Hindenburg Line through heavy ground fire when he saw a German plane 150 yards away in the mist. He dug Devlin Hamilton, his observer, in the ribs and yelled 'Hun'. The German hadn't seen them. 'Kicked on right rudder,' Palstra wrote in his diary, 'doing a flat turn thus giving Ham a chance with his Lewis. Ham, who like myself had been in a blue funk up to now, rose to the occasion and rattled a drum of Lewis fair into the Hun. He appeared to catch fire, large patches of smoke came from his machine and he went down in a sideslip dive. My first Hun.'

THE AMERICAN 27TH Division went out into the mist and fog just before 6 am on September 29, to be at once shot up by machine gunners who had been untouched by any barrage. Thirty-four tanks went with the Americans. Ten ran into an old British minefield, even though the Germans had marked it with signs. Another eighteen were either hit by German field guns or ditched. The heaviest fire was coming from the strong points Butler's III Corps had failed to take: the Knoll, Gillemont Farm and Quennemont Farm. Many of the American officers were soon hit. Men who were lost or confused straggled towards the rear. Soon the American line became a series of groups, often leaderless, cut off from each other and unsure where they were. By mid-morning there was no prospect of them capturing the outpost line, let alone crossing the tunnel. Which meant Gellibrand's 3rd Division, which was supposed to follow the Americans at around 9 am and pass through them, would also be held up.

A few hours after the attack began the American commanders didn't know where their men were. Further back still Monash thought everything was going as it should. Then at 11.12 am he received a message from the 3rd Division saying that the Americans were stalled in front of them. Monash became more and more confused. One report would say that the Americans were across the tunnel, then another would say they were still behind the outpost line. The hamlet of Bony, on the western edge of the canal, was taken, then it wasn't. The attack had become a replay of so many battles in 1916: as soon as the troops left the start line, the generals had no notion of what was happening.

The 3rd Division had blundered into the back of the Americans and joined them in trying to break through the outpost line. The Australians looked down on American dead and wounded in the wheat crop and peered into the fog and smoke, trying to spot the machine guns that had been stuttering since they crossed the old American frontline. They knew something was wrong but they didn't know what. They met small parties of Americans falling back, leaderless and anxious for someone to tell them what to do.

Hubert Wilkins, the official Australian photographer, came on a group of Americans sitting quietly on the floor of a trench. A little further down the trench German stick-bombs were landing. The Americans were doing nothing because they thought the stick-bombs were shells. This was near the Knoll. An Australian lieutenant nearby collected 200 Americans and combined them with his platoon. This was happening all over the front. Americans and Australians were fighting together in isolated groups. And they still hadn't broken through the outpost line.

To the south the men of the 30th American Division, with the advantage of a creeping barrage, had done better. They crossed the line of the tunnel, where they came under flanking fire from the out-post positions that the 27th Division had failed to reach. The Americans took Bellicourt, which had been hit hard by artillery. The task of the 5th Australian Division here was the same as for the 3rd Division to the north: pass through the Americans and go on to the support lines. Machine-gun posts that had been missed held up the 5th Division infantrymen, but they went through the Americans and took Nauroy, just behind the support line at 12.20 pm. They were more than a mile ahead of the 3rd Division, hung up to the north.

Major Blair Wark, a twenty-four-year-old quantity surveyor from Sydney, won the Victoria Cross for his leadership in this bat-tle. He had brought the 32nd Battalion of the 5th Division through the fog and smoke south of Bellicourt, near the mouth of the tun-nel, having picked up 200 Americans who were without officers, and pushed on for Nauroy before turning south-east. Here he saw khaki-clad infantrymen on his right. They were men of the 46th Division from Braithwaite's corps. They had crossed the canal on rafts and lifebelts and seized several bridges. Theirs was the great success of the morning. Wark was delighted to see them: his left flank was still open but the Englishmen made him secure on his right. He pushed on eastwards towards the village of Joncourt, which was still held by the Germans, before halting around 3 pm. He was on the extreme right of the Australian line and, unlike most of his countrymen, close to his final objective. He didn't know it, and Monash certainly didn't, but the Australian frontline, instead of running roughly north–south, was a diagonal running across the main Hindenburg Line at the tunnel. Wark was at the southern end of the diagonal, roughly where the plan said he was supposed to be, and to the north Gellibrand's division was pinned down on the other side of the tunnel, around the outpost line and the hamlet of Bony. Wark would have been in danger of being cut off had it not been for the Englishmen on his right.

THOSE ENGLISHMEN, TERRITORIALS, many of them from the mining and pottery towns of the North Midlands, had not only performed one of the memorable feats of the war in crossing the open canal; they had done so on time and with few casualties. Only when one stands on the near-vertical canal banks south of Bellicourt does one begin to understand the scale of their achievement.

The North Midlanders, shouting and cheering, had surged out of the fog and taken the German trenches on the western side of the canal with bayonet charges. Then they crossed: some swimming, some wading, others floating on rafts, lifebelts and planks. They rushed the high Riqueval bridge as the Germans were about to blow it. One of the most dramatic photographs of the war shows a brigade of the North Midlanders posing on the eastern side of the canal, some still wearing lifebelts, a few wearing captured German helmets, while their brigadier addresses them from the bridge, which is shell-pocked but intact. When this photograph was taken the division's other two brigades had surged eastwards. Of the 5300 prisoners taken by Rawlinson's army this day, the 46th Division took 4200; it penetrated 6000 yards into the Hindenburg defences and lost only 800 men. The North Midlanders had shown rare spirit, but the division also went forward under what was probably the heaviest barrage that had ever accompanied a British division during the Great War. The American division that had failed in the north on the same day had gone out with no barrage. The main tactical lesson of the war was on display again.

BY MID-AFTERNOON RAWLINSON seemed to think the attack was succeeding everywhere. 'I could not have hoped for such good results,' he wrote in his diary. Sometime afterwards he realised the Americans and the 3rd Division were stalled on the outpost line. 'The Americans appear to be in a state of hopeless confusion,' he added to his diary entry. He feared the American casualties had been heavy – 'but it is their own fault'.

Was it? Rawlinson and Monash, both experienced commanders, had sent them off in a fog without an artillery barrage. Here was proof that Pershing, the commander of the American forces and a soldier of modest talents, had been right to insist that, wherever possible, his troops should fight as an independent army and only when they were properly trained. The 27th American Division lost 5000 men in the three days to September 30.

Monash didn't know much more than Rawlinson about how the battle was going; he merely thought he did. He told Bean: 'Well, you see what I expected might happen has happened. The Americans sold us a pup. They're simply unspeakable.' In the official history, published in 1942, Bean argued that Monash should have realised how raw the Americans were. Monash's battle plan, Bean contended, had broken down because he had underestimated the human element. Bean was probably right, but we need to remember that he held Monash to a higher standard than he did Birdwood, Godley and White.

Gellibrand had gone forward just before 10 am to try to discover what was happening to his division. He went so far forward that he came under machine-gun fire. He returned convinced that the Americans on his front could not reach their final objective. Monash, on the other hand, was influenced by an airman's report that Americans had been seen a mile past the Hindenburg Line. Monash believed that the Americans had taken their objectives and had merely failed to mop up, leaving pockets of Germans behind them. Gellibrand and his staff thought those 'pockets' were the main German line, which they were.

Monash told Gellibrand to attack at 3 pm and wipe out the 'pockets'; there would be no artillery support for fear of hitting Americans further forward. Gellibrand demurred. Monash bullied him. Blamey, Monash's chief-of-staff, told Gellibrand: 'We have had the report [the airman's account of where the Americans were] absolutely confirmed from a number of places.'

Gellibrand sent two brigades forward. They eventually captured Gillemont Farm, one of the strong points on the outpost line, but could go no further. Towards evening mixed parties of Americans and Australians drove the Germans off two of the other strong points, Quennemont Farm and the western side of the Knoll. The outpost line had finally fallen, but the main Hindenburg Line on this front was still a mile away and there was no hope of taking it by nightfall.

A little after 4 pm Monash decided on a new tactic: he would try to attack the Germans on Gellibrand's front by sending troops north from the 5th Division's positions on the other side of the Hindenburg Line. He would try to clear Gellibrand's front from behind. He had scrapped his original plan. He also told Rawlinson that the Americans should be withdrawn.

A 'SENSATIONAL REPORT' arrived at 5th Division headquarters from the troops at the southern end of the St Quentin Canal. They had discovered a factory, just inside the tunnel entrance, for boiling down the bodies of dead German soldiers to obtain fats and oils that were to be used to make high explosives.

Allied soldiers in France and civilians in Britain had been speculating about the existence of such a factory for eighteen months. A Berlin newspaper had in 1917 carried a story that mentioned a 'carcase-utilisation establishment'. The item was apparently about a rendering plant for animal carcases. It was mistranslated in Britain to suggest that the Germans were boiling down the bodies of their dead soldiers. Stories spread at the front that trains ran back into Germany after nightfall carrying bodies of dead soldiers, tied neck to heel in pairs.

The Australians and Americans at the tunnel believed they had the evidence. In a stinking chamber just inside the tunnel entrance they found a dozen hacked-up bodies, two coppers and two or three tins of fat. Bean went to see the 'factory' the next day. He entered a chamber that contained two coppers and a table. Twelve Germans lay dead on the floor covered with red brick-dust. One was missing his head; another's skull was 'cracked like an eggshell'; body parts and blood were splattered on the walls. A thirteenth German lay in one of the coppers, his head beneath the surface scum, his exposed shoulder blade showing through the grey of his coat.

The Germans had used the three-and-a-half miles of the tunnel as a shelter and dormitory. Bean promptly concluded that he was in a kitchen. Then he looked up and saw a hole. He could see the marks made by the driving band of a six-inch shell. The shell had penetrated three or four feet of masonry and earth above the tunnel, entered the chamber and exploded on the kitchen floor, throwing one of the Germans into the copper.

American and Australian soldiers were in the chamber with Bean. An American said: 'Well, I never believed it before, but now I have seen it I can write home and tell them that I have seen it with my own eyes.'

A young Australian was more sceptical. 'If this is the way they did it,' he said, 'one man at a time, all I can say is that it must be a bloody long job.'

MONASH'S POSITION AT the end of that first day was not as bad as his flights of caprice would suggest. His plan had gone wrong, communications with the northern front had broken down and he didn't know where the Americans were and hence was limited in his use of artillery. Monash saw all these things as forms of untidiness. This, and his tiredness – he had had only six days off in six months – probably explained his flashes of temper. Mostly he argued with Gellibrand and mostly Gellibrand was right. Yet Monash was hardly presiding over the sort of shambles that had several times visited Birdwood, Godley and White in 1916 and 1917. His front was a diagonal line when the plan said it should have been a vertical line, but he had still breached the main Hindenburg Line across the tunnel. And the Germans lacked the men to mount the furious counter-attacks that had always been part of their way of war.

For September 30, the second day of the battle, Monash decided to attack north-east, rather than from west to east. The 3rd Division would go for the hamlet of Bony, on the western side of the tunnel. The 5th Division would push north-east towards the Beaurevoir Line, the last line of German defences. So began two days of grinding against the Germans during which the line edged east to the crump of bombs and the flashes of bayonets. The attack became a series of small-scale battles in the rain and mud. As Monash later admitted, there could be no methodical advance covered by artillery. 'It was, in a peculiar degree, a private soldier's battle,' he said.

The privates did well. The 3rd Division crept towards Bony and finally took it on October 1. On the same day the 5th Division took Joncourt, on the edge of the Beaurevoir Line. To the north the Australians had sent patrols into Le Catelet.

Norman Dalgleish, a twenty-three-year-old lieutenant in Pompey Elliott's brigade, kept going although wounded. Then a shell fragment hit him in the head, causing fearful wounds that left him speechless. He insisted on personally telling his superiors that his company needed reinforcements. He did so with sign language and by sketching on a sheet of paper that was soon sodden with his blood. At the hospital Dalgleish asked a nurse to help him write commendations for two of his NCOs. Then he collapsed. He died about a week later. Dalgleish's father 'broke down completely and cried like a child' when Elliott's account of Norman's last exploit was read to him.

By the end of October 1 most of the Americans had been gathered in. Monash now had almost all of the ground he had aimed to take and around 3000 prisoners. He decided to relieve the 3rd and 5th divisions, which had run up around 2600 casualties. He would bring in the 2nd Division to take the Beaurevoir Line on October 3.

LIEUTENANT JOE MAXWELL came up with the 2nd Division. He was only twenty-two, a notorious scrapper and reveller. He also owned an impish sense of humour and a winsome smile and didn't take himself too seriously away from the guns. He had twice won the Military Cross, as well as the Distinguished Conduct Medal.

The attack went in at 6.05 am on October 3 under a barrage that fell short on Maxwell's section of the front. The 5th and 7th brigades made the initial assault. They could come up with only 2500 frontline troops between them for a frontage of 6000 yards. Maxwell watched his men go down, first from Australian shells dropping short, then from German fire. The wire was mostly uncut. Maxwell could see steam rising from a German machine gun: the

Ground taken by Monash's Australian Corps, 1918

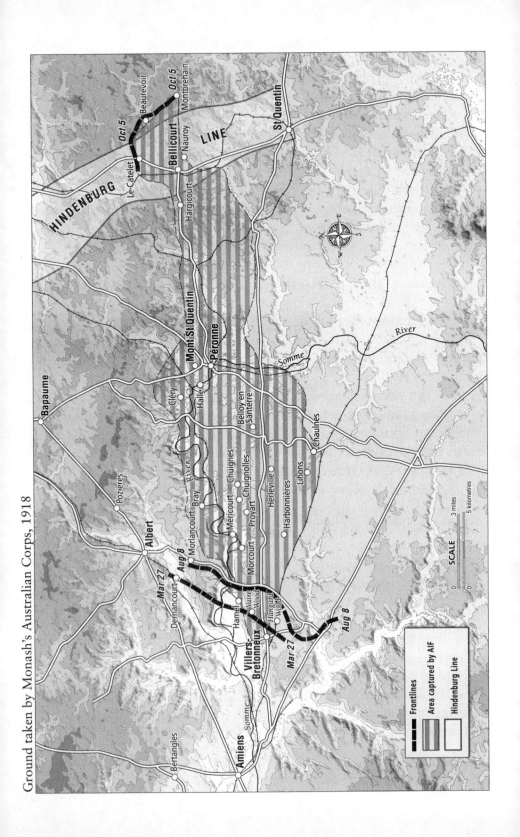

water in the jacket was boiling but the Maxim was still firing. Maxwell rushed the post, firing his revolver as he ran, and landed among the Germans, only to realise that his revolver was empty. 'When the Germans before us shouted "*Kamerad*" I was the most pleased and relieved man in France.'

Maxwell was now in the Beaurevoir Line. A rifle cracked from one of the dugouts. An Australian sank, clutching wildly at his stomach. 'He was dead in two minutes,' Maxwell wrote. 'In that dugout there were seven of the enemy. That cowardly act had to be punished. We shot every one of them.'

Later in the day an 'impetuous' Australian shot a German who was about to surrender. Other Germans nearby hesitated to surrender. Maxwell walked over to their trench with a prisoner as interpreter and two privates. Maxwell realised his error as soon as he arrived there. Some Germans wanted to surrender and some didn't. 'An officer wearing a peaked cap was bitterly opposed to any surrender. He flung gusts of excited German at his men.' Two machine guns were pointed at the Australian trench.

A dead Australian lay among the Germans. Maxwell bent down to identify him. He gazed up into the muzzle of a German pistol. The man was about to shoot him. The officer stopped him and demanded Maxwell's revolver. Maxwell handed it over.

The officer noticed that Maxwell had a cut on the chin and blood smears on his neck. 'You might care for this,' he said in English, offering Maxwell a bottle of schnapps. Maxwell hesitated.

'It is not poisoned. We do not kill defenceless prisoners. We fight cleanly.'

Maxwell took a drink and told the officer he should surrender. 'Our people will blow the trench to smithereens. You have no chance. Be sensible.'

The German said he would fight on. A moment later the Australian barrage fell on the trench. Men flew in the air. The German officer stood bravely in the cloud of smoke and dust. He took a shell-blast in the face and died without a murmur. Maxwell escaped to the Australian line.

THE AUSTRALIANS TOOK their 6000 yards of trench that day; south of them Braithwaite's corps took another 5000 yards. The Hindenburg Line had been breached from front to back. The Australians might have taken Beaurevoir village too but they lacked the numbers. They had taken about 1000 prisoners; next day they rounded up another 800. The Australian casualties for three days at the Beaurevoir Line were close to 1000, a heavy loss for the low numbers involved. The Australian divisions were just about spent.

WHEN JOE MAXWELL crossed the Beaurevoir Line on October 3 he came upon an Australian with a severe head wound. Maxwell stabbed a rifle with bayonet fixed into the ground next to him, so that stretcher-bearers would see the man. 'Two days later,' Maxwell wrote, 'when we passed this spot the poor fellow was still alive, but he was wrapped in the topcoat of a German whose body lay near. The German, apparently seeing his end was near, had taken off his coat to cover the Australian, whom he thought had a chance.'

There was plenty of rum for Maxwell and his men that night. They drank their issue, plus that of the eighty-odd men who had been killed or wounded. They were then ordered to the rear. Hardly a man was sober enough to walk, Maxwell said. Two months later he was told he had won the Victoria Cross.

MONASH NOW DECIDED to withdraw the 2nd Division. It would be replaced by the two American divisions, which had been given a brief rest. The Americans could not take over the front until October 5. Monash said that Rawlinson asked him to hold the front for another day and to use it to push the line further east. Monash decided to attack the village of Montbrehain.

ON THE GROUND south of the tunnel entrance one is still reminded of the weight of the barrage that supported the North Midlanders' attack across the water. It has rained overnight and shrapnel balls, round and dull grey, have been washed into the path leading down to the canal. Near the Riqueval bridge patches of land remain unreclaimed and copses have grown up around shell holes that are filling with pine needles. Here and there are shell fragments and pieces of driving bands. The bridge is much as it was in 1918: a single lane, about fifty-feet across with low concrete sides above a high arch, a modest structure that was the scene for one of the most arresting photographs of the war.

At the entrance to the tunnel, just below Bellicourt, the water is still and slimy green. You start when a fish jumps near the brick banks. A plaque above the entrance says that Napoleon, emperor and king, started the canal in 1802. Just below the sign you see where slits for machine guns have been mortared over. Behind those slits was the kitchen that some thought was a corpse factory.

The American cemetery near Bony is beautifully kept. Instead of headstones, white marble crosses and an occasional Star of David mark the American dead. A notice forbids skateboarding, roller-skating, bicycling, motorcycling and ball playing. Among all the nations with cemeteries on the western front only the Americans see the need to remind people not to do these things.

47

Goodbye to all that

The men of the 24th Battalion of the 2nd Division had been only lightly caught up in the struggle for the Beaurevoir Line. Next day, along with the rest of the division, they were savouring a long rest, preferably near the coast. Apart from the matter of their weariness, there weren't many of them left. In the afternoon they were surprised to learn that they were to be used as part of a scratched-up force to take the village of Montbrehain, on the plateau to the east, the following day. They would be joined by the 21st Battalion, which had not fought at the Beaurevoir Line, the division's pioneers, who were to be used as infantry for the first time, as well as a few men from the brigade's machine-gun company.

After hearing this news, nine officers of the 24th Battalion huddled in a German dugout that smelled of earth and mildew and engaged in a singsong, 'as if war were a huge comedy'. They invented new lyrics for popular songs. Their version of 'Parlez-vous' told how infantrymen ('who "rat" the poor old Huns') were superior to cavalrymen, engineers and gunners. Captains Harry Fletcher and Austin Mahony sang 'I'm Courting Bonnie Lizzy Lindsay Noo' and Fletcher gave a solo rendition of 'The Bells of St Mary's'.

Fletcher and Mahony had been close friends before the war,

when they lived in the same boarding house near Melbourne University. On Sundays they would leave for church, parting on the way. Fletcher was a Protestant and Mahony a Catholic. They would meet up again on the way home. They enlisted together as privates in March, 1915, and received consecutive numbers. They went to Gallipoli together, foregoing chances of promotion to stay together in the same battalion.

Mahony was tall and strongly built, with a broad heavy jaw and brown eyes that looked kindly on the world. In most of his photographs there is the hint of a smile, as though smiling is the most natural thing to do. He grew up at Hansonville, in Victoria's northeast, and was dux of Wangaratta High School and topped the State in French before coming to Melbourne to work as a clerk in the public service. His passion was playing Australian rules football. By the time of the Gallipoli landings he and Fletcher were both sergeants, promoted on the same day.

The following year Mahony, now a lieutenant, won the Military Cross at Pozières. He always carried a walking stick at the front and inspired those around him with his coolness. He was also regarded as lucky. Several times when he should have been killed he walked away swinging his stick.

Football, rather than shellfire, put him in hospital. A sprained ankle took him away from the front for eight months in 1917 and early 1918. Four months after the injury he still had difficulty walking up stairs. He was made a captain in May, 1918, and in September he and Harry Fletcher arranged to spend a weekend together in London, where they stayed with an English family. They followed their old routine on the Sunday: Fletcher and the family went to 'kirk'; Mahony went to Mass. An evening of song followed.

Mahony had set up his headquarters on the new front after the battle for the Beaurevoir Line. Two German runners blundered in after dark and the Australians grabbed for their rifles. The Germans hadn't realised the front had shifted. They had brought dispatches and a tripe stew for the regimental commander who had occupied Mahony's dugout. They became prisoners; the fate of the tripe is unknown.

Harry Fletcher had rejoined the battalion only four days earlier. Photographs of him show a handsome young man with a serious air, intelligent eyes, a neat part in his hair and a dimple on his chin. He grew up at Eaglehawk, a suburb of Bendigo, and had become a teacher at Princes Hill, near Melbourne University, where he was studying for an arts degree. His sister, Annie, who died in 2004 aged 109, said he had a 'good sense of humour' and was 'quite sporty'. He was on the committee of a debating society that argued such topics as 'Is militarism desirable for a nation?' and 'Does the press of Australia exert too much of an influence over the politics of the nation?'

Mahony and Fletcher were in the trenches at Lone Pine when the Turks, late in the campaign, finally brought up howitzers. More than forty men were killed in one barrage that fell on the 24th Battalion. Fletcher was wounded and buried. According to family sources, one side of his face was damaged and he did not afterwards have to shave in that area. Gallipoli seared him but he kept his sense of humour. On the Greek island of Lemnos he took a hot bath. 'After washing about half an hour I found a singlet which I had lost a couple of months ago. On peeling it off I had to start and wash again.'

We know that Lieutenant John Gear from Ballarat was at the singsong before Montbrehain. He was twenty-four and had interrupted his studies for a diploma of education to join up as a private. He was a fine athlete and had earlier been accepted for the Duntroon military academy, only to be rejected because he was an inch too short. He had been wounded at Pozières and had won the Military Cross in 1918. We do not know whether Lieutenant George Ingram was present. He was a building contractor from the Melbourne suburb of Caulfield who had also risen through the ranks and been decorated for bravery.

MONTBREHAIN HAD BEEN a large village of 900 people. The Germans had evacuated some of them but elderly couples, as well as women and children, were sheltering in cellars and battered houses. A quarry and a cemetery stood on the north-west outskirts of the village.

The plan was for the 21st Battalion to go through the village and dig in on its eastern side. The 24th would go through and dig in on the northern side. The pioneers would veer south before the village and set up a defensive flank. In conception it was a nasty little operation. With only two battalions attacking, the front would be narrow, more so because each battalion could only offer about 240 men. If the assault succeeded, it would create a salient that could be hit from three sides. The war was now moving at a terrific pace. Monash probably didn't think too long about what he was ordering.

THE MORNING WAS cold and frosty and a bright moon shone on Australian bayonets and men rubbing their hands against the chill. Some sneezed from the gas they encountered on the way to the start line. The sun was just lighting the horizon as they followed the creeping barrage up the gentle slope to the village. The tanks that were to help them were late.

The 21st Battalion, on the right, broke into the village and a shell killed Captain James Sullivan, a young law clerk from Geelong. He had won the Military Medal on Gallipoli and two Military Crosses on the western front. He had been wounded earlier in 1918 but had returned to fight at Mont St Quentin. The men pushed on up the main street. In a cellar they came on twenty French women and children who later in the day gave them coffee and milk.

South of the village the pioneers fought well in their first essay as infantrymen. Lieutenant Norman Wilkinson, from the brigade's machine-gun company, had joined them with two gun teams. Wilkinson came upon about 100 German machine gunners manning a line on an embankment and firing into the Australians attacking the village. The Germans hadn't seen him. Wilkinson's teams poured fire into the embankment from close range. Each gun fired two belts. That was enough to put fourteen German guns out of action and kill thirty of the gunners and wound another fifty. In the afternoon Wilkinson was carried out with a bullet wound to the leg.

On the north-western side of the village Lieutenant Ingram led his platoon in rushing a machine-gun post, killing more than forty gunners and capturing six guns. (One account has them capturing nine guns: the Germans were short of men and food, but not machine guns.) With help from a tank Ingram next led an attack on the quarry on the north-western edge of the village. He landed among the Germans and shot several. The quarry gave up a large bag of prisoners and forty machine guns. Ingram went on into the village, where he saw a machine gun firing from a cellar ventilator. Ingram shot the gunner and rushed the cellar stairs. His men found him holding thirty prisoners. Ingram lived to be awarded the Victoria Cross.

Lieutenant Gear died, hit in the heart by a machine-gun bullet. He was in Fletcher's company on the extreme left of the attack. Then Harry Fletcher was killed. The Germans fired on a tank with a field gun. One of the shells hit Fletcher.

Mahony's company was going for the village before wheeling to the north-east. It paused at a hedge outside the village. A lieutenant was pushing his head through the hedge to see what was ahead when his helmet clanked against the muzzle of a machine gun. His batman, Private John Blankenberg, known throughout the battalion as 'Russia', shot its crew of four, saying they were 'cowards'. Blankenberg was himself killed later in the day.

French civilians, mostly old people and a few young girls, came out to meet Mahony's company as it moved through the village. An old man walked up the street saying '*Anglais bon! bon!*' Mahony came up to supervise the siting of his posts. He stood in the open and a machine-gun bullet, probably fired from some hundreds of yards away, slapped into his temple. A private who was with him said Mahony quickly lapsed into unconsciousness and did not speak. He died four days later.

Mahony had been hit about 8 am, Fletcher about an hour later. There had always been a symmetry to their military careers. And now, after nearly four years, in this village that really didn't matter that much, the symmetry had continued, except that it had turned black. There would be no more singsongs. The journey that had begun in Melbourne was over.

By early evening the Australians held Montbrehain and its out-skirts. Joe Maxwell went up to the village. Old people were abusing German prisoners. One woman – 'gaunt and as old as one of the witches in *Macbeth*' – shrieked at the prisoners then hoisted her petticoats 'and exposed to them that part of her gaunt old anatomy on which nature had intended her to sit'.

The men here didn't know it, Monash didn't know it, but the Australian infantrymen had fought their last battle of the Great War.

LIEUTENANT NORMAN WILKINSON'S leg wound took him to Wandsworth Hospital in London. He remembered that he had taken a Mauser pistol from a German at Montbrehain. It was in his haversack, which was hanging from the bed head. He rummaged for the pistol. He was going to ask one of the men in the ward to unload it for him. His finger touched the trigger. *Crack*. The bullet went through the floor. Orderlies and patients came running. The two ward sisters 'did handsprings' and a New Zealand officer whose right leg had been amputated fell into shell-shock.

IT WAS SOME time before Fletcher's parents at Bendigo were told of their son's death. They then wondered why his friend Austin had not written to them. The pair's effects were eventually shipped home. Fletcher's included a gold cigarette case, two pocket testa-ments and a Commonwealth Bank chequebook containing twelve unused cheques. Mahony's included a rosary, a crucifix, a pair of football shorts, a red guernsey and two pipes. Both men had left their estates to their mothers. Mahony's father asked the defence authorities if he could wear his son's medals. He was told this was against regulations. Both families eventually held a joint memorial service at Bendigo for their sons.

Nearly eighty years later two photographs of Austin Mahony in uniform were found among the keepsakes of Mrs Celia Ash, who had died in 1996, aged 100. Mrs Ash grew up in the Hansonville–Greta area. She went to Melbourne in her teens to continue her education. When and where she met Austin and the nature of their friendship is unknown; but he meant enough for her to keep his photograph for the rest of her life.

In Royal Parade, Parkville, close to the university and to where Fletcher and Mahony boarded, a memorial was dedicated to the fallen from the district. A slouch-hatted soldier rendered in marble stands above a grey granite pediment. The names of Fletcher and Mahony are there. The monumental mason, Peter Jageurs of Parkville, had to inscribe the name of his son, John, among the dead.

THE LAST OF the Australian infantrymen left the frontline the day after Montbrehain. A few days earlier, Captain Ellis, the historian of the 5th Division, watched Australians leaving.

> Troops more fatigued had rarely been seen and yet, by sheer determination, they overcame the weakness of the body and marched back in excellent order . . . But their strained, pallid faces revealed what they had passed through, and numerous transport units along the road respectfully and in silence pulled their vehicles to one side that the war-worn men might not have an extra step to march. It was the mute and eloquent testimony of brave men to heroes.

CAPTAIN JAMES SULLIVAN, the young law clerk from Geelong, lies in Bellicourt British Cemetery. The main Hindenburg Line once ran through here. A bay thoroughbred horse stands in the paddock next to the graveyard, staring out over the headstones. Harry Fletcher is in the yellowy soil of Calvaire Cemetery at Montbrehain, a short walk from where he died. Austin Mahony is a few miles back in Tincourt New British Cemetery. It seems wrong that the two are not lying side by side.

48

Götterdämmerung

Ludendorff was a Prussian militarist by training and a bully by temperament. He was made for war, not peace. He had embraced the idea of peace – or at least an armistice based on President Wilson's Fourteen Points – as a way of gaining time to make war at some future date on terms more to his liking. It was a matter of tactics, not a flight to pacifism. Every day for weeks he had been forced to react to some fresh crisis. He needed time to think, to work out how he might save the 'honour' of the German military and – no small matter – the honour of himself and Hindenburg.

But there were new difficulties and they were not on the battle-field. The country had been taken by surprise when Ludendorff told the politicians that Germany could not win. This at first brought disbelief and a sense of betrayal: Hindenburg and Ludendorff had previously given no hints of how badly their war was going. Then morale at home, which had held up so well, began to collapse. Many people had accepted starvation and deprivation as part of the price of victory; they were not going to starve for a defeat.

A political frenzy, not unlike that which followed the abdication of Tsar Nicholas, broke out. Self-styled patriots wanted to fight on.

Women wanted food for their children and damn the honour of the army. Bolsheviks, and they were many, wanted to go the way of their brothers in Russia. Moderates wanted some form of constitutional monarchy. Liberals wanted a republic. Anarchists just wanted anarchy. Everything was happening at a terrific pace. There was no time to reflect or consider. The German leaders needed to secure an armistice before their armies were driven back to the frontier.

Wilson now began to add to this ferment. He saw old Europe as degenerate; he was not going to negotiate with Prussian militarists or Kaiser Wilhelm and his flunkeys. If there were to be talks about an armistice, Wilson would need to be convinced that Prince Max, the new Chancellor, and his government spoke for all the people.

Clemenceau and Lloyd George questioned Wilson's right to dictate the terms of the peace. They were bemused, as they were entitled to be, by his high-handedness in sending notes to Berlin without first consulting them. And there were tensions among the allied military leaders. Foch, Pétain and Pershing wanted to impose harsh terms on Germany; Pershing, unlike his president, wanted an unconditional surrender. Haig wanted the war to end in 1918. He was winning on all his fronts but knew he was running out of men. He was worried that if the peace terms presented to Germany were too severe, the war would go into 1919.

By October 5, when the Australians fought their last battle at Montbrehain, Haig's armies had broken the Hindenburg Line at three critical points. With Canadians and New Zealanders in the forefront, they were threatening Lille in the north and Douai and Cambrai in the centre. British and Belgian forces on the Ypres front were working towards Ostend and Bruges. The 5th Army, now under Birdwood, had joined the offensive. Far to the south the Americans were pushing into the Argonne towards Sedan.

THE AUSTRALIANS WERE resting near the coast west of Amiens. Young men with old faces and eyes that had seen too much wrote letters home, scrounged coffee and eggs from French kitchens, raided the *estaminets* of Amiens and Abbeville and sent their crumpled boots off for repairs. The Australians had incurred another 24,162 casualties in the offensive that had begun in front of Villers-Bretonneux on August 8. This was a heavy enough toll but it covered nearly two months' fighting. By the standards of the Great War it was reasonable, especially since the Australians had taken their front forward more than thirty miles. In the advance that ended at Montbrehain they liberated more than 100 villages and took more than 29,000 prisoners. They had fought thirty-nine German divisions and all but wiped out several of them. They had become an elite force, although no-one at Haig's headquarters was going to concede this outside private conversations.

Australians ever since have been prone to overstate their country's contribution to the victories of 1918, partly, one suspects, as a counter to Britain's tendency to understate them. The truth is that the Canadians and New Zealanders had also become elite forces and that Currie, in his different way, was as good a leader as Monash. It is more sensible to say that Haig's force owed more to dominion troops than most of its chroniclers have ever acknowledged. Why did the 'colonials' perform so well? The fact that the Australians were all volunteers made a difference. And the colonials appeared to be physically stronger than their counterparts who had grown up in the grime of Britain's industrial cities. It may also be true that the Great War said something about the 'British' civilisations that had flourished in the dominions. Feudal notions of 'class' didn't play so strongly in the outposts; men were more likely to rise on their worth (as Monash and Currie had done), rather than on who their fathers were or where they had gone to school.

Hamel, Amiens, Mont St Quentin and Bellicourt – these were victories against the main enemy in the main theatre. There is nothing to match them in Australia's military history, yet they were little celebrated in Australia at the time and have been all but forgotten since. The Somme and Passchendaele, both heavy with futility, are better remembered. Gallipoli is remembered best of all. Gallipoli has become a faith and faith is hostile to analysis. Gallipoli is said to embody a spirit, and it does, although there are many interpretations of the nature of that spirit. The journey from Villers-Bretonneux to Montbrehain was the stuff of greatness, and it embodied a spirit too; but the places along that road, if they are remembered at all, are just names.

Churchill wrote in the 1920s that the victories of British and dominion troops in 1918 'will excite the wonder of future generations'. They didn't. Haig and his army are better remembered for their failures.

THE NOTES FLEW back and forth between Berlin and Washington. Prince Max on October 3 asked for an armistice. Wilson replied that he could propose an armistice only if Germany agreed to give up all invaded territory. He also, in effect, asked Prince Max whom he spoke for.

Prince Max said Germany would evacuate occupied territory. He said his new government had the backing of the Reichstag; he spoke for the German people. While this note was being drafted a German submarine torpedoed the mail packet *Leinster* in the Irish Channel with the loss of hundreds of lives, many of them women and children. Wilson quickly raised the price. Germany had to stop sinking passenger ships. Wilson also said, in effect, that there had to be democratic reforms in Germany. Wilson was saying, without actually writing down the words, that the Kaiser had to go.

Wilhelm was outraged. 'You must use it [the note] to arouse the entire people to rally round their emperor in defence of their sacred heritage,' he told the Chancellor. Prince Max was running out of negotiating time. Birdwood's 5th Army had taken Lille and the Belgians were about to take Ostend and Bruges. Prince Rupprecht, who understood the military position better than Ludendorff, told Prince Max the armies could not hold out until Christmas.

The Chancellor called a meeting of the War Cabinet to decide what to do. And here Ludendorff changed his mind. He favoured arming civilians to fight alongside the army, a *levée en masse*. He was playing the warrior again – and also shifting responsibility for defeat to the politicians. This would play well for posterity.

Ludendorff said he was worried about Bolshevism spreading from Russia. The German people, he said, were willing 'to sacrifice the last ounce of their strength to the army'. Prince Max knew this was bluster. He knew the mood of the people was close to revolution.

Prince Max and his government lost confidence in Ludendorff that day. Ludendorff failed to realise this. He was upbeat when he returned to Spa and spoke to Hindenburg, who supported all his First Quartermaster-General had said.

Three days later Prince Max replied to Wilson. He agreed to end the submarine campaign against passenger ships. He repeated that democratic reforms were taking place and that his government was free of 'arbitrariness', which was his way of saying the Kaiser was no more than a figurehead and that Hindenburg and Ludendorff were now responsible to the government. Wilson's reply to this suggested he didn't quite believe the Chancellor. If the United States had to deal with 'military masters' and 'monarchial autocrats', now or in the future, it would demand surrender rather than peace talks. Wilson also said the only armistice that he would consider was one that would make a renewal of hostilities by Germany impossible. The price of peace had risen again. Wilson was really talking about a form of surrender and saying he wanted the Kaiser out.

Hindenburg and Ludendorff now sent a message to 'all troops in the field'. Wilson's note was a demand for unconditional surrender, they said. It was a challenge to 'us soldiers' to keep fighting. 'When our enemies know that no sacrifice will achieve the rupture of the German front, they will be ready for a peace . . .' Hindenburg and Ludendorff were out of touch with 'us soldiers': most of the German rank and file wanted an armistice. Worse, Hindenburg and Ludendorff were defying Prince Max's new government and its liberal spirit. They were acting as if they still ran Germany. It didn't matter that their message didn't reach most troops.

Prince Max came down with the influenza that was killing Germans by the thousands. He offered his resignation to the Kaiser, telling him that he had to choose between the new government and the old militarists. Next day, October 26, Wilhelm summoned Hindenburg and Ludendorff. He chastised them for their message to the troops and said he was tired of their changes of mind. The exchange between the Kaiser and Ludendorff became angry. Hindenburg wrote that at one stage Wilhelm shouted: 'Excellency, I must remind you that you are in the presence of your emperor.' Ludendorff offered his resignation and the Kaiser accepted it. Hindenburg also offered to resign but this was turned down, as Hindenburg knew it would be. Hindenburg apparently did not try to defend Ludendorff. Outside the palace Ludendorff accused Hindenburg of 'treachery' and refused to ride in his car. Audiences at Berlin cinemas that night cheered when Ludendorff's resignation was announced.

Ludendorff worried that revolutionaries might try to kill him. He eventually donned a wig and spectacles and fled to Sweden on false papers.

Prince Max sent a new note to Wilson. The German Government, he said, awaited proposals for an armistice.

THE ALLIED COMMANDERS had met a few days earlier at Foch's head-quarters to discuss what the Fourteen Points meant and what armistice terms they would demand. Haig urged caution. The German army was not yet defeated in the field, he said. If the peace terms were too severe, the Germans might fight on. Foch disagreed. Germany *was* defeated, he said. Pétain spoke of exacting a huge financial indemnity from Germany. Pershing wanted unconditional surrender. He, unlike Haig, had the troop numbers to keep fighting in 1919.

Pershing and Haig were looking ahead and coming to different conclusions. Pershing, as he said later, was concerned that people in Berlin would not realise their army had been beaten, and 'it will have to be done all over again'. Haig wrote to his wife that the allies should not try to humiliate Germany and 'produce a desire for revenge'. Foch and Pétain, it is fair to say, were probably thinking of revenge; if so, this is easy enough to understand.

The commanders decided (with Haig dissenting on some points) that the Germans should leave France and Belgium and hand back

Alsace-Lorraine, which the Germans had taken from France in 1870. They were to surrender 5000 artillery pieces, 30,000 machine guns and 3000 trench mortars. The German army would leave the west bank of the Rhine and the allies would occupy bridgeheads there. The Germans would hand over 5000 locomotives and 150,000 railway trucks, as well as 150 submarines. The blockade of Germany would continue.

All this was close to a call for unconditional surrender.

GENERAL WILHELM GRÖNER replaced Ludendorff at Spa. He was fifty-one years old, a first-rate staff officer and a nice judge of public opinion. He knew that Germany was close to revolution. Gröner made a quick tour of the front and told Prince Max an armistice had to be arranged at once. Prince Max suggested a week's delay. Gröner told him that would be too long.

The Kaiser now arrived at Spa. He said he wanted to be with his fighting men. In truth he had fled Berlin because too many there were demanding his abdication. Gröner didn't favour abdication: he thought it might lead to anarchy. He had a better idea: the Kaiser should go to the front 'to look for death'. Even if he were merely to be wounded, the feelings of his subjects would change towards him. Wilhelm had been a military romantic all his life; he wasn't that romantic.

The clamour for his removal grew. Who would tell him to go? Prince Max fell into a coma with his influenza. A Cabinet minister decided he would tell the Kaiser that he must abdicate. Wilhelm reprimanded him for his 'insolence and effrontery'. He would not go 'because of a few hundred Jews and a thousand workmen. Tell that to your masters in Berlin!'

The Kaiser's troops kept falling back. The Americans and French pushed deeper into the Argonne. The Canadians took Valenciennes, north-east of Cambrai. British divisions headed towards the River Sambre. Here the young poet Wilfred Owen, his best works unpublished, became one of 'those who die as cattle'. He had won the Military Cross a week earlier. Owen wrote of the pity of war. (*Out there, we've walked quite friendly up to Death/Sat down and eaten with him, cool and bland . . .*) Many consider him the finest poet of the Great War.

Near to where Owen died the New Zealanders took the old walled town of Le Quesnoy, climbing the ramparts with scaling ladders. Haig's armies took another 19,000 prisoners in the four days to November 4. Turkey and Austria-Hungary had by then signed armistices. Germany was alone.

The allied leaders looked again at Wilson's Fourteen Points. Back in January, when the President announced them, the European allies had seen them as an abstraction. Now, with Germany lurching towards peace, they needed to give them precise meanings. Points Seven and Eight said France and Belgium were to be evacuated and 'restored'. The European allies decided that 'restored' meant financial compensation – reparations. The price of peace had risen again.

Lloyd George thought the allies might be demanding too much. Foch agreed but wasn't concerned: he now thought he could beat the Germans by Christmas. His rallying cry had been 'Everyone to battle'. And now it was happening. Each day the Germans had to decide where the biggest crisis was. Was it in the Argonne, or on the Sambre, or in Belgium? Or was it at home?

THE GERMAN ADMIRALS had been worrying about their honour. They drew up a plan to take the High Seas Fleet to sea to fight to the death against the British. It was a script for suicide, heroic but pointless, the navy's *Götterdämmerung*. The sailors in Kiel refused to raise steam and mutinied. Soldiers sent to put down the mutiny joined the mutineers. Red flags were soon flying all over Kiel. The port admiral fled the city in disguise.

President Wilson had by now told the Germans that Foch would receive their representatives. Prince Max appointed Matthias Erzberger, who headed the German Catholic Centre Party, to lead the armistice commission. The party left Spa on November 7 and crossed the frontline around 9 pm. The French put the delegates in a railway carriage that early next morning pulled into a siding in the forest of Compiègne, forty miles north of Paris. When dawn broke, the Germans, hungry and confused, noticed another carriage nearby. Around 9 am they were led across to it. Inside they came into the presence of a little man with fierce eyes. They were introduced to Marshal Foch. He noticed that one of the Germans was wearing the *Legion d'Honneur*, which had been awarded to the delegate before the Great War. 'You have my permission not to wear that,' Foch told the German.

The two sides sat down at the conference table. Foch turned to his interpreter. 'Ask these gentlemen what they want,' he said. Foch was no Wilsonian idealist.

BY NOW REVOLUTION had come to Germany. The naval mutiny spread to Hamburg and Bremen. Revolutionaries carrying red flags paraded in the streets of Berlin. A workers' republic was declared in Munich. Soviets sprung up across the land.

Moderates in the Reichstag told Prince Max the emperor had to go. Friedrich Ebert, the prominent Social Democrat and moderate, said a revolutionary gesture was necessary to stall something worse. The Foreign Minister, Admiral von Hintze, was sent to the Kaiser with a compromise: Wilhelm would abdicate once the armistice was signed. No, he wouldn't, said Wilhelm. He had another plan: he would lead his army to Berlin to put down the revolution. He told Gröner to prepare plans. The Kaiser's aide, General Hans von Plessen, arrived to collect the plan for what would have been the German civil war. Gröner said there would be no plan. Plessen left in tears.

This was November 8, the day after the armistice commission had left for France. That night Hindenburg and Gröner, both monarchists, decided the Kaiser had to go. Next morning they set off into the fog and cold to tell him.

They arrived at the château and the Kaiser asked Hindenburg for his report on the military situation. The field-marshal, already unstrung, asked to be allowed to resign. No, said the Kaiser. Tears ran down Hindenburg's cheeks. As Ludendorff well knew,

Hindenburg was good at contriving to make others do his work. And now Gröner did it, as gently as he could.

The Kaiser's aides disputed Gröner's arguments. Wilhelm finally announced his plans. He would not engage in counter-revolution. He would stay at Spa until the armistice was signed, then return home at the head of his army. 'Sire,' Gröner said, 'you no longer have an army.' Shortly after the meeting broke up. Nothing had been decided.

Prince Max had been telephoning Spa from Berlin during the morning. His government was in turmoil. He needed the Kaiser to abdicate at once. So he simply announced that this had happened. 'Treason,' said Wilhelm.

Whatever it was, it had come too late. On the same day revolutionaries seized the Imperial Palace in Berlin, flew a red blanket from it and proclaimed a soviet. Philipp Scheidemann, the leader of the moderate Social Democrats, proclaimed a republic from the Reichstag balcony. Prince Max resigned and Ebert became Chancellor.

Hindenburg told the Kaiser that he should go to Holland for his own safety. Next morning the Kaiser arrived at the Dutch border in his silver train. On arriving at the castle that would become his place of exile he asked for a cup of 'good English tea'.

AT THE RAILWAY carriage at Compiègne the Germans were learning what 'armistice' meant. They had been shocked when Foch asked them, through an interpreter, what they wanted. Matthias Erzberger recovered to reply that he and his party believed that they were there to talk about the armistice terms. 'Tell these gentlemen that I have no proposals to make,' Foch said.

The Germans said they were there because of President Wilson's last note. Erzberger read the note, which said Foch had the authority to disclose the terms of the armistice. Foch said he could make these terms known – if the German delegates asked for an armistice. 'Do you ask for an armistice?' Foch asked.

The first battle of the new war was being fought. Foch had

always taught that a general had to establish a psychological ascendancy over his opponent. He was playing his best game. Yes, the bewildered Germans said, *they* had asked for the armistice. In that case, Foch replied, his aide would read out the terms. The Germans had to leave all occupied territory, including Alsace-Lorraine, remove their troops from the western bank of the Rhine, and hand over battleships, cruisers, submarines, artillery pieces, locomotives, rolling stock and aircraft to the allies. They also had to repudiate the Brest-Litovsk treaty. The Germans might have expected these demands, but not what followed as the aide read on. The Germans had to accept a continuance of the naval blockade. And they had to accept guilt for the war and pay reparations. Foch was handling them almost as roughly as they had the Russians at Brest-Litovsk.

Erzberger asked for an immediate ceasefire. Foch said this couldn't happen until Germany accepted the terms of the armistice. Erzberger sent the allies' demands back to Berlin by courier. The talks continued the next day, November 9, the day the Kaiser was told he wanted to abdicate. By now the Canadians were closing on the Belgian town of Mons, where Britain's war had begun.

On the evening of Sunday, November 10, the German delegates received a reply from Berlin. Germany's new leaders accepted the armistice terms, while pointing out that they would bring famine to the land. At 5 am the following morning the German delegates signed. The war would end at 11 am that morning.

BRIGADIER-GENERAL BERNARD FREYBERG, one of the youngest generals in the British army, had been born in Surrey and had grown up in New Zealand. By Armistice Day he had won the Victoria Cross and been wounded nine times. He wrote to his friend Winston Churchill to tell him about 'the most wonderful finish to my war'. Freyberg explained that he heard at 9.15 am that the ceasefire would begin at 11. 'I decided to get in touch with the Bosche and raid him with my Cavalry and cyclists one last time.' Freyberg knew the Germans were holding a village some miles away. He galloped his cavalry for an hour to burst into the village at 10.55, 'shooting

The line at the end of the Great War, November 11, 1918

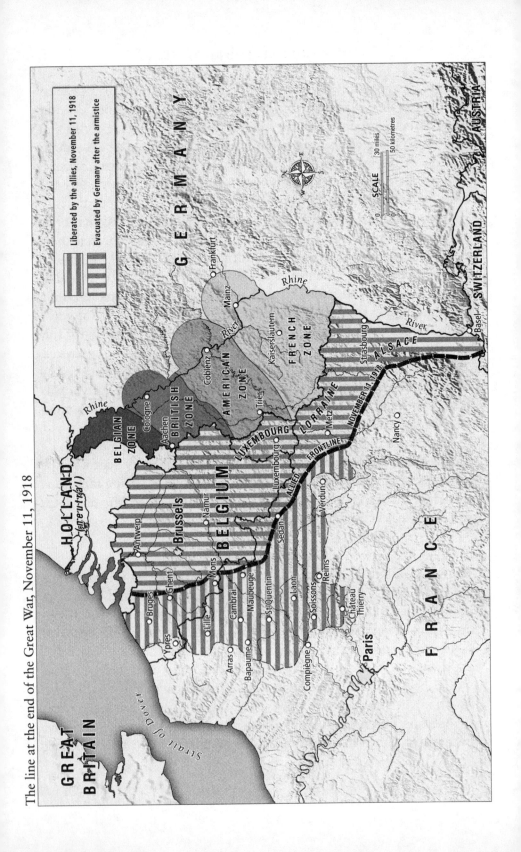

GREAT BRITAIN

HOLLAND (/ˈhɒlənd/)

GERMANY

Legend:
Liberated by the allies, November 11, 1918
Evacuated by Germany after the armistice

SCALE
0   30 miles
0   50 kilometres

Rhine River

Frankfurt

Mainz

Rhine River

Coblenz

BELGIAN ZONE

Cologne

Aachen

BRITISH ZONE

AMERICAN ZONE

Trier

Kaiserslautern

FRENCH ZONE

Strasbourg

ALSACE

River

Basel

SWITZERLAND

AUSTRIA

LUXEMBOURG

Luxembourg

LORRAINE

Metz

NOVEMBER 11, 1918

Nancy

BELGIUM

Brussels

Antwerp

Namur

Mons

Ghent

Bruges

Ypres

Lille

Cambrai

Bapaume

Arras

Maubeuge

St Quentin

Laon

Sedan

Verdun

ALLIED FRONTLINE

Reims

Soissons

Château Thierry

Compiègne

Paris

FRANCE

Strait of Dover

up the streets with revolvers and chasing bosche round blocks of buildings. We captured a bridge head at 2 minutes to eleven and mopped up the village to the tune of 4 officers 102 other ranks and several machine guns. I thought this would amuse you.' The madness of the war apparently still owned Freyberg. His reaction to the coming armistice was atypical. Some 2700 men from both sides died on the last day.

Corporal Adolf Hitler's reaction was also atypical. He had been briefly blinded by mustard gas near Ypres in October and was recovering in a hospital in Prussia. There a clergyman, his voice quavering, told the patients that the Kaiser had abdicated, Germany was a republic and that the war was lost and would soon end. Hitler said he started to go blind again. He buried his head in a pillow. A doctor said Hitler's blindness had returned because he was a 'psychopath with hysterical symptoms'. Soon Hitler would speak on public platforms and show hysterical symptoms of another sort.

American gunners attached long ropes to the lanyards of their guns when the armistice was minutes away. Hundreds of men then took hold of the rope so that all could claim to have fired the last shot of the war. Captain Harry Truman didn't tell the crew of his battery that the armistice was coming. He fired 164 rounds at the Germans that morning. After 11 am, he said, 'it was so quiet it made me feel as if I'd suddenly been deprived of my ability to hear.'

Sydney celebrated the armistice three days before it happened, thanks to a cable report that was wrong. An effigy of the Kaiser was hanged and burned. A magistrate discharged the drunks picked up the previous night. Three days later, after the armistice *had* been signed, Sydney celebrated again. The Kaiser was burned again. In Melbourne the *Age* asked people not to explode fireworks 'in the interests of invalided soldiers and particularly those suffering from shell-shock'.

PRIVATE LYALL HOWARD, the pioneer, wasn't going to change his laconic prose style because something important had happened. For November 11 he wrote two words in his diary: 'Armistice signed.'

Lieutenant Joe Maxwell wasn't going to change his style either. He had always known how to have a good time. He headed south for Paris. 'The city blazed with light and rocked to the sound of delirious rejoicing. Rockets flared; bands crashed; scores of thousands sang in unison; scores of thousands danced in streets, on café tables, anywhere; scores of thousands of war-weary men grabbed bright-eyed mademoiselles in the endless whirl of gaiety that surged through the city from end to end.'

Sergeant Rupert Baldwin of the 2nd Division was recovering from back and shoulder wounds in an English hospital. 'Everyone went mad in hospital last night,' he scribbled in his diary. 'Bloke with crutches and sticks forgot them & walked with broken legs.'

Major Donald Coutts, the medical officer for the 24th Battalion, was working in a hospital at Amiens. 'I was walking down the road to see a sick civilian,' he wrote, 'when all the whistles began to blow, and all the anti-aircraft guns round Amiens began to fire . . . Great celebrations in Amiens and many casualties during the evening.'

Gunner Charles Rea, also at Amiens, told his mother the men seemed lost without the war.

> When it was on we always had something to occupy our minds, but now it is different. Of course we have the horses to look after, but we seem to be living another life . . . Nobody can realise what a cruel war this has been unless he has been in it. I used to tell you it wasn't bad and was all right etc, but now that it is all over and I've come through safely, I can tell you candidly it was a rotten business. There have been times when I would have given anything to get out of it. But now that it is finished I'm not sorry I came. It's been a very dangerous game and I reckon I'm one of the luckiest to be here now . . . I think we must all be homesick, for nothing seems to satisfy us.

Lieutenant 'Mick' Moon, who had won the Victoria Cross at Bullecourt after receiving shocking wounds to the face, was a first-rate horseman. He celebrated the armistice by watching an

Australian rules football match, then drank lots of rum, so much that he rode his horse back to camp 'from head to tail'.

Lyall Howard's reaction to the armistice is perhaps more typical than the others mentioned above. Most frontline soldiers seemed to take the news quietly; civilians far from the front made more noise. A Sydney electrician serving with the 2nd Division in France wrote in his diary: 'We had two victories today. We won the War and defeated the 5th Field Coy @ Soccer. The news of the Armistice was taken very coolly . . . nobody seemed to be able to realise it.'

PRIVATE WILLIAM MCBEATH, from the Melbourne suburb of Preston, had joined up halfway through 1918. He was nineteen. In the early months of 1919, he found himself digging up bodies from temporary graves around Villers-Bretonneux and moving them to permanent cemeteries. McBeath told his mother that his detachment had reburied 200 men for the week.

> Last Wednesday an English lady came here looking for her son's grave, she found out we were reburying him at the Adelaid cemetery, she went round after we'd knocked off & found him lying in a bag on the ground, there was a load just came in & we didn't have time to bury them, she fainted when she saw him & is in hospital suffering from shock, so English people are forbidden to travel in the battle areas now.

AFTERMATH

We must look forward one hundred, two hundred, three hundred years, to the time when the vast continent of Australia will contain an enormous population; and when that great population will look back through the preceding periods of time to the world-shaking episode of the Great War, and when they will seek out with the most intense care every detail of that struggle; when the movements of every battalion, of every company, will be elaborately unfolded to the gaze of all; when every family will seek to trace some connection with the heroes who landed on the Gallipoli Peninsula, or fought on the Somme, or in the other great battles in France . . .

– Winston Churchill, London, December 16, 1918

49

Same war, different name

Signaller Ted Matthews, who had once been a carpenter, heard about the armistice in the Indian Ocean. He was on his way home on leave as one of the original Anzacs. Armistice Day was his twenty-second birthday. He had enlisted in Sydney as a seventeen-year-old. When he arrived in Egypt an officer said: 'Ah, they're sending babies.' Matthews was hit in the chest by shrapnel at the Anzac landing. A heavy notebook in his top pocket softened the blow. In 1918 he fought at Villers-Bretonneux. He had been away from home for four years. He had been to some of the Great War's worst hellholes and survived.

Sergeant Charles Johnson, from the Victorian town of Nagambie, was discharged in Melbourne on July 20, 1919, having enlisted as a fifteen-year-old. Unlike Matthews, Johnson had looked older than his years. He told the recruiting officer he was eighteen. He was only nineteen at the time of his discharge. His discharge papers said he had spent 1388 days abroad. What they do not say is that his sixteenth birthday came on Gallipoli, that he was wounded in France and went to hospital several times with pleurisy, and that one of his brothers, Harry, died from shrapnel wounds during the Passchendaele campaign.

Matthews and Johnson had been on extraordinary journeys, but so had tens of thousands of others, and now they all had to start life again. Matthews was married with two daughters when the Depression came. Twice a week he would walk from his home to Circular Quay to register for work, then on to Railway Square to pick up food parcels, a round trip of about twelve miles. He died in 1997, aged 101, the last of the 'original' Anzacs. Charlie Johnson managed hotels in Darwin and Melbourne, played football, married and brought up four children after his wife died prematurely. He died in 1971, aged seventy-one.

Some 180,000 Australians had come home – from France, Britain and the Middle East – by the end of 1919. These men who returned were not mostly heroes, a word now used carelessly. Nor were they necessarily moral exemplars. But it was surely true – on the basis of what they had done, where they had been and the time they had been away – that they were, as Bean put it, great-hearted men.

What was the nation going to do for great-hearted men? The answer turned out to be: not much. After four years those at home longed for normalcy, for the old orders and routines. Neither in Britain nor Australia did people much want to celebrate the string of victories in 1918 that were the counterpoints to the slaughters on the Somme and at Passchendaele. Only after three or four generations did a perspective start to form on the war. Only then did people begin to realise what their grandfathers and great-grandfathers had endured. By then most of the great-hearted men were dead.

Some 61,700 Australians didn't come home. They were in the ground on Gallipoli and in Palestine and – mostly, about two-thirds of them – along the line that stretched from Villers-Bretonneux to Passchendaele. The wounded ran to 155,000, or about half the 324,000 men who had served overseas, and this figure excludes a large number who were gassed but did not seek treatment and spent the rest of their lives coughing and scratching. The Australian casualty rate was the highest among the British empire forces. Perhaps one-quarter of the original force of about 30,000 that left Australia in 1914 had survived.

The casualties were still being counted during the 1930s. By then another 60,000 had died from wounds or illnesses caused by the war. At least one generation of women and children, and maybe a second, suffered terribly from all this, and it is impossible to count casualty figures here. Many men returned broken and bitter; others turned drunk and violent. This legacy has been little explored. It may explain why many Australians in the thirty years after 1918 did not see the war, and Gallipoli in particular, in the romantic lights that have flickered around it in the new century.

Many men didn't want to talk about where they had been or what they had done. There seemed no point talking about the barrage at Pozières to someone who had not been there. These men also knew that the war had been misrepresented in the Australian press and thus many 'home patriots' didn't know what they were talking about. Australia is still full of families that say of their grandfather: 'He never talked about the war.' There wasn't even much point talking about what to many was the best part, the comradeship. Again, how would someone who had not been present understand the acts of kindness and self-sacrifice that occurred alongside killing and cruelty? In their own conclaves the soldiers talked most about the mateship, the pranks and the jokes, and wrote about them in *Reveille*. These were the sweet memories. Ted Rule dedicated *Jacka's Mob*, his narrative of the war, to 'that grand companionship of great-hearted men, which for most of us, is the one splendid memory of the war'. The men who came back joined returned servicemen's clubs. There at least they could talk to like minds; they didn't have to try to explain the unexplainable.

The soldiers' private memories were mostly bad and sad: friends lost, acts regretted, sights that were unspeakable, sounds that were indescribable, smells that belonged to an abattoir and all the terrible 'what-ifs' of war. (One soldier, Sergeant Andrew Muir, on visiting Belgium years later refused to drink the water: he explained that he had seen too many men dead in puddles there.) Their silences and brooding at least ensured that Australia would never again trip off to war as thoughtlessly as it had in 1914. It wasn't a case of the men, or the nation, doubting the rightness of the cause; rather it was the realisation of how cruel war truly was.

Some men just wanted to be alone with their nightmares. The nightmares became their lives. An officer who had fought with distinction at Fromelles, and who was afterwards promoted to colonel, in the early 1930s threatened to kill his children, then left to live in a cave for a year. This is another aspect of the war that has been little scratched. Bronzed Anzacs are more attractive than bewildered men in caves.

There was no logic to the way the war came to be seen in popular memory. Gallipoli, the foundation story, had an aura and Fromelles did not. Gallipoli was a defeat and Mont St Quentin an unlikely victory, but Mont St Quentin never lodged in the nation's consciousness. Simpson, the man with the donkey, was lionised and Percy Black, crucified on the wire at Bullecourt, was not. Folklore took over the war. The soldiers knew much of the folklore was wrong.

As one historian has noted, the Australians had fighting instincts but not soldierly instincts: to the end they had found the dictatorship of the army hard to accept. Yet it was also hard to be a civilian again. Safer, but anti-climactic. Having tramped around France for two years, scrounging and skylarking, having felt thrillingly alive when the barrage stopped, it was hard to adjust to taking the 7.51 train to the warehouse for a day's paper-shuffling. Those who had left Australia in their late teens had not known any adult life except fighting. Joe Maxwell, the boilermaker's apprentice who won the Victoria Cross, returned and worked as a gardener. He wrote in 1932 that even after more than a decade, city life palled at odd moments – 'the dull struggling routine of tram, train, office, and rule of thumb'. He felt he had lost a sense of freedom – 'the freedom of being unfettered to office or desk'. He missed the faces of the fellows he knew 'in the days of storm' and the faces of those who had gone.

In 1914 Henry Gordon Bennett had been an actuarial clerk with the AMP Society. He finished the war as a brigadier-general, a rank he had reached at twenty-nine, making him then the youngest brigade commander in the British empire armies. He was a man of some achievement. He called on the Melbourne manager of the

AMP on his return. Yes, he could have his 1914 job back, nothing grander. He felt let down. 'I would rather resign,' he told the manager. 'In that case,' the manager said, 'you will have to refund the salary paid to you throughout the war.'

THE GREAT WAR was the worst trauma of the twentieth century for Australia. People back home could explain the loss of a son or a husband with one word. They simply said 'Pozières' or 'Passchendaele'. Many wives of dead soldiers never remarried; women who had lost their fiancés remained spinsters and as sixty-year-olds still opened a drawer and stared at a photo of a young man with bright eyes and wearing a rough woollen tunic. The Australian historian Bill Gammage in 1994 spoke of 'dreams abandoned, lives without purpose, women without husbands, families without family life, one long national funeral for a generation and more after 1918'.

A generation had lost many of its most generous male spirits. Geoffrey Blainey wrote that the worst effect of the war on Australia could never be enumerated. It was the loss of 'all those talented people who would have become prime ministers and premiers, judges, divines, engineers, teachers, doctors, poets, inventors and farmers, the mayors of towns and leaders of trade unions, and the fathers of another generation of Australians'.

The war started off bringing Australians together and ended up dividing them. Almost half the eligible male population had enlisted. Here was the first divide: between those who had gone and those who had not. Another wound had opened up over conscription and it would not heal for generations. Sectarianism was now part of the landscape and both Catholic and Protestant clergymen kept it going long after the war ended. The Labor Party in the decade after Federation had helped make Australia a unique democracy that was perhaps kinder to the working man than any other in the world. Conscription had split Labor so badly that it would not regain government until 1929, and then only briefly.

The war should have modified Australia's view of 'the mother country'. Australians had grown up with an idealised view of Britain and the wisdom of her politicians and military leaders. The soldiers discovered the reality. British soldiers were no better than them. British generals made terrible mistakes and they were called Fromelles and First Bullecourt. British politicians made mistakes and one of the worst was called Gallipoli. British democracy was not the same as Australian democracy; it came with hangovers from feudalism. And there was the country itself: so much of Britain seemed crowded and polluted and grimy. The war had revealed these things to the soldiers. They talked about them among themselves and in their letters home, but not publicly. Billy Hughes should have noticed the same things. If he did, he didn't mention them, but then he was trying to be too many things to too many people. And so, after 1918, a chance was lost for Australia to rethink its relationship with Britain and, without rupturing the bond, without abandoning ties that were sound as well as sentimental, accept that the British empire was not quite what they thought it was in 1914, and that many homespun Australian values were as worthy as those that had been imported. Australia mostly lapsed back into the ways of a self-governing colony.

The country was weary from war overseas and political nastiness at home. Spanish influenza arrived in Australia and killed some 12,000 in 1919. (Around the world it killed more people than the Great War.) The world began the slide towards depression in 1929 and by 1932 unemployment in Australia had reached thirty per cent of the workforce. The historian Michael McKernan found just the right adjective when he called the interlude between the two big wars 'the grey years'. The new identity would be a while coming. It would take the fall of Singapore, another world war, the break-up of the old British empire, the fears of the Cold War and mass migration from Europe to change the 'British' society in the south seas into something nearer to an Australian society.

BILLY HUGHES WAS angry when the armistice was signed. He had not been consulted. He thought President Wilson's Fourteen Points threatened the things Australia had fought for, and high among these was the right to annex German New Guinea and keep Japan as far as possible from the Australian coast. He wanted compensation for war losses and to punish Germany severely. He thought Wilson a dreamer, a liberal who didn't know how deals were done in the grubby conclaves outside universities and definitely not the bloke you would pick to run a waterfront strike. Hughes now reverted to the Australian nationalist and trade-union scrapper. No high-minded Virginian was going to rob him of the spoils he had set out to win. Hughes demanded that Australia be represented in its own right at the peace conference in Paris in 1919 rather than as part of the British empire. He went along and did what he did best: theatrics. But clever theatrics, designed to unsettle his opponents and produce the end he wanted. Impish, cranky, fiddling with his hearing aid and pretending to be deaf when it suited, 'this strange man' (as an English delegate called him) managed to offend and befuddle Wilson. Hughes' cameos – he was, after all, only a bit player – produced a string of anecdotes, some hard to verify.

Wilson wondered if he understood Hughes' attitude on German New Guinea. 'If I do,' Wilson said, 'it is this, that the opinion of the whole civilised world is to be set at nought. This conference, fraught with such infinite consequence to mankind for good or evil, is to break up with results which may well be disastrous to the future happiness or unhappiness of eighteen hundred millions of the human race, in order to satisfy the whim of five million people in the remote southern continent whom you claim to represent.'

Hughes fiddled with his hearing aid and replied: 'Very well put, Mr President, you have guessed it. That's just so.' Everyone laughed, except Wilson.

Hughes agreed with Wilson that in mandated territories (as German New Guinea was to become) natives should be allowed access to missionaries of any denomination. 'By all means, Mr President,' said Hughes, 'I understand that those poor people sometimes go for months together without half enough to eat.'

The allies all had different motives and ends. Clemenceau wanted revenge, to punish Germany so severely that she could never start another war. Hughes' position happened to be close to Clemenceau's. Lloyd George's was subtle and complex. Like Clemenceau, he objected to Wilson, whose country had not suffered as France and Britain had, trying to dictate the terms of the peace and delivering lectures on morality. Lloyd George's coalition had been returned at the general election of December, 1918. It became clear during the campaign that the public (as one politician put it) wanted the German lemon squeezed until the pips squeaked. Lloyd George didn't want to impose a harsh peace on Germany, partly because he thought it might tip the country towards Bolshevism. But he was a politician seeking re-election, so publicly he said the Germans 'must pay to the uttermost farthing, and we shall search their pockets for it'.

Wilson wanted a soft peace. He believed that no country should profit from the war, that spoils should not be divided up, that there should be no punitive damages, that subject people had the right to self-determination and that the League of Nations (the last of his Fourteen Points and the forerunner of the United Nations) should moderate world affairs. Vittorio Orlando, the Italian Prime Minister, came to Paris to collect on the pledges of territory that had been made to draw Italy into the war. A young Vietnamese kitchen hand working in Europe wanted Wilson to consider a proposal for Vietnamese self-determination. Nguyen Ai Quoc was turned away. Much later, and now called Ho Chi Minh, he humiliated another American president.

Here was the trouble: there was no unity of purpose. Deals had already been done. Clemenceau, Lloyd George, Orlando, the Japanese delegation and Billy Hughes didn't much believe in self-determination. Germany had lost her overseas empire as soon as the war began. Turkey had lost the Ottoman empire upon signing the armistice. So by the time Wilson came to Paris the British had taken Palestine and created Iraq out of Mesopotamia, and they didn't care too much if Wilson wanted to call these possessions 'mandates'. Arthur Balfour had promised that Britain would consider setting up a Jewish homeland in Palestine. The French took Syria and Alexandretta. The Greeks took Bulgaria's Aegean coastline and eyed the Turkish heartland. Japan took Germany's island colonies in the Pacific north of the equator. Britain, France and South Africa claimed pieces of the Kaiser's African empire. Poland was reborn and grabbed territory from Germany. And Billy Hughes insisted that Australia should control what had been German New Guinea. He had to settle for a mandate rather than annexation, but that gave Hughes all the power he needed.

Hughes wanted Germany bled white by reparations. The armistice signed at Compiègne simply mentioned 'Reparation for damage done'. The delegates at the peace conference had to decide what this meant and reduce it to a money sum. Was it physical damage to France and Belgium: houses and factories destroyed, livestock stolen, farmland devastated? Did it cover the millions of tons of merchant shipping sunk? Or the allies' costs in waging war? Hughes knew what he wanted: the £354 million that Australia had spent on the war, and another £100 million to cover repatriation and pension costs. Clemenceau pushed for crippling reparations; Lloyd George urged moderation. The demand against Germany came out at £24 billion. If it caused bitterness in Germany and gave pleasure to Clemenceau, it was also academic. The sum was reduced at a string of later conferences. In 1932 the idea of reparations was dropped.

But in 1919 Hughes appeared to have won on this as well as German New Guinea. No Australian Prime Minister since has played the free spirit with such zest among the world's great powers. And if Hughes lacked Wilson's gravitas, he had a better sense of his constituency. Wilson returned home and was unable to sell the treaty or the League of Nations to the Senate. He suffered a stroke late in 1919, possibly caused by overwork, and died five years later.

The Germans had been given no say in the draft of the treaty. They received a document that reduced their territory and population by about ten per cent. They would lose all their colonies and both banks of the Rhine would become a demilitarised zone. Their army would be limited to 100,000 men; they could not manufacture tanks, aircraft and submarines. The 'war guilt' clause made them responsible for the war. They had to pay a fantastic sum in reparations. It was a punitive peace, just like the one the Germans had imposed on Russia. But it might have been worse. Germany had not been invaded or dismembered: it still had its sovereignty.

Moderate Germans felt that Wilson had failed them, that they should never have believed in him and his Fourteen Points. Wilson saw those points as one thing and his allies as another, although much of Wilson's idealism survived in the final treaty. Martin Gilbert, Churchill's biographer, summed up what had happened in two sentences: 'The Treaty of Versailles was not as vindictive as France had hoped; nor was it as moderate as Lloyd George desired. It was certainly not as utopian as Woodrow Wilson envisaged.'

Less moderate Germans, many of them soldiers, corporals as well as generals, began to argue that they had not been beaten in the field and that they had been 'stabbed in the back', not by Wilson but by their own politicians and Jews. This was nonsense. The Germans had been allowed to carry their rifles home and demobilise themselves, but they had still been beaten. For much of the war two soldiers, Hindenburg and Ludendorff, had run Germany; they, rather than the politicians, had lost it. And Jewish casualties in the German army had been disproportionately high. None of these facts mattered. The stabbed-in-the-back explanation was easier to understand.

The treaty was signed in the Hall of Mirrors, seventy-odd yards long and dripping with chandeliers, in the Palace of Versailles on June 28, 1919.

THEY SAID IT was the war to end all wars. It wasn't. They said it was the war to make the world safe for democracy. It didn't. It led, almost in a straight line, to the Nazi Party and its chambers of horrors, to a sideshow run by the Italian impresario Benito Mussolini, who brought a dress code to fascism, and to the rise of Japanese militarism. They said the war would create lands fit for heroes. It didn't. The men who had fought the Great War struggled to find jobs and security as the world headed towards what would be called the Great Depression. It might be said that the new war that broke out in 1939, bigger and much more cruel than the first, was not new at all but the Great War, Part Two.

Some still argue that World War II flowed from the harshness of the Versailles Treaty. By European standards the treaty was not that severe. The fact that many Germans did not believe they had lost the war was a problem. A bigger one was the matter of enforcement of the treaty. This fell mostly to Britain, France and the United States. In 1920 the United States abruptly repudiated Wilsonian idealism, including a guarantee that Wilson had given to defend France. Britain and France, both devastated by the war in a way the United States was not, were left to enforce the treaty. They lacked the will and the means. Germany began to rearm. The Great War would soon resume under a new name.

It is also fashionable to argue that the allies, particularly Britain and her dominions, fought the Great War for nothing of value. If they had not fought, France, an enlightened democracy and a well-spring of liberal ideals, would have fallen to the Kaiser. He and his Prussian militarists would have dominated Europe from the Ukraine to the English Channel and human progress would have been turned back to the absolutism of pre-Enlightenment times. The Kaiser was not Hitler; but like Hitler, he was about brute force.

Australia's casualties were too high for such a small nation, but Australia had to fight, and it is important here to see events as they were seen in 1914. There was a sentimental attachment to Britain. Australia depended on Britain for naval protection. Australia had a vital interest in the Suez Canal, which was being threatened by the Turks. It had a vital interest in ensuring that Japan did not take over German New Guinea. And, as a liberal democracy, it had an interest in seeing France remain free.

THE GREAT WAR produced battle casualties of about thirty-seven million, of whom 8.5 million were dead. It is probable that at least half of these died from artillery fire and fewer than two per cent from bayonet thrusts. This was the first big war fought between industrialised societies. It started off looking back towards Napoleon, French soldiers walking to their death in red-and-blue uniforms, and ended up pointing towards Kursk, tanks lurching ahead of infantry-men in workaday colours and carrying automatic weapons.

The Great War was also the event that determined, perhaps more than any other, the shape of the twentieth century. It helped to bring on the Russian Revolution and the rise of Marxism around the world. It did away with three reactionary monarchies but led to fas-cism in Germany and Italy. It helped turn the United States into a great power and contributed to the economic decline of Britain. It made Japan stronger and tempted it towards expansionism. The Great War was the overture to World War II. This time the corpses were so many that no-one knows how many died, particularly in Russia and China. Estimates of the dead, including civilians, range from thirty-five million to sixty million, including some six million Jews. This time the Passchendaeles and Sommes took place in the east; this time the war would be won from the east.

As the year 2000 approached news organisations across the world tried to decide who had been the most influential man or woman of the century. No-one seemed to think of Gavrilo Princip, the nobody from Bosnia, and the shots he fired at Sarajevo.

NO SOONER HAD the Great War ended than the struggle for its his-tory began. No figure has polarised the chroniclers so well as Douglas Haig. His admirers say he had great gifts as a commander; his detractors say he was a butcher and a muddler. His admirers say he was bright and his detractors insist he was dull. There is no mid-dle ground. Each side claims too much. Haig remains a mystery.

The publication of his war diary and other private papers in 1952 probably did him more harm than anything. He comes across as cold, selfish and literal-minded, although much of the apparent coldness may simply be his natural taciturnity. Hardly ever does he pause to acknowledge the young men who are dying for him. It is as though it is their duty to do so and no more needs to be said. He is suspicious of Frenchmen and other 'foreigners', the Irish,

Catholics, politicians, the working classes and Australians. He stood too far back from the war, more like a king than a general, and delegated too much. His judgement of men was often poor.

But he had nerve, impressive nerve. He was always clear-eyed. Whatever the setback, he kept his poise. He had moral courage and a profound sense of duty. He fixed on his objectives and never wavered, never seemed to doubt himself. In 1918 Haig's armies did more than the French or the Americans to secure victory. Unlike those of the French, Italians and Russians, his armies never came close to mutiny. Haig did what no British soldier had ever done before: commanded an army of one million men on a front of more than 100 miles in a new form of war for which no rule books had been written. The mistakes Haig made are easy to identify ninety years later, but Haig had no precedents to guide him. And, in the end, he did what generals are supposed to do: he won. He was proof of Noël Coward's observation that the secret of success is the ability to survive failure. One cannot help but wonder whether some of the obloquy that has been heaped against Haig's name comes down to the fact that, as an individual, he was hard to like and, ultimately, unknowable.

Churchill wrote that Haig was like 'a great surgeon before the days of anaesthetics, versed in every detail of such science as was known to him, sure of himself, steady of poise, knife in hand, intent upon the operation, entirely removed in his professional capacity from the agony of his patient, the anguish of relations, or the doctrines of rival schools, the devices of quacks, or the first-fruits of new learning. He would operate without excitement, or he would depart without being affronted; and if the patient died, he would not reproach himself.'

Haig was offered no work after 1920. Lloyd George was not going to forgive him for being Haig. But the field-marshal did well from the war. He received an earldom and a grant of £100,000 (a 'comfortable' annual salary at this time was £200 a year). A public subscription was launched so that Haig might buy Bemersyde, the ancestral home of his family, on a hill above the Tweed.

Haig spent most of the rest of his life working for ex-servicemen and seemed to mellow. He died suddenly in 1928, aged sixty-six. A simple wagon drawn by farm horses carried his body to Dryburgh Abbey, Scotland, where he was buried under gloomy skies. His headstone is identical to those on the war graves in France. He had wanted it that way.

Hubert Gough was a pallbearer at Haig's funeral. Lloyd George had refused to give Gough a chance to clear himself before a court of inquiry in 1918 and he left the army in 1922 and went into business. If it was true that Gough was the scapegoat for the British retreat during the German offensive of March, 1918, it was also true that, before that, he had been promoted far beyond his abilities. He lacked quiet judgement. Yet in 1937 Gough was awarded the Order of the Bath and one may only wonder why. Gough lived to be ninety-three.

William Birdwood lived to be eighty-five. He received a baronetcy and £10,000 for his war service. He toured Australia in 1920 to warm applause. His affection for the men he had led was obvious. He wanted to be Governor-General of Australia, and probably would have been, but the Labor Government decided an Australian should have the job, and it went to Sir Isaac Isaacs. Birdwood, typically, thought the decision correct. Birdwood was no tactician or organiser. His gift, and it was considerable, lay in building morale. The Australians knew him by sight. He had much physical courage. He was forever out just behind the frontline, shaking hands with privates from Bendigo and Dubbo, who, if slightly bewildered, decided he 'wasn't a bad sort of cove'. Birdwood was one of the most popular generals of the Great War.

David Lloyd George fell in 1922 when he recklessly confronted Mustafa Kemal, the new Turkish leader, over the Dardanelles neutral zone and almost dragged Britain into a needless war. Lloyd George resigned. By all the obvious measuring sticks he had been a good wartime leader. He could inspire with words and cut a dramatic figure with his wayward hair and mesmerising eyes. He understood the rhetoric of war and the temper of the people. He united the nation behind him in a way that Billy Hughes did not. He had energy: more than anyone he harnessed Britain's industrial resources to win the war. What was not apparent to the public at the time was that since 1915 his war strategy had been muddle-headed. To the end he had believed that the war could be won in the east. Also unknown was his weakness in dealing with Haig. He would shun and humiliate him; he thought him a 'butcher'. But he would not replace him, or even confront him. There was something feeble about this. Lloyd George devoted himself to writing from 1931. He married Frances Stevenson, his secretary, after the death of his wife. He died in 1945.

ERICH LUDENDORFF WROTE his memoirs in Sweden. He claimed the military had been 'stabbed in the back' by politicians and likened himself to Siegfried. He returned to Berlin, a hero of the Right, and marched with his one-time corporal, Adolf Hitler, in the Munich *putsch*, and soon after became a Nazi member of the Reichstag. He divorced his wife to marry a neurologist who was also an amateur philosopher, and the pair worshipped ancient gods and blamed Germany's troubles on Jews and Freemasons. Ludendorff began to criticise Hitler's methods in the 1930s, but by then many thought him a crank. He died in 1937.

Paul von Hindenburg endured. His position as a national hero and father figure seemed unassailable. He too fostered the stabbed-in-the-back explanation. Hindenburg became President of the German republic in 1925. He was still there when the Great Depression hit. Hindenburg knew little of economics. Crisis followed crisis and suddenly Hitler's Nazi Party had a mass following. The Nazis, communists and democrats brawled for Germany's soul. In 1932, though in his eighties and showing signs of senility, Hindenburg ran again for president against Hitler. The field-marshal beat the corporal, but the following year, as the crises continued, Hindenburg appointed Hitler as Chancellor, and the Weimar Republic became the corporal's first victim. Hindenburg at this time showed some warmth towards Hitler. That had always been his way: he accommodated. Hindenburg died in 1934.

The Dutch Government refused demands by the allies for the extradition of Kaiser Wilhelm to face charges as a war criminal.

Wilhelm lived as a country gentleman. Photographs show him saw-
ing firewood and feeding ducks. He liked to read; P. G. Wodehouse
was his favourite author. Wilhelm died in 1941. He had been at his
best when the going was good.

In 1921 Right-wing extremists in Berlin assassinated Matthias
Erzberger, who had signed the armistice at Compiègne. Hermann
Goering, who took over the flying circus from the dead Richthofen,
headed the Luftwaffe for Hitler in World War II. He was condemned to death at the Nuremberg war crimes trials but committed
suicide the night before he was due to be hanged. Rudolf Hess was
wounded three times as an infantryman in the Great War before
becoming a pilot. Hess was Hitler's deputy until 1941, when he
flew to Scotland with a bizarre peace proposal. He was given a life
sentence at Nuremberg. Heinz Guderian began the Great War commanding a wireless section. He became 'the father of the panzer
divisions' and an exponent of *blitzkrieg*. Guderian spearheaded the
drive to the French coast in 1940 and the following year took his
panzer group to the outskirts of Moscow. Erwin Rommel led the
Afrika Korps in North Africa in World War II and acquired a reputation among allied troops there that perhaps exaggerated his
talents.

DOUGLAS MACARTHUR WENT on his first trench raid with the
American forces in March, 1918. Instead of a helmet, he wore an
officer's cap with the wire removed and set at a jaunty angle.
Instead of a tunic, he wore a sweater with a black 'A' for Army
emblazoned on the front. A long scarf knitted by his mother topped
the outfit. He was armed with only a riding crop. Asked why he
was not in regulation dress, he said: 'It's the orders you disobey that
make you famous.' He was sacked during the Korean War for, in
effect, disobeying orders and became even more famous. The man
who sacked him was Harry Truman, the plain-speaking artillery
officer who had become President of the United States.

George Patton was as vain as MacArthur, and more flamboyant,
less talented as a strategist but a quick thinker. He came into the

Great War as a cavalryman and left it convinced that tanks were the future. Patton covered more ground than any other allied commander in the race across western Europe after D-Day; he also committed more indiscretions. He died in a traffic accident in Germany in 1945.

'Black Jack' Pershing returned home heavy with honours and was given the unusual rank of 'General of the Armies'. His best achievement had been to keep most of his army under his control, rather than having it farmed out to Haig and Pétain. America's contribution to the Great War is often misunderstood. It is not so much what American troops did in 1918, but what was promised: three million Americans on the ground in 1919. This changed the arithmetic of the war and led to Ludendorff's wild throws of 1918.

FERDINAND FOCH, THE fiery little Frenchman, was one of the truly great figures thrown up by the war and his reputation, unlike Haig's, has endured well. No man imposed his personality on the war more dramatically than Foch. To some the war was about firepower: whoever had most, and in the right places, would win. To Foch the war was also about faith. He was indomitable; he believed in himself and the power of will. Most of the power came not from his office but his personality. He inspired, prodded, nagged, cajoled and encouraged the French, British, Belgian and American armies. Rebuffed here, he would try there. His catch-cry roughly translated to 'Everyone to battle'. Foch declined to enter politics after the war. He visited the United States and was taken to a baseball game at Yankee Stadium. He was introduced to Babe Ruth, the legendary player, who looked at his shoes as he tried to think of something friendly to say. Eventually he looked up at Foch and smiled. 'You were in the war, weren't you?' Babe said amiably.

Foch died in Paris in 1929 and is buried close to Napoleon in the church of Saint-Louis-des-Invalides. Clemenceau died in the same year. He had asked to be buried without ceremony. He wanted an iron railing around his grave, but no inscription.

Like Foch, Henri-Philippe Pétain, the hero of Verdun and the

767

French army commander at war's end, was made a Marshal of France. At the age of eighty-four, and with the French armies defeated by Hitler, Pétain became head of the Vichy regime. The pessimist in him saw this as the best compromise – or at least this is the kindest interpretation of what he did. Pétain was sentenced to death for treason in 1945. Pétain had once described the young Charles de Gaulle as 'an officer of real worth'. De Gaulle, another veteran of Verdun, commuted Pétain's sentence to solitary confinement for life. Pétain died in 1951, aged ninety-five. His name was removed from the memorial to those who served at Verdun.

IN VOLUME IV of his memoirs Lloyd George wrote that, after the war, he discovered that the only man who might have replaced Haig 'was a dominion general'. Did he mean Currie or Monash? In a later volume Lloyd George answered the question: it was Monash, the 'most resourceful general in the whole of the British army'. Lloyd George was of course using Monash to diminish the reputation of Haig and others. When Haig needed replacing, Monash was only a divisional general and little known outside the Australian force. In 1918, when Monash was a corps commander and known for Hamel, Amiens and Mont St Quentin, the need to dump Haig had passed: the allies were winning the war.

Lloyd George *could* have been referring to Currie, an outstanding soldier who was at least the equal of Monash. Currie retired from the army and became a university vice-chancellor but could find no peace. A Canadian politician used parliamentary privilege to accuse Currie of being cavalier with the lives of his men while seeking glory for himself. Currie sued for defamation when an Ontario newspaper repeated the allegations years later. He won the case but it was said that the ordeal affected his health. He died in 1933, aged fifty-seven.

Monash lived to be sixty-six. Vic, his wife, and Bertha, his daughter, joined him in London in 1919. That year he wrote the 115,000 words of *The Australian Victories in France in 1918* in one frantic month. It is sad that he wrote hurriedly and with the main purpose of correcting press reports that had undersold Australia's – and his – part in Germany's defeat. The tone of the book showed the less attractive side of Monash's character: a sense of self-importance and a tendency to exaggerate. Nor did the prose reflect Monash's unusual gifts as a writer.

He arrived back in Australia on Boxing Day, 1919. Vic died of cancer shortly after. Unlike Currie, Monash enjoyed the warmth of public affection without controversies, but his homecoming, particularly when viewed from this distance, was anti-climactic. The Australian Government did nothing to honour him, although he was eventually promoted to full general. He was offered no high posts. He was still the outsider, somehow not quite right for the Establishment. He eventually ran the State Electricity Commission of Victoria. This was important work; but it was not to be compared to breaking the Hindenburg Line. Lizzie Bentwitch returned to Australia and became his companion. Monash had always loved children; now he enjoyed playing with Bertha's youngsters, teaching them to read and play draughts and giving them piggy-backs. He built a doll's house for his grand-daughter, Elizabeth. It was a typical Monash production: nearly five-feet high, double-storeyed, every piece of furniture made to scale and complete with a toilet bowl and electric light.

He developed high blood pressure and began to tire easily. In 1931 he suffered a series of heart attacks over about a week. He died of pneumonia shortly afterwards. His state funeral brought out a crowd of 250,000, maybe 300,000, on a cold and cloudy day. Monash appealed across the spectrum. He was not of the Establishment, nor a 'professional' soldier; he was not 'political'. Monash was not like other people, but he was a man of the people. Geoffey Serle, his biographer, wrote that soldiers needed a representative hero who was a volunteer; Monash was acceptable as 'a seemingly unpretentious outsider . . . His commanding intellect was sensed as well as his basic honesty and decency. He was one tall poppy who was never cut down . . . No-one in Australian history, perhaps, crammed more effective work into a life . . .' Few Australians have better claims to greatness than Monash.

Pompey Elliott committed suicide a few months before Monash died. Monash was saddened: the two had got on well. Elliott found no peace after the war. He had never recovered for being passed over for a divisional command. The 'supercession', he admitted in 1929, 'has actually coloured all my post-war life'. He became a Nationalist senator and used the parliament and the press to attack Birdwood and White and the British high command. He was bothered by nightmares about the war and haunted by the deaths of those who had served under him. His blood pressure rose, he developed diabetes and received a head injury while horse riding. In 1930 he broke down and wept while opening a war memorial at Ararat. Earlier the following year he attempted suicide by turning on a gas oven. He was eventually admitted to a private hospital. During the night he opened up his left elbow with a razor blade and bled to death. Each year, on the anniversary of his death, the Friends of the 15th Brigade gather around his grave in Burwood Cemetery. A eulogy is delivered and at the end of the service the mourners walk to his grave one by one and place a poppy on it. The inscription on his headstone says: 'This was a man.'

Bert Jacka was badly gassed in 1918 and underwent two operations in England. He returned home a hero late in 1919, by which time a cult had grown up around him. He went into business and became mayor of St Kilda. His business collapsed during the Depression. Jacka's health broke down, partly because of his war wounds. He died of chronic nephritis early in 1932, aged thirty-nine.

No cult developed around Harry Murray: he was a modest man and it would have embarrassed him. He ended up the most decorated infantry soldier in the British empire armies of the Great War. He bought a grazing property near Roma in south-eastern Queensland and told Bean he was teaching his 10,000 sheep to march in fours. He married and six years later was divorced. He remarried and moved to an even more remote sheep property north of Winton. The marriage was happy and produced a son and a daughter. Murray loved the solitude: he enjoyed reading and listening to cricket broadcasts. And he began to write for *Reveille*. Few ex-servicemen wrote sweeter prose. Murray was without swagger.

He died in 1966, aged eighty-five. In 2006 a bronze statue of Murray by Peter Corlett (sculptor of the poignant 'Cobbers' statue at Fromelles) was unveiled at Evandale in northern Tasmania. Murray's son and daughter were present.

Brudenell White was coaxed from retirement to become Australia's Chief of the General Staff in World War II. He was killed, along with three federal ministers, in a plane crash near Canberra in 1940. White was courteous, modest and a fine staff officer. One may only wonder how successful Birdwood would have been without him. Tom Blamey, Monash's former chief-of-staff, commanded the Australian army in World War II. His leadership was controversial, but he eventually became a field-marshal. Leslie Morshead, who had led the 33rd Battalion at Messines, Passchendaele and Villers-Bretonneux, commanded the 9th Australian Division at Tobruk and El Alamein. Talbot Hobbs, the architect who succeeded Monash as commander of the Australian Corps, helped design memorials to Australians in France and Belgium. William Glasgow, the pastoralist famous for his part in the counter-attack at Villers-Bretonneux and later commander of the 1st Division, became Minister for Defence in 1927. Charles Rosenthal, commander of the 3rd Division, returned to his architecture practice, served in the New South Wales parliament, and led the Sydney Anzac Day march for many years. John Gellibrand, leader of the 3rd Division, served three years in the federal parliament and helped found Legacy, which looks after the families of ex-servicemen.

Cyril Lawrence, one of the finest Australian chroniclers of the war, returned to work for the State Rivers and Water Supply Commission of Victoria. He became a brigadier during World War II, then held senior positions with the Commonwealth Department of Postwar Reconstruction and the Snowy Mountains Authority. Upon the death of his wife he left to live with his daughter, Margaret, in South Africa. He died in 1981, aged ninety-two.

William Donovan Joynt, the Victoria Cross winner, went farming after the war, then founded a printing and publishing business in Melbourne. He wrote *Saving the Channel Ports* and lived to be ninety-seven. Joe Maxwell worked as a gardener, wrote *Hell's Bells and Mademoiselles* and enlisted for World War II under an alias. 'Mick' Moon became managing director of a large woolbroking and pastoral house. Ted Rule went back to being an orchardist. Private Martin O'Meara, a stretcher-bearer who won the Victoria Cross at Mouquet Farm and was wounded twice afterwards, returned to Western Australia and spent the rest of his life in a mental hospital. Corporal Arthur Thomas, the tailor who wrote so affectingly of Pozières, turned forty in the trenches during 1918. 'I have had a damned long run and should be out of it by now, but men are wanted . . . so will stick it to the end,' he wrote. He was killed three months later. Walter Howard and his son Lyall opened a petrol station at Dulwich Hill, Sydney. Lyall never recovered from his gassing: he suffered from chronic bronchitis and skin rashes. He died in 1955, aged fifty-nine. John, his son, became Prime Minister of Australia in 1996.

In 1920 Billy Hughes received a cheque for £25,000 – a 'subscription' – in recognition of his services to Australia and the British empire. The presumption was that 'grateful citizens' had raised the money, but the nation was never told who they were. This touched on something that was starting to bother people. Where did Hughes' allegiances lie? With the workers' party that had spawned him? Or with his new friends, some of them rich and powerful, on the conservative side of politics?

The conservative parties won the election of 1922 but the Country Party said it would not serve with Hughes. He resigned the prime ministership and spent the rest of his life waiting for calls: to be prime minister again, to be re-embraced by the Labor Party, to be seen as the natural leader of the nation. For the next thirty years he remained a force in Australian politics, a bundle of nervous energy forever plotting, manoeuvring and intriguing, offending one group as he charmed another, conducting vendettas, pretending to be deaf when it suited, sacking secretaries and eventually playing the grand old man, frail and indestructible.

Hughes almost single-handedly brought down the Nationalist Prime Minister Stanley Melbourne Bruce, a twice-decorated veteran of the Great War, in 1929. Expelled from the Nationalist Party, Hughes, aged sixty-eight, formed his own party. Then he joined the United Australia Party that had replaced the Nationalists and held a string of ministerial posts. Aged eighty-two, he was expelled from the United Australia Party in 1944. After World War II Hughes joined the Liberals. This was his sixth party. The story goes that when Sir Robert Menzies observed that Hughes had never joined the Country Party, Hughes replied: 'You had to draw the line somewhere.'

Hughes died in 1952, aged ninety. Archbishop Mannix died eleven years later. There had been a reconciliation of sorts between the two. Like Haig, Hughes still polarises people. He is a patriot to some and a 'Labor rat' to others; there is no middle ground.

KEITH MURDOCH HAD been Hughes' secret agent during the Great War. The relationship had begun to curdle in 1918 when Murdoch tried to undermine Monash and Hughes went along with the plot until he discovered that hardly anyone agreed with Murdoch, except Bean. Murdoch and Hughes finally fell out at the Paris peace conference. Murdoch in 1921 became editor of the Melbourne *Herald*. At this he was truly gifted: he had an uncanny sense of his audience. The paper prospered and Murdoch prospered even more. He still played the kingmaker but there were now better candidates than Hughes. Around the time that Hughes lost the prime ministership Murdoch put out a memorandum to staff. 'We should be careful of W. M. Hughes,' it said. 'His motives are ugly – vindictiveness, jealousy, self-interest. His dominant idea is not to help the country but to destroy [Stanley] Bruce.' Like Hughes, Murdoch polarised opinions. Some said he was a fine newspaperman and a high-minded citizen; others said he was a seeker of power and wealth. Murdoch died in 1952.

Charles Bean didn't polarise. He was admired for his industry, modesty and decency. He wrote six volumes of war history, two on

Gallipoli and four on France and Belgium. He favoured infantry-men rather than artillerymen, White and Gellibrand and McCay rather than Monash, country boys rather than those from the cities. He sometimes joined one sentence to another to create jungles in which the reader had to trudge on, past tangle after tangle, until finally a shaft of sunlight broke through the canopy, and you under-stood why four men were running down a trench. But his volumes are also remarkable for their accuracy, their detail and democratic temper. Bean, a man of integrity and quiet courage, died in 1968. Long before that he had refused a knighthood. He told a friend that he could not imagine his wife (he married at forty-one) going to the butcher and asking for the meat for Sir Charles Bean.

50

Known Unto God

The land in the foreground is low lying and throws up rust-coloured weeds that say something sour lies underneath. Heaps of clay dominate the middle distance. They seem to be following the line of something. Beneath these heaps men with shovels prod and peer. Their movements are delicate: the men are too careful to be navvies. In the background is an industrial building that looks like a grey briefcase tipped on its side, the sort of prefabricated box you might see on the outskirts of any town anywhere in the world.

This town – or, more accurately, village – is Boesinghe, about three miles north of Ypres. Boesinghe was part of the old British frontline in the Great War. Edmund Blunden, the poet and critic, served here and told how the village looked then: jutting roof-timbers, roomless doorways, rubble everywhere. John McCrae, the Canadian doctor, came here to treat soldiers who had been gassed. One morning he walked out of his dressing station, looked at the rows of wooden crosses that each day became thicker, and wrote the deathless poem *In Flanders Fields*.

The men working in the shadows of those heaps of clay call themselves battlefield archaeologists. This is their dig. They are following the line of a trench from the Great War, rummaging for its secrets before another box of a factory is erected over the ground. They wear shorts and gumboots and work with narrow-bladed shovels. They cut a slice of clay from the face, deposit it gently, knead the shovel through it even more gently, then reach down to pick up a spent cartridge or a scrap of uniform.

Two weeks ago these men came upon a body. 'He was there,' one of the diggers says. 'Blown to pieces.' The skeleton was in two parts.

Earlier this Saturday morning, with police present and in the heavy air of a cloudy summer's day, they lifted it out. All that the diggers know about this man is that he was probably from the Rifle Brigade. A shoulder badge, with the words still legible, lay among the bones.

Now the diggers are searching beyond the triangular patch where the body lay for whatever the soldier left in this world. One by one his possessions come out of the clay. A brass belt buckle. Rifle rounds stained with soft green mould. Scraps of a woollen uniform that have endured so well in this wet ground that they do not tear when pulled. Leather strapping, the rivets covered with a lurid green. Small shards of bones, like grey pumice. Buttons. And the driving band from the shell that probably killed the soldier.

All of this goes into plastic bags. But, as usually happens, there is nothing that can establish who this man was.

THEY BURIED HIM the following Friday afternoon in one of the 155 cemeteries that loop around Ypres like a necklace of well-kept sorrow. Buglers from the Menin Gate sounded the Last Post over his bones and the standard of the Royal British Legion was raised under an overcast sky. Some seventy-five people attended, including a representative of the British Government. The Reverend Ray Jones of St George's Memorial Church in Ypres led the service, which was non-denominational. Brief reports of the burial appeared in local papers the next day.

One day soon they will put a headstone over his grave. Known Unto God, it will say.

YOU KEEP THINKING about this man, or rather that huddle of clay-smeared bones, during the next few weeks, which is absurd because you know nothing about him and never will. Maybe that's why you keep thinking about him. What was he doing when the shell hit? Was he on sentry duty, scratching away at lice as he stared into a black night, or was he hopping the bags? Did he hear the shell coming? Was he young or old? Did he have a wife and children? What did he think about the war? Who wept when he was reported missing?

The Great War is long ago and far away. And in the clay that is soft and springy under your feet at Boesinghe it is still with us, loaded with mysteries and heavy with sadness and thoughts of things that are unspeakable. All the Australians who fought on the western front are gone now. There were so many of them, and we never really saw them.

Australian divisions in France and Belgium 1916–18

1st Division (commanded, successively, by H. B. Walker and
T. W. Glasgow):
1st Brigade: 1st, 2nd, 3rd, 4th battalions.
2nd Brigade: 5th, 6th, 7th, 8th btns.
3rd Brigade: 9th, 10th, 11th, 12th btns.

2nd Division (commanded, successively, by J. G. Legge,
N. M. Smyth and C. Rosenthal):
5th Brigade: 17th, 18th, 19th, 20th btns.
6th Brigade: 21st, 22nd, 23rd, 24th btns.
7th Brigade: 25th, 26th, 27th, 28th btns.

3rd Division (commanded, successively, by J. Monash and
J. Gellibrand):
9th Brigade: 33rd, 34th, 35th, 36th btns.
10th Brigade: 37th, 38th, 39th, 40th btns.
11th Brigade: 41st, 42nd, 43rd, 44th btns.

4th Division (commanded, successively, by H. V. Cox, W. Holmes and E. G. Sinclair-MacLagan):
4th Brigade: 13th, 14th, 15th, 16th btns.
12th Brigade: 45th, 46th, 47th, 48th btns.
13th Brigade: 49th, 50th, 51st, 52nd btns.

5th Division (commanded, successively, by J. W. McCay and J. J. T. Hobbs):
8th Brigade: 29th, 30th, 31st, 32nd btns.
14th Brigade: 53rd, 54th, 55th, 56th btns.
15th Brigade: 57th, 58th, 59th, 60th btns.

Australian and British formations in 1916–18

Section: eight to ten men, commanded by a corporal.
Platoon: four sections, commanded by a lieutenant.
Company: four platoons, perhaps 200 men, commanded by a captain.
Battalion: four companies, around 1000 men, commanded by a lieutenant-colonel or colonel.
Brigade: four battalions, around 4000 men, commanded by a brigadier or brigadier-general.
Division: three brigades, plus artillery, commanded by a major-general.
Corps: three or four divisions, commanded by a lieutenant-general.
Army: three or four corps, commanded by a general.

Endnotes

PROLOGUE

Page
6.   'Hell, I can't go back . . .': Major Sidney Rogerson, 'Australia in France: Some Candid Recollections', *Reveille*, April, 1937.
6.   'By jove . . .': *Bulletin*, August 1, 1918.
10. 'I have one puttee . . .': John Raws, letter July 25, 1916, Australian War Memorial.
11. 'They'd been trained to identify . . .': Pat Barker, *Regeneration*, p. 48.
12. 'I hope the officers . . .': quoted in Tim Travers, *The Killing Ground: The British Army, the Western Front and the Emergence of Modern War 1900–1918*, p. 39, from *Napoleon as a General*, by Major W.H. James (ed), Vol 1, p. v, by Count Yorck von Warlenburg (1902).
14. 'Each day . . .': Robin Corfield, *Don't forget me, cobber*, p. 404.

PART ONE: 1916

Chapter 1
Page
24. 'dear, bright eyes . . .' and 'our dear little pets': Pompey Elliott letters December 1, 1914, and July 19, 1916, AWM.
26. 'born soldier . . .': *Bulletin*, October 8, 1930.
27. 'completely lost' and 'wanted to know . . .': quoted in Denis Winter, *25 April 1915: The Inevitable Tragedy*, p. 166.
29. 'old woman': Earl Sir Douglas Haig Diary, August 13, 1914, National Library of Scotland.

30. 'most backward in training . . .': C.E.W. Bean, *Official History of Australia in the War 1914–18*, Vol III, p. 62.

34. 'For days I have seen nothing . . .': quoted in Martin Gilbert, *First World War*, p. 233.

36. 'From Marseilles . . .': Arthur Thomas, letter April 3, 1916, AWM.

37. 'We wanted to climb out of the train . . .': Gordon Maxfield, letter April 29, 1916, AWM.

37. 'the only hope . . .', 'It seemed such a pity . . .' and 'a frightful amount of dog . . .': Raws, letters July 12, 1915, May 29, 1916 and June 6, 1916, AWM.

37. 'Beautiful match': Ivor Margetts, diary entry, December 6, 1915.

38. 'You pull up at a large farm house . . .': F.M. Cutlack (ed), *War Letters of General Monash*, letter, June 12, 1915.

38. 'with any amount of ladies aboard' and 'God! Sergeant . . .': Cyril Lawrence (ed Peter Yule), *Sergeant Lawrence Goes to France*, p. 4, p. 26.

38. 'and one good thing about the beer . . .': William Barry, diary entry, AWM.

39. 'This is a most gorgeous country . . .': Geoffrey McCrae, letter July 13, 1916, AWM.

Chapter 2
Page

42. Commanding generals were not even spectators: John Keegan, *The First World War*, p. 341.

42. 'I don't know what is to be done . . .': quoted in J.F.C. Fuller, *The Decisive Battles of the Western World*, Vol III, p. 233.

43. 'We would rather have a classically educated . . .': quoted in Travers, p. 41, from Evidence of Lt-Col A.M. Murray to *Report of the Committee Appointed to Consider the Education and Training of Officers of the Army*, Cmnd Paper 983 (1902).

44. 'With affected calm . . .': Charles de Gaulle quoted in Richard Holmes, *The Western Front*, p. 38.

44. 'No-one would have described . . .': Robert Rhodes James, *A Spirit Undaunted: The Political Role of George VI*, p. 36.

45. 'for the sake of the empire': Haig Diary, October 24, 1915, NLS.

45. 'was not to expend itself . . .': Sir John Monash, *Australian Victories in France 1918*, p. 96.

46. 'Bloody lot of use that is . . .': Robert Graves, *Goodbye to All That*, p. 103.

47. 'You bloody cowards . . .': Graves, p. 140.

47. 'a much over-rated weapon': quoted in A.J.P. Taylor (ed), *History of World War I*, p. 107.

48.   'unreasoning brain': Haig Diary, October 2, 1915, NLS.
48.   'I therefore thought . . .': Haig Diary, October 24, 1915, NLS.
48.   'duty' to refrain from visiting casualty clearing stations: in Robert Blake, *The Private Papers of Douglas Haig*, p. 9.
51.   Philip Game's opinion of Richard Haking, Game Papers, IWM.
52.   'no doubt to render the maps . . .' and 'At this moment . . .': Edmund Blunden, *Undertones of War*, p. 60 and p. 67.
53.   'It is a mixture of damp earth . . .': A.D. Ellis, *The Story of the Fifth Australian Division*, p. 78.
53.   '. . . it remained only in the vague rumour . . .': C.E.W. Bean, *OH*, Vol III, p. 109.
54.   'I hate these unprepared little shows . . .': C.E.W. Bean, *OH*, Vol III, p. 443.
54.   'and so get a big splash': Elliott, letter August 26, 1916, AWM.
57.   'The Commander-in-Chief wishes . . .': C.E.W. Bean, *OH*, Vol III, pp. 349–50.
57.   'did nothing to relieve . . .': Brig-Gen James Edmonds, *British Official History of the Great War: Military Operations France and Belgium 1916*, p. 125.

Chapter 3
Page
59.   Walter Downing in France and moving to the front line: Walter Downing, *To the Last Ridge*, pp. 6–8.
61.   'Boys, you won't find a German . . .': C.E.W. Bean, *OH*, Vol III, p. 362.
62.   'The row was deafening . . .' and 'One or two of the chaps . . .': privately held letter of Leslie Martin, July 31, 1916.
65.   'standing out shoulder high . . .': quoted in Corfield, p. 156.
66.   'Today I lead my battalion . . .': Geoff McCrae, letter July 19, 1916, AWM.
66.   '. . . we hope to so pound the enemy's trenches . . .': Elliott, letter July 19, 1916, AWM.
66.   'Some operations are pending': Tom Elliott, letter July 19, 1916, AWM.
66.   Elliott letters to Geoff McCrae's parents, July 21 and 23, 1916, AWM.
67.   'Here, I'm done . . .': Ignatius Norris in Corfield, p. 147.
69.   'was the man in front of me blown to atoms . . .': Richard Kennedy in Corfield, pp. 238–39.
69.   Message from Frederick Toll, in C.E.W. Bean, *OH*, Vol III, p. 377.
70.   'You could hear the moans of the wounded . . .': Martin, letter July 31, 1916.
72.   'Am attacking at 9 pm . . .': Message from General Carter in Bean, *OH*, Vol III, p. 392.

72. 'At the enemy wire . . .': A.D. Ellis, *The Story of the Fifth Australian Division*, p. 101.

73. 'Under instructions from corps commander . . .': C.E.W. Bean, *OH*, Vol III, p. 394.

74. 'They asked for the assistance . . .': Ross McMullin, p. 233.

74. 'Men of all battalions are coming back . . .': Charles Denehy in C.E.W. Bean, *OH*, Vol III, pp. 397–98.

75. 'The interminable hours wore on . . .': Downing, p. 10.

75. 'Especially in front of the 15th Brigade . . .': C.E.W. Bean, *OH*, Vol III, p. 437.

76. 'What had been ordinary sandbagged trenches . . .': J. Schroder in Bean Papers, AWM.

76. 'This was when Pompey Elliott . . .': William Boyce in Corfield, p. 223.

77. 'Old Elliot was dead asleep . . .': Bean Diary, July 20, 1916, AWM.

Chapter 4
Page

79. Story of wounded Australian soldier wandering in front of German lines in Bean Notebook 122, AWM.

81. 'we were told to read a verse . . .': quoted in R. McNicoll, *The Royal Australian Engineers 1902–1919: Making or Breaking*, p. 65.

81. 'I was in "no-man's land" . . .': William Barry, Diary, AWM.

82. 'Frontline cannot be held . . .': C.E.W. Bean, *OH*, Vol III, p. 401.

83. Story of William Barry's capture by Germans in his Diary, AWM.

84. 'Dawn showed our trenches to be a shambles . . .': M. Purser, 'Memories of Fromelles', *Reveille*, July, 1935.

84. 'Poor old Tivey . . .': Bean Diary, July 20, 1916, AWM.

84. 'picked his way carefully . . .': Ellis, p. 105.

84. 'Col Toll's head was covered in blood . . .': quoted in Corfield, p. 131.

84. 'Well, men, no-one could ask you . . .': William Miles in Bean Papers, AWM.

84. 'Several bodies I passed . . .': Miles, letter July 31, 1916, AWM.

85. '. . . we lost the man on the right . . .': Strode quoted in McNicoll, p. 66.

86. 'Position almost desperate . . .': Walter Cass in C.E.W. Bean, *OH*, Vol III, p. 419.

87. Privately held letters from Walter Cass to his future wife, Helena, June 16, 1916, and July 12, 1916.

88. 'Oh, cruel, cruel!': Norman Gibbins in C.E.W. Bean, *OH*, Vol III, p. 431fn.

88. 'The German flares were the best display . . .': William Smith, 'Leaves from a Sapper's Diary', *Reveille*, July, 1936.

90. 'Dear we got such a "strafing" . . .': Cass, letter July 29, 1916.
90. 'Some damned politician-cum-soldier . . .': family interview with Angela, daughter of Walter Cass.
91. Carrying in the wounded from the battle at Fromelles: Downing, pp. 11–13.
91. 'One foggy morning in particular . . .': Simon Fraser in C.E.W. Bean, *OH*, Vol III, p. 441.
91. 'Should I fall . . .': Harry Williams in C.E.W. Bean, *OH*, Vol III, p. 118.
92. Story of 'Rowley' Lording in A.G. Butler, *Official History of the Australian Army Medical Corps 1914–18*, Vol III, p. 842.
92. 'For sixteen hours we worked . . .': privately held letter of Alfred Langan, July 22, 1916.
92–4. William Miles and the attempted truce: Bean Papers, C.E.W. Bean, *OH*, Vol III, pp 438–40. For an excellent account, see Corfield, pp. 260–70.
94. 'With about half of his division dead . . .': Corfield, p. 268.
95. 'It was McCay's neglect . . .': Corfield, p. 403.
95. 'The mistake made . . .': letter from Brig-Gen Sir James Edmonds to Charles Bean, November 3, 1927, Bean Papers, AWM.
95. 'The losses amongst our troops . . .': *Sydney Morning Herald*, July 24, 1916.
95. 'Yesterday evening, south of Armentières, . . .': C.E.W. Bean, *OH*, Vol III, p. 446.
96. 'What is the good of deliberate lying like that?': Bean Diary, July 20, 1916, AWM.
96. 'The artillery preparation . . .': Haking in C.E.W. Bean, *OH*, Vol III, pp. 444–45fn.
97. 'In viewing 1914–14 I feel . . .': Edmonds to Bean, letter September 11, 1928, Bean Papers, AWM.
97. 'God knows why this enterprise . . .': Elliott, letter July 23, 1916, AWM.

Chapter 5

Page

102. 'When you fall, Eamonn . . .' and 'We have done right . . .': quoted in Michael Foy and Brian Barton, *The Easter Rising*, pp. 243 and 238.
103. 'His loss, popularly regarded as a national tragedy . . .': John Keegan and Andrew Wheatcroft, *Who's Who in Military History*, p. 154.
105. 'recoiled from illness . . .': John Grigg, *Lloyd George: From Peace to War 1912–1916*, p. 384.
111. 'life is a constant horrible struggle': from Adolf Hitler, *Monologe im Fuhrerhauptquartier 1941–44* (ed Heinrich Heims), p. 71.

115. 'The weather report is favourable for tomorrow . . .': Haig Diary, June 30, 1916, NLS.
117. 'Very successful attack . . .': Haig to Lady Haig, July 1, 1916, Haig Papers, NLS.
119. 'as if expecting to find nothing . . .': Edmonds, *History of the Great War: Military Operations, France and Belgium, 1916*, p. 393.
121–2 'Things are going well . . .' and 'In another fortnight . . .': Haig to Lady Haig, July 2 and 8, 1916, Haig Papers, NLS.
124. 'This was the biggest bombardment . . .': C.E.W. Bean, *OH*, Vol III, p. 461.
127. 'The dead Newfoundlanders . . .': quoted in Stephen Bull, *Aspects of War: Trench Warfare*, p. 80.

Chapter 6
Page

129. 'The melodrama of it rose strongly . . .': 'Charles Edmonds', *A Subaltern's War*, p. 38.
132. 'Both were men of the left . . .': John Grigg, *Lloyd George: War Leader 1916–1918*, p. 538.
132. William Johnson's quip to Billy Hughes in C.E.W. Bean, *OH*, Vol III, p. 471.
132. 'had shown that through self-sacrifice . . .': quoted in Donald Horne, *Billy Hughes*, p. 109.
132. 'I have been rather busy writing . . .': Ivor Margetts, letter February 11, 1916, AWM.
133. '. . . we realised that at last we were in a war . . .': Ben Champion, diary entries July 19 and 23, 1916, AWM.
135. Charles Carrington's experiences at the front: 'Charles Edmonds', pp. 42, 49, and 52.
136. 'The Australians were going in the line there . . .': Edmonds, p.83.
136. 'part of a serious offensive . . .': Haig Diary, July 22, 1916, NLS.
136. 'The men were looking splendid . . .': Haig Diary, late March, 1916, NLS.
137. 'I want you to go into the line . . .': C.E.W. Bean, *OH*, Vol III, p. 468.
137. 'too rash and headstrong' and 'first class as divisional and corps commander . . .': Letters from James Edmonds to Charles Bean, September 15, 1930, and July 3, 1928, Bean Papers, AWM.
137. 'perfectly infatuated': Edmonds to Bean, July 2, 1928, Bean Papers, AWM.
138. 'Scrappy and unsatisfactory orders . . .': letter from Walker to Bean, August 13, 1928, Bean Papers, AWM.
138. 'in terms which could have jeopardised . . .': Robert Rhodes James, *Gallipoli*, p. 129.

139. 'a small man dressed in light khaki . . .': Cyril Lawrence (ed Ronald East), *The Gallipoli Diary of Sergeant Lawrence*, p. 66.
139. 'I can hardly believe a word . . .': Gough's letter attached to Edmond's letter to Bean, November 16, 1927, Bean Papers, AWM.
140. 'It was at the Conference . . .': Walker letter to Bean, August 13, 1928, Bean Papers, AWM.

Chapter 7
Page
145. Robert Graves' near-death experience: Robert Graves, *Goodbye to All That*, pp. 190, 193, 196 and 199.
146. German letter: in C.E.W Bean, *OH*, Vol III, p. 522.
147. 'Every now and then . . .': in C.E.W. Bean, *OH*, Vol III, p. 494.
147. 'In the tumult it was impossible . . .': Harold Preston, 'John Leak VC', *Reveille*, August, 1935.
147. 'All tiredness was forgotten, . . .': Champion, diary entry July 23, 1916, AWM.
148. 'A and B Coy were supposed to stay in this trench . . .': Archie Barwick, diary entry July 23, 1916, quoted in Bill Gammage, *The Broken Years*, p. 163.
148. 'terrified and shrieking' Germans: C.E.W. Bean, *OH*, Vol III, p. 514.
148. 'shaky and rattled . . .': Champion diary, July 23, 1916, AWM.
149. 'Shells came in about 1 or 2 a second . . .': Frank Shoobridge, diary entry July 23, 1916, AWM.

Chapter 8
Page
151. 'the usual inappropriate message . . .': Graves, p. 189.
152. 'A number of cases . . .': C.E.W Bean, *OH*, Vol III, p. 537fn.
153. Jack Bourke and the cake boxes: C.E.W. Bean, *OH*, Vol III, p. 249.
153. 'I heard him . . .': C.E.W. Bean, *OH*, Vol III, p. 541.
154. Alan Vowles captures Germans: C.E.W. Bean, *OH*, Vol III, p. 542fn.
154. Lt-Col Elliott's letter to Ivor Margetts' parents, November 24, 1916, AWM.
155. G.A. McKenzie's letter, September 22, 1916, AWM.
156. Story of Edward Jenkins: in C.E.W. Bean, *OH*, Vol III, p. 554
157. Letter from Philip Howell-Price, August 1, 1916, AWM.
157. 'Of course, Fritz has his own late trenches . . .': Champion, diary entry, July 24, 1916, AWM.
158. 'It seems probable that his courage . . .': Dominic Hibberd, *Wilfred Owen: The Last Year*, p. 10.

158. 'They have to stay there . . .': Bean Diary, August 4, 1916, AWM.
159. 'Has that message been delivered?': C.E.W. Bean, *OH*, Vol III, p. 598.
159. 'I don't mind a joke . . .' and 'We passed a cartful of maimed kiddies':
     Bernhardt Walther, diary entries May 1 and June 19, 1916, AWM.
160. 'competent Jew': quoted in John Robertson, *Anzac and Empire*, p. 35.
162. 'Bodies of hundreds of Australians . . .': Frank Legg, *The Gordon
     Bennett Story*, p. 104.
163. 'Buried were you?': C.E.W. Bean, *OH*, Vol III, p. 580.
163. 'For Christ's sake write a book . . .': Thomas, diary entry July 25,
     1916, AWM.
163. 'All day long the ground rocked & swayed . . .': Barwick, diary entry
     July 24. 1916.
164. 'and we simply had to walk over them': Preston, *Reveille*, August 1935.
164. Arthur Thomas on Pozières: letters August 1 and 3, 1916, AWM.
165. 'My men are being unmercifully shelled . . .': Bennett in C.E.W. Bean,
     OH, Vol III, p. 590.
165. 'mortally afraid': in Frank Legg, *The Gordon Bennett Story*, p. 108.
165. 'The heaviest fire yet faced': C.E.W. Bean, *OH*, Vol III, p. 592.
165. 'What a mess of a Battalion . . .': Champion, diary entry July 26,
     1916.
165. 'We were taken out today . . .': Thomas, diary entry, July 27, 1916,
     AWM.
166. 'Last week I was fighting dirty . . .': Philip Howell-Price, letter August
     1, 1916, AWM.
166. '. . . we had our eyes opened . . .': Edgar Rule, *Jacka's Mob*, p. 25.
166. 'They were like boys . . .': C.E.W. Bean, *OH*, Vol III, p. 599.

Chapter 9

Page

169. John Raws explains his duties, and gives his views on saluting, French
     girls and the war: in letters, June 20, 22, 27, and July 16 and 20,
     1916, AWM.
172. 'did not have Walker's sure touch . . .': John Coates, *An Atlas of
     Australia's Wars*, p. 56.
173. 'Blancmange Trench': Clarence Wallach in C.E.W. Bean, *OH*, Vol III,
     p. 619.
173. 'There were only blackened dead . . .': C.E.W. Bean, *OH*, Vol III,
     pp. 616–17.
174. 'generosity in sport . . .': C.E.W. Bean, *With the Flagship in the South*,
     p. 129–30.
176. Bean wounded at Gallipoli: K. Fewster, *Gallipoli Correspondent*,
     p. 147.

180. 'I went with the first line myself . . .': Walter Boys, letter August 2, 1916, AWM.

180. 'so complete in its stark tragedy . . .': Arnold Brown, 'The Old Windmill: Pozières' Tragic Landmark', *Reveille*, October, 1932.

181. 'an almost impossible task': Edmonds, *History of the Great War 1916*, p. 155.

182. 'inflamed with alcohol': C.E.W. Bean, *OH*, Vol III, p. 639fn.

182. 'As they neared our kitchens . . .': W. Ambrose Cull, *At All Costs*, p. 34.

183. John Raws and his missing brother, Goldy: letters home, August 3 and 12, 1916, AWM.

Chapter 10

Page

185. 'From several reports . . .': Haig Diary, July 29, 1916, NLS.

186. 'You're not fighting Bashi-Bazouks . . .': C.E.W. Bean, *OH*, Vol III, p. 643.

186. 'I dare say you are right, young man': C.E.W. Bean, *OH*, Vol III, p. 644.

187. 'We were shelled all the way up . . .': Raws, letter August 8, 1916, AWM.

188. Attack postponed: C.E.W. Bean, *OH*, p. 664 and fn.

188. 'From what he said . . .': Haig Diary, August 3, 1916, NLS.

188. 'The Powers that be . . .': Robertson quoted in John Grigg, *Lloyd George: From Peace to War 1912–1916*, p. 378.

189. 'shifty and unreliable': Haig Diary, January 30, 1916, NLS.

190. 'From every point of view . . .': Winston Churchill, *The World Crisis 1911–1918*, p. 1058.

190. Haig optimistic and explains the situation to the King: diary entries August 3 and 8, 1916, NLS.

191. 'I expect to get a decoration out of it': Boys, letter August 2, 1916, AWM.

191. Percy Cherry and George O'Neill: in C.E.W. Bean, *OH*, Vol III, pp. 694fn and 696.

193. 'we had to sit and suffer . . .': Arnold Brown, *Reveille*, October, 1932.

193. 'My party capture . . .': Eric Edgerton, privately held diary, entry August 4, 1916.

194. 'We have just come out of a place . . .': Maxfield, letter August 15, 1916, AWM.

195. 'We are lousy, . . .' and 'Before going into this next affair . . .': Raws, letters July 22 and August 19, 1916, AWM.

Chapter 11

Page

198. 'one of those crotchety . . .': John Monash, letter to wife, May 8, 1916, Monash Papers, NLA.
199. 'I managed to get the beggars, sir': C.E.W. Bean, *OH*, Vol II, p. 150.
199. 'To me, he looked the part . . .': Rule, pp. 2–3.
200. I have nothing to thank him for': quoted in George Franki and Clyde Slatyer, *Mad Harry: Australia's Most Decorated Soldier*, p. 5.
200. 'He might have been Diomed . . .': Harry Murray, 'The First Three Weeks on Gallipoli', *Reveille*, April, 1939.
200. 'some bad lads with white hides': quoted in Jeff Hatwell, *No Ordinary Determination: Percy Black and Harry Murray of the First A.I.F.*, p. 30.
200. 'Harry Murray and I have a walk . . .': quoted in *Mad Harry*, p. 116.
200. 'I fought many a hard battle . . .': Harry Murray, 'His Hardest Battle When Discipline Mastered Fear', *Reveille*, December, 1935.
201 'Jacka is killed . . .', and 'I could see some of our boys . . .': Rule, p. 29.
203. 'I can't face it anymore': C.E.W. Bean, *OH*, Vol III, p. 710fn.
204. Story of Albert Jacka's wounding: Rule, pp. 29–30
205. Jacka's recovery in hospital: Rule, pp 48–49.

Chapter 12

Page

209. Casualties of the 4th Army: Robin Prior and Trevor Wilson, *Command on the Western Front: The Military Career of Sir Henry Rawlinson*, p. 204.
210. 'You can have no idea of what the ground is like . . .': Allan Leane, letter August 9, 1916, AWM.
211. 'A nice old man . . .' and 'Derek is enjoying himself so much . . .': Haig Diary, July 29 and August 2, 1916, NLS.
212. 'He is most enthusiastic . . .': Haig Diary, August 2 and September 11, 1916, NLS.
213. 'such confusion and loss . . .': Edmonds, *History of the Great War, 1916*, p. 219.
213. 'We cannot move . . .' and 'Both 13th C.O. thinks . . .': C.E.W. Bean, *OH*, Vol III, p. 763.
215. Harry Murray's near escape: Harry Murray, 'His Hardest Battle When Discipline Mastered Fear', *Reveille*, December, 1935.
216. 'one of the most skilfully conducted fights': C.E.W. Bean, *OH*, Vol III, p. 769.
216. Monash on discipline: General Sir John Monash, *Australian Victories in France in 1918*, p. 292.

Chapter 13
Page
219. 'We appeared to be sniped . . .': Champion, diary entry August, 1916.
220. 'You will all be in a serious action . . .': Champion, diary entry, August, 1916.
220. 'invigorating tone': C.E.W. Bean, *OH*, Vol III, p. 771.
221. 'which is very nice of him . . .': Owen Howell-Price, letter August 14, 1916, AWM.
222. 'I am doubtful . . .': Owen Howell-Price in C.E.W. Bean, *OH*, Vol III, p. 789.
223. 'induced to come forward': C.E.W. Bean, *OH*, Vol III, p. 790.
223. 'by a sort of bicycle . . .': 'Squatter' Preston, 'To Do Or Die', *Reveille*, January, 1936.
224. Bert Crowle, letter August 24, 1916, AWM.

Chapter 14
Page
228. 'Get up, you loafer . . .': Cull, p. 53.
228. Quotation marks around the word 'tank': Haig Diary, August 11, 1916, NLS.
229. Haig watches the tanks: Haig Diary, August 26, 1916, NLS.
230. 'the whole area now resembled . . .': C.E.W. Bean, *OH*, Vol III, p. 812.
231. 'I thought the first show was worse . . .': Maxfield, letter August 31, 1916, AWM.
234. Food shortages in Leipzig: Caroline Cooper, *Behind the Lines: One Woman's War 1914–18*, pp. 113, 130 and 136.
234. Australian and German duel: C.E.W. Bean, *OH*, Vol III, p. 816.

Chapter 15
Page
237. Ted Rule receives his orders: Rule, pp. 37–40.
239. Attack on Mouquet Farm: Rule, pp. 43, 47.
240. 'Subject to extraction of stumps': Hatwell, p. 24.
240. 'The bravest man I ever knew . . .': Harry Murray, 'Experimental Stage: Tanks at Bullecourt', *Reveille*, April, 1933.
242. 'But the climax that surpassed all horrors . . .': Joseph Trotman, 'Account of the battle at Mouquet Farm 1–4 September, 1916', AWM.
243. 'I'll reach that trench . . .': C.E.W. Bean, *OH*, Vol III, p. 848.

Chapter 16

Page

246. 'There is indescribable enthusiasm . . .': Ernest Scott, *Official History of Australia in the War: Australia During the War,* Vol XI, p. 13.

246. 'Would it not be well . . .': Scott, p. 8.

246. 'in a time of emergency . . .': Scott, p. 22.

248. 'He is a little man . . .': Scott, pp. 331–32.

249. 'Good night, Will . . .': quoted in Donald Horne, *Billy Hughes,* p. 72.

251. 'splashing and threshing . . .': John Hetherington, (ed Matthew Ricketson), *The Best Australian Profiles,* p. 110.

253. 'staggering demand': C.E.W. Bean, *OH,* Vol III, p. 868.

254. 'In no circumstances . . .': Scott, p. 337.

Chapter 17

Page

255. 'For myself . . .': Scott, p. 348.

256. 'Hughes allowed himself to be deceived . . .': Donald Horne, *Billy Hughes,* p. 123.

256. 'As a sheer feat of physical and mental exertion . . .': Scott, p. 349.

256. 'Are you in favour . . .': Scott, p. 341.

257. 'Progressively it was used . . .': Joan Beaumont (ed), *Australia's War 1914–18,* p. 39.

258. 'muddy-mettled wastrels . . .': Scott, p. 348.

258. 'Australia in September . . .': L.L. Robson, *The First A.I.F.: A Study of its Recruitment 1914–18,* p. 95.

258. Cartoon in the *Bulletin,* February 10, 1916.

259. 'quite certain . . .': cable from Hughes to Murdoch, August 30, 1916, AWM.

260. 'please arrange widest . . .': cable from Hughes to Murdoch, September 30, 1916, AWM.

260. Manifesto 'excellent': cable from Murdoch to Hughes, October 7, 1916, AWM.

260. 'It is absolutely imperative . . .': cable from Hughes to Murdoch, October 10, 1916, AWM.

260. 'tremendous excitement . . .': cable from Murdoch to Hughes, October 11, 1916, AWM.

261. 'Strongly urge you to prevent publication . . .': cable from Murdoch to Hughes, October 21, 1916, AWM.

261. Bean's thoughts on conscription voting: C.E.W. Bean, *OH,* Vol III, pp. 891–92.

262. 'The result was remarkable . . .': Rule, p. 52.

262. Newton Wanliss on conscription vote: Newton Wanliss, *The History of the 14th Battalion*, p. 164.
263. 'The poor little man . . .': quoted in Gavin Souter, *Lion and Kangaroo*, p. 319.
264. 'For the moment the anarchist . . .': quoted in Souter, p. 325–26.

Chapter 18
Page
266. Haig risk: Prior and Wilson, *Command on the Western Front*, p. 232.
266. 'When we climbed up to the lines . . .': Prior and Wilson, p. 238.
266. 'did not speak with confidence . . .': Haig Diary, September 15, 1916, NLS.
267. 'a conspiracy against the public . . .': Grigg, *Lloyd George: From Peace to War 1912–1916*, p. 383.
268. The day's casualties: Prior and Wilson, *Command on the Western Front*, p. 243.
268. Haig impressed with tanks: Haig Diary, September 15, 1916, NLS.
268. Story of Basil Henriques: in Patrick Wright, *Tank*, p. 49.
269. 'for the mere petty purpose . . .': Winston Churchill, *The World Crisis 1911–1918*, p. 525.
269. 'The PM was not discomposed . . .': John Joliffe (ed), *Raymond Asquith: Life and Letters*, p. 294.
272. 'The British position will doubtless . . .': Haig Diary, November 12, 1916, NLS.

Chapter 19
Page
273. 'My poor old horse . . .': Elliott, letter October 28, 1916, AWM.
274. 'The dead lay everywhere . . .' and 'There was a foot of slush . . .': Downing, pp. 17 and 20.
274. 'I cannot understand it . . .': Elliott, letter November 9, 1916, AWM.
275. Death of Owen Howell-Price: Red Cross report, February 6, 1917, AWM.
275. 'This was the turning point . . .': Philip Howell-Price in Bean, *OH*, Vol III, p. 907.
277. 'the most trying period . . .': C.E.W Bean, *OH*, Vol III, p. 918.
278. 'merely a matter of discipline': C.E.W. Bean, *OH*, Vol III, p. 921.
279. 'One or two' cases of desertion: C.E.W. Bean, *OH*, Vol III, p. 940.
281. 'nothing more would be done . . .': David Lloyd George, *War Memoirs*, Ch XXXII.
281. 'We are in a great political muddle . . .': Haig Diary, December 4, 1916, NLS.

281. 'Asquith resigned . . .': Haig Diary, December 6, 1916, NLS.
282. 'This morning the A.G. brought me . . .': Haig Diary, December 6, 1916, NLS.
282. 'to carry around the fiery cross': from H.H. Asquith, *Letters to Venetia Stanley (ed Michael and Eleanor Brock)*, p. 201.
283. 'irresponsible spectator': in Grigg, *Lloyd George: From Peace to War 1911–1916*, p. 460.
283. 'get rid of the Asquith incubus': in Grigg, p. 468.
283. 'That is the only kind of loyalty . . .': John Monash in October, 1916, Monash Papers, AWM.
284 King was 'chatty and breezy and merry . . .': Cutlack (ed), *War Letters of General Monash*, September 30, 1916.
284. 'On parting he put his arm . . .': Cutlack (ed), December 21, 1916.
284. 'The men looked splendid . . .': Hiag Diary, December 21, 1916, NLS.
287. Christmas a 'splendiferous affair', and 'heavy going, isn't it': Lawrence, pp. 55 and 64.

PART TWO: 1917

Chapter 20
Page

291. 'Gets quite cross if I do anything . . .': Lawrence, p. 78.
292. 'Gad it is awful, too awful': Thomas, letter 20 January, 1917, AWM.
292. 'lovely clear water': C.E.W. Bean, *OH*, Vol IV, p. 21.
292. 'I now swank round with the General . . .': Maxfield, letters January 20 and February 12, 1917, AWM.
293. 'and the whole country looks sweet . . .': Allan Leane, letter January 18, 1917.
293. 'They say we did 24 miles an hour . . .' and 'each man gets a quarter small loaf': David Whinfield, diary entries January 16 and 30, 1917.
294. 'Much of our losses . . .': Haig Diary, January 15, 1917, NLS.
294. Grave weakness in government: John Grigg, *Lloyd George: War Leader, 1916–1918*, p. 35.
295. 'both in the letter and in the spirit': War Cabinet, January 17, 1917.
295. 'hastily considered': Haig Diary, January 16, 1917, NLS.
296. 'It is, indeed a calamity . . .': Haig Diary, February 7, 1917, NLS.
296. 'Certain officers . . .': C.E.W. Bean, *OH*, Vol IV, p. 23.
298. Harry Murray's determination to fight: R.Winn, 'Stormy Trench', *Reveille*, February, 1938.
299. Stormy Trench: Harry Murray, 'Stormy Trench: Aussies in Grim Duel Against Worthy Foes', *Reveille*, December, 1937.

301. 'My getting the VC was all rot': quoted in D. Chalk, 'The Great Harry Murray', *Wartime*, Issue 8, 1999.
301. 'Harry Murray was not recommended . . .': Hatwell, p. 150.
302. 'Important developments have been taking place . . .': Haig Diary, February 25, 1917, NLS.

Chapter 21
Page
304. 'such measures as might appear . . .': in Grigg, *Lloyd George: War Leader 1916–1918*, p. 41.
304. 'Tell him to keep nothing back . . .': Haig Diary, February 26, 1917, NLS.
305. Lloyd Gearge was 'extremely brutal': quoted in Grigg, p. 42.
305. 'And so we went to bed . . .': Haig Diary, February 26, 1917, NLS.
306. Twice-flawed plan at Calais: Grigg, p. 43.
306. 'I think, as the actual document stands . . .': Haig Diary, February 28, 1917, NLS.
309. 'But it could not be helped': quoted in Robert Asprey, *The German High Command at War*, p. 305.
310. 'mad with delight': Lawrence, p. 98.
310. 'spiritual thrill': A.D. Ellis, *The Story of the Fifth Division*, p. 177.
311. 'In places they lie around . . .': privately held letter of Eric West, 1917.
312. 'No building is a quarter sound . . .': Whinfield, diary entry March 18, 1917.
312. 'What we want is a republic . . .': quoted in Martin Gilbert, *First World War*, p. 315.
314. 'My Dear Knox . . .': quoted in Gilbert, p. 316.
315. 'It is a long, long time . . .': Walter Adcock, *Genuine War Letters*, letter March 17, 1917.
316. 'required holding': C.E.W. Bean, *OH*, Vol IV, p. 154.
316. 'even one distant rifle shot . . .': George Wieck to Bean, October 7, 1929, Bean Papers, AWM.
316. 'They've even bashed the poor kiddies' toys . . .': Elliott, letter April 9, 1917, AWM.
317. 'Napoleonic ideas': Elliott to Bean, Bean Papers, AWM.
317. 'amusing figure . . .': White to Bean, Bean Papers, AWM.
317. 'Counter-attack me, would they?': Wieck to Bean, Bean Papers, and C.E.W. Bean, *OH*, Vol IV, p. 169.
317. 'The old Bosche cannot fight . . .': Elliott, letter March 29, 1917, AWM.
318. Prince Frederick Charles of Prussia in C.E.W. Bean, *OH*, Vol IV, p. 189–90.

Chapter 22

Page
321. Bullecourt: Eric West, letter 1917.
324. 'Well, goodbye, colonel . . .': C.E.W Bean, *OH*, Vol IV, p. 295.
324. 'Harry, this will be my last fight . . .': C. Longmore, 'Major Percy Black', *Reveille*, October, 1936.
324. 'Tell them the first objective is gained . . .': C.E.W. Bean, *OH*, Vol IV, p. 297.
325. 'Very good, sir . . .': quoted in Denis Winter, *Haig's Command: A Reassessment*, p. 261. 20
325. 'as a Christmas present . . .': quoted in Grigg, p. 150.
327. 'It was galling . . .': Cyril Falls, *History of the Great War*, 1917, p. 360.
327 Plan to use the tanks: C.E.W. Bean, *OH*, Vol IV, pp. 272–74.
329. 'materially changed the situation . . .': C.E.W. Bean, *OH*, Vol IV, p. 278.
330. Jacka captures two Germans: Rule, p. 75.
330. 'I think there is just time . . .': C.E.W. Bean, *OH*, Vol IV, p. 282.
331. 'Cold, and fed up . . .': Ray Leane, 'Hindenburg Line Break: First Bullecourt Memories', *Reveille*, April, 1933.
331. April 10 called a 'fiasco': Falls, p. 362.
333. 'I don't think I should have given way . . .': Bean Notebook, May, 1918, and C.E.W. Bean, *Two Men I Knew*, p. 154.
334. 'Of what use would I be . . .': C.E.W. Bean, *OH*, Vol IV, p. 289.
336. Eric West's journey to a dressing station: letter, 1917.
336. Percy Black: Longmore, *Reveille*, October, 1936.
337. 'Come on, boys . . .': C.E.W. Bean, *OH*, Vol IV, p. 295.
337. 'How we got through the remaining wire . . .': Harry Murray, 'Memories of First Bullecourt', *Reveille*, December, 1936.
338. 'Anywhere, where men were grouped . . .': Bert Knowles, 'Bullecourt Tragedy Retrospect', *Reveille*, April, 1931.
340. 'With artillery support . . .': Knowles, April, 1931.
341. 'The ground was a carpet of dead . . .': G.D. Mitchell, 'When Discipline Overcame Fear', *Reveille*, February, 1936.
341. 'We were being raked by machine-gun fire': C.E.W. Bean, *OH*, Vol IV, p. 308.
342. 'What are you doing, lad?': Harry Murray, *Reveille*, December, 1936.
342. 'A most aggravating . . .': C.E.W. Bean, *OH*, Vol IV, p. 327.
344. 'Situation appears to be . . .': C.E.W. Bean, *OH*, Vol IV, p. 329.
344. Story of Henry Eibel in C.E.W. Bean, *OH*, Vol IV, p. 326fn.
344. 'Oh for that barrage . . .': Harry Murray, *Reveille*, December, 1936.
345. 'I do not know what time it was then . . .': Knowles, *Reveille*, April, 1931.

345. Murray makes it back to safety: Harry Murray, *Reveille*, December, 1936.
346. Story of William Evans in C.E.W. Bean, *OH*, Vol IV, p. 337fn.
346. 'So I shook my fist . . .': G.D. Mitchell, Diary, AWM.
346. 'as strong as it could be made': C.E.W. Bean, *OH*, Vol IV, p. 337.
347. 'the luckiest man alive': Allan Leane, letter January 18, 1917.
347. 'They looked up at us but said nothing': G.D. Mitchell, Diary, AWM.
347. 'I saw a tall non-com . . .': W.H. Nicholson, 'Capt G.D. Mitchell', *Reveille*, March, 1936.
348. Unofficial truce, in C.E.W. Bean, *OH*, Vol IV, p. 341.
348. Capture of Bert Knowles: Knowles, *Reveille*, April, 1931.
349. Birdwood speech: Rule, p. 81.
349. Eric West at the casualty-clearing station: letter, 1917.
351. 'In the whole course of the War . . .': Falls, *History of the Great War, 1917*, p. 366.
351. 'experiment of extreme rashness' and 'satisfied that the effect upon the whole situation . . .': C.E.W. Bean, *OH*, Vol IV, pp. 349–51.
353. Edmond's letter to Bean enclosing Gough's letter: August 31, 1930, Bean Papers, AWM.
353. 'I expect that I shall be in full accord . . .': Edmonds to Bean, June 25, 1930, Bean Papers, AWM.
353. Edmond's opinion of Gough: letter to Bean, July 2, 1928, Bean Papers, AWM.
353. Neill Malcolm's response to Bean's proofs: letter, September 9, 1930, Bean Papers, AWM.
353. Edmonds on Gough and Malcolm: letter, September 15, 1930, Bean Papers, AWM.
354. Edmond's letter enclosing D.K. Bernard's memories of the time: letter, November 18, 1930, Bean Papers, AWM

Chapter 23
Page

359. Nivelle had aroused exaggerated hopes: Correlli Barnett, *The Swordbearers: Studies in Supreme Command in the First World War*, p. 199.
359. 'Nivelle has fallen into disgrace . . .': diary entry May 12, 1917, Frances Stevenson, *Lloyd George: A Diary*, (ed A.J.P.Taylor).
360. 'the victim of his over-elaborate promises': Sir Hubert Gough, *The Fifth Army*, p. 186.
361. 'Their stares seemed to be fixed . . .': Marshal Philippe Pétain, *La Bataille de Verdun*, quoted in Barnett, p. 222.
361. 'I found him businesslike . . .': Haig on Pétain, Haig Diary, May 18, 1917, NLS.

362. 'broadcast as far as the soldier . . .': Pétain in Barnett, p. 221.
363. Trust in Pétain: John Terraine, *Douglas Haig: The Educated Soldier*, p. 297.
364. The answer came as 'swift as lightning': C.E.W. Bean, *OH*, Vol IV, p. 394.
365. Pope's death: C.E.W. Bean, *OH*, Vol IV, p. 373.
365. 'a very ugly situation': Falls, *History of the Great War, 1917*, p. 378.
366. 'When I was 15 years and 5 months . . .': Billy Williams, privately held letter July 8, 1980.
371. 'What time is zero?': C.E.W. Bean, *OH*, Vol IV, p. 429.

Chapter 24
Page

374. 'I was told to shut up . . .': John Wright to Bean, letter dated September 14, 1937, Bean Papers, AWM.
376. Gellibrand asleep on the table: C.E.W. Bean, *OH*, Vol IV, p. 483.
376. Stanley Savige at Bullecourt: S.G. Savige, 'A Soldier's Battle: Second Bullecourt', *Reveille*, May, 1933.
377. 'I am still in an undamaged condition . . .': Maxfield, letter April 29, 1917, AWM.
378. Maxfield message: C.E.W. Bean, *OH*, Vol IV, p. 442.
379. 'All they want is a leader': C.E.W. Bean, *OH*, Vol IV, p. 448.
379. 'We were 1,600 yards out . . .': Savige, *Reveille*, May, 1933.
380. Letters from Sister Jean Simpson, May 25, June 24, June 30, 1917, and January 21, 1918.
381. '. . . men fought until they dropped . . .': Savige, *Reveille*, May, 1933.
382. 'Give the bastards hell': C.E.W. Bean, *OH*, Vol IV, p. 484.

Chapter 25
Page

387. 'The Army seems to be doing nothing . . .': Bean Diary, May 6, 1917, Bean Papers, AWM.
388. William Joynt on Percy Lay: *Reveille*, July, 1933.
388. 'Here I witnessed the most tragic episode . . .': Walter Hill, privately held letter, July 21, 1980.
389. Jimmy Downing goes into the line: Downing, p. 65 and 67.
389. 'A terrible time . . .': Rupert Moon, in John Lahey, 'The Last of the Anzacs', *Age*, April 21, 1984.
390. 'You've got the tough one, Mickey,': in Ross McMullin, p. 286.
391. 'I've got three cracks . . .': C.E.W. Bean, *OH*, Vol IV, p. 531fn.
391. 'It is easy to see . . .': Falls, *History of the Great War*, 1917, p. 481.
392. Bean on Bullecourt: C.E.W. Bean, *OH*, Vol VI, p. 544, and *Two Men I Knew*, p. 155.

392. Bean's account of Second Bullecourt: E.M. Andrews, 'Bean and Bullecourt', *Revue Internationale d'Histoire Militaire*, No. 72, Canberra, June, 1990.
394. 'Bullecourt represents . . .': Downing, p. 62.

Chapter 26
Page
397. Jellicoe an 'old woman': Haig Diary, May 7, 1917, NLS.
399. 'Just as if they had stepped . . .': Cutlack, March 24, 1917.
399. 'Wonderful detail . . .': in Roland Perry, *Monash: The Outsider Who Won a War*, p. 277.
399. 'Any attempt to desert . . .': Monash letter, April 29, 1917.
400. 'His Jewish blood . . .': C.E.W. Bean, *OH*, Vol IV, p. 562.
400. 'most thorough and capable commander': Haig Diary, July 1, 1918.
400. 'What did they come back to?': in Mark Baker, 'Schuler's War, *Age*, April 23, 2005.
401. Schuler's engagement: Roy Bridges, *That Yesterday Was Home*, p. 219, and Robin Denholm, *Paperman* (family memoir), p. 57.
401. 'Can you be too much of a gentleman?': in Denis Winter, *Haig's Command: A Reassessment*, p. 293.
403. 'In appearance . . .': Philip Gibbs quoted in John Terraine, *Douglas Haig: The Educated Soldier*, p. 308.
403. Plumer lacking the 'real offensive spirit': Haig Diary, May 22, 1917, NLS.
403. 'Plumer and Harington . . .': Charteris quoted in Terraine, p. 318.
403. Philip Gibbs on Harington, quoted in Terraine, p. 318.
405. 'do all I can to crush . . .': George Davies, Diary p. 93–94, AWM.
405. 'If I live I shall stand . . .': George Davies, letter, June 6, 1917, AWM.
405. Walde Fisher, Diary entries April 14 and May 29, 1917, AWM.
406. 'Have to wear box respirators . . .': William Palstra, from *Great Heart*, privately held diary and letters, p. 90.
407. 'Evidently he had heard of Ned Kelly': quoted in Franki and Slatyer, *Mad Harry*, p. 114.
408. 'All the trenches . . .': quoted in Richard Holmes, *The Western Front*, p. 159.
408. 'The most diabolical splendour . . .': Philip Gibbs in Holmes, p. 159.
408. 'Debris of all description . . .': Bob Grieve, 'Messines', AWM.
408. 'Nineteen gigantic roses . . .': quoted in Terraine, *Douglas Haig*, p. 314.
409. 'like a volcano . . .': Palstra, *GreatHeart*, p. 92–93.
409. 'Pretty strong . . .': Bean Diary, June 6–7, 1917, Bean Papers, AWM.
410. 'I have never seen men so demoralised': C.E.W. Bean, *OH*, Vol IV, p. 595.
411. 'Digging away for all they were worth . . .': Grieve, 'Messines', AWM.
412. 'When they have been racked . . .': C.E.W. Bean *OH*, Vol IV, p. 624.

412. 'There was a noise . . .': Wilfred Gallwey, diary, AWM.

413. Australians 'maddened': C.E.W. Bean, *OH*, Vol IV, p. 627.

414. 'I was covered in dirt and mud . . .': Grieve, 'Messines', AWM.

414. 'Soon after 4 pm . . .': Haig Diary, June 7, 1917, NLS.

414. 'More c-attacks . . .': Bean Diary, June 7, 1917, AWM.

Chapter 27

Page

416. 'Almost the first one we looked at . . .': Consett Carre Riddell, *Thoughts of a Soldier in Two World Wars and Peace* (ed John Carre Riddell), letter to John Carre Riddell, 1945.

416. 'You know that for a long time . . .': Carre Riddell, letter October 29, 1917.

417. 'I fired from first to last . . .': Monash, letter June 7, 1917.

417. 'He sent some H.E. over and luckily . . .': Joseph Trotman, letter August, 1917, AWM.

417. Walde Fisher diary entries, June 12 and 14, 1917.

418. 'I've been knocked over by a shell . . .': George Carson, letter June 14, 1917, AWM.

418. Bean on cavalry, Godley, the 3rd Division and the French mutinies: Bean Diary, June 11, 1917, Bean Papers, AWM.

419. Phillip Schuler 'won much credit for his gallantry': C.E.W. Bean, *OH*, Vol IV, p. 562fn.

419. 'His head was all bandaged up . . .': Richard Dowse, letter to Bean, May 1, 1947, Bean Papers, AWM

419. 'Your letter . . . has made me feel very bad.': Sir Ian Hamilton's reply to Richard Dowse, July 2, 1917.

420. 'All his friends knew him . . .': Bean's tribute to Phillip Schuler, in War Services Old Melburnians, 1914–1918.

420. Plaque to Phillip Schuler in a Cairo church: Robin Denholm, *Paperman*, p. 57.

423. 'Haig, in short, had arranged matters . . .': Robin Prior and Trevor Wilson, *Passchendaele*, p. 73.

424. 'trouble in the land . . .'; Haig Diary, June 15, 1917, NLS.

425. Jellicoe: 'We cannot go on': Haig Diary, June 20, 1917, NLS.

425. Haig refuses a peerage: Haig Diary, June 24, 1917, NLS.

425. 'He is a worthy little man . . .': Haig Diary, July 10, 1917, NLS.

426. Haig on John Pershing: Haig Diary, July 20, 1917, NLS.

426. Sending troops to Italy was 'the act of a lunatic': Haig Diary, July 21, 1917, NLS.

427. 'My God, it's a wonder . . .': Philip Gibbs quoted in Leon Wolff, *In Flanders Fields*, p. 103.

Chapter 28
Page

433. Edmund Blunden at the front: Edmund Blunden, *Undertones of War*, pp. 200–1, 205.
433. Officers sent to casualty-clearing stations: Haig Diary, July 31, 1917, NLS.
434. 'the next advance will be made as soon as possible': Haig Diary, July 31, 1917, NLS.
434. 'terrible day of rain'; Haig Diary, August 1, 1917, NLS.
434. 'It was a medical miracle . . .': T.A. White, *The Fighting Thirteenth: The History of the Thirteenth Battalion*, p. 103.
435. 'the place was like a circus . . .': Blunden, p. 191.
435. The word 'Diggers' becomes popular: C.E.W. Bean, *OH*, Vol IV, p. 732.
436. 'You read of "drum fire" . . .': Lawrence, letter July 31, 1917.
436. 'It has rained for two days . . .': Lawrence, letter August 1, 1917.
437. 'They seem to have gone forward . . .': Haig Diary, August 17, 1917.
437. Comment seems superfluous: Prior and Wilson, *Passchendaele*, p. 103.
438. Gough threatens to court-martial 'glaring instances': Prior and Wilson, p. 105.
438. 'Gentlemen, I have just come from an interview . . .': C.D. Baker-Carr, *From Chauffeur to Brigadier*.
438. Gough wanted to abandon the attack: Sir Hubert Gough, *The Fifth Army*, p. 205.
438. Prince Rupprecht's diary entry: C.E.W. Bean, *OH*, Vol IV, p. 728.
439. Baker-Carr told off: Baker-Carr, *From Chauffeur to Brigadier*.
440. 'Not unnaturally the Cabinet ask me . . .': Robertson quoted in Grigg, *Lloyd George: War Leader 1916–1918*, p. 223–24.
440. Lloyd George 'a real bad 'un': Haig Diary, August 9, 1917, NLS.
441. 'I have no doubt that Winston . . .': Haig Diary, September 14, 1917, NLS.

Chapter 29
Page

445. 'I can see him now . . .': Lady Clementine Waring in Stephen Snelling, *VCs of the First World War*, pp. 170–1.
446. 'the race knocked me out': and 'Am handing this to Frank tonight': privately held diary, entries September 3 and 12, 1917.
446. 'Very interesting it was too . . .': A.M. McGrigor, diary entry September 14, 1917, Imperial War Museum.
447. 'He calculated the distance . . .': Prior and Wilson, *Passchendaele*, p. 116.
449. 'I crawled a few yards . . .' and 'And among that wilderness . . .': Joe Maxwell, *Hell's Bells and Mademoiselles*, pp. 113–14.

449. 'I came out on the right side . . .': Maxwell, p. 130.

449. Walter Bradby in 'Polygon Wood and Broodseinde', *Stand-To*, September/October, 1963.

450. 'we could have got to Berlin . . .': Percy Lay, diary entry, September 20, 1917.

450. 'All the tenants received . . .': Stanley Calderwood, privately held diary, entry September 20, 1917.

451. 'Get out of the way, sergeant . . .': C.E.W. Bean, *OH*, Vol IV, p. 766.

451. Ivon Murdoch and Maurice Wilder-Neligan in C.E.W. Bean, *OH*, Vol IV, p. 763fn and 764.

452. Fred Moore and Donovan Joynt in C.E.W. Bean, *OH*, Vol IV, p. 772.

452. Bean on war: Vol IV, p. 772fn.

453. Seabrook Brothers: Red Cross Reports.

453. William Tooney, letters February 22, 1918, and November 21, 1917, AWM.

454. 'Some of them didn't seem to understand . . .': Donald Coutts, privately held diary, entry September 19, 1917.

454. 'one Australian whom the General spoke to . . .': A.M. McGrigor, diary entry September 20, 1917, IWM.

454. 'complete success': C.E.W. Bean, *OH*, Vol IV, p. 788.

455. 'We have done a good offensive . . .': Lord Bertie in C.E.W. Bean, *OH*, Vol IV, p. 790.

455. 'I found there an atmosphere . . .': David Lloyd George, *War Memoirs*, Vol 4, p. 412 (Nicolson and Watson edition).

456. Lloyd George visits war prisoners: Lloyd George, *War Memoirs*, Vol 4, p. 414.

456. 'I was struck by the discourtesy . . .': Sir Hubert Gough, *The Fifth Army*, p. 211.

Chapter 30
Page

462. 'not a very helpful sight': William Gamble, privately held *A Gamble of Gambletown: Memoirs of Corporal William Gamble*, p. 11.

462. 'There was a crash close by . . .': Downing, pp. 76–77.

463. George Elliott in Ross McMullin, *Pompey Elliott*, p. 295.

464. 'Dumps were going up in all directions . . .': Talbot Hobbs, diary entry September 25, 1917, AWM.

465. 'We passed many killed . . .': David Whinfield, privately held diary, entry September 25, 1917.

466. 'was the acme of perfection . . .': Newton Wanliss, *The History of the 14th Battalion*, p. 240.

466. Aurora Borealis: Downing, p. 78–79.

467. Sinclair Hunt, 'The Operation at Polygon Wood', p. 3 and 6–8, AWM.
468. 'dressed as they were in sloppy fitting tunics . . .': Gamble, p. 12.
469. 'Many brave men – many good men have I met . . .': C.E.W. Bean, *OH*, Vol IV, p. 828fn.
469. John Turnour and Patrick Bugden in C.E.W. Bean, *OH*, Vol IV, p. 814fn and 815fn.
470. 'Your men are up there . . .': from Ross McMullin, *Pompey Elliott*, p. 327.
471. Elliott goes to the frontline: McMullin, pp. 327–28.
471. 'I never saw such a scene of confusion . . .': Elliott, letter October 2, 1917 AWM.
471. Pompey writes of brother's death: McMullin, p. 380.
472. 'Poor old Geordie . . .': Elliott, letter October 2, 1917, AWM.
472. 'Pardon, brother, you don't need it': Downing, p. 82.
473. 'chopped into lumps' and 'We were a pathetic band . . .': Downing, pp. 83–84.
473. 'until some puffing hero . . .': Hunt, p. 12, AWM.
474. 'I pointed out how favourable . . .': Haig Diary, October 2, 1917, NLS.
474. 'Gardiner says . . .': Haig Diary, September 24, 1917, NLS.

Chapter 31
Page
475. 'Probably the truth': Cutlack, letter July 26, 1917.
477. 'the apotheosis of banality . . .': Monash, letter September 24, 1917, Monash Papers, NLA.
477. 'For three years . . .': Cutlack, letter dated October 1, 1917.
479. 'bonzer nick . . .': privately held letter, Jarvis Fuller to his sister Ruby, August 8, 1917.
479. Worried about Les Darcy: Jarvis Fuller, letter May 31, 1917.
479. 'I feel in bonzer health . . .': Jarvis Fuller to his sister Pearl, September 29, 1917.
480. 'Some old men . . .': Philip Howell-Price, letter September 25, 1917, AWM.
480. 'About seven minutes later, or less . . .': Bean Diary, October 4, 1917, AWM.
481. 'We were formed up on the tapes . . .': Paul Johanessen, letter September 17, 1918, AWM.
481. 'We met Fritz attacking . . .': Percy Lay diary, October 4, 1917.
482. 'The accepted included some exceptionally fine men . . .': *Wangaratta Chronicle*, February 12, 1916.

482. Frank Handcock wounded: family history, and Neil Wilson, 'Brothers in Arms', *Herald Sun*, April 23, 2005.
483. 'most of its defenders were shot down': C.E.W. Bean, *OH*, Vol IV, p. 855.
483. 'About six of us had some fun . . .': Lay diary, October 4, 1917.
484. No-one could shoot the wounded German: Charles Edmonds, pp. 120–21.
484. 'a grand monument to the desolation . . .': Will Palstra, p. 110.
484. 'Your men are funny . . .': Bean Diary, October 4, 1917, AWM.
485. 'As we gazed back over the country . . .': W.J. Harvey, *The Red and White Diamond: Authorised History of the Twenty-fourth Battalion*, p. 188.
485. 'Every 20 paces or less lay a body . . .': Frank Hurley, *Hurley at War*, p. 52.
486. Roy Fuller continues to search for brother, Jarvis: privately held letters, November 30, December 10 and 30, 1917.
486. 'Your son, Private Fuller . . .': letter to Mrs Fuller confirming the death of Jarvis, February 10, 1918.
487. Broodseinde an 'overwhelming blow': C.E.W. Bean, *OH*, Vol IV, p. 875.
487. Harington letter, December 12, 1932, Bean papers, AWM.
488. 'Robertson comes badly out of this': Haig Diary, October 3, 1917, NLS.

Chapter 32

Page

491. 'Great happenings are possible': Monash, letter October 7, 1917.
491. Germans were 'staggering': Monash, letter October 6, 1917, Monash Papers, NLA.
491. Australians were being 'sacrificed': Monash, letter October 18, 1917.
493. 'I believe the official attitude . . .': Bean Diary, October 8, 1917.
496. 'The results were very successful' and Robertson disillusioned: Haig Diary, October 9, 1917, NLS.
496. 'I cannot think why the War Office . . .': Haig Diary, October 15, 1917, NLS.
496. Charteris realises there can be no success in 1917: C.E.W. Bean, *OH*, Vol IV, p. 908fn.
496. 'Never have I seen . . .': Fisher, diary entry October 24, 1917, AWM.
497. Bean interviews Haig: Bean Diary, October, 1917, AWM.
498. Haig mentions the need for an Australian corps commander: Bean Diary, October, 1917, AWM.
498. Sister Elsie Grant: letter, August 23, 1917, AWM.

499. Crown Prince Rupprecht rejoices in the rain: C.E.W. Bean, *OH*, Vol IV, p. 928.
500. 'a hopeless tangle . . .': Palstra, p. 113.
500. 'I don't think I shall ever forget . . .': John Hardie, letter October 30, 1917, AWM.
501. 'There was really nothing to conform to': C.E.W. Bean, *OH*, Vol IV, p. 912.
502. 'What am I to do?': C.E.W. Bean, *OH*, Vol IV, p. 918.
503. 'Things are bloody, very bloody': Morshead Papers, AWM.
503. 'In the vicinity . . .': Palstra, p. 114.
503. Death of Elsie Grant's brother: letter October 20, 1917.
504. 'Our men gave all their food . . .': Fisher, diary entry October 24, 1917, AWM.
504. 'During the afternoon . . .': George Watkins, diary entry October 13, 1917.
505. 'Are you dead, sir?': letter of unknown, but possibly an Australian, medical officer with the British 18th Division, PR84/068, AWM.
506. Telegram from Lloyd George to Haig: Haig Diary, October 16, 1917.
506. 'I carried my protest to the extreme limit': A.M.J. Hyatt, 'Sir Arthur Currie at Passchendaele', *Stand-To*, Jan/Feb, 1965.
507. 'Here we stayed four days . . .': Fisher, diary entry October 24, 1917, AWM.
508. 'Dante would never have condemned . . .': C.E.L. Lyne, diary entries November 4 and 6, 1917, IWM.
509. 'It was no longer life at all . . .': Erich Ludendorff, *My War Memories 1914–1918*, Vol II, p. 491.
509. 'Today was a very important success': Haig Diary, October 6, 1917, NLS.
510. 'We have won great victories . . .': Lloyd George quoted in Grigg, *Lloyd George: War Leader 1916–1918*, p. 288.

Chapter 33
Page
513. John Fuller on Douglas Haig: Introduction to Leon Wolff, *In Flanders Fields*, pXIII.
516. Low point of Haig's career: John Terraine, *Douglas Haig: The Educated Soldier*, p. 379.
517. Lloyd George 'well on the warpath': Haig Diary, December 6, 1917, NLS.
517. 'I gather that the PM is dissatisfied . . .': Haig Diary, December 8, 1917, NLS.

518. Haig did not want to affect Gough's self-confidence: Haig Diary, December 14, 1917, NLS.

518. 'He was essentially a cloistered soldier . . .': John Fuller in Wolff, p. xiv.

518. 'Though (Haig) often insisted . . .': Grigg, p. 317.

520. 'flashed the brutality . . .': Robert Asprey, *The German High Command at War*, p. 361.

520. Lloyd George on Clemenceau: Lloyd George, *War Memoirs*, p. 2678–79.

520. Churchill on Clemenceau: Winston Churchill, *Great Comtemporaries*, p. 310–11.

Chapter 34
Page

524. Referendum question: Scott, p. 414.

524. 'did not speak as a priest . . .': Scott, p. 420.

526. 'Those of you who have relatives in the trenches . . .': Hughes in the *Argus*, November 13, 1917.

526. 'The wealthy classes would be very glad . . .': Mannix in *The Advocate*, December 8, 1917.

527. Cables between Hughes and Murdoch before federal election: March 16 and April 11, 1917, and Birdwood letter, March 24, 1917, Murdoch Papers, AWM.

527. 'Anzac vote vital to success': cable, November 6, 1917, AWM.

527. 'This would have a striking effect . . .': Murdoch to Hughes, cable dated November 8, 1917.

527. 'Lives are to be drawn for . . .': *Australian Worker*, November 15, 1917.

528. Nellie Melba's message: quoted in C.M.H. Clark, *A History of Australia, Vol VI*, p. 74.

528. 'the little Tsar': Mannix, in Scott, p. 420.

528. Billy Hughes in scuffle: *Brisbane Courier*, November 30, 1917.

528. 'Did *youse* ever do any fightin?': *Bulletin*, December 20, 1917.

529. 'We can't go on forever . . .': Lawrence, p. 146.

529. 'Will I vote – will I what!': Lawrence, p. 148–49.

529. 'Another cold day . . .': privately held diary of Sapper F.X. Heerey, *A Tasmanian Story of the Great War*, diary entry December 11, 1917.

530. 'Well father you asked me some time ago . . .': Roy Brewer, letter May 27, 1918.

530. 'We've just heard the result . . .': *Bulletin*, March 7, 1918.

530. 'Tell me all about the wee people . . .': Elliott, letter June 22, 1917.

530. Pompey Elliott feeling the strain: letter, January 7, 1918.

531. 'What am I fighting for?': Carre Riddell, letter December 28, 1917.
531. Murdoch cable to Hughes: July 12, 1917, Murdoch Papers, AWM.
532. Australians had revolutionary ideas: Haig to Lady Haig, February 28, 1918, NLS.
533. Monash on Godley: letter November 14, 1917, Monash Papers, NLA.

Part Three: 1918

Chapter 35
Page
539. 'All were most friendly . . .': Haig Diary, January 7, 1918, NLS.
540. 'I felt I had made a horrible mistake . . .': Adcock, letter January 31, 1918.
541. 'It is too quiet . . .': Lawrence, p. 147.
541. 'It was the funniest collection . . .': Lay diary, November 27, 1917.
541. 'It was quite pleasant . . .': Monash, letter December 30, 1917.
541. Monash knighted: letters January 13 and March 15, 1918, Monash Papers, NLA.
541. 'My darling . . .': Vic to Monash, letter January 4, 1918, Monash Papers, NLA.
541. 'and it rained very hard . . .': Johanessen, letter August 17, 1918.
541. Joe Maxwell shot at by sentry, and goes to church: Maxwell, p. 161 and 163.
542. Christmas in Leipzig: Cooper, pp. 221 and 234.
542. 'dipping his toes . . .': *Bulletin*, January 17, 1918.
542. 'Ludendorff never possessed . . .': Frau Mathilde Ludendorff, *My Married Life with Ludendorff*, p. 232.
543. 'We must not imagine . . .': Erich Ludendorff, *My War Memories*, p. 588.
548. 'it was his duty to go . . .': Haig Diary, February 11, 1918.
548. 'I have never seen him . . .': Wilson, quoted in John Toland, *No Man's Land: 1918, the Last Year of the Great War*, p. 47.
548. 'D. is a very weak-minded fellow': Haig to Lady Haig, January 14, 1918, NLS.
549. 'We have a lot of new men . . .': Thomas, letter March 20, 1918, AWM.
549. 'we didn't lose any sleep . . .': Whinfield, February 3 and 4, 1918.
549. 'Wait 'till the spring offensive': Maxwell, p. 170.
552. British instruction to the Americans: William S. Triplet, *A Youth in the Meuse-Argonne*, p. 56.
552. 'Met Dad at WC Club . . .': Lyall Howard, diary entry March 7, 1918.

552. 'Inoculated again', 'First day in trenches', 'Shoved in old barn' and
     'Will wounded and dies': Lyall Howard, diary entries August 28,
     December 1, December 27, 1917, and August 27, 1918.
553. 'Slightly gassed': Lyall Howard, diary entry July 30, 1917.
553. 'I must say that I feel quite confident . . .': Haig to Lady Haig,
     February 28, 1918, NLS.
553. 'In any case we must be prepared . . .': Haig Diary, March 14, 1918,
     NLS.
554. 'like a damn foreigner': John Charteris, *Field-Marshal Earl Haig*,
     p. 313.
554. 'Everyone is in good spirits . . .': Haig to Lady Haig, March 20, 1918,
     NLS.

Chapter 36
Page
555. '. . . the silence was broken . . .': Winston Churchill, *The World Crisis
     1911–1918*, p. 1250–51.
557. 'It swept around us . . .': Churchill, p. 1251.
558. 'Philip – not in bed yet?': Charteris, p. 206.
558. 'Before 8 am . . .': Haig Diary, March 21, 1918, NLS.
559. 'so sustained and steady . . .': Gough, p. 260.
560. Haig's dislike of telephones: Charteris, p. 205.
560. 'did not seem to grasp . . .': Gough, p. 271.
561. 'The first to be affected . . .': quoted in Martin Middlebrook, *The
     Kaiser's Battle*, p. 161.
562. Story of J.H. Dimmer in Middlebrook, p. 254.
563. 'He spoke to us in good English . . .': quoted in Middlebrook, p. 291.
564. Estimate of casualties: Middlebrook, p. 322.

Chapter 37
Page
566. 'our men are in great spirits . . .': Haig Diary, March 22, 1918, NLS.
566. 'On the first day . . .': Haig Diary, March 23, 1918, NLS.
567. 'What is the use of all these decorations?': in John Wheeler-Bennett,
     Hindenburg: The Wooden Titan, p. 148–49.
567. Interval for recruiting at the races: in Moonee Valley Racing Club
     Members' Magazine, *On Track*, Spring, 2005.
567. 'very much upset . . .': Haig Diary, March 24, 1918, NLS.
568. 'General Foch or some other determined General . . .': Haig Diary,
     March 25, 1918, NLS.
569. 'He had the appearance of a Commander . . .': Haig Diary, March 26,
     1918, NLS.

569. 'we must not retire a single inch . . .': Foch in Edmonds, *History of the Great War, France and Belgium 1918*, p. 542.
570. 'Well, you've got the job you so much wanted . . .': quoted in Terraine, p. 424.
570. 'most impertinently': Haig Diary, March 26, 1918, NLS.
570. Experiences of Henry Sandilands in letter to James Edmonds, August 14, 1923, PRO.
573. 'I cannot get my men out of this cellar without bloodshed': Rudolph Binding, *A Fatalist at War*, pp. 209–10.
573. 'Here I found General Ruggles-Brise . . .': Gough, p. 315.
574. Haig on Gough: Haig Diary, April 3, 1918, NLS.
574. 'Don't worry about me': Gough, p. 325.
574. 'As regards Gough . . .': Haig to Lady Haig, June 16, 1918, NLS.
576. Refugees near Albert: John Barton, diary entry March 28, 1918, AWM.
576. Millencourt empty: Coutts, diary entry April 7, 1918.
576. French leave everything behind: Roy Brewer, letter May 24, 1918, AWM.

Chapter 38
Page
580. Stolen wine confiscated: C.E.W. Bean, *OH*, Vol V, p. 315.
580. Frank Wormald at Corbie: stories on tape recorded by Billy Wines.
583. 'uselessly entrenched in queer places . . .': C.E.W. Bean, *OH*, Vol V, p. 304.
583. Young officer wants a cavalry charge: C.E.W. Bean, *OH*, Vol V, p. 307.
584. Gilbert Coghill in C.E.W. Bean, *OH*, Vol V, pp. 313 and 319.
585. 'went off his head with the strain': Haig Diary, March 29, 1918, NLS.
585. 'These Tommy divisions . . .': Monash, letter April 4, 1918, Monash Papers, NLA.
587. Bean meets stragglers: C.E.W. Bean, *OH*, Vol V, p. 331–32.
587. John Milne in C.E.W. Bean, *OH*, Vol V, p. 340.
588. Bean and Wilkins at Villers-Bretonneux: C.E.W. Bean, *OH*, Vol V, p. 350.
589. 'Here lies a brave English warrior': C.E.W. Bean, *OH*, Vol V, p. 418.
589. 'the Australians and Canadians . . .': C.E.W. Bean, *OH*, Vol V, p. 417.
589. 'They are the means to the end of strategy . . .': Correlli Barnett, p. 329.

Chapter 39
Page
591. 'Terrible stories were told . . .': William Donovan Joynt, diary entry April 6, 1918, AWM.

591. 'The people of Amiens . . .': Lawrence, p. 150.
593. 'most selfish and obstinate': Haig Diary, April 9, 1918, NLS.
593. 'There is no other course . . .': C.E.W. Bean, *OH*, Vol V, p. 437.
594. Donovan Joynt moves to near Vieux Berguin: Joynt diary, entry April 12–14, 1918, AWM.
595. 'Their officer was very apologetic . . .': Joynt diary, entry April 15, 1918, AWM.
596. 'But what help are all orders to attack . . .': quoted in Asprey, pp. 395–96.
596. 'What Allies to fight with': Haig Diary, April 26, 1918, NLS.
596. 'used by Divisions . . .': Haig Diary, April 18, 1918, NLS.
596. 'living like lords': Lawrence, pp. 160 and 162.
596. 'If this is true . . .': Lawrence, pp. 161.
596. 'piled them up . . .' and 'Gee, it makes a fellow thankful . . .': Lawrence, pp. 161–62.
597. Joynt holding his front: Joynt diary, April 15, 16 and 18, 1918.

Chapter 40

Page
601. 'Nothing of note . . .': Clarence Wallach, privately held diary, entry 27–28 September, 1915.
602. 'awkward situation': C.E.W. Bean, *OH*, Vol III, p. 511.
602. Clarence Wallach's injuries: dossier from National Archives.
602. Death of Neville Wallach: Red Cross report.
603. 'a most glorious house': Elliott, letter April 11, 1918.
604. Elliott's edict: C.E.W. Bean, Vol V, p. 550fn.
604. 'Eighty – that is really a decent number': Floyd Gibbons, *The Red Knight of Germany*, p. 363.
606. 'For two days companies of infantry . . .': C.E.W. Bean, *OH*, Vol V, p. 540.
607. 'enormous and terrifying iron pillbox': C.E.W. Bean, *OH*, Vol V, p. 552.
608. 'All British troops . . .': C.E.W. Bean, *OH*, Vol V, p. 549.
609. 'I can't be sure of it': C.E.W. Bean, *OH*, Vol V, p. 572.
609. Glasgow and Heneker: C.E.W. Bean, *OH*, Vol V, p. 574–5.
610. 'Such a day – I never want to see any more like it . . .': Whinfield diary, April 24, 1918.
610. 'There were houses burning . . .': Downing, p. 117.
610. 'Into the bastards, boys.': C.E.W. Bean, *OH*, Vol V, p. 603.
611. The Australians 'killed and killed . . .': Downing, p. 119.
611. A more explicit letter courtesy of Downing's sons: William, John, David and the late James.

612. 'The Monument is your goal . . .': C.E.W. Bean, *OH*, Vol V, p. 580.
612. 'Carry out the order . . .': C.E.W. Bean, *OH*, Vol V, p. 583.
613. Friendly fire: C.E.W. Bean, *OH*, Vol V, p. 583.
614. 'No prisoners . . .': C.E.W. Bean, *OH*, Vol V, p. 590.
614. Birdwood congratulates Elliott: letter, April 28, 1918, AWM.
615. 'the brilliant idea of the III Corps . . .': Ellis, p. 302.
615. 'Our people have had very trying experience . . .': Talbot Hobbs, diary entry April 27, 1918, AWM.
615. 'It will ever be remembered . . .': G. Grogan, 'Villers-Bretonneux April 24, 1918', *Reveille*, August, 1936.
616. 'I can't rhapsodise . . .': Whinfield diary, April 25, 26, 28 and 30, 1918.
616. Charlie Stokes in Allan Blankfield and Robin Corfield, *Never Forget Australia*, p. 70.
618. Dr Levit's death: in Martin Gilbert, *First World War*, p. 419.

Chapter 41

Page

619. 'from his first word . . .': Bean on White: C.E.W. Bean, *Two Men I Knew*, p. 3.
620. Bean's reaction to news on Monash: C.E.W. Bean, *OH*, Vol VI, p. 185.
620. 'There was immediately a great consternation . . .': Bean Diary, May 17, 1918, AWM.
621. White 'universally considered greatest . . .': Geoffrey Serle, *John Monash: A Biography*, p. 322.
621. 'very fine and typical . . .': Eric Edgerton, diary entry January 12, 1918.
621. 'The villages around here are pitiful . . .': Edgerton, diary entry May 1, 1918.
622. 'Had they talked to ordinary people . . .': Robert Asprey, p. 404.
623. 'Retreat?': quoted in Asprey, p. 423.
624. Monash's letters to Vic on the size of his corps, his Rolls-Royce and his château: Cutlack, letters May 31, June 25 and August 14, 1918.
624. Bean convinces Murdoch that White should be corps commander: C.E.W. Bean, *OH*, Vol VI, p. 197, and in *Two Men I Knew*, p. 172.
624. 'who believed that their views . . .': C.E.W. Bean, *OH*, Vol VI, p. 197fn.
624. Murdoch cable to Hughes: May 20, 1918, AWM.
624. 'strong unanimous view': Serle, p. 322.
625. 'the designer of the new': Corfield, p. 151.
625. Bean believed he was stopping a 'tragic mistake': C.E.W. Bean, *Two Men I Knew*, p. 170.

626. 'irresponsible pressman': Serle, 323.
626. Bean changes his mind on Monash: Bean Diary, June I, 1918, AWM.
626. Birdwood to Munro-Ferguson: letter May 27, 1918, Novar Papers, NLA. Murdoch to Monash: letter May 21, 1918, Monash Papers, NLA. Monash to Vic: letter May 31, 1918. Monash Papers, NLA.
627. Bean to White: letter June 26, 1918, Bean Papers, AWM.
627. 'to regard me with suspicion . . .': Murdoch to Monash, June 6, 1918, Monash Papers, NLA.
627. 'It is a poor compliment . . .': Monash to Birdwood, but not sent, Monash Papers, AWM.
627. 'Monash is a man of very ordinary ideals . . .': Bean Diary, June 16, 1918.
628. Birdwood to Murdoch: Bean Diary, June 10, 1918, AWM.
628. 'Of course, he can do it much more ably than I': Serle, p. 325.
628. 'a mischievous and persistent villain': Rawlinson in Birdwood Papers, letter June 27, 1918, AWM.
628. Monash letter to Vic: Cutlack, June 25, 1918.
629. 'if the conspirators . . .': letter to Monash, Monash Papers, AWM.
629. White rebukes Murdoch: C.E.W. Bean, *Two Men I Knew*, p. 173.
630. 'Then as to yourself . . .': White to Elliott, letter May 22, 1918, AWM.
630. 'supersession': Ross McMullin, *Pompey Elliott*, p. 453.
630. 'So much for our high-intentioned . . .': C.E.W. Bean, *Two Men I Knew*, p. 173.
631. 'It is a great nuisance . . .': Monash letter to Vic, June 25, 1918, Monash Papers, NLA.
631. 'It is perhaps the outstanding case . . .': Serle, p. 328.

Chapter 42

Page

634. 'He was so badly damaged . . .': courtesy of Bruce Mellor, and also Red Cross report.
635. Five Davey brothers: *Bulletin*, August 29, 1918.
637. 'These Yanks view things . . .': Rule, p. 131.
638. 'There is a great feeling of comradeship . . .': Edgerton, diary entry June 15, 1918.
638. 'The swing of them . . .': C.E.W. Bean, *OH*, Vol VI, p. 261.
639. 'The troops were going to count them out . . .': Adcock, p. 249 and 250.
639. 'seemed wrapped up in the men . . .': C.E.W. Bean, *OH*, Vol VI, p. 273.
640. 'Well, I haven't met a single one of them . . .': Bean Diary, June 14, 1918, AWM.

640. Monash and Rawlinson: C.E.W. Bean, *OH*, Vol VI, p. 279.
641. 'I find this occupation . . .': Monash, letter July 4, 1918.
642. Australians killed 'right and left' here: C.E.W. Bean, *OH*, Vol VI, p. 290.
643. 'Do you think Fitzroy'll beat Carlton . . .': C.E.W Bean, *OH*, Vol VI, p. 300.
643. 'When I yelled out . . .': Rule, p. 133.
644. 'What a harvest for our boys . . .': Rule, p. 134.
645. 'standing in those unmistakable . . .': C.E.W. Bean, *OH*, Vol VI, p. 306.
645. 'Never have I seen . . .': Edgerton, diary entry July 7, 1918.
645. Poor lot of prisoners: C.E.W. Bean, *OH*, Vol VI, p. 327.
646. Clemenceau's speech in C.E.W. Bean, *OH*, Vol VI, p. 335.
646. Race meeting at Allonville: A.W. Hyman, 'An Australian Race Meeting in France', *Reveille*, July, 1931.
647. 'I'm all right – get the badly wounded boys out': C.E.W. Bean, *OH*, Vol VI, p. 110fn.

Chapter 43
Page
649. 'a mastery over the enemy . . .': C.E.W. Bean, *OH*, Vol VI, p. 479.
651. 'orchestral composition': General Sir John Monash, *Australian Victories in France in 1918*, p. 56.
651. Battle of firepower: Prior and Wilson, *Command on the Western Front*, p. 314.
653. 'no football, no wandering, but sleep': John Monash, battle notes, August 3, 1918, AWM.
653. 'deadly anxious not to do anything . . .': White to Bean, June 27, 1935, White Papers, AWM.
654. Borden: 'largely due to lack of foresight . . .': Imperial War Cabinet, June 13, 1918.
654. 'wasted for want of proper leadership . . .': Billy Hughes quoted in Grigg, p. 541.
655. 'all was right behind them': C.E.W. Bean, *OH*, Vol VI, p. 525.
656. 'Sir, I have nothing to do . . .': Serle, p. 346.
656. Donald Coutts couldn't see ten yards: diary entry August 8, 1918.
656. David Whinfield said he couldn't see five yards: diary entry August 8, 1918.
657. German officer 'gone through' by a 'horde of drunken Australians': C.E.W. Bean, *OH*, Vol VI, p. 539fn.
657. John Barton, diary, p. 62, AWM.
657. 'so we merely directed them back . . .': Carre Riddell, letter August 27, 1918.

658. 'Not shoot, not kill me . . .': James Armitage, diary entry, p. 26, AWM.

659. 'As we watched during a halt': Barton, diary entry p. 62, AWM.

659. 'It was all a most wonderful sight . . .': Carre Riddell, letter August 27, 1918.

659. 'Round and round they flew . . .': Percy Lucas, 'The Victory of August 8, 1918', *Reveille*, August, 1936.

660. 'There were few of the usual depressing . . .': Downing, pp. 142 and 145.

661. Story of E.J. Rollings: C.E.W. Bean, *OH*, Vol VI, p. 578.

661. 'all over their anatomy': Monash, letter August 15, 1918.

662. 'neither morally nor materially . . .': John Terraine, p. 454.

663. 'the British had to have a success': White in C.E.W. Bean, *Two Men I Knew*, p. 178.

663. 'I was told of deeds of glorious valour . . .': Ludendorff, Vol II, p. 683.

664. 'the situation had developed more favourably . . .': Haig Diary, August 8, 1918, NLS.

664. 'You do not know what the Australians . . .': John Hetherington, *Blamey*, p. 47.

665. Harington letter to James Edmonds, December 15, 1932, Bean Papers, AWM.

665. Pompey Elliot shot in the buttock: Ross McMullin, p. 468.

667. 'an appalling sense of *déjà vu*': Prior and Wilson, p. 330.

667. 'We took 150 prisoners . . .': Whinfield diary, August 9, 1918.

669. 'The fields are covered . . .': Eric Edgerton, letter July 22, 1918.

669. Edgerton thanks his sister for a pair of socks: letter July 25, 1918.

670. Sid Horton at Edgerton's funeral: letter August 14, 1918.

670. Sid Horton remembers Edgerton in 'A Pal's Appreciation', written in the 1930s.

670. Battalion commander upset by Edgerton's death: Coutts, diary entries August 11 and 12, 1918.

670. Unrest in the German army: Edmonds, *History of the Great War 1918*, pp. 149 and 439.

670. Kaiser says war must be ended: Edmonds, p. 140.

Chapter 44

Page

674. Haig 'had at last divined the manner of proceeding . . .': Trevor Wilson, *The Myriad Faces of War: Britain and the Great War; 1914–1918*, p. 595.

675. Churchill believed war would continue till mid-1919: Haig Diary, August 21, 1918, NLS.

675. 'Risks which a month ago . . .': Haig Diary, August 22, 1918, NLS.

675. Lawrence McCarthy in C.E.W. Bean, *OH*, Vol VI, p. 742.

676. 'Let's go and have a look': Joynt in C.E.W. Bean, *OH*, Vol VI, p. 745.

676. Joynt at Plateau Wood: Joynt diary, August 23, 1918, AWM.

677. Joynt wounded and taken to England: diary, August 24, 1918, AWM.

678. 'These are great days . . .': *Times* correspondent report, August 26, 1918, in John Terraine, *To Win a War*, p. 127.

679. 'and advantage will be taken . . .': Monash adding to Rawlinson's orders, Monash Papers, AWM.

681. Cecil Healy: Harry Gordon, "From Track to Trenches', *Weekend Australian*, April 25, 1998.

681. A plan 'vaguely forming': Monash, *Australian Victories in France 1918*, p. 176.

682. 'So you think you're going to take . . .': Rawlinson in Monash, *Australian Victories . . .*, p. 181.

683. 'Most of us are a dilapidated-looking lot . . .': Robert Mactier, letter May 3, 1918, AWM.

684. Robert Mactier goes on leave, greets General Birdwood, is gassed and made a company runner: letters September, 1917, December 30, 1917, July 25, 1918 and August 22, 1918, and Tony Ford, *Our Heroes: Tatura's WWI Roll of Honour*, p. 64.

685. 'a regular old-fashioned charge': C.E.W. Bean, *OH*, Vol VI, p. 815.

686. 'He wore his monocle . . .': Maxwell. p. 217.

686. 'As . . . I was dressing . . .': Rawlinson diary entry August 31, 1918.

686. 'a magnificent feat of arms': Edmonds, *History of the Great War 1918*, p. 374fn.

687. 'Casualties no longer matter': C.E.W. Bean, *OH*, Vol VI, p. 822.

688. 'There was a big day in London . . .': Roy Brewer, letter August 4, 1918, AWM.

688. 'We were kept going continuously . . .': Coutts, diary entry August 31, 1918.

689. 'he tried to speak to me . . .': Red Cross report on Robert Mactier, December 17, 1918.

689. Letter from Mactier's father in Tony Ford, *Our Heroes: Tatura's WWI Roll of Honour*, p. 65.

689. Mont St Quentin looked 'impregnable': W.J. Harvey, *The Red and White Diamond: Authorised History of the Twenty-fourth Battalion, A.I.F.*, p. 277.

691. Lyall Howard diary entries March 30–May 10, August 30 and September 3, 1918.

692. 'There were machine guns everywhere': Coutts, diary entries September 5 and 7–17, 1918.

693. Charles Repington interview with Foch in John Terraine, *To Win a War*, p. 143.
694. 'He had only worked, worried . . .': in W. Foerster, *De Feldherr Ludendorff*, p. 73.

Chapter 45
Page

695. Monash makes an impression on English journalists: Arthur Doyle, *The British Campaign in Europe*, p. 104, and Arthur O'Conner, *Weekly Despatch*, June 18, 1948.
696. 'a little footsore': C.E.W. Bean, *OH*, Vol VI, p. 875.
697. David Whinfield resting near Péronne: diary entry, September 14, 1918.
698. Paton and MacArthur: quoted in William Manchester, *American Caesar*, p. 115.
699. Germans asking 'Which way?': C.E.W. Bean, *OH*, Vol VI, p. 906.
699. Refusal to fight: C.E.W. Bean, *OH*, Vol VI, p. 983.
701. 'I have done a thing . . .': N.G. McNicol, *The Thirty Seventh: History of the Thirty Seventh Battalion A.I.F.*, p. 252.
701. '(Colonel Scanlan) ordered slope arms . . .': Whinfield diary, September 26, 1918.
702. Disbandment of the 60th Battalion: McMullin pp. 489–90.
703. 'wild Irish and German Catholics': R. Ferrell, *The Autobiography of Harry S. Truman*, p. 46.
703. 'I never heard a man cuss so well . . .': Laurence Stallings, *The Story of the Doughboys*, pp. 133–34.
704. 'revolution from above': in Asprey, p. 468.

Chapter 46
Page

705. 'I am pretty sure . . .': Rawlinson diary, September 16, 1918.
710. 'It was contrary to the policy . . .': Monash, *Australian Victories in France 1918*, p. 251.
710. Monash diary entry, September 27, 1918.
712. 'he is a good, honest fellow . . .': Haig Diary, September 28, 1918, NLS.
712. Will Palstra shoots down his first plane: Palstra, p. 157.
715. 'I could not have hoped . . .' and 'The Americans appear . . .': Rawlinson diary, September 29, 1918.
716. 'Well, you see what I expected . . .': Bean Diary, September, 1918, AWM.
716. 'We have had the report . . .': Operational Records, 1.10 pm, September 29, 1918.

717. 'Boiling down factory': C.E.W. Bean, 'Corpse Factory: Short-Lived Mystery', *Reveille*, May, 1930.
719. Norman Dalgleish: letter January 18, 1919, AWM and McMullin, p. 494.
721. Maxwell in the Beaurevoir Line: Maxwell, pp. 225–28.
722. Wounded Australian wrapped in German overcoat: Maxwell, p. 229.
722. Extra rum ration: Maxwell, p. 230–31.

Chapter 47
Page

725. Harry Fletcher and Austin Mahony the night before Montbrehain: Harvey, *The Red and White Diamond*, p. 293.
726. Information on Fletcher and Mahony: from family sources and NAA files.
727. 'After washing about half an hour . . .': privately held letter, January 1, 1916.
728. Norman Wilkinson in W. Carne, *History of the 6th Machine Gun Company*, p. 376.
729. John Blankenberg in C.E.W. Bean, *OH*, Vol VI, p. 1037fn.
730. Old woman 'hoisted her petticoats': Maxwell, p. 232.
730. Norman Wilkinson in hospital: Norman Wilkinson, *Travel Trimmings*, p. 188.
731 'Troops more fatigued . . .': Ellis, p. 380.

Chapter 48
Page

736. 'You must use it . . .': in G. Ritter, *The Sword and the Sceptre: The Problem of Militarism in Germany*, Vol IV, p. 361.
737. 'military masters' and 'monarchial autocrats': C.E.W. Bean, *OH*, Vol VI, p. 1050.
737. 'When our enemies know that no sacrifice . . .': Ludendorff, Vol II, p. 761.
738. 'Excellency, I must remind you . . .': in Asprey, p. 484.
738. 'produce a desire for revenge': Haig to Lady Haig, October 26, 1918, NLS.
739. 'to look for death': Wheeler-Bennett, p. 186.
739. 'because of a few hundred Jews . . .': in Martin Gilbert, *First World War*, p. 490.
741. Meeting German delegates: Marshal Foch, *Memoirs* (trans Col. T. Bentley Mott), p. 546.
742. Armistice request: Foch, p. 546.
743. Bernard Freyberg before the Armistice: in Martin Gilbert, *Winston Churchill*, Vol IV, *Companion Part I*, pp. 416–17.

745. 'it was so quiet . . .': Harry Truman, letter November 11, 1918.
745. 'Armistice signed': Lyall Howard diary, November 11, 1918.
746. 'The city blazed with light . . .': Maxwell, p. 236–37.
746. 'Everyone went mad . . .': Rupert Baldwin diary, November 12, 1918.
746. 'I was walking down the road . . .': Coutts diary, November 11, 1918.
746. 'When it was on . . .': Charles Rea, letter December 2, 1918, AWM.
746. 'Mick' Moon at a football match: John Lahey, 'The Last of the Anzacs', *Age*, April 21, 1984.
747. 'We had two victories today . . .': D. Cleary in Bill Gammage, *The Broken Years*, p. 265.
747. William McBeath: *Diaries of Graves Detachment Digger*, letter April 19, 1919, AWM.

AFTERMATH

749. From a speech given by Winston Churchill, December 16, 1918.

Chapter 49
Page
751. 'Ah, they're sending babies': Tony Stephens, *The Last Anzacs: Gallipoli 1915*, p. 60.
751. Charles Johnson: privately held family papers.
753. Sergeant Andrew Muir refusing to drink the water: Muir family source.
754. Maxwell finds civilian life difficult: Maxwell, p. 1.
754. Gordon Bennett seeking work: Legg, p. 142.
755. 'dreams abandoned': Bill Gammage in *The Great War, Gains and Losses: ANZAC and Empire* (ed Craig Wilcox), p. 6.
755. 'all those talented people . . .': Geoffrey Blainey, *A Shorter History of Australia*, p. 159.
756. 'the grey years': Michael McKernan, *The Australian People and the Great War*, p. 201.
757. 'If I do, it is this . . .': Wilson in Scott, p. 786fn.
757. Hughes and Wilson: Scott, p. 787fn.
758. 'must pay to the uttermost farthing . . .': quoted in Martin Gilbert, *The Treaty of Versailles*, in *The History of World War I* (ed A.J.P. Taylor), p. 274.
760. 'The Treaty of Versailles . . .': Martin Gilbert, *History of World War I*, p. 276.
763. Churchill on Haig: Winston Churchill, *Great Contemporaries*.
766. 'It's the orders you disobey . . .': Manchester, p. 101.

767. Foch and Babe Ruth: Red Smith (ed), *Press Box*, p. 44.
768. Monash could have replaced Haig: Lloyd George, Vol VI, p. 3424.
769. Monash's doll's house: Monash family sources.
769. Geoffrey Serle's entry on John Monash in *The Dictionary of Biography.*
770. 'The supercession . . .': Elliott letter to Talbot Hobbs, July 23, 1929.
772. 'I have had a damned long run . . .': Thomas, letter March 12, 1918.
773. 'You had to draw the line somewhere': quoted in Donald Horne, *Billy Hughes*, p. 13.
773. 'We should be careful . . .': Desmond Zwar, *In Search of Keith Murdoch*, p. 86.

Select bibliography

BOOKS

Adcock, W.F., *Genuine War Letters*.
Aitken, Sir Max, *Canada in Flanders: The Official Story of the Canadian Expeditionary Force, Vol I*, Hodder and Stoughton, 1916.
Aiton, Doug, and Lane, Terry, *The First Century: Australia's Federal Elections since Federation*, Information Australia, 2000.
Arminius (trans. by Gerald Griffin), *From Serajevo to the Rhine*, Hutchinson, 1933.
Asprey, Robert, *The German High Command at War*, Warner Books, 1994.
Asquith, Raymond, (ed John Joliffe), *Life and Letters*, Century Hutchinson, 1987.
Austin, Ron, *As Rough As Bags: The History of the 6th Battalion, 1st A.I.F, 1914–1919*, R.J. and S.P. Austin, 1992.
—— *Our Dear Old Battalion: The Story of the 7th Battalion, A.I.F., 1914–1919*, Slouch Hat Publications, 2004.
—— *Cobbers in Khaki: The History of the 8th Battalion, 1914–1918*, Slouch Hat Publications, 1997.
Australian Dictionary of Biography, Melbourne University Press.
Baker-Carr, Brigadier-General C.D., *From Chauffeur to Brigadier*, Benn, 1930.
Barker, Pat, *Regeneration*, Viking, 1991.
Barnett, Correlli, *The Swordbearers: Studies in Supreme Command in the First World War*, Eyre & Spottiswoode, 1963.
Barton, Peter, *The Battlefields of the First World War: The Unseen Panoramas of the Western Front*, Constable, 2005.
Bassett, Jan, *Guns and Brooches: Australian Army Nursing from the Boer War to the Gulf War*, Oxford University Press, 1992.

Bean, C.E.W., *Official History of Australia in the War 1914–18, Vol I and Vol II, The Story of Anzac*, Angus and Robertson, 1940.
—— *Official History of Australia in the War 1914–18, Vol III, The A.I.F in France 1916*, Angus and Robertson, 1940.
—— *Official History of Australia in the War 1914–18, Vol IV, The A.I.F. in France 1917*, Angus and Robertson, 1933.
—— *Official History of Australia in the War 1914–18, Vol V and Vol VI, The A.I.F. in France 1918*, Angus and Robertson, 1937 and 1942.
—— *Two Men I Knew*, Angus and Robertson, 1957.
—— *Anzac to Amiens*, Penguin, 1993.
—— *With the Flagship in the South*, Werner Laurie, 1915.
—— *On the Wool Track*, Hodder & Stoughton, 1916.
Bean, C.E.W., and Gullett, H.S., *Official History of Australia in the War, Vol XII, Photographic Record of the War*, Angus and Robertson, 1923.
Beaumont, Joan (ed), *Australia's War 1914–1918*, Allen & Unwin, 1995.
Birdwood, Field-Marshal Lord William, *Khaki and Gown*, Ward, Lock & Co, 1941.
Bishop, Alan, and Little, M. (eds), *Letters From A Lost Generation – First World War Letters of Vera Brittain and Four Friends*, Brown and Company, 1998.
Blainey, Geoffrey, *A Short History of the 20th Century*, Penguin, 2005.
—— *Black Kettle and Full Moon*, Penguin, 2003.
—— *A Shorter History of Australia*, Heinemann, 1994.
—— *A Short History of the World*, Penguin, 2000.
—— *The Causes of War*, Sun Books, 1998.
Blake, Robert, *The Private Papers of Douglas Haig 1914–1919*, Eyre & Spottiswoode, 1952.
Blankfield, Allan, and Corfield, Robin S., *Never Forget Australia: Australia and Villers-Bretonneux 1918–1993*, The Villers-Bretonneux 75th Anniversary Pilgrimage Project Committee, 1994.
Blunden, Edmund, *Undertones of War*, Penguin, 1937.
Bond, Brian, *The Unquiet Western Front*, Cambridge University Press, 2002.
Brown, Malcolm, *The Imperial War Museum Book of the First World War*, Sidgwick & Jackson, 1991.
Bull, Stephen, *Aspects of War:Trench Warfare*, PRC Publishing, 2003.
Burne, Jerome (ed), *Chronicles of the World*, Chronicle Australasia, 1991.
Butler, Col. A.G., *Official History of the Australian Army Medical Services 1914–1918, Vol I–III*, AWM, 1938
Carlyon, Les, *Gallipoli*, Macmillan, 2001.
Carne, Lt W., *In Good Company: Being a Record of the 6th Machine Gun Company, A.I.F. 1915–1919*, John Burridge, 1937.

Carver, Lord Michael (Field-Marshal), *Twentieth Century Warriors*, Weidenfeld and Nicolson, 1987.

Cecil, Hugh, and Liddle, Peter, *At the Eleventh Hour*, Leo Cooper, 1998.

Charlton, Peter, *Pozières 1916*, Methuen Haynes, 1986.

Charteris, Brig-Gen. John, *Field-Marshal Earl Haig*, Cassell, 1929.

Churchill, Winston, *The World Crisis 1911–1918, 4 Vols*, Odhams, 1938.

—— *Great Contemporaries*, W.W. Norton and Company, 1990.

Clark, Alan, *The Donkeys*, Pimlico, 2000.

Clark, C.M.H., *A History of Australia, Vol VI*, MUP, 1987.

Coates, John, *An Atlas of Australia's Wars*, Oxford University Press, 2001.

Cooper, Ethel, (ed Decie Denholm), *Behind the Lines: One Woman's War 1914–18*, Jill Norman & Hobhouse, 1982.

Corfield, Robin, *Don't forget me, cobber*, Corfield and Company, 2000.

Cull, W. Ambrose, *At All Costs*, Australian Authors' Agency.

Cutlack, F.M. (ed), *War Letters of General Monash*, Angus and Robertson, 1935.

—— *Official History of Australia in the War 1914–18, Vol VIII, The Australian Flying Corps*, Angus and Robertson, 1923.

Dennis, Peter, et al, *The Oxford Companion to Australian Military History*, Oxford University Press, 1995.

Desegneaux, Henri, *A French Soldier's War Diary 1914–18*, Elmford Press, 1975.

Devine, W., *The Story of a Battalion (History of the 48th)*, Melville & Mullen, 1919.

De Vries, Susanna, *Heroic Australian Women in War*, HarperCollins, 2004.

Downing, Walter, *To the Last Ridge*, Duffy & Snellgrove, 1998

Dyer, Geoff, *The Missing of the Somme*, Hamish Hamilton, 1994.

'Edmonds, Charles' (Charles Carrington), *A Subaltern's War*, Icon Books, 1964.

Edmonds, Brig-Gen. Sir James, *History of the Great War: Military Operations, France and Belgium 1916, Vol I*, IWM and Battery Press, 1932.

—— *History of the Great War: Military Operations, France and Belgium, Vol II, 1917*, IWM and Battery Press, 1948.

—— *History of the Great War: Military Operations, France and Belgium, Vol IV, 1918*, IWM and Battery Press, 1947.

Eisenhower, John S.D. with Eisenhower, Joanne Thompson, *Yanks*, Simon & Schuster, 2001.

Ellis, Capt A.D., *The Story of the Fifth Australian Division*, Hodder and Stoughton, 1920.

Ellis, John, *Eye-Deep in Hell: Trench Warfare in World War 1*, John Hopkins University Press, 1989.

Evans, Martin Marix, *1918: The Year of Victories*, Arcturus Publishing, 2002.

Evans, Michael and Ryan, Alan, *From Breitenfeld to Baghdad*, Land Warfare Studies Centre, Working Paper, 122.

Falls, Capt. Cyril, *History of the Great War: Military Operations, France and Belgium 1917, Vol I*, IWM and Battery Press.

Falls, Cyril, *The Great War*, Perigee Books, 1959.

Farrar-Hockley, A.H., *The Somme*, Pan Books, 1983.

Foch, Ferdinand, *The Memoirs of Marshal Foch* (trans. T. Mott), Heinemann, 1931.

Ford, Tony, *Our Heroes – Tatura's World War 1 Roll of Honour*, 2003.

Foy, Michael, and Barton, Brian, *The Easter Rising*, Sutton Publishing, 2000.

Franki George, and Slatyer, Clyde, *Mad Harry: Australia's Most Decorated Soldier*, Kangaroo Press, 2003.

Franks, Norman, and Bennett, Alan, *The Red Baron's Last Flight: A Mystery Investigated*, Macmillan, 1998.

Fuller, J.F.C., *Decisive Battles of the Western World, Vol 3*, Eyre & Spottiswoode, 1956.

Gammage, Bill, *The Broken Years*, Penguin, 1975.

Gaunson, A.B., *College Street Heroes: Old Sydneians in the Great War*, Sydney Grammar School Press, 1998.

'GSO', *G.H.Q.*, Philip Allen & Co, 1920.

General Staff, *Notes on Trench Warfare for Infantry Officers*, His Majesty's Stationery Office, 1916.

Gilbert, Martin, *First World War Atlas*, Weidenfeld and Nicolson, London, 1970.

—— *First World War*, HarperCollins, 1995.

—— *The Routledge Atlas of the First World War*, Routledge, 2002.

—— *Winston S. Churchill, Vol IV, Companion Part 1*, Heinemann, 1977.

Gleichen, Lord Edward (ed), *Chronology of the Great War 1914–18*, Greenhill Books, 2000.

Gough, Sir Hubert, *The Fifth Army*, Hodder and Stoughton, 1931.

Graves, Robert, *Goodbye to All That*, Folio Society, 1981.

Griffith, Paddy, *Battle Tactics of the Western Front: The British Army's Art of Attack 1916–18*, Yale University Press, 1996.

Grigg, John, *Lloyd George: The Young Lloyd George*, HarperCollins, 1997.

—— *Lloyd George: The People's Champion 1902–1911*, HarperCollins, 1997.

—— *Lloyd George: From Peace to War 1912–1916*, HarperCollins, 1997

—— *Lloyd George: War Leader 1916–1918*, Allen Lane, 2002.

Groom, Winston, *A Storm In Flanders*, Cassell, 2002.

Hamilton, John, *Goodbye Cobber, God Bless You*, Pan Macmillan, 2004.

Harrison, Charles Yale, *Generals Die in Bed*, Penguin, 2003.

Harvey, Sgt W.J., *The Red and White Diamond: Authorised History of the Twenty-fourth Battalion, A.I.F.*, Alexander McCubbin, 1920.

Hatwell, Jeff, *No Ordinary Determination: Percy Black and Harry Murray of the First A.I.F.*, Fremantle Arts Centre Press, 2005.

Haythornthwaite, Philip J., *The World War One Source Book*, Brockhampton Press, 1998.

Helprin, Mark, *A Soldier of the Great War*, Arrow, 1993.

Hetherington, John, *Blamey: Controversial Soldier*, Australian War Memorial, 1973.

Hibberd, Dominic, *Wilfred Owen: The Last Year*, Constable, 1992.

Hinckfuss, Harold, *Memories of a Signaller: The First World War 1914–18*, University of Queensland Press, 1983.

Holmes, Richard, *The Western Front*, BBC Worldwide Ltd, 1999.

—— (ed), *The Oxford Companion to Military History*, Oxford University Press, 2001.

Horne, Donald, *Billy Hughes*, Black Inc, 2000.

Horner, David, *The Gunners: A History of Australian Artillery*, Allen & Unwin, 1995.

—— *The Commanders*, Allen & Unwin, 1984.

Hurley, Frank, *Hurley at War*, Fairfax Library, 1986.

Hyatt, Albert, *The Military Career of Sir Arthur Currie*, 1985, AWM MSS1088.

Inglis, Ken, *Sacred Places*, Miengunyah Press, 1999.

Johnson, Paul, *Napoleon*, Weidenfeld & Nicolson, 2002.

Johnson, Carl and Barnes, Andrew (eds), *Jacka's Mob: A Narrative of the Great War*, by Edgar John Rule, Military Melbourne, 1999.

Joynt, W.D., VC, *Saving the Channel Ports 1918*, Wren Publishing, 1975.

Kearney, Robert, *Silent Voices: The Story of the 10th Battalion*, New Holland, 2005.

Keatinge, M.B.B., *War Book of the Third Pioneer Battalion*, Specialty Press.

Keegan, John, *The First World War*, Hutchinson, 1998.

—— *The Face of Battle*, Pimlico, 1998.

Keegan, John, and Wheatcroft, Andrew, *Who's Who in Military History*, Routledge, 2002.

Kelly, Paul, *The End of Certainty*, Allen & Unwin, 1992.

Kershaw, Ian, *Hitler 1889–1936: Hubris*, Penguin, 2001.

Knightley, Phillip, *The First Casualty*, Harcourt Brace Jovanovich, 1975.

Kyle, Roy, (ed Bryce Courtenay), *An Anzac's Story*, Penguin, 2003.

Laffin, John, *Guide to Australian Battlefields of the Western Front 1916–1918*, Kangaroo Press and Australian War Memorial, 1992.

—— *The Battle of Hamel*, Kangaroo Press, 1999.

—— *A Western Front Companion 1914–1918*, Sutton Publishing, 1997.

Lawrence, Cyril, (ed Peter Yule), *Sergeant Lawrence Goes to France*, MUP, 1987.

Legg, Frank, *The Gordon Bennett Story*, Angus and Robertson, 1965.

Liddle, Peter, *Passchendaele in Perspective: The Third Battle of Ypres*, Leo Cooper, 1997.

Likeman, Lt-Col. Robert, *Men of the Ninth: A History of the Ninth Australian Field Ambulance 1916–1994*, Slouch Hat Publications, 2003.

Lloyd George, David, *War Memoirs, 6 Vols*, Odhams, 1933-6.

Ludendorff, General E., *My War Memories 1914–1918*, Hutchinson, 1919.

MacArthur, Douglas, *Reminiscences*, McGraw Hill, 1964.

McCarthy, Chris, *The Somme: The Day-to-Day Account*, Cassell, 1993.

Macdonald, Lyn, *1914–1918: Voices and Images of the Great War*, Michael Joseph, 1988.

—— *They Called It Passchendaele*, Penguin, 1993.

Macdougall, A.K., *War Letters of General Sir John Monash*, Duffy & Snellgrove, 2002.

McKernan, Michael, *The Australian People and the Great War*, Collins, 1984.

Mackenzie, K.W., *The Story of the 17th Battalion*, 1946.

McMullin, Ross, *Pompey Elliott*, Scribe Publications, 2002.

McNicol, N.G., *The Thirty Seventh: History of the Thirty Seventh Battalion, A.I.F.*, Modern Printing Co, 1936.

McNicol, Ronald, *The Royal Australian Engineers 1902 to 1919: Making and Breaking*, Committee of the Royal Australian Engineers, Canberra, 1979.

Malthus, Cecil, *Armentières and the Somme*, Reed, 2002.

Manchester, William, *American Caesar: Douglas MacArthur 1880–1964*, Dell, 1978.

Manning, Frederic, *The Middle Parts of Fortune*, Text, 2000.

Martin, Christopher, *Battle of the Somme*, Wayland, Sussex, 1987.

Masefield, John, *The Battle of the Somme*, Cedric Chivers Ltd, 1968.

Maxwell, Joseph, VC, *Hell's Bells and Mademoiselles*, Angus and Robertson, 1941.

Middlebrook, Martin, *The Kaiser's Battle*, Penguin, 2000.

—— *The First Day of the Somme*, Penguin, 2001.

Miles, Captain Wilfrid, *History of the Great War: Military Operations, France and Belguim 1916, Vol II*, IWM and Battery Press, 1938.

Mitford, Nancy, *The Sun King*, Hamish Hamilton, 1966.

Monash, General Sir John, *The Australian Victories in France in 1918*, IWM and Battery Press, 1993.

Moore, John, *Morshead*, Haldane, 1976.

Morris, Eric, et al, *Weapons & Warfare of the 20th Century*, Octopus Books, 1976.

Mosier, John, *The Myth of the Great War*, Profile Books, 2002.

Murdoch, Walter, *Alfred Deakin*, Constable, 1923.

Nasht, Simon, *The Last Explorer: Hubert Wilkins – Australia's Unknown Hero*, Hodder, 2005.

Neillands, Robin, *The Great War Generals*, Robinson, 1999.

Newton, L.M., *The Story of the Twelfth*, J. Walch & Sons, 1925.

Nicholson, G.W.L., *Official History of the Canadian Army in the First World War*, 1962.

Nicholson, G. Harvey (ed), *First Hundred Years: Scotch College Melbourne 1851–1951*, 1952.

Northcliffe, Lord, *At the War*, Hodder and Stoughton, 1916.

North-Eastern Historical Society, *Worthy of Mention*, 1992.

Nott, David, *Somewhere in France*, Harper Perennial, 1996.

Palmer, Alan, *The Kaiser*, Weidenfeld and Nicolson, 1978.

Parsons, I.M. (ed), *Men Who March Away: Poems of the First World War*, Heinemann, 1987.

Partridge, Eric, *Frank Honywood, Private: A Personal Record of the 1914–1918 War*, Introduced and annotated by Geoffrey Serle, MUP, 1987.

Pedersen, P.A., *Monash as Military Commander*, MUP, 1992.

Perry, F.W., *Order of Battle of Divisions: Part 5a*, Ray Westlake Military Books, 1992.

Perry, Roland, *Monash: The Outsider Who Won a War*, Random House, 2004.

Persico, Joseph E., *11th Month, 11th Day, 11th Hour*, Random House, 2004.

Piggott, Michael, *A Guide to the Personal Family and Official Papers of C.E.W. Bean*, Australian War Memorial, 1983.

Pimlott, John, *The Guinness History of the British Army*, Guinness Publishing, 1993.

Pitt, Barrie, *Great Battles of the 20th Century*, Hamlyn, 1977.

Pope, Stephen, and Elizabeth-Anne Wheal, *Dictionary of the First World War*, Pen & Sword, 2003.

Prior, Robin, and Wilson, Trevor, *Passchendaele: The Untold Story*, Yale University Press, 1996.

—— *The First World War*, Cassell & Co, 2001.

—— *Command on the Western Front: The Military Career of Sir Henry Rawlinson 1914–1918*, Pen & Sword, 2004.

—— *The Somme*, Yale University Press, 2005.

Purdom, C.B. (ed), *Everyman at War*, J.M. Dent & Sons, 1930.

Reed, Paul, *Walking the Somme*, Leo Cooper, 1997.

—— *Walking the Salient*, Leo Cooper, 2001.

Rhodes James, Robert, *A Spirit Undaunted: The Political Role of George VI*, Little, Brown & Co, 1998.

Rice, Grantland, (ed Red Smith), *Press Box*, W.W. Norton & Company, 1976.

Ricketson, Matthew, *The Best Australian Profiles*, Black Inc, 2004.

Robertson, John, *Anzac and Empire*, Hamlyn, 1980.

Robson, L.L., *The First A.I.F.: A Study of its Recruitment 1914–18*, MUP, 1970.

—— *Australia & the Great War*, Macmillan, 1970.

Roze, Anne, *Fields of Memory: A Testimony to the Great War*, Cassell & Co.

Schuler, Phillip, *Australia in Arms*, T. Fisher Unwin, 1916.

Scott, Ernest, *Official History of Australia in the War, Vol XI, Australia During the War*, Angus and Robertson, 1936.

Serle, Geoffrey, *John Monash: A Biography*, MUP, 1985.

Shawcross, William, *Murdoch*, Random House, 1992.

Sheffield, Gary, *The Somme*, Cassell, 2004.

Sloan, Lt-Col. H., *The Purple and Gold – A History of the 30th Battalion*, John Burridge, 1990s.

Souter, Gavin, *Lion and Kangaroo*, Text Publishing, 2000.

Smith, Neil, *The Red and Black Diamond: The History of the 21st Battalion 1915–1918*

Snelling, Stephen, *VCs of the First World War: Gallipoli*, Sutton Publishing, 1999.

Staunton, Anthony, *Victoria Cross: Australia's Finest and the Battles They Fought*, Hardie Grant, 2005.

Stephens, Tony, *The Last Anzacs*, Allen and Kemsley, 1996.

Stevenson, Frances, (ed A.J.P. Taylor), *Lloyd George: A Diary*, Hutchinson, 1971.

Strachan, Huw, *The First World War*, Simon & Schuster, 2003.

Sulzberger, C.L., *The Fall of Eagles*, Crown Publishers, 1977.

Taylor, A.J.P., *The First World War: An Illustrated History*, George Rainbird, 1963.

—— *Revolutions and Revolutionaries*, Hamish Hamilton, 1980.

—— (ed) *History of World War 1*, Macdonald & Co, 1988.

Terraine, John, *The Western Front 1914–18*, Arrow Books, 1970.

—— *To Win a War*, Sidgwick & Jackson, 1978.

—— *White Heat: The New Warfare 1914–18*, Guild Publishing, 1982.

—— *Douglas Haig: The Educated Soldier*, Leo Cooper, 1990.

Thomas, Nigel, *The German Army in World War 1, 1914–18*, Osprey Publishing, 2003.

Thomson, Alistair, *Anzac Memories: Living with the Legend*, Oxford University Press, 1995.

Tilton, May, *The Grey Battalion*, Angus & Robertson, 1934.

Toland, John, *No Man's Land: 1918, The Last Year of the Great War*, Doubleday, 1980.
Travers, Tim, *The Killing Ground: The British Army, the Western Front & the Emergence of Modern War 1900–1918*, Pen & Sword, 2003.
Triplet, William, (ed Robert Ferrell), *A Youth in the Meuse-Argonne*, University of Missouri Press, 2000.
Tuchman, Barbara, *August 1914*, Constable, 1962.
Wanliss, Newton, *The History of the 14th Battalion*, The Arrow Printery, 1929.
Warner, Philip, *Field Marshall Earl Haig*, Cassell & Co, 2001.
Westwell, Ian, *World War 1 Day by Day*, Brown Partworks, 2002.
Wheeler-Bennett, John, *Hindenburg: The Wooden Titan*, Macmillan, 1936.
White, T.A., *The Fighting Thirteenth: The History of the Thirteenth Battalion*.
Wilkinson, Norman, *Travel Trimmings*, Robertson & Mullins.
Williams, John F., *Anzacs, the Media and the Great War*, UNSW Press, 1999.
—— *German Anzacs and the First World War*, UNSW Press, 2003.
Winter, Denis, *Making the Legend: The War Writings of C.E.W. Bean*, University of Queensland Press, 1992.
—— *Death's Men*, Penguin, 1979.
—— *Haig's Command: A Reassessment*, Penguin, 2001.
—— *25th April 1915: The Inevitable Tragedy*, QUP, 1994.
Witkop, Philipp (ed), *German Students' War Letters*, Pine Street Books, 2002.
Wolff, Leon, *In Flanders Fields*, Longmans, 1959.
Woodward, David, *Armies of the World 1854–1914*, Sidgwick & Jackson, 1978.
Wright, Patrick, *Tank*, Faber and Faber, 2001.
Younger, R.M., *Keith Murdoch: Founder of a Media Empire*, HarperCollins, 2003.
Zwar, Desmond, *In Search of Keith Murdoch*, Macmillan, 1980.

ARTICLES

Andrews, E. and Jordan, B.G., 'Hamel', *Journal of the Australian War Memorial*, April 1991, and 'Second Bullecourt revisited: The Australians in France, 3 May 1917, *Journal of the Australian War Memorial*, 1989.
Aarons, Capt. D.S., 'Terrible Tragedy: 16th Bn's Black Day', *Reveille*, April 1933.
A.W.B., 'Vale! "Dolly" Durrant', *Stand-To*, Sep/Oct 1963.
Baker, Mark, 'Schuler's War', the *Age*, April 23, 2005.

Bean, C.E.W., 'Corpse Factory: Short-Lived Mystery', *Reveille*, May 1930, and 'Writing the War History', *Reveille*, June 1933.

Berry, Maj W, 'Sir John Monash: Knighted in Field', *Reveille*, June 1937.

Blamey, Maj-Gen T.A., 'Disliked Show: Sir John Monash's Simple Tastes', *Reveille*, Oct 1931.

Bradby, Pte W.J., 'Polygon Wood and Broodseinde', *Stand-To*, Sept/Oct 1963.

Brown, Maj. Arnold, 'The Old Windmill: Pozières' Tragic Landmark', *Reveille*, Oct 1932.

The *Bulletin* magazine, all issues 1916–1918

Burness, Peter, 'Pozières hell', *Wartime*, Issue 22.

Bruche, Maj-Gen J.H., 'War Memorials: Somme Battles', *Reveille*, Aug 1931.

Brand, Brig-Gen C.H., 'Who Broke the Hindenburg Line? : Many Claims', *Reveille*, April 1933.

Blackburn, Sgt D.W., 'Tank Opens Fire: Shock for 14th Battalion', *Reveille*, April 1933.

Barrie, Rupert, 'Monument Wood: 48th's Stunt', *Reveille*, May 1933.

Bishop of Amiens, 'Address to 1st Div in Memory of the Australian Fallen', 4th Nov, 1918.

Chalk, David, 'The great Harry Murray', *Wartime*, Issue 8.

Churchill, Winston, Speech at the Australia and New Zealand Club, London, 16th Dec 1918.

Crawford, Robert, 'Propaganda Artist', *Wartime*, Issue 24.

Dawson, Capt F.C., 'Lieut Moon's VC: 58th Bn at Bullecourt', *Reveille*, May 1933.

Donald, W.F., 'A Small World', *Reveille*, May 1936.

Denham, Lt-Col H.K., 'Barbed Wire Belts: Bullecourt Defences', *Reveille*, April 1933.

Dunworth, Lt-Col David, 'Muddle on Muddle: 4th Bde at Bullecourt', *Reveille*, April 1933.

Dutton, Phillip, 'For Services Rendered', *Wartime*, Issue 24.

Ekins, Ashley, 'The Australians at Passchendaele', in Peter Liddle (ed), *Passchendaele in Perspective*, Leo Cooper, 1997.

—— 'Australians at the End of the Great War', in Hugh Cecil and Peter Liddle (eds), *At the Eleventh Hour*, Leo Cooper, 1998.

—— 'The Battle of Fromelles: A Bloody Initiation', unpublished paper.

—— 'The Unknown Australian Soldier', *Wartime*, Issue 25.

Emma Gee, 'Fragmentary Memories – Polygon Wood and Around Ypres', *Reveille*, Sept 1936, and 'A Fragmentary Memory – Broodseinde', *Reveille*, Oct 1934.

Evans, J.E., 'Battle for Mont St Quentin', *Reveille*, Sept 1932.

Gledhill, Capt. A.J., 'Dernancourt – A Recollection', *Reveille*, Oct 1933.

Gopnik, Adam, 'The Big One', *The New Yorker*, 23rd Aug, 2004.

Gordon, Harry, 'From Track to Trenches', *Weekend Australian*, 25 April, 1998.

The *Great War Magazine*, H.W. Wilson and J.A. Hammerton (eds), various issues 1916–1919.

Grogan, Brig-Gen G.W. St G., 'Villers-Bretonneux April 24, 1918', *Reveille*, Aug 1936.

Harris, Lt Russell, 'The 27th in the Menin Road Battle', *Stand-To*, Jan/Mar 1966.

Hodge, Ian, 'Spectacle preserved', *Wartime*, Issue 24.

Hughes, Prime Minister William, 'The whole world lies bleeding and exhausted . . .' Speech to Parliament, on the Treaty of Versailles, 10th Sept, 1919.

Hyman, Lt-Col A.W., 'An Australian Race Meeting in France', *Reveille*, July 1931.

Jackson, Pte Dudley, 'Flanders 1917', *Stand-To*, Jul/Sep 1967.

Kinchington, Pte P., 'Heavy Death Toll', *Reveille*, date unknown.

Knowles, Bert, 'Bullecourt Tragedy Retrospect', *Reveille*, April 1931.

Lahey, John, 'The last of the Anzacs . . .', the *Age*, 21st April 1984.

Leane, Brig-Gen R., ' Hindenburg Line Break: First Bullecourt Memories', *Reveille*, April 1933.

Lecky, J., 'The German Stampede', *Reveille*, Aug 1936.

Longmore, Capt C., 'Lieut-Gen Sir J. Talbot Hobbs', *Reveille*, Jan 1935, 'Major Percy Black', *Reveille*, Oct 1936, and 'Lieut J. B. Minchin', *Reveille*, July 1935.

Lucas, P.F., 'The Victory of August 8, 1918', *Reveille*, Aug 1936, and 'The Attack at Bellicourt', *Reveille*, Sep 1935.

Macarthur-Onslow, Lt J.A., 'The Fifth Army in the Battle of St Quentin March 1918', *Reveille*, Mar/June/July 1937.

Maynard, Jim, 'Around the Menin Road', *Reveille*, Aug 1936.

Mitchell, Capt. G.D., 'The Winter of 1916–17', *Reveille*, Dec 1934, Jan/Feb 1935, 'When Discipline Overcame Fear', *Reveille*, Feb 1936, and 'And on to Messines', *Reveille*, Sep/Oct 1936.

Murray, Lieut-Col. Harry, 'Experimental Stage: Tanks at Bullecourt', *Reveille*, April 1933, 'Captain Ralph Kell', *Reveille*, May 1933, 'Training Juniors: Field Ranks', *Reveille*, June 1933, 'His Hardest Battle When Discipline Mastered Fear', *Reveille*, Dec 1935, 'Memories of First Bullecourt', *Reveille*, Dec 1936, 'Capture of Stormy Trench: Aussies in Grim Duel Against Worthy Foes', *Reveille*, Dec 1937, and 'The First Three Weeks on Gallipoli', *Reveille*, April 1939.

Nichols, Robert, 'The Capture of the Amiens Gun', *Wartime*, Issue 23.

Nicholson, W.H., 'Capt. G.D. Mitchell', *Reveille*, Mar 1936.

Orchard, A.A., 'Second Bullecourt Inferno', *Reveille*, Aug 1937.

Preston, Sgt. H., 'To Do or Die', *Reveille*, Jan 1936, and 'John Leak's VC', *Reveille*, Aug 1935.

Pugsley, Christopher, 'Those Other "Diggers" in 1918', AWM History Conference, 27–29 Sep 1993.

Purser, Lt-Col. M., 'Memories of Fromelles', *Reveille*, July 1935.

Reveille, Jan 1931, 'Heavy Blows: Three Brothers Killed'.

Rogerson, Maj. Sidney, 'Australia in France', *Reveille*, April 1937

Savige, Lt-Col. S.G., 'A Soldier's Battle: Second Bullecourt', *Reveille*, May 1933.

Scott, Capt. Alex, 'I Remember', *Reveille*, Aug 1937.

Simkins, Peter, 'Co-Stars or Supporting Cast? British Divisions in the Hundred Days' 1918', AWM History Conference, 28–29 Sep, 1993.

Smith, Spr William, 'Leaves from a Sapper's Diary', *Reveille*, July 1936

Staunton, Anthony, 'The "other" man', *Wartime*, Issue 21.

Tambling, Capt. R., 'Etinehem and Corbie-Bray Road', *Reveille*, Aug 1937.

Untitled, 'Truth from the Trenches', *The Spectator*, 14th Jan, 2005.

Viney, Lt-Col H., 'Anzac Last Fight', *Reveille*, Sep 1935, 'Sir H.B. (Hooky) Walker', *Reveille*, Dec 1934 and 'Walker, Lt-Gen Sir H.B.: Celebrities of the A.I.F No 52', *Reveille*, Dec 1934.

Wanliss, Newton, 'We Shall Remember Him – Capt. Albert Jacka, V.C., M.C', *Reveille*, Jan 1936.

White, Capt T.A., 'On to Messines', *Reveille*, June 1937.

Wilson, Maj. B.C., 'Celebrities of the A.I.F. (27): Lt-Col. O. G. Howell-Price', *Reveille*, Nov 1932.

Wilson, Neil, 'Brothers-in-Arms', *Herald Sun*, April 23, 2005.

Winn, Maj. R. C., 'Stormy Trench', *Reveille*, Feb 1938.

Private Papers and Material Relating to Individuals

Australian War Memorial, Canberra
Cpl. Robert Addison   PR00442
Gnr. James Armitage   PR00420
Sgt. R.J. Baldwin   PR00557
Pte. William Barry PR00814
Lt. J.H. Barton   PR00261
Bean Papers
Cpl. Alfred Binskin   PR83/047
Capt. Walter Boys   1DRL0142
Pte. Roy Brewer   PR02010/2
L/Cpl. P.R. and Sig. S.R. Candy   3DRL6673
Sgt. R. Capel   PR00658
Lt. B. Champion   2DRL0512

L/Cpl. Leonard Clyde   PR00142
Lt. G.M. Carson   2DRL0185
Lt. H.W. Crowle   1DRL0227
Lt. A. Davey   1DRL0234
L/Cpl P Davey, VC
Pte. George Davies   2DRL789
Capt. K. Doig   PR00317
Gnr. K. Downes   3DRL6987
Lt-Col. R. Dowse   AWM 27 113/4
Brig-Gen. H.E. Elliott   1DRL427, 2DRL0513, 3DRL3297, 3DRL3856,
   3DRL6673.
Maj. Tom Elliott   3DRL 2872
Lt. D. Falconer   2DRL0524
Lt. W.G. Fisher   2DRL0113
Lt. S. Fraser   1DRL0300
Sister Elsie Grant   PR00596
Capt. R.C. Grieve, VC   2DRL0260
Sgt. W.C. Groves   2DRL0268
Lt. W.H. Guard   2DRL0879
Pte. John Hardie   PR00519
Gen. Talbot Hobbs   PR82/153/3
Lt. A. Hollyhoke   3DRL0277
Lt-Col. O.G. Howell-Price   1DRL0362
Maj. P.L. Howell-Price   1DRL0363
Lt. S.E. Hunt   2DRL0277
Pte. S.L. Huntingdon   PR00654
Maj. A.J. Hutchinson   1DRL0371
Pte. Paul Johanesen   PR87/018
W.D. Joynt, VC   2DRL0765
Capt. Percy Lay   PR83/058
Capt. A.E. Leane   1DRL 0411
Lynch, Phyllis   PR00716
Pte. W. McBeath   PR00675)
Maj. G.G. McCrae   1DRL0427
Pte. Robert Mactier, VC   2DRL0144, PR83/210
Capt. Ivor Margetts   1DRL0478
Capt. G. Maxfield   1DRL0489
Capt. G.D. Mitchell   2DRL0928
Lt-Col. J. Mott   ExDoc 004
Keith Murdoch   3DRL2925, 3DRL 6673/62
Lts. J.A. & R.G. Raws   2DRL0481
Gnr. C. Rea   PR00184

Sig. G. Ridgway   3DRL3986
Lt. Schonemann   PR89/003
Pte. F. Shoobridge PRO0626
Pte. Walter Smyth   PR00927
Cpl. Arthur Thomas 3DRL2206
Toll Papers   AWM26 34/1
Pte. William Tooney   PR02027
Sgt. Joseph Trotman   PR00511
Maj. Fred Tubb, VC   ExDoc036
Cpl. Henry Turnbull PR91/015
Pte. W. Vincent   PR84/261
Gnr. F. Wormald   PR00816
Capt. B. Walther   PR00837

Papers and photographs privately held
Lt. E.A.C. Atkinson
Pte. H.D. Burness
Capt. Stanley Calderwood
Cpl. Fred Carpenter
Lt. Consett Carre Riddell
Lt-Col.Walter Cass
Maj. Donald Coutts
Sgt. Walter Downing
Lt-Col. H. Duigan
Lt. Eric Edgerton
Pte. S.L. Filer
Capt. John Harry Fletcher
Pte. Jarvis Fuller
L/Cpl. Roy Fuller
Cpl. William Gamble
Pte. Henry Gibb
Pte. R.M. Gunn
Handcock Brothers
Cpl. William Hart
Sapper Frank Heerey
Pte. Walter Hill
Pte. Walter Howard
Pte. Lyall Howard
Sgt. S. Horton
Sgt. Charles Johnson
Maj. Alfred Langan
Sgt. Cyril Lawrence

Capt. Percy Lay
Lt. Sydney Leigh
Pte. Robert Mactier, VC
Capt. John Austin Mahony
Capt. Ivor Margetts
Lt. Leslie Martin
Sgt. Andrew Muir
Pte. Myles O'Reilly
Lt. William Palstra
Pte. Leslie Pezet
Lt. Phillip Schuler
Maj. Fred Tubb, VC
Wallach Brothers
Sgt. George Watkins
Pte. Eric West
Pte. D.H. Whinfield
Lt. Norman Wilkinson
Pte. Fawkner Yeates

National Archives of Australia
L/Cpl. Phillip Davey, VC
Capt. John Harry Fletcher
Pte. Jarvis Fuller
Capt. Albert Jacka, VC
Lt-Col. W. D. Joynt, VC
Pte. R. Mactier, VC
Capt. John Austin Mahony
Capt. R. Moon, VC
Lt. Phillip Schuler
Maj. Fred Tubb, VC
Capt. Clarence Wallach
Pte. Henry Wallach
Capt. Neville Wallach

Overseas papers
Birdwood Papers, Imperial War Museum
Lt-Col. C.E.L. Lyne, Imperial War Museum
Capt. A.M. McGrigor, Imperial War Museum
Brig-Gen. Henry Sandilands, PRO
Haig Papers, National Library of Scotland
Rawlinson Papers, Churchill College, Cambridge
Philip Game Papers

Acknowledgements

Acknowledgements are written last, when one is weary from toiling over the preceding 800-odd pages and inclined to overlook things. So my first concern, and it mortifies me, is that I will forget to acknowledge someone. It has been a long journey and so many people have helped along the way: digging out family documents and photographs, advising on technical matters, steering me around the battlefields of France and Belgium. My second concern is to say at once that, despite the size and generosity of the supporting cast, should this book contain any errors of fact or judgement, I alone am responsible.

This book, I suppose, grew out of *Gallipoli*. Ashley Ekins, a senior historian at the Australian War Memorial, helped me enormously with that book and he has done the same with this one, pointing me towards promising material, giving generously of his time (even though he was caught up with writing the official history of the Vietnam War) and, best of all, his wisdom. I owe him a great deal. Peter Burness, another historian at the AWM, has an expert knowledge of the western front battlefields, and he was kind enough to point me towards the right places and people in France. Also at the AWM, I should thank Mal Booth, David Joliffe and Lee-Anne McConchie at the Research Centre, and Ian Kelly.

In France, Paul Reed, who has written several fine books on the western front, took me around many of the Somme killing grounds; Paul's friend Jacky Platteeuw helped me navigate the Ypres salient. Paul and Jacky not only gave me good advice but also the pleasure of their company. Martial Delebarre took me around Fromelles, which is a hard battlefield to understand. Claude and Colette Durand showed me around Bullecourt, put on a barbeque and couldn't do enough to assist. Also at Bullecourt, Jean Letaille led me through his museum, which is a thing of wonder. Pierre Jubault was kind enough to guide me around the beautiful village of Bussy-les-Daours, where Clemenceau in 1918 came to see the Australians. Jean-Pierre Thierry pointed me in the right directions at Villers-Bretonneux. Dr Ross Bastiaan gave me advice on places to visit. My son, Patrick, drove me for thousands of kilometres up and down the battlefields and developed a taste that he cannot afford for French cuisine and Belgian beer.

Back home I received help, advice and encouragement from old friends from newspaper days, notably John Hamilton, Garry Linnell, Patrick Walters, Cameron Forbes, Neil Mitchell, Peter Cole-Adams, Creighton Burns, Mark Baker, Colin Bennett (who also happens to be John Monash's grandson), Michael Leunig and Andrew Rule. Rod Cameron again helped me find books, as did Coleman and Sylvia Johnson. Ian Clarke, who assisted with *Gallipoli*, again provided lots of books and documents. Lieutenant-General John Coates and Major-General Des Mueller helped me with technical matters. I am also grateful to Professor Robin Prior for allowing me to test a few ideas on him. Lambis Englezos of The Friends of the 15th Brigade went to extraordinary lengths to find letters and documents for me. Ross McMullin and Robin Corfield were gracious with their time and knowledge. The library staff at the *Bulletin*, Sydney, was exceptionally helpful with material on the home front between 1916 and 1918.

It is impossible to write a book such as this without relying on the work of earlier authors. Some books are more important than others. Charles Bean's official histories are in a category of their own for detail and accuracy. John Coates' *An Atlas of Australia's Wars* is just about the finest single volume ever produced on Australia's military history. The books by Robin Prior and Trevor Wilson on the Somme and Passchendaele are remarkable for their clarity, economy and hardheaded analysis. Robin Corfield's *Don't forget me, cobber* is the definitive work on Fromelles. Martin Middlebrook's *The First Day of the Somme* and *The Kaiser's Battle* are brilliant reconstructions. One cannot write about Australia's Victoria Cross winners without reading Anthony Staunton's *Victoria Cross*. Geoffrey Serle's *John Monash* is an outstanding biography, as is John Grigg's four-volume series on David Lloyd George. Correlli Barnett's *The Swordbearers* is not only good history but also a lovely piece of writing.

For permission to quote from collections, my thanks to the Australian War Memorial, the Imperial War Museum, the National Archives of Australia; to Colin Bennett and the late Betty Durre, for permission to quote from the Monash Papers, and Earl Haig and the Trustees of the National Library of Scotland, for permission to quote from the Earl Sir Douglas Haig Papers.

I am grateful to the following people and organisations who gave so willingly of their time to provide information for this book: Alan Bennett; Lesle Berry (ed *Ancestor*); Ian Black (Hamilton History Centre Inc); Bendigo Regional Genealogical Society; Butch Calderwood; Dr John Carre-Riddell;

ACKNOWLEDGEMENTS

Brigid Cole-Adams and Harold Love; Pearl Collins (Echuca–Moama Family History Group); Helen Cole; Diana Cousens; Val Craig and Billy Wines; Dr Selwin Crick; Roslyn Devine, Joyce Wallach and Meg Doyle; William, John, David and the late James Downing; Jean Dugan and Zandra Thomas; James Fellows; Tony Ford; Dr Bruce Gaunson and Ily Benedek; Colin, Neville and Nancy Handcock; Robert Hannah; J. Murray Hamilton; Norma Harrison; Brett Hart; Jeff Hatwell; Prof. John Hayman; Mr Justice Peter Heerey; Dr Margaret Heese; Michael Hiscock; John and Janette Howard; Rod Johnson; Robyn Johnson; Greg Kirk; Lurline Knee (Tatura and District Historical Society); Michael Leunig; Jarvis McBean and Dorothy Seers; Pauline McIntyre; Jim Mactier; John Mahony, Cec O'Brien, Michael Dwyer and Val Gleeson; Douglas, Andrew, Barrie and Marj Margetts; Jim Martin; Bruce Mellor; P. McGrigor; Jack Mensforth; Betty and Neil Morrison; Sir Laurence Muir; Russell and Ann O'Sullivan; Jan Parker; Mabel and Doug Parry; Patrick Regan; Cecilia Thornton; Fred Tubb; Unley Genealogical Society; William Van der Kloot; Arthur West; Max Whinfield; Peter Wilkinson; Ross Watts; and Ron Yeates.

Extracts from the following books have been produced with permission: from Robert Asprey, *The German High Command at War*, Warner Books, 1994, with permission of the William Morris Agency; from Pat Barker, *Regeneration*, Viking, 1991, with permission of the Penguin Group, UK; from Correlli Barnett, *The Swordbearers: Studies in Supreme Command in the First World War*, Eyre & Spottiswoode, 1963, with permission of Correlli Barnett; from Charles Bean, *Two Men I Knew*, Angus and Robertson, 1957, and Frank Legg, *The Gordon Bennett Story*, Angus and Robertson, 1965, with permission of Harper Collins Publishers Ltd; from Joan Beaumont (ed.), *Australia's War 1914–1918*, 1995, with permission of Allen & Unwin; from Edmund Blunden, *Undertones of War*, Penguin, 1937, with permission of Harper Collins Publishers Ltd; from Winston Churchill, *The World Crisis 1911–1918*, Odhams, 1938, and *Great Contemporaries*, W. W. Horton and Company, 1990, with permission of Curtis Brown on behalf of the Estate of Sir Winston Churchill; from Robin Corfield, *Don't forget me, cobber*, Corfield and Company, 2000, with permission of Robin Corfield; from Walter Downing, *To the Last Ridge*, Duffy and Snellgrove, 1998, with permission of William, John, David and the late James Downing; from Martin Gilbert, *The Treaty of Versailles in History of World War I* (ed A.J.P. Taylor), Macdonald and Co, 1988, with permission of Martin Gilbert and A.P. Watt; from Martin Gilbert, *Winston S. Churchill. Vol IV, Companion Part I*, Heinemann, 1977, with permission of the Random House Group; from John Grigg, *Lloyd George: From Peace to War 1912–1916*, Harper Collins, 1977, and *Lloyd George: War Leader 1916–1918*, Allen Lane, 2002, with permission of the Penguin Group, UK; from Robert Graves, *Goodbye to All That*,

Folio Society, 1981, with permission of Carcanet Press Ltd; from Donald Horne, *Billy Hughes*, Black Inc, 2000, with permission of Myfanwy Horne; from Jeff Hatwell, *No Ordinary Determination: Percy Black and Harry Murray of the First A.I.F.*, Fremantle Arts Centre, 2005, with permission of Jeff Hatwell; from John Keegan and Andrew Wheatcroft, *Who's Who in Military History*, Routledge, 2002, with permission of the Thomson Publishing Service; from Cyril Lawrence, *Sergeant Lawrence Goes to France* (ed Peter Yule), MUP, 1987, with permission of Dr Margaret Heese; from Ross McMullin, *Pompey Elliott*, Scribe Publications, 2002, with permission of Ross McMullin; from Martin Middlebrook, *The Kaiser's Battle*, Penguin, 2000, with permission of Martin Middlebrook; from Robin Prior and Trevor Wilson, *Passchendaele: The Untold Story*, Yale University Press, 1996, and *Command on the Western Front: The Military Career of Sir Henry Rawlinson 1914–1918*, Pen & Sword, 2004, with permission of Robin Prior; from William Triplet, *A Youth in the Meuse-Argonne: A Memoir 1917–1918* (ed Robert Ferrell), with permission of the University of Missouri Press, copyright 2000 by Curators of the University of Missouri; from Robert Rhodes James, *A Spirit Undaunted: The Political Role of George VI*, Little, Brown and Co, 1998, with permission of Little, Brown Book Group; from Frances Stevenson, *Lloyd George: A Diary*, Hutchinson, 1971, with permission of David Higham Associates; from John Terraine, *Douglas Haig: The Educated Soldier*, Leo Cooper, 1990, with permission of the Orion Publishing Group; from Tim Travers, *The Killing Ground: The British Army, the Western Front and the Emergence of Modern War*, 2003, with permission of Pen & Sword.

I owe an enormous debt to Deborah Callaghan, my literary agent, who has looked after me so well for so long, and whose judgement is unerringly good. Tom Gilliatt, the director of non-fiction publishing at Pan Macmillan, nursed *The Great War* through every stage, as he did with *Gallipoli*. I am also grateful to Jon Gibbs, Chris Mattey, Jane Novak and many others at Macmillan.

I owe much to my grandchildren – Belinda, Matthew and James – who managed to keep me sane, more or less, as I wrote this book, and who, by their presence, reminded me of what was truly important.

As with *Gallipoli*, my biggest debt is to my wife, Denise. This is her book as much as mine, simply because it could not have been written without her.

Index

Argonne Forest 697, 703, 734, 739,
740
Armentières 52, 110, 129, 130, 405,
593
armistice *see* peace negotiations; truce
Armistice Day 743
Armitage, Gunner James 658
Arras 293, 307, 310, 316, 324, 325,
327, 332, 369, 390
allied attack 1918 679, 680, 686
battle of the Scarpe 680
German attempt to recapture 538,
550, 568, 589
Artois 31
Ash, Celia 730–1
Ashmead-Bartlett, Ellis 251
Asprey, Robert 622
Asquith, Herbert 102, 131, 211, 269,
281, 282, 283, 360, 426
Asquith, Lieutenant Raymond 269,
280
Aubercourt 581, 583
Aubers Ridge 17, 31, 46, 48, 53, 112
Auchonvillers 568
Australian army
Anzac Corps *see* Anzac Corps
Australian Corps 531–3, 580
Battalions
1st 157, 384, 385, 386, 779
2nd 384, 779
3rd 157, 221, 222, 275, 384, 779
4th 161, 223, 599, 779
5th 161, 779
6th 676, 779
7th 161, 445, 479, 675, 779
8th 153, 161, 448, 483, 591, 779
9th 223, 387, 779
10th 223, 224, 386, 451, 779
11th 161, 384–6, 451, 779
12th 155, 223, 224, 384, 385,
386, 779
13th 198, 213–5, 240, 241, 298,
337, 348
14th 198, 199, 201, 213, 240
15th 206, 298, 344, 346, 389
16th 240, 324, 337, 349, 661,
662, 698
17th 374, 448, 685, 779
18th 685, 779
19th 374, 685, 699, 779
20th 685, 779

21st 173, 230, 699, 725, 728,
779
22nd 230, 378, 380, 383, 779
23rd 171, 194, 230, 378, 688,
689, 779
24th 230, 376–8, 382, 383, 540,
576, 689, 692, 725, 727,
728, 746, 779
25th 180, 194, 699, 779
26th 779
27th 779
28th 381, 779
29th 64, 82, 469
30th 64, 84
31st 64, 69, 70, 469
32nd 64, 69, 82, 714
33rd 583, 585, 586, 588, 686,
771, 779
34th 583, 586, 779
35th 583, 584–6, 588, 779
36th 583, 586–8, 779
37th 699, 700, 701, 779
38th 779
39th 779
40th 779
41st 779
42nd 699, 779
43rd 779
44th 779
45th 206
46th 335, 336, 340, 341, 342,
346
47th 342
48th 202, 206, 323, 331, 335,
340, 341, 346, 347, 349,
355, 589
49th 213, 243
50th 213
51st 213–5, 612
52nd 90, 242, 243
53rd 64, 67, 68, 81, 86, 87
54th 64, 67, 68, 81, 86, 699
55th 64, 68, 81, 86
56th 64, 463
57th 59, 60, 64, 462, 465, 610,
612
58th 64, 72, 464, 465
59th 60, 65, 72–5, 466, 469, 470,
608, 610, 701
60th 60, 64, 65, 72–5, 465, 608,
610, 701, 702